**Nominated for 3 EISNER AWARDS including
Best New Series and Best Ongoing Series**

"For fans of literature (from classics to contemporary) this series is worth a read. . . .
The Unwritten is **a roller-coaster ride through a library, weaving famous authors
and characters into a tale of mystery** that is, at once, oddly familiar yet highly original."
– USA TODAY

"*The Unwritten* makes a leap from being just a promising new Vertigo title to being on-track to
become the best ongoing Vertigo book since *Sandman*. And given that Vertigo has delivered
the likes of *100 Bullets*, *Y: The Last Man*, and *Fables* since *Sandman* ended,
that's saying something… A-"
–THE A.V. CLUB

"In a time where periodical comics are often being ignored in favor of waiting for the collected
edition, Carey and Gross haven't forgotten how a strong periodical can keep people's interest.
This is a serial that makes me want to read it monthly, because I just have to know
what happens next. Now that's good stuff."
– BOOK RESOURCES

the Unwritten
TOMMY TAYLOR AND THE WAR OF WORDS

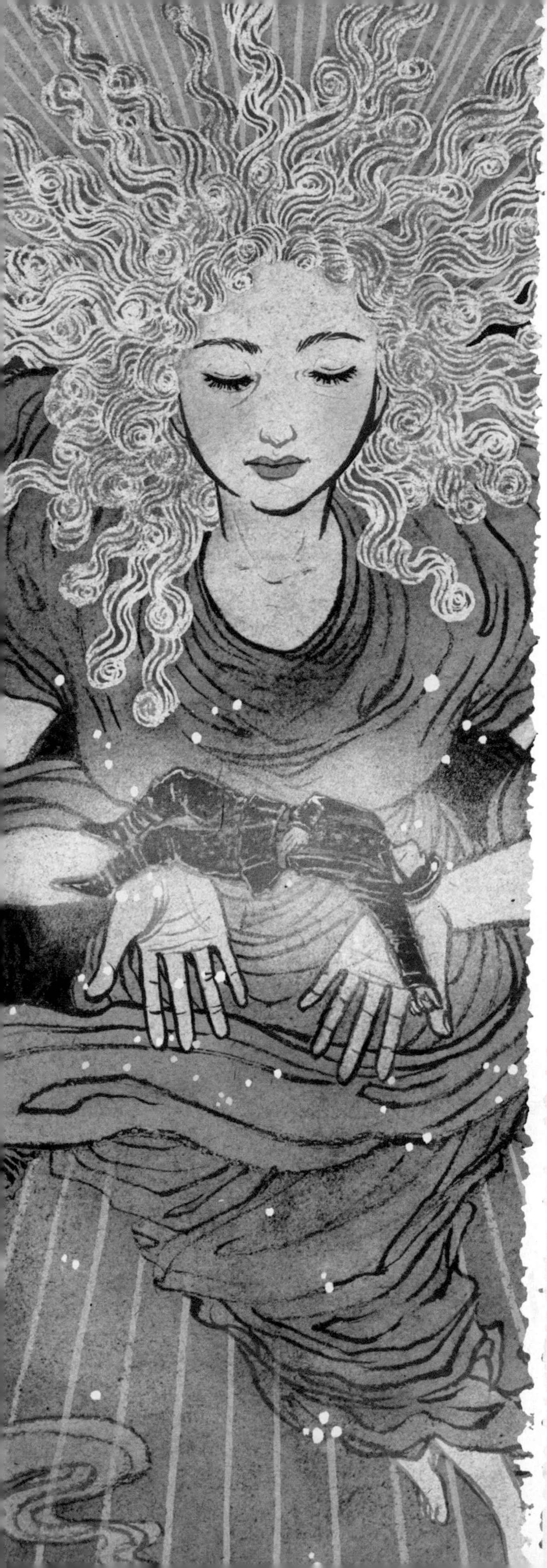

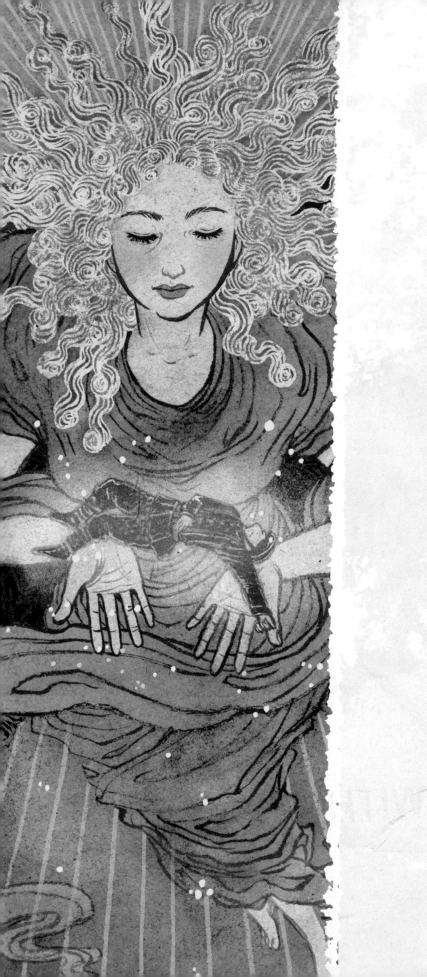

the unwritten

TOMMY TAYLOR AND THE WAR OF WORDS

Mike Carey & Peter Gross Script – Story – Art

M.K. Perker Dean Ormston Vince Locke Finishes

Michael WM. Kaluta Gary Erskine Gabriel Hernandez Walta Rick Geary Bryan Talbot Additional art

Chris Chuckry Fiona Stephenson Lee Loughrige Colorists

Todd Klein Letterer Yuko Shimizu Cover Artist

THE UNWRITTEN created by Gross and Carey

Karen Berger Editor – Original Series
Joe Hughes Assistant Editor – Original Series
Jeb Woodard Group Editor – Collected Editions
Rowena Yow Editor – Collected Edition
Steve Cook Design Director – Books
Louis Prandi Publication Design

Shelly Bond VP & Executive Editor – Vertigo

Diane Nelson President
Dan DiDio and Jim Lee Co-Publishers
Geoff Johns Chief Creative Officer
Amit Desai Senior VP – Marketing & Global Franchise Management
Nairi Gardiner Senior VP – Finance
Sam Ades VP – Digital Marketing
Bobbie Chase VP – Talent Development
Mark Chiarello Senior VP – Art, Design & Collected Editions
John Cunningham VP – Content Strategy
Anne DePies VP – Strategy Planning & Reporting
Don Falletti VP – Manufacturing Operations
Lawrence Ganem VP – Editorial Administration & Talent Relations
Alison Gill Senior VP – Manufacturing & Operations
Hank Kanalz Senior VP – Editorial Strategy & Administration
Jay Kogan VP – Legal Affairs
Derek Maddalena Senior VP – Sales & Business Development
Jack Mahan VP – Business Affairs
Dan Miron VP – Sales Planning & Trade Development
Nick Napolitano VP – Manufacturing Administration
Carol Roeder VP – Marketing
Eddie Scannell VP – Mass Account & Digital Sales
Courtney Simmons Senior VP – Publicity & Communications
Jim (Ski) Sokolowski VP – Comic Book Specialty & Newsstand Sales
Sandy Yi Senior VP – Global Franchise Management

Library of Congress Cataloging-in-Publication Data

Carey, Mike, 1959-
  The unwritten : Tommy Taylor and the war of words / Mike Carey, Peter
Gross, M.K. Perker.
      p. cm.
  "Originally published in single magazine form in The Unwritten 31-35,
31.5-35.5."
  ISBN 978-1-4012-3560-4 (alk. paper)
  1. Characters and characteristics in literature--Comic books, strips, etc.
2. Fame--Psychological aspects--Comic books, strips, etc. 3. Identity
(Philosophical concept)--Comic books, strips, etc. 4. Fiction--Comic
books, strips, etc. 5. Graphic novels. I. Gross, Peter, 1958- II. Perker, M.
K., 1972- III. Title.
  PN6727.C377U68 2012
  741.5'973--dc23
                                    2012022581

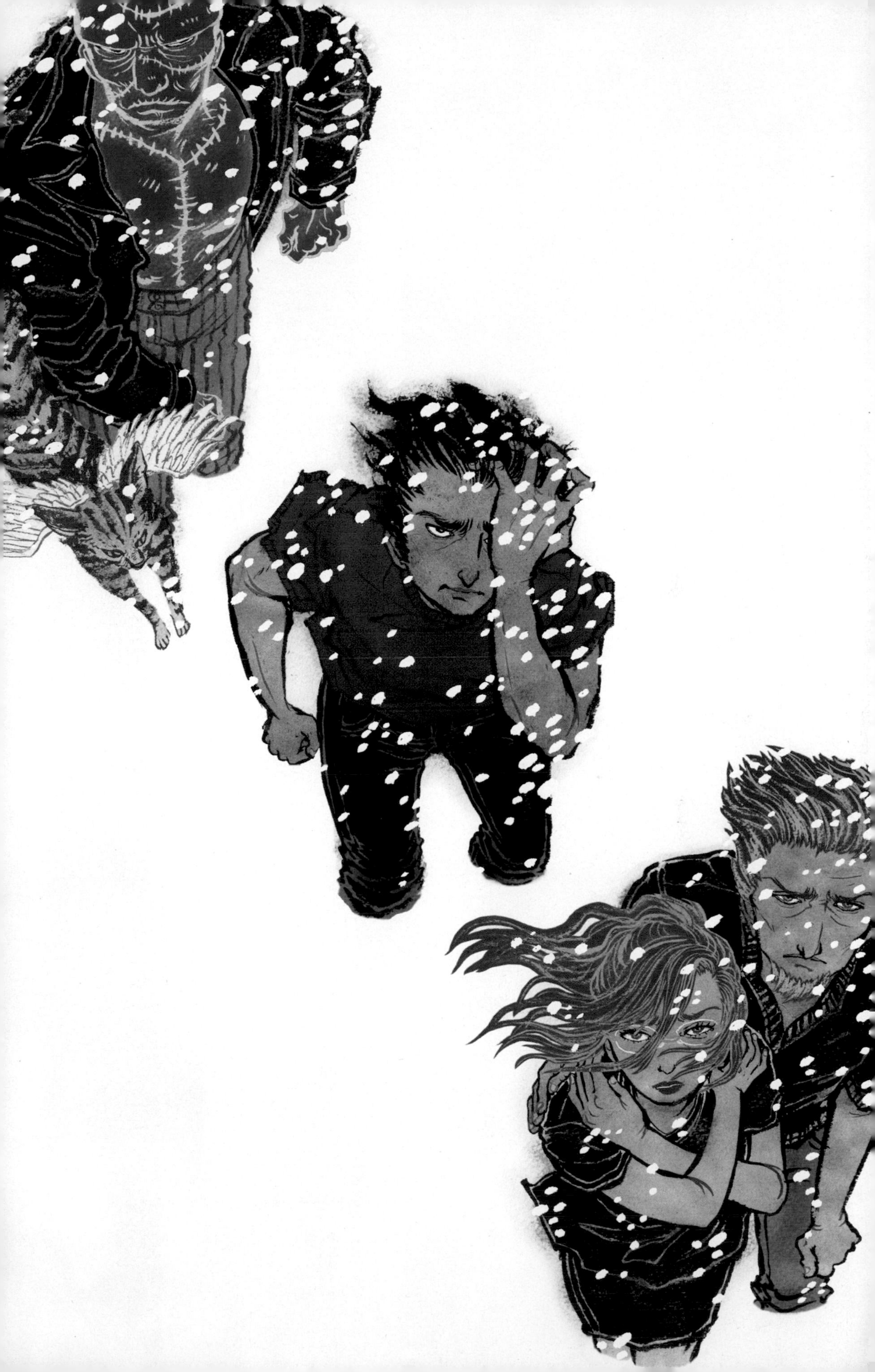

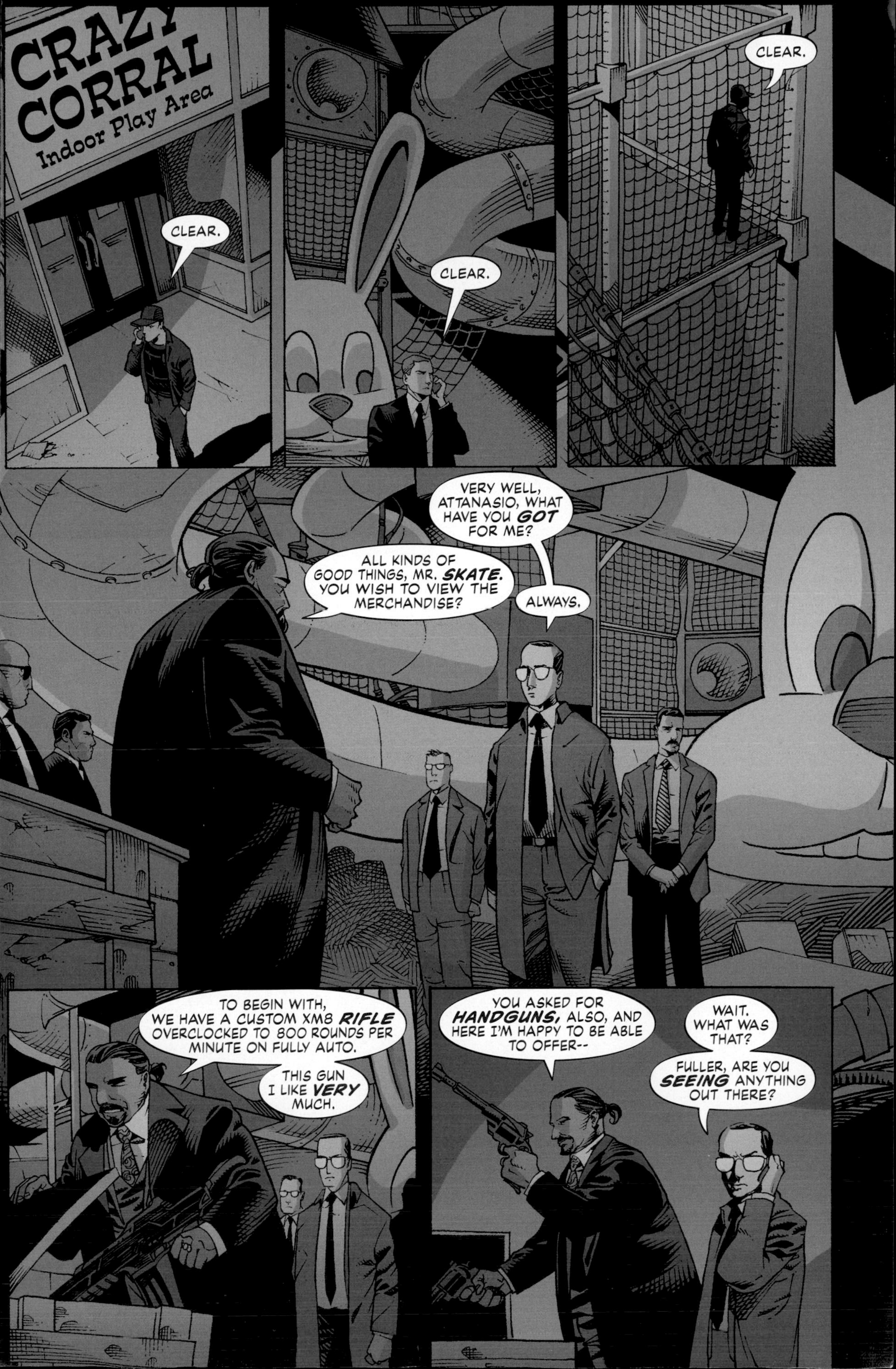
CRAZY CORRAL
Indoor Play Area
CLEAR.
CLEAR.
CLEAR.
VERY WELL, ATTANASIO, WHAT HAVE YOU GOT FOR ME?
ALL KINDS OF GOOD THINGS, MR. SKATE. YOU WISH TO VIEW THE MERCHANDISE?
ALWAYS.
TO BEGIN WITH, WE HAVE A CUSTOM XM8 RIFLE OVERCLOCKED TO 800 ROUNDS PER MINUTE ON FULLY AUTO.
THIS GUN I LIKE VERY MUCH.
YOU ASKED FOR HANDGUNS, ALSO, AND HERE I'M HAPPY TO BE ABLE TO OFFER--
WAIT. WHAT WAS THAT?
FULLER, ARE YOU SEEING ANYTHING OUT THERE?

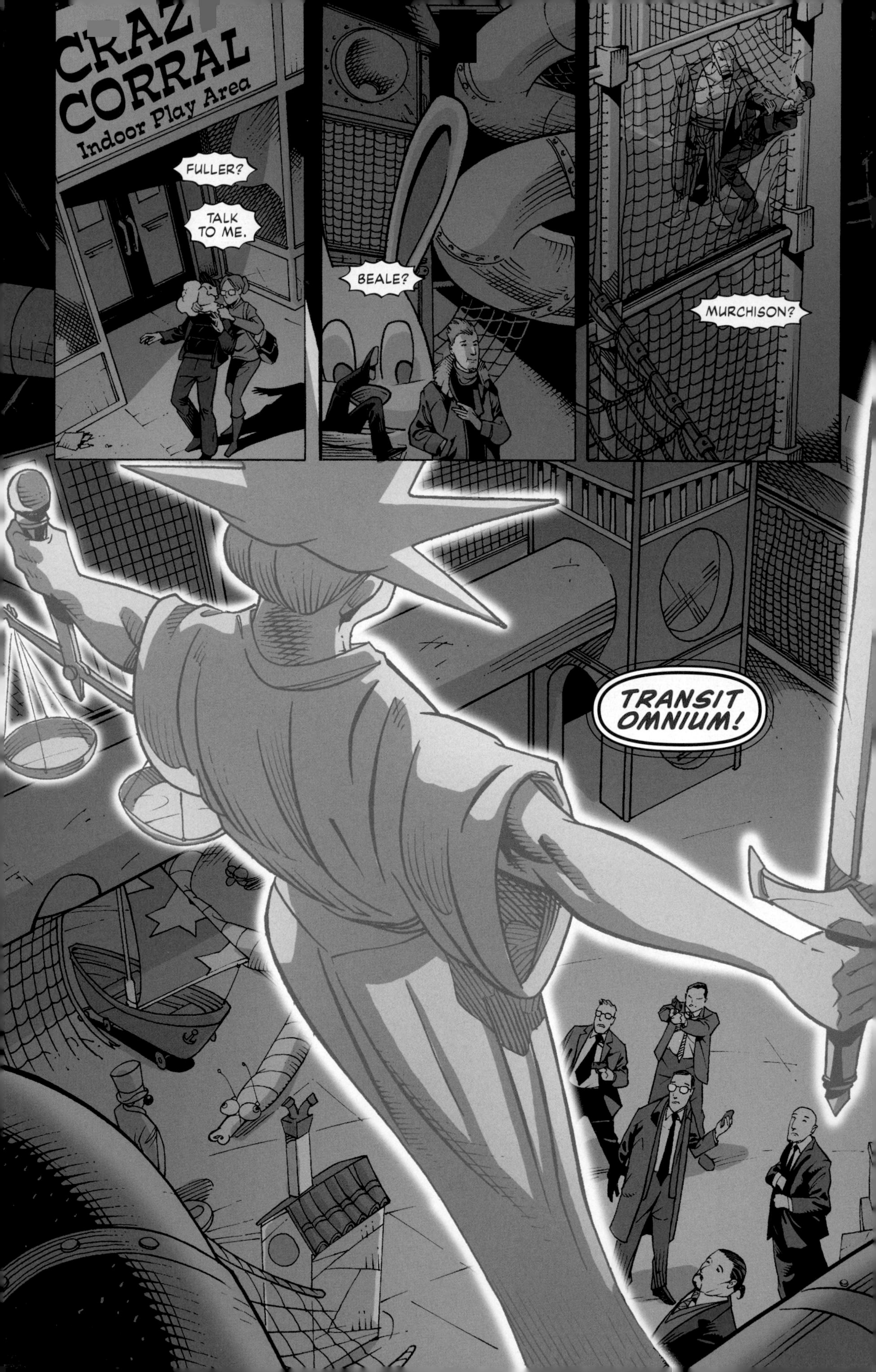
CRAZ
CORRAL
Indoor Play Area
FULLER?
TALK TO ME.
BEALE?
MURCHISON?
TRANSIT OMNIUM!

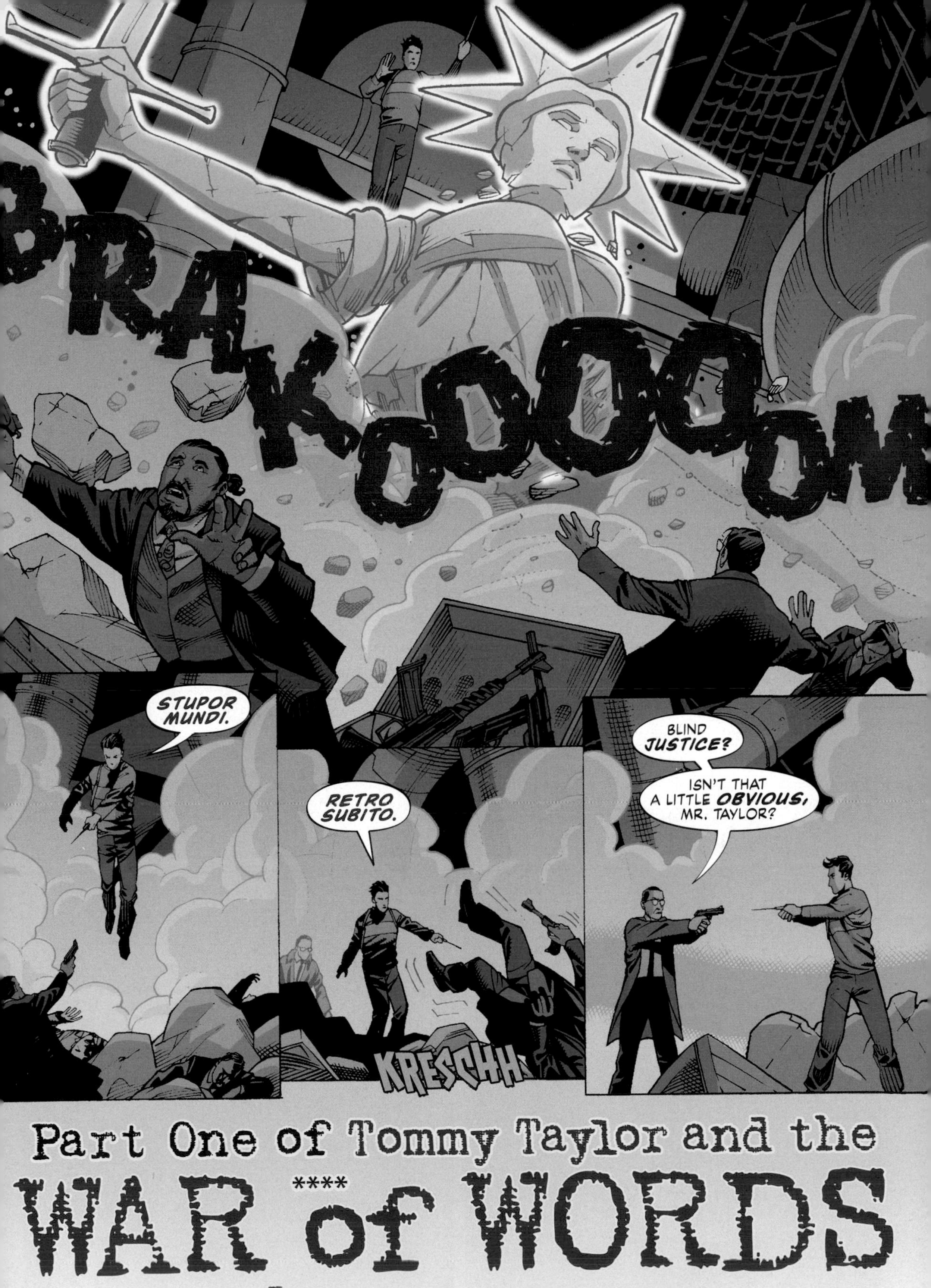
BRAKOOOOM
STUPOR MUNDI.
RETRO SUBITO.
KRESCHH
BLIND JUSTICE?
ISN'T THAT A LITTLE OBVIOUS, MR. TAYLOR?

Part One of Tommy Taylor and the WAR **** of WORDS

By **** Mike Carey **** and **** Peter Gross

M.K. Perker, finishes
Chris Chuckry, colors
Todd Klein, letters
Yuko Shimizu, cover

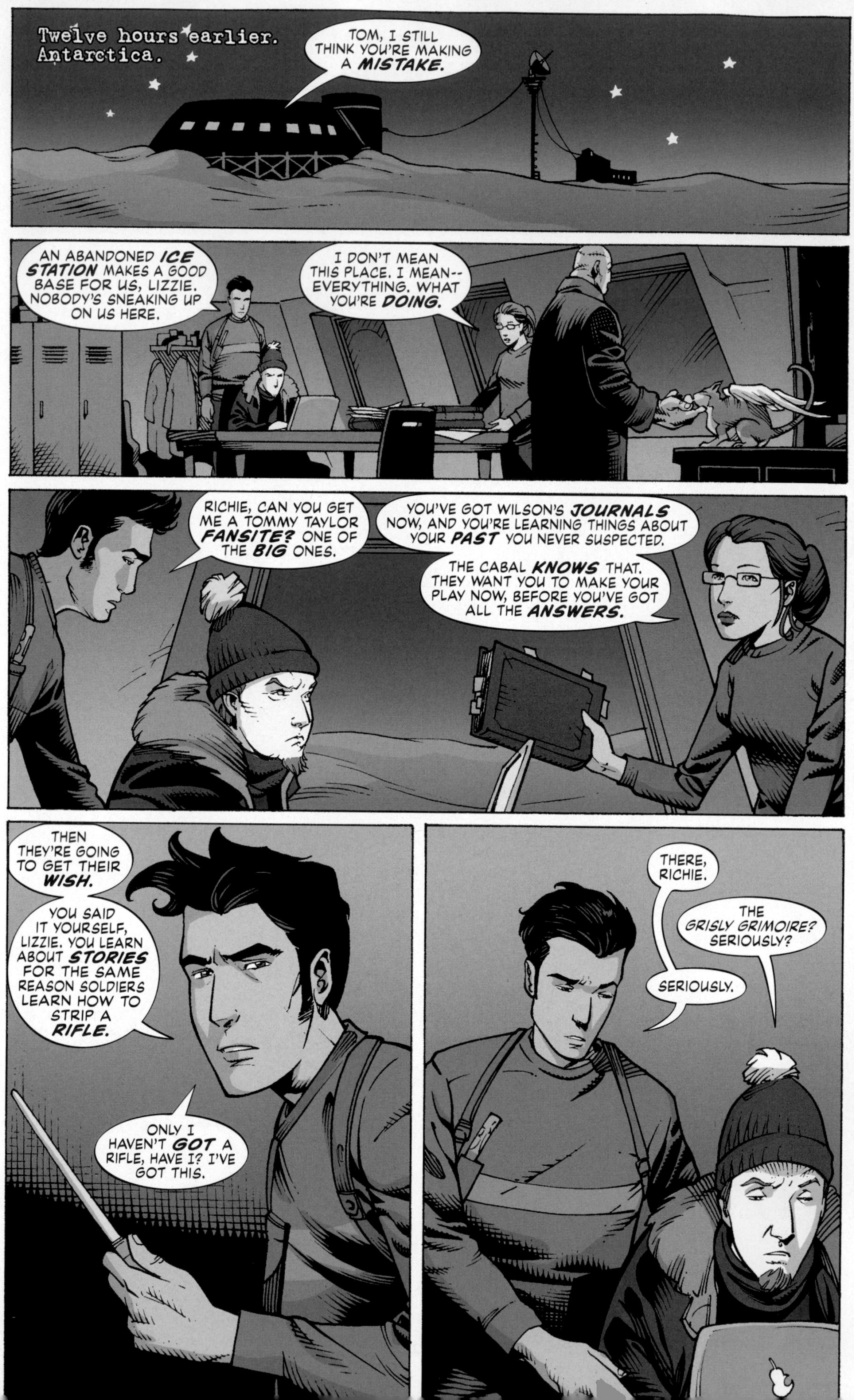

Twelve hours earlier. Antarctica.
TOM, I STILL THINK YOU'RE MAKING A MISTAKE.
AN ABANDONED ICE STATION MAKES A GOOD BASE FOR US, LIZZIE. NOBODY'S SNEAKING UP ON US HERE.
I DON'T MEAN THIS PLACE. I MEAN-- EVERYTHING. WHAT YOU'RE DOING.
RICHIE, CAN YOU GET ME A TOMMY TAYLOR FANSITE? ONE OF THE BIG ONES.
YOU'VE GOT WILSON'S JOURNALS NOW, AND YOU'RE LEARNING THINGS ABOUT YOUR PAST YOU NEVER SUSPECTED.
THE CABAL KNOWS THAT. THEY WANT YOU TO MAKE YOUR PLAY NOW, BEFORE YOU'VE GOT ALL THE ANSWERS.
THEN THEY'RE GOING TO GET THEIR WISH.
YOU SAID IT YOURSELF, LIZZIE. YOU LEARN ABOUT STORIES FOR THE SAME REASON SOLDIERS LEARN HOW TO STRIP A RIFLE.
ONLY I HAVEN'T GOT A RIFLE, HAVE I? I'VE GOT THIS.
THERE, RICHIE.
THE GRISLY GRIMOIRE? SERIOUSLY?
SERIOUSLY.

GRISLY GRIMOIRE

This is a comprehensive listing of all the spells used in the Tommy Taylor novels, broken down by first appearance and with notes on proper usage, variants and side effects. Most of the material here was compiled by Jemima and OneTrueKing, with thanks to Ludo.

ALL WHO HAVE THE SPARK MUST PROTECT AND STAND BY THE SPARK!

SPELL	DESCRIPTION
Dermis obduro	Makes flesh as hard as plate armour. Not actually used, but mentioned by Tommy when he's testing Sue on her spell homework (Ship That Sank Twice, p84).
Lux liquescat	Makes a ball of light that explodes on impact, harmlessly but distractingly. Sue initially has problems with this spell: her light blasts tend to have a greenish tinge and taste of mint (Ship That Sank Twice, p89). Later used by Sue to get Ambrosio's attention when Tommy wants to lure him away from the Academy.
Terram resurgus	Makes a small, localised earthquake. Used by Peter when he helps Tom against Hexley and his cronies. Later, mind-controlled by Ambrosio, Peter tries to use the same spell against Tommy, only to be stymied by Tommy's use of protectus omnium (qv).
Obfuscus oculi	Causes temporary blindness. Used by Hexley against Sue in the scene already mentioned. Despite the Sue versus Harpies scene in Last Gorgon, it's made very clear elsewhere that the effects are not permanent, and that no organic damage is done to the eyes of the person hit by the spell. "Her vision clouded, and when she tried to blink them clear the clouds only got darker." (Ship That Sank Twice, p114).
The House Wants Water	We don't know whether this is a real spell or not, but since it's the first bit of magic we ever see Tommy do, it has to be here. The big water wheel at the Academy responds to a human voice, but only if the command is correctly worded. Tommy memorably uses this in his first fight against Ambrosio (Ship That Sank Twice, p227).
Metamorphicus	The basic shape-changing spell used by Tom, Sue and Peter at several points in Ship That Sank Twice. Usually, the spell-caster has to add an additional word, naming the thing that he intends to change into (eg, "Metamorphicus avis"), but it doesn't seem to be necessary to specify the target.
Frigidari	Freezes the victim in place. Professor Tulkinghorn uses this spell to break up the fight between Tommy and Hexley when

---

latest video cards on DirectPuma

Bright Sparks

THE GREAT CONCORDANCE

The notes below cover Tommy Taylor novels one to thirteen, and the eight additional works in the canon that Wilson Taylor wrote for benefit books and anthologies. Notes for last year's *Tommy Taylor and the Day of Judgment* will be coming soon!

Tommy Taylor and the Ship That Sank Twice
Tommy Taylor and the Magic Doorknob
Tommy Taylor and the Cave of Silence
Tommy Taylor and the Everything Box
Tommy Taylor and the Last Gorgon
Tommy Taylor and the Glass Sword
Tommy Taylor and the Rain of Salt
Tommy Taylor and the Tower of Always
Tommy Taylor and the Nine-fold Curse
Tommy Taylor and the Palace of Bone
Tommy Taylor and the Undead King
Tommy Taylor and the Unicorn's Prophecy
Tommy Taylor and the Golden Trumpet

Three Ways to Kill a Basilisk
Tommy's Unlucky Day
The World Without Tommy
Sue Sparrow's Magnificent Abecedary
Wonderbuss's Tale
The Prince of Lyonesse
Count Ambrosio: A History
Tommy Fetches Water: An Epic Poem

The finest teas brewed by man or magic
Take an inspiring journey through the worlds of Tommy Taylor with our newest collection of fine loose leaf teas.

Tommy Taylor Tea of the Month Club

Bright Sparks

EIGHTFOLD MAGIC!

In *Tommy Taylor and the Ship That Sank Twice*, Sue (with Tommy's help) lists the seven types of offensive magic as follows:-

Pyrotics
Physical missiles
Elemental magics
Sundering forces
Metamorphoses
Compulsions and coercions
Temporal and causal breaches

This essay attempts to assign the most important Tommy Taylor spells to their rightful place in the magical taxonomy, and ultimately suggests that there may be an eighth category of spell invented by Tommy himself in the course of the later books.

Despite the apparent simplicity of this schematic division, some of the spells of the first novel remain notoriously difficult to classify under the offered headings. C. Whelan is surely wrong in identifying Sue's lux liquescat as a pyrotic spell. It produces light, not heat, and there is never any suggestion that it is intended to do any harm. Tommy uses it to light the cavern of the Gorgons, and again to find his way in the Palace of Bone. Nor is it a physical missile, since the light has neither mass nor momentum. Is light an element, perhaps? Some have certainly argued for this, taking

---

Bright Sparks

Learn about upcoming projects, fanworks, films, collections and Taylormore by joining millions of others sparks worldwide. Information so fast it comes to you by Mingus

Sign up for our newsletter! | Your Email

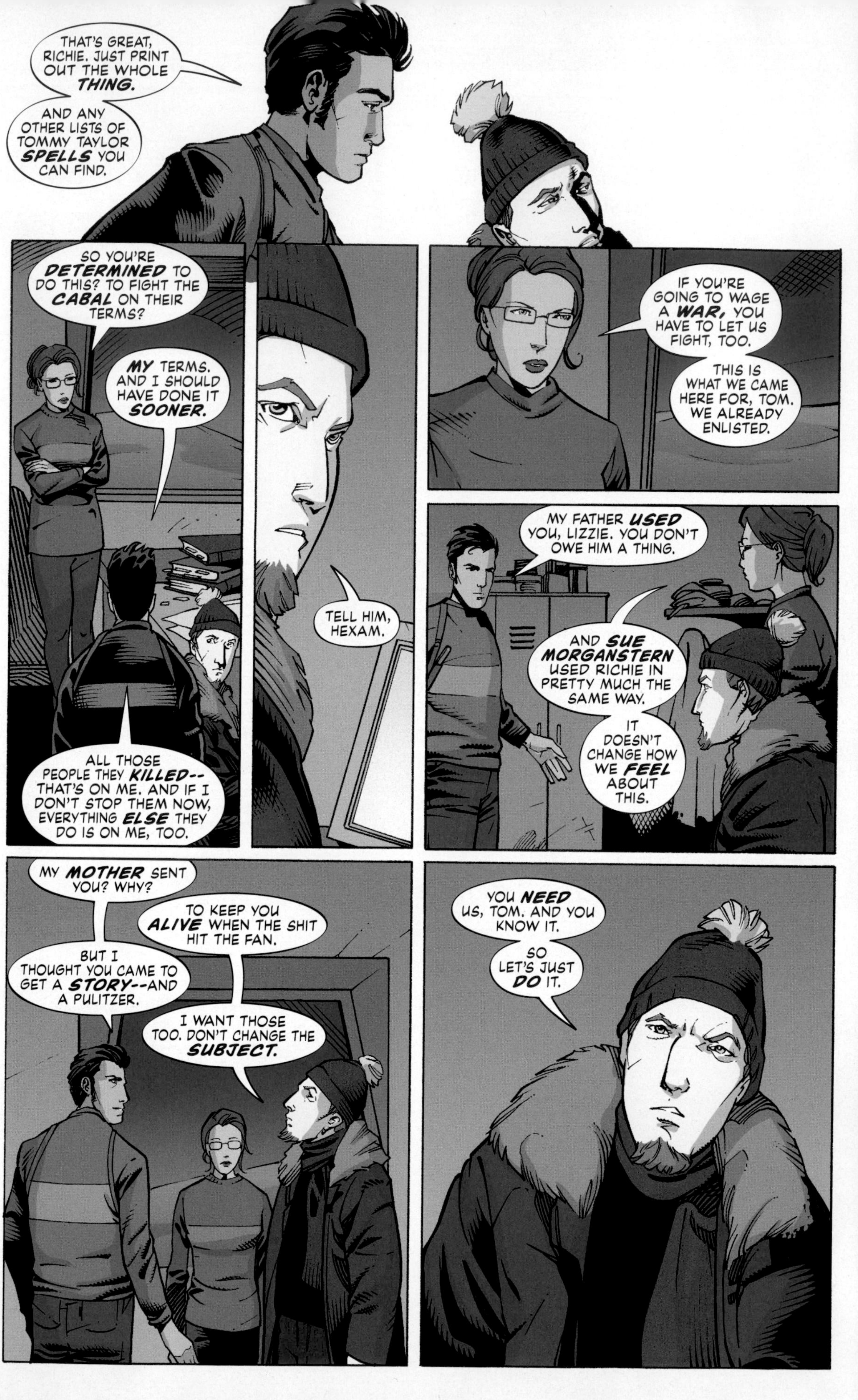
THAT'S GREAT, RICHIE. JUST PRINT OUT THE WHOLE THING.
AND ANY OTHER LISTS OF TOMMY TAYLOR SPELLS YOU CAN FIND.
SO YOU'RE DETERMINED TO DO THIS? TO FIGHT THE CABAL ON THEIR TERMS?
MY TERMS. AND I SHOULD HAVE DONE IT SOONER.
ALL THOSE PEOPLE THEY KILLED--THAT'S ON ME. AND IF I DON'T STOP THEM NOW, EVERYTHING ELSE THEY DO IS ON ME, TOO.
TELL HIM, HEXAM.
IF YOU'RE GOING TO WAGE A WAR, YOU HAVE TO LET US FIGHT, TOO.
THIS IS WHAT WE CAME HERE FOR, TOM. WE ALREADY ENLISTED.
MY FATHER USED YOU, LIZZIE. YOU DON'T OWE HIM A THING.
AND SUE MORGANSTERN USED RICHIE IN PRETTY MUCH THE SAME WAY.
IT DOESN'T CHANGE HOW WE FEEL ABOUT THIS.
MY MOTHER SENT YOU? WHY?
TO KEEP YOU ALIVE WHEN THE SHIT HIT THE FAN.
BUT I THOUGHT YOU CAME TO GET A STORY--AND A PULITZER.
I WANT THOSE TOO. DON'T CHANGE THE SUBJECT.
YOU NEED US, TOM. AND YOU KNOW IT.
SO LET'S JUST DO IT.

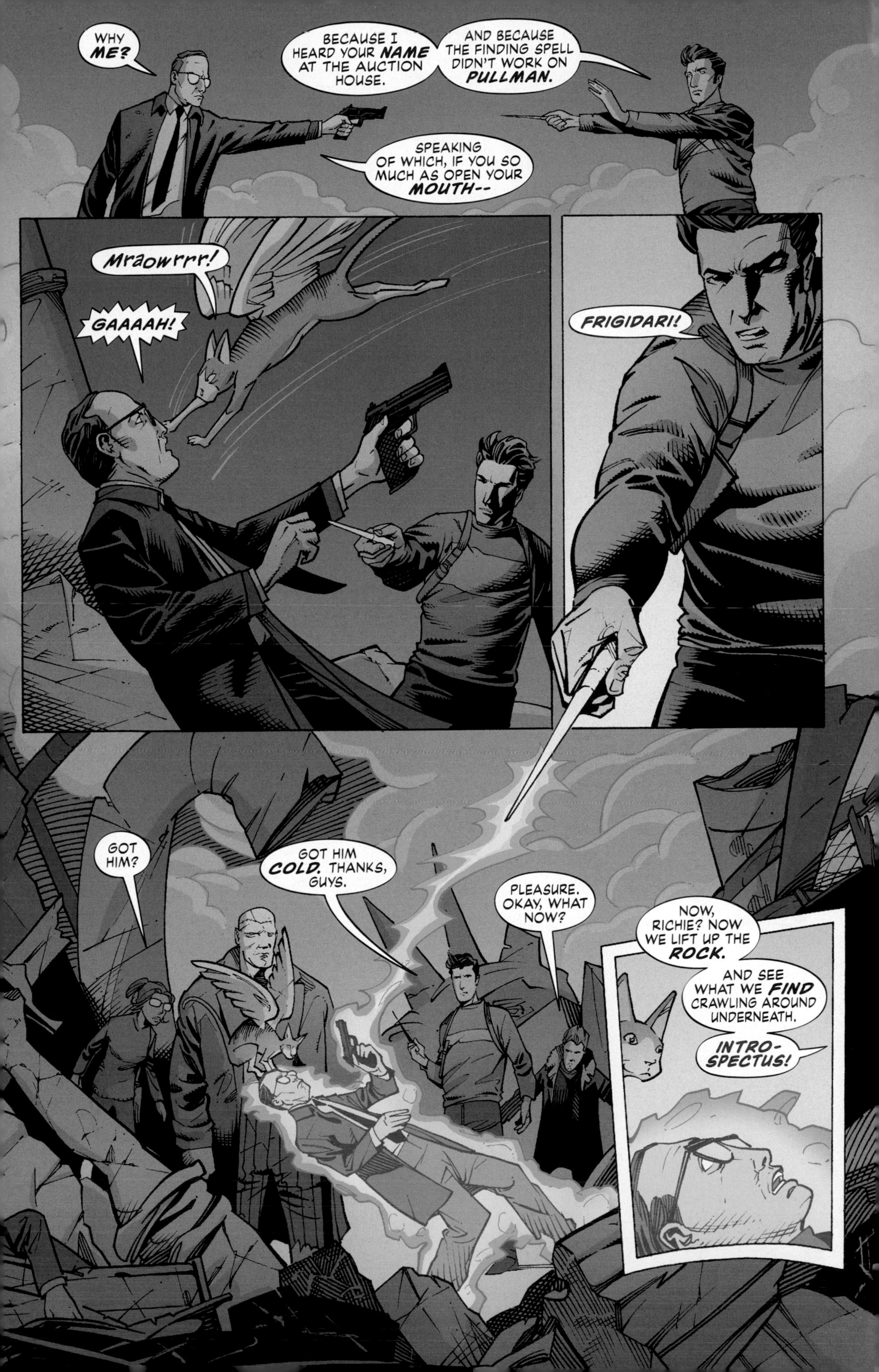

WHY ME?
BECAUSE I HEARD YOUR NAME AT THE AUCTION HOUSE.
AND BECAUSE THE FINDING SPELL DIDN'T WORK ON PULLMAN.
SPEAKING OF WHICH, IF YOU SO MUCH AS OPEN YOUR MOUTH--
Mraowrrr!
GAAAAH!
FRIGIDARI!
GOT HIM?
GOT HIM COLD. THANKS, GUYS.
PLEASURE. OKAY, WHAT NOW?
NOW, RICHIE? NOW WE LIFT UP THE ROCK.
AND SEE WHAT WE FIND CRAWLING AROUND UNDERNEATH.
INTRO-SPECTUS!

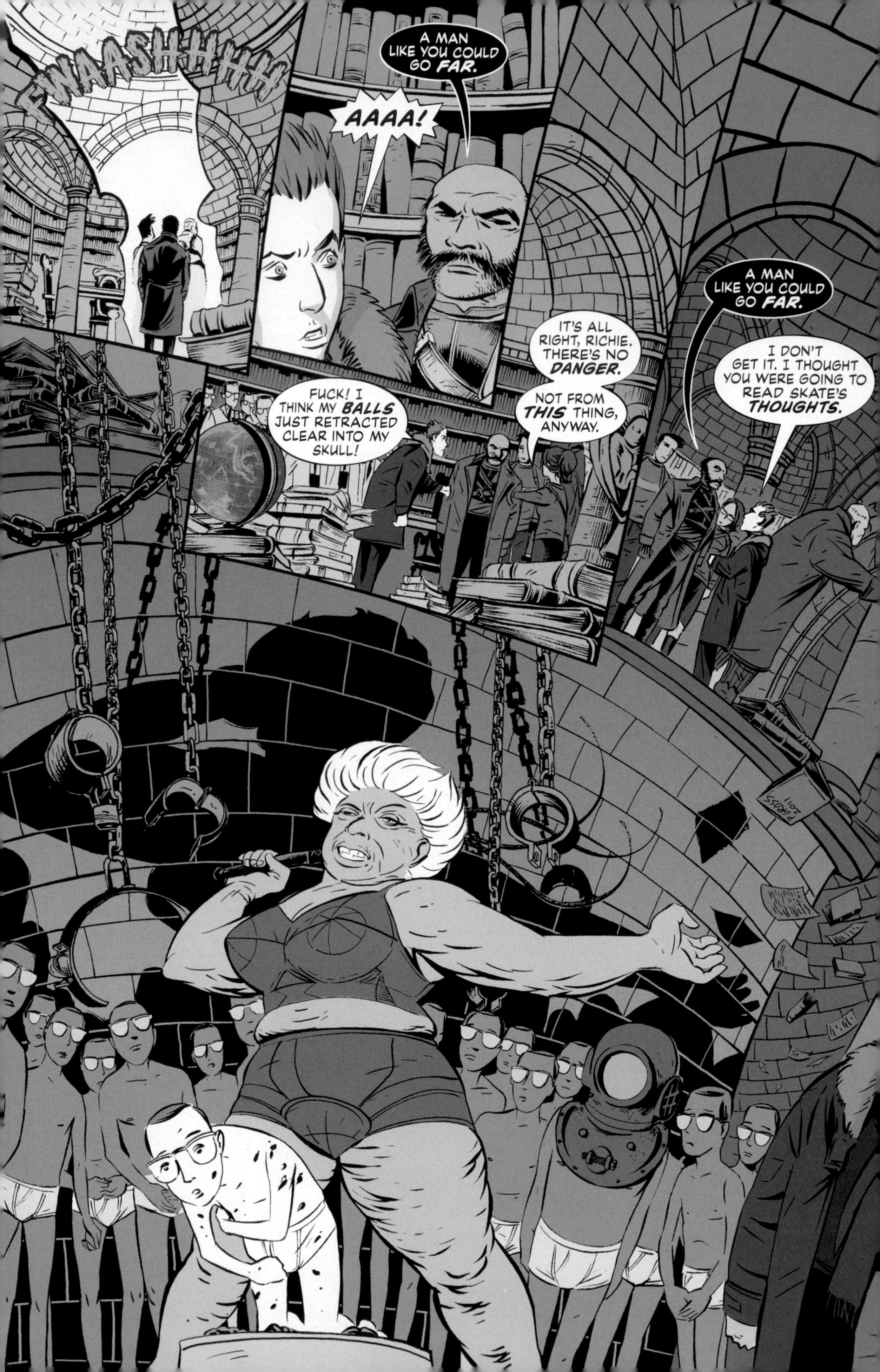
FWASHHHHH
A MAN LIKE YOU COULD GO FAR.
AAAA!
FUCK! I THINK MY BALLS JUST RETRACTED CLEAR INTO MY SKULL!
IT'S ALL RIGHT, RICHIE. THERE'S NO DANGER.
NOT FROM THIS THING, ANYWAY.
A MAN LIKE YOU COULD GO FAR.
I DON'T GET IT. I THOUGHT YOU WERE GOING TO READ SKATE'S THOUGHTS.
PAROSS 2011

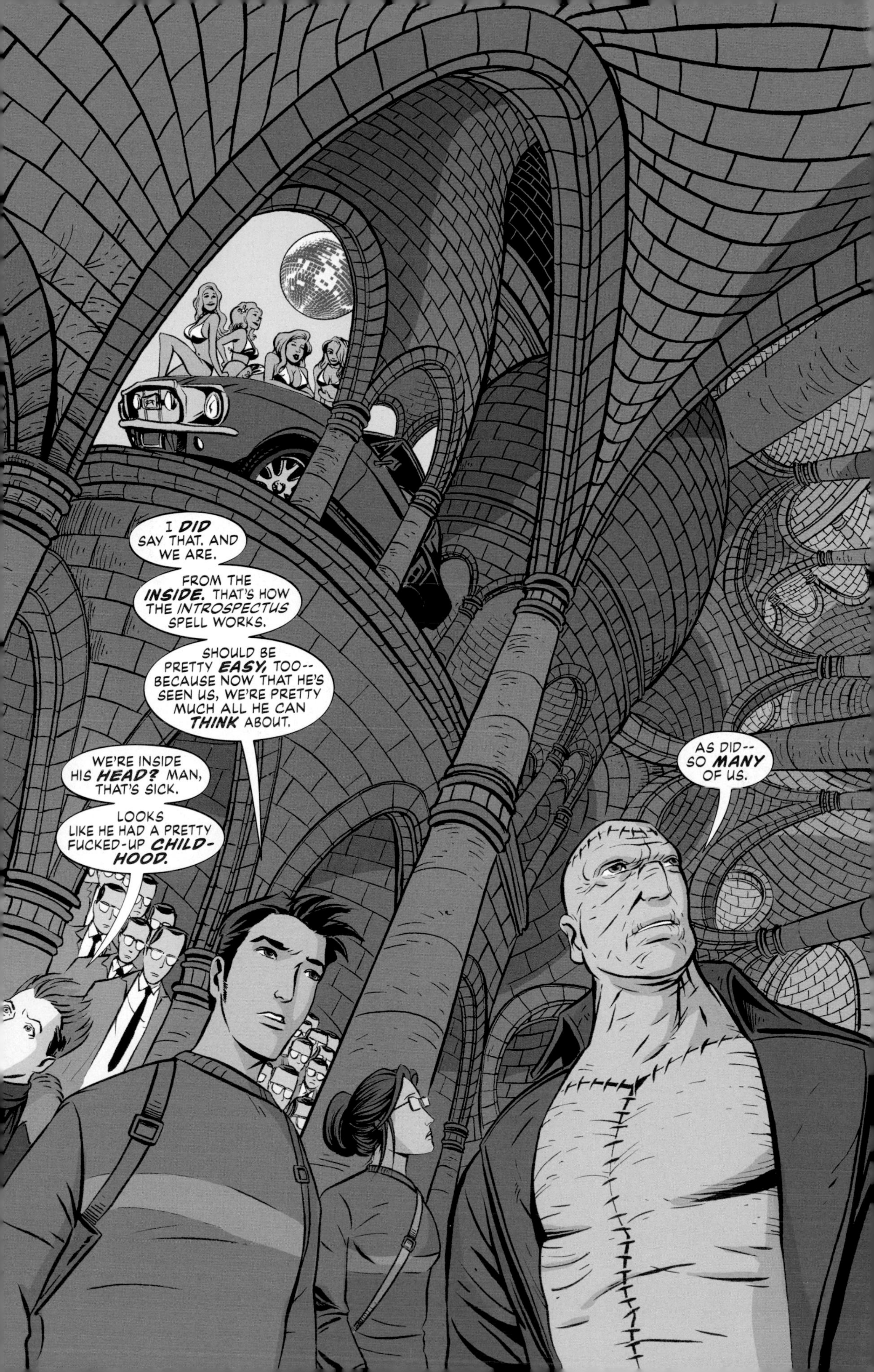
I DID SAY THAT. AND WE ARE.
FROM THE INSIDE. THAT'S HOW THE INTROSPECTUS SPELL WORKS.
SHOULD BE PRETTY EASY, TOO-- BECAUSE NOW THAT HE'S SEEN US, WE'RE PRETTY MUCH ALL HE CAN THINK ABOUT.
WE'RE INSIDE HIS HEAD? MAN, THAT'S SICK.
LOOKS LIKE HE HAD A PRETTY FUCKED-UP CHILD-HOOD.
AS DID-- SO MANY OF US.

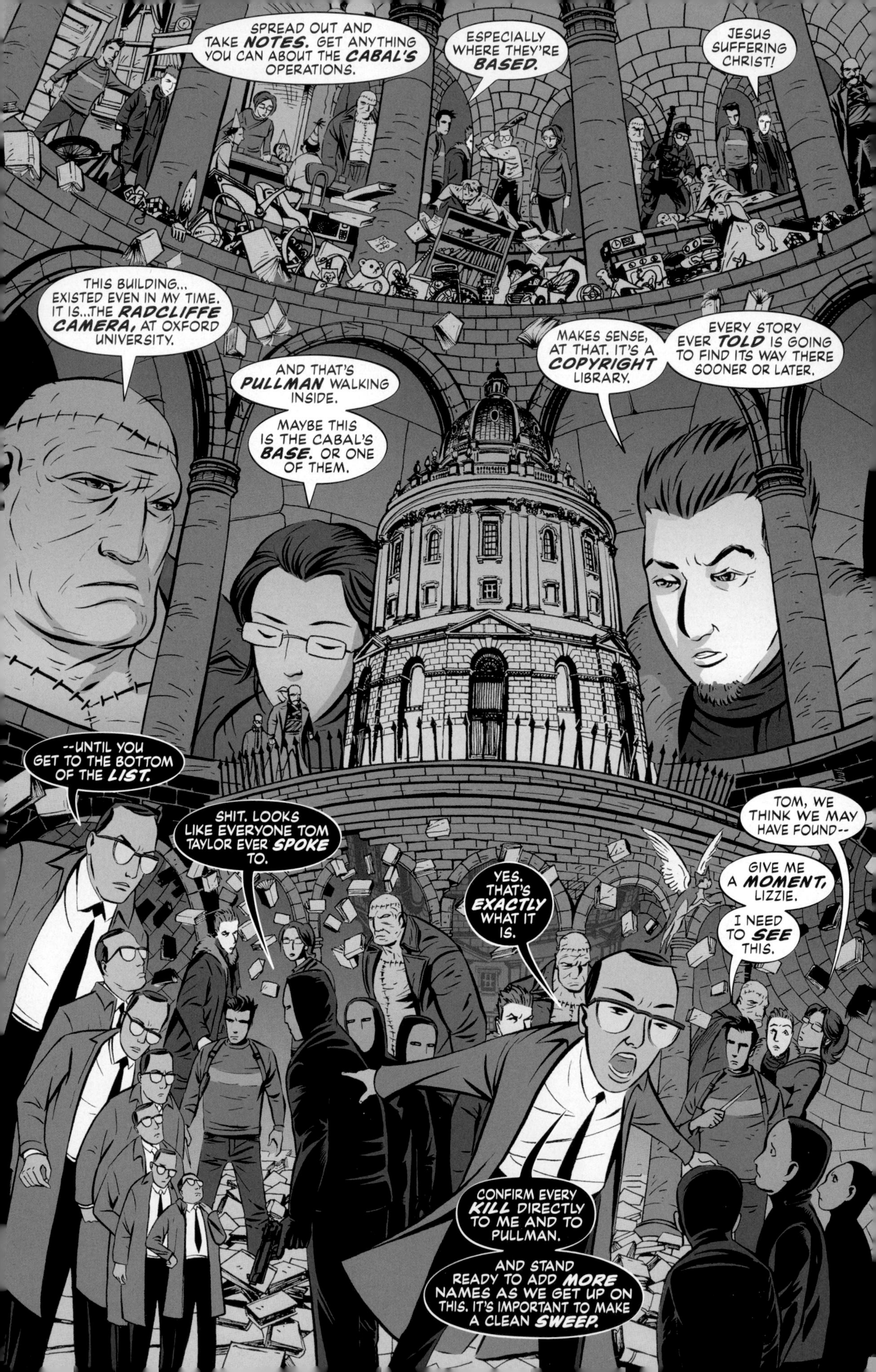
SPREAD OUT AND TAKE NOTES. GET ANYTHING YOU CAN ABOUT THE CABAL'S OPERATIONS.
ESPECIALLY WHERE THEY'RE BASED.
JESUS SUFFERING CHRIST!
THIS BUILDING... EXISTED EVEN IN MY TIME. IT IS...THE RADCLIFFE CAMERA, AT OXFORD UNIVERSITY.
AND THAT'S PULLMAN WALKING INSIDE.
MAYBE THIS IS THE CABAL'S BASE. OR ONE OF THEM.
MAKES SENSE, AT THAT. IT'S A COPYRIGHT LIBRARY.
EVERY STORY EVER TOLD IS GOING TO FIND ITS WAY THERE SOONER OR LATER.
--UNTIL YOU GET TO THE BOTTOM OF THE LIST.
SHIT. LOOKS LIKE EVERYONE TOM TAYLOR EVER SPOKE TO.
YES. THAT'S EXACTLY WHAT IT IS.
TOM, WE THINK WE MAY HAVE FOUND--
GIVE ME A MOMENT, LIZZIE.
I NEED TO SEE THIS.
CONFIRM EVERY KILL DIRECTLY TO ME AND TO PULLMAN.
AND STAND READY TO ADD MORE NAMES AS WE GET UP ON THIS. IT'S IMPORTANT TO MAKE A CLEAN SWEEP.

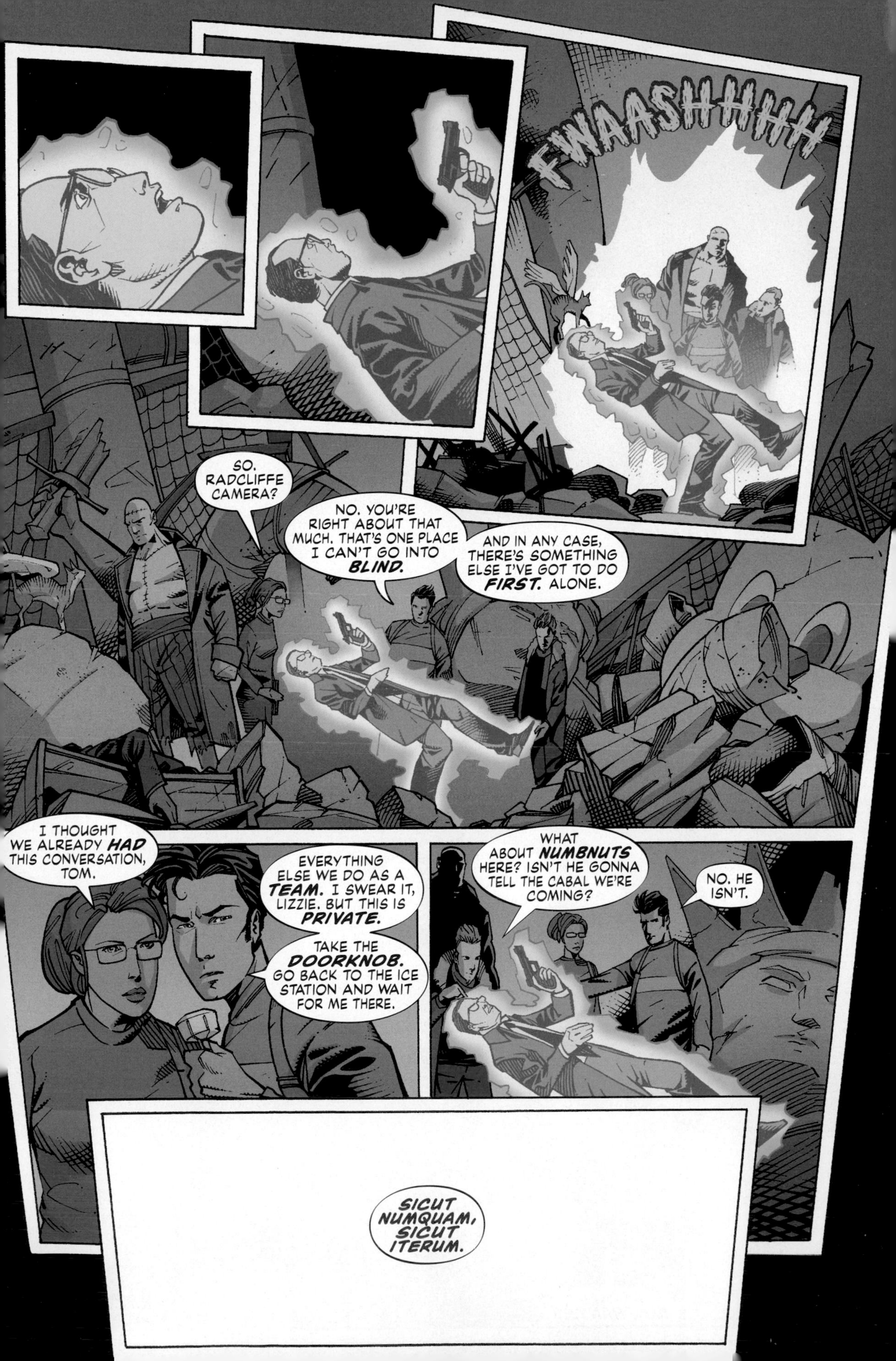
FWAASHHHH
SO. RADCLIFFE CAMERA?
NO. YOU'RE RIGHT ABOUT THAT MUCH. THAT'S ONE PLACE I CAN'T GO INTO BLIND.
AND IN ANY CASE, THERE'S SOMETHING ELSE I'VE GOT TO DO FIRST. ALONE.
I THOUGHT WE ALREADY HAD THIS CONVERSATION, TOM.
EVERYTHING ELSE WE DO AS A TEAM. I SWEAR IT, LIZZIE. BUT THIS IS PRIVATE.
TAKE THE DOORKNOB. GO BACK TO THE ICE STATION AND WAIT FOR ME THERE.
WHAT ABOUT NUMBNUTS HERE? ISN'T HE GONNA TELL THE CABAL WE'RE COMING?
NO. HE ISN'T.
SICUT NUMQUAM, SICUT ITERUM.

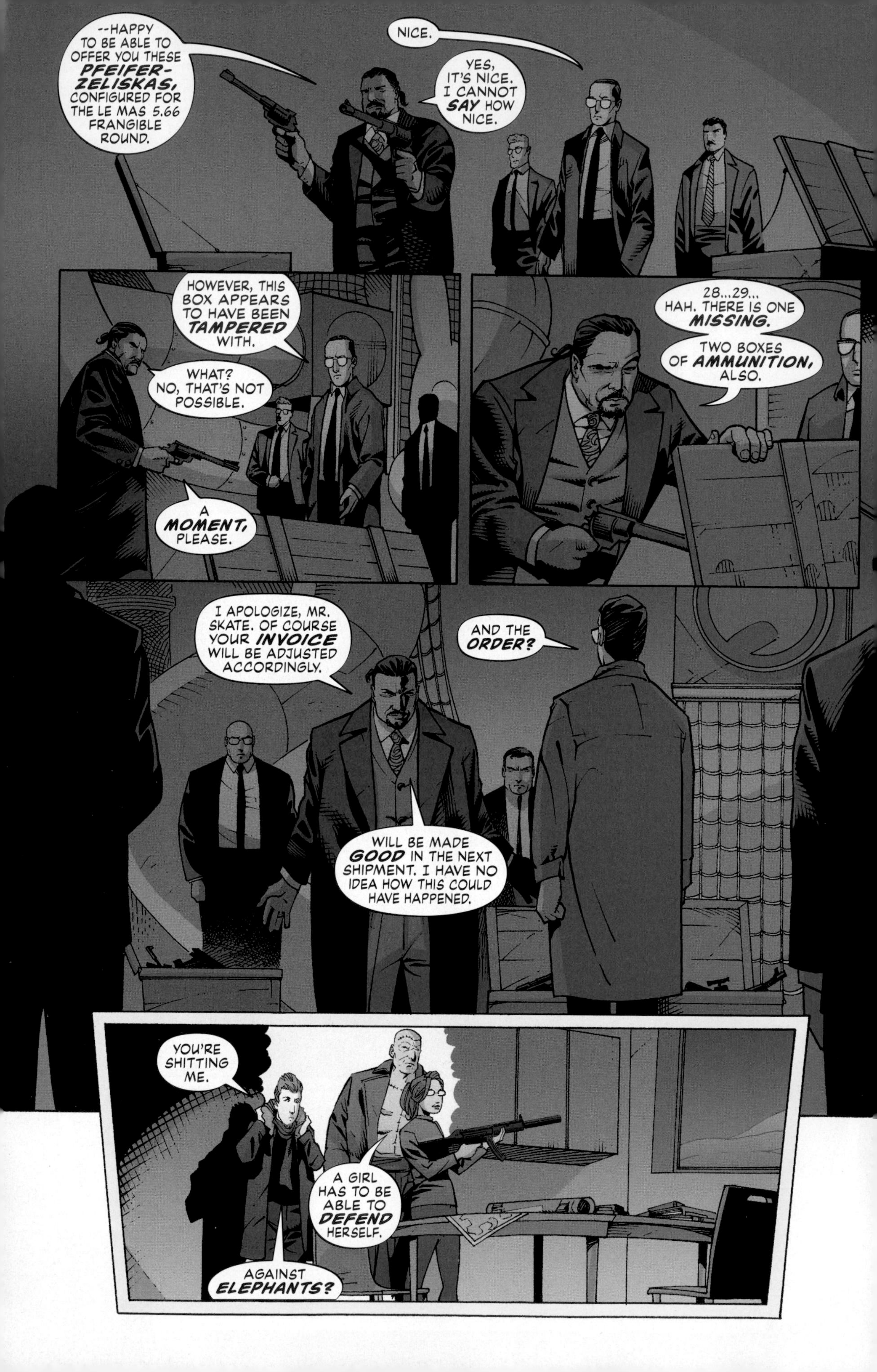
--HAPPY TO BE ABLE TO OFFER YOU THESE PFEIFER-ZELISKAS, CONFIGURED FOR THE LE MAS 5.66 FRANGIBLE ROUND.
NICE.
YES, IT'S NICE. I CANNOT SAY HOW NICE.
HOWEVER, THIS BOX APPEARS TO HAVE BEEN TAMPERED WITH.
WHAT? NO, THAT'S NOT POSSIBLE.
A MOMENT, PLEASE.
28...29... HAH. THERE IS ONE MISSING.
TWO BOXES OF AMMUNITION, ALSO.
I APOLOGIZE, MR. SKATE. OF COURSE YOUR INVOICE WILL BE ADJUSTED ACCORDINGLY.
AND THE ORDER?
WILL BE MADE GOOD IN THE NEXT SHIPMENT. I HAVE NO IDEA HOW THIS COULD HAVE HAPPENED.
YOU'RE SHITTING ME.
A GIRL HAS TO BE ABLE TO DEFEND HERSELF.
AGAINST ELEPHANTS?

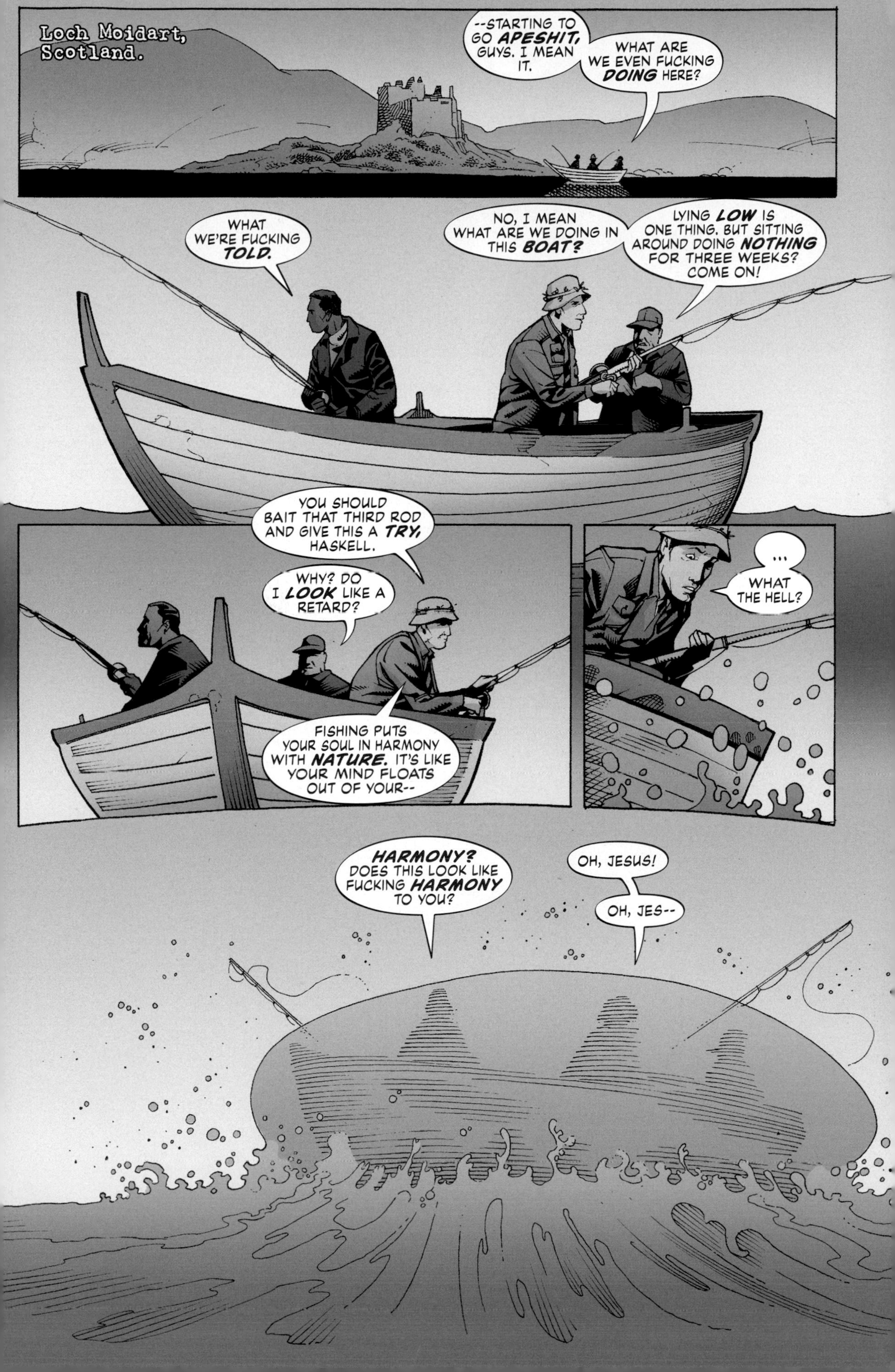
Loch Moidart, Scotland.
--STARTING TO GO APESHIT, GUYS. I MEAN IT.
WHAT ARE WE EVEN FUCKING DOING HERE?
WHAT WE'RE FUCKING TOLD.
NO, I MEAN WHAT ARE WE DOING IN THIS BOAT?
LYING LOW IS ONE THING. BUT SITTING AROUND DOING NOTHING FOR THREE WEEKS? COME ON!
YOU SHOULD BAIT THAT THIRD ROD AND GIVE THIS A TRY, HASKELL.
WHY? DO I LOOK LIKE A RETARD?
FISHING PUTS YOUR SOUL IN HARMONY WITH NATURE. IT'S LIKE YOUR MIND FLOATS OUT OF YOUR--
...
WHAT THE HELL?
HARMONY? DOES THIS LOOK LIKE FUCKING HARMONY TO YOU?
OH, JESUS!
OH, JES--

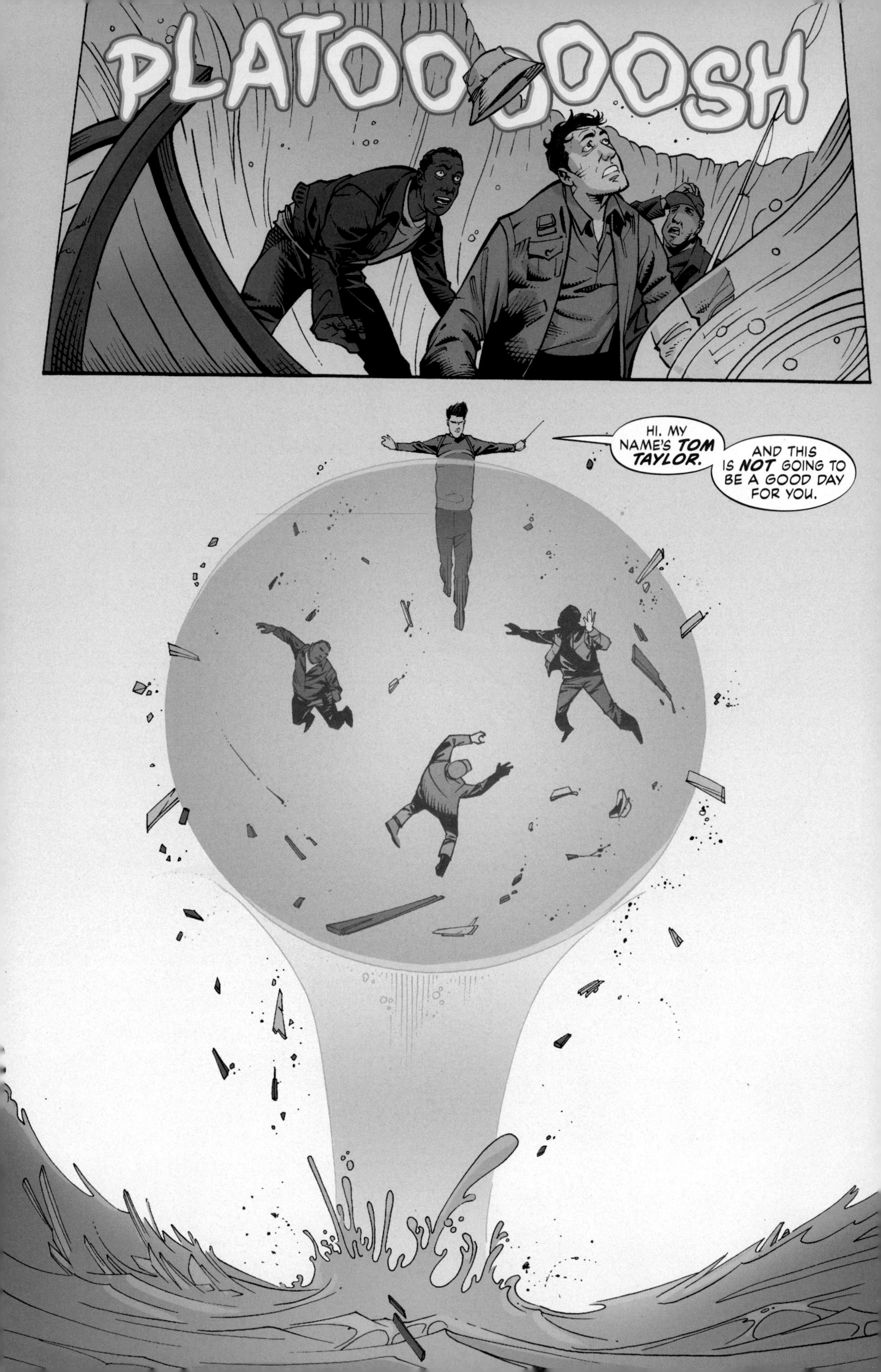
PLATOOOOOOSH
HI. MY NAME'S TOM TAYLOR.
AND THIS IS NOT GOING TO BE A GOOD DAY FOR YOU.

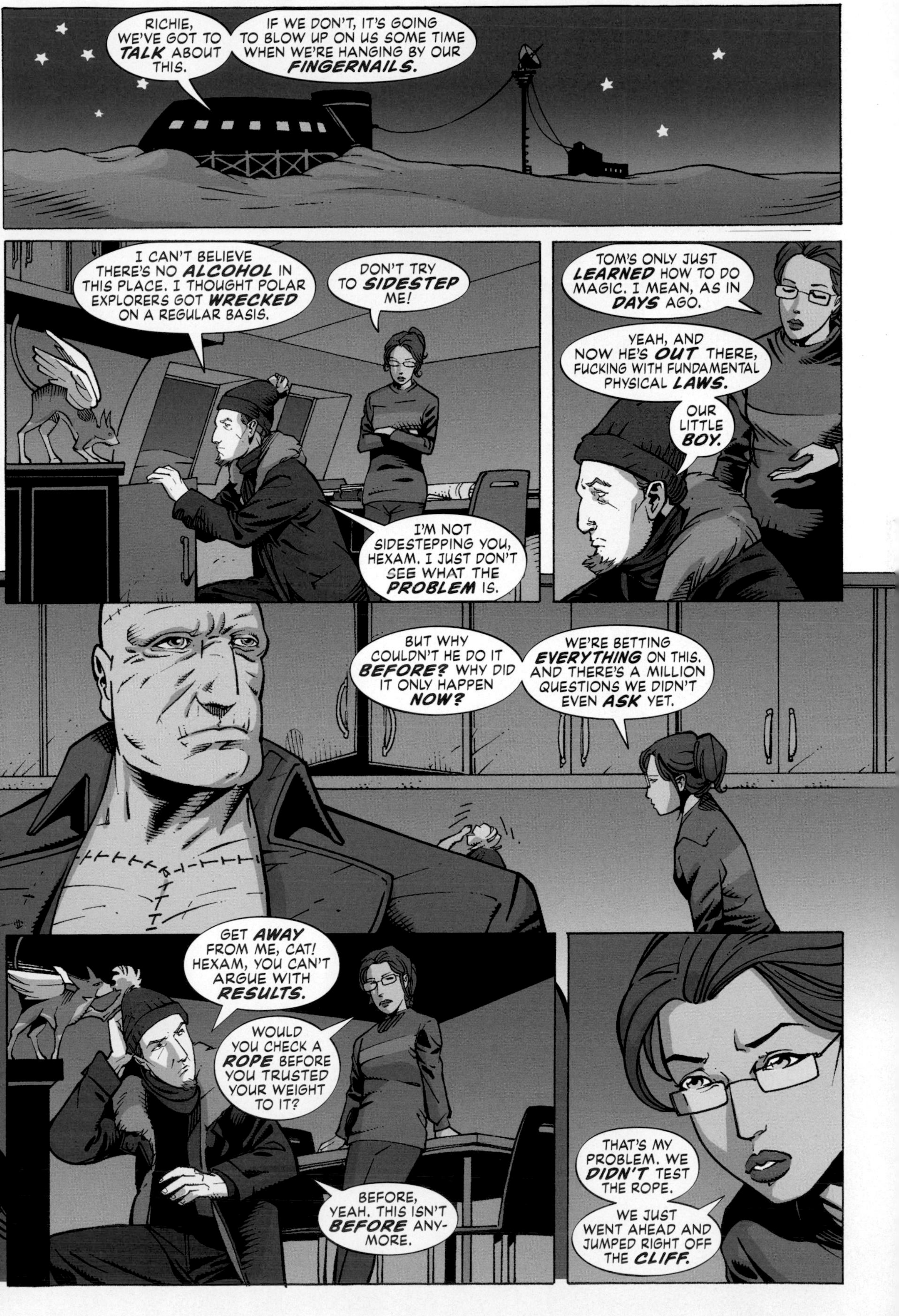
RICHIE, WE'VE GOT TO TALK ABOUT THIS.
IF WE DON'T, IT'S GOING TO BLOW UP ON US SOME TIME WHEN WE'RE HANGING BY OUR FINGERNAILS.
I CAN'T BELIEVE THERE'S NO ALCOHOL IN THIS PLACE. I THOUGHT POLAR EXPLORERS GOT WRECKED ON A REGULAR BASIS.
DON'T TRY TO SIDESTEP ME!
I'M NOT SIDESTEPPING YOU, HEXAM. I JUST DON'T SEE WHAT THE PROBLEM IS.
TOM'S ONLY JUST LEARNED HOW TO DO MAGIC. I MEAN, AS IN DAYS AGO.
YEAH, AND NOW HE'S OUT THERE, FUCKING WITH FUNDAMENTAL PHYSICAL LAWS.
OUR LITTLE BOY.
BUT WHY COULDN'T HE DO IT BEFORE? WHY DID IT ONLY HAPPEN NOW?
WE'RE BETTING EVERYTHING ON THIS. AND THERE'S A MILLION QUESTIONS WE DIDN'T EVEN ASK YET.
GET AWAY FROM ME, CAT! HEXAM, YOU CAN'T ARGUE WITH RESULTS.
WOULD YOU CHECK A ROPE BEFORE YOU TRUSTED YOUR WEIGHT TO IT?
BEFORE, YEAH. THIS ISN'T BEFORE ANY-MORE.
THAT'S MY PROBLEM. WE DIDN'T TEST THE ROPE.
WE JUST WENT AHEAD AND JUMPED RIGHT OFF THE CLIFF.

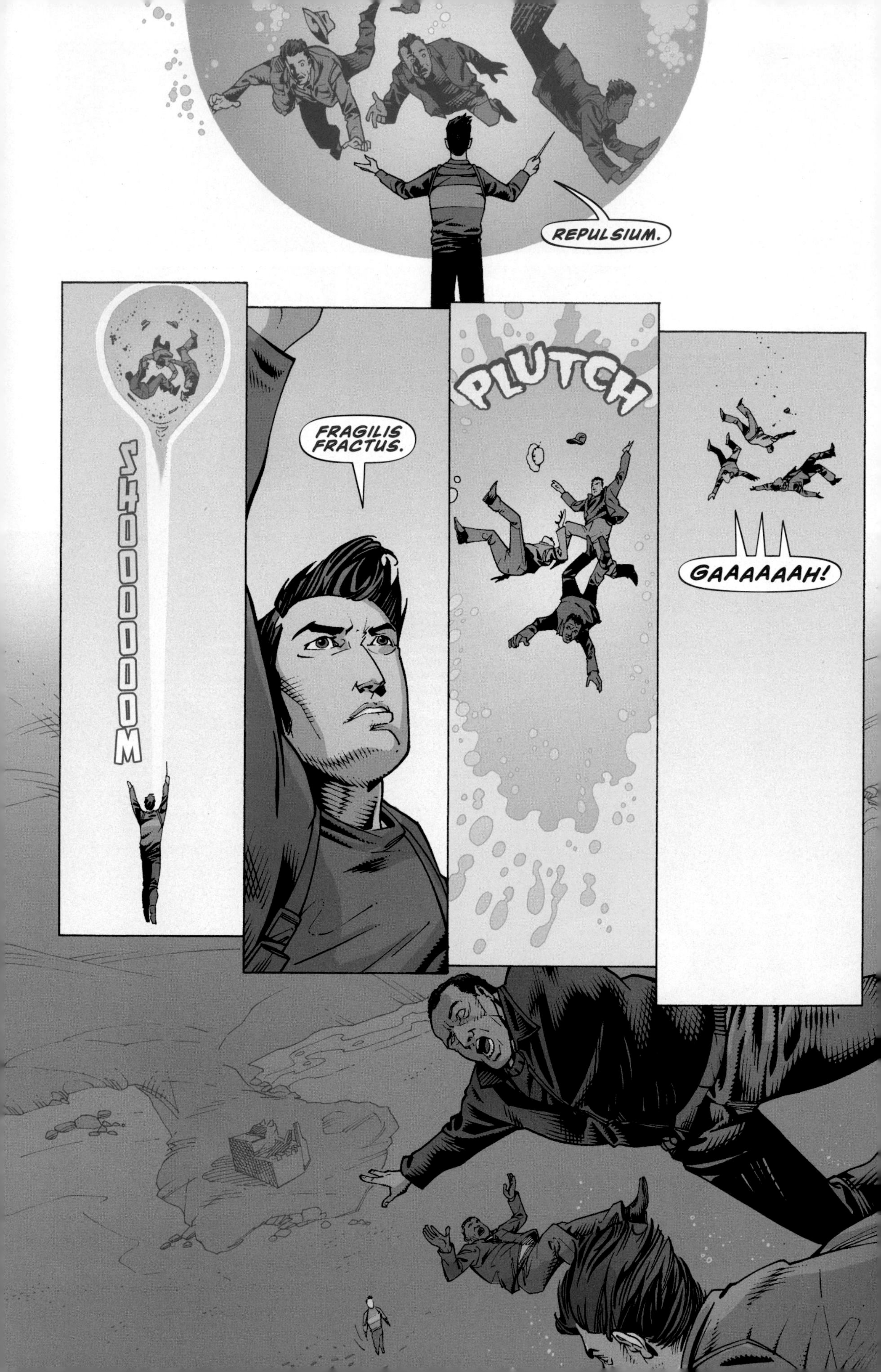
REPULSIUM.
SHOOOOOOOOM
FRAGILIS FRACTUS.
PLUTCH
GAAAAAAH!

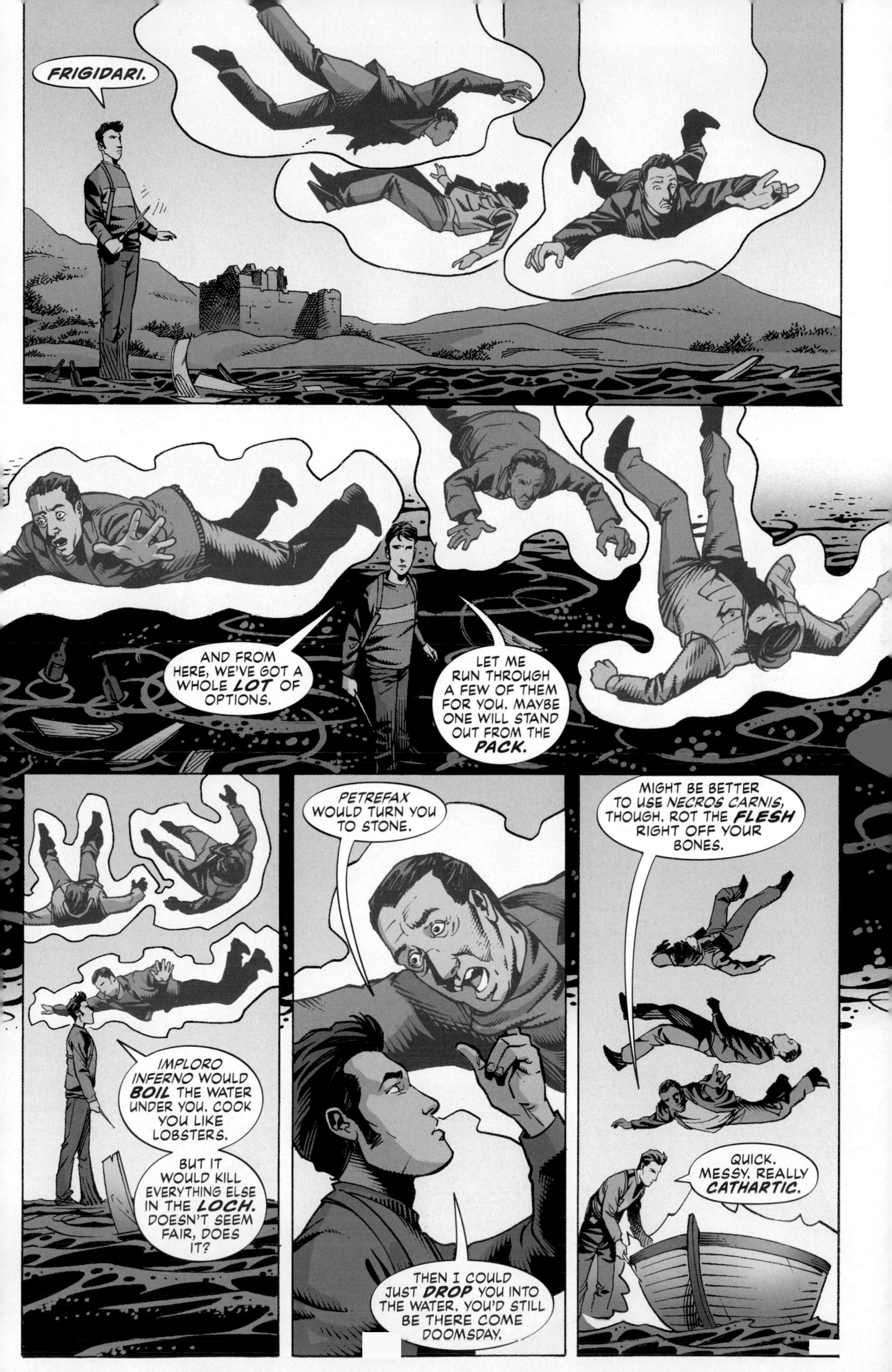
FRIGIDARI.
AND FROM HERE, WE'VE GOT A WHOLE LOT OF OPTIONS.
LET ME RUN THROUGH A FEW OF THEM FOR YOU. MAYBE ONE WILL STAND OUT FROM THE PACK.
IMPLORO INFERNO WOULD BOIL THE WATER UNDER YOU. COOK YOU LIKE LOBSTERS.
BUT IT WOULD KILL EVERYTHING ELSE IN THE LOCH. DOESN'T SEEM FAIR, DOES IT?
PETREFAX WOULD TURN YOU TO STONE.
THEN I COULD JUST DROP YOU INTO THE WATER. YOU'D STILL BE THERE COME DOOMSDAY.
MIGHT BE BETTER TO USE NECROS CARNIS, THOUGH. ROT THE FLESH RIGHT OFF YOUR BONES.
QUICK. MESSY. REALLY CATHARTIC.

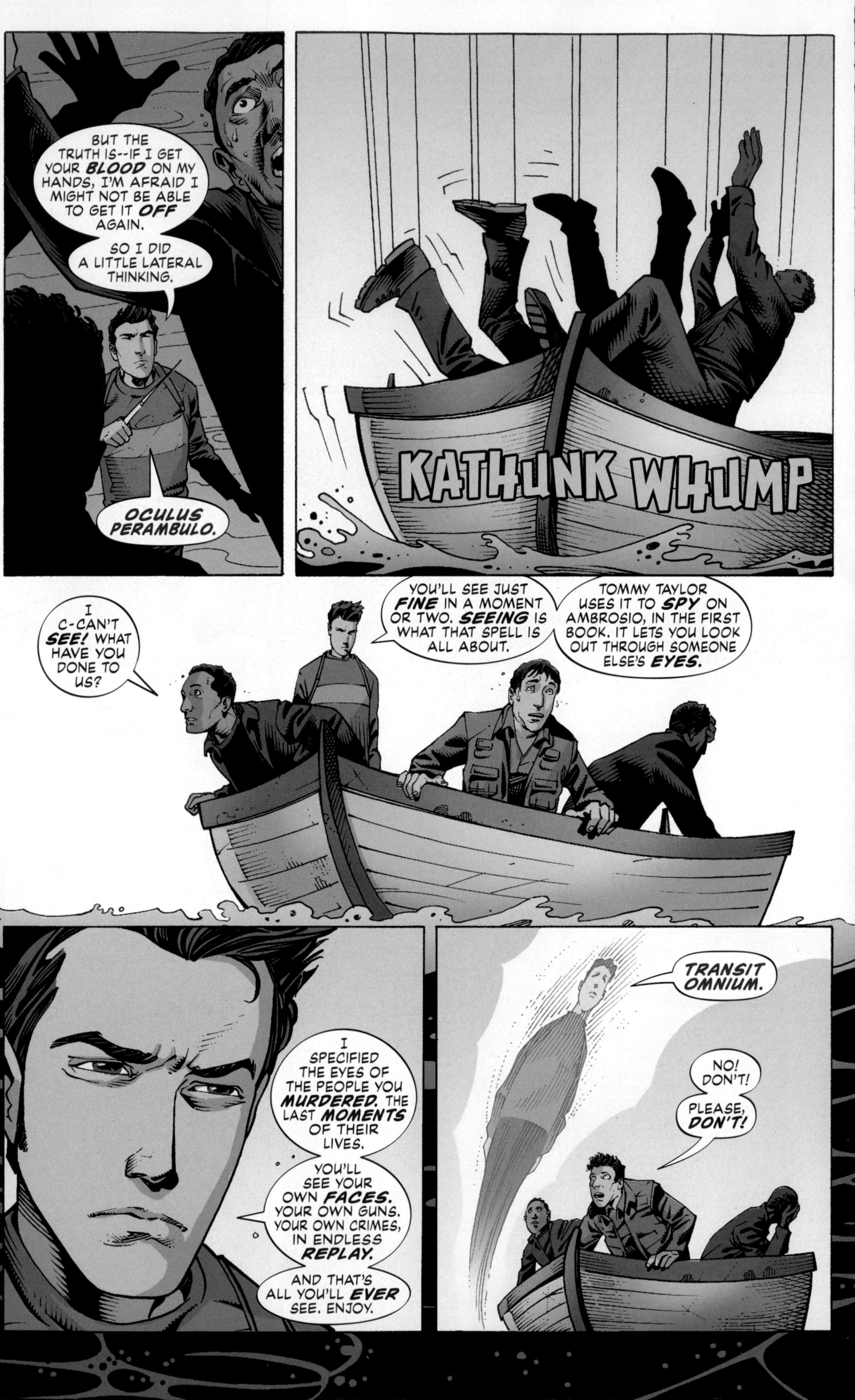
BUT THE TRUTH IS--IF I GET YOUR BLOOD ON MY HANDS, I'M AFRAID I MIGHT NOT BE ABLE TO GET IT OFF AGAIN.
SO I DID A LITTLE LATERAL THINKING.
OCULUS PERAMBULO.
KATHUNK WHUMP
I C-CAN'T SEE! WHAT HAVE YOU DONE TO US?
YOU'LL SEE JUST FINE IN A MOMENT OR TWO. SEEING IS WHAT THAT SPELL IS ALL ABOUT.
TOMMY TAYLOR USES IT TO SPY ON AMBROSIO, IN THE FIRST BOOK. IT LETS YOU LOOK OUT THROUGH SOMEONE ELSE'S EYES.
I SPECIFIED THE EYES OF THE PEOPLE YOU MURDERED. THE LAST MOMENTS OF THEIR LIVES.
YOU'LL SEE YOUR OWN FACES. YOUR OWN GUNS. YOUR OWN CRIMES, IN ENDLESS REPLAY.
AND THAT'S ALL YOU'LL EVER SEE. ENJOY.
TRANSIT OMNIUM.
NO! DON'T!
PLEASE, DON'T!

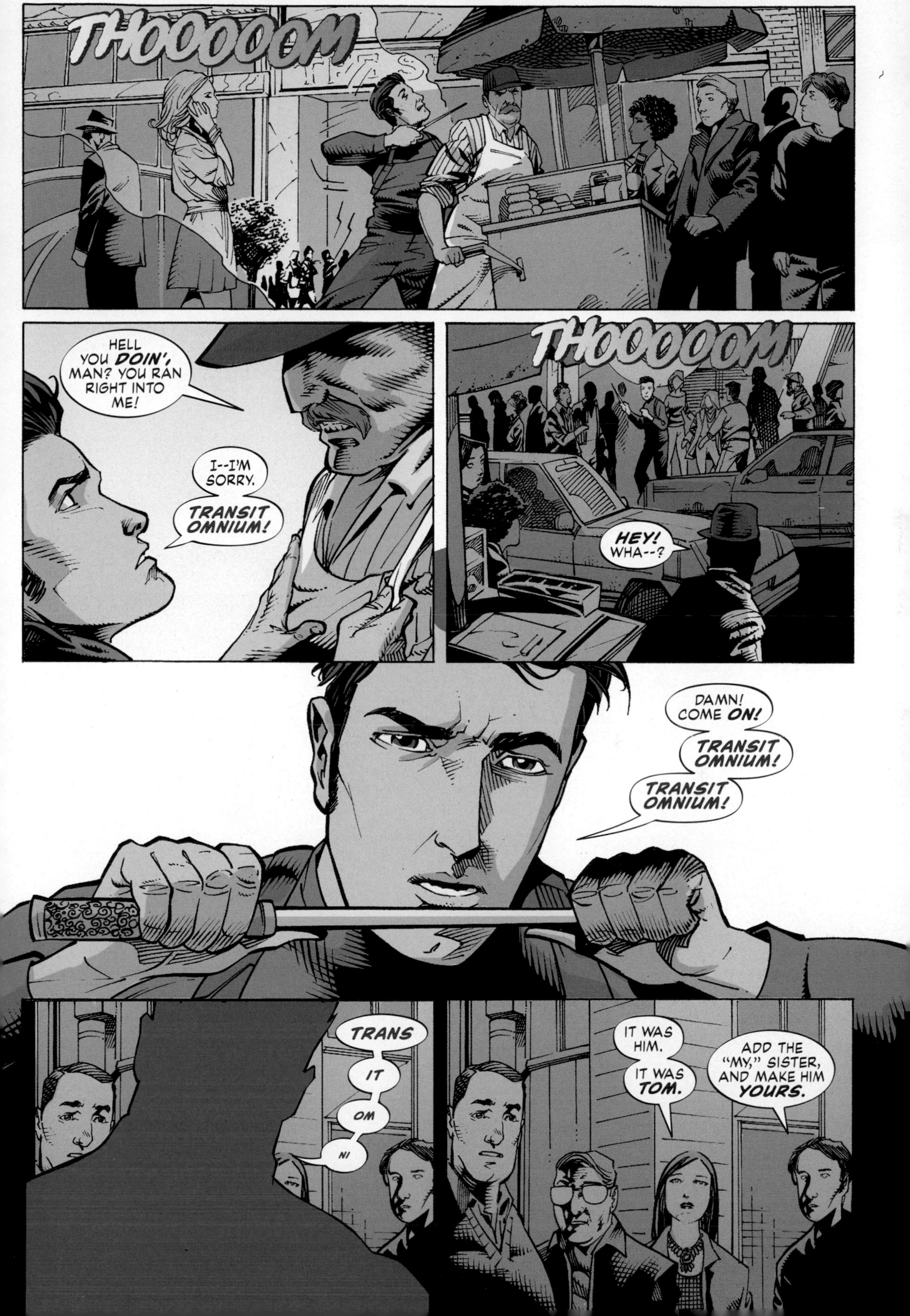
THOOOOOM
HELL YOU DOIN', MAN? YOU RAN RIGHT INTO ME!
I--I'M SORRY.
TRANSIT OMNIUM!
THOOOOOM
HEY! WHA--?
DAMN! COME ON!
TRANSIT OMNIUM!
TRANSIT OMNIUM!
TRANS
IT
OM
NI
IT WAS HIM.
IT WAS TOM.
ADD THE "MY," SISTER, AND MAKE HIM YOURS.

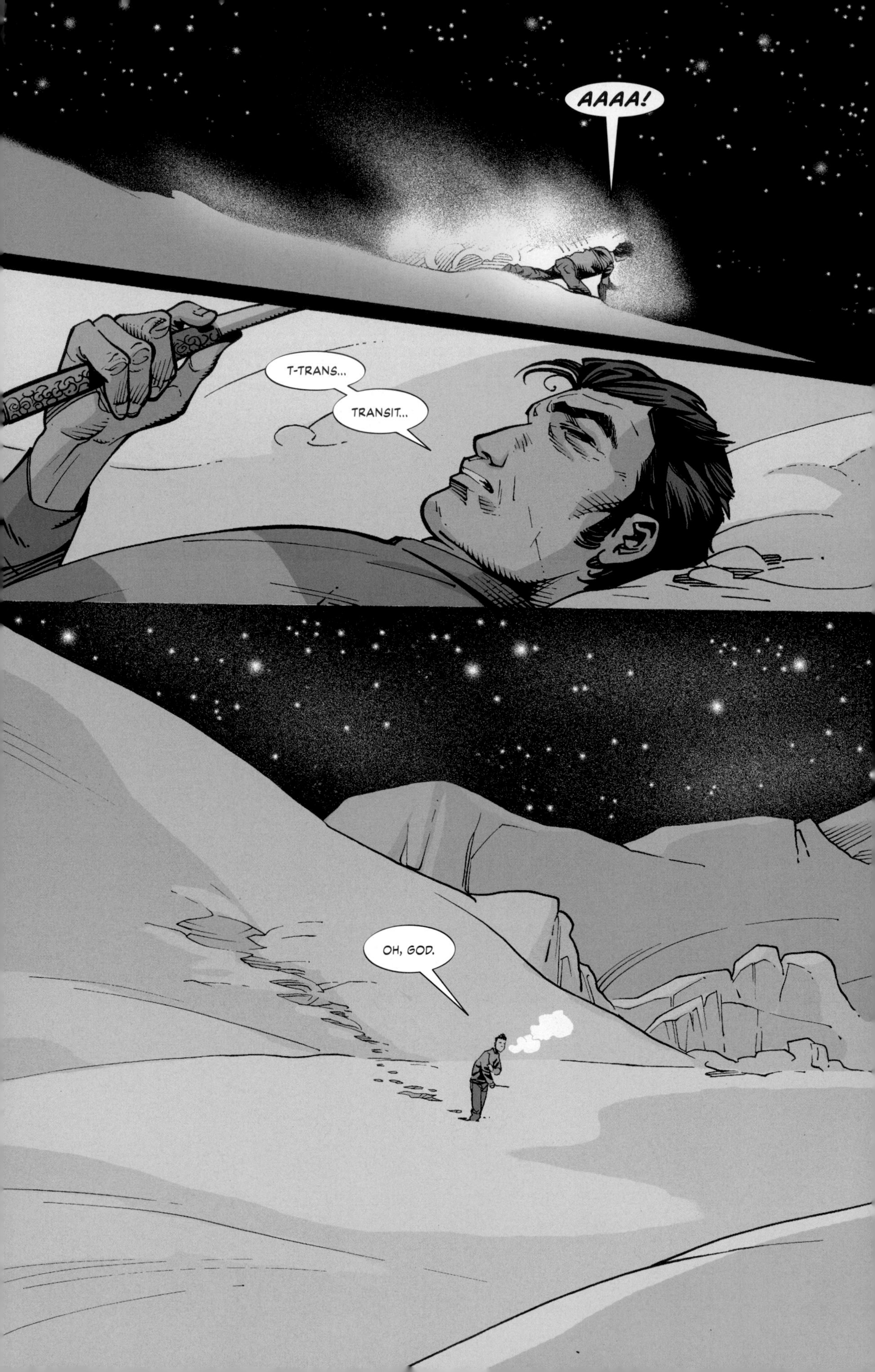
AAAA!
T-TRANS...
TRANSIT...
OH, GOD.

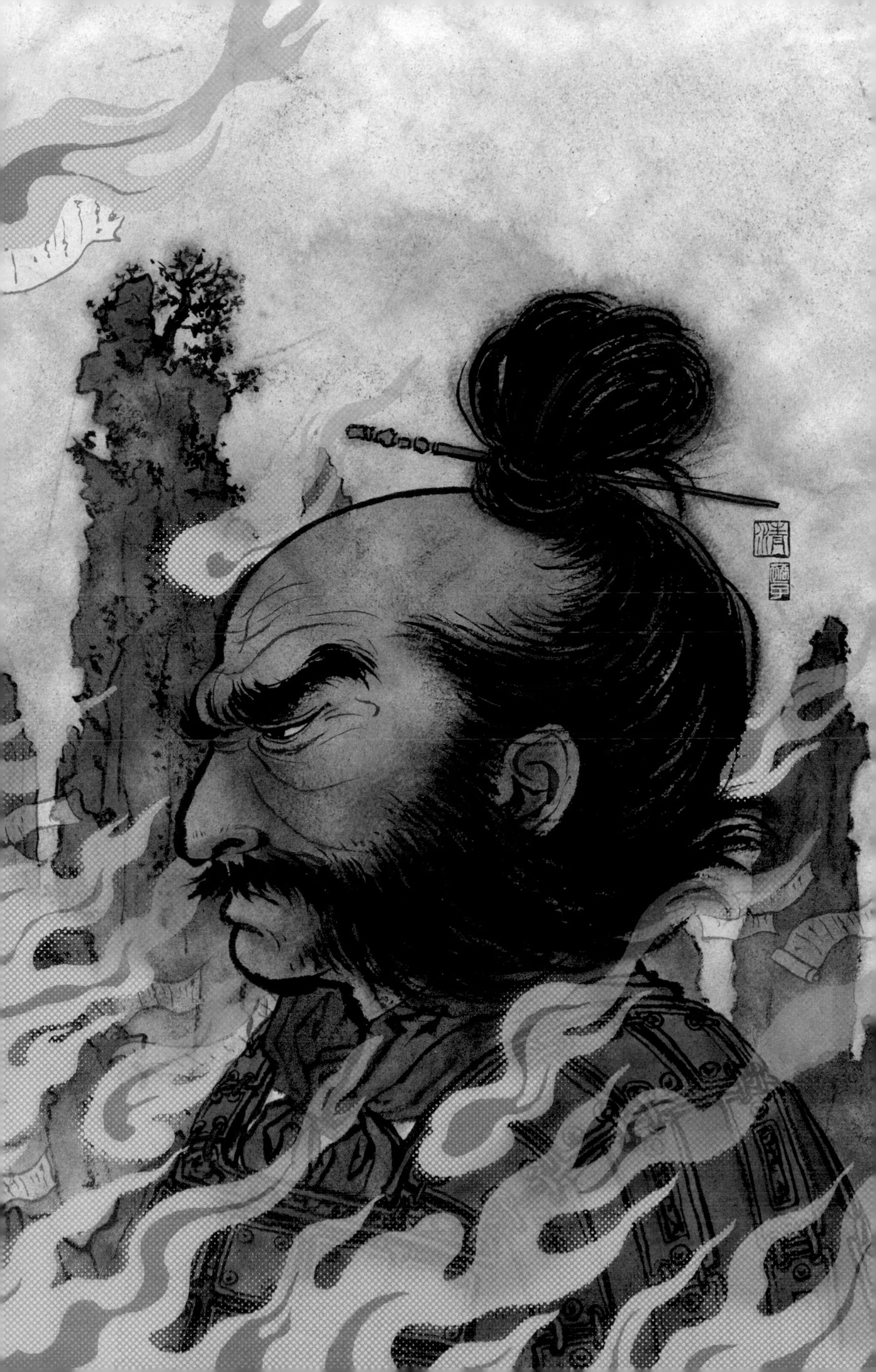

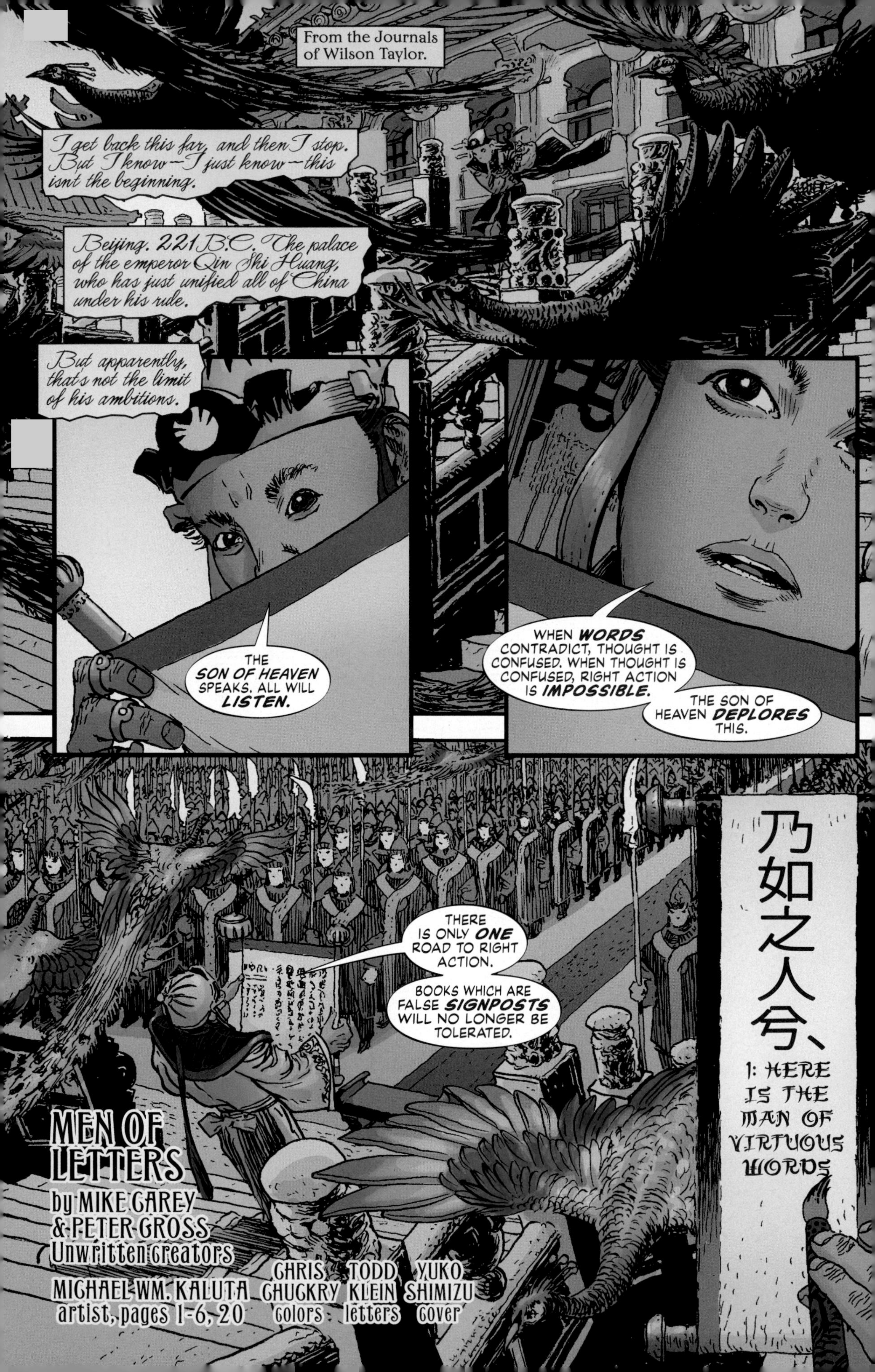
From the Journals of Wilson Taylor.
I get back this far, and then I stop. But I know--I just know--this isn't the beginning.
Beijing. 221 B.C. The palace of the emperor Qin Shi Huang, who has just unified all of China under his rule.
But apparently, that's not the limit of his ambitions.
THE SON OF HEAVEN SPEAKS. ALL WILL LISTEN.
WHEN WORDS CONTRADICT, THOUGHT IS CONFUSED. WHEN THOUGHT IS CONFUSED, RIGHT ACTION IS IMPOSSIBLE.
THE SON OF HEAVEN DEPLORES THIS.
THERE IS ONLY ONE ROAD TO RIGHT ACTION.
BOOKS WHICH ARE FALSE SIGNPOSTS WILL NO LONGER BE TOLERATED.
乃如之人兮、
1: HERE IS THE MAN OF VIRTUOUS WORDS
MEN OF LETTERS
by MIKE CAREY & PETER GROSS Unwritten creators
MICHAEL WM. KALUTA artist, pages 1-6, 20
CHRIS CHUCKRY colors
TODD KLEIN letters
YUKO SHIMIZU cover

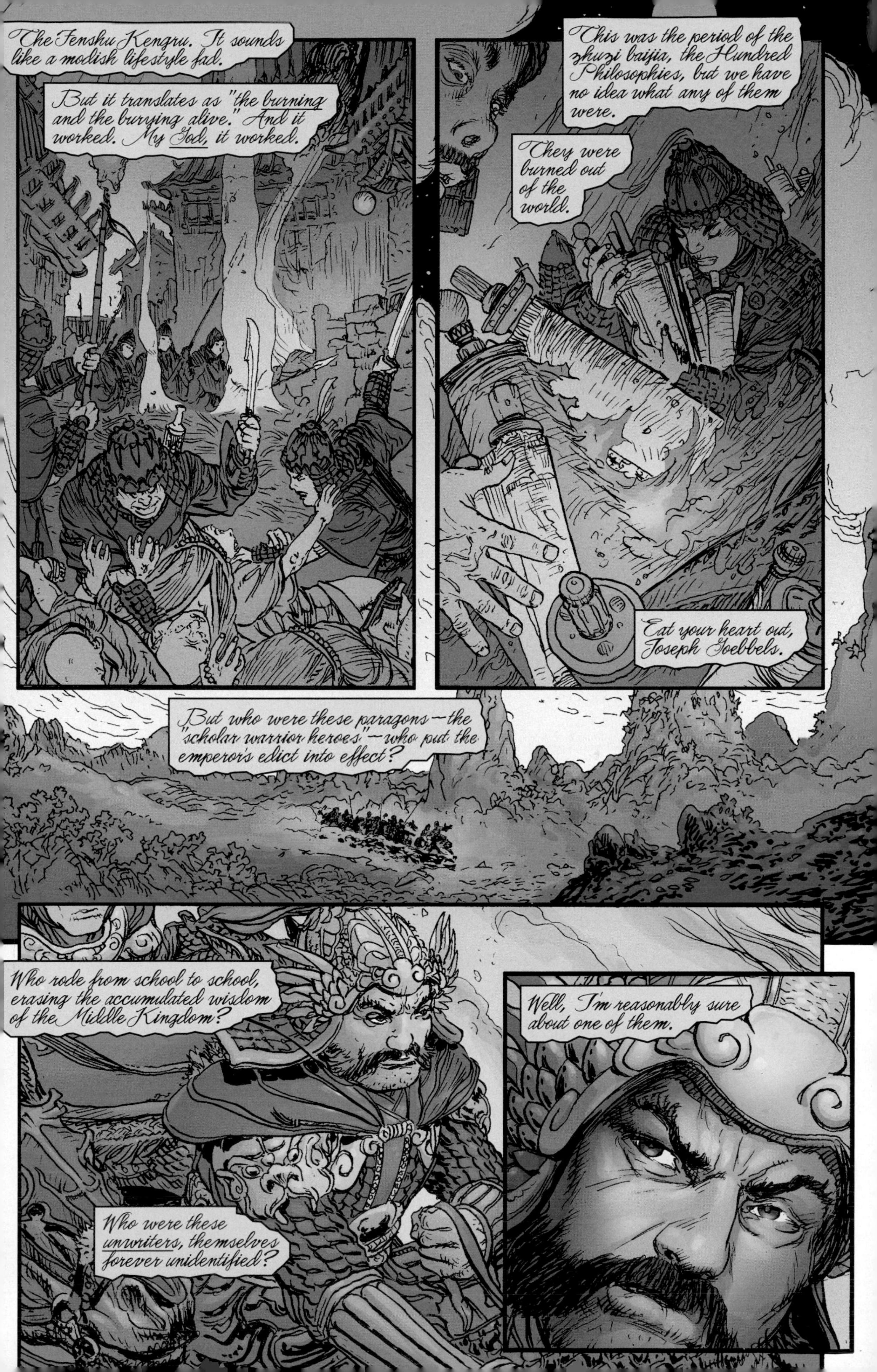
The Fenshu Kengru. It sounds like a modish lifestyle fad.
But it translates as "the burning and the burying alive." And it worked. My God, it worked.
This was the period of the zhuzi baijia, the Hundred Philosophies, but we have no idea what any of them were.
They were burned out of the world.
Eat your heart out, Joseph Goebbels.
But who were these paragons—the "scholar warrior heroes"—who put the emperor's edict into effect?
Who rode from school to school, erasing the accumulated wisdom of the Middle Kingdom?
Who were these unwriters, themselves forever unidentified?
Well, I'm reasonably sure about one of them.

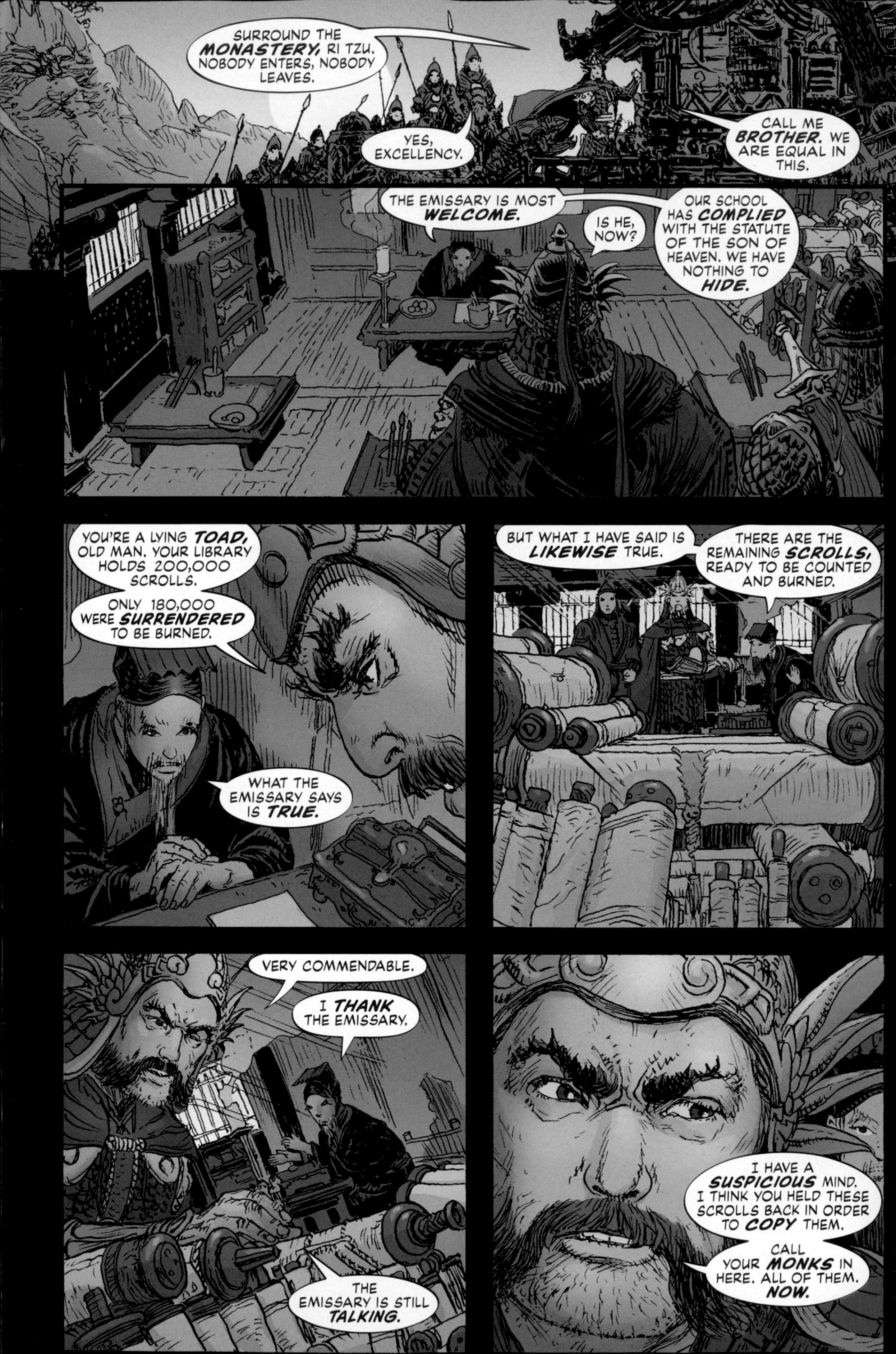
SURROUND THE MONASTERY, RI TZU. NOBODY ENTERS, NOBODY LEAVES.
YES, EXCELLENCY.
CALL ME BROTHER. WE ARE EQUAL IN THIS.
THE EMISSARY IS MOST WELCOME.
IS HE, NOW?
OUR SCHOOL HAS COMPLIED WITH THE STATUTE OF THE SON OF HEAVEN. WE HAVE NOTHING TO HIDE.
YOU'RE A LYING TOAD, OLD MAN. YOUR LIBRARY HOLDS 200,000 SCROLLS.
ONLY 180,000 WERE SURRENDERED TO BE BURNED.
WHAT THE EMISSARY SAYS IS TRUE.
BUT WHAT I HAVE SAID IS LIKEWISE TRUE.
THERE ARE THE REMAINING SCROLLS, READY TO BE COUNTED AND BURNED.
VERY COMMENDABLE.
I THANK THE EMISSARY.
THE EMISSARY IS STILL TALKING.
I HAVE A SUSPICIOUS MIND. I THINK YOU HELD THESE SCROLLS BACK IN ORDER TO COPY THEM.
CALL YOUR MONKS IN HERE. ALL OF THEM. NOW.

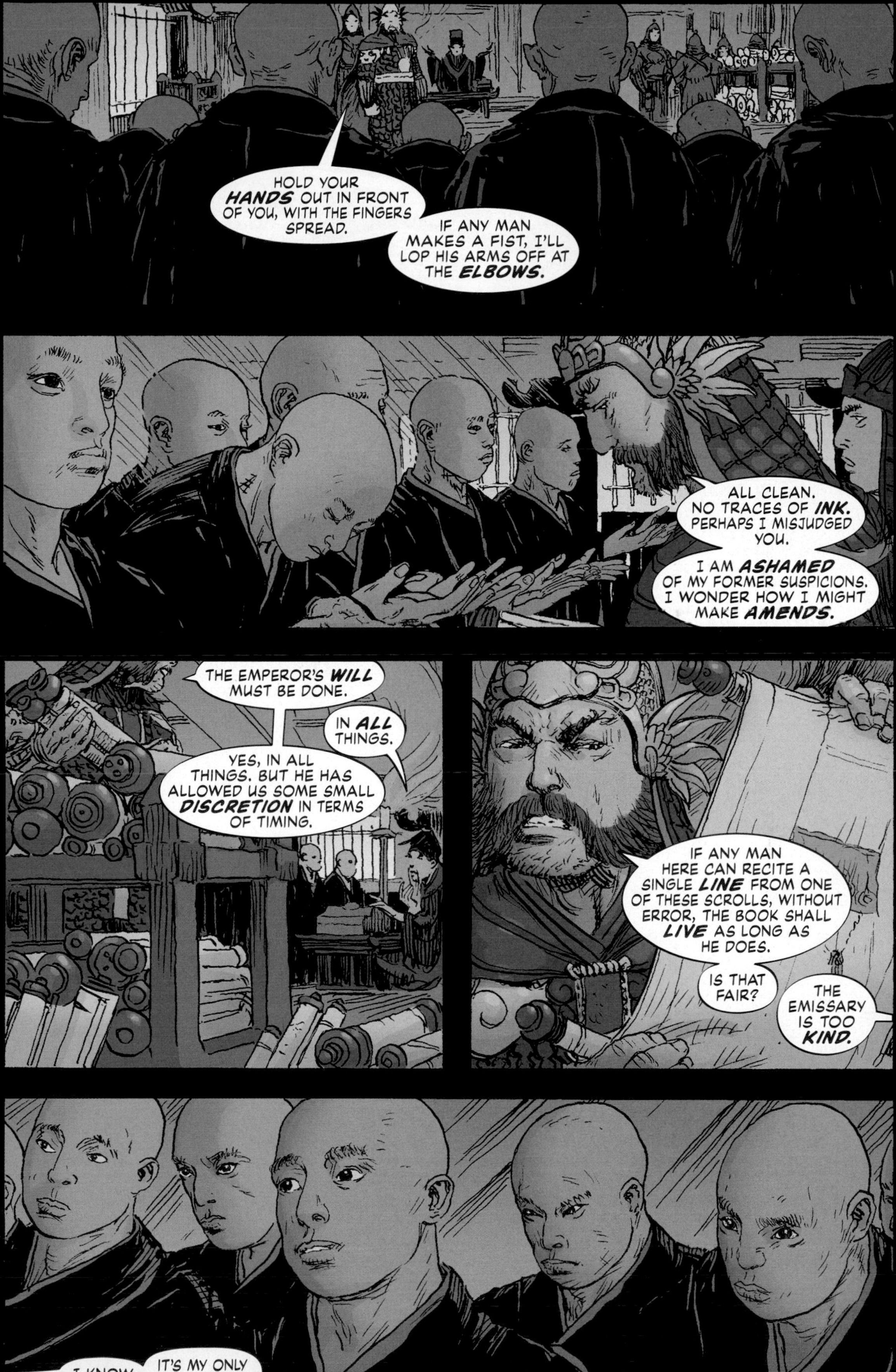
HOLD YOUR HANDS OUT IN FRONT OF YOU, WITH THE FINGERS SPREAD.
IF ANY MAN MAKES A FIST, I'LL LOP HIS ARMS OFF AT THE ELBOWS.
ALL CLEAN. NO TRACES OF INK. PERHAPS I MISJUDGED YOU.
I AM ASHAMED OF MY FORMER SUSPICIONS. I WONDER HOW I MIGHT MAKE AMENDS.
THE EMPEROR'S WILL MUST BE DONE.
IN ALL THINGS.
YES, IN ALL THINGS. BUT HE HAS ALLOWED US SOME SMALL DISCRETION IN TERMS OF TIMING.
IF ANY MAN HERE CAN RECITE A SINGLE LINE FROM ONE OF THESE SCROLLS, WITHOUT ERROR, THE BOOK SHALL LIVE AS LONG AS HE DOES.
IS THAT FAIR?
THE EMISSARY IS TOO KIND.
I KNOW.
IT'S MY ONLY FAILING.

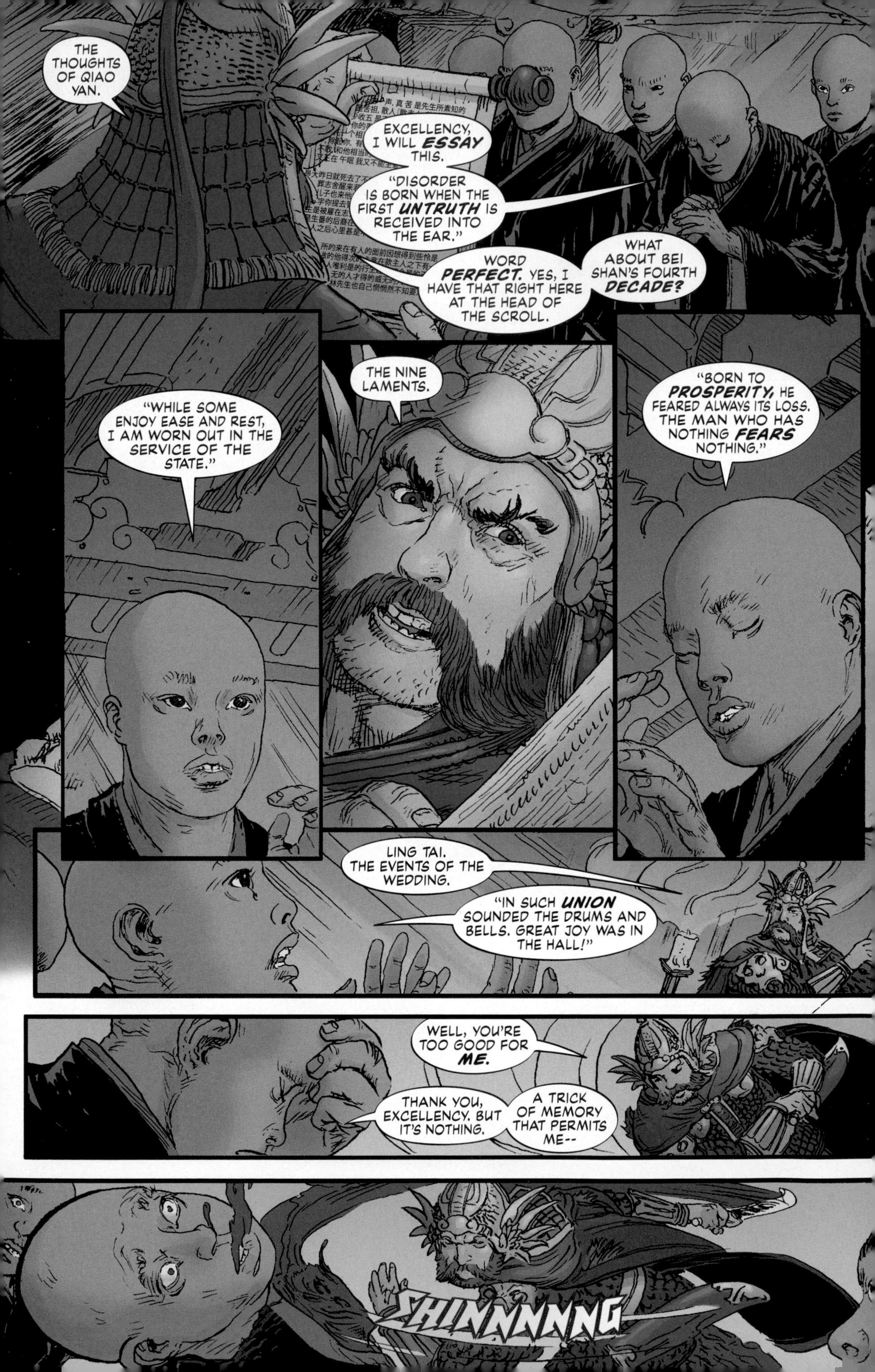
THE THOUGHTS OF QIAO YAN.
EXCELLENCY, I WILL ESSAY THIS.
"DISORDER IS BORN WHEN THE FIRST UNTRUTH IS RECEIVED INTO THE EAR."
WORD PERFECT. YES, I HAVE THAT RIGHT HERE AT THE HEAD OF THE SCROLL.
WHAT ABOUT BEI SHAN'S FOURTH DECADE?
"WHILE SOME ENJOY EASE AND REST, I AM WORN OUT IN THE SERVICE OF THE STATE."
THE NINE LAMENTS.
"BORN TO PROSPERITY, HE FEARED ALWAYS ITS LOSS. THE MAN WHO HAS NOTHING FEARS NOTHING."
LING TAI. THE EVENTS OF THE WEDDING.
"IN SUCH UNION SOUNDED THE DRUMS AND BELLS. GREAT JOY WAS IN THE HALL!"
WELL, YOU'RE TOO GOOD FOR ME.
THANK YOU, EXCELLENCY. BUT IT'S NOTHING.
A TRICK OF MEMORY THAT PERMITS ME--
SHINNNNNG

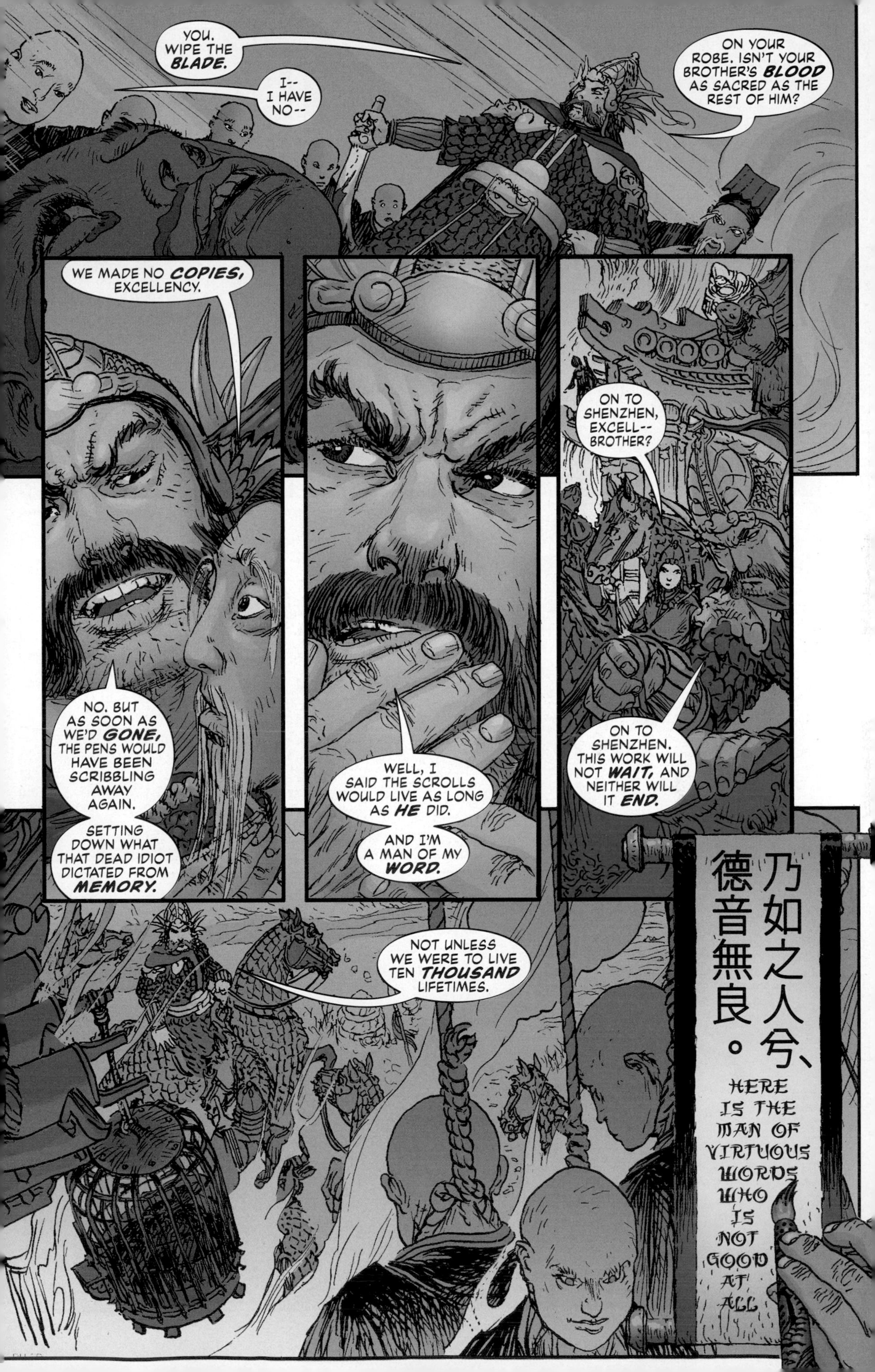
YOU. WIPE THE BLADE.
I-- I HAVE NO--
ON YOUR ROBE. ISN'T YOUR BROTHER'S BLOOD AS SACRED AS THE REST OF HIM?
WE MADE NO COPIES, EXCELLENCY.
NO. BUT AS SOON AS WE'D GONE, THE PENS WOULD HAVE BEEN SCRIBBLING AWAY AGAIN.
SETTING DOWN WHAT THAT DEAD IDIOT DICTATED FROM MEMORY.
WELL, I SAID THE SCROLLS WOULD LIVE AS LONG AS HE DID.
AND I'M A MAN OF MY WORD.
ON TO SHENZHEN, EXCELL-- BROTHER?
ON TO SHENZHEN. THIS WORK WILL NOT WAIT, AND NEITHER WILL IT END.
NOT UNLESS WE WERE TO LIVE TEN THOUSAND LIFETIMES.
乃如之人兮、德音無良。
HERE IS THE MAN OF VIRTUOUS WORDS WHO IS NOT GOOD AT ALL

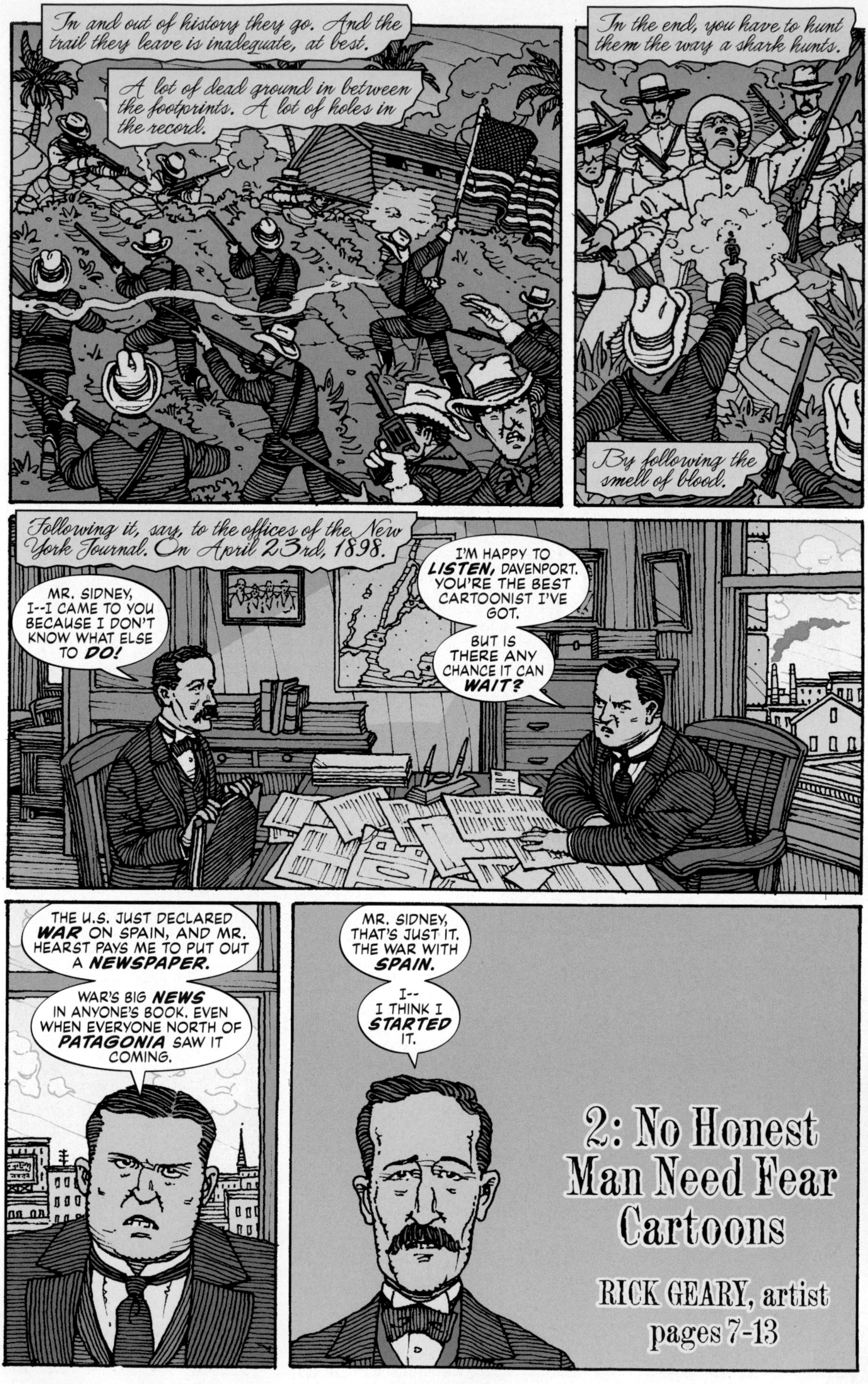
In and out of history they go. And the trail they leave is inadequate, at best.
A lot of dead ground in between the footprints. A lot of holes in the record.
In the end, you have to hunt them the way a shark hunts.
By following the smell of blood.
Following it, say, to the offices of the New York Journal. On April 23rd, 1898.
MR. SIDNEY, I--I CAME TO YOU BECAUSE I DON'T KNOW WHAT ELSE TO DO!
I'M HAPPY TO LISTEN, DAVENPORT. YOU'RE THE BEST CARTOONIST I'VE GOT.
BUT IS THERE ANY CHANCE IT CAN WAIT?
THE U.S. JUST DECLARED WAR ON SPAIN, AND MR. HEARST PAYS ME TO PUT OUT A NEWSPAPER.
WAR'S BIG NEWS IN ANYONE'S BOOK. EVEN WHEN EVERYONE NORTH OF PATAGONIA SAW IT COMING.
MR. SIDNEY, THAT'S JUST IT. THE WAR WITH SPAIN.
I-- I THINK I STARTED IT.
2: No Honest Man Need Fear Cartoons
RICK GEARY, artist
pages 7-13

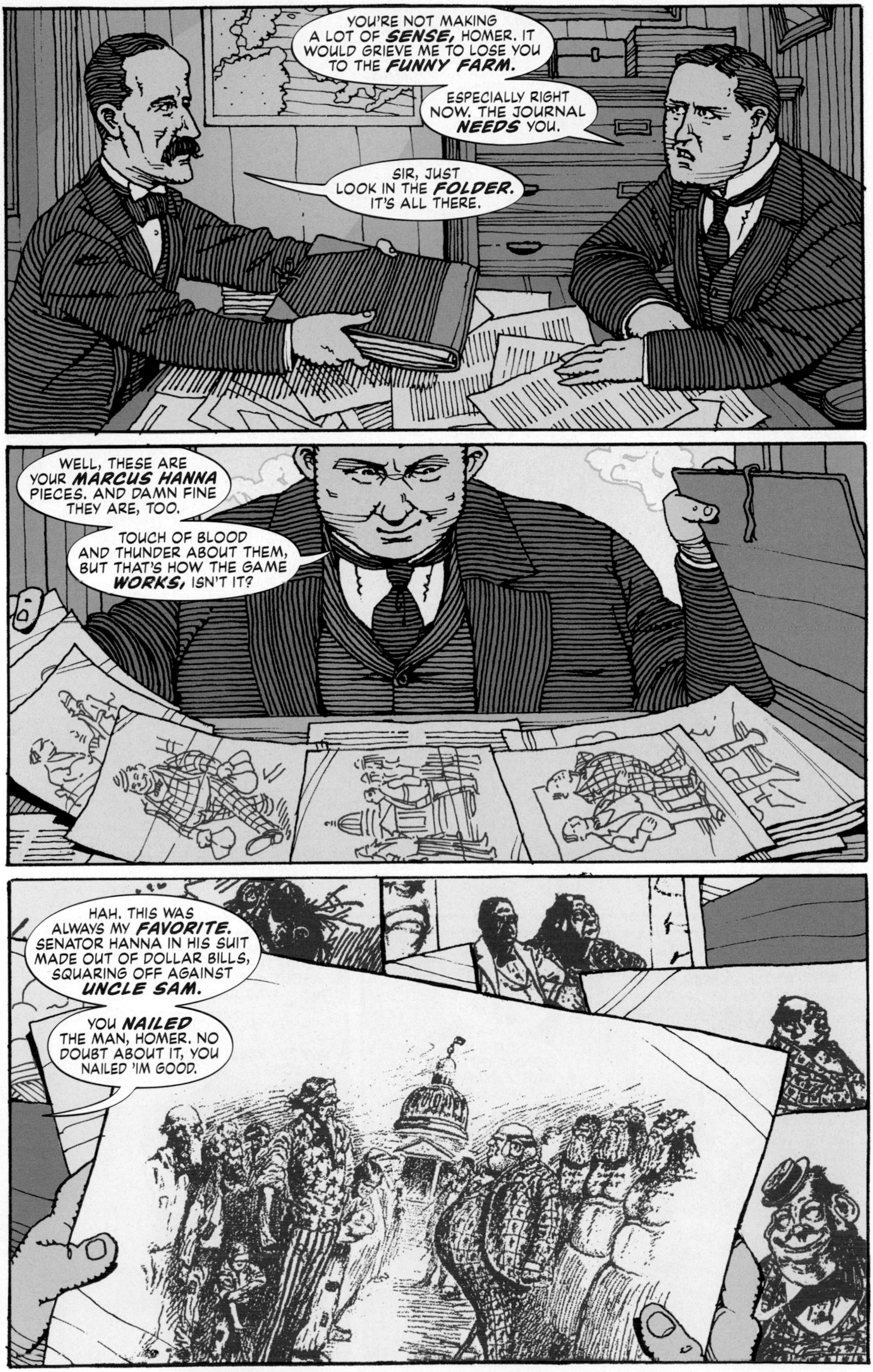
YOU'RE NOT MAKING A LOT OF SENSE, HOMER. IT WOULD GRIEVE ME TO LOSE YOU TO THE FUNNY FARM.
ESPECIALLY RIGHT NOW. THE JOURNAL NEEDS YOU.
SIR, JUST LOOK IN THE FOLDER. IT'S ALL THERE.
WELL, THESE ARE YOUR MARCUS HANNA PIECES. AND DAMN FINE THEY ARE, TOO.
TOUCH OF BLOOD AND THUNDER ABOUT THEM, BUT THAT'S HOW THE GAME WORKS, ISN'T IT?
HAH. THIS WAS ALWAYS MY FAVORITE. SENATOR HANNA IN HIS SUIT MADE OUT OF DOLLAR BILLS, SQUARING OFF AGAINST UNCLE SAM.
YOU NAILED THE MAN, HOMER. NO DOUBT ABOUT IT, YOU NAILED 'IM GOOD.

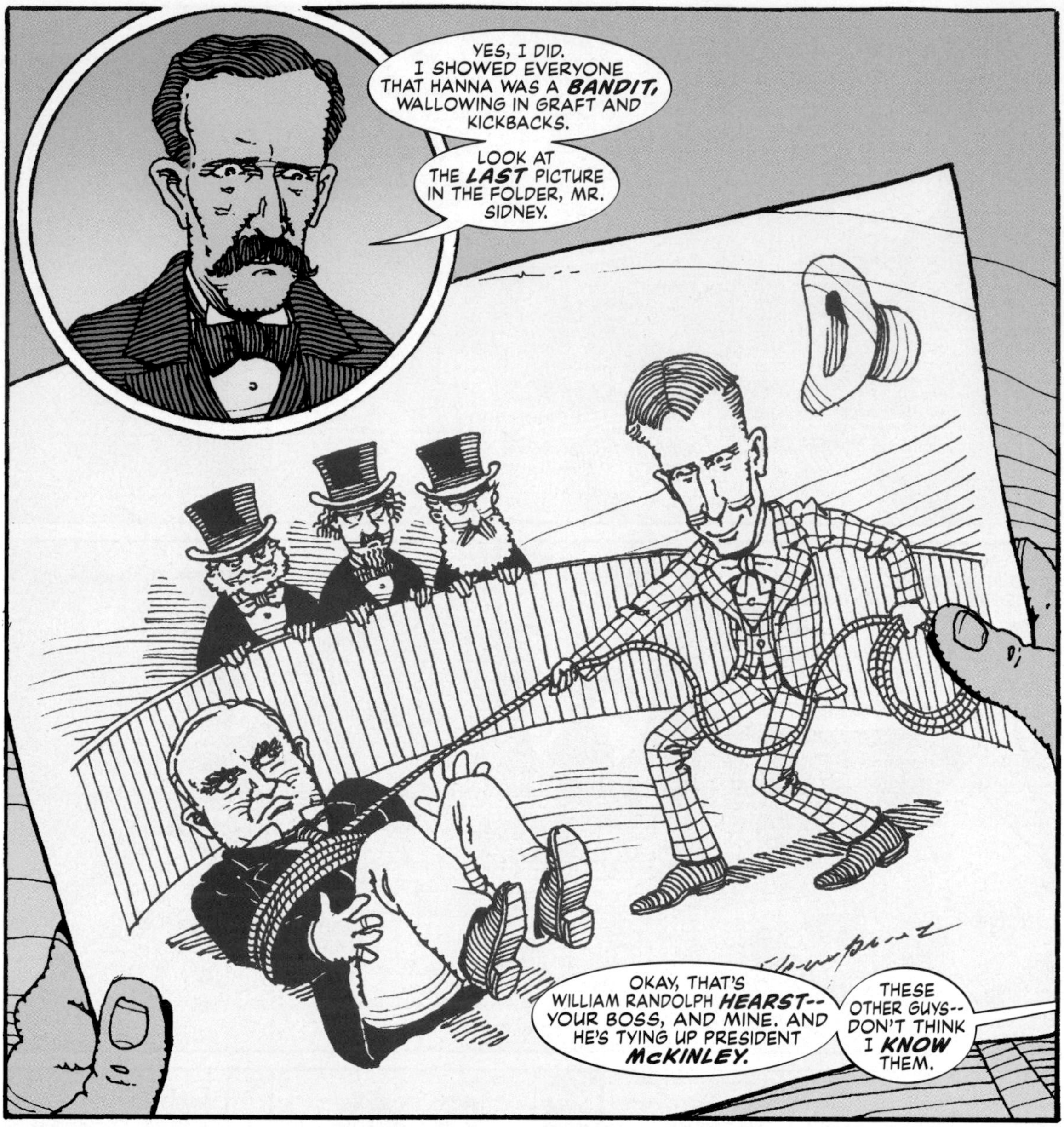
YES, I DID. I SHOWED EVERYONE THAT HANNA WAS A BANDIT, WALLOWING IN GRAFT AND KICKBACKS.
LOOK AT THE LAST PICTURE IN THE FOLDER, MR. SIDNEY.
OKAY, THAT'S WILLIAM RANDOLPH HEARST-- YOUR BOSS, AND MINE. AND HE'S TYING UP PRESIDENT McKINLEY.
THESE OTHER GUYS-- DON'T THINK I KNOW THEM.

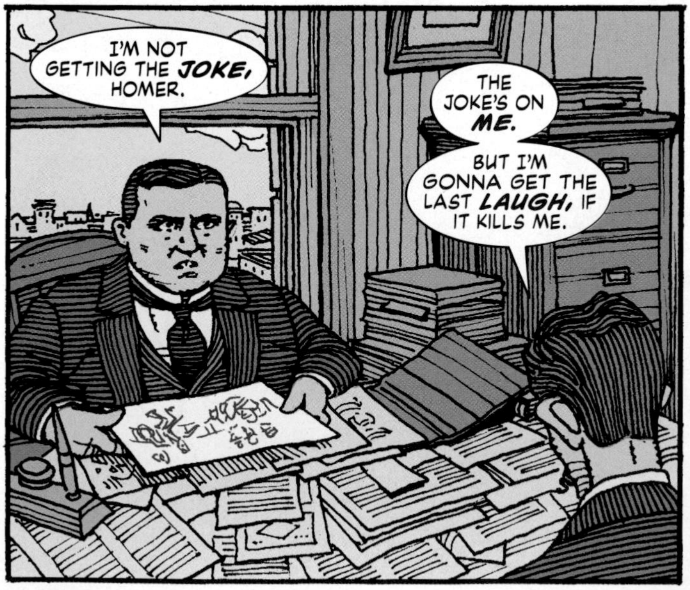
I'M NOT GETTING THE JOKE, HOMER.
THE JOKE'S ON ME.
BUT I'M GONNA GET THE LAST LAUGH, IF IT KILLS ME.

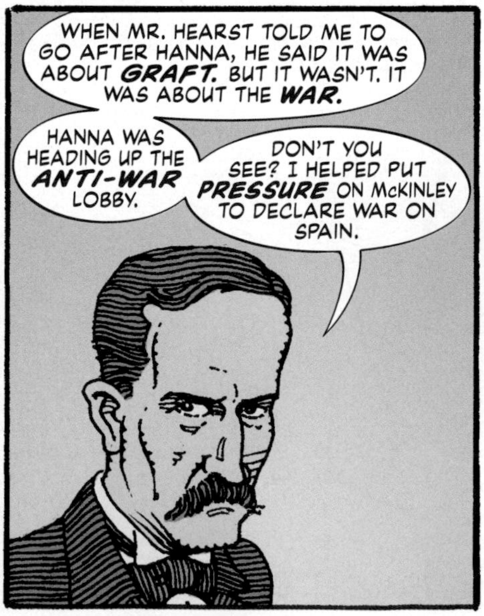
WHEN MR. HEARST TOLD ME TO GO AFTER HANNA, HE SAID IT WAS ABOUT GRAFT. BUT IT WASN'T. IT WAS ABOUT THE WAR.
HANNA WAS HEADING UP THE ANTI-WAR LOBBY.
DON'T YOU SEE? I HELPED PUT PRESSURE ON McKINLEY TO DECLARE WAR ON SPAIN.

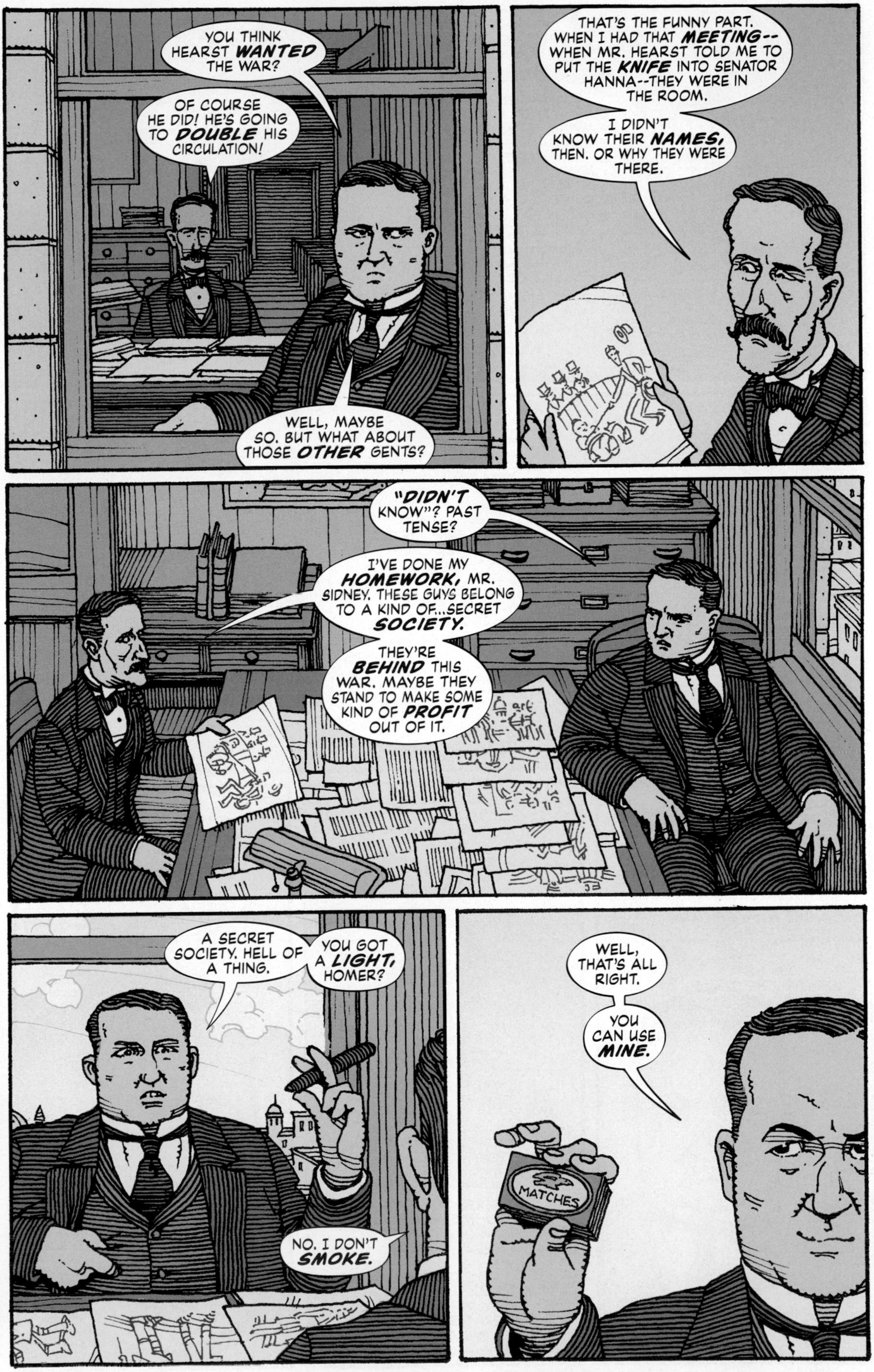
YOU THINK HEARST WANTED THE WAR?
OF COURSE HE DID! HE'S GOING TO DOUBLE HIS CIRCULATION!
WELL, MAYBE SO. BUT WHAT ABOUT THOSE OTHER GENTS?
THAT'S THE FUNNY PART. WHEN I HAD THAT MEETING-- WHEN MR. HEARST TOLD ME TO PUT THE KNIFE INTO SENATOR HANNA--THEY WERE IN THE ROOM.
I DIDN'T KNOW THEIR NAMES, THEN. OR WHY THEY WERE THERE.
"DIDN'T KNOW"? PAST TENSE?
I'VE DONE MY HOMEWORK, MR. SIDNEY. THESE GUYS BELONG TO A KIND OF...SECRET SOCIETY.
THEY'RE BEHIND THIS WAR. MAYBE THEY STAND TO MAKE SOME KIND OF PROFIT OUT OF IT.
A SECRET SOCIETY. HELL OF A THING.
YOU GOT A LIGHT, HOMER?
NO. I DON'T SMOKE.
WELL, THAT'S ALL RIGHT.
YOU CAN USE MINE.
MATCHES

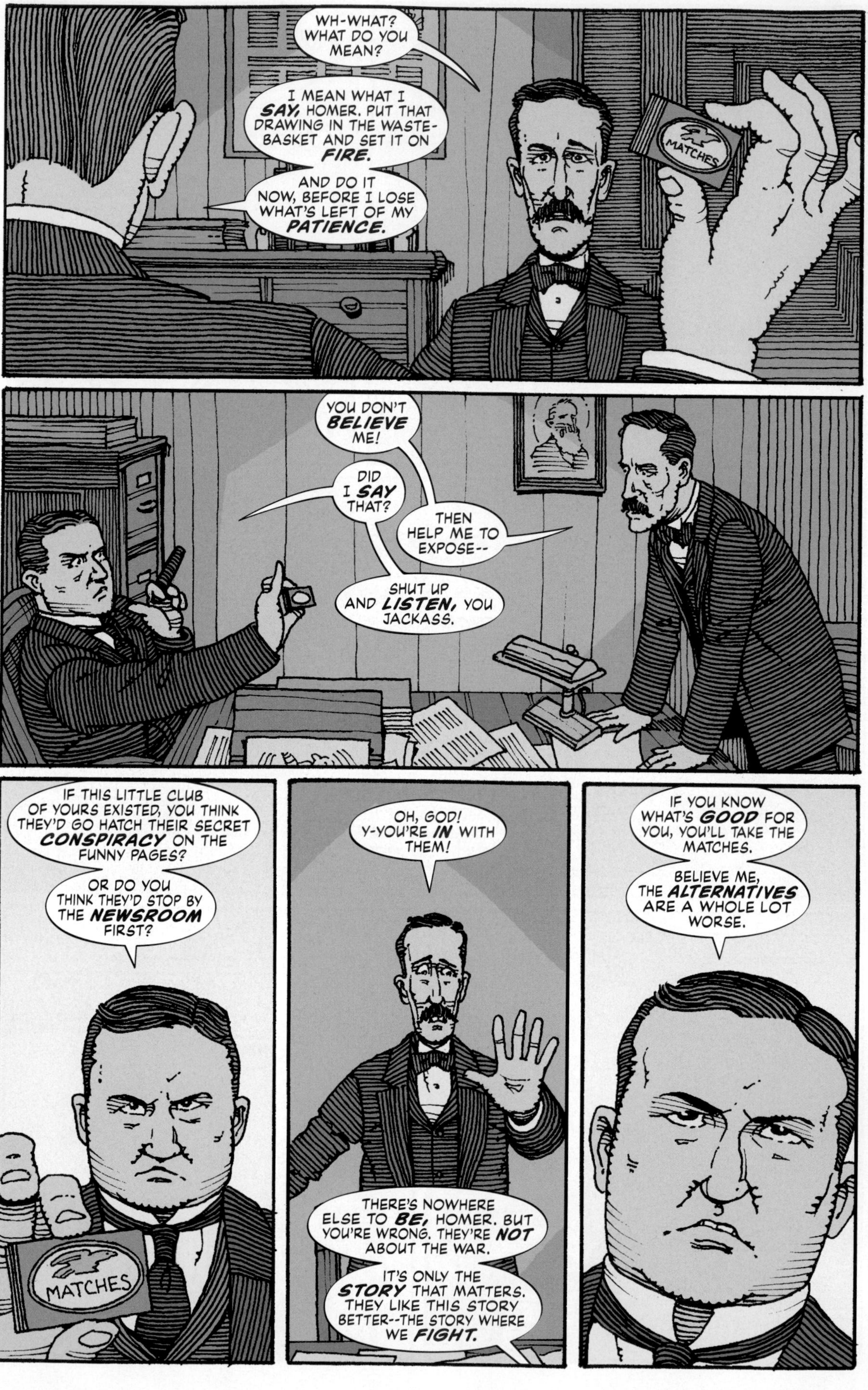
WH-WHAT? WHAT DO YOU MEAN?
I MEAN WHAT I SAY, HOMER. PUT THAT DRAWING IN THE WASTE-BASKET AND SET IT ON FIRE.
AND DO IT NOW, BEFORE I LOSE WHAT'S LEFT OF MY PATIENCE.
MATCHES
YOU DON'T BELIEVE ME!
DID I SAY THAT?
THEN HELP ME TO EXPOSE--
SHUT UP AND LISTEN, YOU JACKASS.
IF THIS LITTLE CLUB OF YOURS EXISTED, YOU THINK THEY'D GO HATCH THEIR SECRET CONSPIRACY ON THE FUNNY PAGES?
OR DO YOU THINK THEY'D STOP BY THE NEWSROOM FIRST?
MATCHES
OH, GOD! Y-YOU'RE IN WITH THEM!
THERE'S NOWHERE ELSE TO BE, HOMER. BUT YOU'RE WRONG. THEY'RE NOT ABOUT THE WAR.
IT'S ONLY THE STORY THAT MATTERS. THEY LIKE THIS STORY BETTER--THE STORY WHERE WE FIGHT.
IF YOU KNOW WHAT'S GOOD FOR YOU, YOU'LL TAKE THE MATCHES.
BELIEVE ME, THE ALTERNATIVES ARE A WHOLE LOT WORSE.

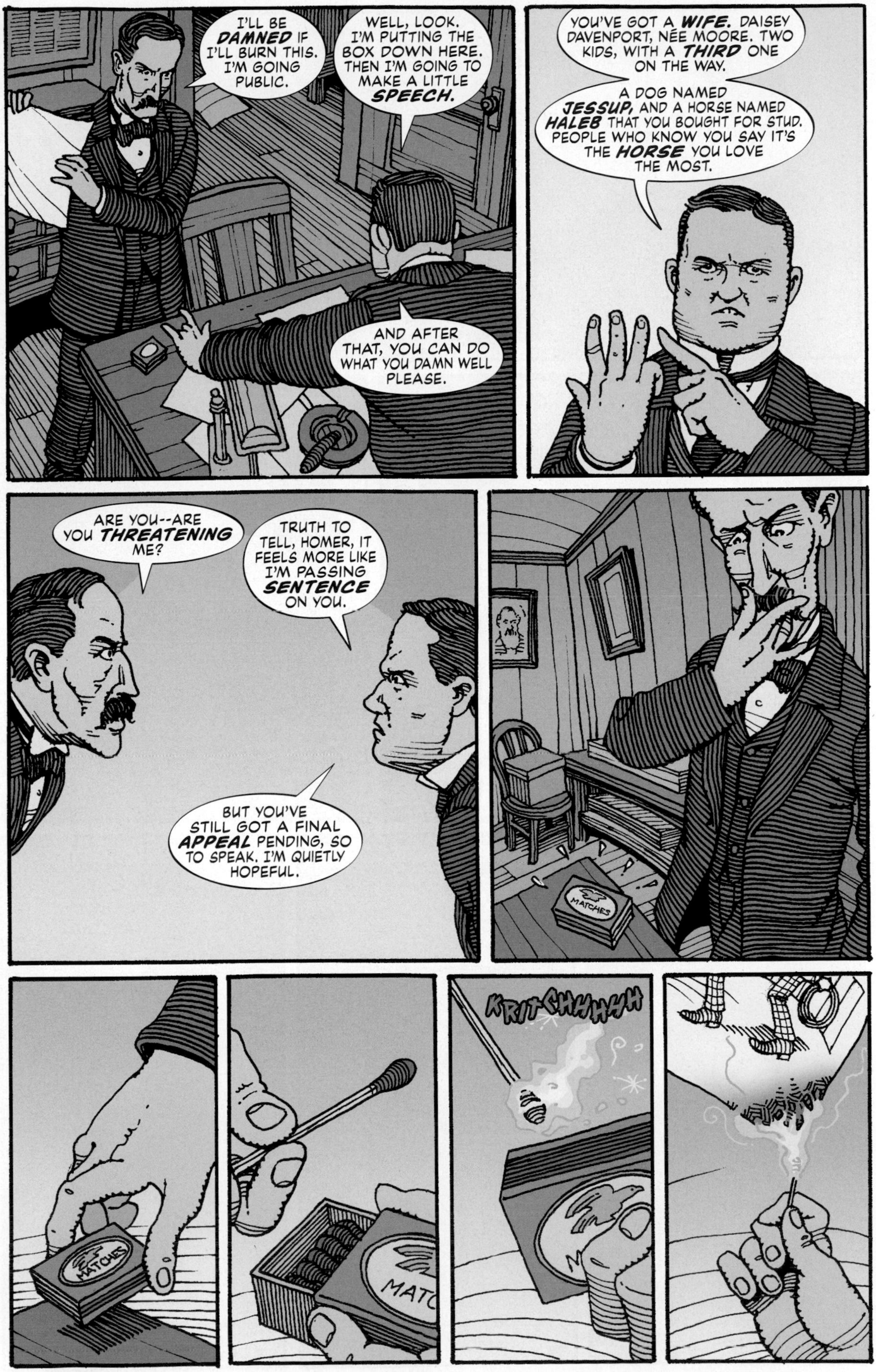
I'LL BE DAMNED IF I'LL BURN THIS. I'M GOING PUBLIC.
WELL, LOOK. I'M PUTTING THE BOX DOWN HERE. THEN I'M GOING TO MAKE A LITTLE SPEECH.
AND AFTER THAT, YOU CAN DO WHAT YOU DAMN WELL PLEASE.
YOU'VE GOT A WIFE. DAISEY DAVENPORT, NÉE MOORE. TWO KIDS, WITH A THIRD ONE ON THE WAY.
A DOG NAMED JESSUP, AND A HORSE NAMED HALEB THAT YOU BOUGHT FOR STUD. PEOPLE WHO KNOW YOU SAY IT'S THE HORSE YOU LOVE THE MOST.
ARE YOU--ARE YOU THREATENING ME?
TRUTH TO TELL, HOMER, IT FEELS MORE LIKE I'M PASSING SENTENCE ON YOU.
BUT YOU'VE STILL GOT A FINAL APPEAL PENDING, SO TO SPEAK. I'M QUIETLY HOPEFUL.
MATCHES
MATCHES
MATCHES
KRITCHHHHH

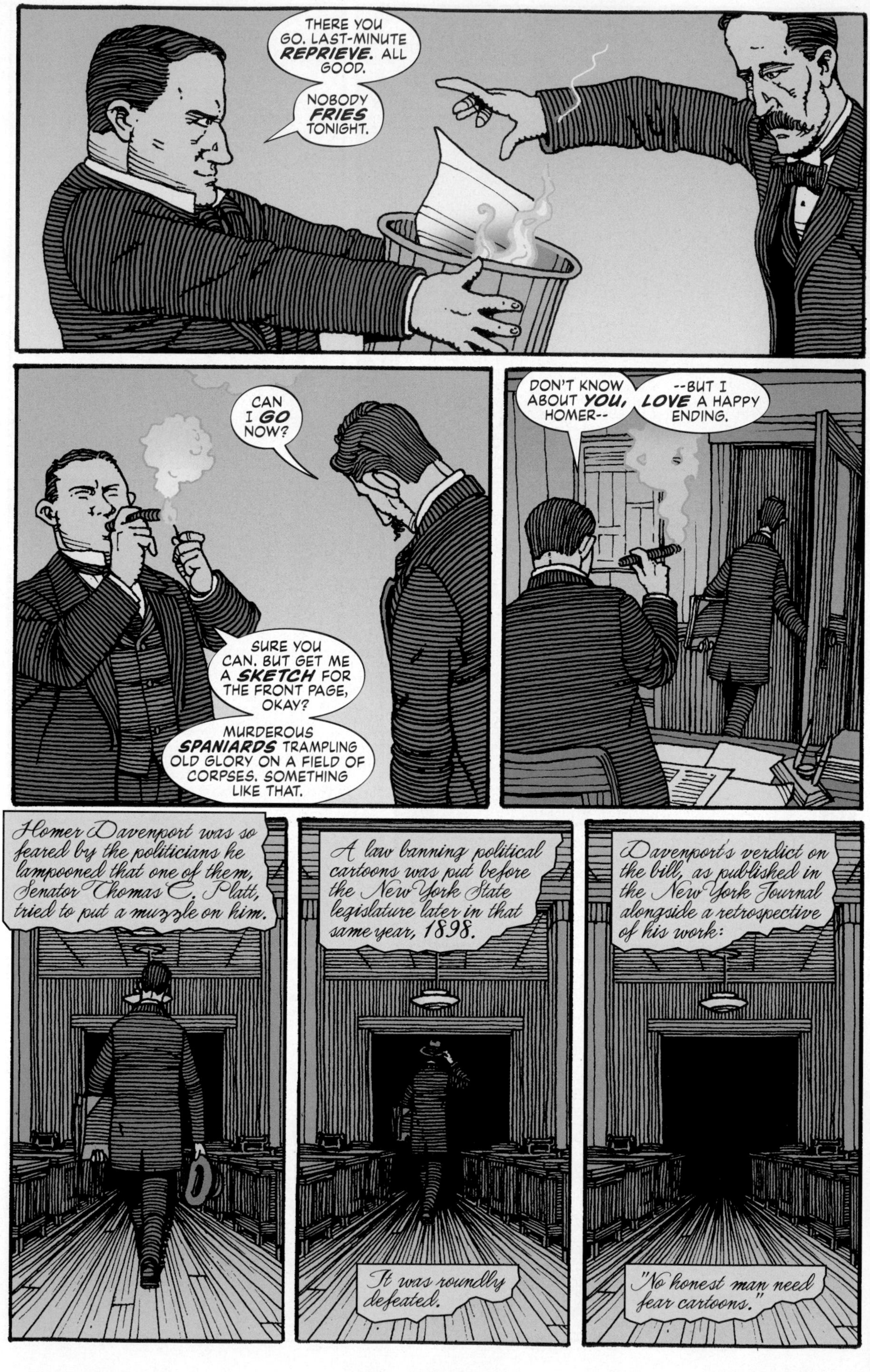
THERE YOU GO. LAST-MINUTE REPRIEVE. ALL GOOD.
NOBODY FRIES TONIGHT.
CAN I GO NOW?
SURE YOU CAN. BUT GET ME A SKETCH FOR THE FRONT PAGE, OKAY?
MURDEROUS SPANIARDS TRAMPLING OLD GLORY ON A FIELD OF CORPSES. SOMETHING LIKE THAT.
DON'T KNOW ABOUT YOU, HOMER--
--BUT I LOVE A HAPPY ENDING.
Homer Davenport was so feared by the politicians he lampooned that one of them, Senator Thomas C. Platt, tried to put a muzzle on him.
A law banning political cartoons was put before the New York State legislature later in that same year, 1898.
It was roundly defeated.
Davenport's verdict on the bill, as published in the New York Journal alongside a retrospective of his work:
"No honest man need fear cartoons."

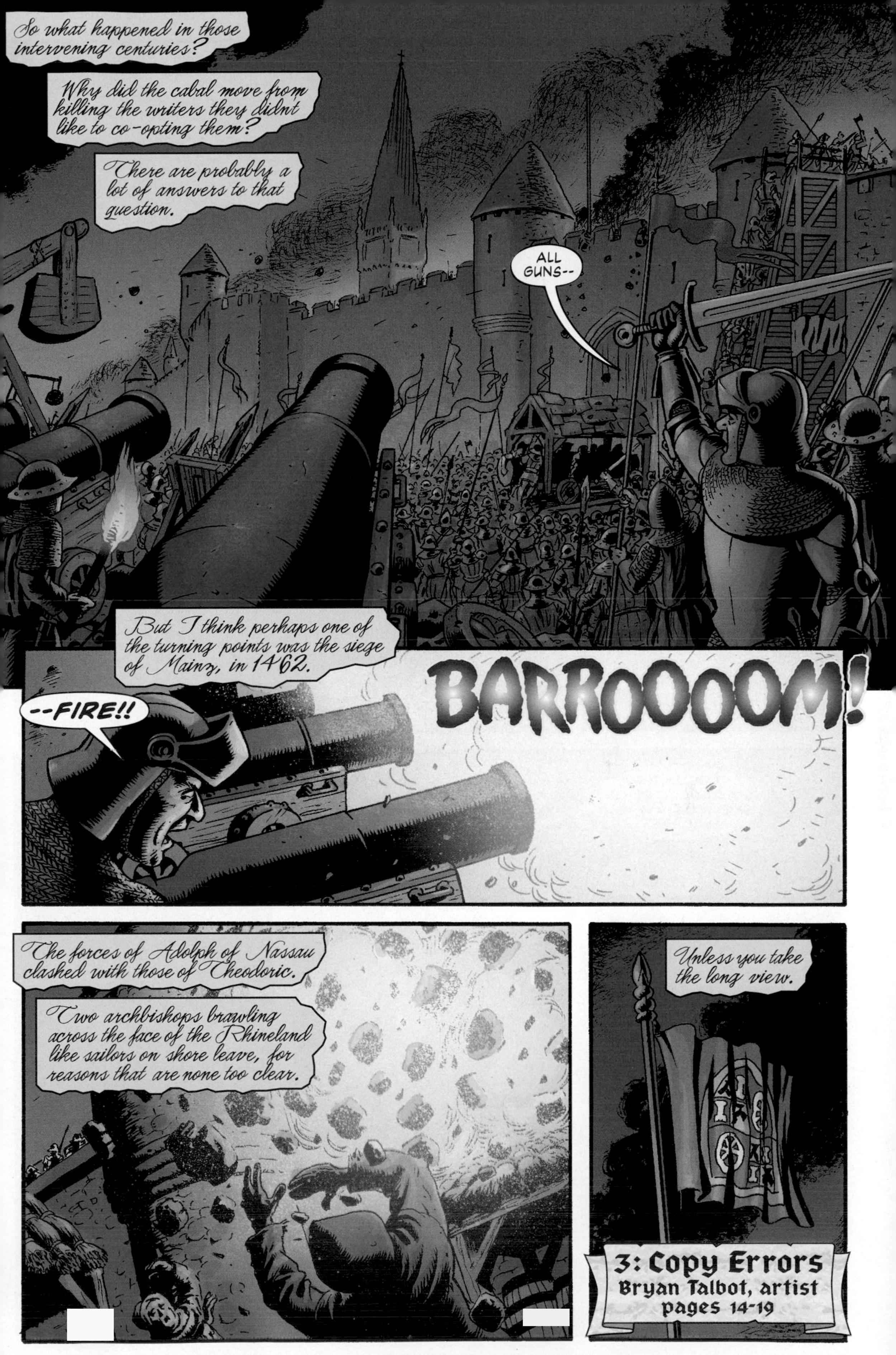

So what happened in those intervening centuries?
Why did the cabal move from killing the writers they didn't like to co-opting them?
There are probably a lot of answers to that question.
ALL GUNS--
But I think perhaps one of the turning points was the siege of Mainz, in 1462.
--FIRE!!
BARROOOOM!
The forces of Adolph of Nassau clashed with those of Theodoric.
Two archbishops brawling across the face of the Rhineland like sailors on shore leave, for reasons that are none too clear.
Unless you take the long view.
3: Copy Errors
Bryan Talbot, artist
pages 14-19

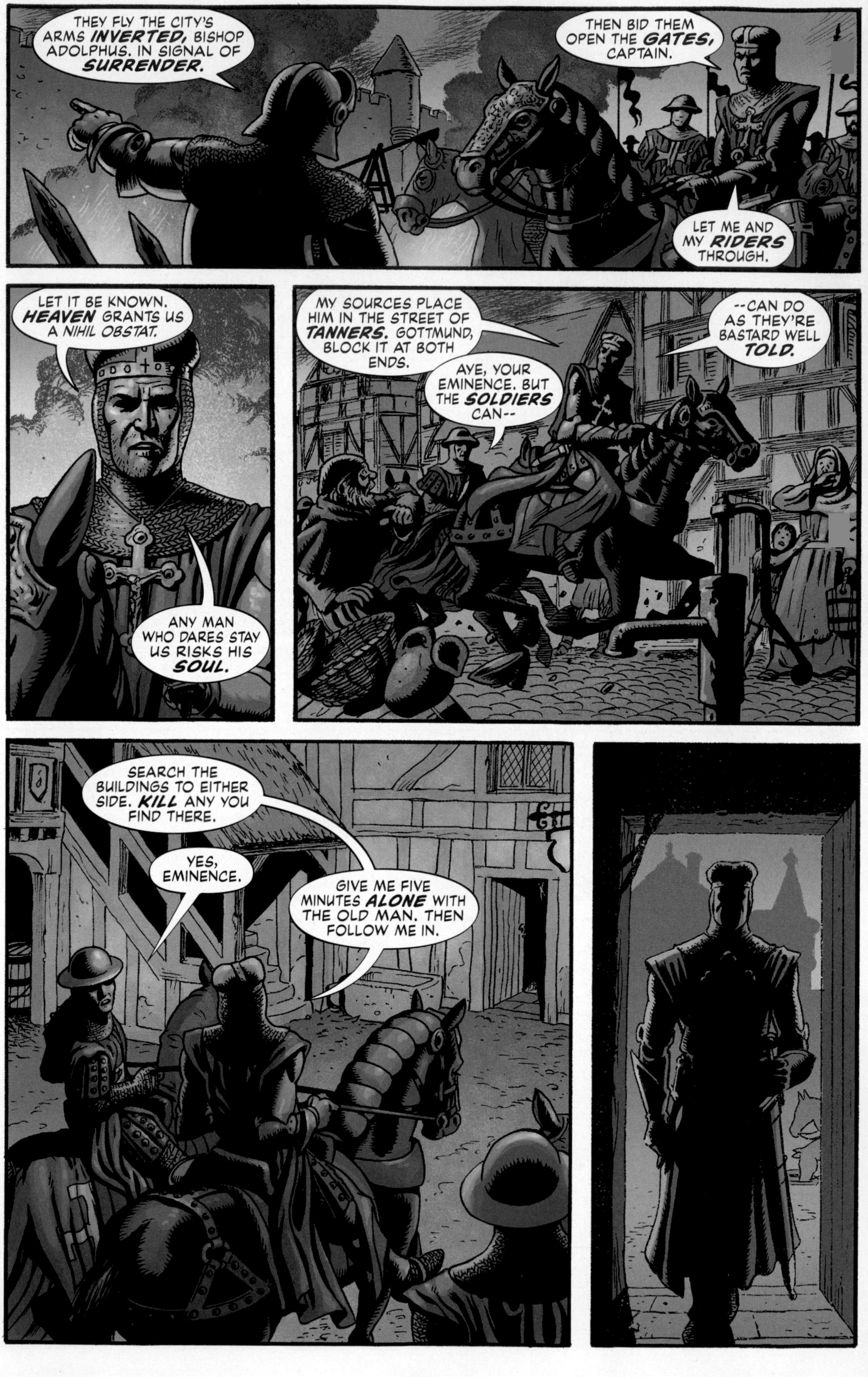
THEY FLY THE CITY'S ARMS INVERTED, BISHOP ADOLPHUS. IN SIGNAL OF SURRENDER.
THEN BID THEM OPEN THE GATES, CAPTAIN.
LET ME AND MY RIDERS THROUGH.
LET IT BE KNOWN. HEAVEN GRANTS US A NIHIL OBSTAT.
ANY MAN WHO DARES STAY US RISKS HIS SOUL.
MY SOURCES PLACE HIM IN THE STREET OF TANNERS. GOTTMUND, BLOCK IT AT BOTH ENDS.
AYE, YOUR EMINENCE. BUT THE SOLDIERS CAN--
--CAN DO AS THEY'RE BASTARD WELL TOLD.
SEARCH THE BUILDINGS TO EITHER SIDE. KILL ANY YOU FIND THERE.
YES, EMINENCE.
GIVE ME FIVE MINUTES ALONE WITH THE OLD MAN. THEN FOLLOW ME IN.

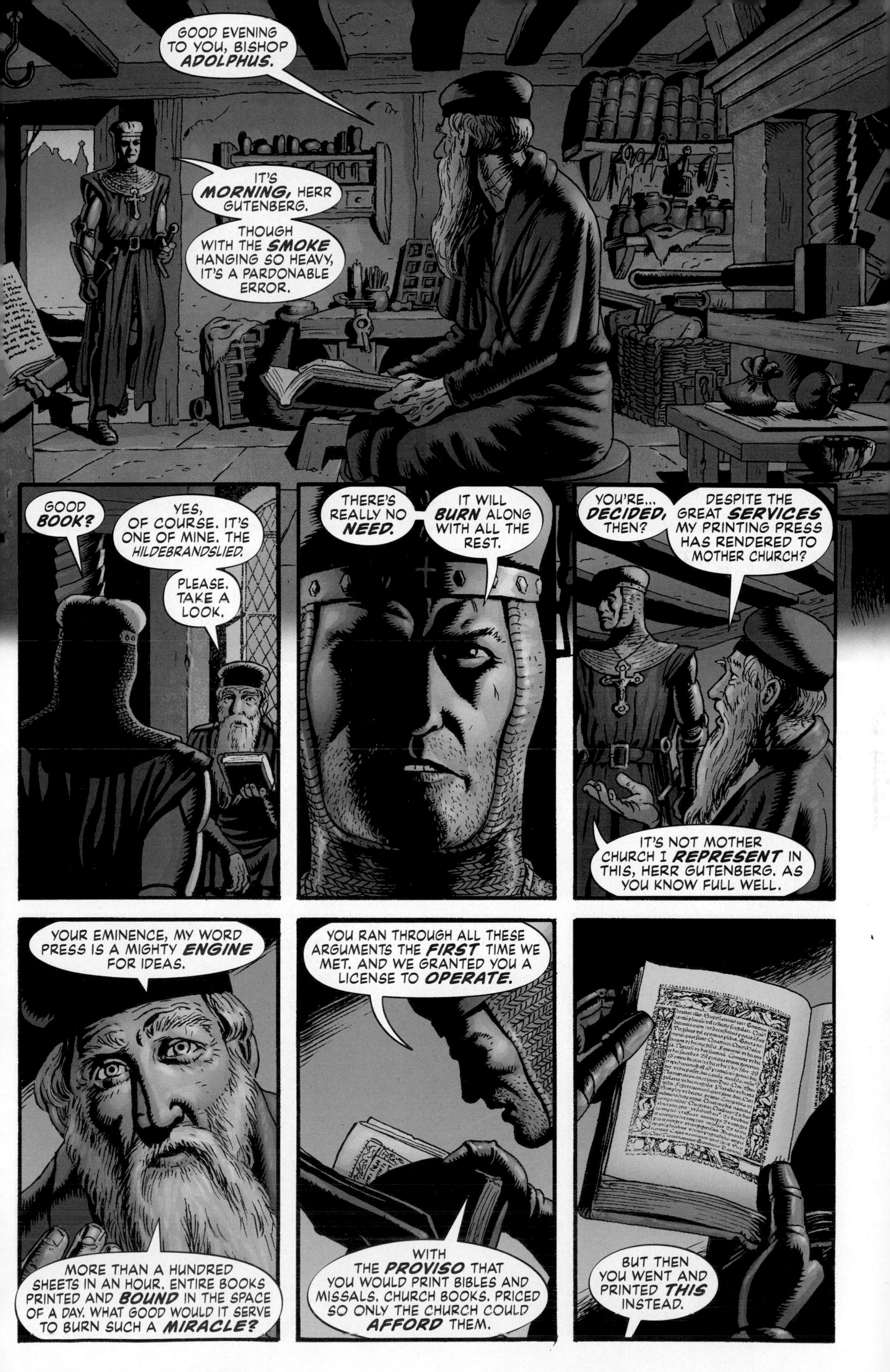
GOOD EVENING TO YOU, BISHOP ADOLPHUS.
IT'S MORNING, HERR GUTENBERG.
THOUGH WITH THE SMOKE HANGING SO HEAVY, IT'S A PARDONABLE ERROR.
GOOD BOOK?
YES, OF COURSE. IT'S ONE OF MINE. THE HILDEBRANDSLIED.
PLEASE. TAKE A LOOK.
THERE'S REALLY NO NEED.
IT WILL BURN ALONG WITH ALL THE REST.
YOU'RE... DECIDED, THEN?
DESPITE THE GREAT SERVICES MY PRINTING PRESS HAS RENDERED TO MOTHER CHURCH?
IT'S NOT MOTHER CHURCH I REPRESENT IN THIS, HERR GUTENBERG. AS YOU KNOW FULL WELL.
YOUR EMINENCE, MY WORD PRESS IS A MIGHTY ENGINE FOR IDEAS.
MORE THAN A HUNDRED SHEETS IN AN HOUR. ENTIRE BOOKS PRINTED AND BOUND IN THE SPACE OF A DAY. WHAT GOOD WOULD IT SERVE TO BURN SUCH A MIRACLE?
YOU RAN THROUGH ALL THESE ARGUMENTS THE FIRST TIME WE MET. AND WE GRANTED YOU A LICENSE TO OPERATE.
WITH THE PROVISO THAT YOU WOULD PRINT BIBLES AND MISSALS. CHURCH BOOKS. PRICED SO ONLY THE CHURCH COULD AFFORD THEM.
BUT THEN YOU WENT AND PRINTED THIS INSTEAD.

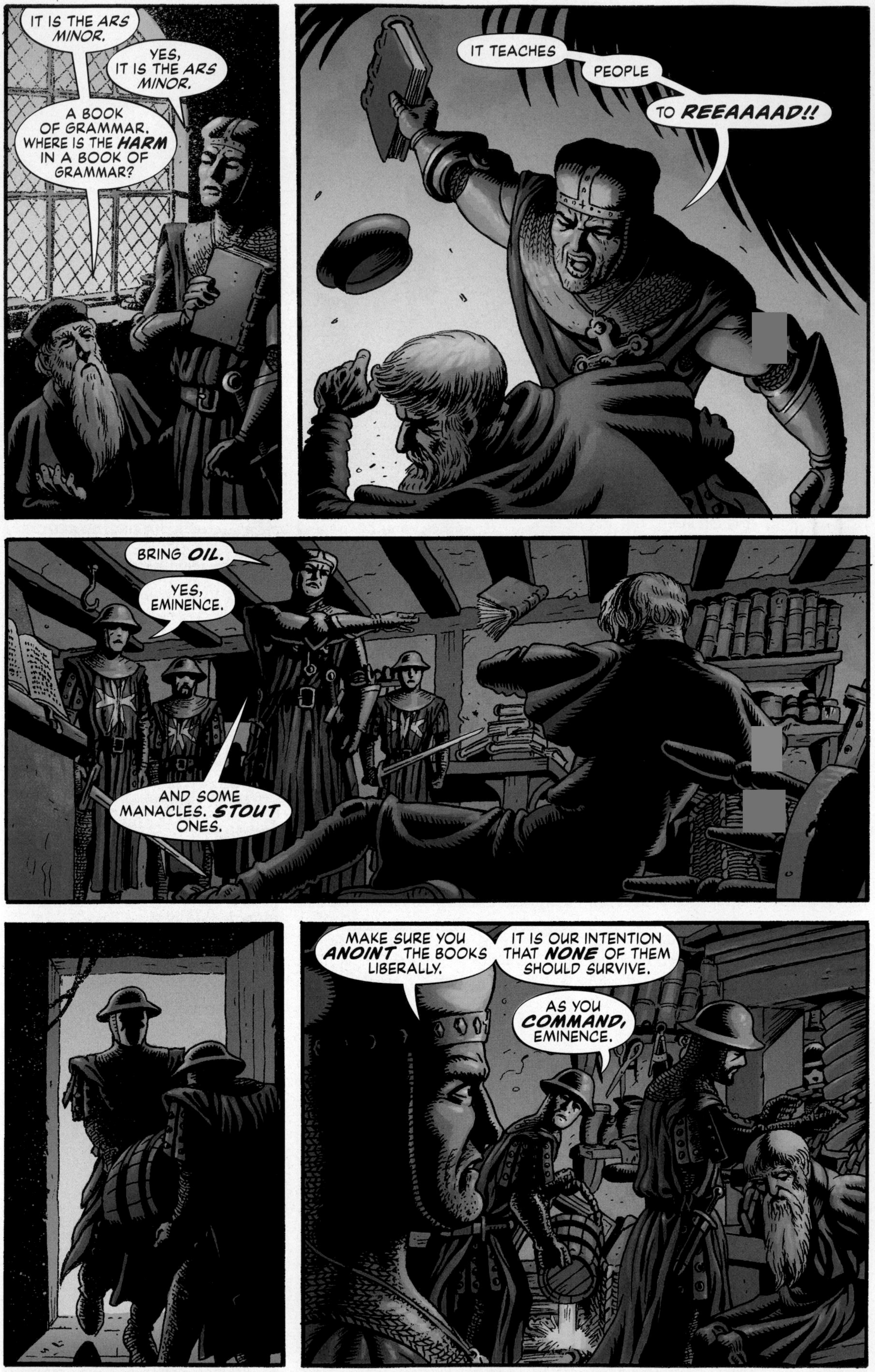
IT IS THE *ARS MINOR.*
YES, IT IS THE *ARS MINOR.*
A BOOK OF GRAMMAR. WHERE IS THE ***HARM*** IN A BOOK OF GRAMMAR?
IT TEACHES
PEOPLE
TO ***REEAAAAAD!!***
BRING ***OIL.***
YES, EMINENCE.
AND SOME MANACLES. ***STOUT*** ONES.
MAKE SURE YOU ***ANOINT*** THE BOOKS LIBERALLY.
IT IS OUR INTENTION THAT ***NONE*** OF THEM SHOULD SURVIVE.
AS YOU ***COMMAND,*** EMINENCE.

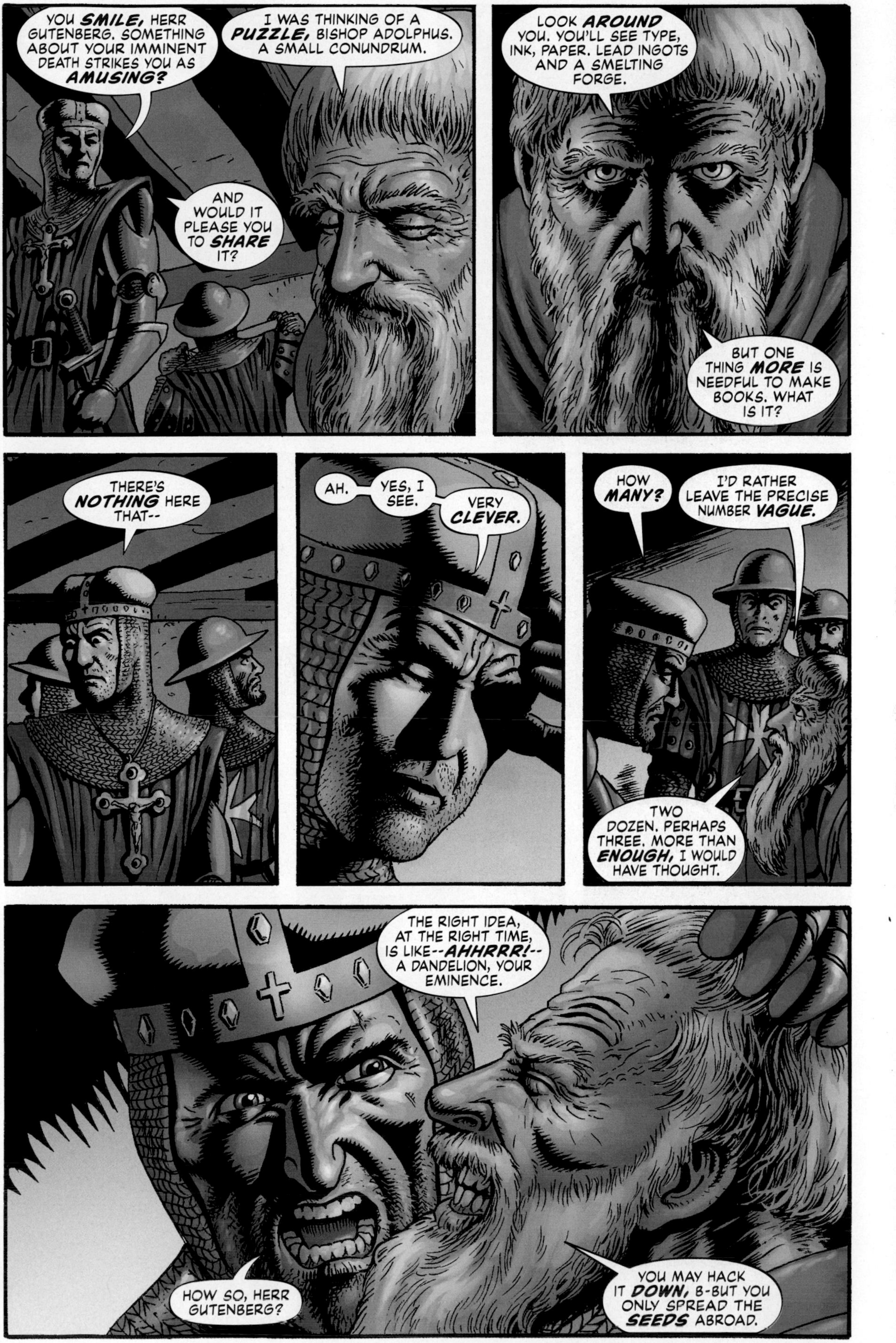
YOU SMILE, HERR GUTENBERG. SOMETHING ABOUT YOUR IMMINENT DEATH STRIKES YOU AS AMUSING?
I WAS THINKING OF A PUZZLE, BISHOP ADOLPHUS. A SMALL CONUNDRUM.
AND WOULD IT PLEASE YOU TO SHARE IT?
LOOK AROUND YOU. YOU'LL SEE TYPE, INK, PAPER. LEAD INGOTS AND A SMELTING FORGE.
BUT ONE THING MORE IS NEEDFUL TO MAKE BOOKS. WHAT IS IT?
THERE'S NOTHING HERE THAT--
AH.
YES, I SEE.
VERY CLEVER.
HOW MANY?
I'D RATHER LEAVE THE PRECISE NUMBER VAGUE.
TWO DOZEN. PERHAPS THREE. MORE THAN ENOUGH, I WOULD HAVE THOUGHT.
THE RIGHT IDEA, AT THE RIGHT TIME, IS LIKE--AHHRRR!-- A DANDELION, YOUR EMINENCE.
HOW SO, HERR GUTENBERG?
YOU MAY HACK IT DOWN, B-BUT YOU ONLY SPREAD THE SEEDS ABROAD.

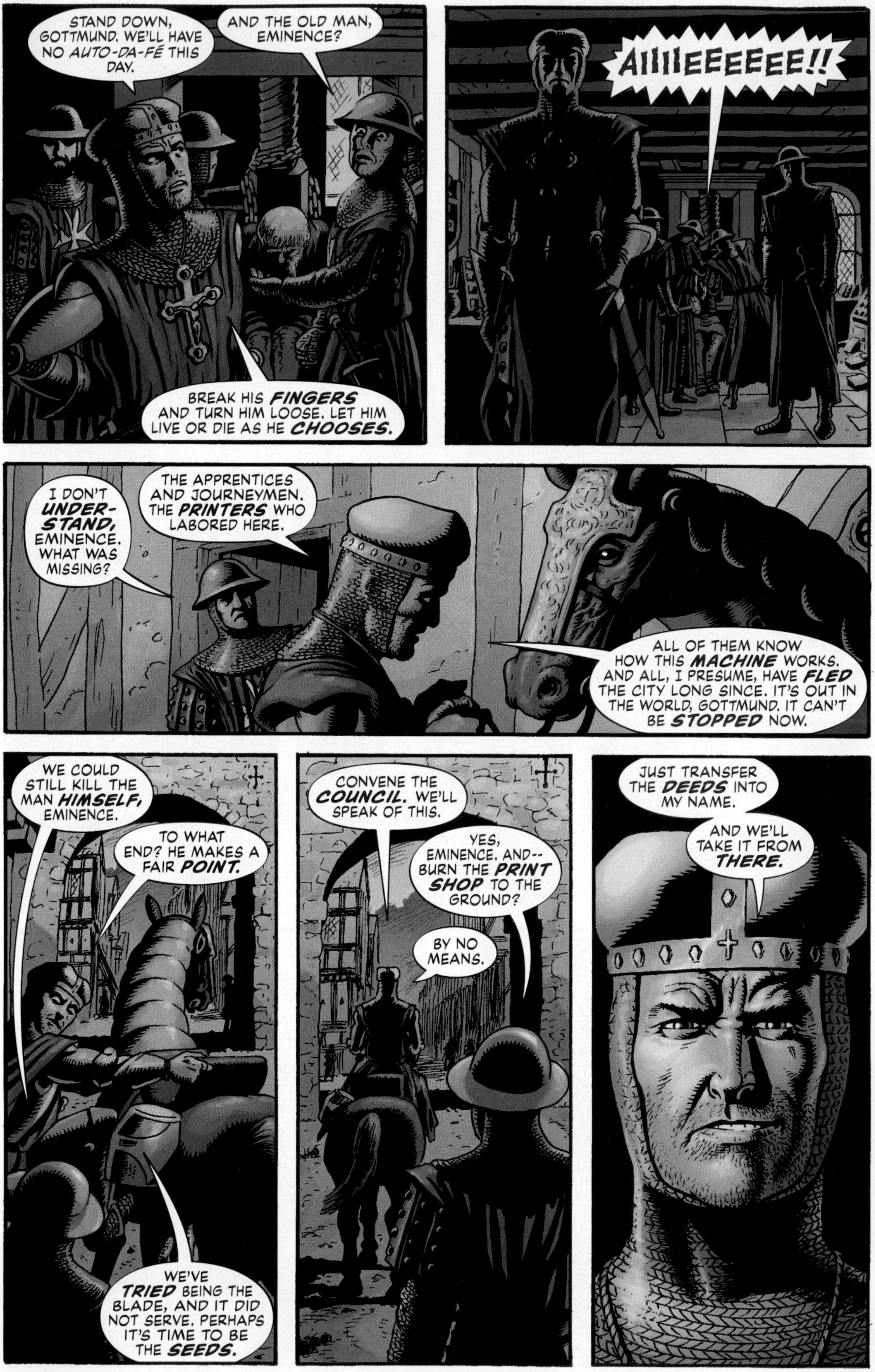
STAND DOWN, GOTTMUND. WE'LL HAVE NO AUTO-DA-FÉ THIS DAY.
AND THE OLD MAN, EMINENCE?
BREAK HIS FINGERS AND TURN HIM LOOSE. LET HIM LIVE OR DIE AS HE CHOOSES.
AIIIIEEEEEE!!
I DON'T UNDERSTAND, EMINENCE. WHAT WAS MISSING?
THE APPRENTICES AND JOURNEYMEN. THE PRINTERS WHO LABORED HERE.
ALL OF THEM KNOW HOW THIS MACHINE WORKS. AND ALL, I PRESUME, HAVE FLED THE CITY LONG SINCE. IT'S OUT IN THE WORLD, GOTTMUND. IT CAN'T BE STOPPED NOW.
WE COULD STILL KILL THE MAN HIMSELF, EMINENCE.
TO WHAT END? HE MAKES A FAIR POINT.
WE'VE TRIED BEING THE BLADE, AND IT DID NOT SERVE. PERHAPS IT'S TIME TO BE THE SEEDS.
CONVENE THE COUNCIL. WE'LL SPEAK OF THIS.
YES, EMINENCE. AND-- BURN THE PRINT SHOP TO THE GROUND?
BY NO MEANS.
JUST TRANSFER THE DEEDS INTO MY NAME.
AND WE'LL TAKE IT FROM THERE.

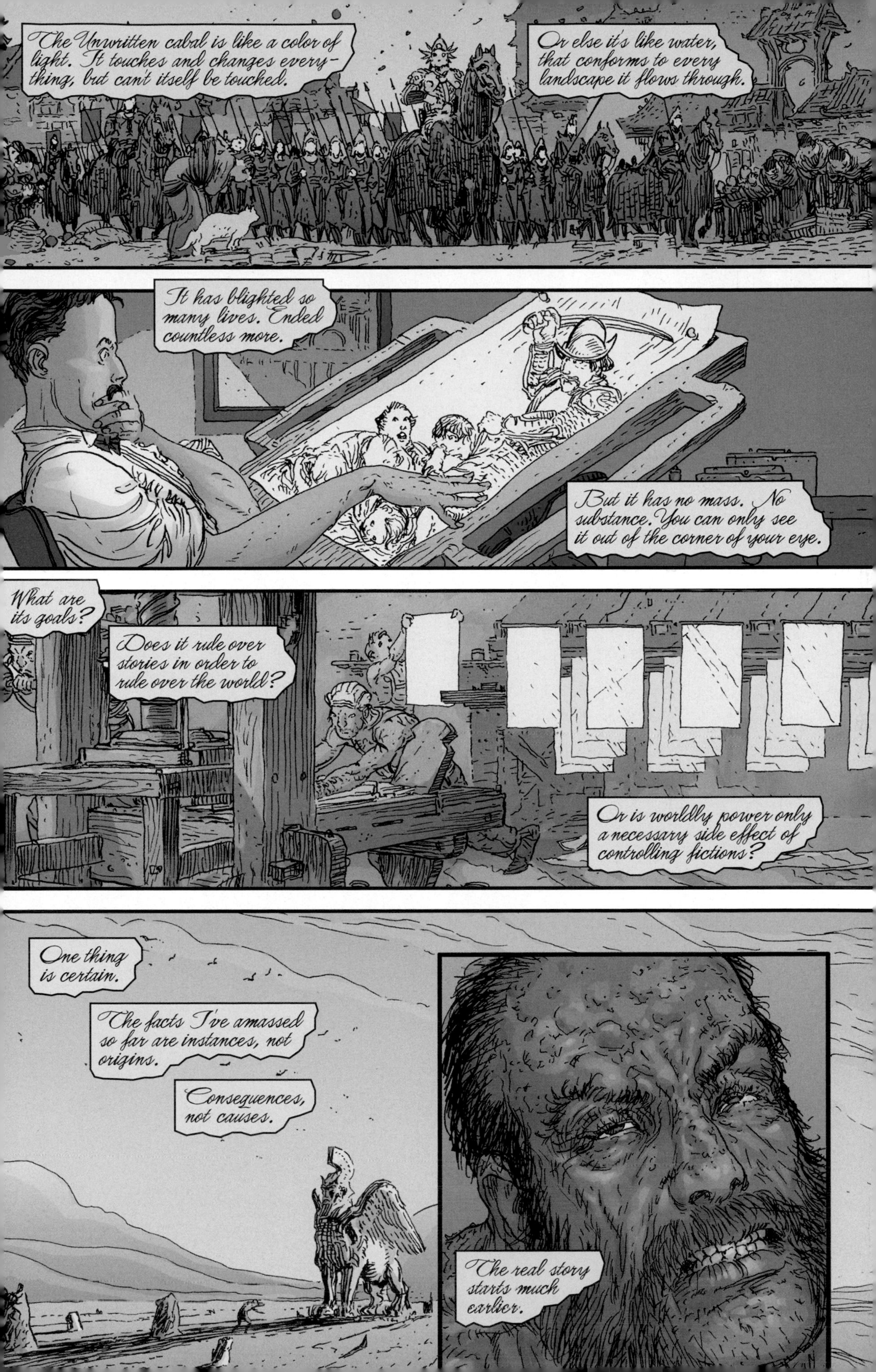
The Unwritten cabal is like a color of light. It touches and changes everything, but can't itself be touched.
Or else it's like water, that conforms to every landscape it flows through.
It has blighted so many lives. Ended countless more.
But it has no mass. No substance. You can only see it out of the corner of your eye.
What are its goals?
Does it ride over stories in order to rule over the world?
Or is worldly power only a necessary side effect of controlling fictions?
One thing is certain.
The facts I've amassed so far are instances, not origins.
Consequences, not causes.
The real story starts much earlier.

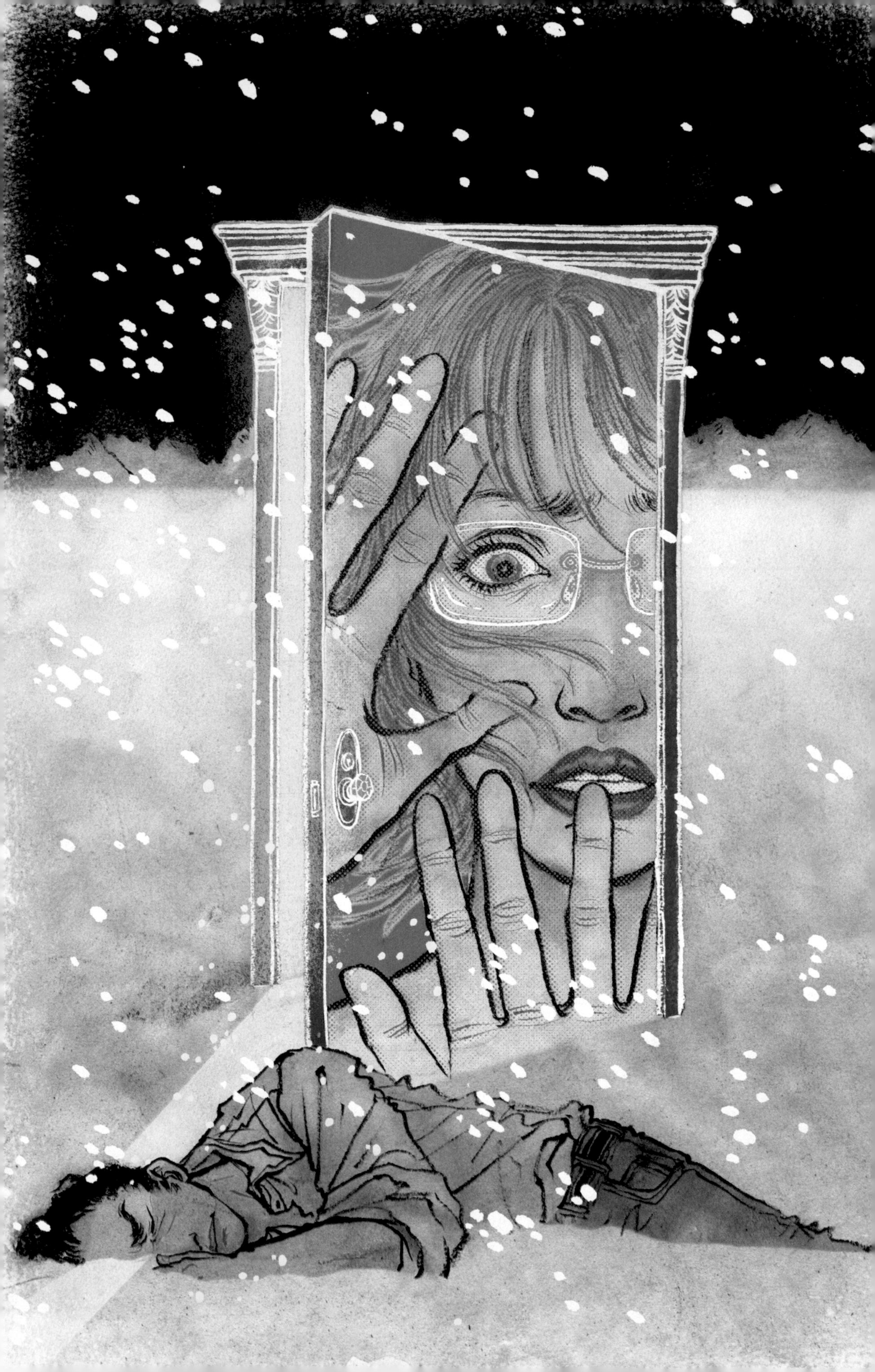

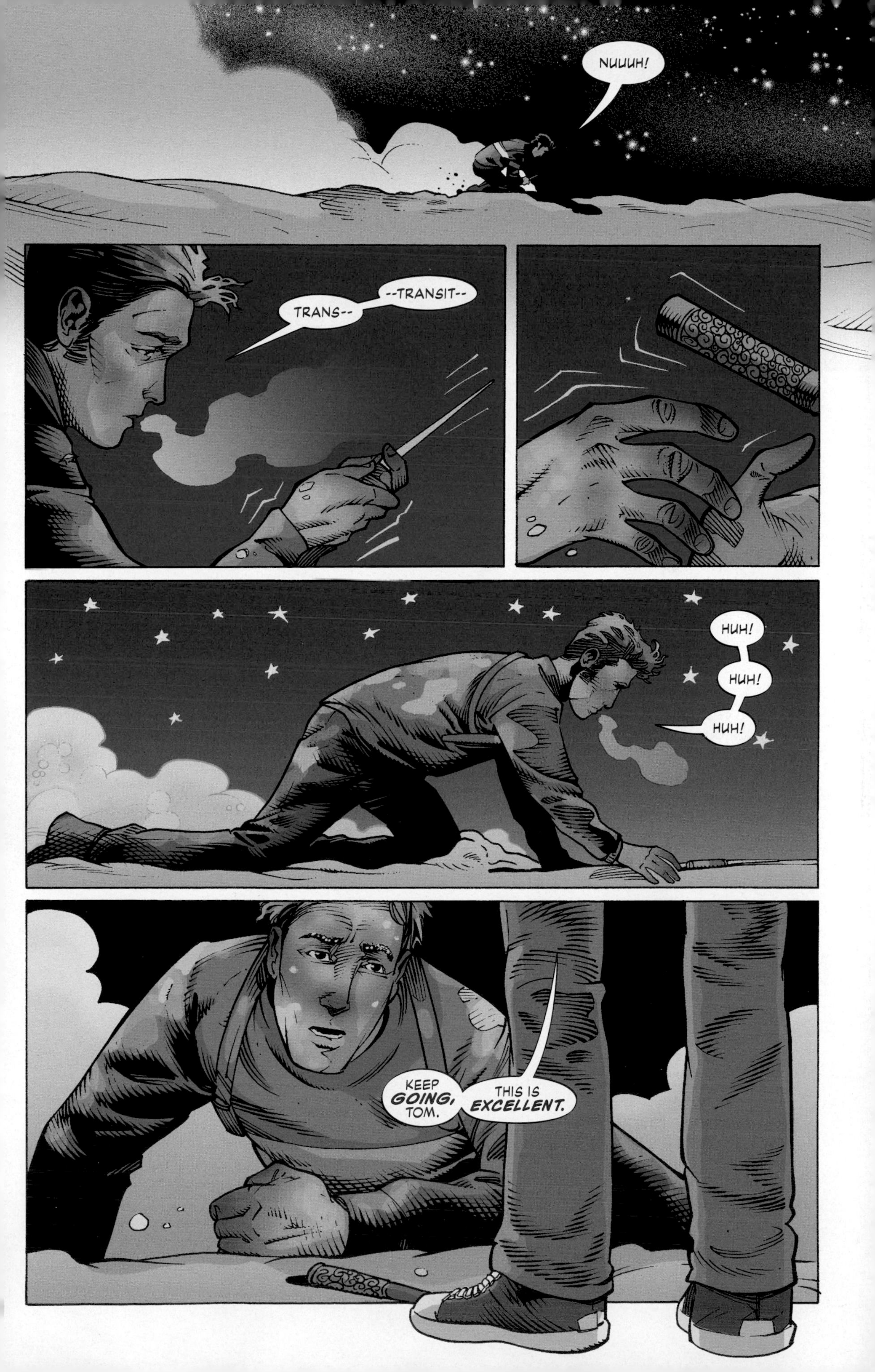
NUUUH!
TRANS--
--TRANSIT--
HUH!
HUH!
HUH!
KEEP GOING, TOM.
THIS IS EXCELLENT.

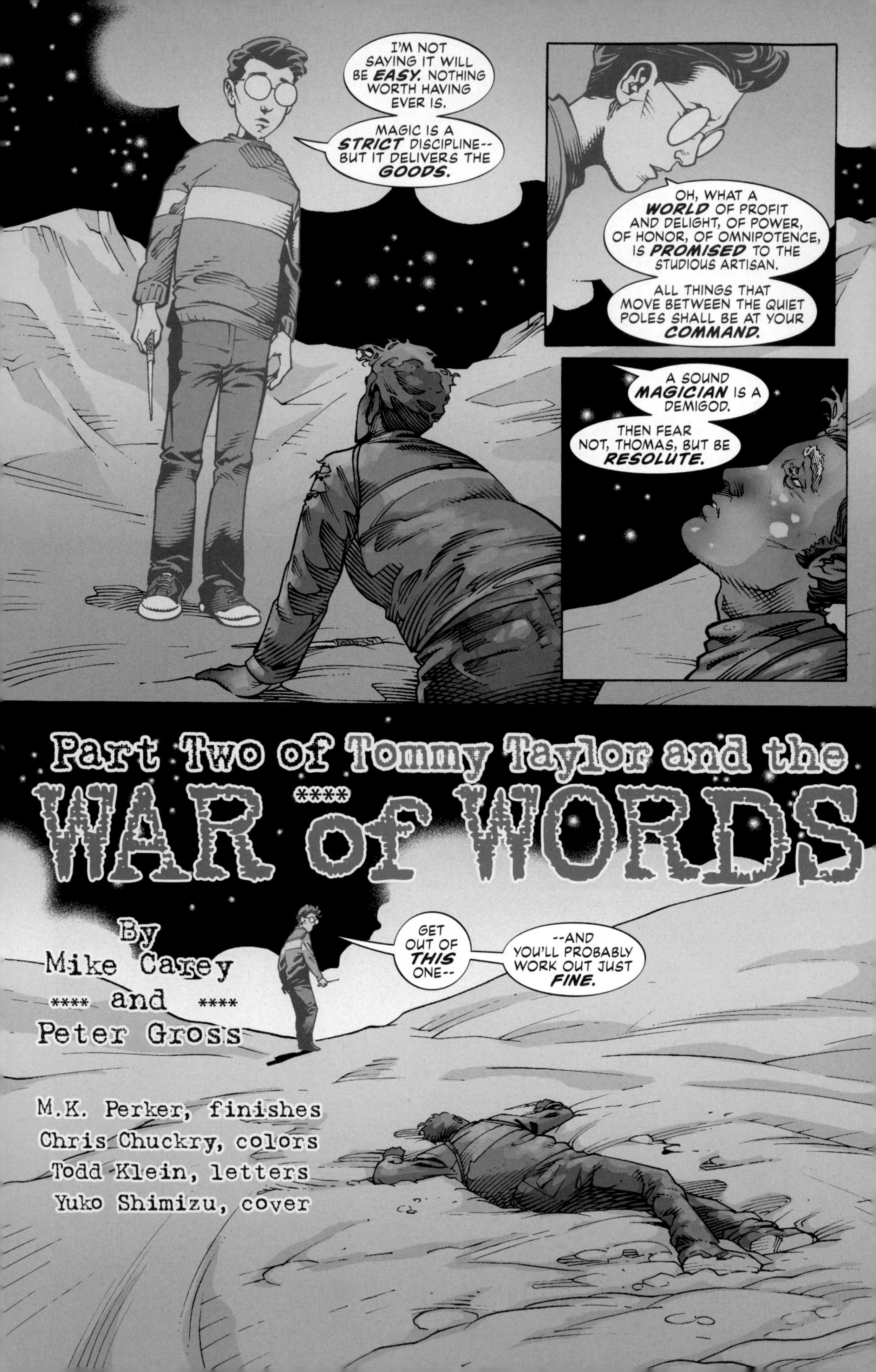
I'M NOT SAYING IT WILL BE EASY. NOTHING WORTH HAVING EVER IS.
MAGIC IS A STRICT DISCIPLINE-- BUT IT DELIVERS THE GOODS.
OH, WHAT A WORLD OF PROFIT AND DELIGHT, OF POWER, OF HONOR, OF OMNIPOTENCE, IS PROMISED TO THE STUDIOUS ARTISAN.
ALL THINGS THAT MOVE BETWEEN THE QUIET POLES SHALL BE AT YOUR COMMAND.
A SOUND MAGICIAN IS A DEMIGOD.
THEN FEAR NOT, THOMAS, BUT BE RESOLUTE.
Part Two of Tommy Taylor and the
WAR of WORDS
By
Mike Carey
and
Peter Gross
GET OUT OF THIS ONE--
--AND YOU'LL PROBABLY WORK OUT JUST FINE.
M.K. Perker, finishes
Chris Chuckry, colors
Todd Klein, letters
Yuko Shimizu, cover

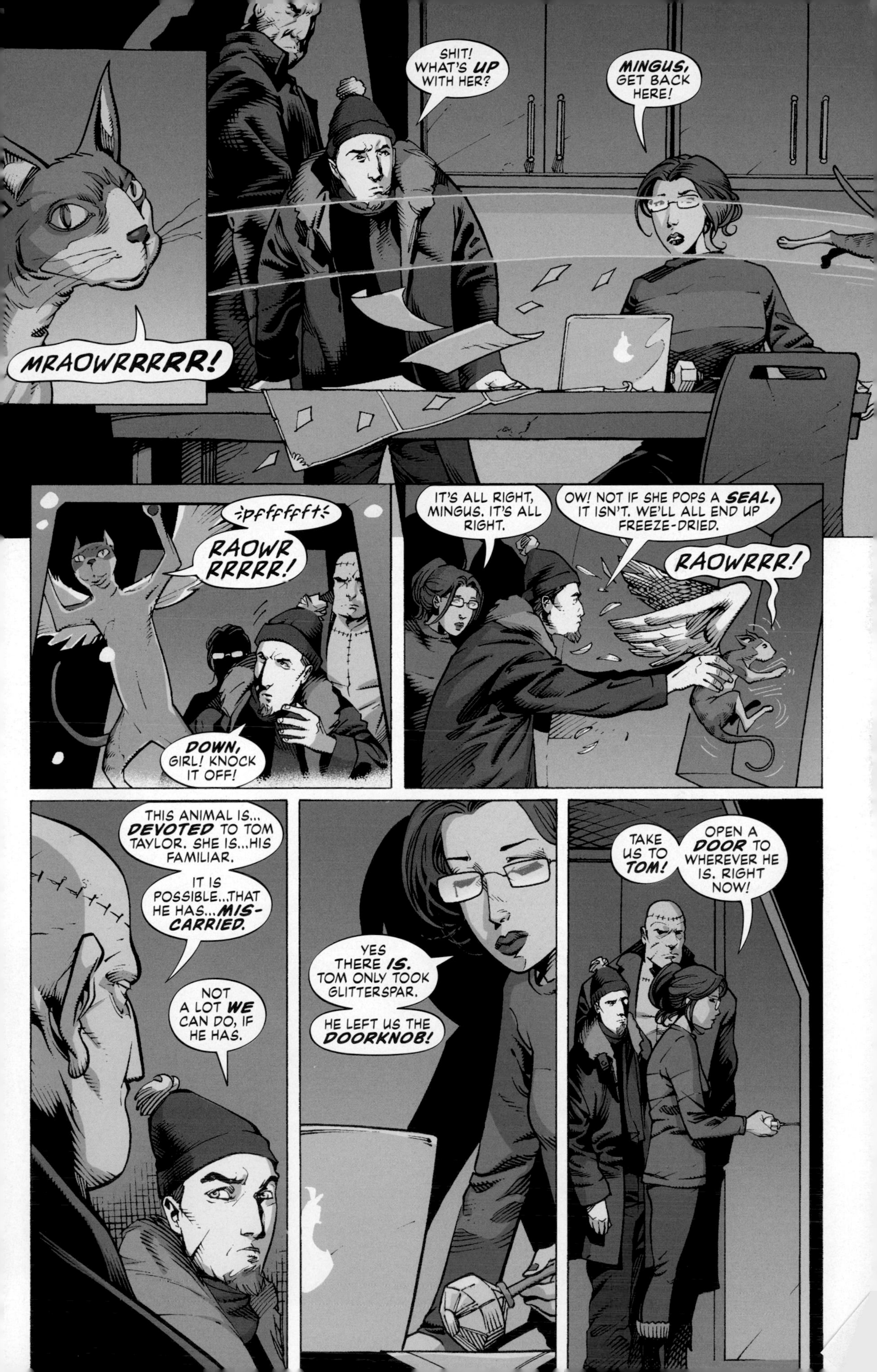
MRAOWRRRRR!
SHIT! WHAT'S UP WITH HER?
MINGUS, GET BACK HERE!
pfffffft
RAOWR RRRRR!
DOWN, GIRL! KNOCK IT OFF!
IT'S ALL RIGHT, MINGUS. IT'S ALL RIGHT.
OW! NOT IF SHE POPS A SEAL, IT ISN'T. WE'LL ALL END UP FREEZE-DRIED.
RAOWRRR!
THIS ANIMAL IS... DEVOTED TO TOM TAYLOR. SHE IS...HIS FAMILIAR.
IT IS POSSIBLE...THAT HE HAS...MIS-CARRIED.
NOT A LOT WE CAN DO, IF HE HAS.
YES THERE IS. TOM ONLY TOOK GLITTERSPAR.
HE LEFT US THE DOORKNOB!
TAKE US TO TOM!
OPEN A DOOR TO WHEREVER HE IS. RIGHT NOW!

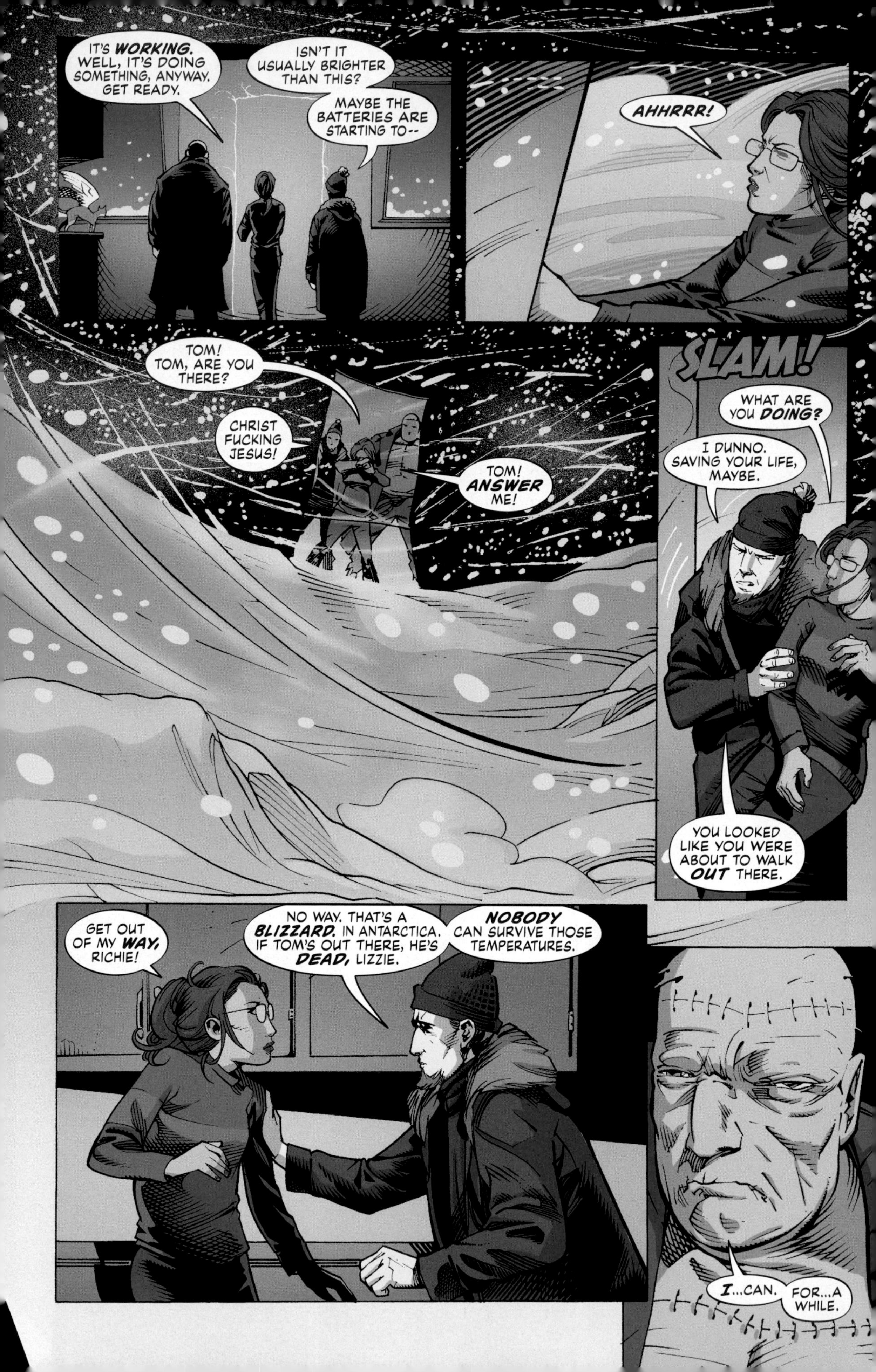

IT'S **WORKING.** WELL, IT'S DOING SOMETHING, ANYWAY. GET READY.
ISN'T IT USUALLY BRIGHTER THAN THIS?
MAYBE THE BATTERIES ARE STARTING TO--
AHHRRR!
TOM! TOM, ARE YOU THERE?
CHRIST FUCKING JESUS!
TOM! **ANSWER** ME!
SLAM!
WHAT ARE YOU **DOING?**
I DUNNO. SAVING YOUR LIFE, MAYBE.
YOU LOOKED LIKE YOU WERE ABOUT TO WALK **OUT** THERE.
GET OUT OF MY **WAY,** RICHIE!
NO WAY. THAT'S A **BLIZZARD.** IN ANTARCTICA. IF TOM'S OUT THERE, HE'S **DEAD,** LIZZIE.
NOBODY CAN SURVIVE THOSE TEMPERATURES.
I...CAN.
FOR...A WHILE.

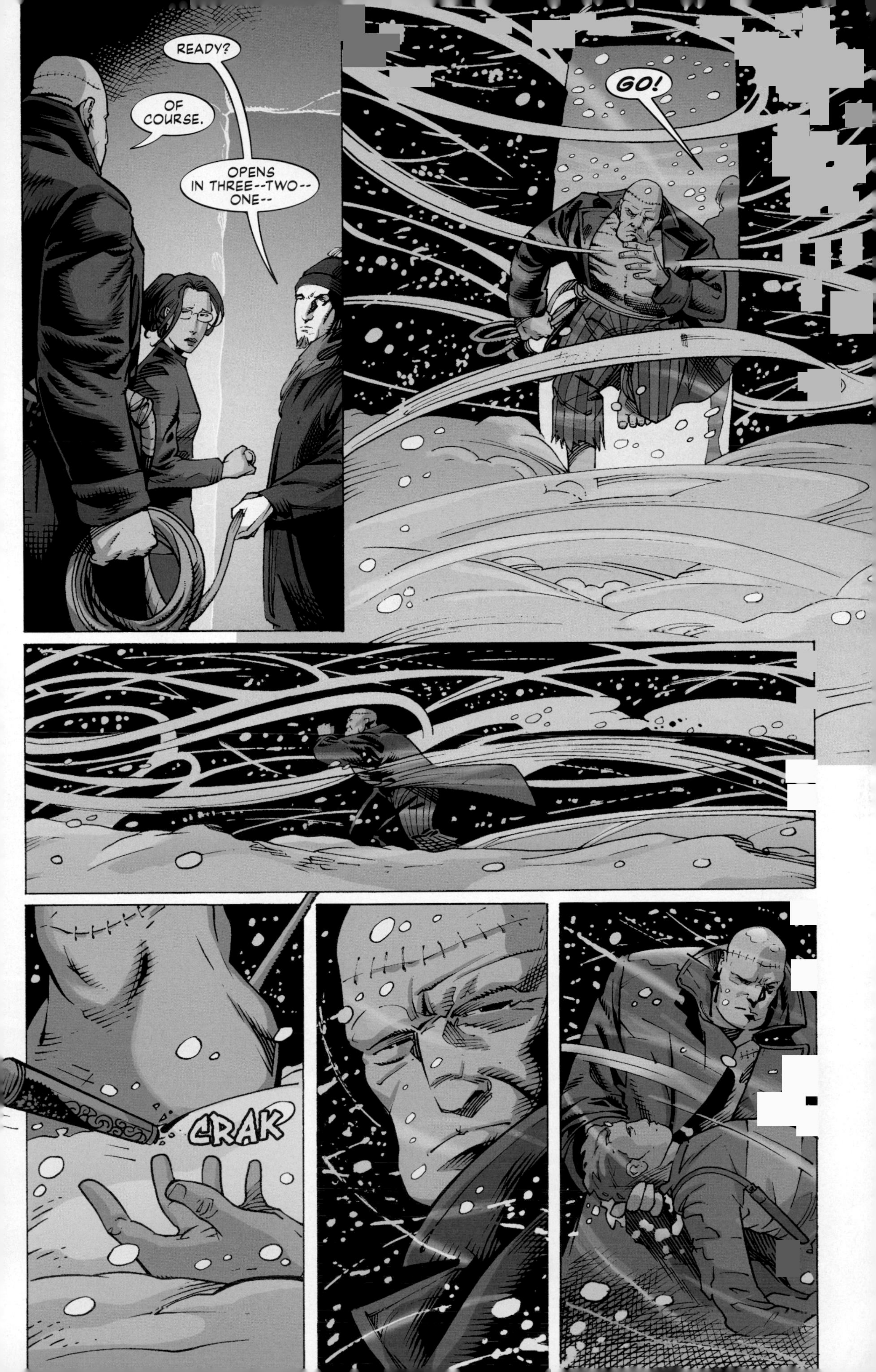
READY?
OF COURSE.
OPENS IN THREE--TWO--ONE--
GO!
CRAK

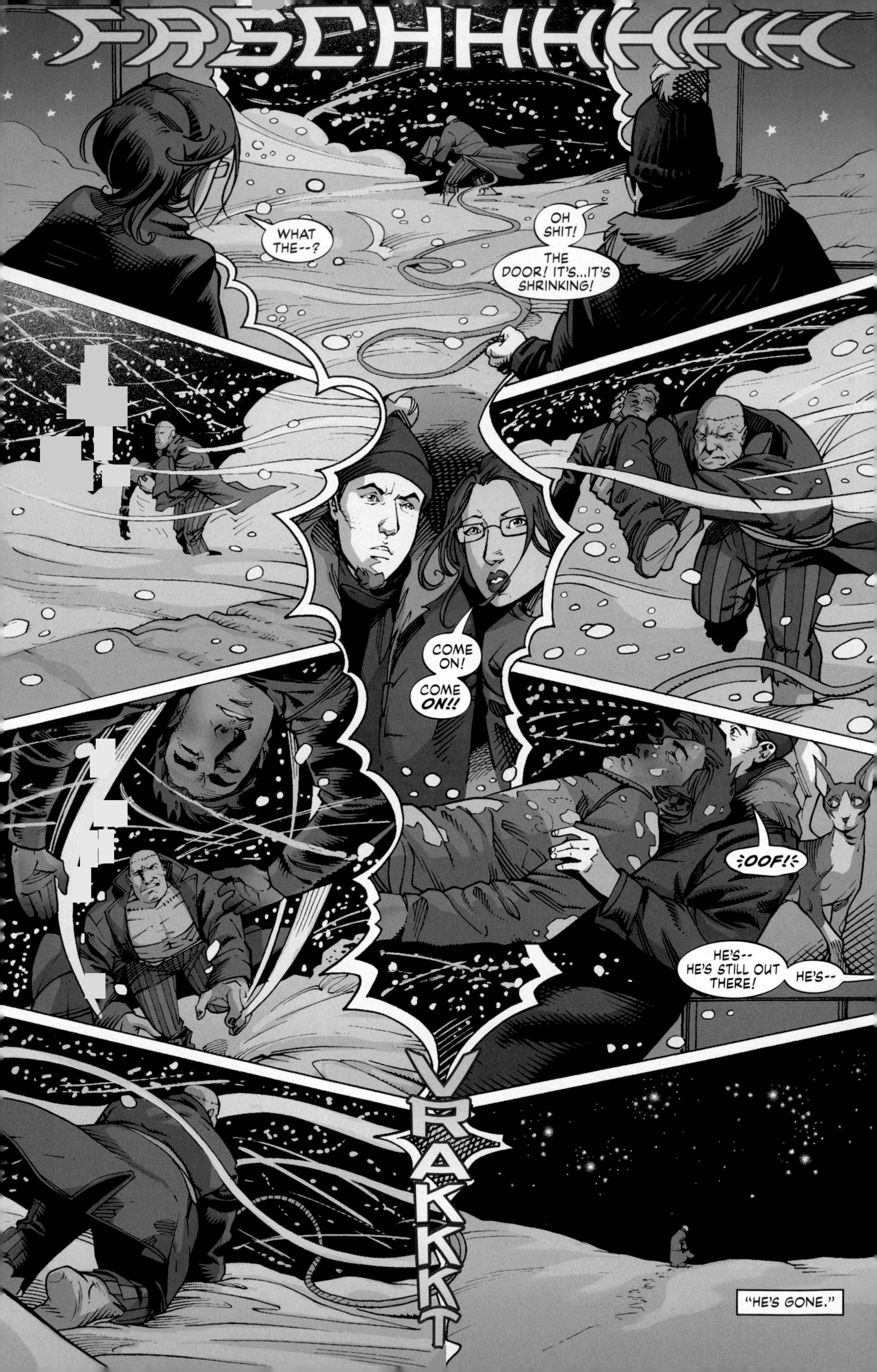
FASCHHHHHH
WHAT THE--?
OH SHIT!
THE DOOR! IT'S...IT'S SHRINKING!
COME ON!
COME ON!!
OOF!
HE'S-- HE'S STILL OUT THERE!
HE'S--
VRAKKT
"HE'S GONE."

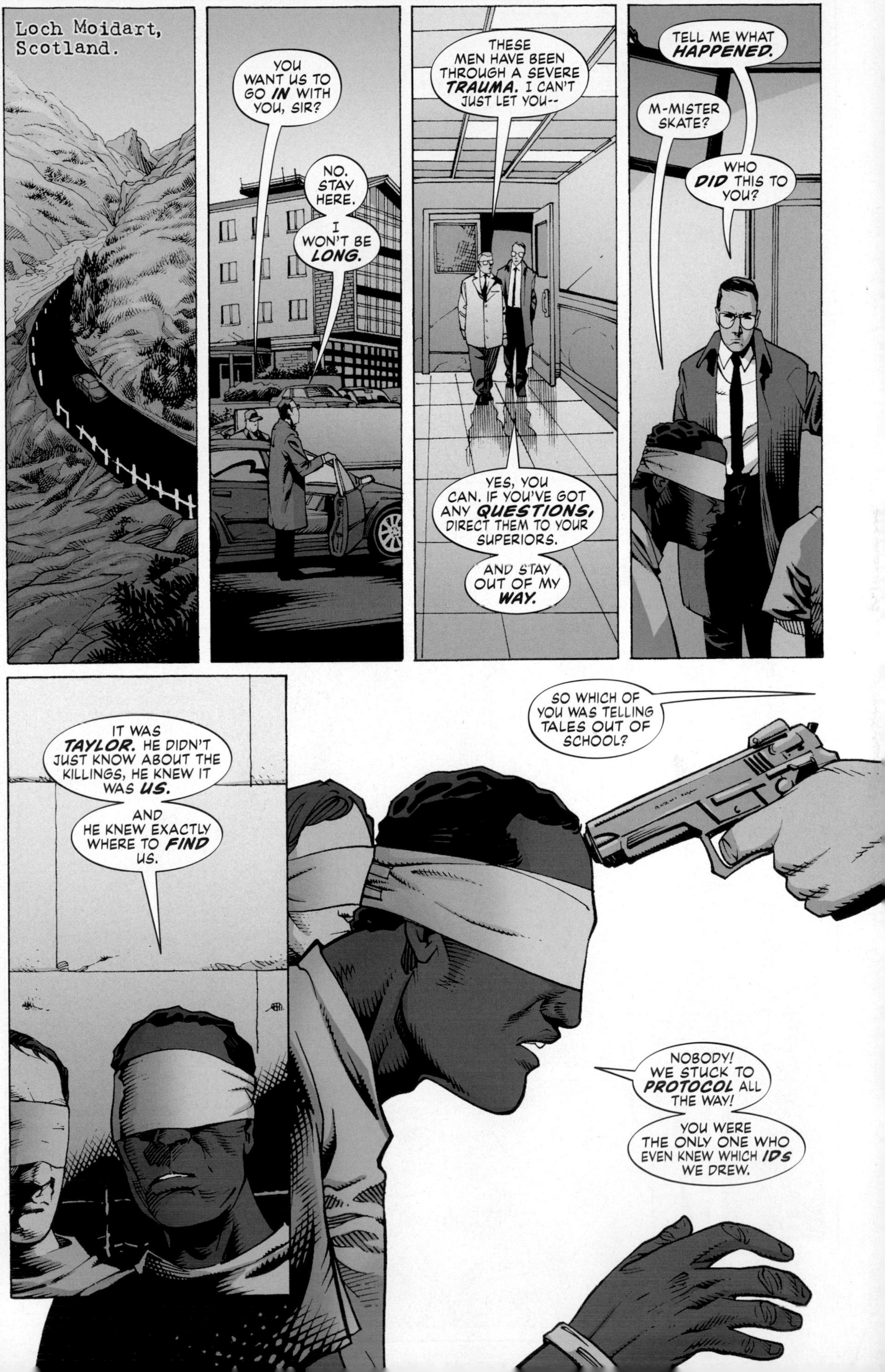
Loch Moidart, Scotland.
YOU WANT US TO GO IN WITH YOU, SIR?
NO. STAY HERE.
I WON'T BE LONG.
THESE MEN HAVE BEEN THROUGH A SEVERE TRAUMA. I CAN'T JUST LET YOU--
YES, YOU CAN. IF YOU'VE GOT ANY QUESTIONS, DIRECT THEM TO YOUR SUPERIORS.
AND STAY OUT OF MY WAY.
TELL ME WHAT HAPPENED.
M-MISTER SKATE?
WHO DID THIS TO YOU?
IT WAS TAYLOR. HE DIDN'T JUST KNOW ABOUT THE KILLINGS, HE KNEW IT WAS US.
AND HE KNEW EXACTLY WHERE TO FIND US.
SO WHICH OF YOU WAS TELLING TALES OUT OF SCHOOL?
NOBODY! WE STUCK TO PROTOCOL ALL THE WAY!
YOU WERE THE ONLY ONE WHO EVEN KNEW WHICH IDS WE DREW.

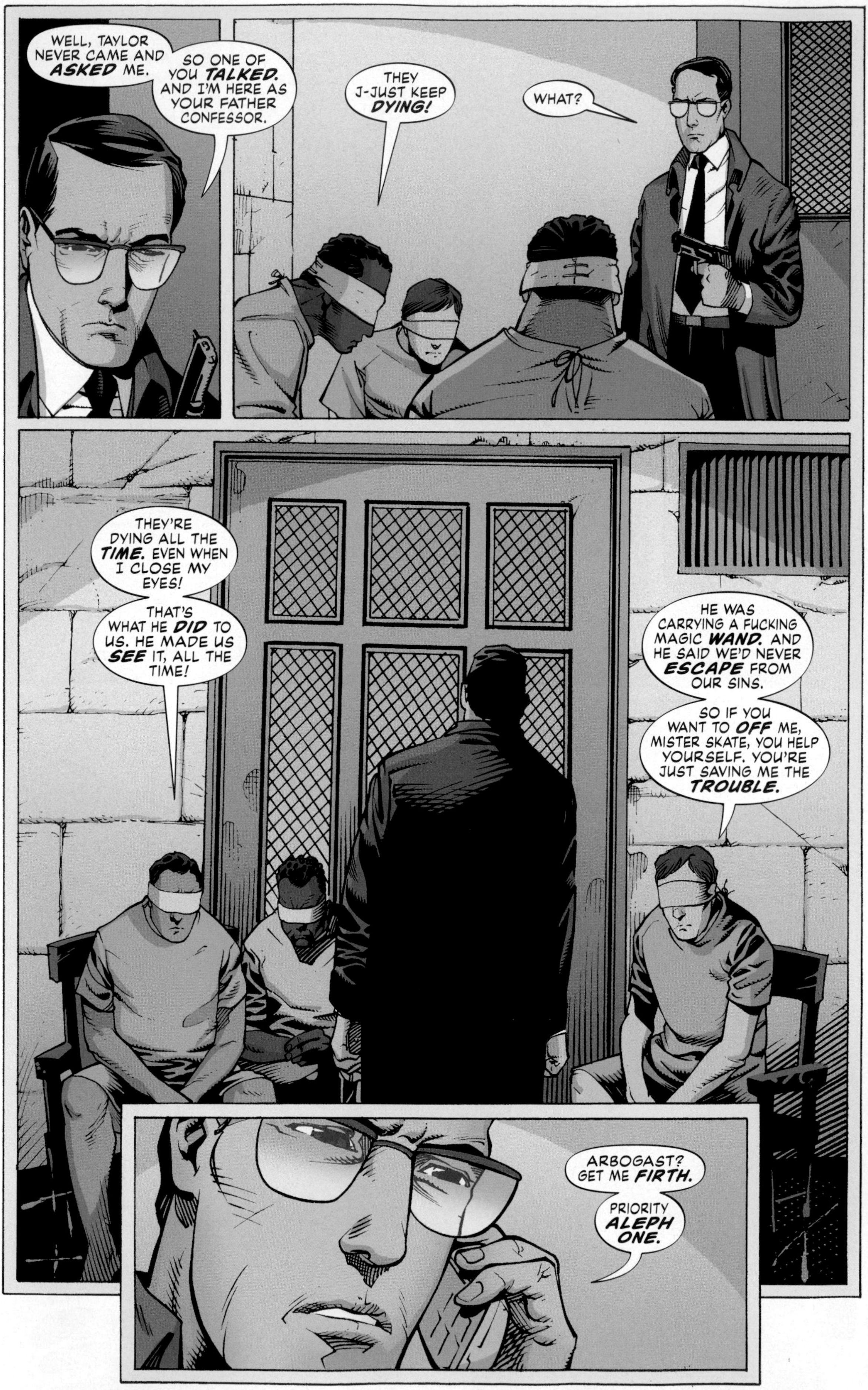
WELL, TAYLOR NEVER CAME AND ASKED ME.
SO ONE OF YOU TALKED. AND I'M HERE AS YOUR FATHER CONFESSOR.
THEY J-JUST KEEP DYING!
WHAT?
THEY'RE DYING ALL THE TIME. EVEN WHEN I CLOSE MY EYES!
THAT'S WHAT HE DID TO US. HE MADE US SEE IT, ALL THE TIME!
HE WAS CARRYING A FUCKING MAGIC WAND. AND HE SAID WE'D NEVER ESCAPE FROM OUR SINS.
SO IF YOU WANT TO OFF ME, MISTER SKATE, YOU HELP YOURSELF. YOU'RE JUST SAVING ME THE TROUBLE.
ARBOGAST? GET ME FIRTH.
PRIORITY ALEPH ONE.

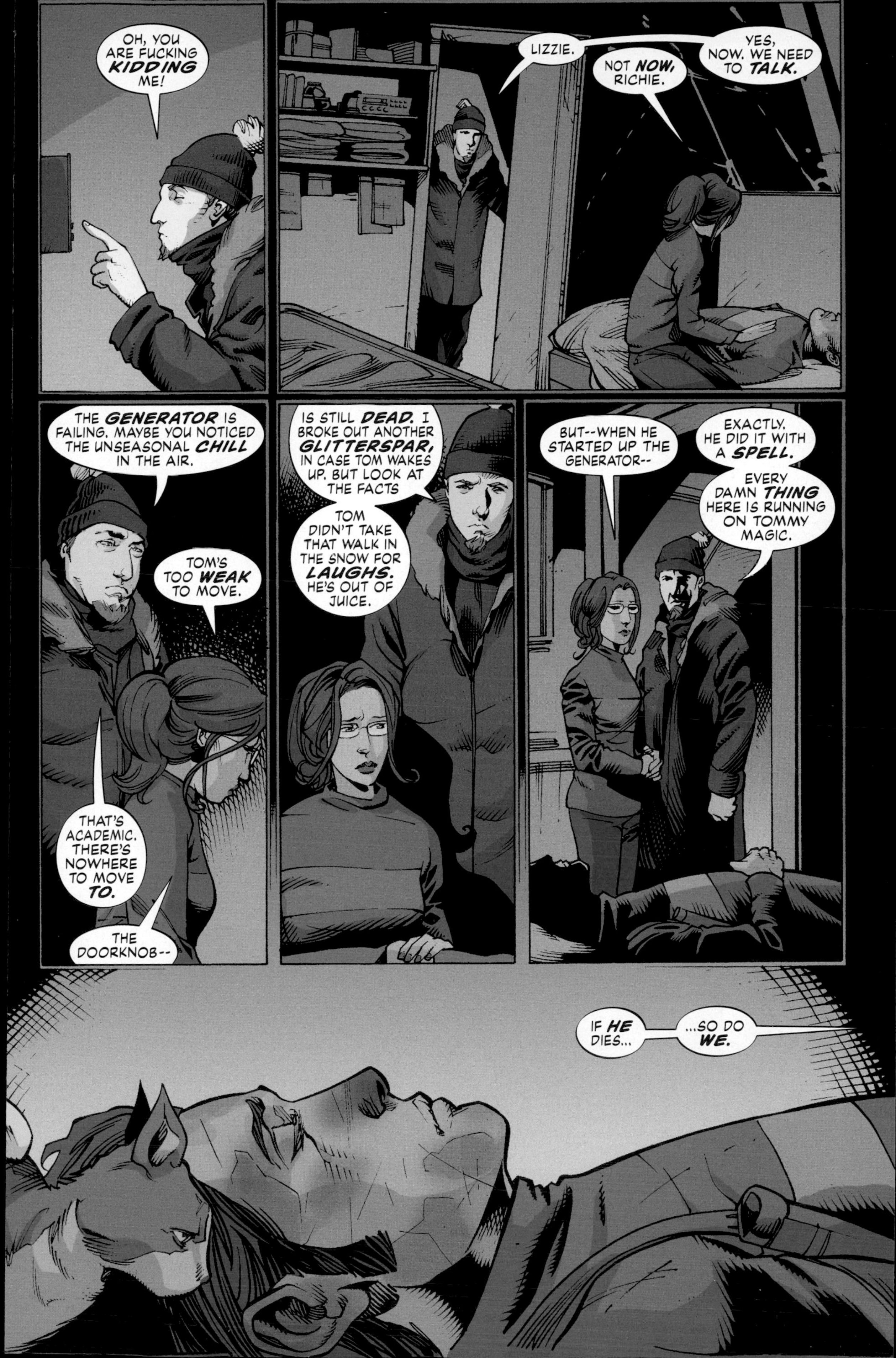

OH, YOU ARE FUCKING KIDDING ME!
LIZZIE.
NOT NOW, RICHIE.
YES, NOW. WE NEED TO TALK.
THE GENERATOR IS FAILING. MAYBE YOU NOTICED THE UNSEASONAL CHILL IN THE AIR.
TOM'S TOO WEAK TO MOVE.
THAT'S ACADEMIC. THERE'S NOWHERE TO MOVE TO.
THE DOORKNOB--
IS STILL DEAD. I BROKE OUT ANOTHER GLITTERSPAR, IN CASE TOM WAKES UP. BUT LOOK AT THE FACTS
TOM DIDN'T TAKE THAT WALK IN THE SNOW FOR LAUGHS. HE'S OUT OF JUICE.
BUT--WHEN HE STARTED UP THE GENERATOR--
EXACTLY. HE DID IT WITH A SPELL.
EVERY DAMN THING HERE IS RUNNING ON TOMMY MAGIC.
IF HE DIES...
...SO DO WE.

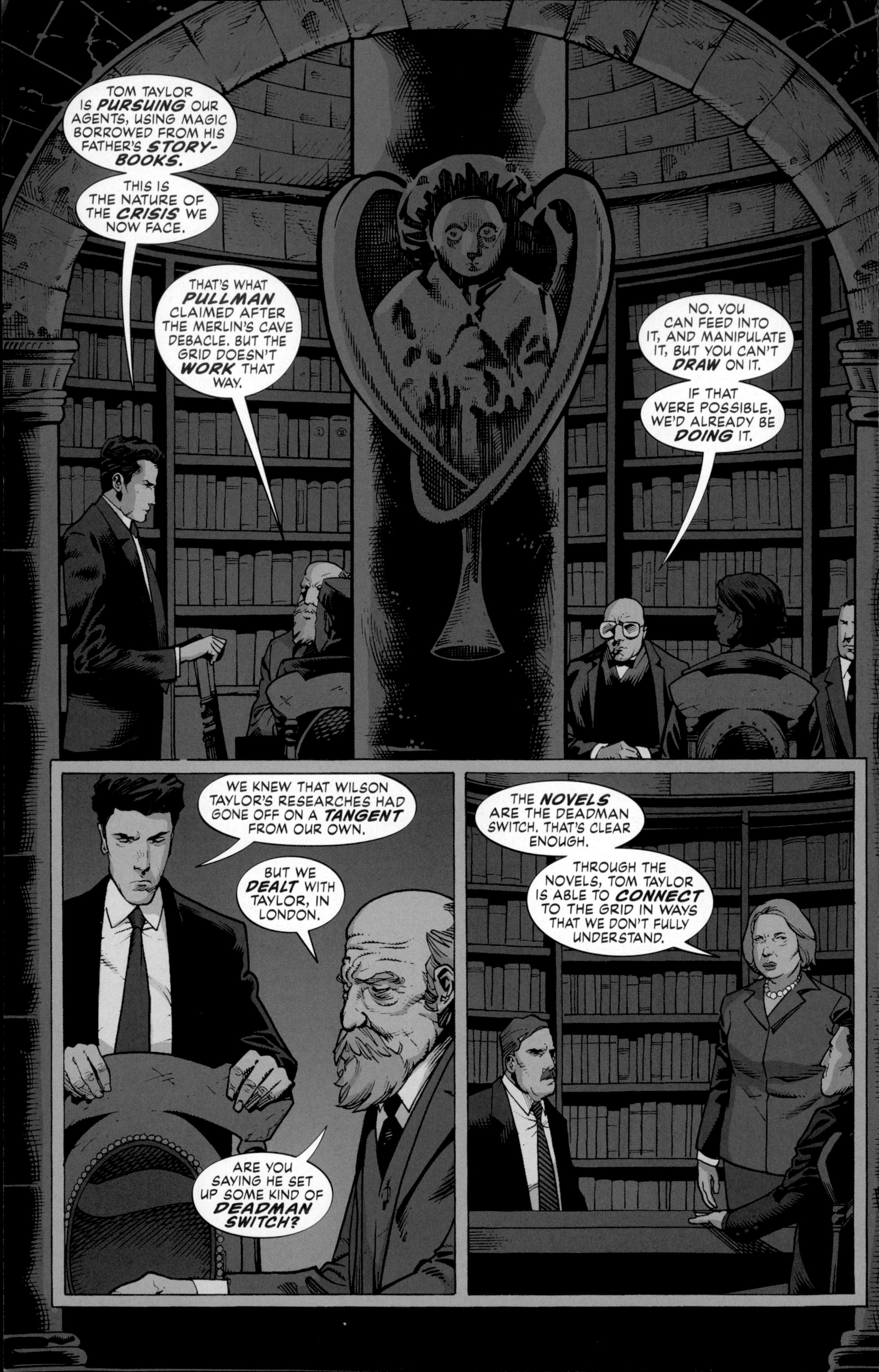
TOM TAYLOR IS PURSUING OUR AGENTS, USING MAGIC BORROWED FROM HIS FATHER'S STORY-BOOKS.
THIS IS THE NATURE OF THE CRISIS WE NOW FACE.
THAT'S WHAT PULLMAN CLAIMED AFTER THE MERLIN'S CAVE DEBACLE. BUT THE GRID DOESN'T WORK THAT WAY.
NO. YOU CAN FEED INTO IT, AND MANIPULATE IT, BUT YOU CAN'T DRAW ON IT.
IF THAT WERE POSSIBLE, WE'D ALREADY BE DOING IT.
WE KNEW THAT WILSON TAYLOR'S RESEARCHES HAD GONE OFF ON A TANGENT FROM OUR OWN.
BUT WE DEALT WITH TAYLOR, IN LONDON.
ARE YOU SAYING HE SET UP SOME KIND OF DEADMAN SWITCH?
THE NOVELS ARE THE DEADMAN SWITCH. THAT'S CLEAR ENOUGH.
THROUGH THE NOVELS, TOM TAYLOR IS ABLE TO CONNECT TO THE GRID IN WAYS THAT WE DON'T FULLY UNDERSTAND.

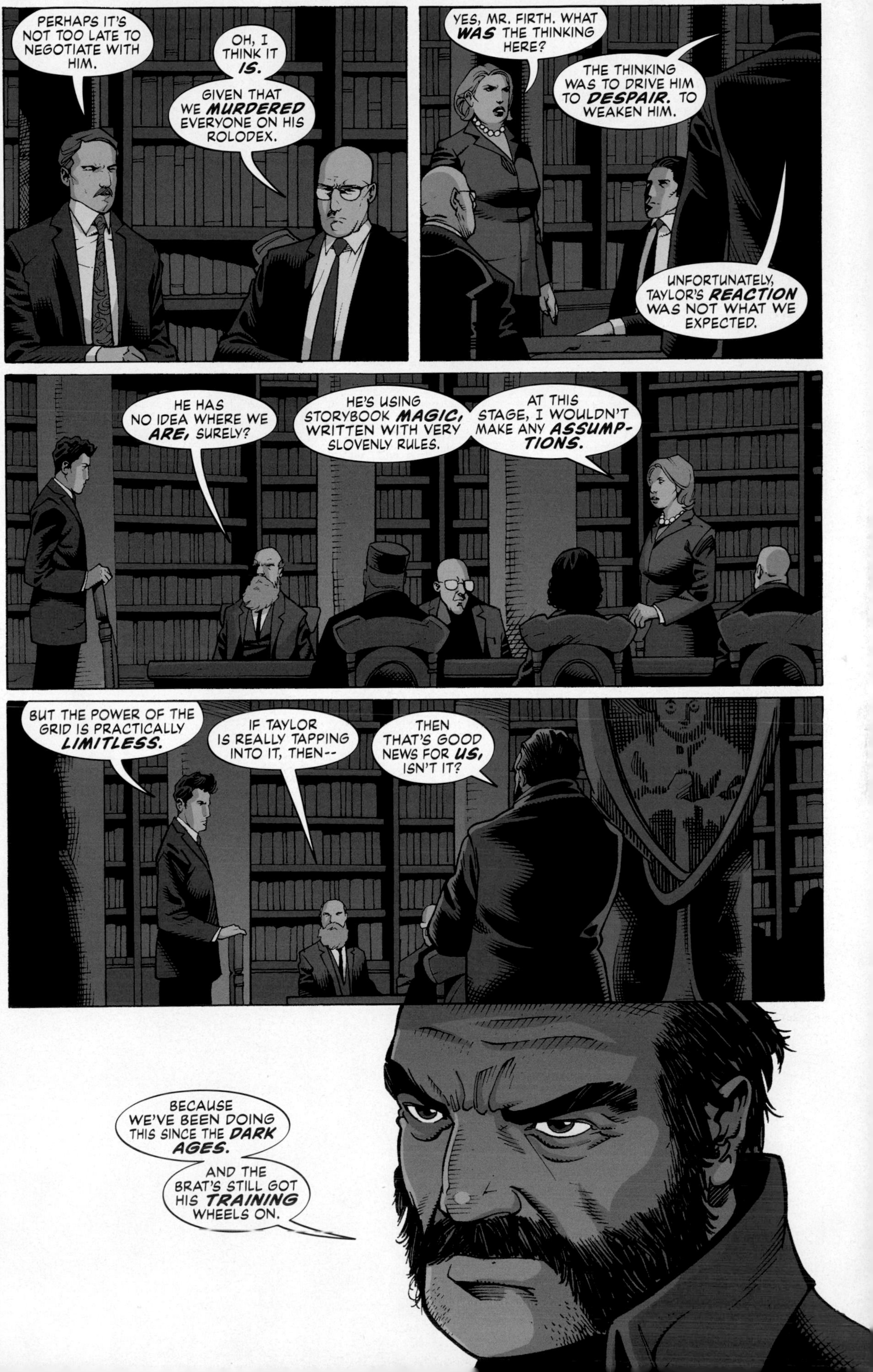
PERHAPS IT'S NOT TOO LATE TO NEGOTIATE WITH HIM.
OH, I THINK IT *IS.*
GIVEN THAT WE *MURDERED* EVERYONE ON HIS ROLODEX.
YES, MR. FIRTH. WHAT *WAS* THE THINKING HERE?
THE THINKING WAS TO DRIVE HIM TO *DESPAIR.* TO WEAKEN HIM.
UNFORTUNATELY, TAYLOR'S *REACTION* WAS NOT WHAT WE EXPECTED.
HE HAS NO IDEA WHERE WE *ARE,* SURELY?
HE'S USING STORYBOOK *MAGIC,* WRITTEN WITH VERY SLOVENLY RULES.
AT THIS STAGE, I WOULDN'T MAKE ANY *ASSUMP-TIONS.*
BUT THE POWER OF THE GRID IS PRACTICALLY *LIMITLESS.*
IF TAYLOR IS REALLY TAPPING INTO IT, THEN--
THEN THAT'S GOOD NEWS FOR *US,* ISN'T IT?
BECAUSE WE'VE BEEN DOING THIS SINCE THE *DARK AGES.*
AND THE BRAT'S STILL GOT HIS *TRAINING* WHEELS ON.

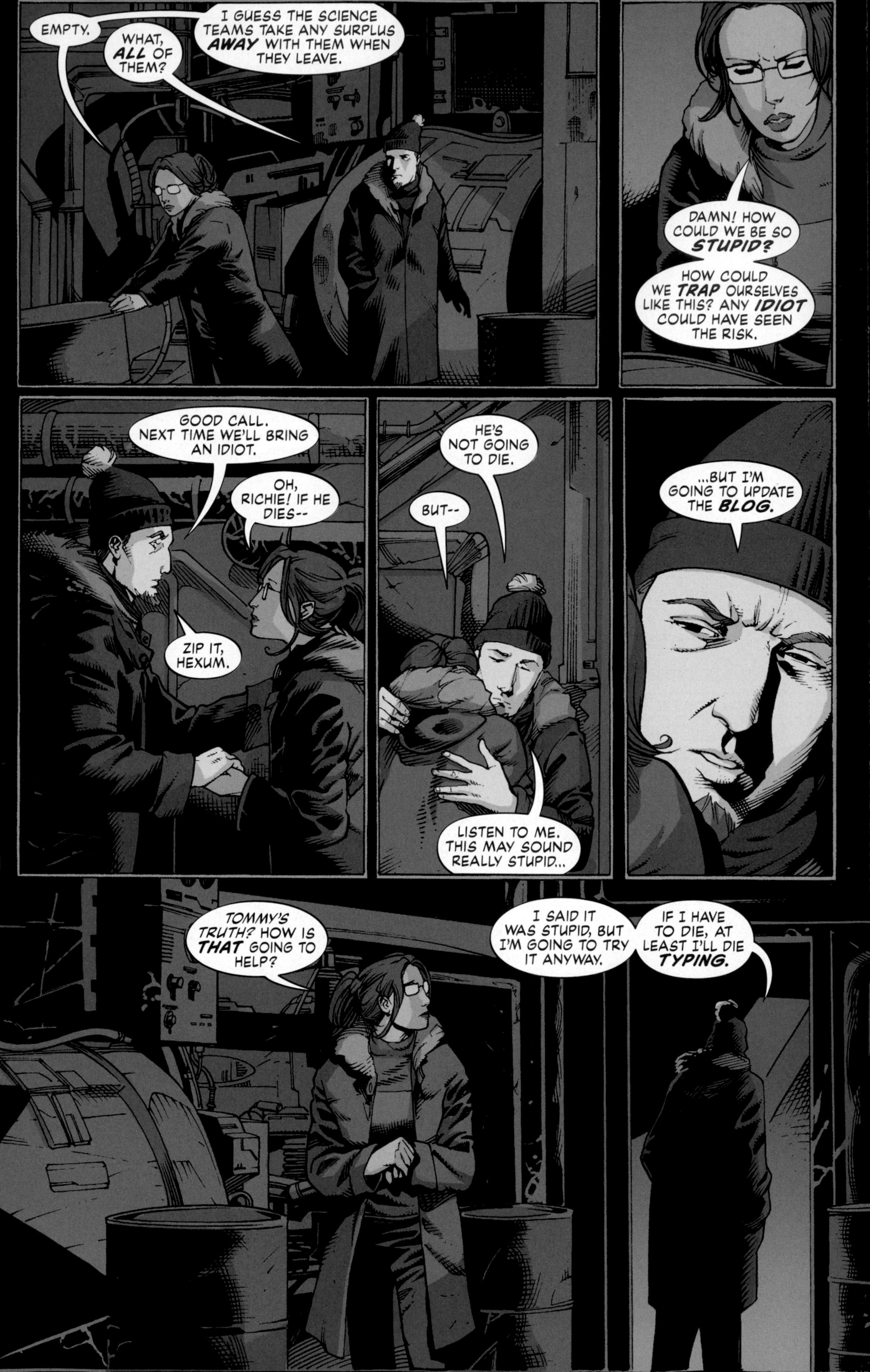

EMPTY.
WHAT, ALL OF THEM?
I GUESS THE SCIENCE TEAMS TAKE ANY SURPLUS AWAY WITH THEM WHEN THEY LEAVE.
DAMN! HOW COULD WE BE SO STUPID?
HOW COULD WE TRAP OURSELVES LIKE THIS? ANY IDIOT COULD HAVE SEEN THE RISK.
GOOD CALL. NEXT TIME WE'LL BRING AN IDIOT.
OH, RICHIE! IF HE DIES--
ZIP IT, HEXUM.
HE'S NOT GOING TO DIE.
BUT--
LISTEN TO ME. THIS MAY SOUND REALLY STUPID...
...BUT I'M GOING TO UPDATE THE BLOG.
TOMMY'S TRUTH? HOW IS THAT GOING TO HELP?
I SAID IT WAS STUPID, BUT I'M GOING TO TRY IT ANYWAY.
IF I HAVE TO DIE, AT LEAST I'LL DIE TYPING.

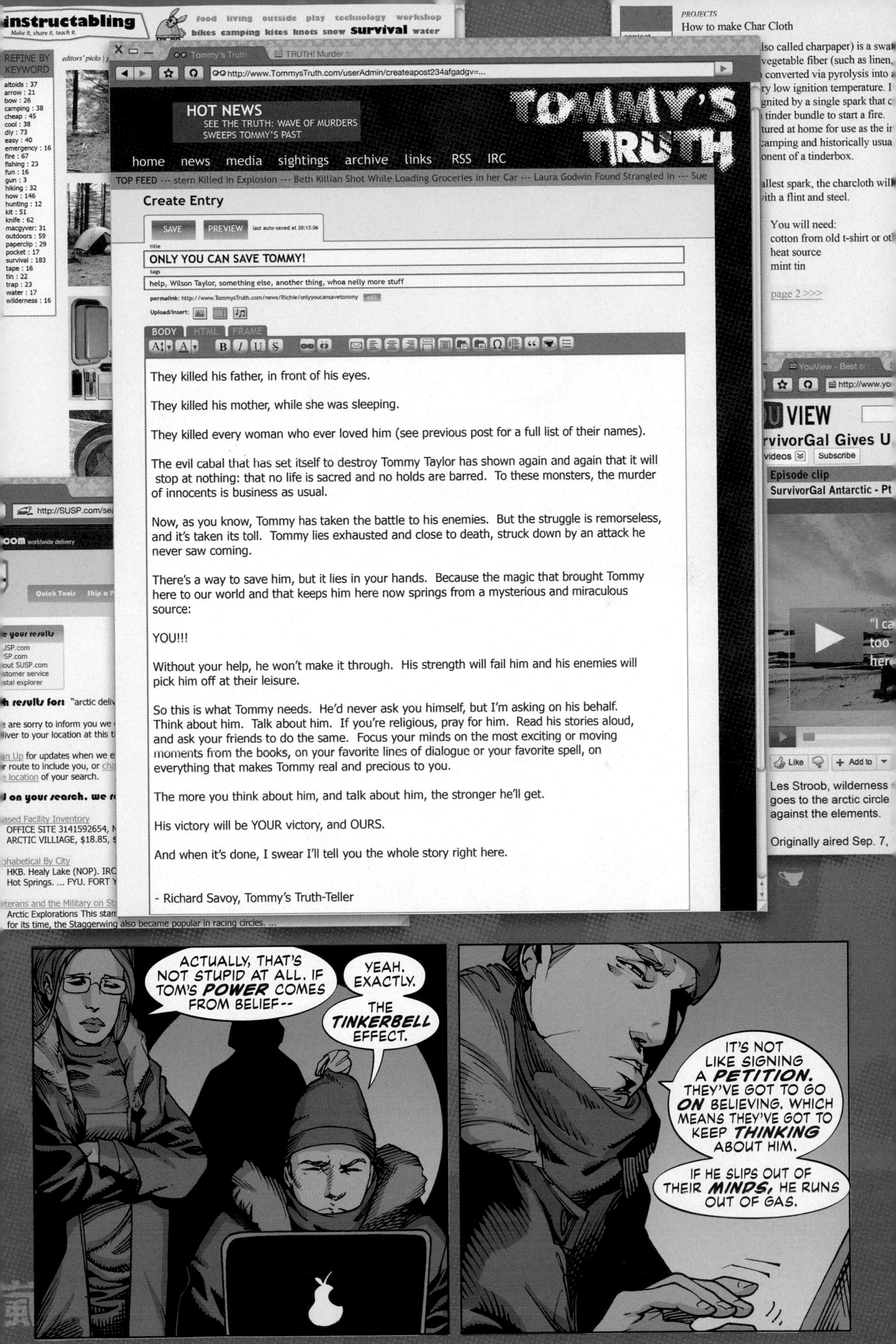
TOMMY'S TRUTH
HOT NEWS
SEE THE TRUTH: WAVE OF MURDERS SWEEPS TOMMY'S PAST
home news media sightings archive links RSS IRC
TOP FEED --- stern Killed in Explosion --- Beth Killian Shot While Loading Groceries in her Car --- Laura Godwin Found Strangled in --- Sue
Create Entry
SAVE PREVIEW last auto-saved at 20:13:06
ONLY YOU CAN SAVE TOMMY!
help, Wilson Taylor, something else, another thing, whoa nelly more stuff
permalink: http://www.TommysTruth.com/news/Richie/onlyyoucansavetommy
They killed his father, in front of his eyes.
They killed his mother, while she was sleeping.
They killed every woman who ever loved him (see previous post for a full list of their names).
The evil cabal that has set itself to destroy Tommy Taylor has shown again and again that it will stop at nothing: that no life is sacred and no holds are barred. To these monsters, the murder of innocents is business as usual.
Now, as you know, Tommy has taken the battle to his enemies. But the struggle is remorseless, and it's taken its toll. Tommy lies exhausted and close to death, struck down by an attack he never saw coming.
There's a way to save him, but it lies in your hands. Because the magic that brought Tommy here to our world and that keeps him here now springs from a mysterious and miraculous source:
YOU!!!
Without your help, he won't make it through. His strength will fail him and his enemies will pick him off at their leisure.
So this is what Tommy needs. He'd never ask you himself, but I'm asking on his behalf. Think about him. Talk about him. If you're religious, pray for him. Read his stories aloud, and ask your friends to do the same. Focus your minds on the most exciting or moving moments from the books, on your favorite lines of dialogue or your favorite spell, on everything that makes Tommy real and precious to you.
The more you think about him, and talk about him, the stronger he'll get.
His victory will be YOUR victory, and OURS.
And when it's done, I swear I'll tell you the whole story right here.
- Richard Savoy, Tommy's Truth-Teller
ACTUALLY, THAT'S NOT STUPID AT ALL. IF TOM'S POWER COMES FROM BELIEF--
YEAH. EXACTLY.
THE TINKERBELL EFFECT.
IT'S NOT LIKE SIGNING A PETITION. THEY'VE GOT TO GO ON BELIEVING. WHICH MEANS THEY'VE GOT TO KEEP THINKING ABOUT HIM.
IF HE SLIPS OUT OF THEIR MINDS, HE RUNS OUT OF GAS.

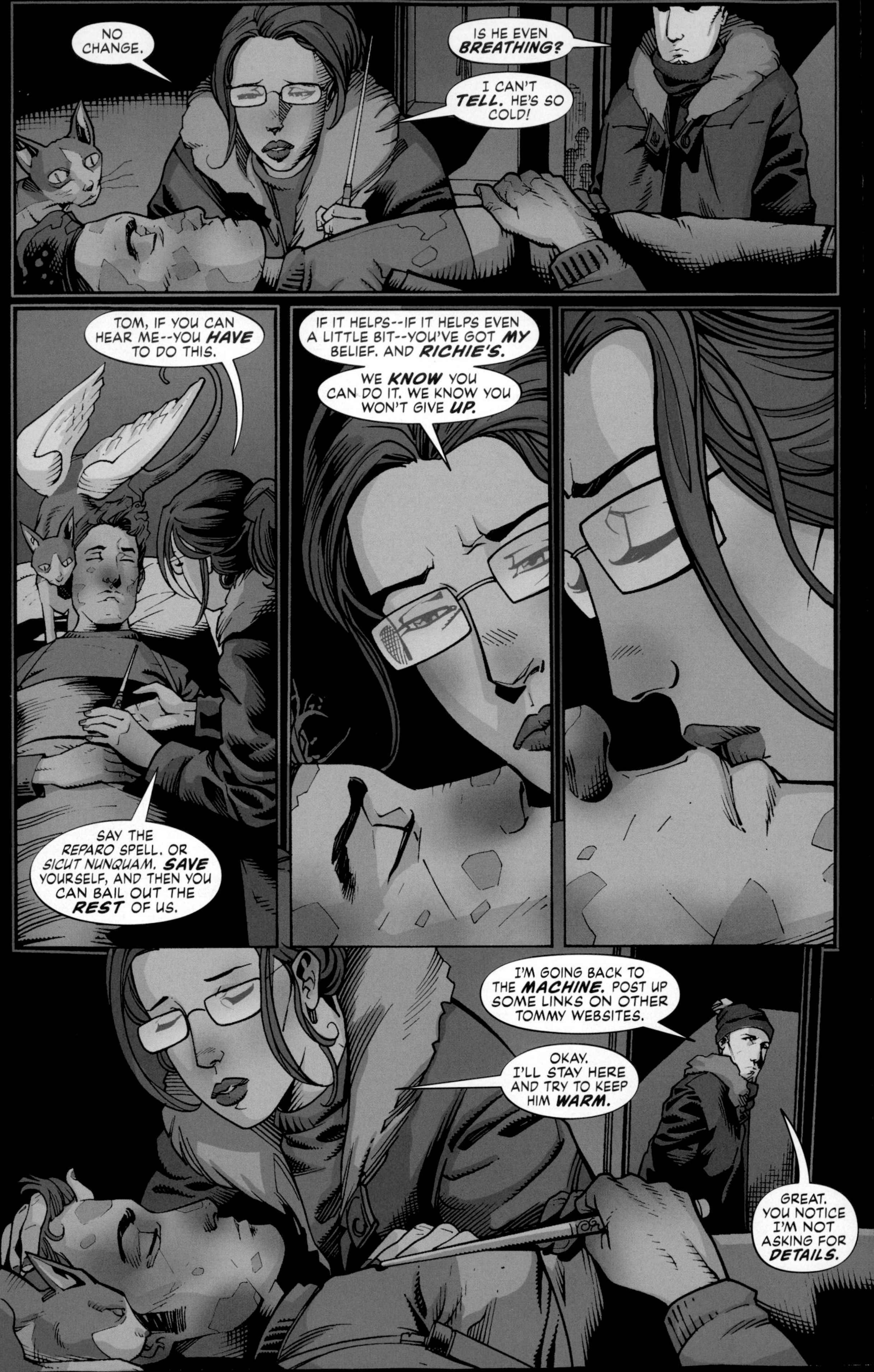
NO CHANGE.
IS HE EVEN BREATHING?
I CAN'T TELL. HE'S SO COLD!
TOM, IF YOU CAN HEAR ME--YOU HAVE TO DO THIS.
SAY THE REPARO SPELL. OR SICUT NUNQUAM. SAVE YOURSELF, AND THEN YOU CAN BAIL OUT THE REST OF US.
IF IT HELPS--IF IT HELPS EVEN A LITTLE BIT--YOU'VE GOT MY BELIEF. AND RICHIE'S.
WE KNOW YOU CAN DO IT. WE KNOW YOU WON'T GIVE UP.
I'M GOING BACK TO THE MACHINE. POST UP SOME LINKS ON OTHER TOMMY WEBSITES.
OKAY. I'LL STAY HERE AND TRY TO KEEP HIM WARM.
GREAT. YOU NOTICE I'M NOT ASKING FOR DETAILS.

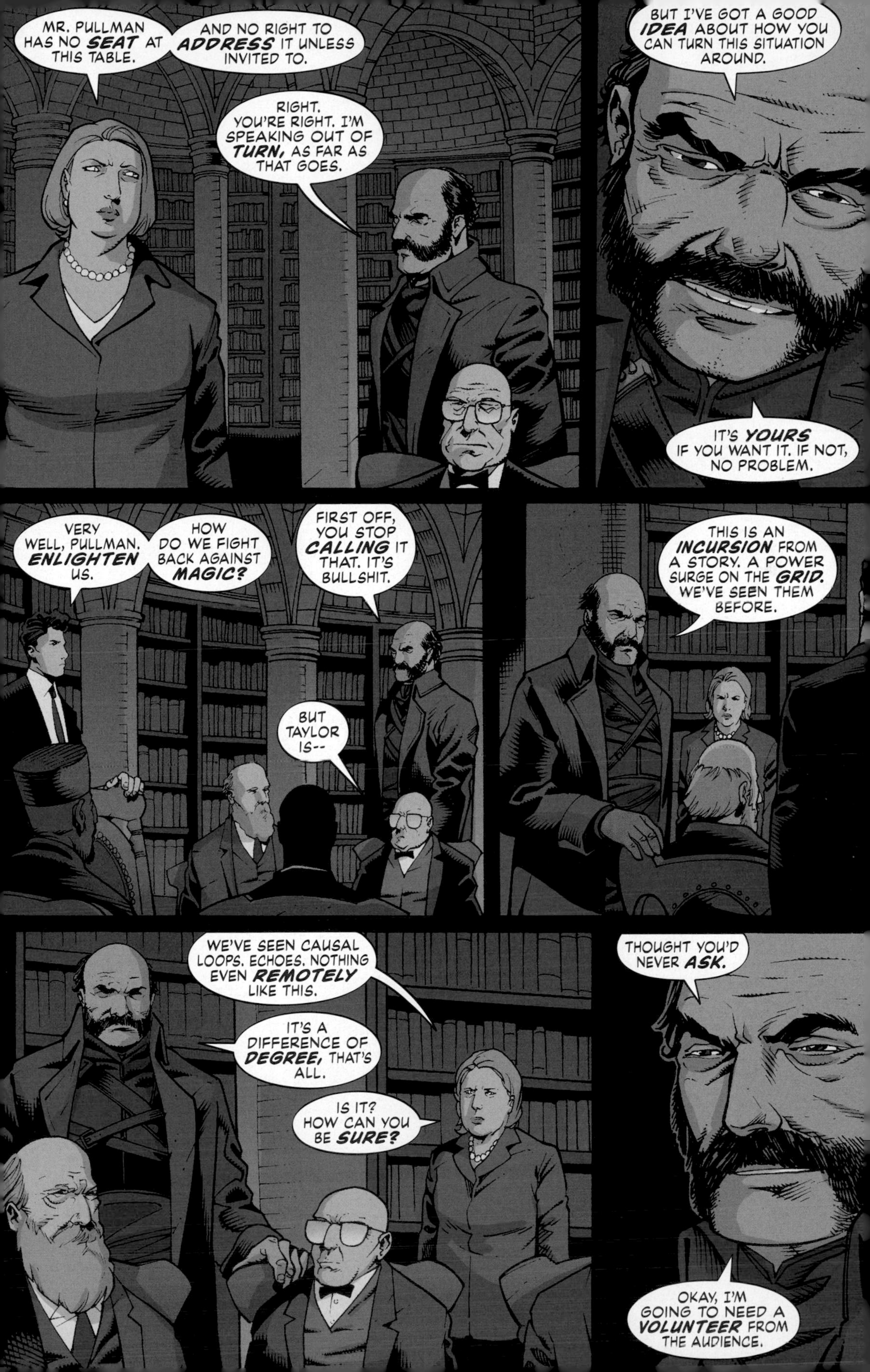

MR. PULLMAN HAS NO SEAT AT THIS TABLE.
AND NO RIGHT TO ADDRESS IT UNLESS INVITED TO.
RIGHT. YOU'RE RIGHT. I'M SPEAKING OUT OF TURN, AS FAR AS THAT GOES.
BUT I'VE GOT A GOOD IDEA ABOUT HOW YOU CAN TURN THIS SITUATION AROUND.
IT'S YOURS IF YOU WANT IT. IF NOT, NO PROBLEM.
VERY WELL, PULLMAN. ENLIGHTEN US.
HOW DO WE FIGHT BACK AGAINST MAGIC?
FIRST OFF, YOU STOP CALLING IT THAT. IT'S BULLSHIT.
BUT TAYLOR IS--
THIS IS AN INCURSION FROM A STORY. A POWER SURGE ON THE GRID. WE'VE SEEN THEM BEFORE.
WE'VE SEEN CAUSAL LOOPS. ECHOES. NOTHING EVEN REMOTELY LIKE THIS.
IT'S A DIFFERENCE OF DEGREE, THAT'S ALL.
IS IT? HOW CAN YOU BE SURE?
THOUGHT YOU'D NEVER ASK.
OKAY, I'M GOING TO NEED A VOLUNTEER FROM THE AUDIENCE.

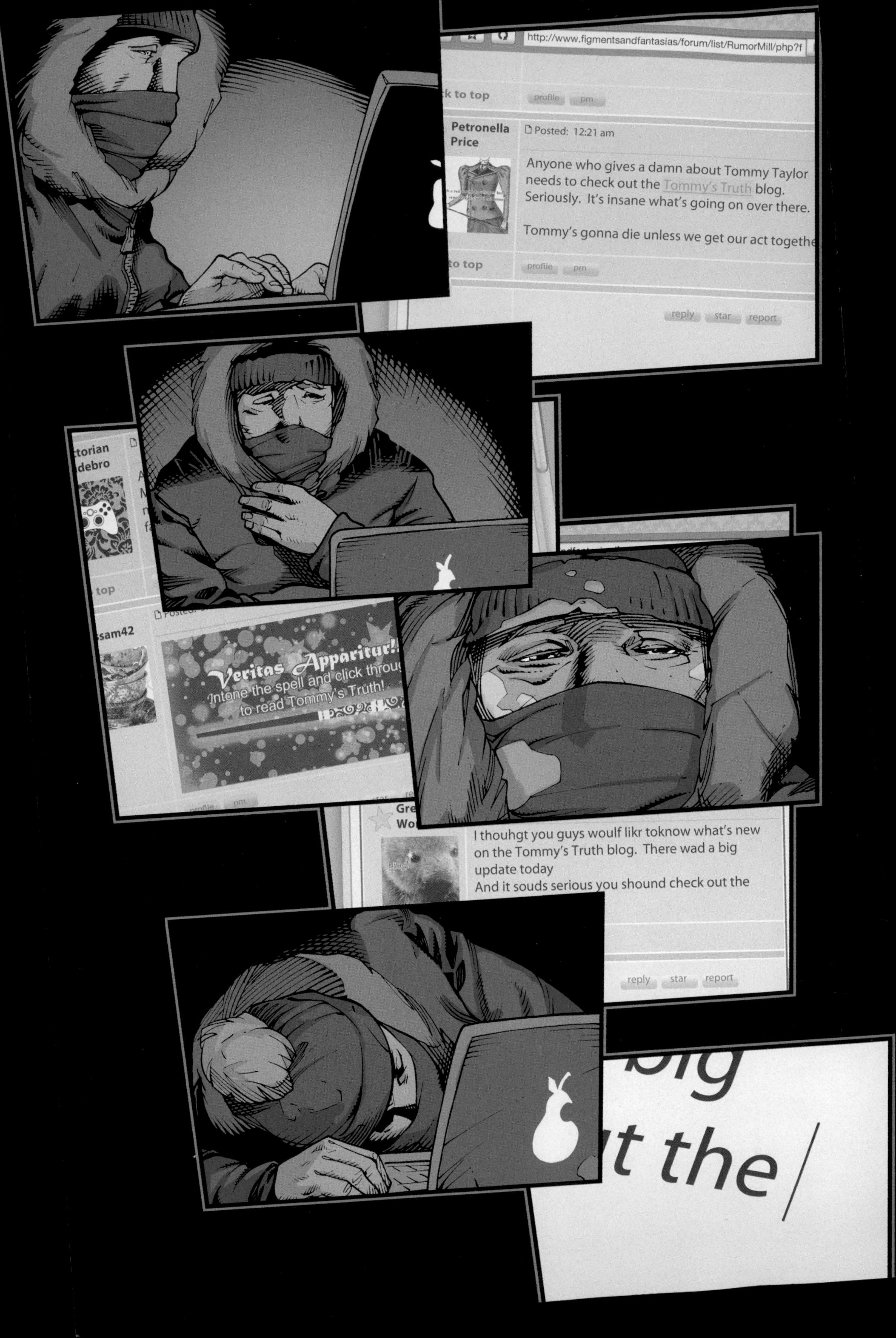
http://www.figmentsandfantasias/forum/list/RumorMill/php?f
ck to top
profile
pm
Petronella Price
Posted: 12:21 am
Anyone who gives a damn about Tommy Taylor needs to check out the Tommy's Truth blog. Seriously. It's insane what's going on over there.
Tommy's gonna die unless we get our act togethe
to top
profile
pm
reply
star
report
ctorian
ndebro
top
ssam42
Veritas Apparitur!!
Intone the spell and click throug
to read Tommy's Truth!
profile
pm
Gre
Wo
I thouhgt you guys woulf likr toknow what's new on the Tommy's Truth blog. There wad a big update today
And it souds serious you shound check out the
reply
star
report
big
t the

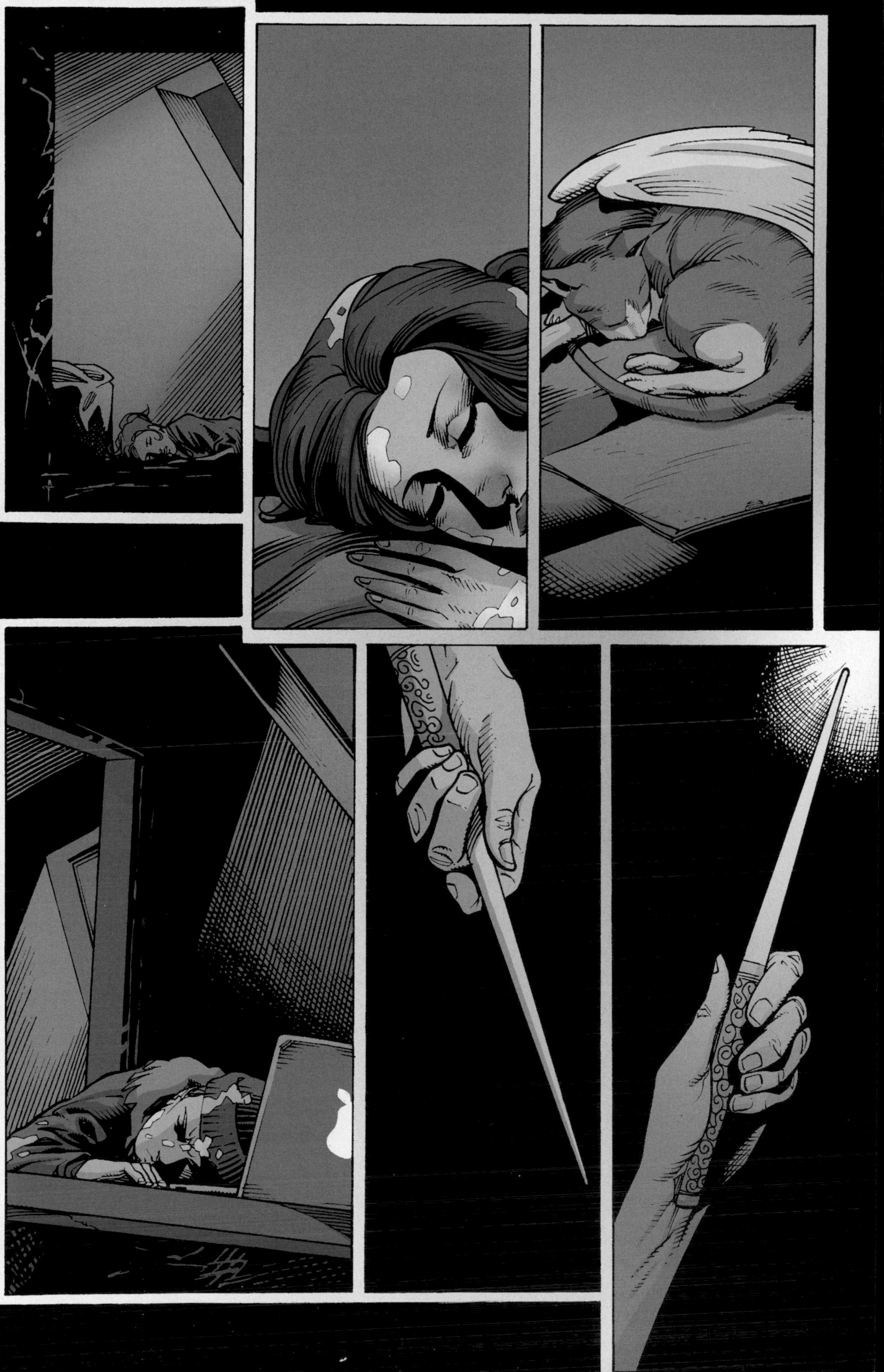

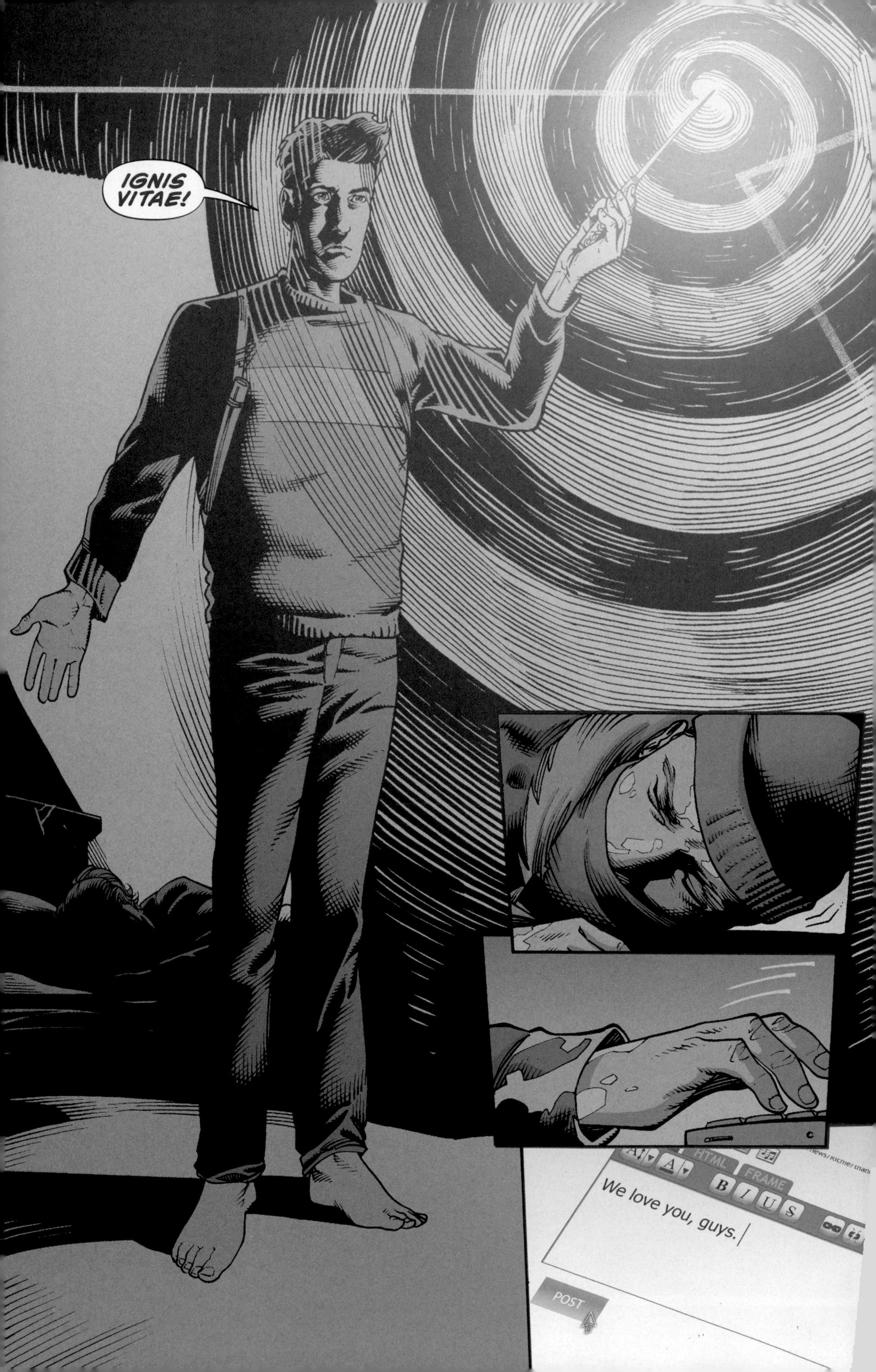
IGNIS VITAE!
HTML
FRAME
We love you, guys.
POST

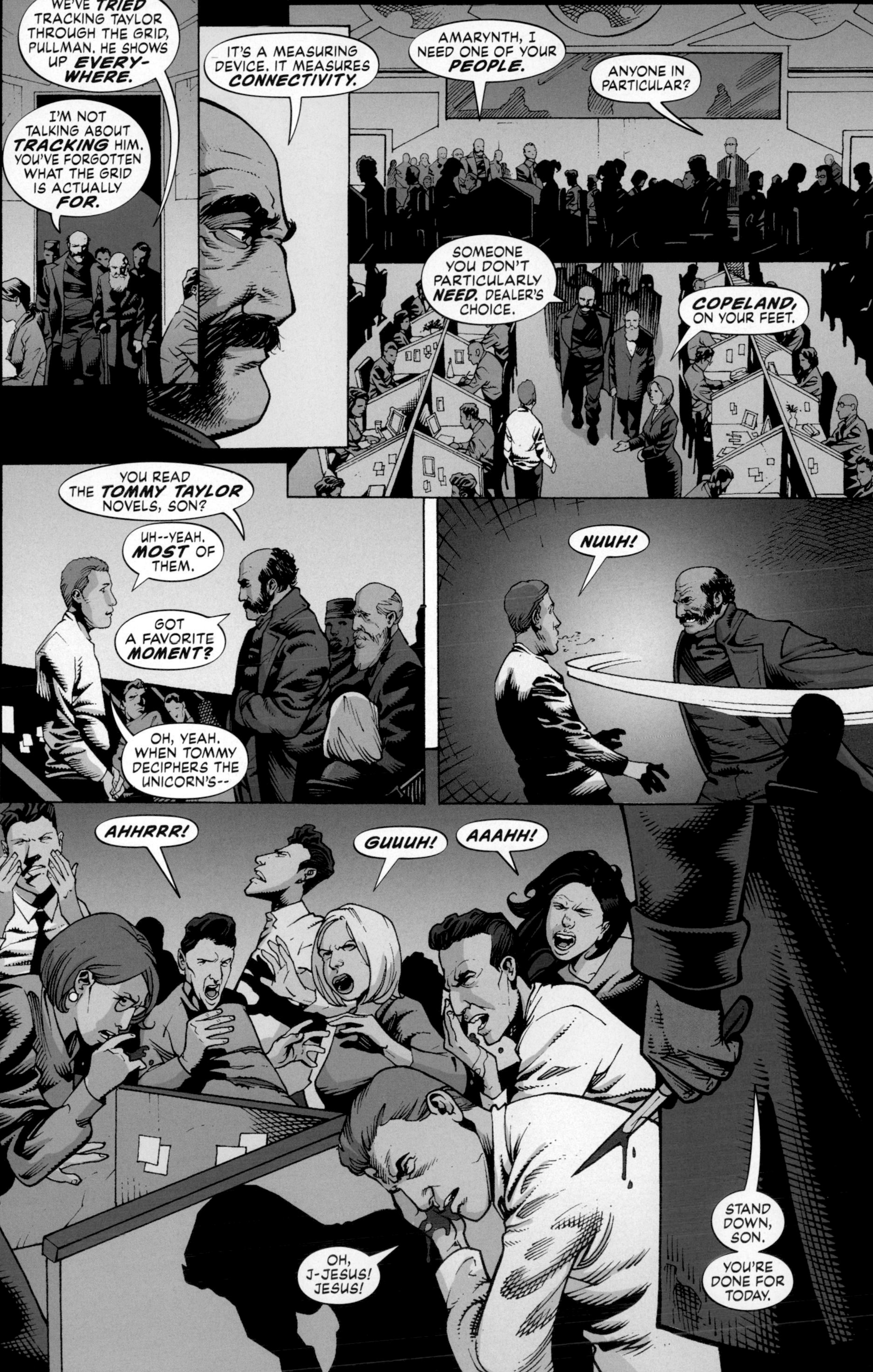
WE'VE TRIED TRACKING TAYLOR THROUGH THE GRID, PULLMAN. HE SHOWS UP EVERY-WHERE.
I'M NOT TALKING ABOUT TRACKING HIM. YOU'VE FORGOTTEN WHAT THE GRID IS ACTUALLY FOR.
IT'S A MEASURING DEVICE. IT MEASURES CONNECTIVITY.
AMARYNTH, I NEED ONE OF YOUR PEOPLE.
ANYONE IN PARTICULAR?
SOMEONE YOU DON'T PARTICULARLY NEED. DEALER'S CHOICE.
COPELAND, ON YOUR FEET.
YOU READ THE TOMMY TAYLOR NOVELS, SON?
UH--YEAH. MOST OF THEM.
GOT A FAVORITE MOMENT?
OH, YEAH. WHEN TOMMY DECIPHERS THE UNICORN'S--
NUUH!
AHHRRR!
GUUUH!
AAAHH!
OH, J-JESUS! JESUS!
STAND DOWN, SON.
YOU'RE DONE FOR TODAY.

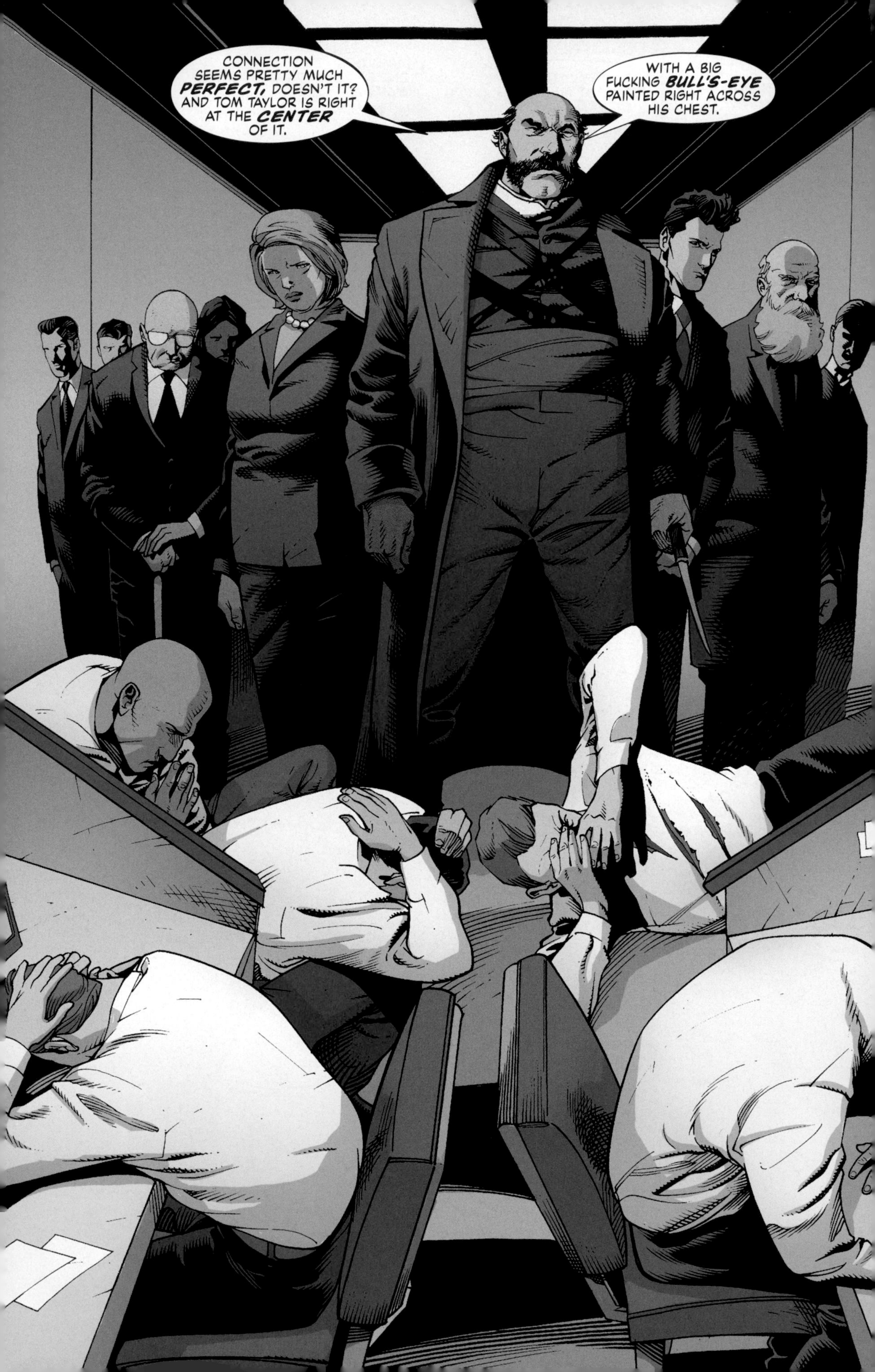
CONNECTION SEEMS PRETTY MUCH PERFECT, DOESN'T IT? AND TOM TAYLOR IS RIGHT AT THE CENTER OF IT.
WITH A BIG FUCKING BULL'S-EYE PAINTED RIGHT ACROSS HIS CHEST.

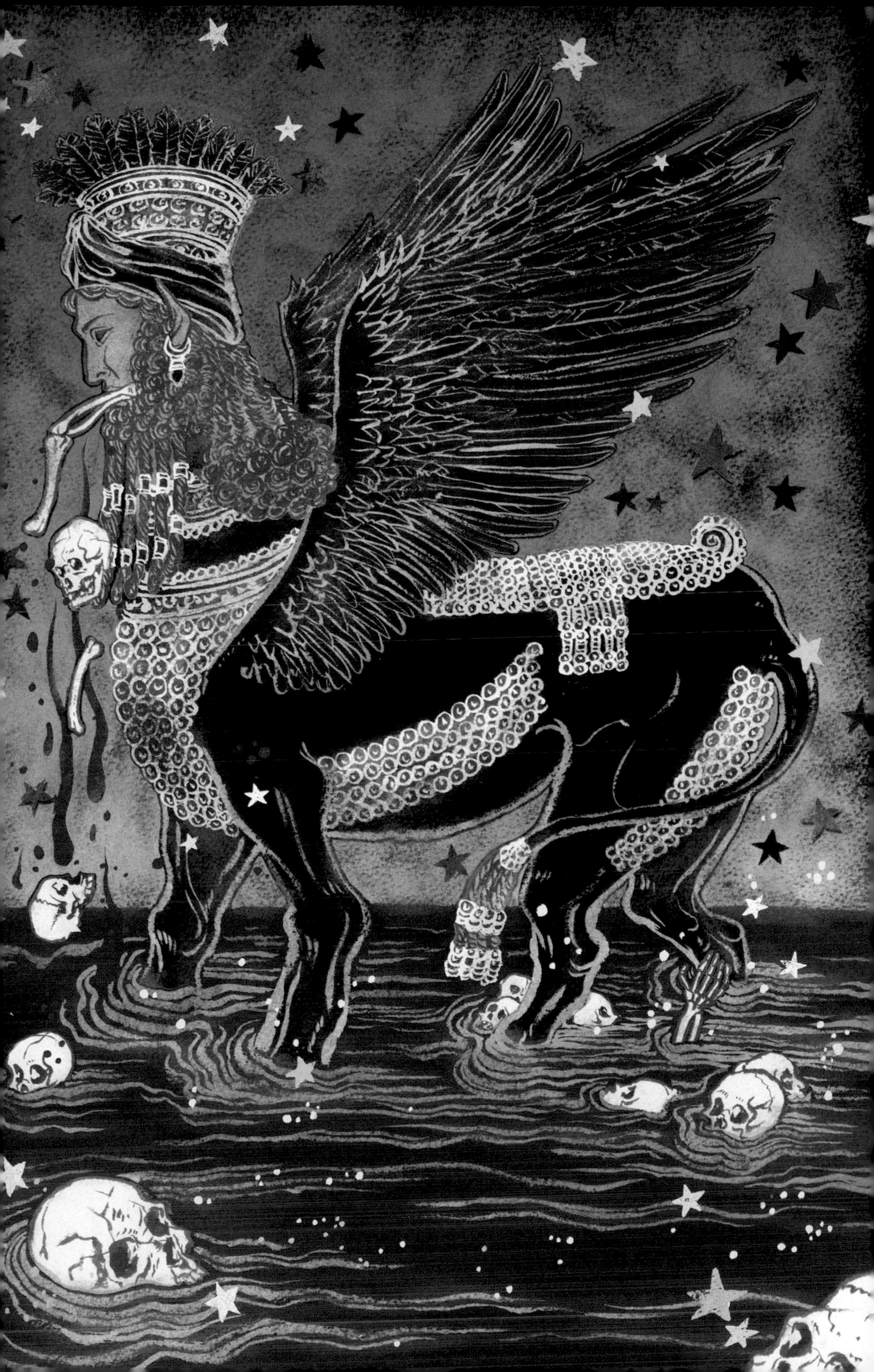

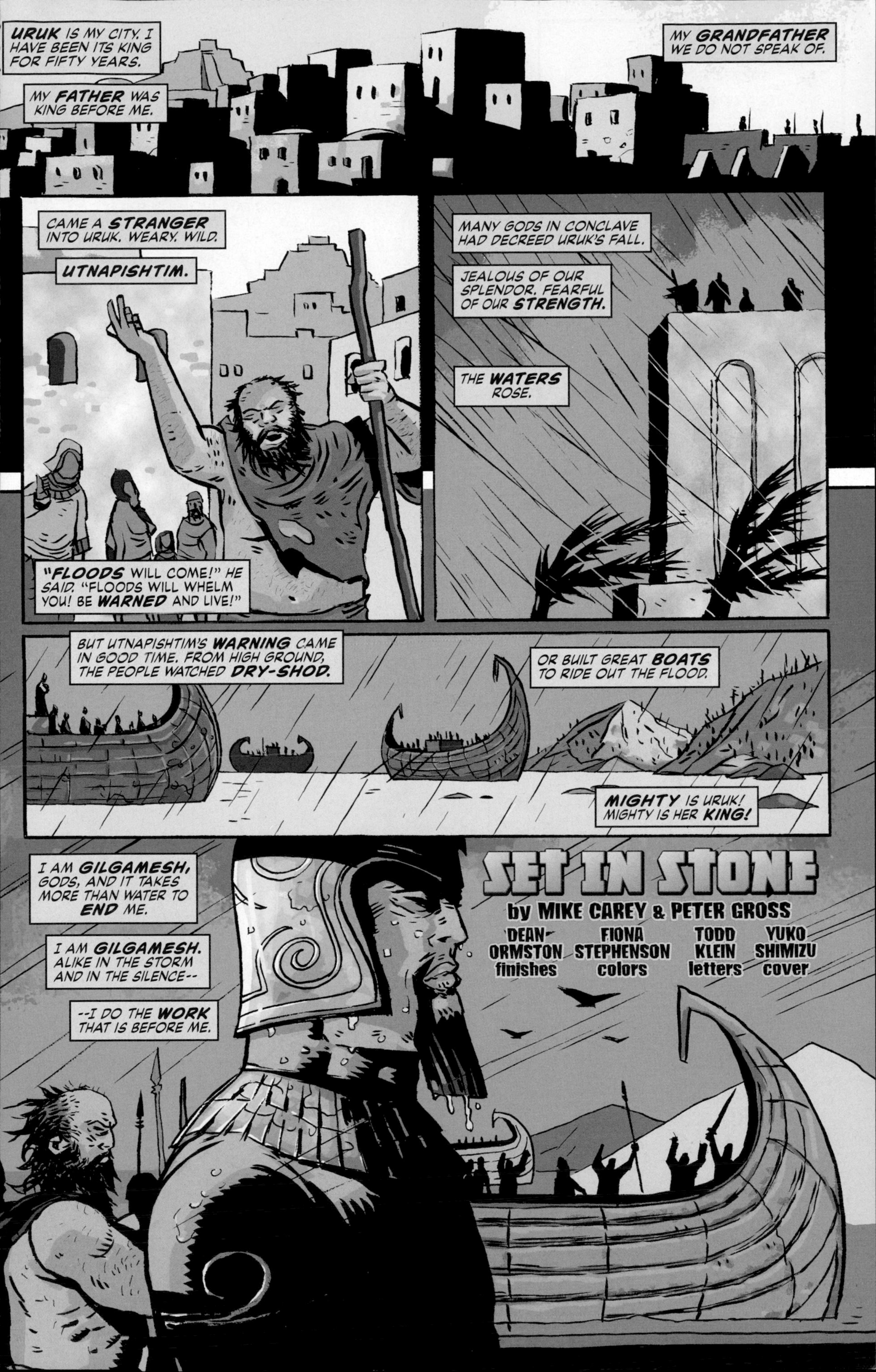
URUK IS MY CITY. I HAVE BEEN ITS KING FOR FIFTY YEARS.
MY FATHER WAS KING BEFORE ME.
MY GRANDFATHER WE DO NOT SPEAK OF.
CAME A STRANGER INTO URUK. WEARY. WILD.
UTNAPISHTIM.
"FLOODS WILL COME!" HE SAID. "FLOODS WILL WHELM YOU! BE WARNED AND LIVE!"
MANY GODS IN CONCLAVE HAD DECREED URUK'S FALL.
JEALOUS OF OUR SPLENDOR. FEARFUL OF OUR STRENGTH.
THE WATERS ROSE.
BUT UTNAPISHTIM'S WARNING CAME IN GOOD TIME. FROM HIGH GROUND, THE PEOPLE WATCHED DRY-SHOD.
OR BUILT GREAT BOATS TO RIDE OUT THE FLOOD.
MIGHTY IS URUK! MIGHTY IS HER KING!
I AM GILGAMESH, GODS, AND IT TAKES MORE THAN WATER TO END ME.
I AM GILGAMESH. ALIKE IN THE STORM AND IN THE SILENCE--
--I DO THE WORK THAT IS BEFORE ME.
SET IN STONE
by MIKE CAREY & PETER GROSS
DEAN ORMSTON finishes
FIONA STEPHENSON colors
TODD KLEIN letters
YUKO SHIMIZU cover

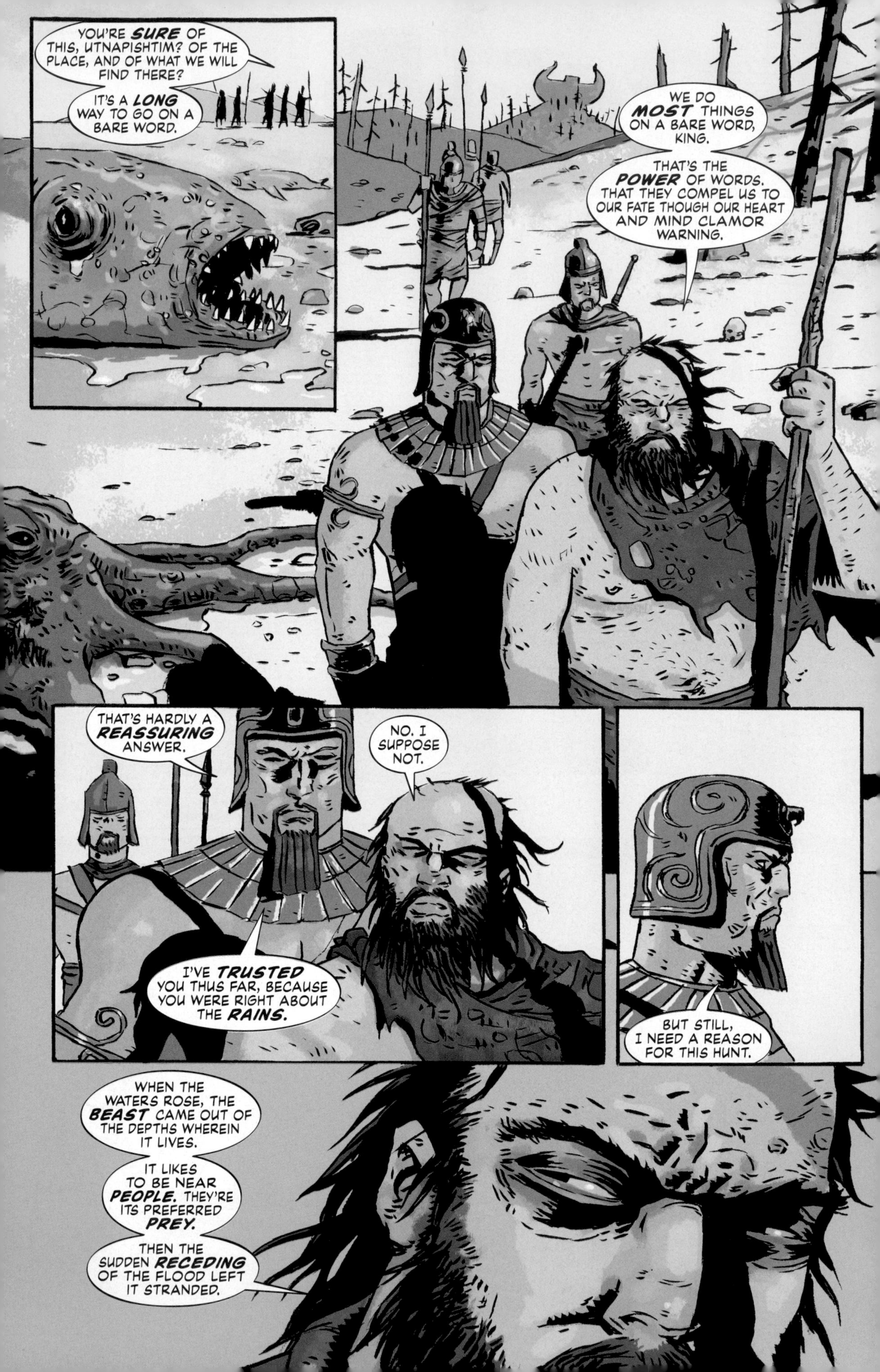
YOU'RE SURE OF THIS, UTNAPISHTIM? OF THE PLACE, AND OF WHAT WE WILL FIND THERE?
IT'S A LONG WAY TO GO ON A BARE WORD.
WE DO MOST THINGS ON A BARE WORD, KING.
THAT'S THE POWER OF WORDS. THAT THEY COMPEL US TO OUR FATE THOUGH OUR HEART AND MIND CLAMOR WARNING.
THAT'S HARDLY A REASSURING ANSWER.
NO. I SUPPOSE NOT.
I'VE TRUSTED YOU THUS FAR, BECAUSE YOU WERE RIGHT ABOUT THE RAINS.
BUT STILL, I NEED A REASON FOR THIS HUNT.
WHEN THE WATERS ROSE, THE BEAST CAME OUT OF THE DEPTHS WHEREIN IT LIVES.
IT LIKES TO BE NEAR PEOPLE. THEY'RE ITS PREFERRED PREY.
THEN THE SUDDEN RECEDING OF THE FLOOD LEFT IT STRANDED.

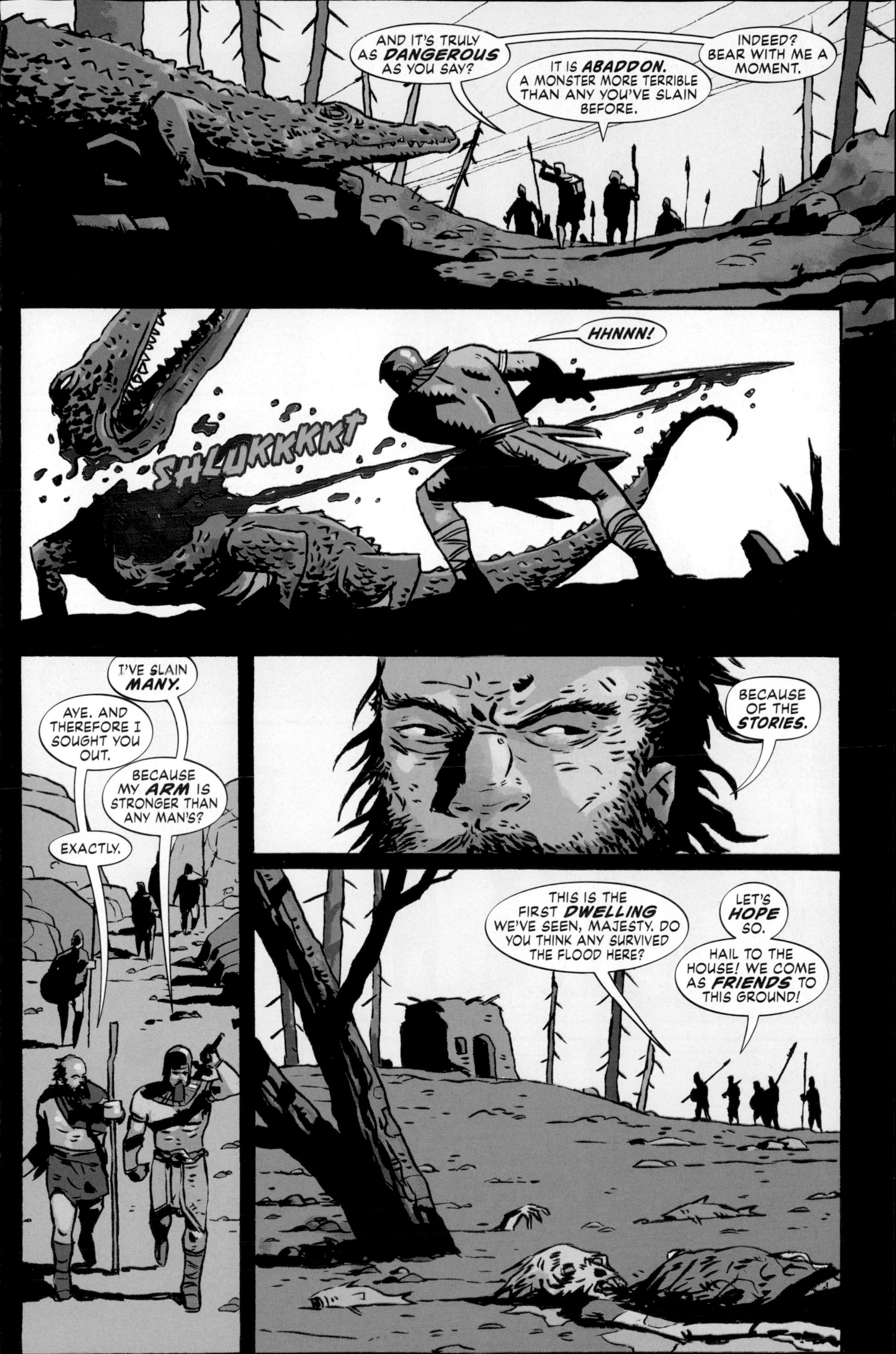

AND IT'S TRULY AS DANGEROUS AS YOU SAY?
IT IS ABADDON. A MONSTER MORE TERRIBLE THAN ANY YOU'VE SLAIN BEFORE.
INDEED? BEAR WITH ME A MOMENT.
HHNNN!
SHLUKKKKT
I'VE SLAIN MANY.
AYE. AND THEREFORE I SOUGHT YOU OUT.
BECAUSE MY ARM IS STRONGER THAN ANY MAN'S?
EXACTLY.
BECAUSE OF THE STORIES.
THIS IS THE FIRST DWELLING WE'VE SEEN, MAJESTY. DO YOU THINK ANY SURVIVED THE FLOOD HERE?
LET'S HOPE SO.
HAIL TO THE HOUSE! WE COME AS FRIENDS TO THIS GROUND!

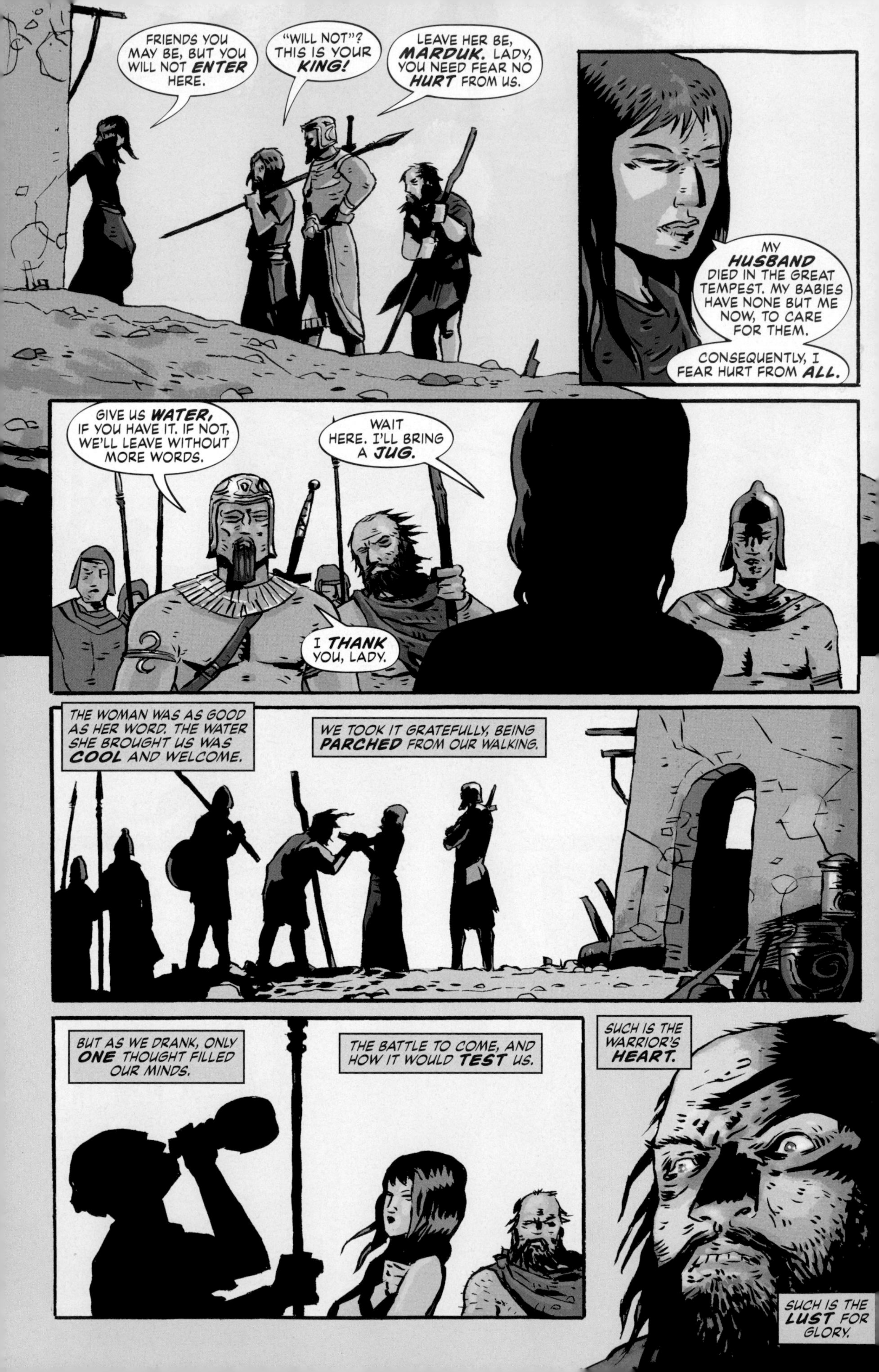
FRIENDS YOU MAY BE, BUT YOU WILL NOT ENTER HERE.
"WILL NOT"? THIS IS YOUR KING!
LEAVE HER BE, MARDUK. LADY, YOU NEED FEAR NO HURT FROM US.
MY HUSBAND DIED IN THE GREAT TEMPEST. MY BABIES HAVE NONE BUT ME NOW, TO CARE FOR THEM.
CONSEQUENTLY, I FEAR HURT FROM ALL.
GIVE US WATER, IF YOU HAVE IT. IF NOT, WE'LL LEAVE WITHOUT MORE WORDS.
WAIT HERE. I'LL BRING A JUG.
I THANK YOU, LADY.
THE WOMAN WAS AS GOOD AS HER WORD. THE WATER SHE BROUGHT US WAS COOL AND WELCOME.
WE TOOK IT GRATEFULLY, BEING PARCHED FROM OUR WALKING.
BUT AS WE DRANK, ONLY ONE THOUGHT FILLED OUR MINDS.
THE BATTLE TO COME, AND HOW IT WOULD TEST US.
SUCH IS THE WARRIOR'S HEART.
SUCH IS THE LUST FOR GLORY.

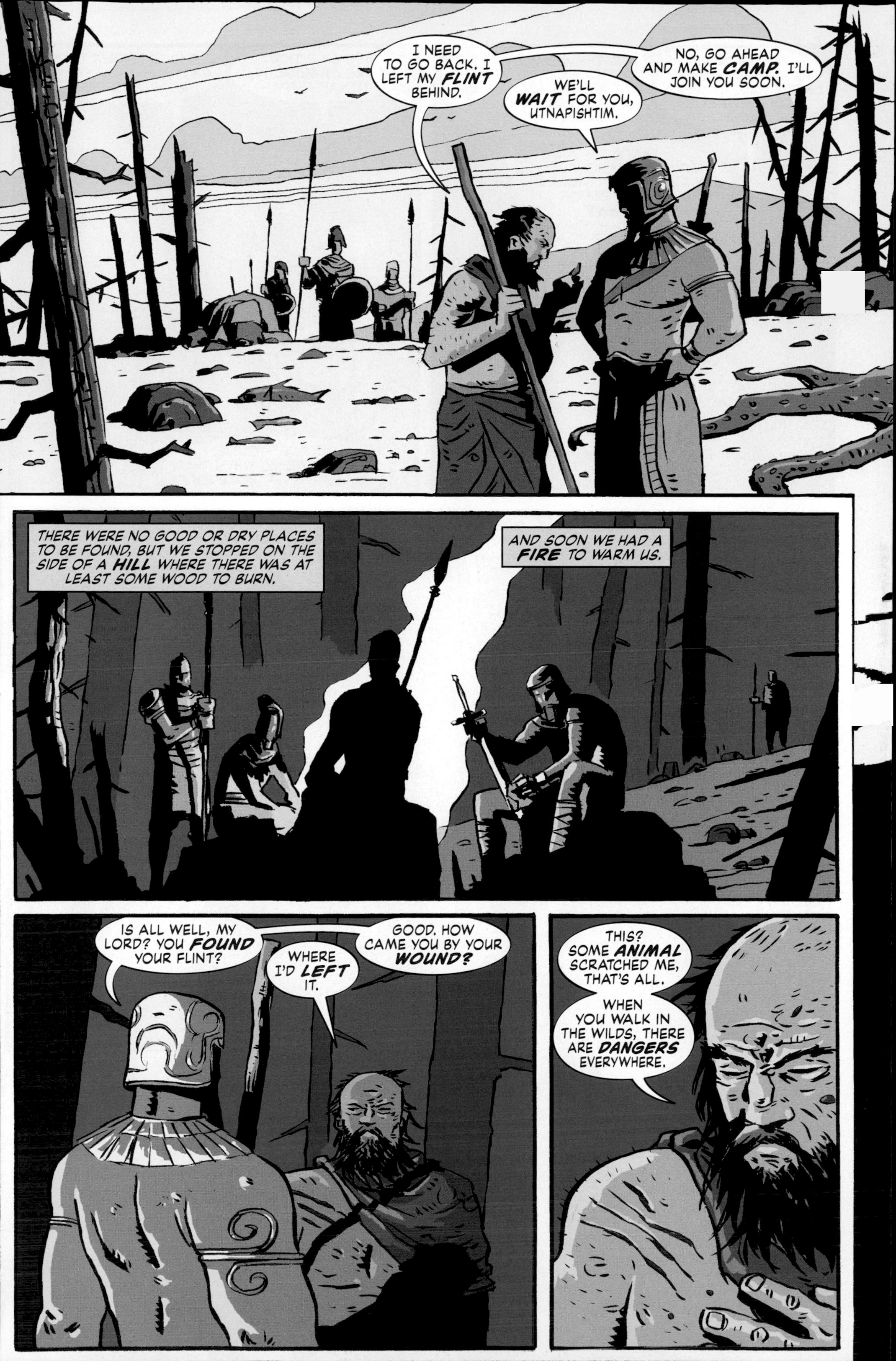

I NEED TO GO BACK. I LEFT MY FLINT BEHIND.
WE'LL WAIT FOR YOU, UTNAPISHTIM.
NO, GO AHEAD AND MAKE CAMP. I'LL JOIN YOU SOON.
THERE WERE NO GOOD OR DRY PLACES TO BE FOUND, BUT WE STOPPED ON THE SIDE OF A HILL WHERE THERE WAS AT LEAST SOME WOOD TO BURN.
AND SOON WE HAD A FIRE TO WARM US.
IS ALL WELL, MY LORD? YOU FOUND YOUR FLINT?
WHERE I'D LEFT IT.
GOOD. HOW CAME YOU BY YOUR WOUND?
THIS? SOME ANIMAL SCRATCHED ME, THAT'S ALL.
WHEN YOU WALK IN THE WILDS, THERE ARE DANGERS EVERYWHERE.

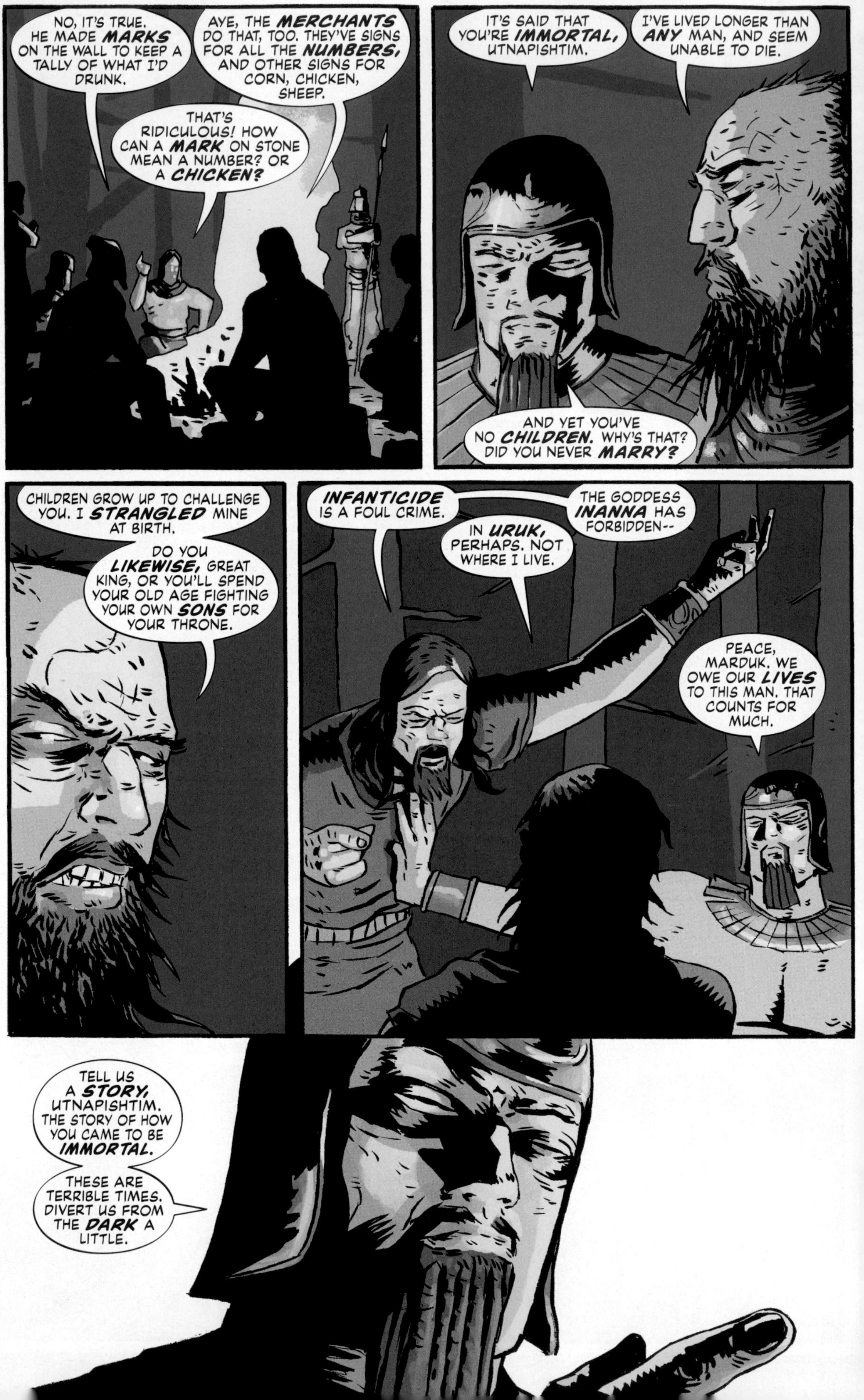

NO, IT'S TRUE. HE MADE MARKS ON THE WALL TO KEEP A TALLY OF WHAT I'D DRUNK.
AYE, THE MERCHANTS DO THAT, TOO. THEY'VE SIGNS FOR ALL THE NUMBERS, AND OTHER SIGNS FOR CORN, CHICKEN, SHEEP.
THAT'S RIDICULOUS! HOW CAN A MARK ON STONE MEAN A NUMBER? OR A CHICKEN?
IT'S SAID THAT YOU'RE IMMORTAL, UTNAPISHTIM.
I'VE LIVED LONGER THAN ANY MAN, AND SEEM UNABLE TO DIE.
AND YET YOU'VE NO CHILDREN. WHY'S THAT? DID YOU NEVER MARRY?
CHILDREN GROW UP TO CHALLENGE YOU. I STRANGLED MINE AT BIRTH.
DO YOU LIKEWISE, GREAT KING, OR YOU'LL SPEND YOUR OLD AGE FIGHTING YOUR OWN SONS FOR YOUR THRONE.
INFANTICIDE IS A FOUL CRIME.
THE GODDESS INANNA HAS FORBIDDEN--
IN URUK, PERHAPS. NOT WHERE I LIVE.
PEACE, MARDUK. WE OWE OUR LIVES TO THIS MAN. THAT COUNTS FOR MUCH.
TELL US A STORY, UTNAPISHTIM. THE STORY OF HOW YOU CAME TO BE IMMORTAL.
THESE ARE TERRIBLE TIMES. DIVERT US FROM THE DARK A LITTLE.

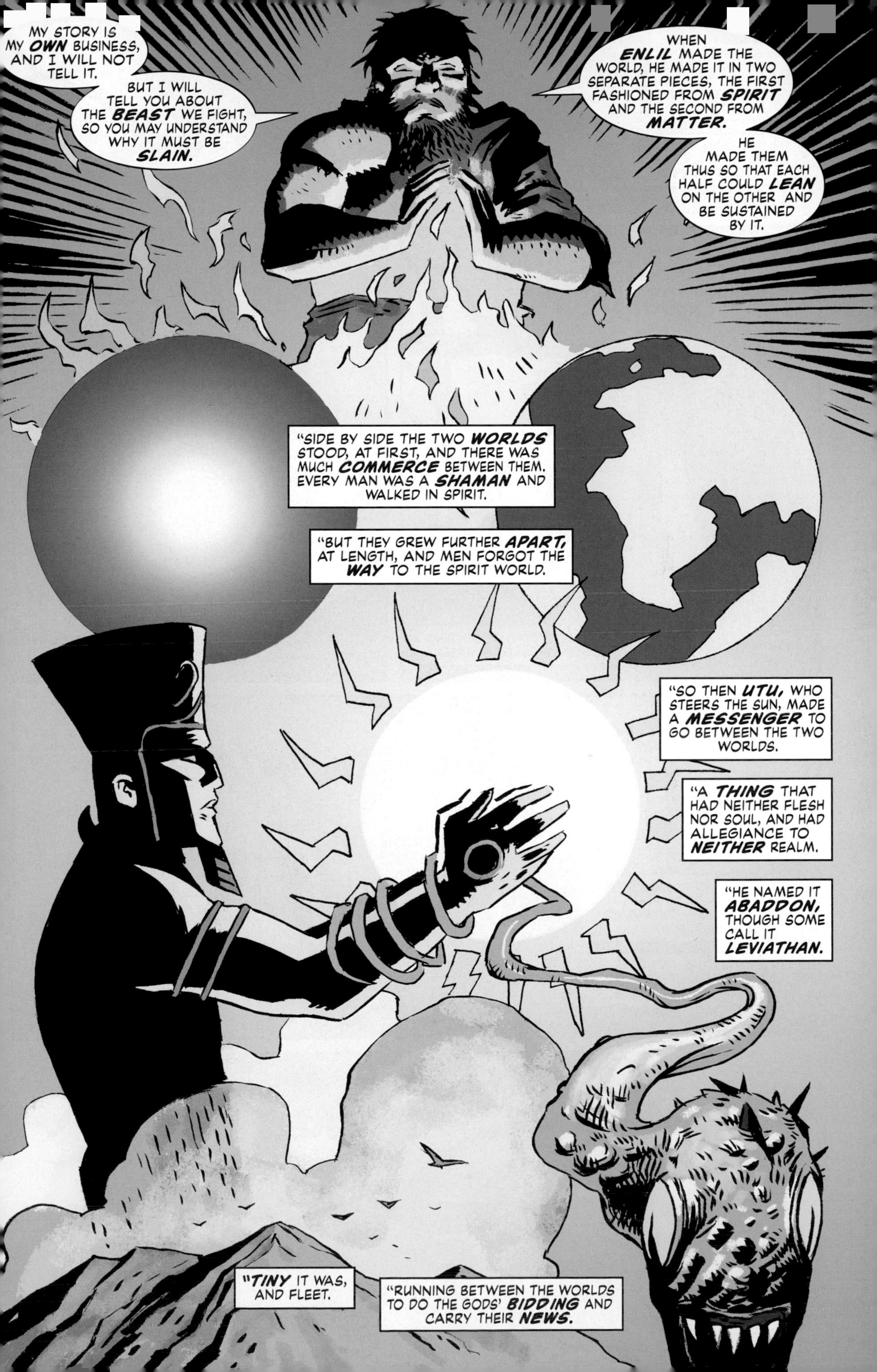
MY STORY IS MY OWN BUSINESS, AND I WILL NOT TELL IT.
BUT I WILL TELL YOU ABOUT THE BEAST WE FIGHT, SO YOU MAY UNDERSTAND WHY IT MUST BE SLAIN.
WHEN ENLIL MADE THE WORLD, HE MADE IT IN TWO SEPARATE PIECES, THE FIRST FASHIONED FROM SPIRIT AND THE SECOND FROM MATTER.
HE MADE THEM THUS SO THAT EACH HALF COULD LEAN ON THE OTHER AND BE SUSTAINED BY IT.
"SIDE BY SIDE THE TWO WORLDS STOOD, AT FIRST, AND THERE WAS MUCH COMMERCE BETWEEN THEM. EVERY MAN WAS A SHAMAN AND WALKED IN SPIRIT.
"BUT THEY GREW FURTHER APART, AT LENGTH, AND MEN FORGOT THE WAY TO THE SPIRIT WORLD.
"SO THEN UTU, WHO STEERS THE SUN, MADE A MESSENGER TO GO BETWEEN THE TWO WORLDS.
"A THING THAT HAD NEITHER FLESH NOR SOUL, AND HAD ALLEGIANCE TO NEITHER REALM.
"HE NAMED IT ABADDON, THOUGH SOME CALL IT LEVIATHAN.
"TINY IT WAS, AND FLEET.
"RUNNING BETWEEN THE WORLDS TO DO THE GODS' BIDDING AND CARRY THEIR NEWS.

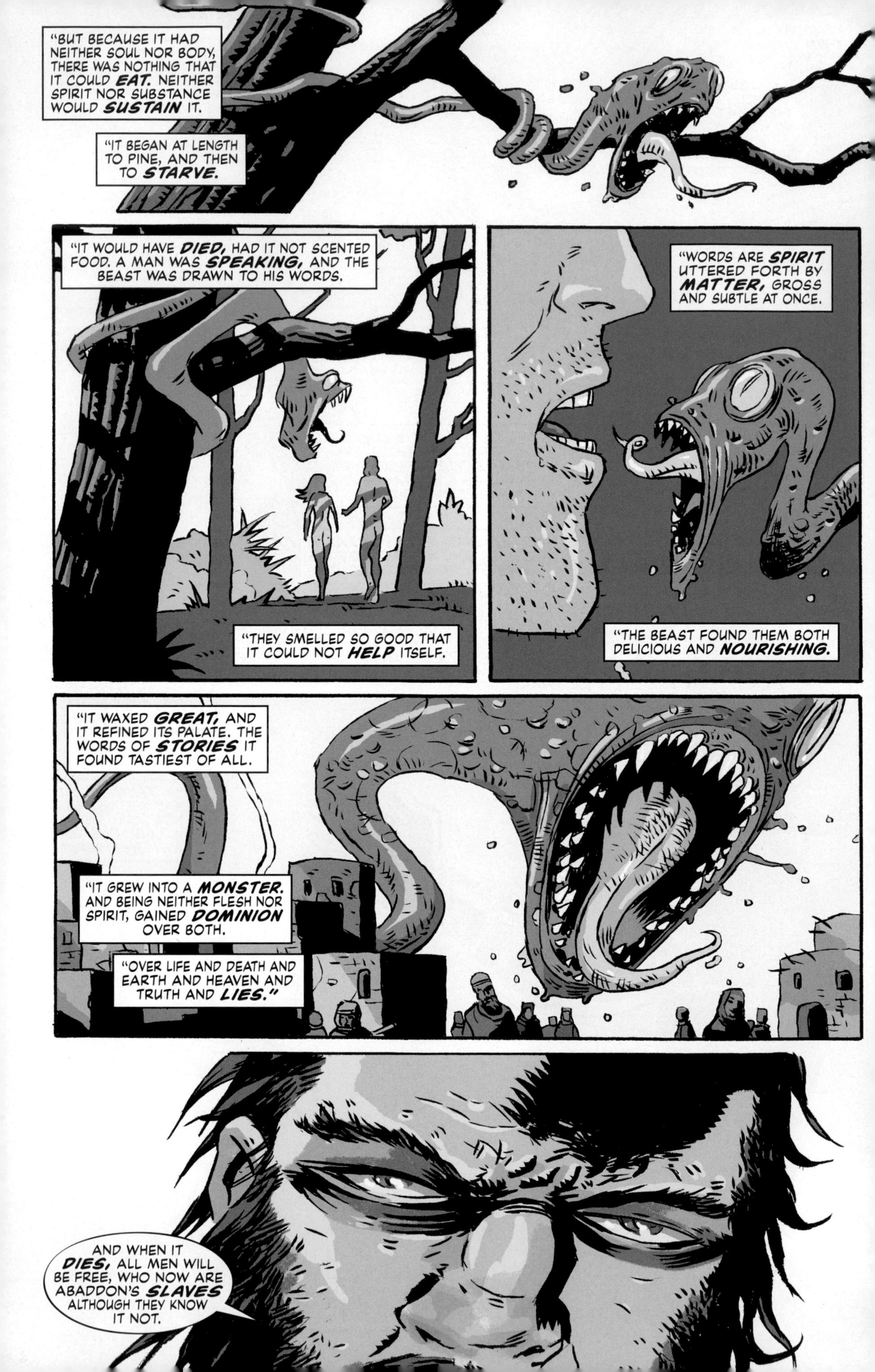

"BUT BECAUSE IT HAD NEITHER SOUL NOR BODY, THERE WAS NOTHING THAT IT COULD EAT. NEITHER SPIRIT NOR SUBSTANCE WOULD SUSTAIN IT.
"IT BEGAN AT LENGTH TO PINE, AND THEN TO STARVE.
"IT WOULD HAVE DIED, HAD IT NOT SCENTED FOOD. A MAN WAS SPEAKING, AND THE BEAST WAS DRAWN TO HIS WORDS.
"THEY SMELLED SO GOOD THAT IT COULD NOT HELP ITSELF.
"WORDS ARE SPIRIT UTTERED FORTH BY MATTER, GROSS AND SUBTLE AT ONCE.
"THE BEAST FOUND THEM BOTH DELICIOUS AND NOURISHING.
"IT WAXED GREAT, AND IT REFINED ITS PALATE. THE WORDS OF STORIES IT FOUND TASTIEST OF ALL.
"IT GREW INTO A MONSTER. AND BEING NEITHER FLESH NOR SPIRIT, GAINED DOMINION OVER BOTH.
"OVER LIFE AND DEATH AND EARTH AND HEAVEN AND TRUTH AND LIES."
AND WHEN IT DIES, ALL MEN WILL BE FREE, WHO NOW ARE ABADDON'S SLAVES ALTHOUGH THEY KNOW IT NOT.

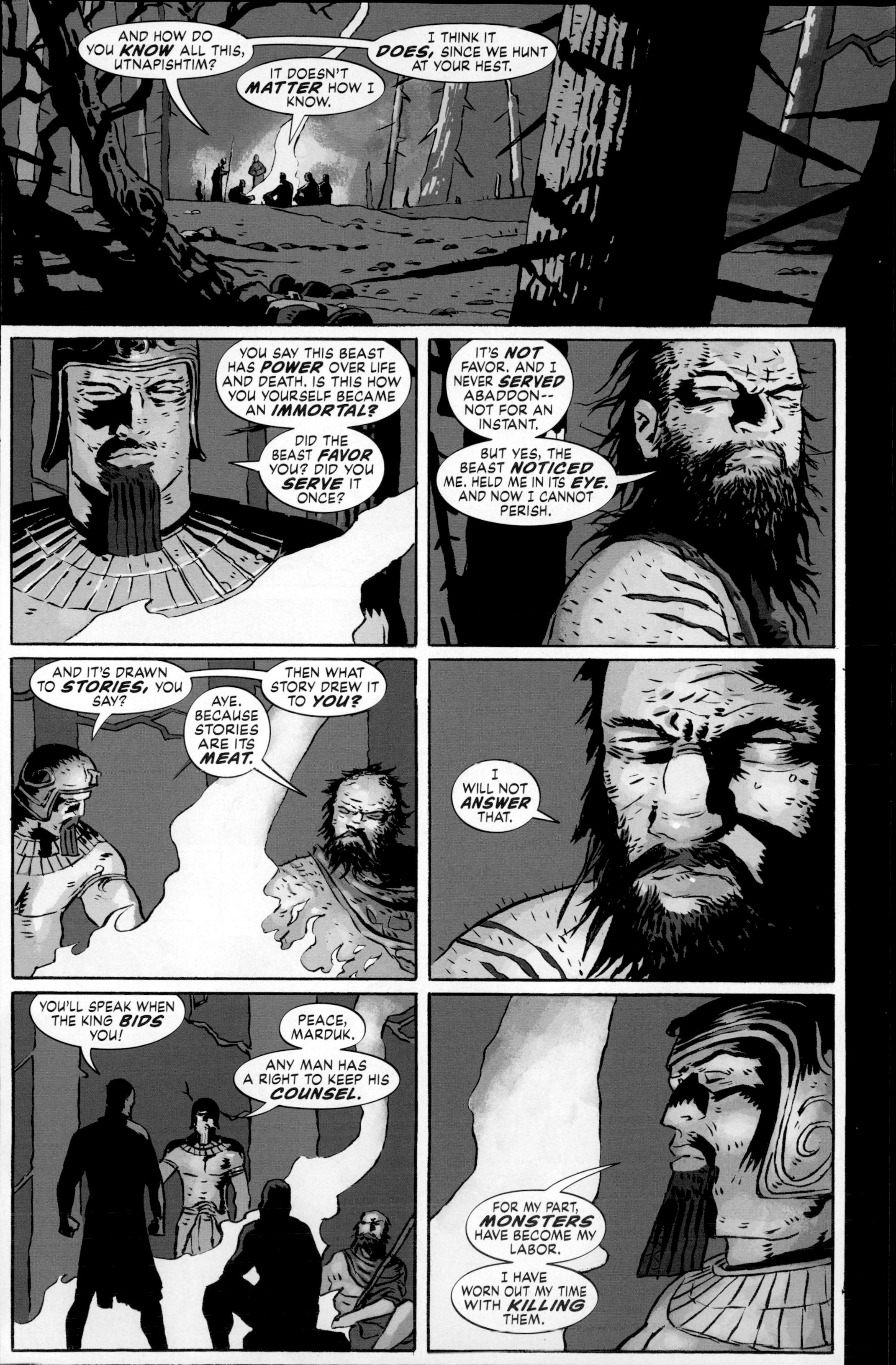

AND HOW DO YOU KNOW ALL THIS, UTNAPISHTIM?
IT DOESN'T MATTER HOW I KNOW.
I THINK IT DOES, SINCE WE HUNT AT YOUR HEST.
YOU SAY THIS BEAST HAS POWER OVER LIFE AND DEATH. IS THIS HOW YOU YOURSELF BECAME AN IMMORTAL?
DID THE BEAST FAVOR YOU? DID YOU SERVE IT ONCE?
IT'S NOT FAVOR. AND I NEVER SERVED ABADDON-- NOT FOR AN INSTANT.
BUT YES, THE BEAST NOTICED ME. HELD ME IN ITS EYE. AND NOW I CANNOT PERISH.
AND IT'S DRAWN TO STORIES, YOU SAY?
AYE. BECAUSE STORIES ARE ITS MEAT.
THEN WHAT STORY DREW IT TO YOU?
I WILL NOT ANSWER THAT.
YOU'LL SPEAK WHEN THE KING BIDS YOU!
PEACE, MARDUK.
ANY MAN HAS A RIGHT TO KEEP HIS COUNSEL.
FOR MY PART, MONSTERS HAVE BECOME MY LABOR.
I HAVE WORN OUT MY TIME WITH KILLING THEM.

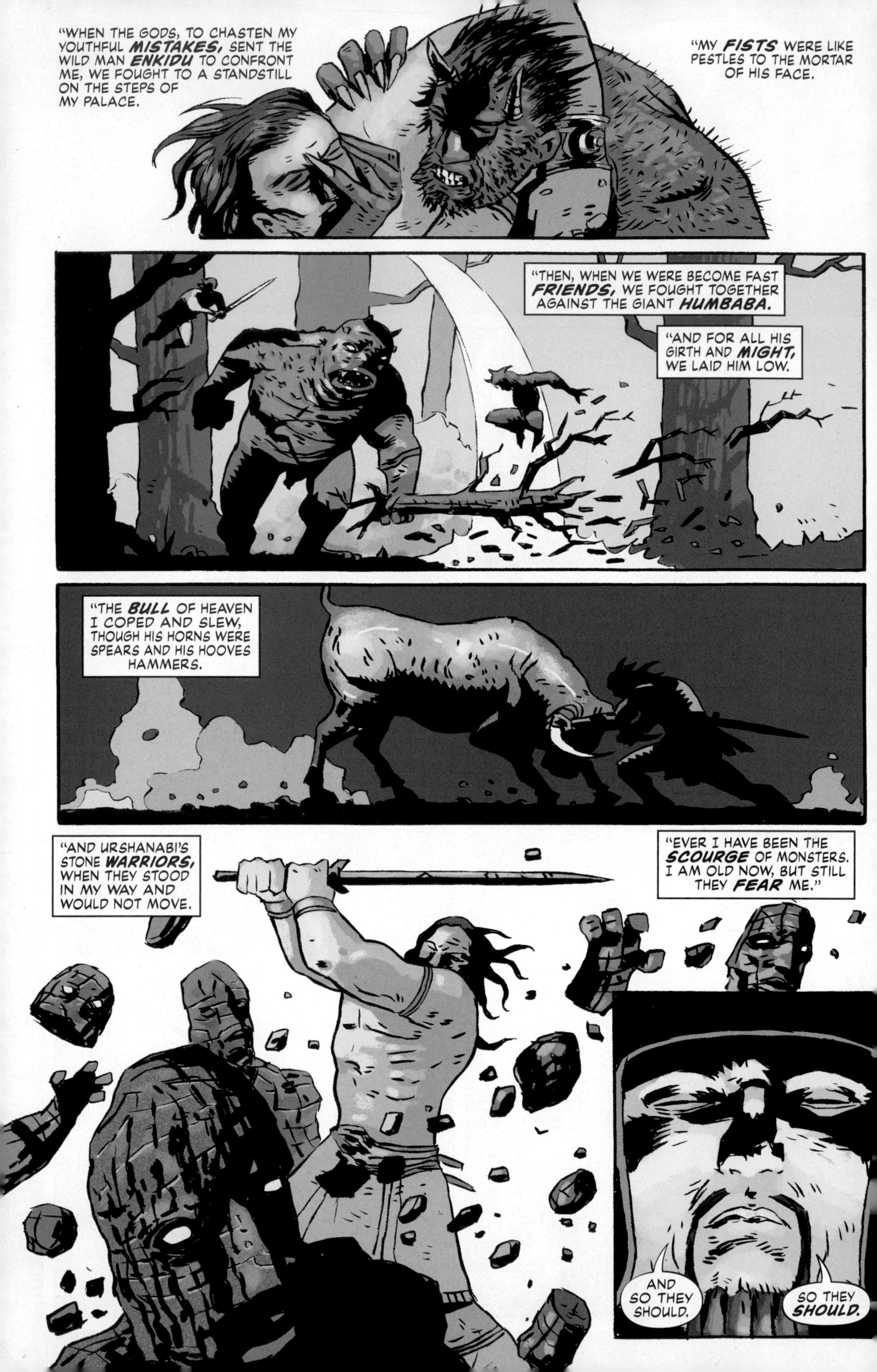
"WHEN THE GODS, TO CHASTEN MY YOUTHFUL MISTAKES, SENT THE WILD MAN ENKIDU TO CONFRONT ME, WE FOUGHT TO A STANDSTILL ON THE STEPS OF MY PALACE.
"MY FISTS WERE LIKE PESTLES TO THE MORTAR OF HIS FACE.
"THEN, WHEN WE WERE BECOME FAST FRIENDS, WE FOUGHT TOGETHER AGAINST THE GIANT HUMBABA.
"AND FOR ALL HIS GIRTH AND MIGHT, WE LAID HIM LOW.
"THE BULL OF HEAVEN I COPED AND SLEW, THOUGH HIS HORNS WERE SPEARS AND HIS HOOVES HAMMERS.
"AND URSHANABI'S STONE WARRIORS, WHEN THEY STOOD IN MY WAY AND WOULD NOT MOVE.
"EVER I HAVE BEEN THE SCOURGE OF MONSTERS. I AM OLD NOW, BUT STILL THEY FEAR ME."
AND SO THEY SHOULD.
SO THEY SHOULD.

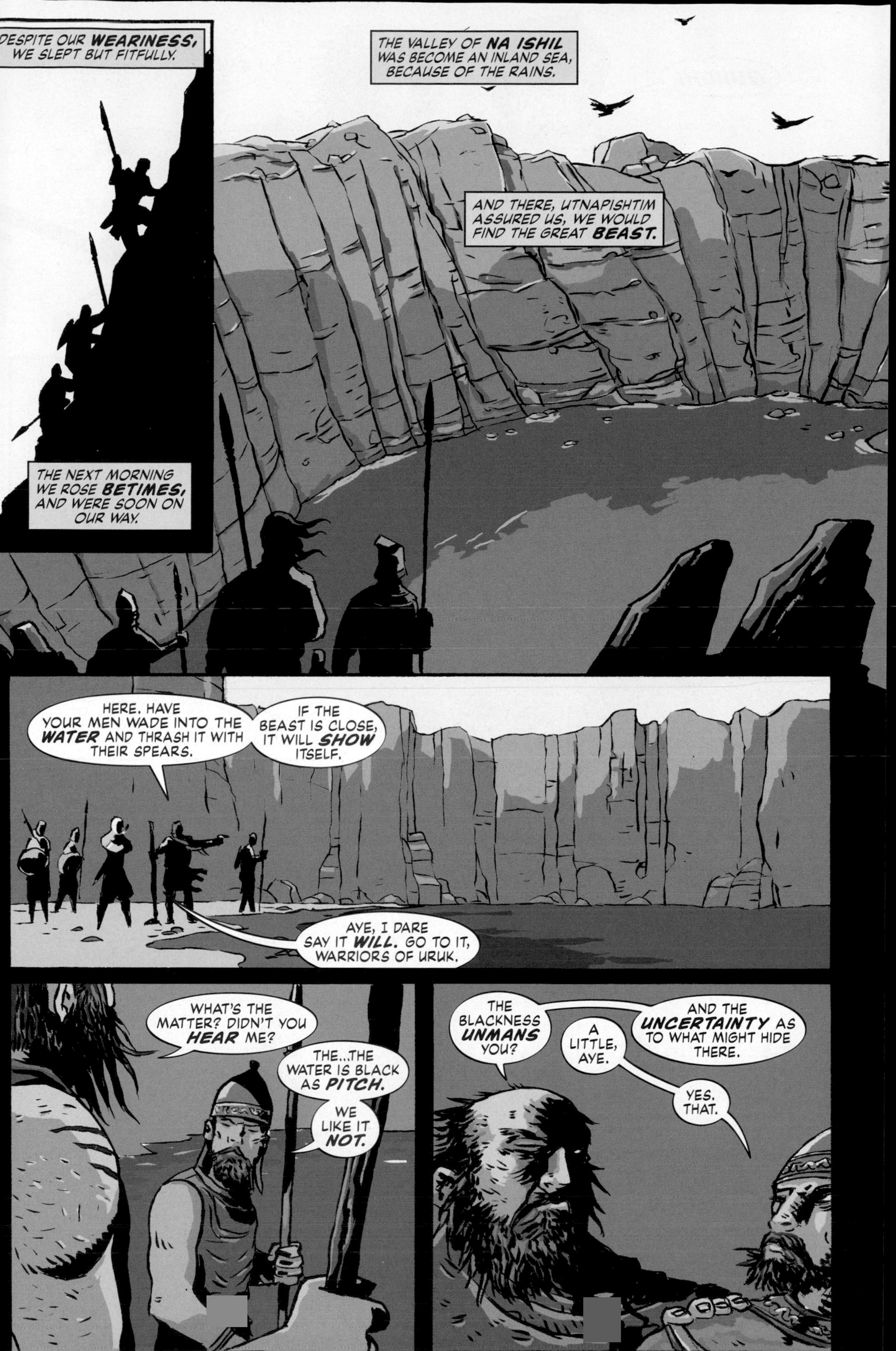
DESPITE OUR WEARINESS, WE SLEPT BUT FITFULLY.
THE VALLEY OF NA ISHIL WAS BECOME AN INLAND SEA, BECAUSE OF THE RAINS.
AND THERE, UTNAPISHTIM ASSURED US, WE WOULD FIND THE GREAT BEAST.
THE NEXT MORNING WE ROSE BETIMES, AND WERE SOON ON OUR WAY.
HERE. HAVE YOUR MEN WADE INTO THE WATER AND THRASH IT WITH THEIR SPEARS.
IF THE BEAST IS CLOSE, IT WILL SHOW ITSELF.
AYE, I DARE SAY IT WILL. GO TO IT, WARRIORS OF URUK.
WHAT'S THE MATTER? DIDN'T YOU HEAR ME?
THE...THE WATER IS BLACK AS PITCH.
WE LIKE IT NOT.
THE BLACKNESS UNMANS YOU?
A LITTLE, AYE.
AND THE UNCERTAINTY AS TO WHAT MIGHT HIDE THERE.
YES. THAT.

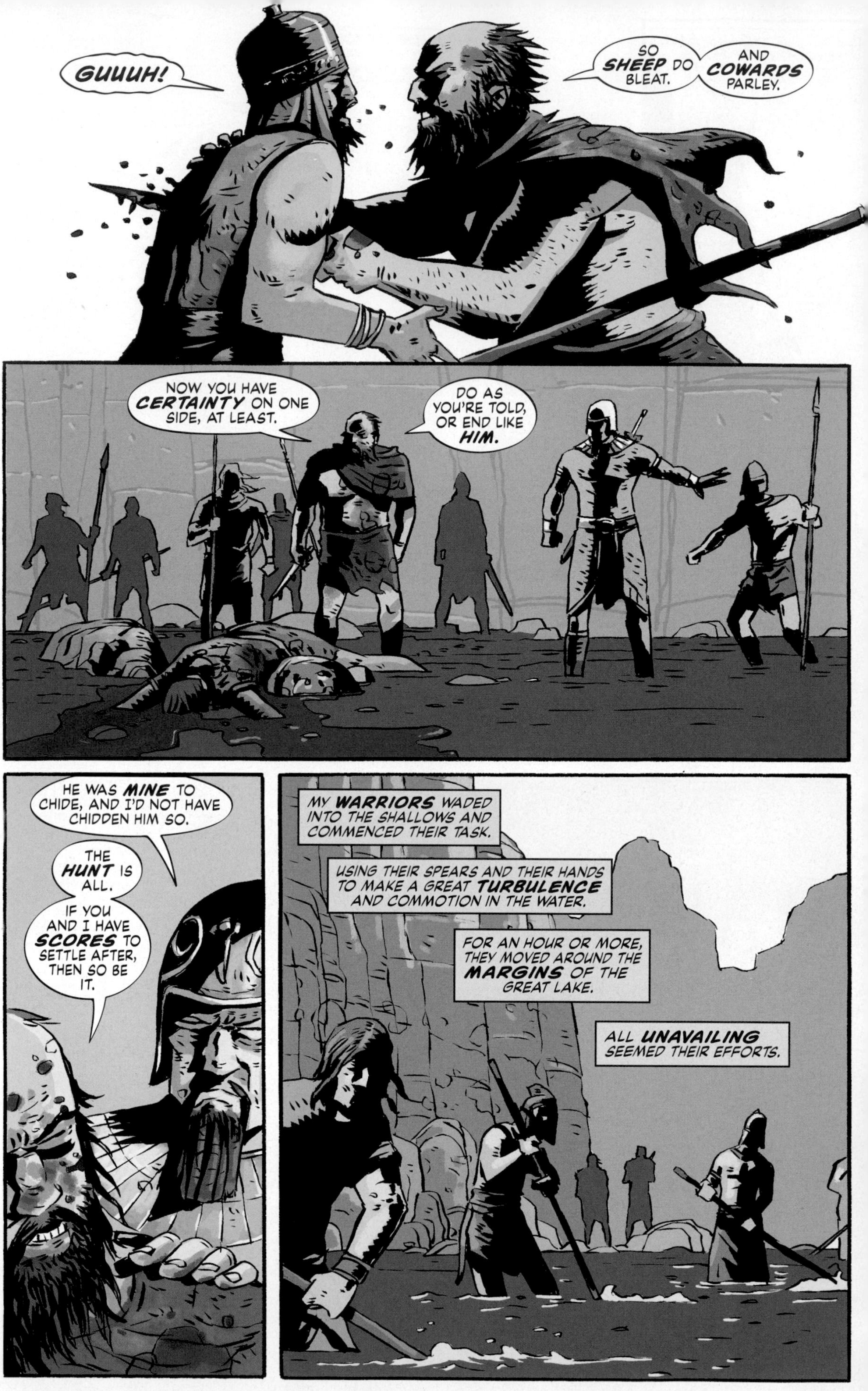

GUUUH!
SO SHEEP DO BLEAT.
AND COWARDS PARLEY.
NOW YOU HAVE CERTAINTY ON ONE SIDE, AT LEAST.
DO AS YOU'RE TOLD, OR END LIKE HIM.
HE WAS MINE TO CHIDE, AND I'D NOT HAVE CHIDDEN HIM SO.
THE HUNT IS ALL.
IF YOU AND I HAVE SCORES TO SETTLE AFTER, THEN SO BE IT.
MY WARRIORS WADED INTO THE SHALLOWS AND COMMENCED THEIR TASK.
USING THEIR SPEARS AND THEIR HANDS TO MAKE A GREAT TURBULENCE AND COMMOTION IN THE WATER.
FOR AN HOUR OR MORE, THEY MOVED AROUND THE MARGINS OF THE GREAT LAKE.
ALL UNAVAILING SEEMED THEIR EFFORTS.

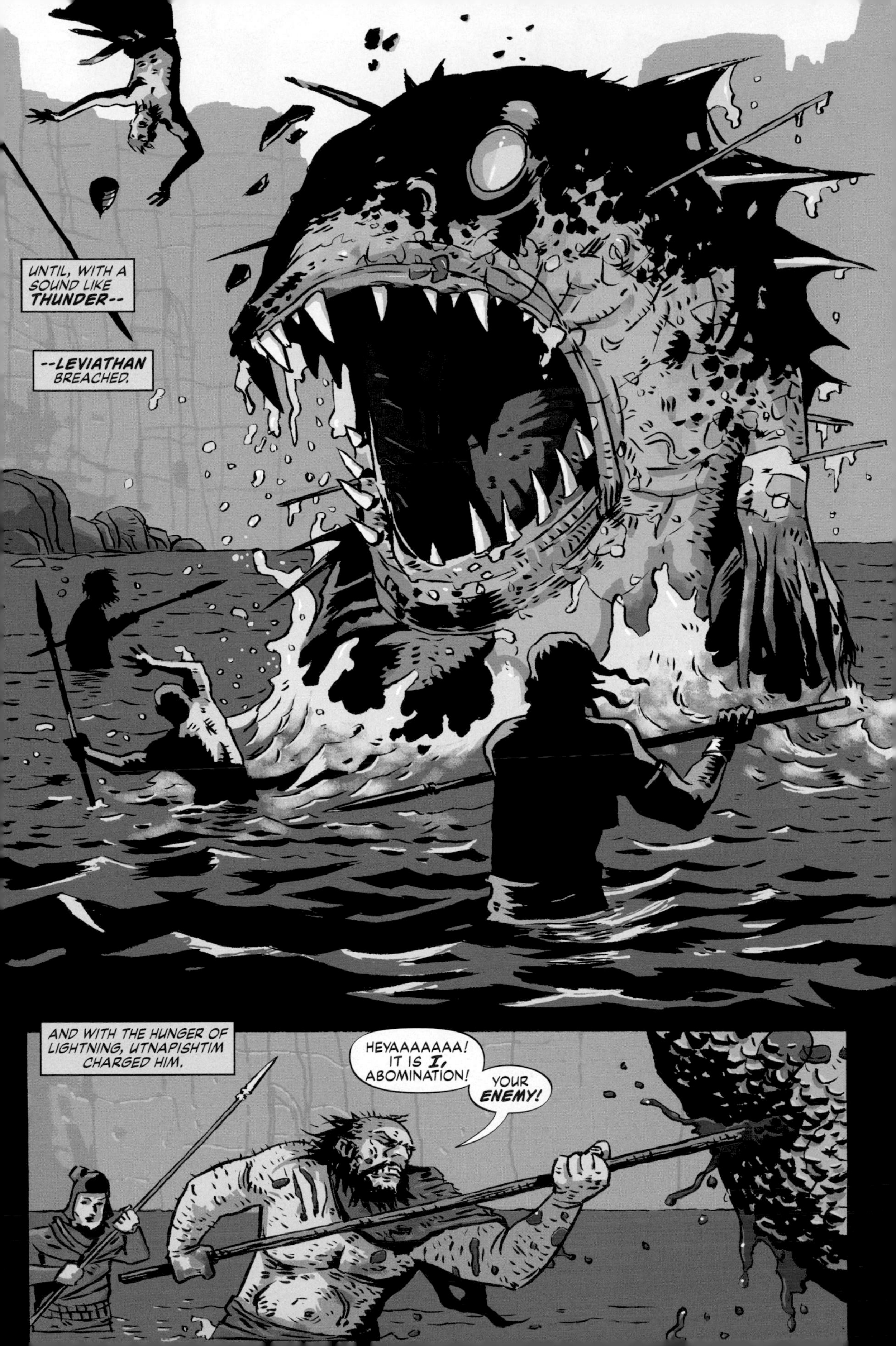
UNTIL, WITH A SOUND LIKE THUNDER--
--LEVIATHAN BREACHED.
AND WITH THE HUNGER OF LIGHTNING, UTNAPISHTIM CHARGED HIM.
HEYAAAAAAA! IT IS I, ABOMINATION!
YOUR ENEMY!

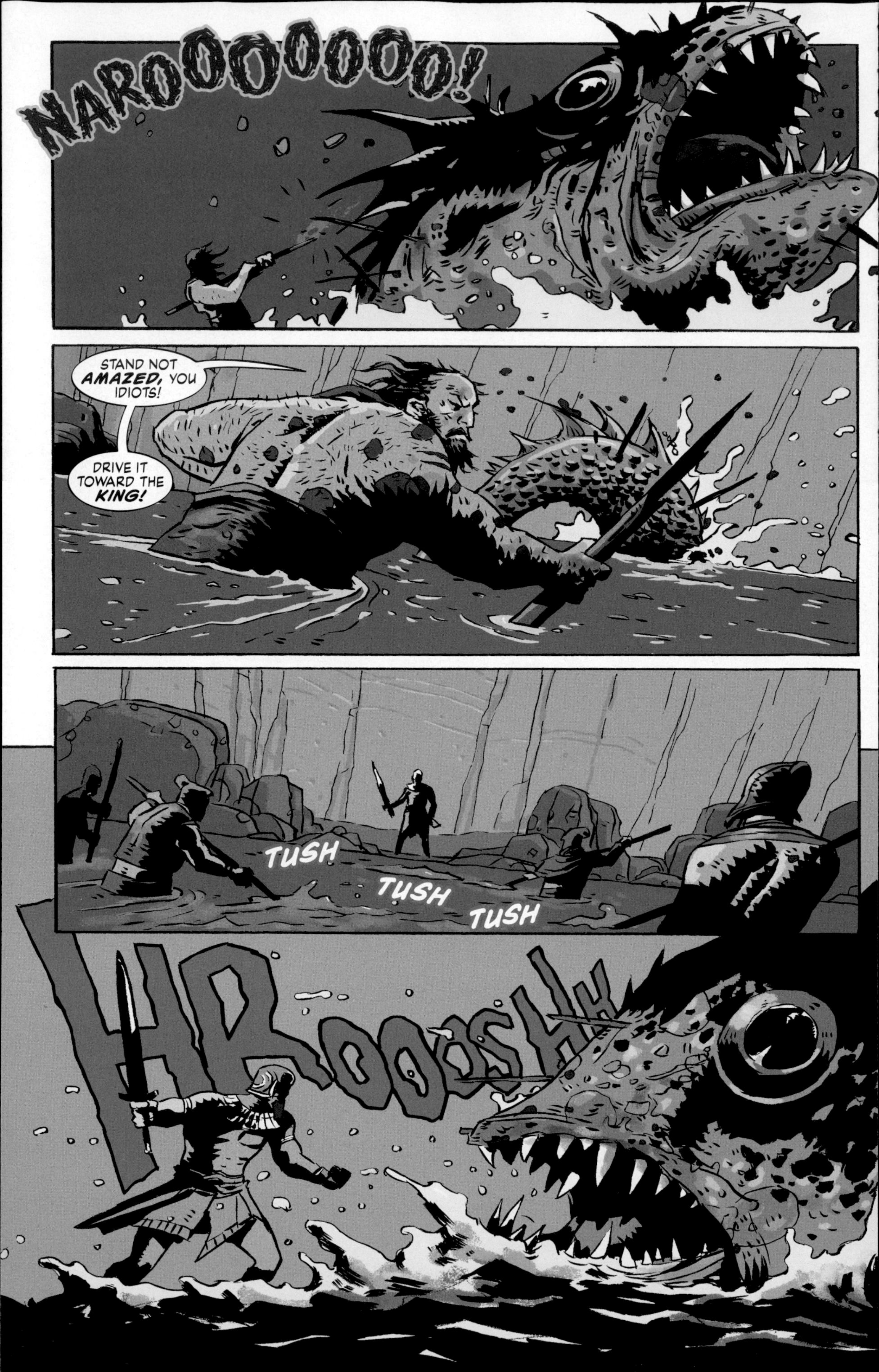
NAROOOOOOOO!
STAND NOT AMAZED, YOU IDIOTS!
DRIVE IT TOWARD THE KING!
TUSH
TUSH
TUSH
HROOOSHH

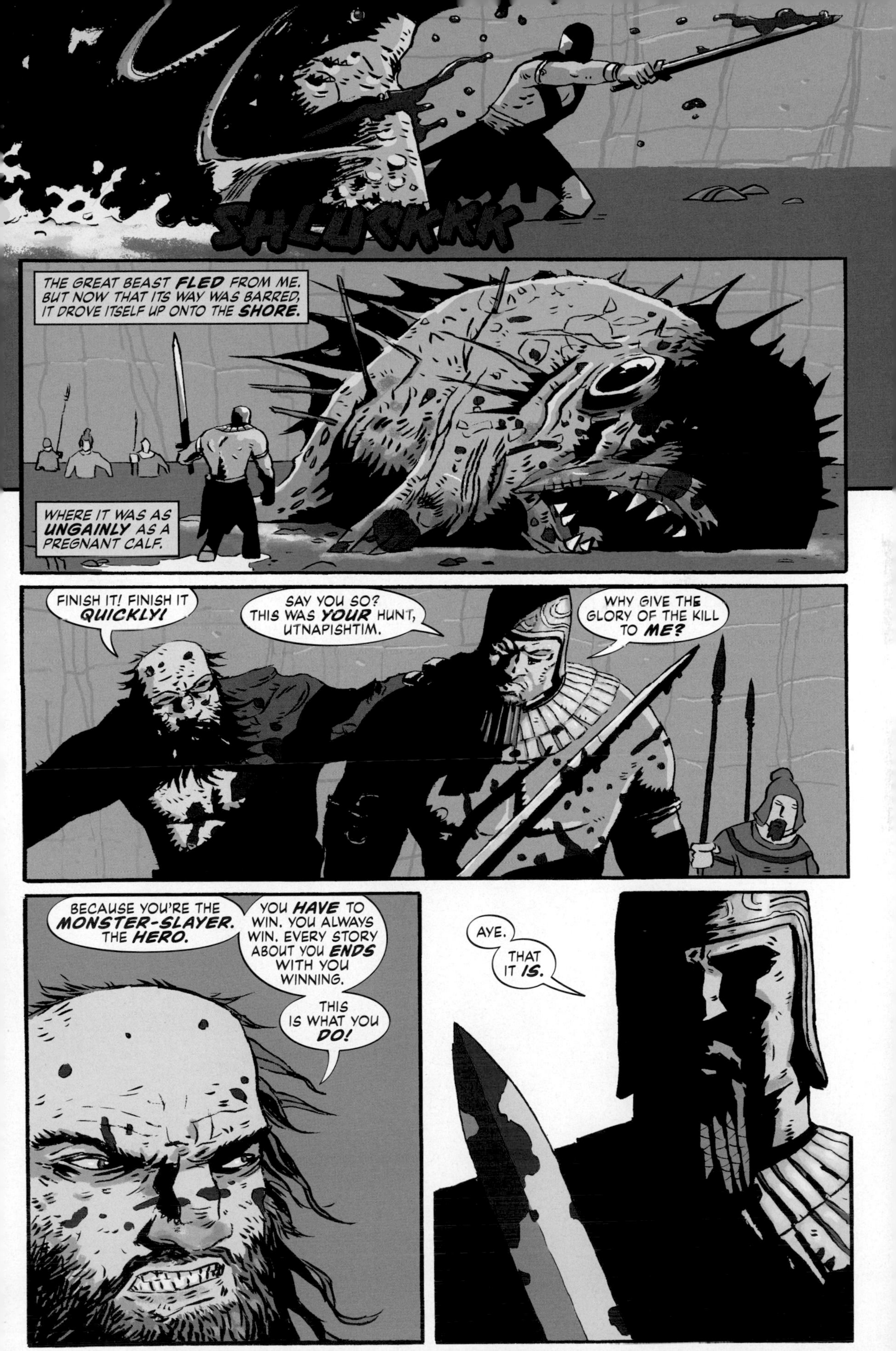
SHLUCKKK
THE GREAT BEAST FLED FROM ME. BUT NOW THAT ITS WAY WAS BARRED, IT DROVE ITSELF UP ONTO THE SHORE.
WHERE IT WAS AS UNGAINLY AS A PREGNANT CALF.
FINISH IT! FINISH IT QUICKLY!
SAY YOU SO? THIS WAS YOUR HUNT, UTNAPISHTIM.
WHY GIVE THE GLORY OF THE KILL TO ME?
BECAUSE YOU'RE THE MONSTER-SLAYER. THE HERO.
YOU HAVE TO WIN. YOU ALWAYS WIN. EVERY STORY ABOUT YOU ENDS WITH YOU WINNING.
THIS IS WHAT YOU DO!
AYE.
THAT IT IS.

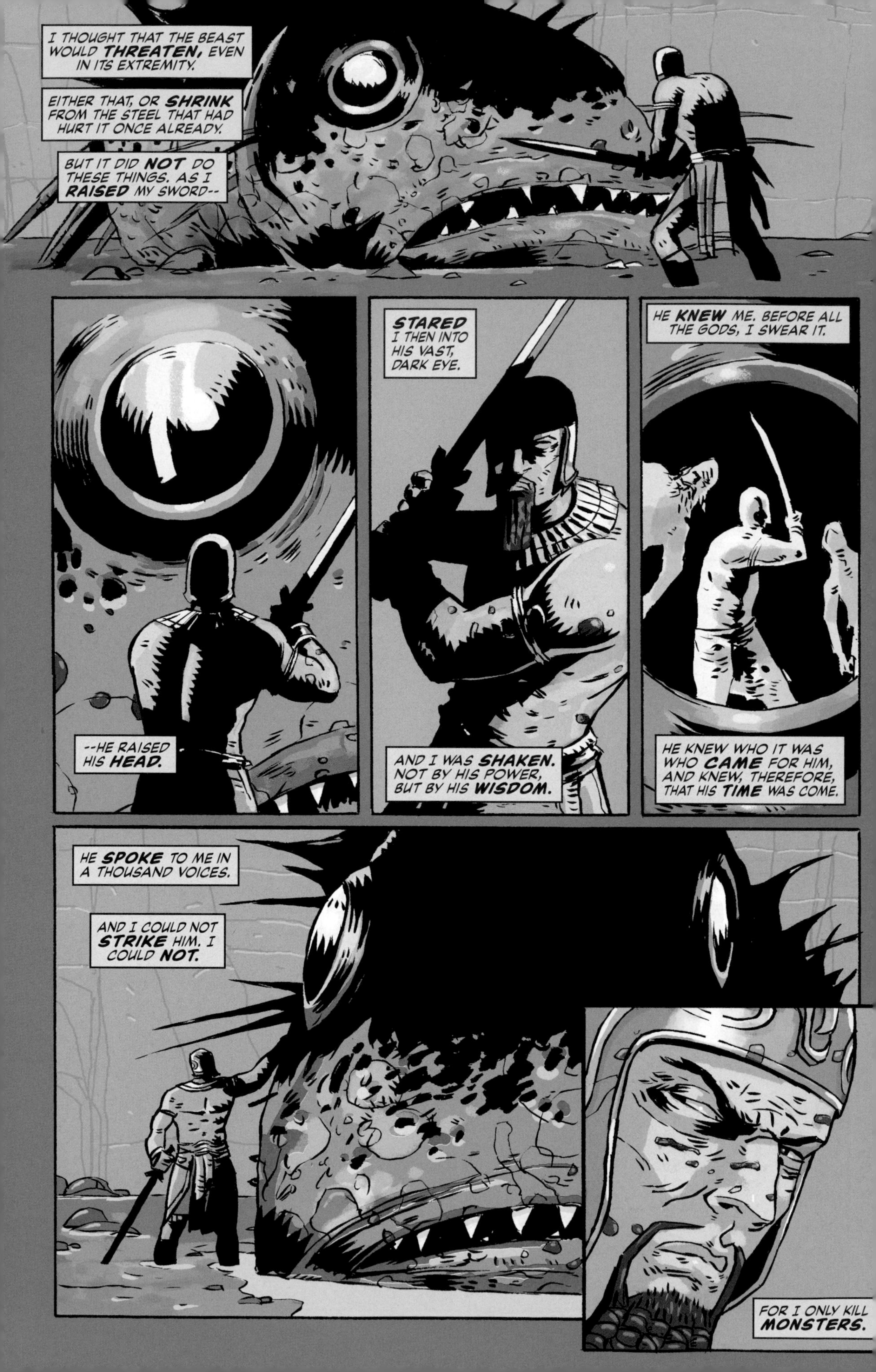
I THOUGHT THAT THE BEAST WOULD **THREATEN,** EVEN IN ITS EXTREMITY.
EITHER THAT, OR **SHRINK** FROM THE STEEL THAT HAD HURT IT ONCE ALREADY.
BUT IT DID **NOT** DO THESE THINGS. AS I **RAISED** MY SWORD--
--HE RAISED HIS **HEAD.**
STARED I THEN INTO HIS VAST, DARK EYE.
AND I WAS **SHAKEN.** NOT BY HIS POWER, BUT BY HIS **WISDOM.**
HE **KNEW** ME. BEFORE ALL THE GODS, I SWEAR IT.
HE KNEW WHO IT WAS WHO **CAME** FOR HIM, AND KNEW, THEREFORE, THAT HIS **TIME** WAS COME.
HE **SPOKE** TO ME IN A THOUSAND VOICES.
AND I COULD NOT **STRIKE** HIM. I COULD **NOT.**
FOR I ONLY KILL **MONSTERS.**

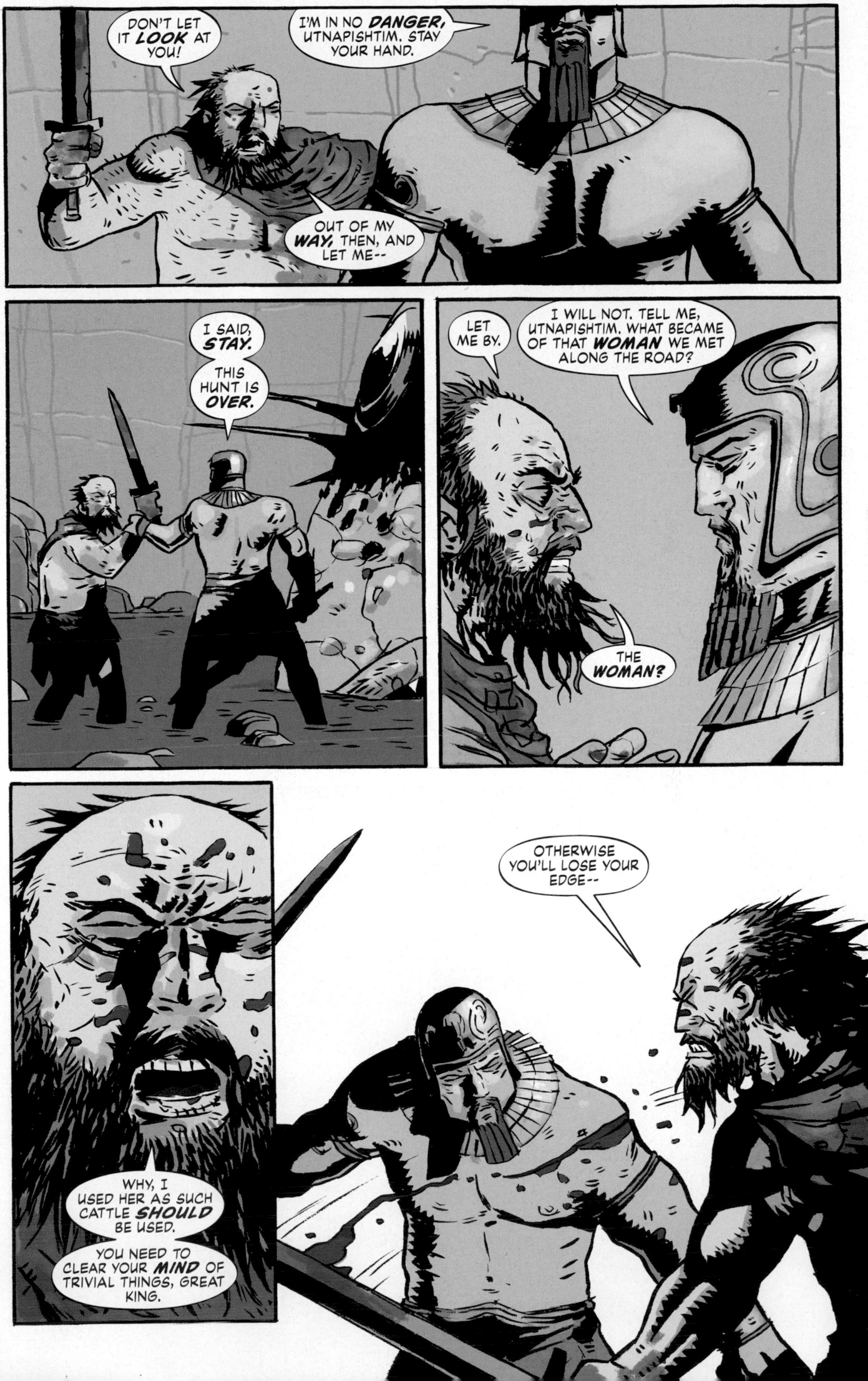
DON'T LET IT LOOK AT YOU!
I'M IN NO DANGER, UTNAPISHTIM. STAY YOUR HAND.
OUT OF MY WAY, THEN, AND LET ME--
I SAID, STAY.
THIS HUNT IS OVER.
LET ME BY.
I WILL NOT. TELL ME, UTNAPISHTIM. WHAT BECAME OF THAT WOMAN WE MET ALONG THE ROAD?
THE WOMAN?
WHY, I USED HER AS SUCH CATTLE SHOULD BE USED.
YOU NEED TO CLEAR YOUR MIND OF TRIVIAL THINGS, GREAT KING.
OTHERWISE YOU'LL LOSE YOUR EDGE--

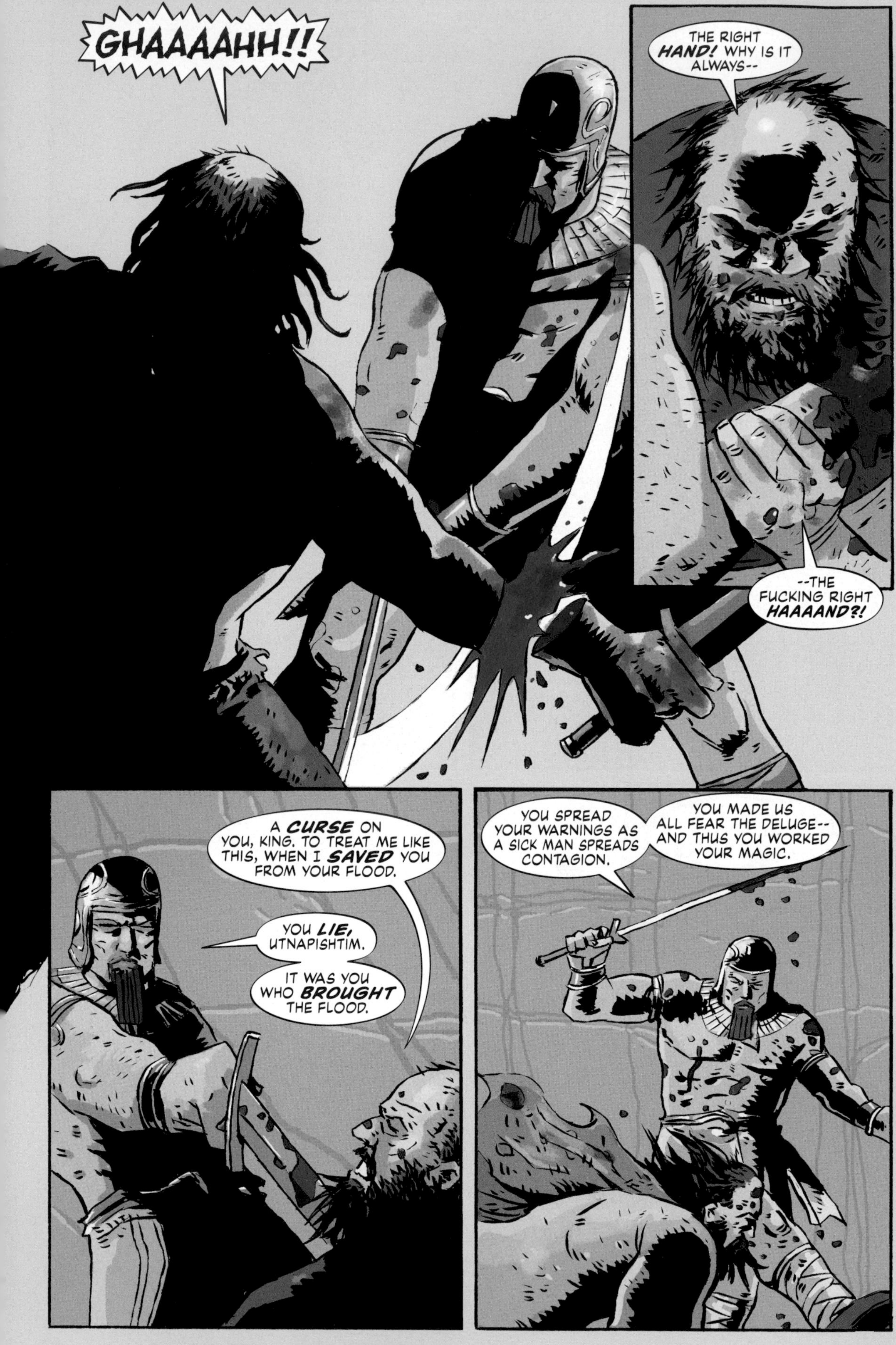
GHAAAAHH!!
THE RIGHT HAND! WHY IS IT ALWAYS--
--THE FUCKING RIGHT HAAAAND?!
A CURSE ON YOU, KING. TO TREAT ME LIKE THIS, WHEN I SAVED YOU FROM YOUR FLOOD.
YOU LIE, UTNAPISHTIM.
IT WAS YOU WHO BROUGHT THE FLOOD.
YOU SPREAD YOUR WARNINGS AS A SICK MAN SPREADS CONTAGION.
YOU MADE US ALL FEAR THE DELUGE-- AND THUS YOU WORKED YOUR MAGIC.

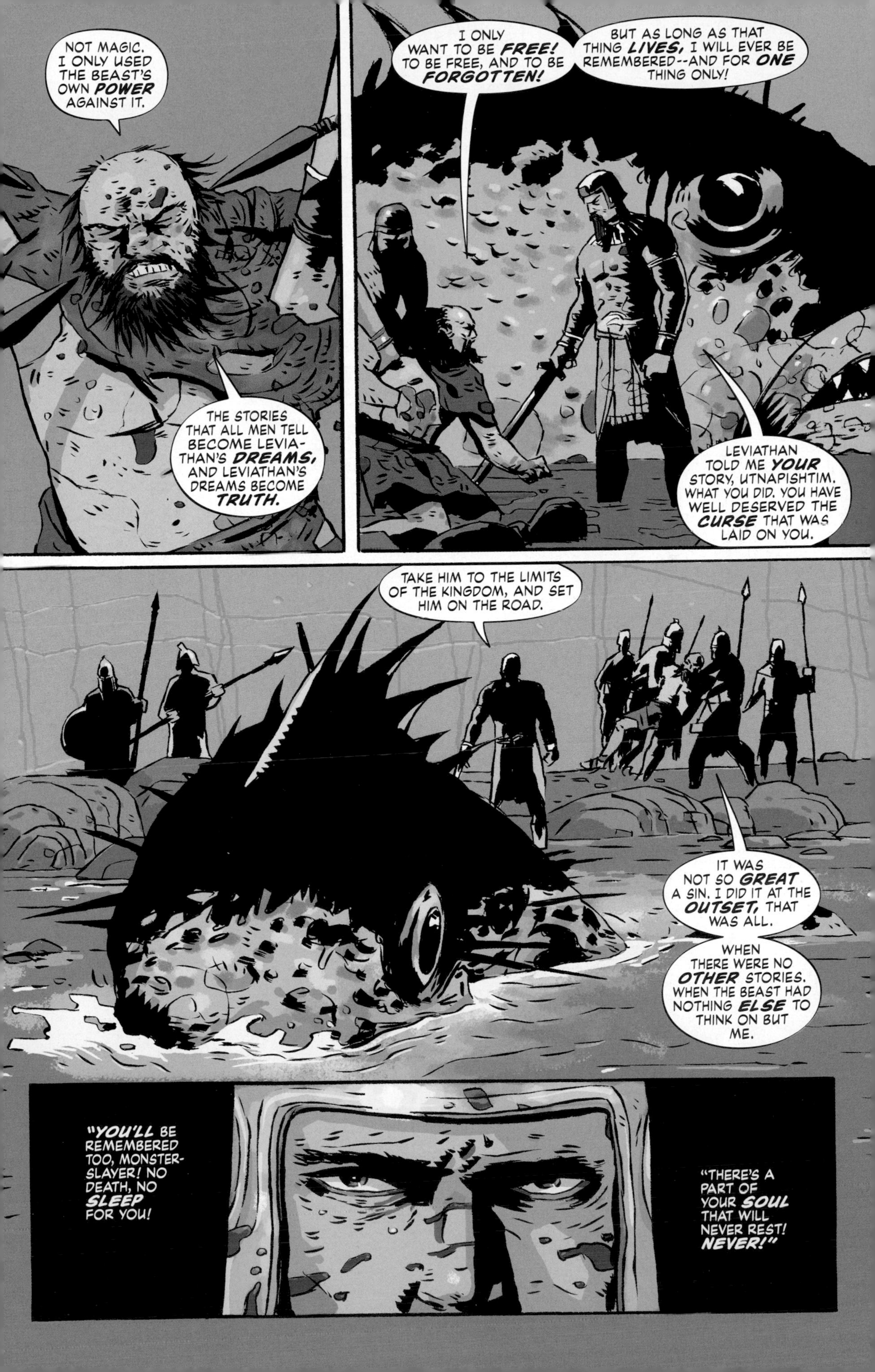
NOT MAGIC. I ONLY USED THE BEAST'S OWN POWER AGAINST IT.
THE STORIES THAT ALL MEN TELL BECOME LEVIA-THAN'S DREAMS, AND LEVIATHAN'S DREAMS BECOME TRUTH.
I ONLY WANT TO BE FREE! TO BE FREE, AND TO BE FORGOTTEN!
BUT AS LONG AS THAT THING LIVES, I WILL EVER BE REMEMBERED--AND FOR ONE THING ONLY!
LEVIATHAN TOLD ME YOUR STORY, UTNAPISHTIM. WHAT YOU DID. YOU HAVE WELL DESERVED THE CURSE THAT WAS LAID ON YOU.
TAKE HIM TO THE LIMITS OF THE KINGDOM, AND SET HIM ON THE ROAD.
IT WAS NOT SO GREAT A SIN. I DID IT AT THE OUTSET, THAT WAS ALL.
WHEN THERE WERE NO OTHER STORIES. WHEN THE BEAST HAD NOTHING ELSE TO THINK ON BUT ME.
"YOU'LL BE REMEMBERED TOO, MONSTER-SLAYER! NO DEATH, NO SLEEP FOR YOU!
"THERE'S A PART OF YOUR SOUL THAT WILL NEVER REST! NEVER!"

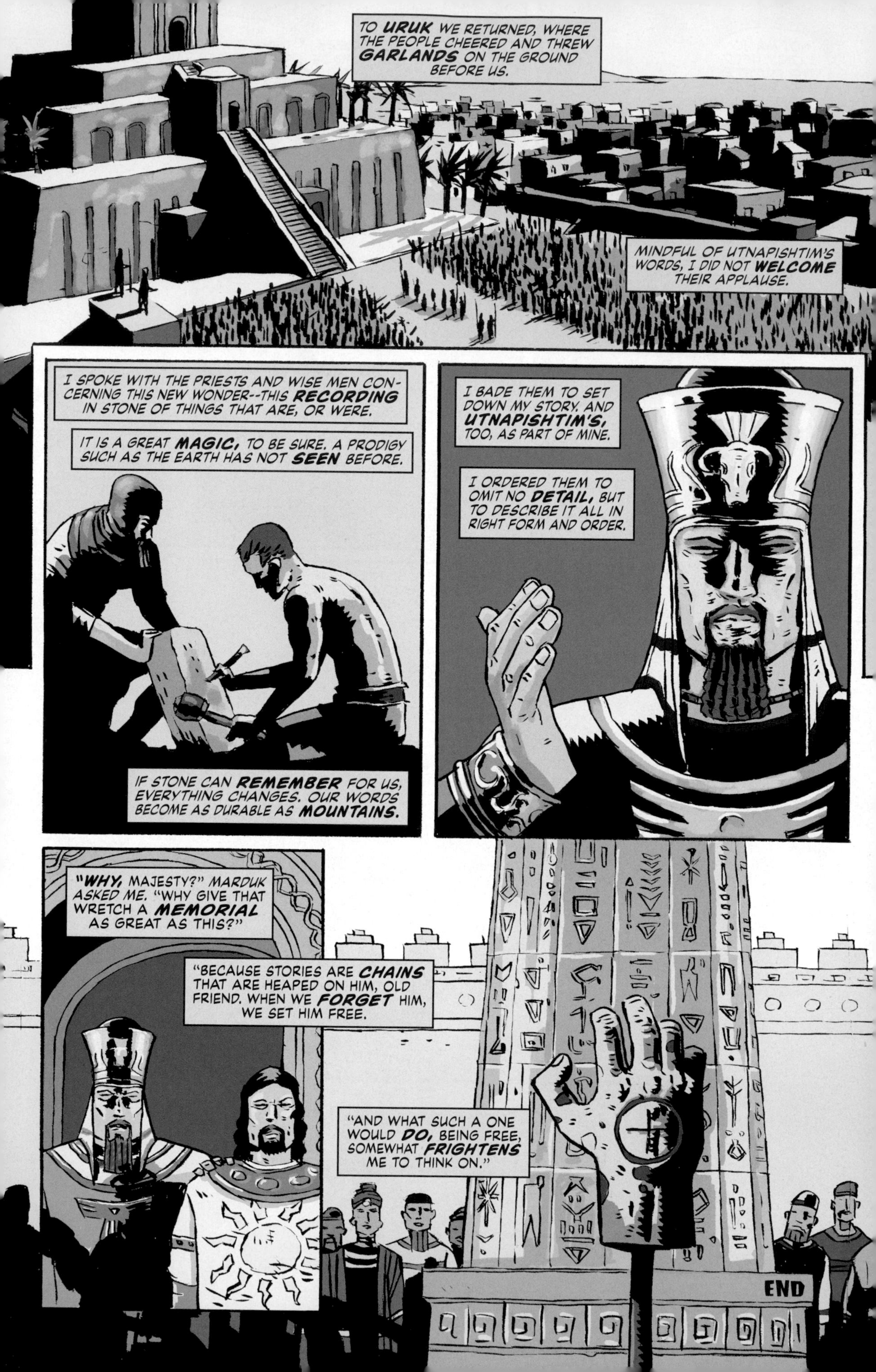
TO URUK WE RETURNED, WHERE THE PEOPLE CHEERED AND THREW GARLANDS ON THE GROUND BEFORE US.
MINDFUL OF UTNAPISHTIM'S WORDS, I DID NOT WELCOME THEIR APPLAUSE.
I SPOKE WITH THE PRIESTS AND WISE MEN CONCERNING THIS NEW WONDER--THIS RECORDING IN STONE OF THINGS THAT ARE, OR WERE.
IT IS A GREAT MAGIC, TO BE SURE. A PRODIGY SUCH AS THE EARTH HAS NOT SEEN BEFORE.
IF STONE CAN REMEMBER FOR US, EVERYTHING CHANGES. OUR WORDS BECOME AS DURABLE AS MOUNTAINS.
I BADE THEM TO SET DOWN MY STORY. AND UTNAPISHTIM'S, TOO, AS PART OF MINE.
I ORDERED THEM TO OMIT NO DETAIL, BUT TO DESCRIBE IT ALL IN RIGHT FORM AND ORDER.
"WHY, MAJESTY?" MARDUK ASKED ME. "WHY GIVE THAT WRETCH A MEMORIAL AS GREAT AS THIS?"
"BECAUSE STORIES ARE CHAINS THAT ARE HEAPED ON HIM, OLD FRIEND. WHEN WE FORGET HIM, WE SET HIM FREE.
"AND WHAT SUCH A ONE WOULD DO, BEING FREE, SOMEWHAT FRIGHTENS ME TO THINK ON."
END

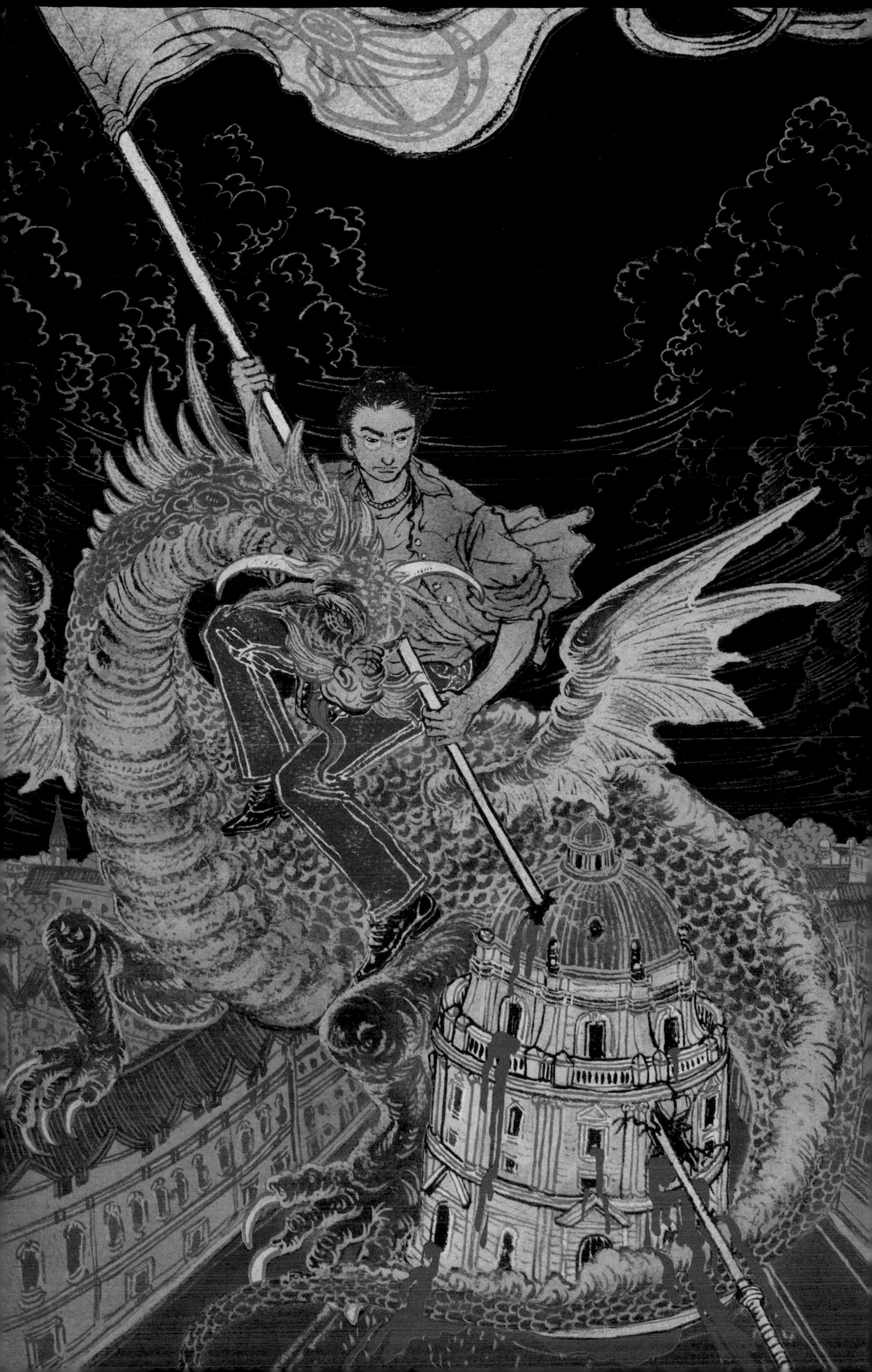

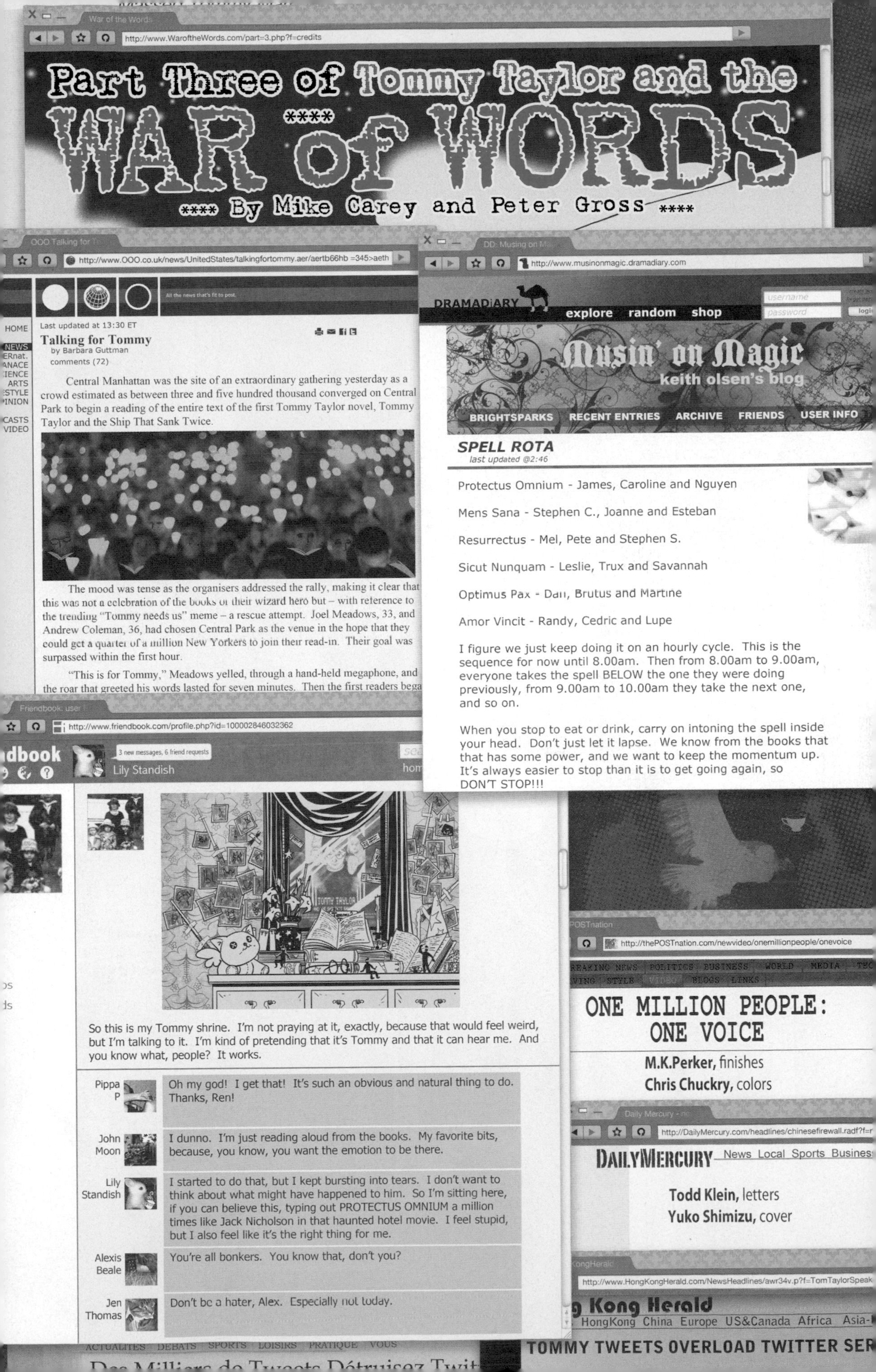
War of the Words
http://www.WaroftheWords.com/part=3.php?f=credits
Part Three of Tommy Taylor and the
WAR **** of WORDS
**** By Mike Carey and Peter Gross ****
OOO Talking for T
http://www.OOO.co.uk/news/UnitedStates/talkingfortommy.aer/aertb66hb =345>aeth
All the news that's fit to post.
HOME
NEWS
ERnat.
ANACE
IENCE
ARTS
STYLE
INION
CASTS
VIDEO
Last updated at 13:30 ET
Talking for Tommy
by Barbara Guttman
comments (72)
Central Manhattan was the site of an extraordinary gathering yesterday as a crowd estimated as between three and five hundred thousand converged on Central Park to begin a reading of the entire text of the first Tommy Taylor novel, Tommy Taylor and the Ship That Sank Twice.
The mood was tense as the organisers addressed the rally, making it clear that this was not a celebration of the books or their wizard hero but – with reference to the trending "Tommy needs us" meme – a rescue attempt. Joel Meadows, 33, and Andrew Coleman, 36, had chosen Central Park as the venue in the hope that they could get a quarter of a million New Yorkers to join their read-in. Their goal was surpassed within the first hour.
"This is for Tommy," Meadows yelled, through a hand-held megaphone, and the roar that greeted his words lasted for seven minutes. Then the first readers bega
DD: Musing on M
http://www.musinonmagic.dramadiary.com
DRAMADIARY
explore random shop
username
password
login
Musin' on Magic
keith olsen's blog
BRIGHTSPARKS RECENT ENTRIES ARCHIVE FRIENDS USER INFO
SPELL ROTA
last updated @2:46
Protectus Omnium - James, Caroline and Nguyen
Mens Sana - Stephen C., Joanne and Esteban
Resurrectus - Mel, Pete and Stephen S.
Sicut Nunquam - Leslie, Trux and Savannah
Optimus Pax - Dan, Brutus and Martine
Amor Vincit - Randy, Cedric and Lupe
I figure we just keep doing it on an hourly cycle. This is the sequence for now until 8.00am. Then from 8.00am to 9.00am, everyone takes the spell BELOW the one they were doing previously, from 9.00am to 10.00am they take the next one, and so on.
When you stop to eat or drink, carry on intoning the spell inside your head. Don't just let it lapse. We know from the books that that has some power, and we want to keep the momentum up. It's always easier to stop than it is to get going again, so DON'T STOP!!!
Friendbook: user
http://www.friendbook.com/profile.php?id=100002846032362
dbook
3 new messages, 6 friend requests
Lily Standish
hom
TOMMY TAYLOR
So this is my Tommy shrine. I'm not praying at it, exactly, because that would feel weird, but I'm talking to it. I'm kind of pretending that it's Tommy and that it can hear me. And you know what, people? It works.
Pippa P
Oh my god! I get that! It's such an obvious and natural thing to do. Thanks, Ren!
John Moon
I dunno. I'm just reading aloud from the books. My favorite bits, because, you know, you want the emotion to be there.
Lily Standish
I started to do that, but I kept bursting into tears. I don't want to think about what might have happened to him. So I'm sitting here, if you can believe this, typing out PROTECTUS OMNIUM a million times like Jack Nicholson in that haunted hotel movie. I feel stupid, but I also feel like it's the right thing for me.
Alexis Beale
You're all bonkers. You know that, don't you?
Jen Thomas
Don't be a hater, Alex. Especially not today.
POSTnation
http://thePOSTnation.com/newvideo/onemillionpeople/onevoice
REAKING NEWS POLITICS BUSINESS WORLD MEDIA TEC
VING STYLE VIDEO BLOGS LINKS
ONE MILLION PEOPLE: ONE VOICE
M.K.Perker, finishes
Chris Chuckry, colors
Daily Mercury
http://DailyMercury.com/headlines/chinesefirewall.radf?f=r
DAILYMERCURY News Local Sports Busines
Todd Klein, letters
Yuko Shimizu, cover
KongHerald
http://www.HongKongHerald.com/NewsHeadlines/awr34v.p?f=TomTaylorSpeak
g Kong Herald
HongKong China Europe US&Canada Africa Asia
TOMMY TWEETS OVERLOAD TWITTER SER
ACTUALITES DEBATS SPORTS LOISIRS PRATIQUE VOUS

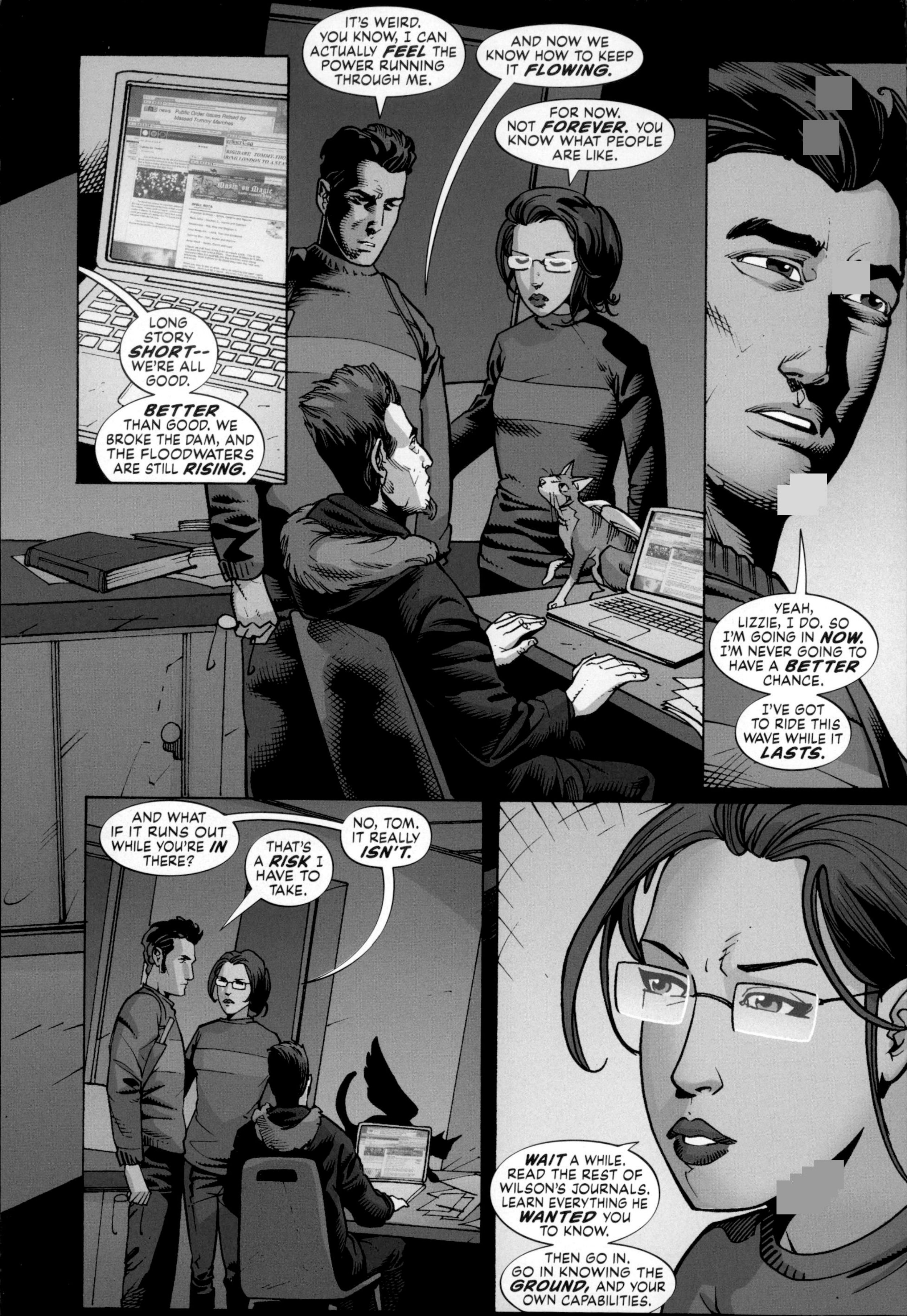

Public Order Issues Raised by Massed Tommy Marches
LONG STORY SHORT-- WE'RE ALL GOOD.
BETTER THAN GOOD. WE BROKE THE DAM, AND THE FLOODWATERS ARE STILL RISING.
IT'S WEIRD. YOU KNOW, I CAN ACTUALLY FEEL THE POWER RUNNING THROUGH ME.
AND NOW WE KNOW HOW TO KEEP IT FLOWING.
FOR NOW. NOT FOREVER. YOU KNOW WHAT PEOPLE ARE LIKE.
YEAH, LIZZIE, I DO. SO I'M GOING IN NOW. I'M NEVER GOING TO HAVE A BETTER CHANCE.
I'VE GOT TO RIDE THIS WAVE WHILE IT LASTS.
AND WHAT IF IT RUNS OUT WHILE YOU'RE IN THERE?
THAT'S A RISK I HAVE TO TAKE.
NO, TOM. IT REALLY ISN'T.
WAIT A WHILE. READ THE REST OF WILSON'S JOURNALS. LEARN EVERYTHING HE WANTED YOU TO KNOW.
THEN GO IN. GO IN KNOWING THE GROUND, AND YOUR OWN CAPABILITIES.

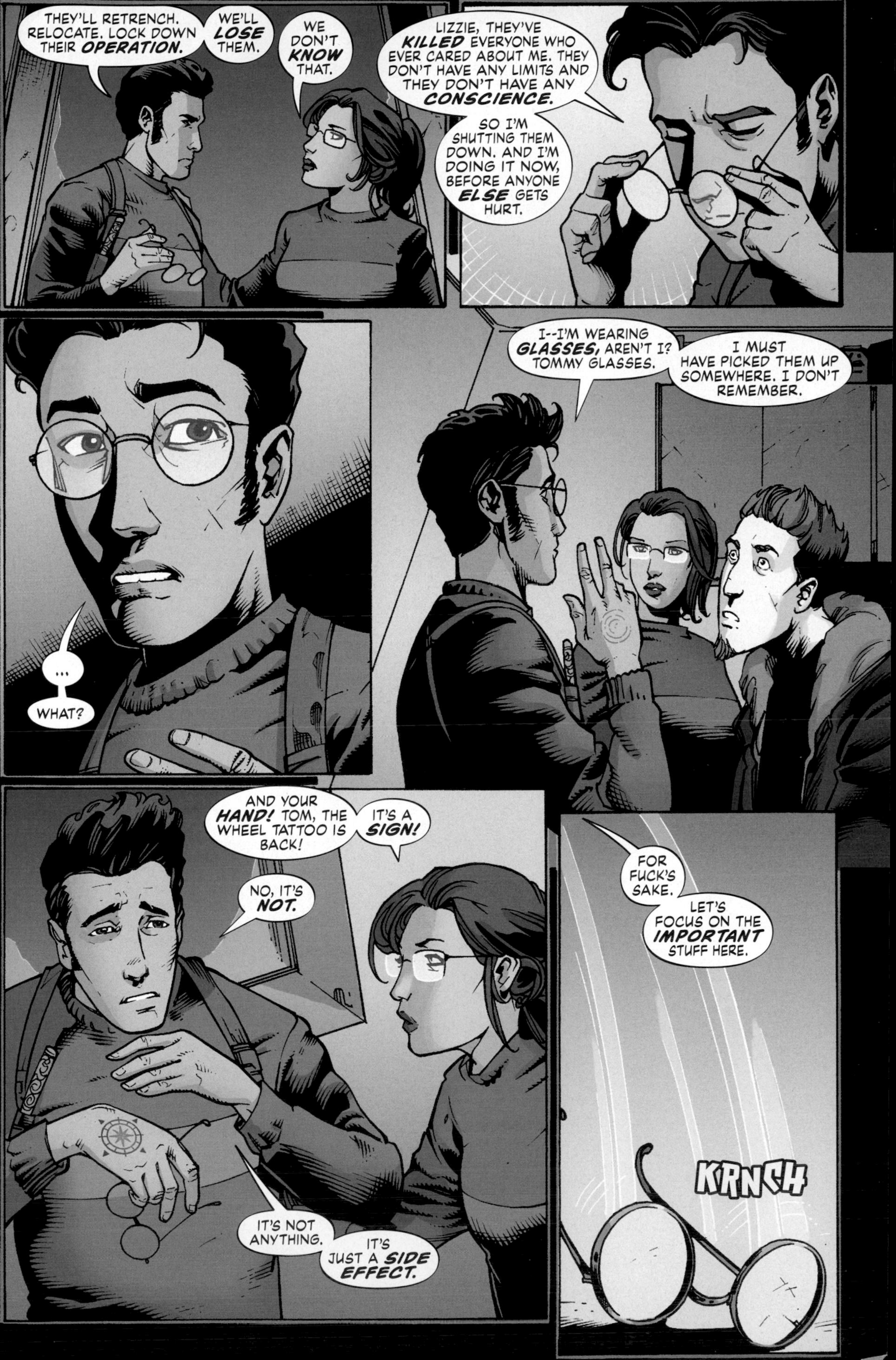
THEY'LL RETRENCH. RELOCATE. LOCK DOWN THEIR *OPERATION.*
WE'LL *LOSE* THEM.
WE DON'T *KNOW* THAT.
LIZZIE, THEY'VE *KILLED* EVERYONE WHO EVER CARED ABOUT ME. THEY DON'T HAVE ANY LIMITS AND THEY DON'T HAVE ANY *CONSCIENCE.*
SO I'M SHUTTING THEM DOWN. AND I'M DOING IT NOW, BEFORE ANYONE *ELSE* GETS HURT.
...
WHAT?
I--I'M WEARING *GLASSES,* AREN'T I? TOMMY GLASSES.
I MUST HAVE PICKED THEM UP SOMEWHERE. I DON'T REMEMBER.
AND YOUR *HAND!* TOM, THE WHEEL TATTOO IS BACK!
IT'S A *SIGN!*
NO, IT'S *NOT.*
IT'S NOT ANYTHING.
IT'S JUST A *SIDE EFFECT.*
FOR FUCK'S SAKE.
LET'S FOCUS ON THE *IMPORTANT* STUFF HERE.
KRNCH

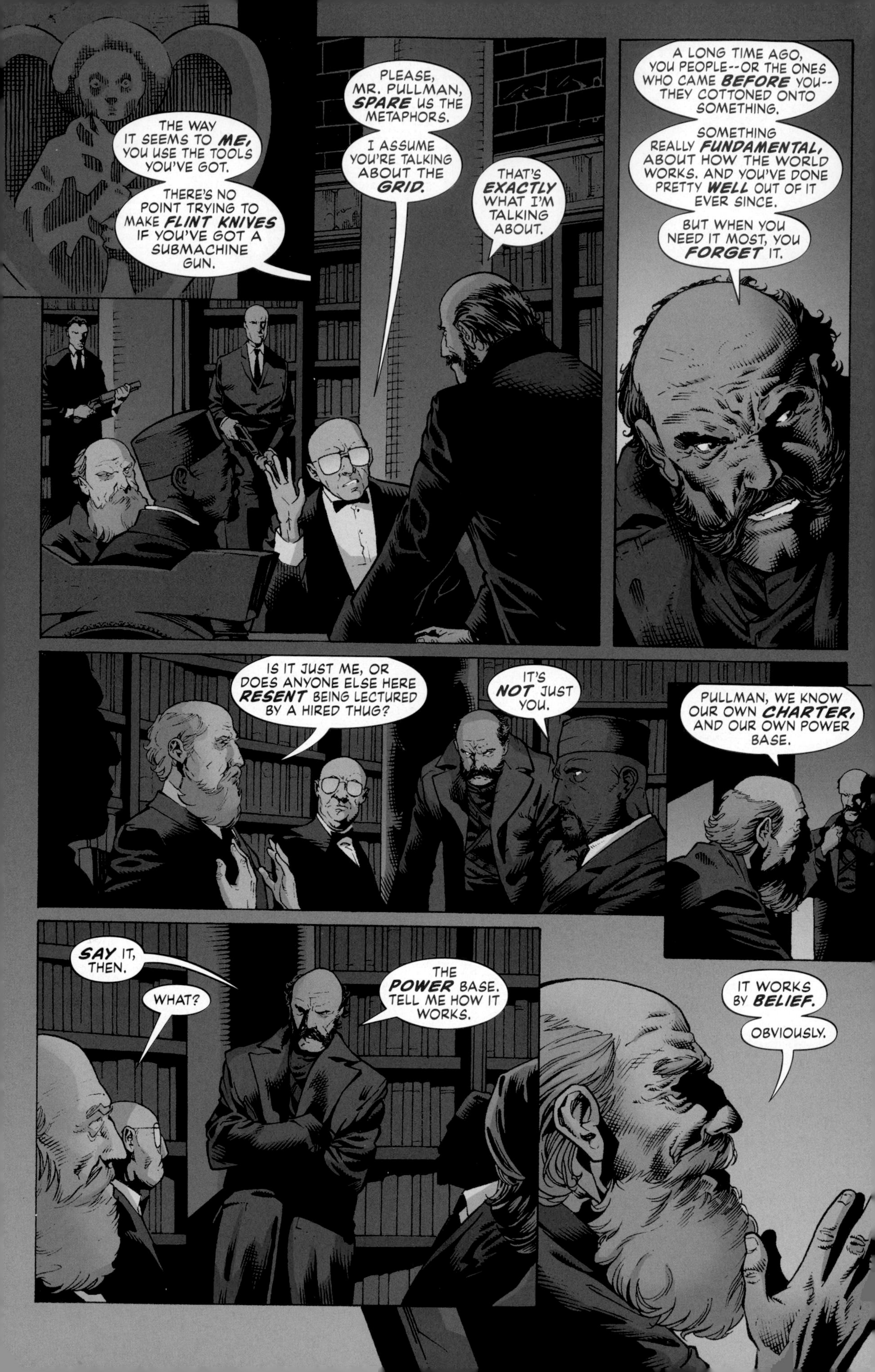
THE WAY IT SEEMS TO ME, YOU USE THE TOOLS YOU'VE GOT.
THERE'S NO POINT TRYING TO MAKE FLINT KNIVES IF YOU'VE GOT A SUBMACHINE GUN.
PLEASE, MR. PULLMAN, SPARE US THE METAPHORS.
I ASSUME YOU'RE TALKING ABOUT THE GRID.
THAT'S EXACTLY WHAT I'M TALKING ABOUT.
A LONG TIME AGO, YOU PEOPLE--OR THE ONES WHO CAME BEFORE YOU--THEY COTTONED ONTO SOMETHING.
SOMETHING REALLY FUNDAMENTAL, ABOUT HOW THE WORLD WORKS. AND YOU'VE DONE PRETTY WELL OUT OF IT EVER SINCE.
BUT WHEN YOU NEED IT MOST, YOU FORGET IT.
IS IT JUST ME, OR DOES ANYONE ELSE HERE RESENT BEING LECTURED BY A HIRED THUG?
IT'S NOT JUST YOU.
PULLMAN, WE KNOW OUR OWN CHARTER, AND OUR OWN POWER BASE.
SAY IT, THEN.
WHAT?
THE POWER BASE. TELL ME HOW IT WORKS.
IT WORKS BY BELIEF.
OBVIOUSLY.

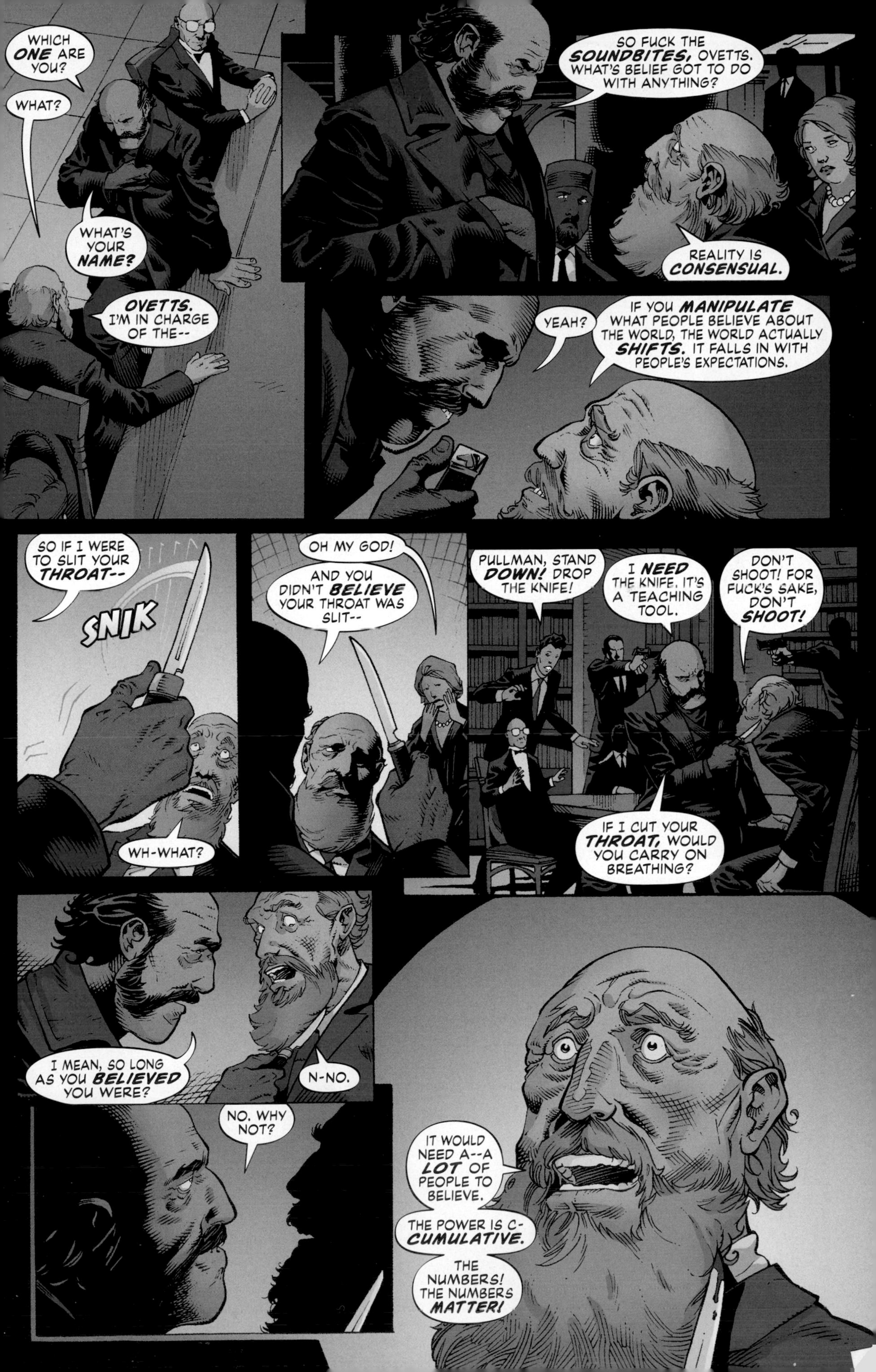
WHICH ONE ARE YOU?
WHAT?
WHAT'S YOUR NAME?
OVETTS. I'M IN CHARGE OF THE--
SO FUCK THE SOUNDBITES, OVETTS. WHAT'S BELIEF GOT TO DO WITH ANYTHING?
REALITY IS CONSENSUAL.
YEAH?
IF YOU MANIPULATE WHAT PEOPLE BELIEVE ABOUT THE WORLD, THE WORLD ACTUALLY SHIFTS. IT FALLS IN WITH PEOPLE'S EXPECTATIONS.
SO IF I WERE TO SLIT YOUR THROAT--
SNIK
WH-WHAT?
OH MY GOD!
AND YOU DIDN'T BELIEVE YOUR THROAT WAS SLIT--
PULLMAN, STAND DOWN! DROP THE KNIFE!
I NEED THE KNIFE. IT'S A TEACHING TOOL.
DON'T SHOOT! FOR FUCK'S SAKE, DON'T SHOOT!
IF I CUT YOUR THROAT, WOULD YOU CARRY ON BREATHING?
I MEAN, SO LONG AS YOU BELIEVED YOU WERE?
N-NO.
NO. WHY NOT?
IT WOULD NEED A--A LOT OF PEOPLE TO BELIEVE.
THE POWER IS C-CUMULATIVE.
THE NUMBERS! THE NUMBERS MATTER!

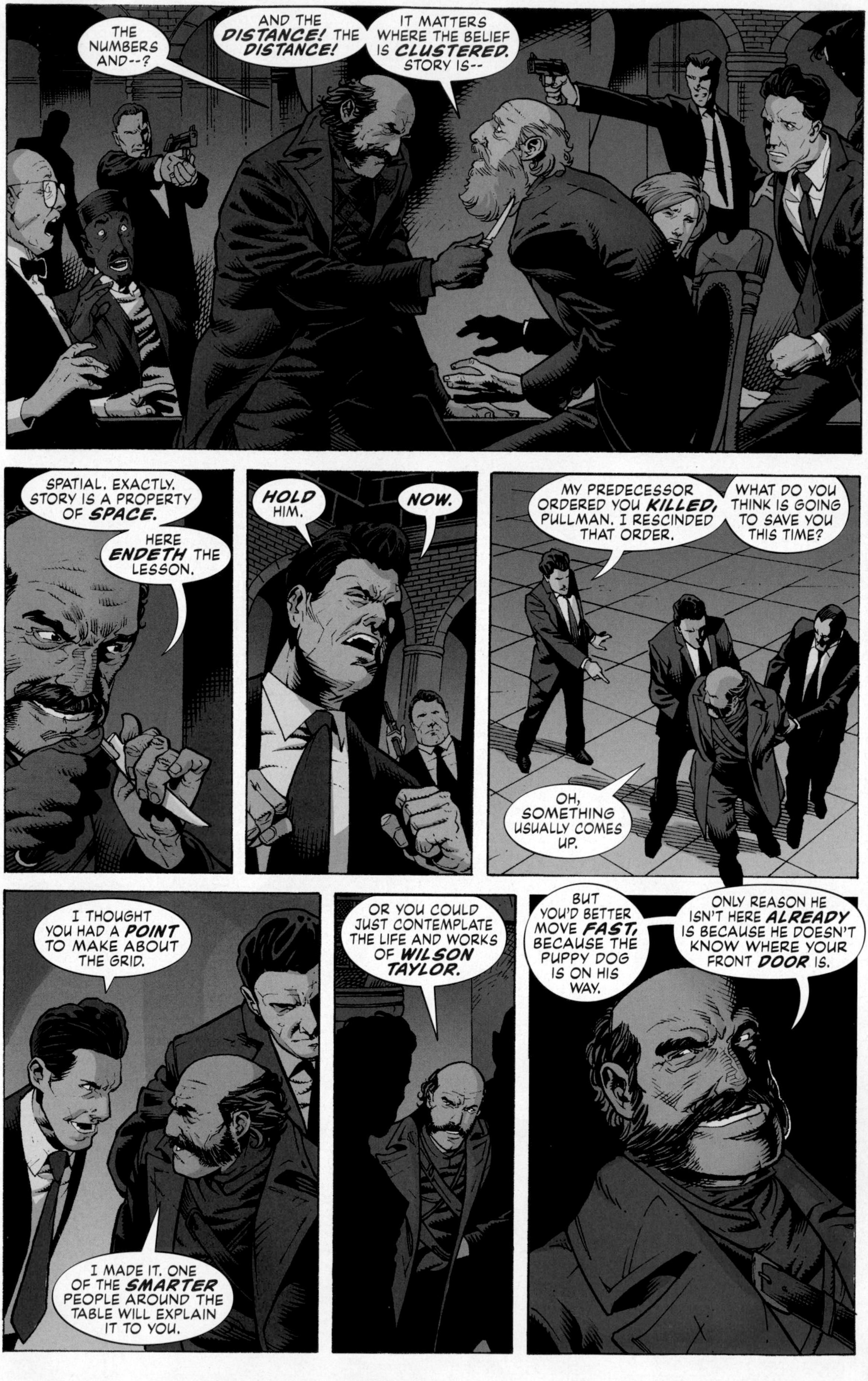
THE NUMBERS AND--?
AND THE DISTANCE! THE DISTANCE!
IT MATTERS WHERE THE BELIEF IS CLUSTERED. STORY IS--
SPATIAL. EXACTLY. STORY IS A PROPERTY OF SPACE.
HERE ENDETH THE LESSON.
HOLD HIM.
NOW.
MY PREDECESSOR ORDERED YOU KILLED, PULLMAN. I RESCINDED THAT ORDER.
WHAT DO YOU THINK IS GOING TO SAVE YOU THIS TIME?
OH, SOMETHING USUALLY COMES UP.
I THOUGHT YOU HAD A POINT TO MAKE ABOUT THE GRID.
I MADE IT. ONE OF THE SMARTER PEOPLE AROUND THE TABLE WILL EXPLAIN IT TO YOU.
OR YOU COULD JUST CONTEMPLATE THE LIFE AND WORKS OF WILSON TAYLOR.
BUT YOU'D BETTER MOVE FAST, BECAUSE THE PUPPY DOG IS ON HIS WAY.
ONLY REASON HE ISN'T HERE ALREADY IS BECAUSE HE DOESN'T KNOW WHERE YOUR FRONT DOOR IS.

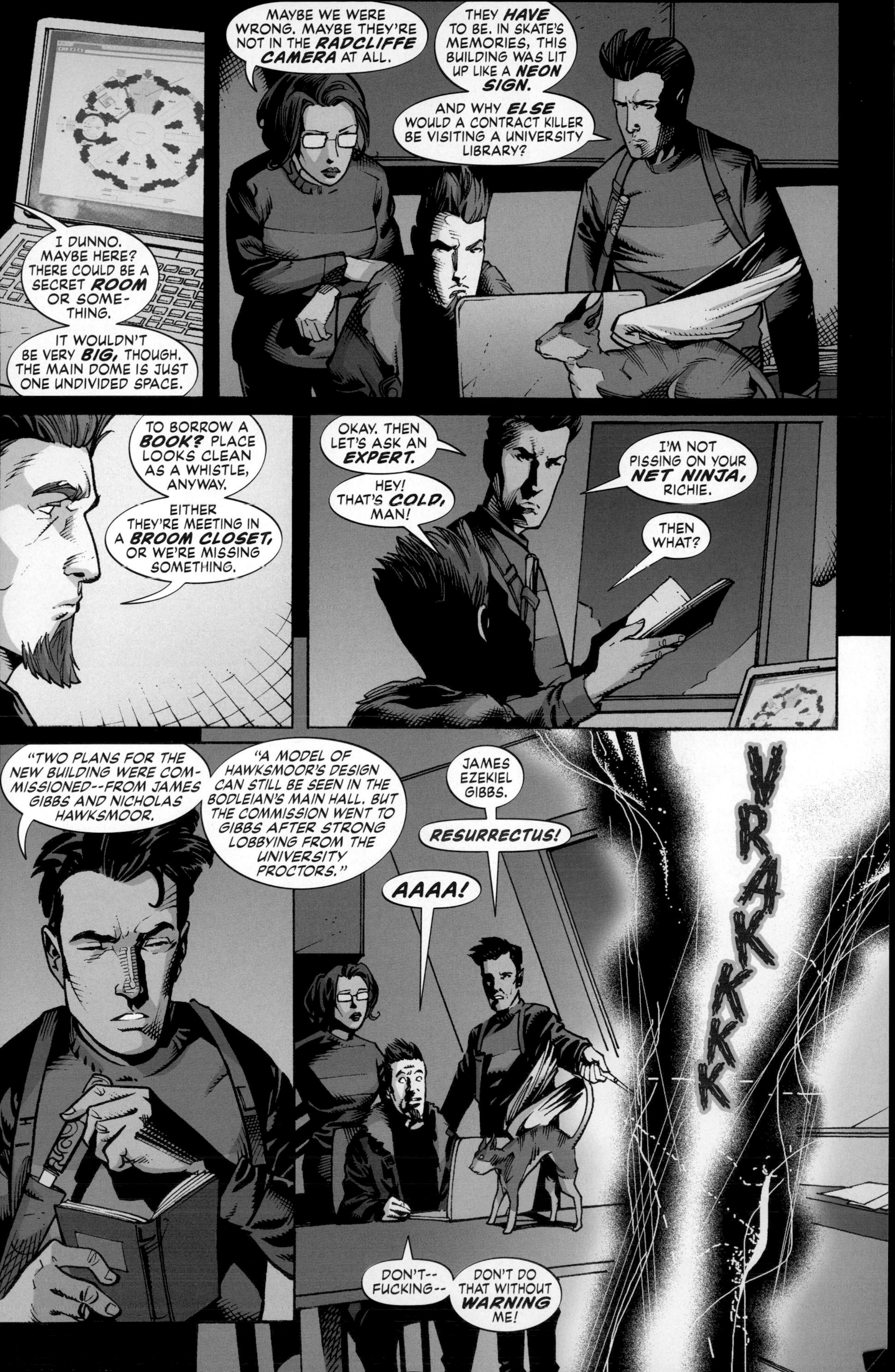
MAYBE WE WERE WRONG. MAYBE THEY'RE NOT IN THE RADCLIFFE CAMERA AT ALL.
THEY HAVE TO BE. IN SKATE'S MEMORIES, THIS BUILDING WAS LIT UP LIKE A NEON SIGN.
AND WHY ELSE WOULD A CONTRACT KILLER BE VISITING A UNIVERSITY LIBRARY?
I DUNNO. MAYBE HERE? THERE COULD BE A SECRET ROOM OR SOME-THING.
IT WOULDN'T BE VERY BIG, THOUGH. THE MAIN DOME IS JUST ONE UNDIVIDED SPACE.
TO BORROW A BOOK? PLACE LOOKS CLEAN AS A WHISTLE, ANYWAY.
EITHER THEY'RE MEETING IN A BROOM CLOSET, OR WE'RE MISSING SOMETHING.
OKAY. THEN LET'S ASK AN EXPERT.
HEY! THAT'S COLD, MAN!
I'M NOT PISSING ON YOUR NET NINJA, RICHIE.
THEN WHAT?
"TWO PLANS FOR THE NEW BUILDING WERE COM-MISSIONED--FROM JAMES GIBBS AND NICHOLAS HAWKSMOOR.
"A MODEL OF HAWKSMOOR'S DESIGN CAN STILL BE SEEN IN THE BODLEIAN'S MAIN HALL. BUT THE COMMISSION WENT TO GIBBS AFTER STRONG LOBBYING FROM THE UNIVERSITY PROCTORS."
JAMES EZEKIEL GIBBS.
RESURRECTUS!
AAAA!
VRAKKKK
DON'T--FUCKING--
DON'T DO THAT WITHOUT WARNING ME!

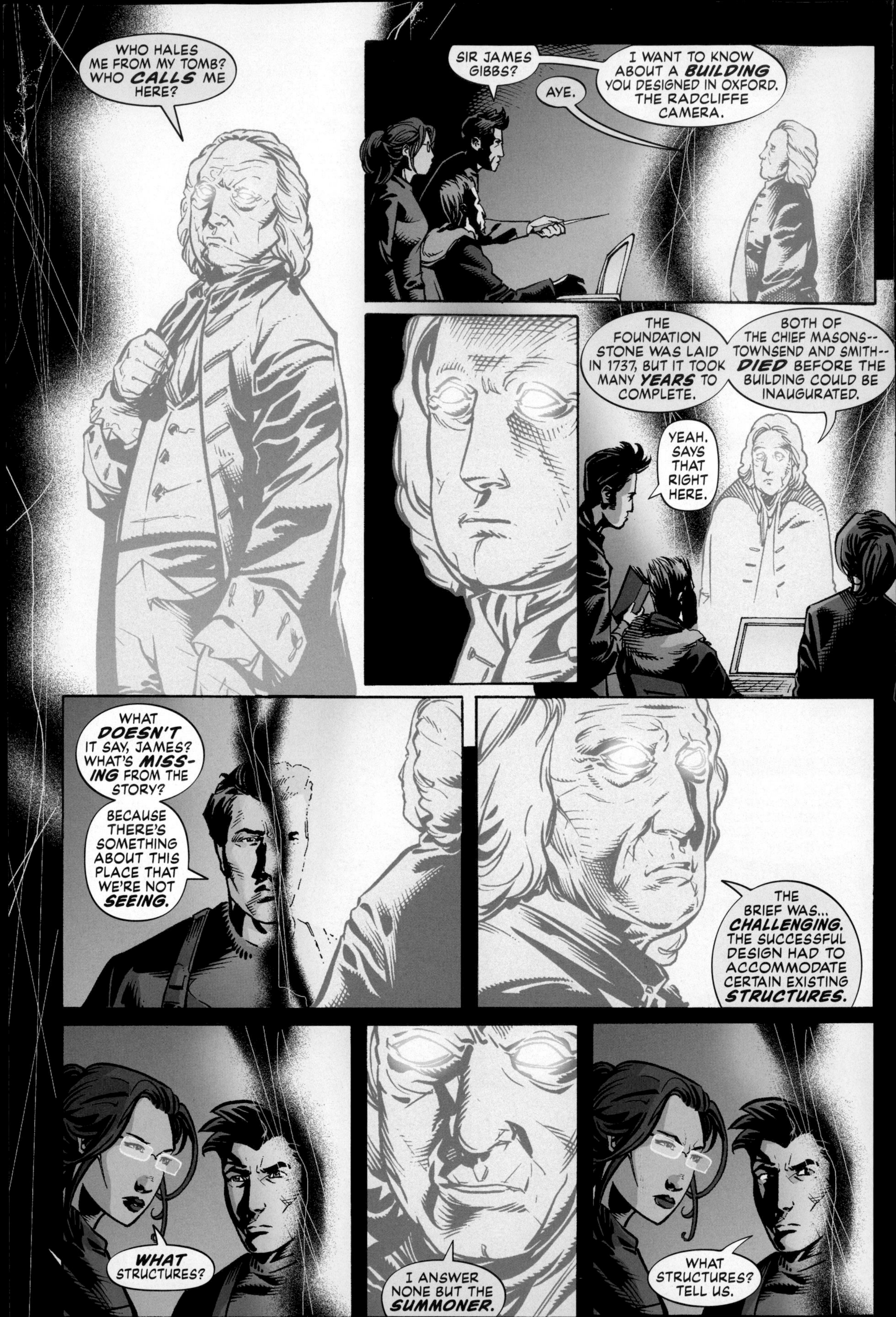
WHO HALES ME FROM MY TOMB? WHO CALLS ME HERE?
SIR JAMES GIBBS?
AYE.
I WANT TO KNOW ABOUT A BUILDING YOU DESIGNED IN OXFORD. THE RADCLIFFE CAMERA.
THE FOUNDATION STONE WAS LAID IN 1737, BUT IT TOOK MANY YEARS TO COMPLETE.
BOTH OF THE CHIEF MASONS--TOWNSEND AND SMITH--DIED BEFORE THE BUILDING COULD BE INAUGURATED.
YEAH. SAYS THAT RIGHT HERE.
WHAT DOESN'T IT SAY, JAMES? WHAT'S MISSING FROM THE STORY?
BECAUSE THERE'S SOMETHING ABOUT THIS PLACE THAT WE'RE NOT SEEING.
THE BRIEF WAS... CHALLENGING. THE SUCCESSFUL DESIGN HAD TO ACCOMMODATE CERTAIN EXISTING STRUCTURES.
WHAT STRUCTURES?
I ANSWER NONE BUT THE SUMMONER.
WHAT STRUCTURES? TELL US.

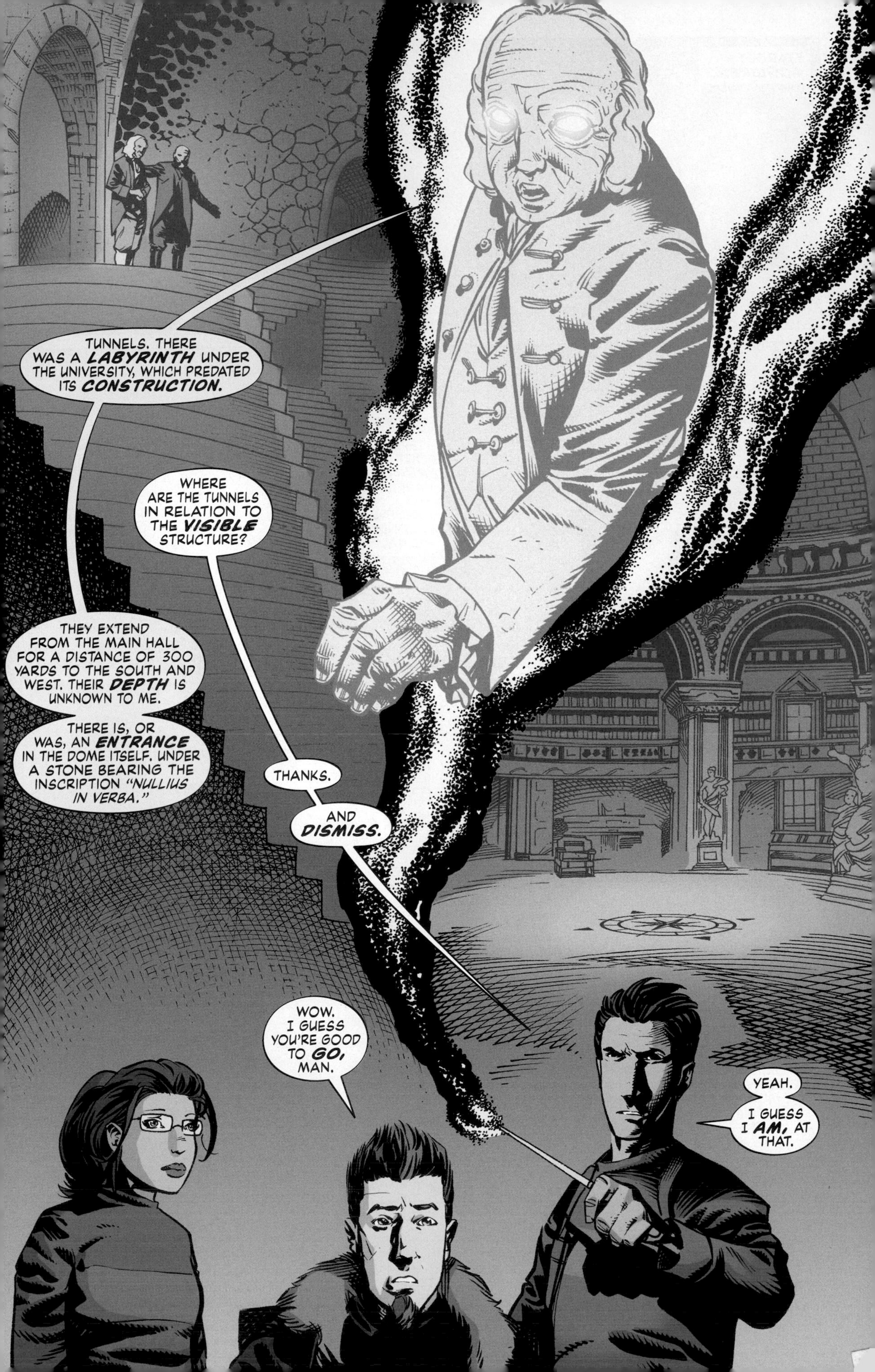
TUNNELS. THERE WAS A LABYRINTH UNDER THE UNIVERSITY, WHICH PREDATED ITS CONSTRUCTION.
WHERE ARE THE TUNNELS IN RELATION TO THE VISIBLE STRUCTURE?
THEY EXTEND FROM THE MAIN HALL FOR A DISTANCE OF 300 YARDS TO THE SOUTH AND WEST. THEIR DEPTH IS UNKNOWN TO ME.
THERE IS, OR WAS, AN ENTRANCE IN THE DOME ITSELF. UNDER A STONE BEARING THE INSCRIPTION "NULLIUS IN VERBA."
THANKS.
AND DISMISS.
WOW. I GUESS YOU'RE GOOD TO GO, MAN.
YEAH.
I GUESS I AM, AT THAT.

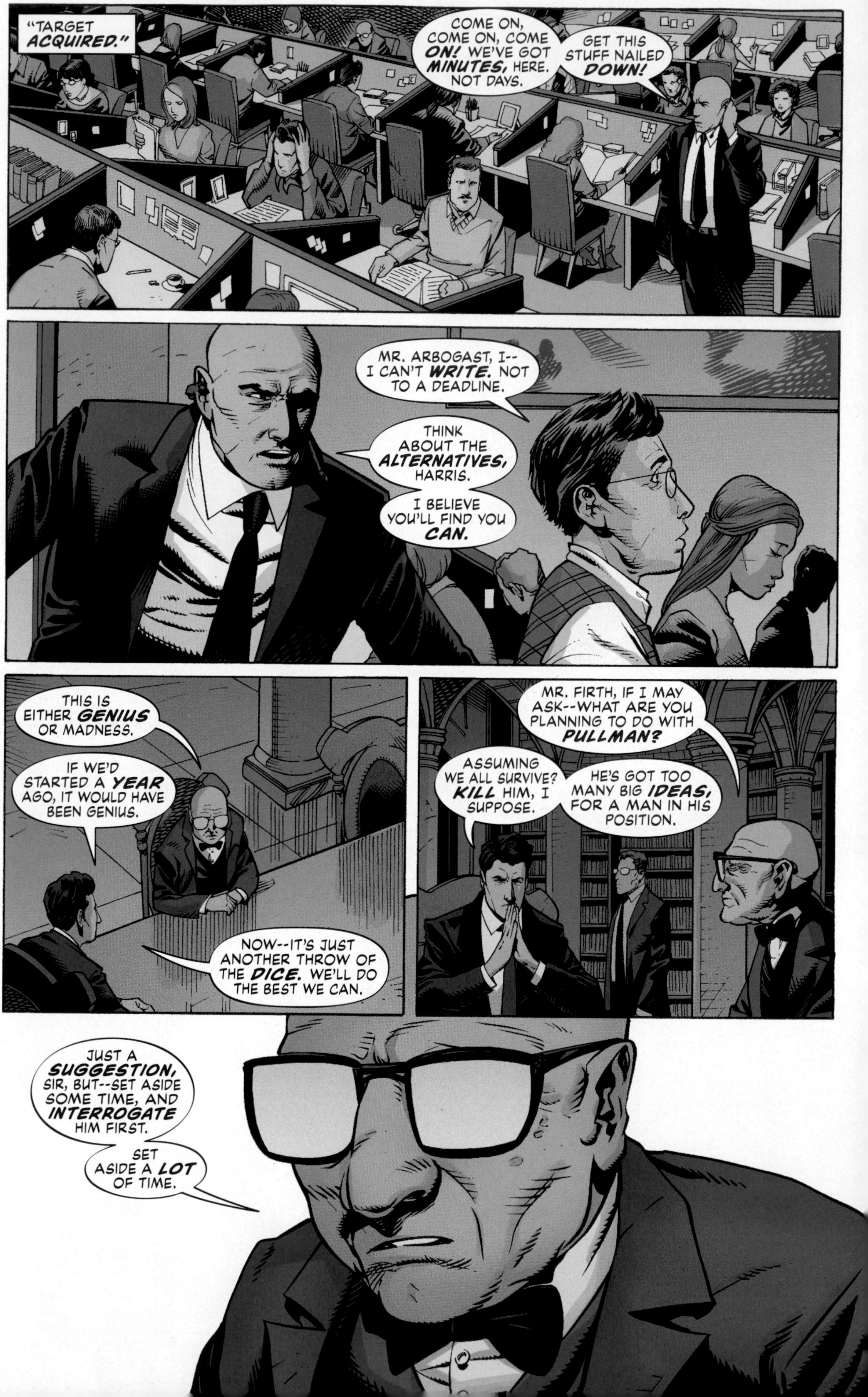
"TARGET ACQUIRED."
COME ON, COME ON, COME ON! WE'VE GOT MINUTES, HERE. NOT DAYS.
GET THIS STUFF NAILED DOWN!
MR. ARBOGAST, I-- I CAN'T WRITE. NOT TO A DEADLINE.
THINK ABOUT THE ALTERNATIVES, HARRIS.
I BELIEVE YOU'LL FIND YOU CAN.
THIS IS EITHER GENIUS OR MADNESS.
IF WE'D STARTED A YEAR AGO, IT WOULD HAVE BEEN GENIUS.
NOW--IT'S JUST ANOTHER THROW OF THE DICE. WE'LL DO THE BEST WE CAN.
MR. FIRTH, IF I MAY ASK--WHAT ARE YOU PLANNING TO DO WITH PULLMAN?
ASSUMING WE ALL SURVIVE? KILL HIM, I SUPPOSE.
HE'S GOT TOO MANY BIG IDEAS, FOR A MAN IN HIS POSITION.
JUST A SUGGESTION, SIR, BUT--SET ASIDE SOME TIME, AND INTERROGATE HIM FIRST.
SET ASIDE A LOT OF TIME.

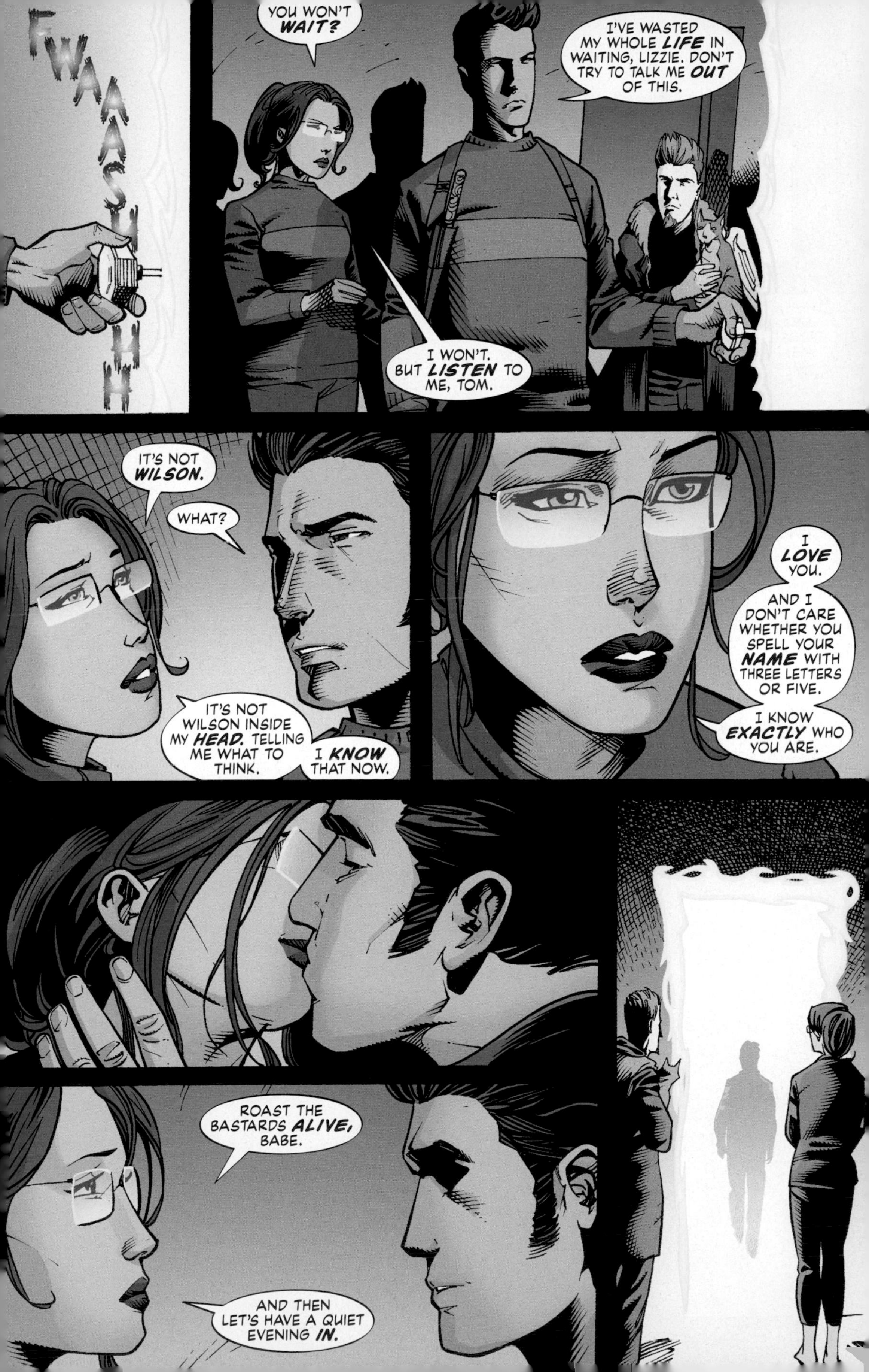
FWAASHHH
YOU WON'T WAIT?
I'VE WASTED MY WHOLE LIFE IN WAITING, LIZZIE. DON'T TRY TO TALK ME OUT OF THIS.
I WON'T. BUT LISTEN TO ME, TOM.
IT'S NOT WILSON.
WHAT?
IT'S NOT WILSON INSIDE MY HEAD. TELLING ME WHAT TO THINK.
I KNOW THAT NOW.
I LOVE YOU.
AND I DON'T CARE WHETHER YOU SPELL YOUR NAME WITH THREE LETTERS OR FIVE.
I KNOW EXACTLY WHO YOU ARE.
ROAST THE BASTARDS ALIVE, BABE.
AND THEN LET'S HAVE A QUIET EVENING IN.

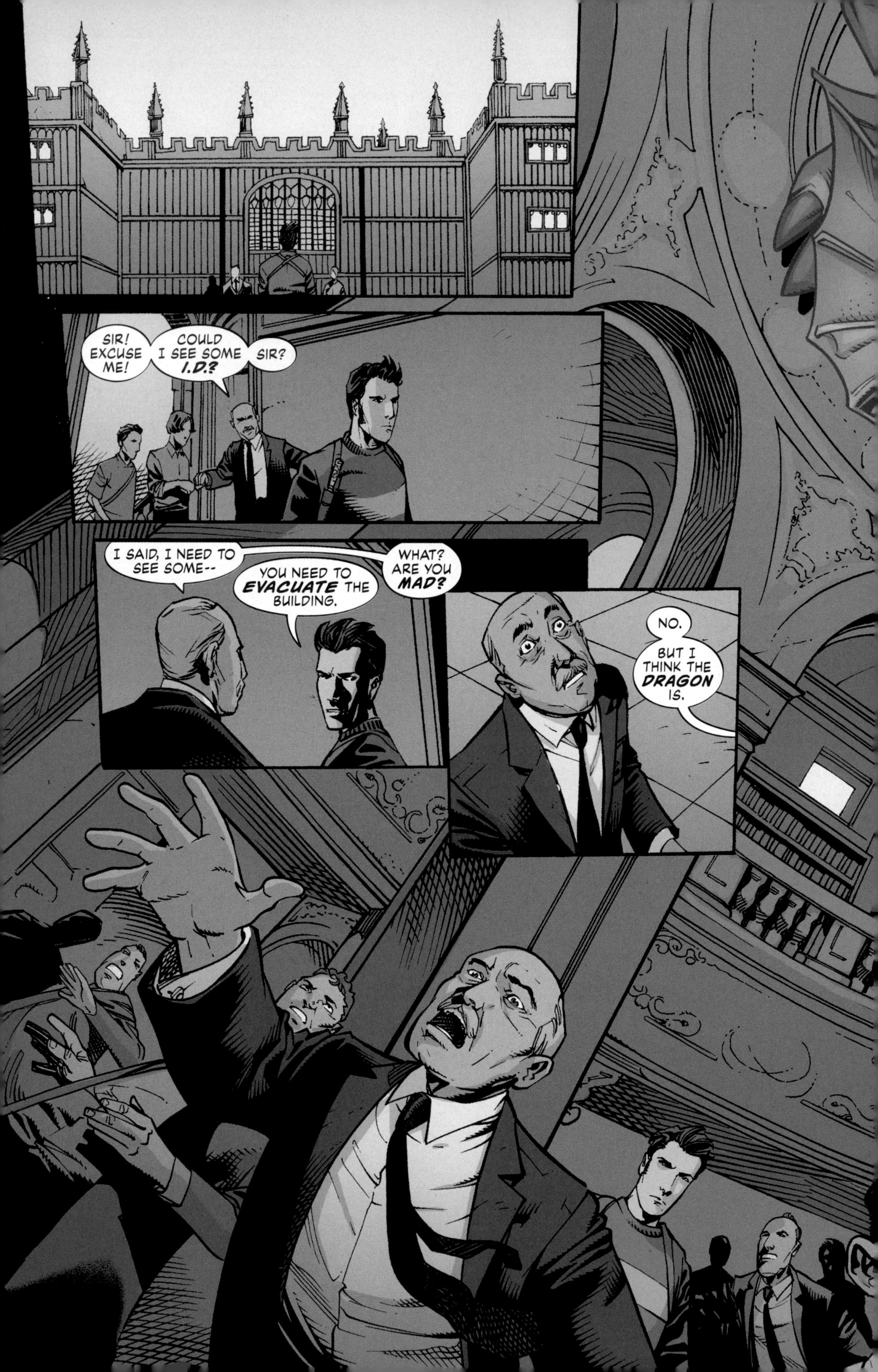

SIR! EXCUSE ME!
COULD I SEE SOME I.D.?
SIR?
I SAID, I NEED TO SEE SOME--
YOU NEED TO EVACUATE THE BUILDING.
WHAT? ARE YOU MAD?
NO.
BUT I THINK THE DRAGON IS.

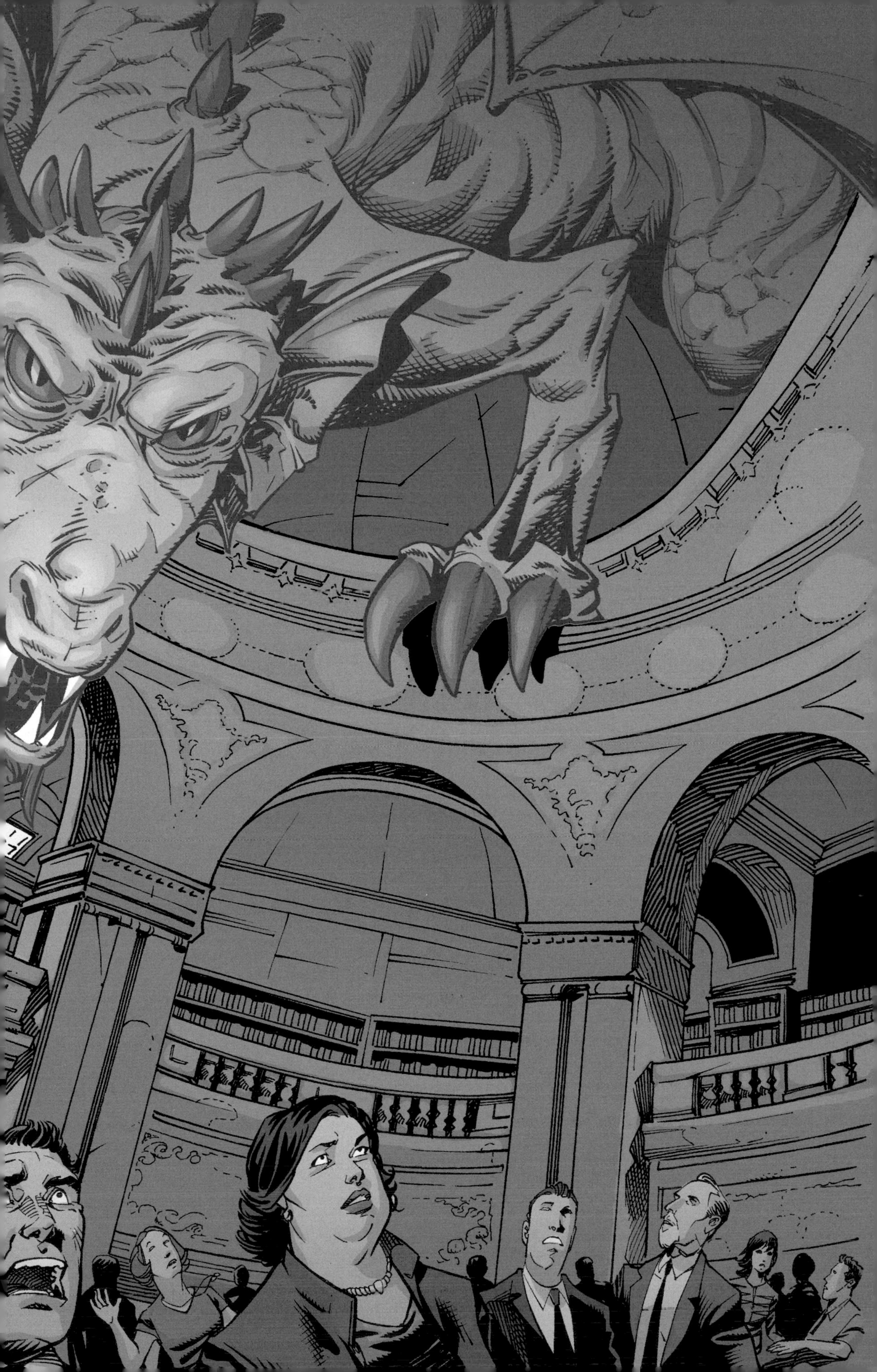

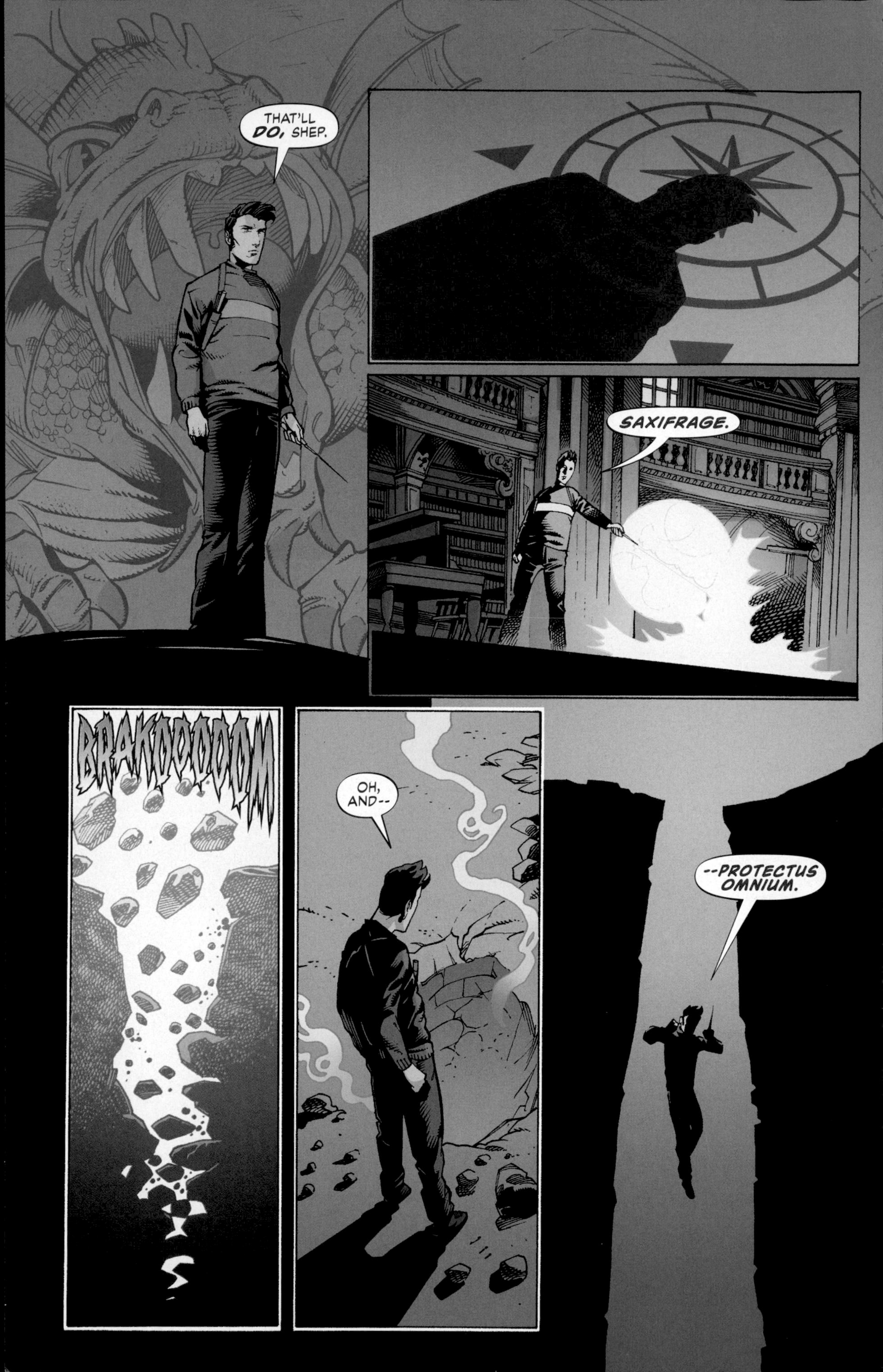
THAT'LL DO, SHEP.
SAXIFRAGE.
BRAKOOOOOM
OH, AND--
--PROTECTUS OMNIUM.

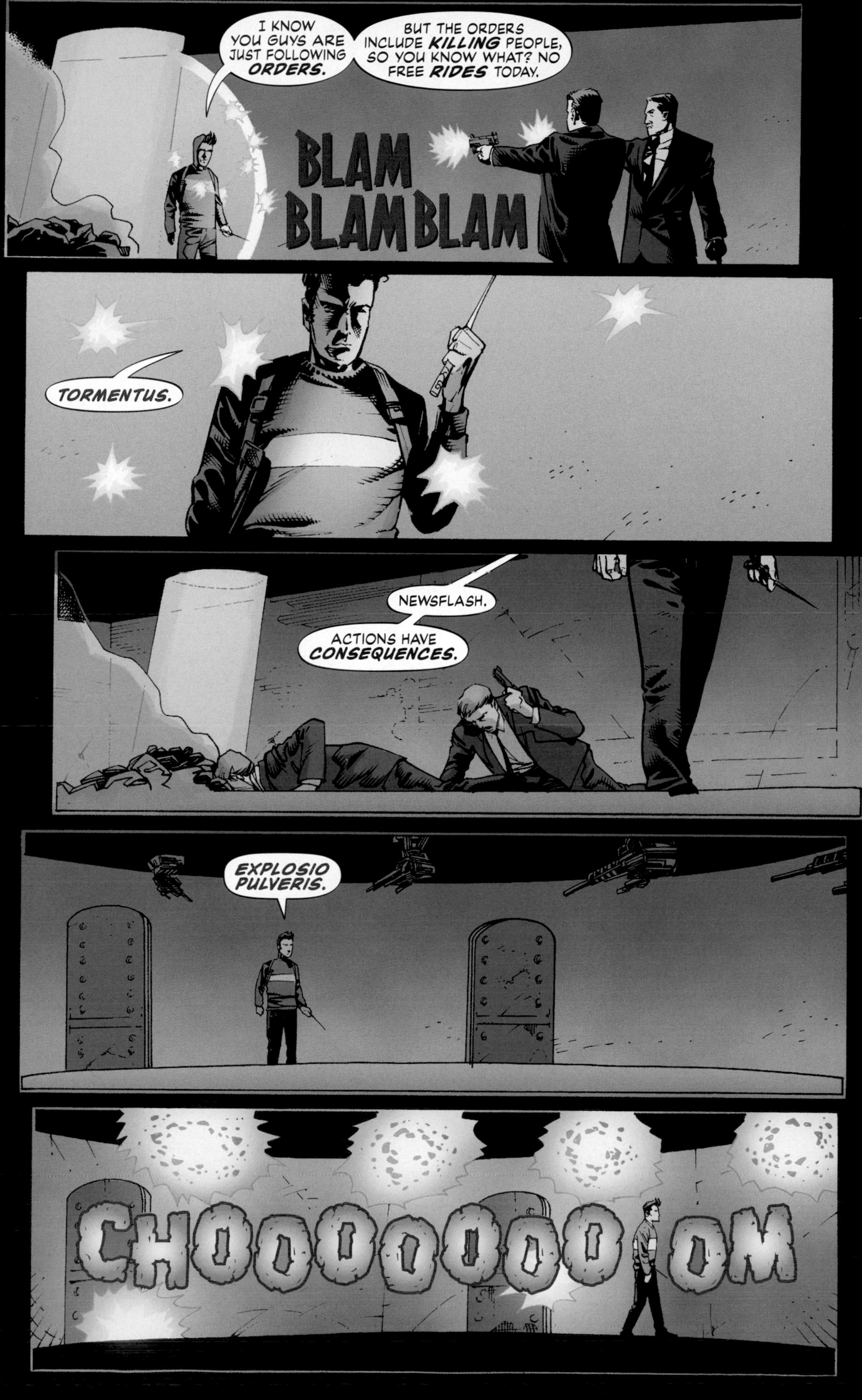
I KNOW YOU GUYS ARE JUST FOLLOWING ORDERS.
BUT THE ORDERS INCLUDE KILLING PEOPLE, SO YOU KNOW WHAT? NO FREE RIDES TODAY.
BLAM BLAMBLAM
TORMENTUS.
NEWSFLASH.
ACTIONS HAVE CONSEQUENCES.
EXPLOSIO PULVERIS.
CHOOOOOOO OM

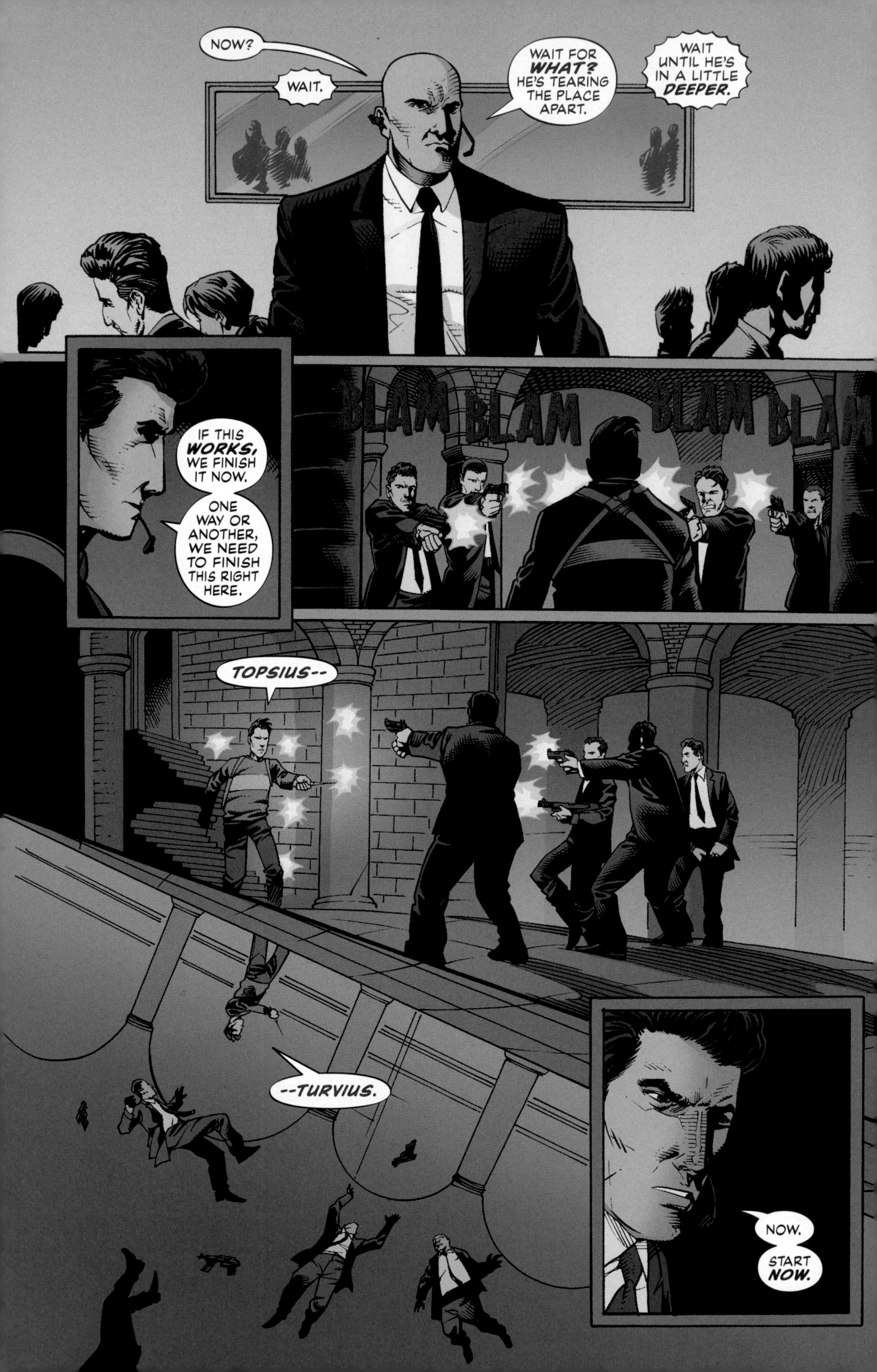
NOW?
WAIT.
WAIT FOR *WHAT?* HE'S TEARING THE PLACE APART.
WAIT UNTIL HE'S IN A LITTLE *DEEPER.*
IF THIS *WORKS,* WE FINISH IT NOW.
ONE WAY OR ANOTHER, WE NEED TO FINISH THIS RIGHT HERE.
BLAM BLAM
BLAM BLAM
TOPSIUS--
--TURVIUS.
NOW.
START *NOW.*

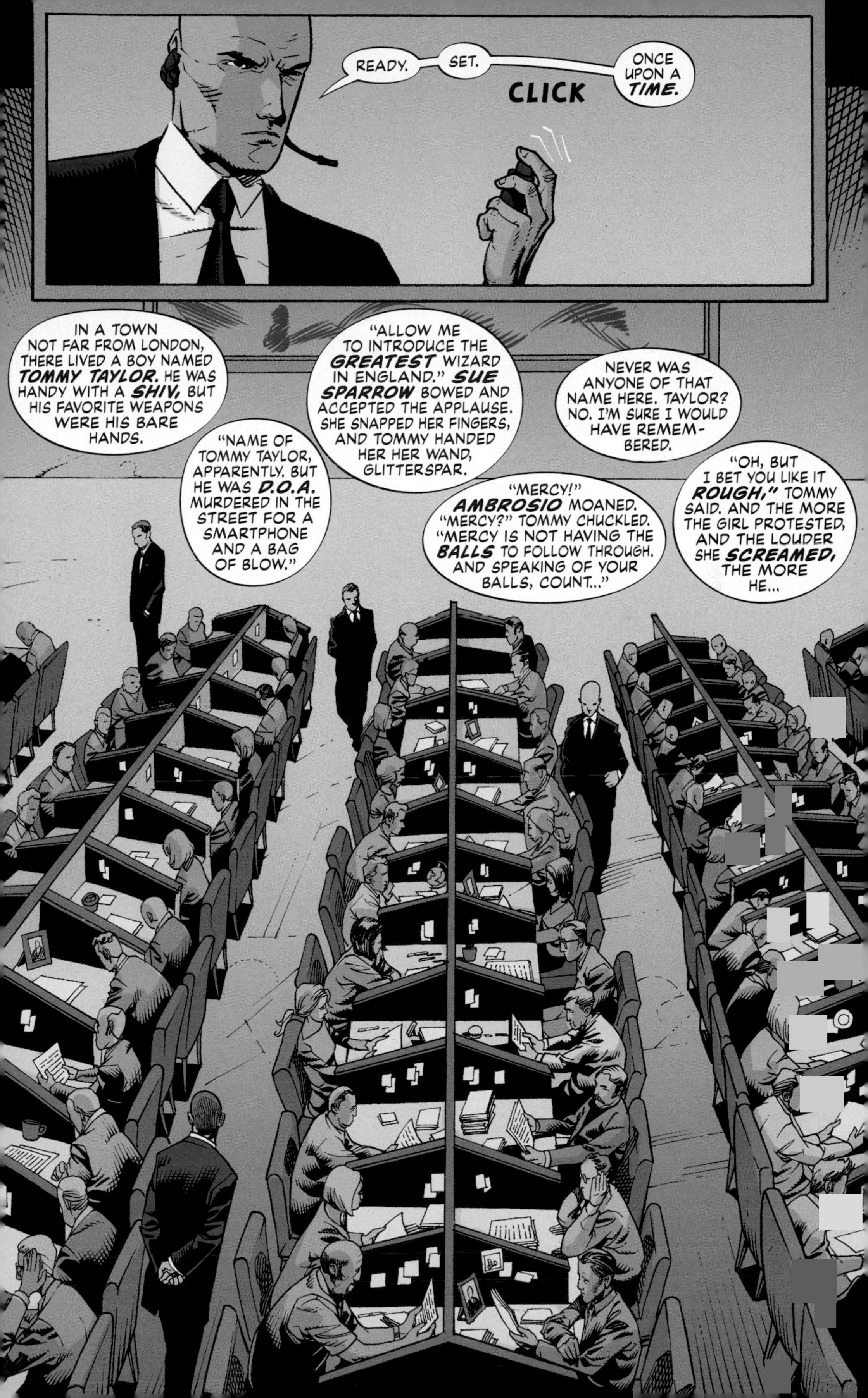
READY.
SET.
CLICK
ONCE UPON A TIME.
IN A TOWN NOT FAR FROM LONDON, THERE LIVED A BOY NAMED TOMMY TAYLOR. HE WAS HANDY WITH A SHIV, BUT HIS FAVORITE WEAPONS WERE HIS BARE HANDS.
"NAME OF TOMMY TAYLOR, APPARENTLY. BUT HE WAS D.O.A. MURDERED IN THE STREET FOR A SMARTPHONE AND A BAG OF BLOW."
"ALLOW ME TO INTRODUCE THE GREATEST WIZARD IN ENGLAND." SUE SPARROW BOWED AND ACCEPTED THE APPLAUSE. SHE SNAPPED HER FINGERS, AND TOMMY HANDED HER HER WAND, GLITTERSPAR.
"MERCY!" AMBROSIO MOANED. "MERCY?" TOMMY CHUCKLED. "MERCY IS NOT HAVING THE BALLS TO FOLLOW THROUGH. AND SPEAKING OF YOUR BALLS, COUNT..."
NEVER WAS ANYONE OF THAT NAME HERE. TAYLOR? NO. I'M SURE I WOULD HAVE REMEM-BERED.
"OH, BUT I BET YOU LIKE IT ROUGH," TOMMY SAID. AND THE MORE THE GIRL PROTESTED, AND THE LOUDER SHE SCREAMED, THE MORE HE...

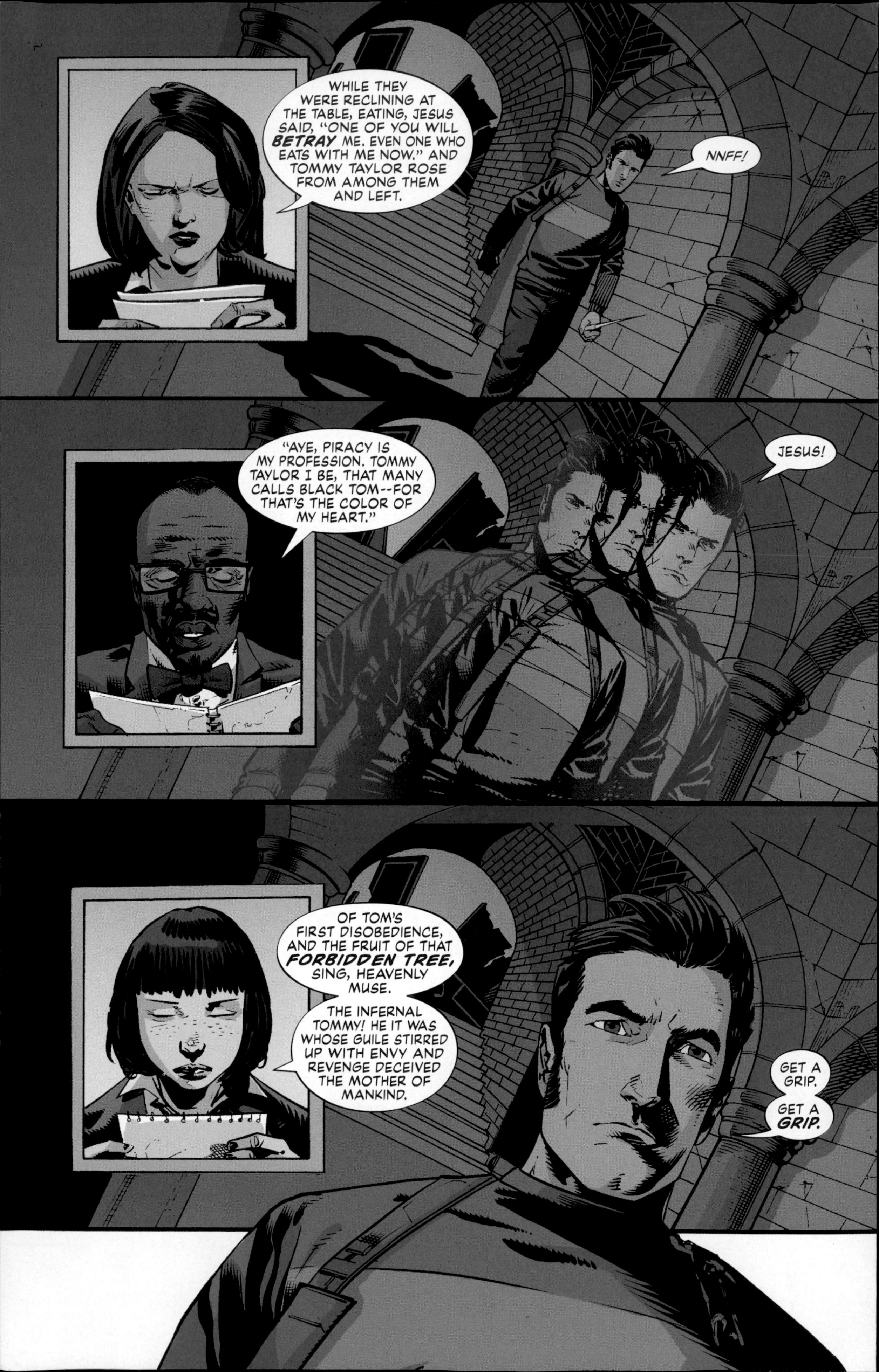

WHILE THEY WERE RECLINING AT THE TABLE, EATING, JESUS SAID, "ONE OF YOU WILL **BETRAY** ME. EVEN ONE WHO EATS WITH ME NOW." AND TOMMY TAYLOR ROSE FROM AMONG THEM AND LEFT.
NNFF!
"AYE, PIRACY IS MY PROFESSION. TOMMY TAYLOR I BE, THAT MANY CALLS BLACK TOM--FOR THAT'S THE COLOR OF MY HEART."
JESUS!
OF TOM'S FIRST DISOBEDIENCE, AND THE FRUIT OF THAT **FORBIDDEN TREE,** SING, HEAVENLY MUSE.
THE INFERNAL TOMMY! HE IT WAS WHOSE GUILE STIRRED UP WITH ENVY AND REVENGE DECEIVED THE MOTHER OF MANKIND.
GET A GRIP.
GET A **GRIP.**

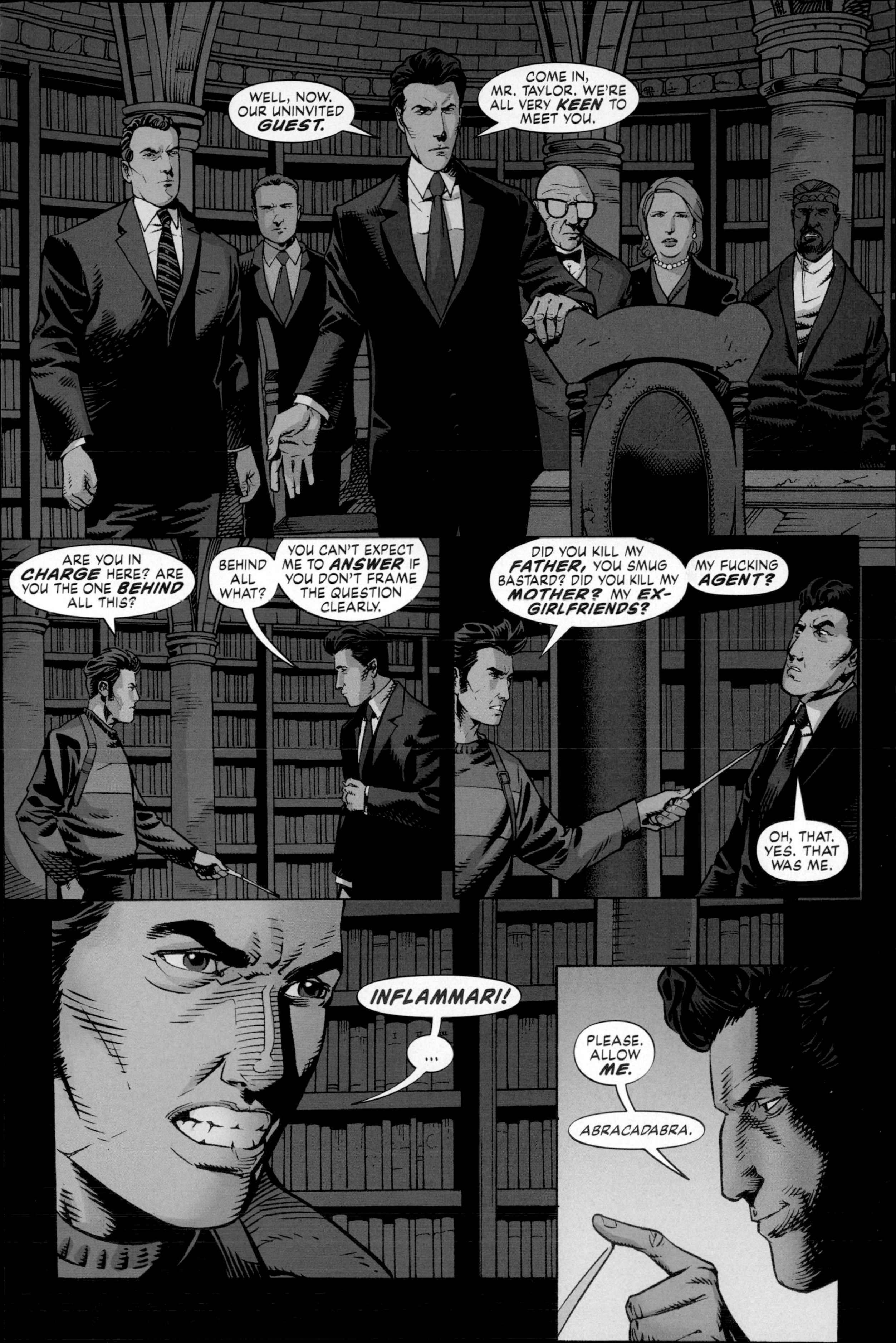
WELL, NOW. OUR UNINVITED GUEST.
COME IN, MR. TAYLOR. WE'RE ALL VERY KEEN TO MEET YOU.
ARE YOU IN CHARGE HERE? ARE YOU THE ONE BEHIND ALL THIS?
BEHIND ALL WHAT?
YOU CAN'T EXPECT ME TO ANSWER IF YOU DON'T FRAME THE QUESTION CLEARLY.
DID YOU KILL MY FATHER, YOU SMUG BASTARD? DID YOU KILL MY MOTHER? MY EX-GIRLFRIENDS?
MY FUCKING AGENT?
OH, THAT. YES. THAT WAS ME.
INFLAMMARI!
...
PLEASE. ALLOW ME.
ABRACADABRA.

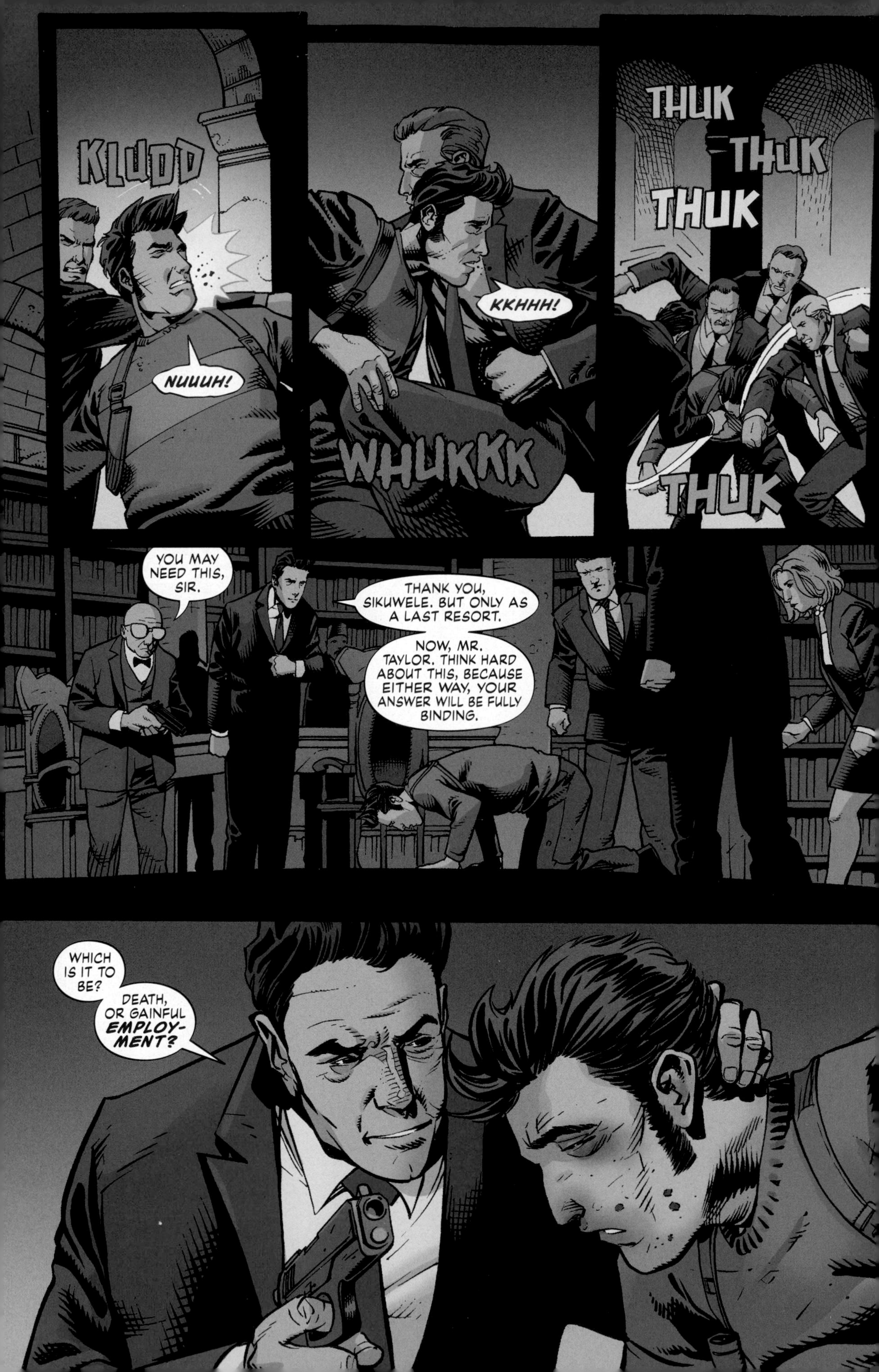
KLUDD
NUUUH!
KKHHH!
WHUKKK
THUK
THUK
THUK
THUK
YOU MAY NEED THIS, SIR.
THANK YOU, SIKUWELE. BUT ONLY AS A LAST RESORT.
NOW, MR. TAYLOR. THINK HARD ABOUT THIS, BECAUSE EITHER WAY, YOUR ANSWER WILL BE FULLY BINDING.
WHICH IS IT TO BE?
DEATH, OR GAINFUL *EMPLOYMENT?*

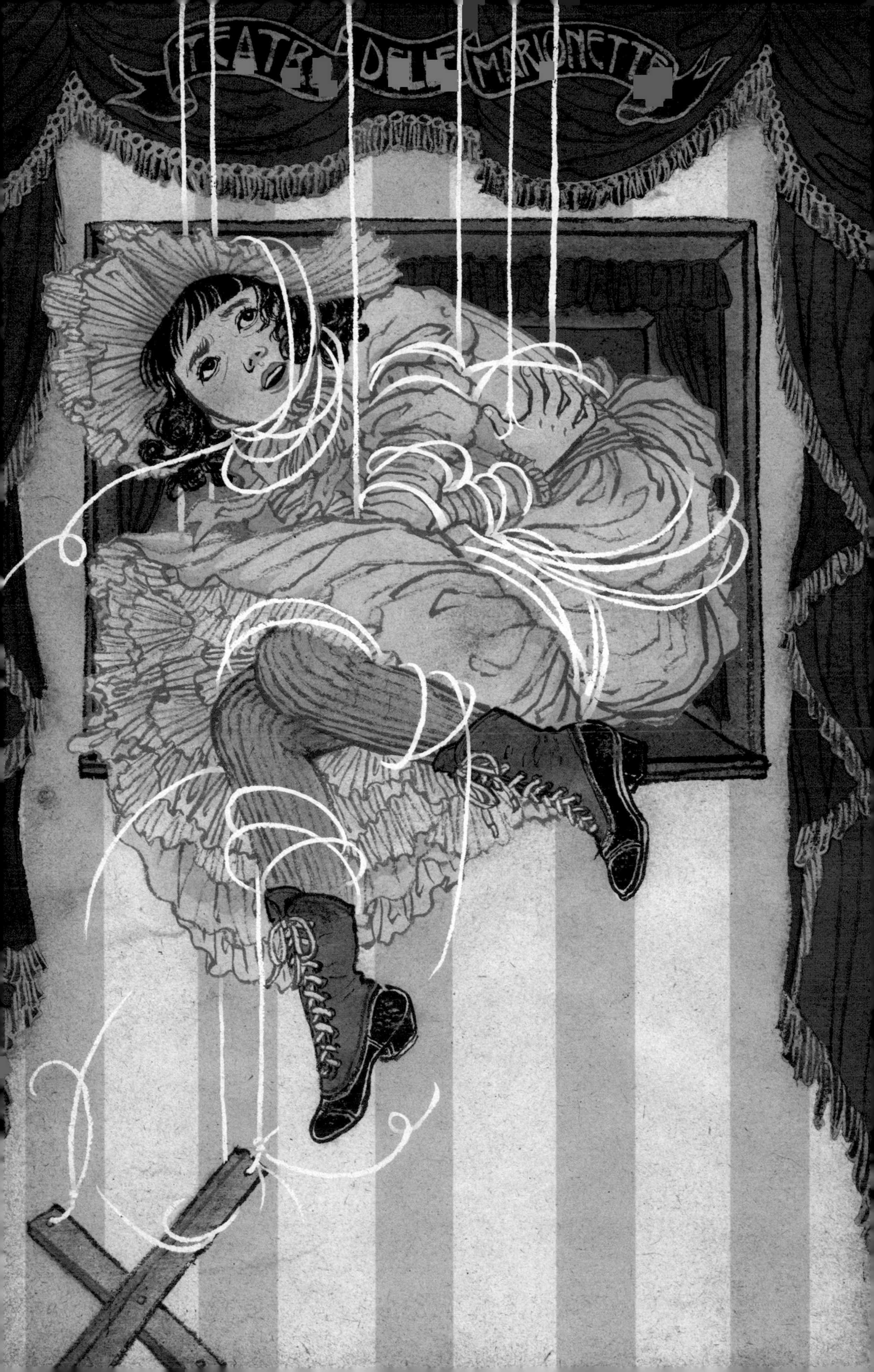

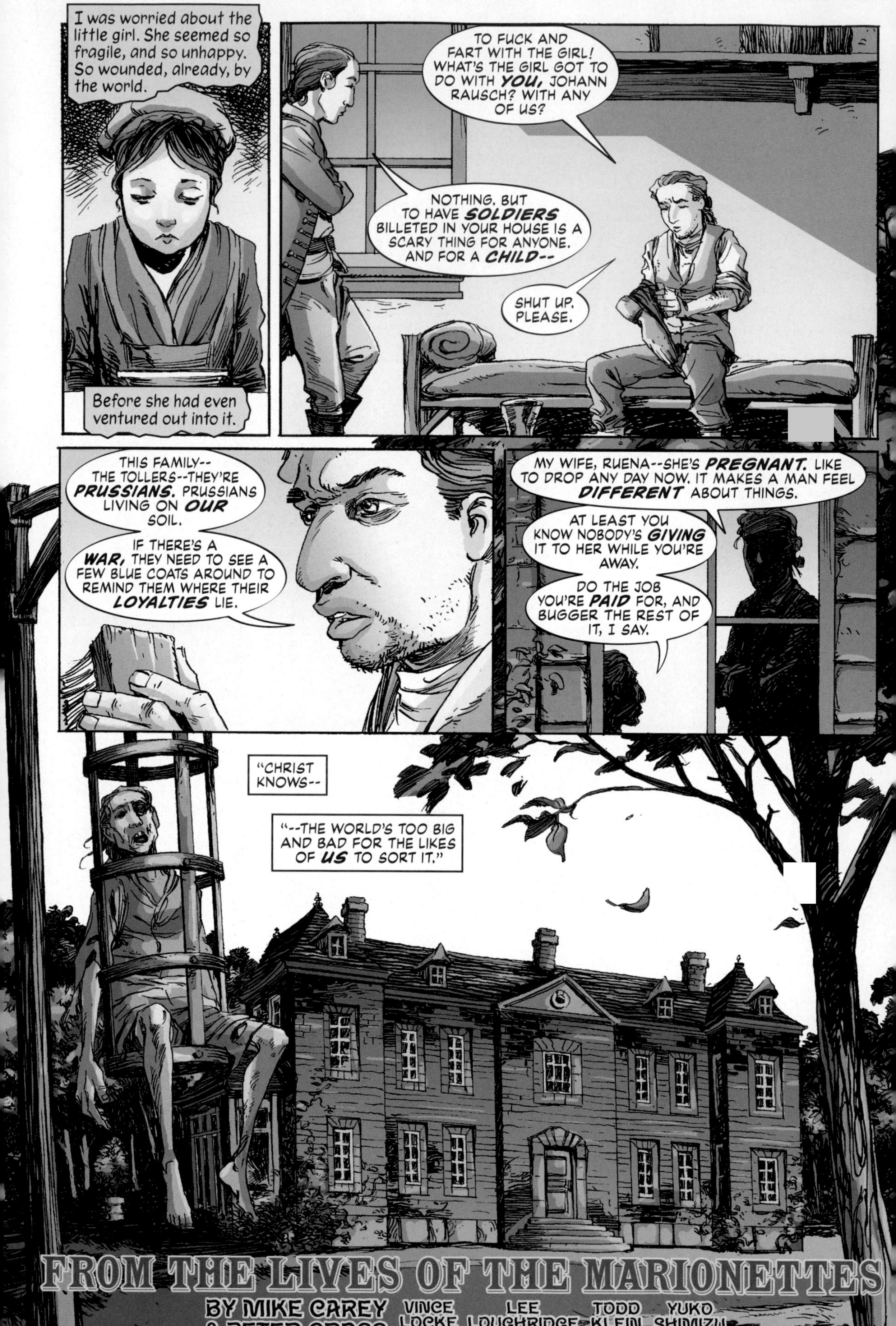
I was worried about the little girl. She seemed so fragile, and so unhappy. So wounded, already, by the world.
Before she had even ventured out into it.
TO FUCK AND FART WITH THE GIRL! WHAT'S THE GIRL GOT TO DO WITH YOU, JOHANN RAUSCH? WITH ANY OF US?
NOTHING. BUT TO HAVE SOLDIERS BILLETED IN YOUR HOUSE IS A SCARY THING FOR ANYONE. AND FOR A CHILD--
SHUT UP, PLEASE.
THIS FAMILY-- THE TOLLERS--THEY'RE PRUSSIANS. PRUSSIANS LIVING ON OUR SOIL.
IF THERE'S A WAR, THEY NEED TO SEE A FEW BLUE COATS AROUND TO REMIND THEM WHERE THEIR LOYALTIES LIE.
MY WIFE, RUENA--SHE'S PREGNANT. LIKE TO DROP ANY DAY NOW. IT MAKES A MAN FEEL DIFFERENT ABOUT THINGS.
AT LEAST YOU KNOW NOBODY'S GIVING IT TO HER WHILE YOU'RE AWAY.
DO THE JOB YOU'RE PAID FOR, AND BUGGER THE REST OF IT, I SAY.
"CHRIST KNOWS--
"--THE WORLD'S TOO BIG AND BAD FOR THE LIKES OF US TO SORT IT."
FROM THE LIVES OF THE MARIONETTES
BY MIKE CAREY & PETER GROSS
VINCE LOCKE finishes
LEE LOUGHRIDGE colors
TODD KLEIN letters
YUKO SHIMIZU cover

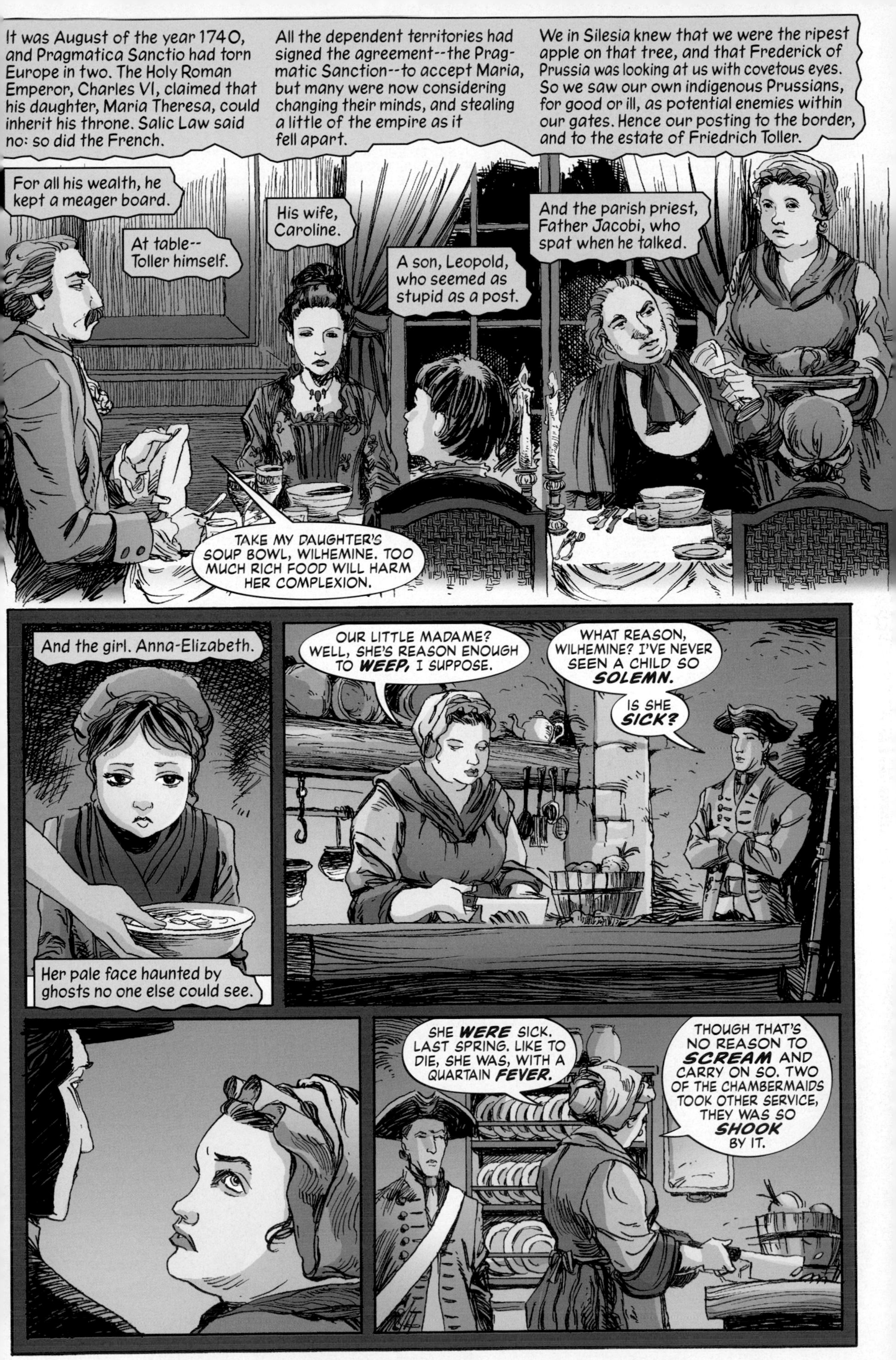
It was August of the year 1740, and Pragmatica Sanctio had torn Europe in two. The Holy Roman Emperor, Charles VI, claimed that his daughter, Maria Theresa, could inherit his throne. Salic Law said no: so did the French.
All the dependent territories had signed the agreement--the Pragmatic Sanction--to accept Maria, but many were now considering changing their minds, and stealing a little of the empire as it fell apart.
We in Silesia knew that we were the ripest apple on that tree, and that Frederick of Prussia was looking at us with covetous eyes. So we saw our own indigenous Prussians, for good or ill, as potential enemies within our gates. Hence our posting to the border, and to the estate of Friedrich Toller.
For all his wealth, he kept a meager board.
At table-- Toller himself.
His wife, Caroline.
A son, Leopold, who seemed as stupid as a post.
And the parish priest, Father Jacobi, who spat when he talked.
TAKE MY DAUGHTER'S SOUP BOWL, WILHEMINE. TOO MUCH RICH FOOD WILL HARM HER COMPLEXION.
And the girl. Anna-Elizabeth.
Her pale face haunted by ghosts no one else could see.
OUR LITTLE MADAME? WELL, SHE'S REASON ENOUGH TO WEEP, I SUPPOSE.
WHAT REASON, WILHEMINE? I'VE NEVER SEEN A CHILD SO SOLEMN.
IS SHE SICK?
SHE WERE SICK. LAST SPRING. LIKE TO DIE, SHE WAS, WITH A QUARTAIN FEVER.
THOUGH THAT'S NO REASON TO SCREAM AND CARRY ON SO. TWO OF THE CHAMBERMAIDS TOOK OTHER SERVICE, THEY WAS SO SHOOK BY IT.

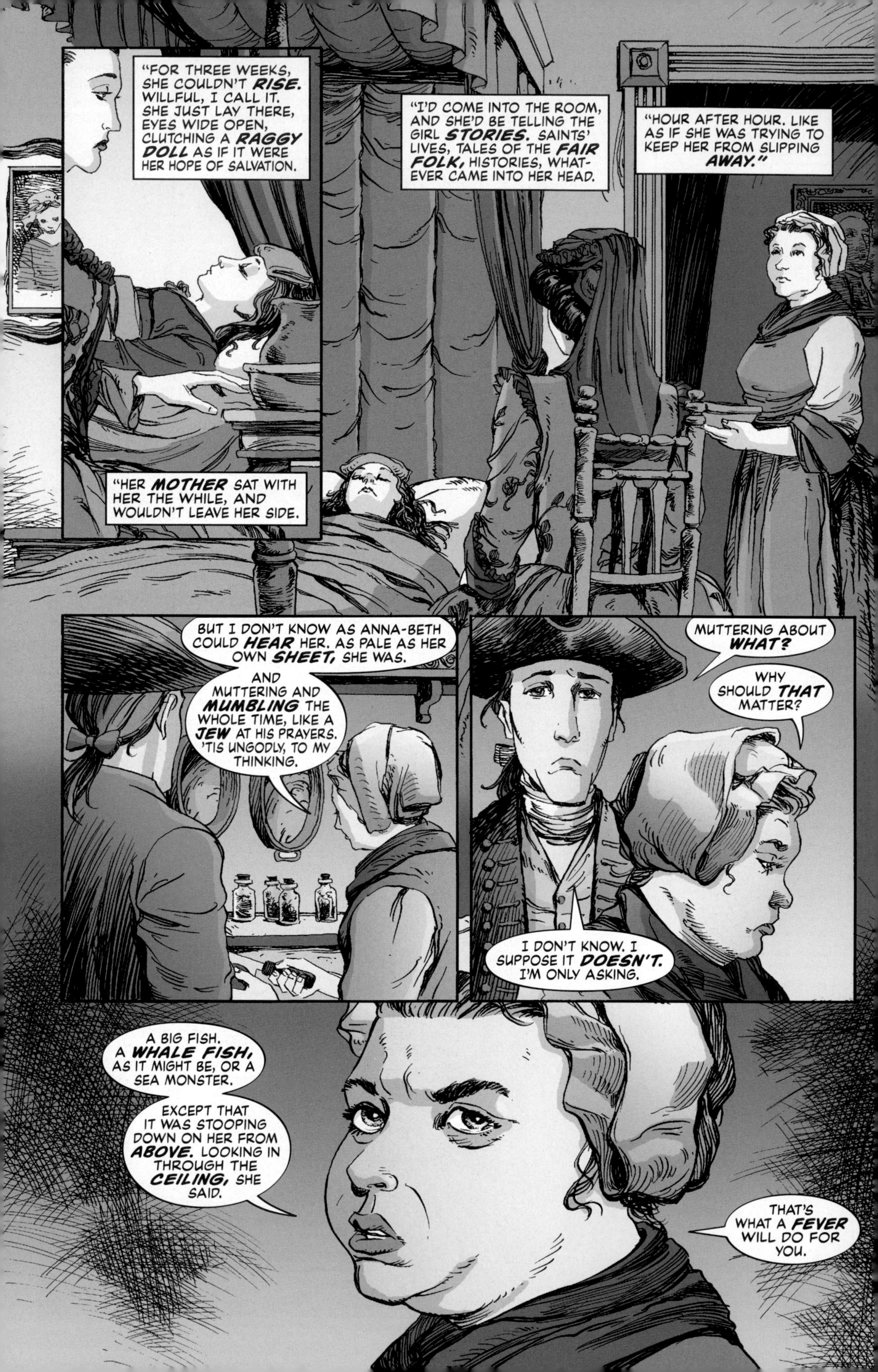
"FOR THREE WEEKS, SHE COULDN'T RISE. WILLFUL, I CALL IT. SHE JUST LAY THERE, EYES WIDE OPEN, CLUTCHING A RAGGY DOLL AS IF IT WERE HER HOPE OF SALVATION.
"HER MOTHER SAT WITH HER THE WHILE, AND WOULDN'T LEAVE HER SIDE.
"I'D COME INTO THE ROOM, AND SHE'D BE TELLING THE GIRL STORIES. SAINTS' LIVES, TALES OF THE FAIR FOLK, HISTORIES, WHATEVER CAME INTO HER HEAD.
"HOUR AFTER HOUR. LIKE AS IF SHE WAS TRYING TO KEEP HER FROM SLIPPING AWAY."
BUT I DON'T KNOW AS ANNA-BETH COULD HEAR HER. AS PALE AS HER OWN SHEET, SHE WAS.
AND MUTTERING AND MUMBLING THE WHOLE TIME, LIKE A JEW AT HIS PRAYERS. 'TIS UNGODLY, TO MY THINKING.
MUTTERING ABOUT WHAT?
WHY SHOULD THAT MATTER?
I DON'T KNOW. I SUPPOSE IT DOESN'T. I'M ONLY ASKING.
A BIG FISH. A WHALE FISH, AS IT MIGHT BE, OR A SEA MONSTER.
EXCEPT THAT IT WAS STOOPING DOWN ON HER FROM ABOVE. LOOKING IN THROUGH THE CEILING, SHE SAID.
THAT'S WHAT A FEVER WILL DO FOR YOU.

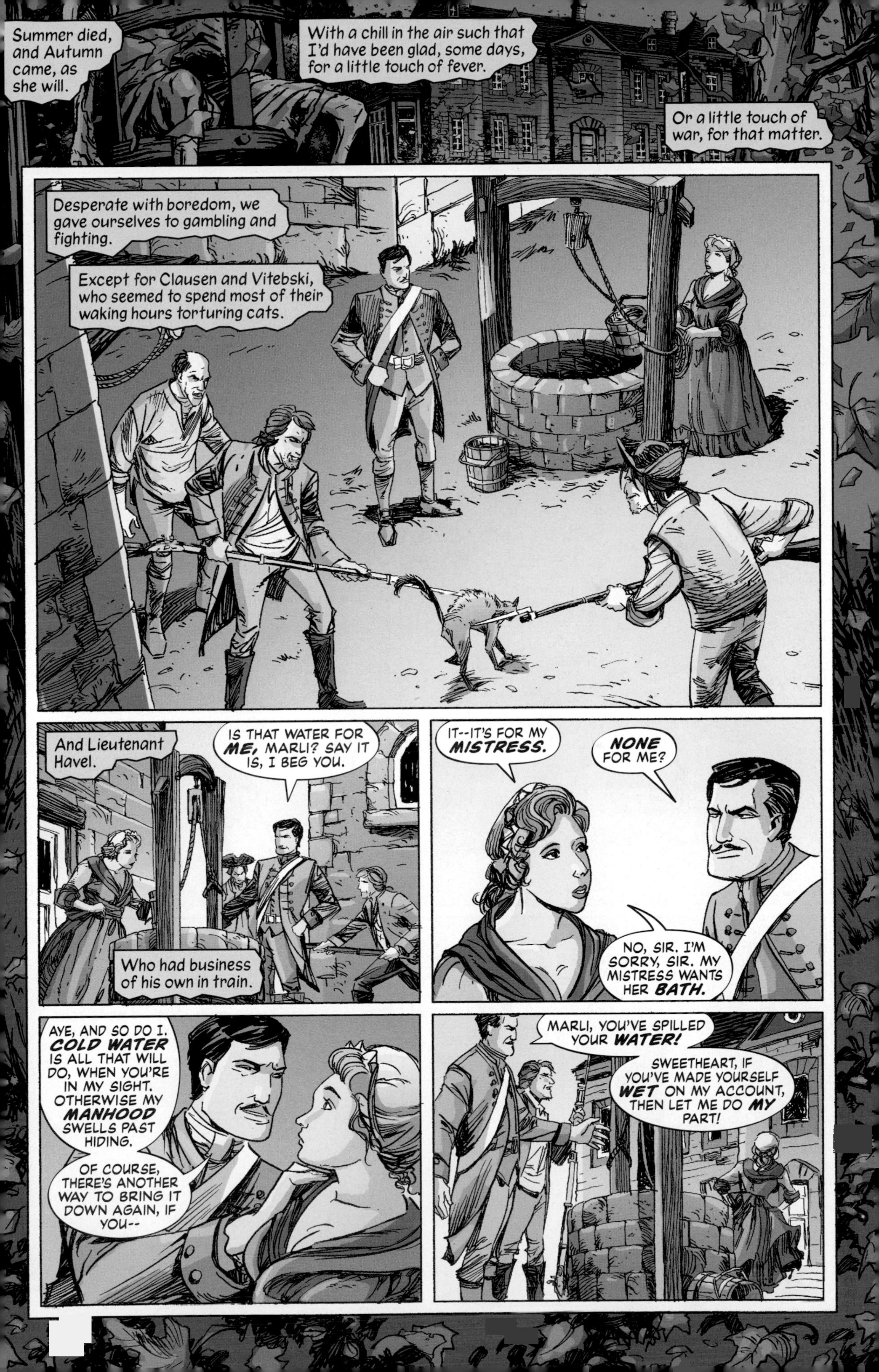

Summer died, and Autumn came, as she will.
With a chill in the air such that I'd have been glad, some days, for a little touch of fever.
Or a little touch of war, for that matter.
Desperate with boredom, we gave ourselves to gambling and fighting.
Except for Clausen and Vitebski, who seemed to spend most of their waking hours torturing cats.
And Lieutenant Havel.
IS THAT WATER FOR ME, MARLI? SAY IT IS, I BEG YOU.
Who had business of his own in train.
IT--IT'S FOR MY MISTRESS.
NONE FOR ME?
NO, SIR. I'M SORRY, SIR. MY MISTRESS WANTS HER BATH.
AYE, AND SO DO I. COLD WATER IS ALL THAT WILL DO, WHEN YOU'RE IN MY SIGHT. OTHERWISE MY MANHOOD SWELLS PAST HIDING.
OF COURSE, THERE'S ANOTHER WAY TO BRING IT DOWN AGAIN, IF YOU--
MARLI, YOU'VE SPILLED YOUR WATER!
SWEETHEART, IF YOU'VE MADE YOURSELF WET ON MY ACCOUNT, THEN LET ME DO MY PART!

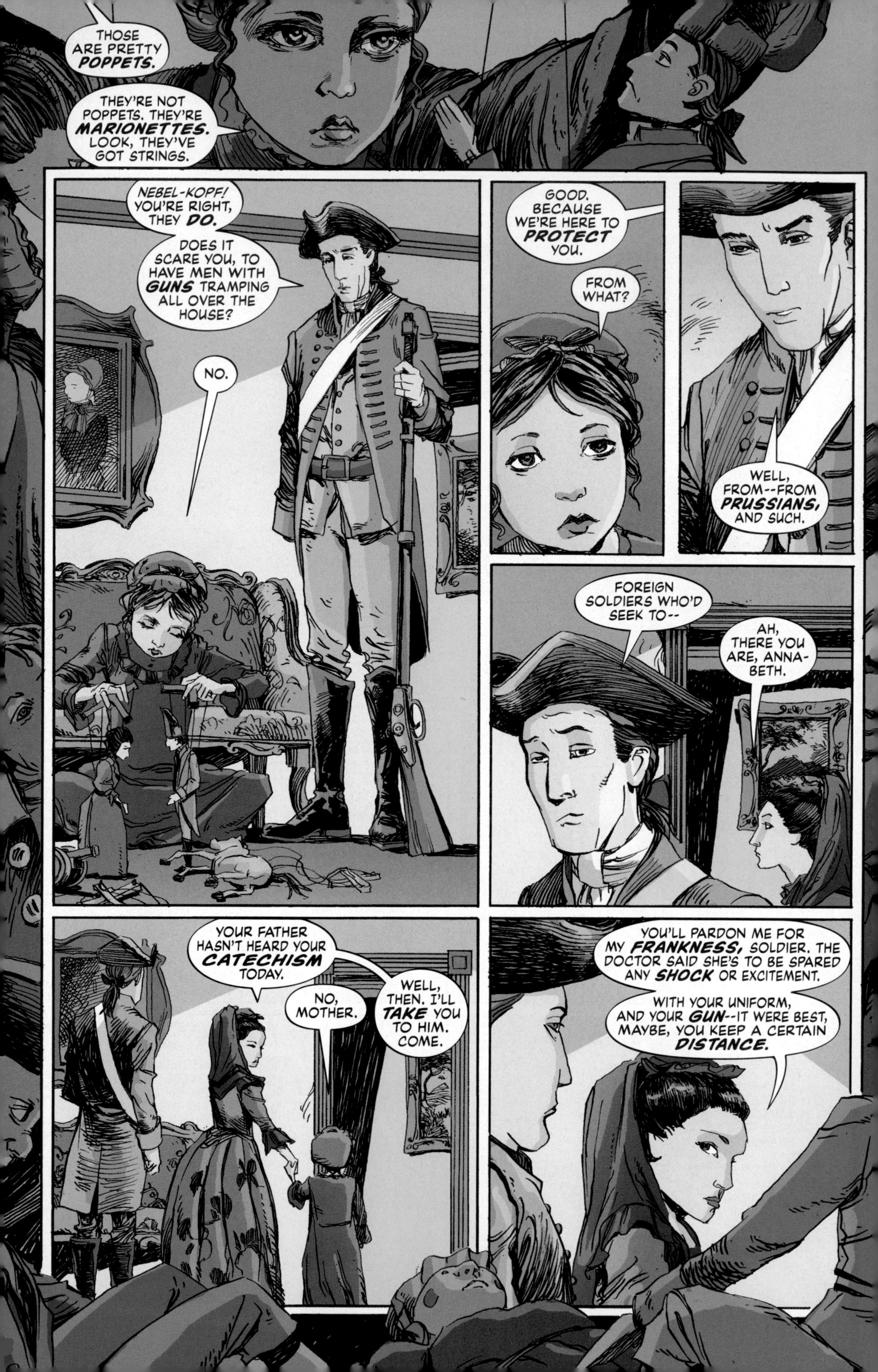
THOSE ARE PRETTY POPPETS.
THEY'RE NOT POPPETS. THEY'RE MARIONETTES. LOOK, THEY'VE GOT STRINGS.
NEBEL-KOPF! YOU'RE RIGHT, THEY DO.
DOES IT SCARE YOU, TO HAVE MEN WITH GUNS TRAMPING ALL OVER THE HOUSE?
NO.
GOOD. BECAUSE WE'RE HERE TO PROTECT YOU.
FROM WHAT?
WELL, FROM--FROM PRUSSIANS, AND SUCH.
FOREIGN SOLDIERS WHO'D SEEK TO--
AH, THERE YOU ARE, ANNA-BETH.
YOUR FATHER HASN'T HEARD YOUR CATECHISM TODAY.
NO, MOTHER.
WELL, THEN. I'LL TAKE YOU TO HIM. COME.
YOU'LL PARDON ME FOR MY FRANKNESS, SOLDIER. THE DOCTOR SAID SHE'S TO BE SPARED ANY SHOCK OR EXCITEMENT.
WITH YOUR UNIFORM, AND YOUR GUN--IT WERE BEST, MAYBE, YOU KEEP A CERTAIN DISTANCE.

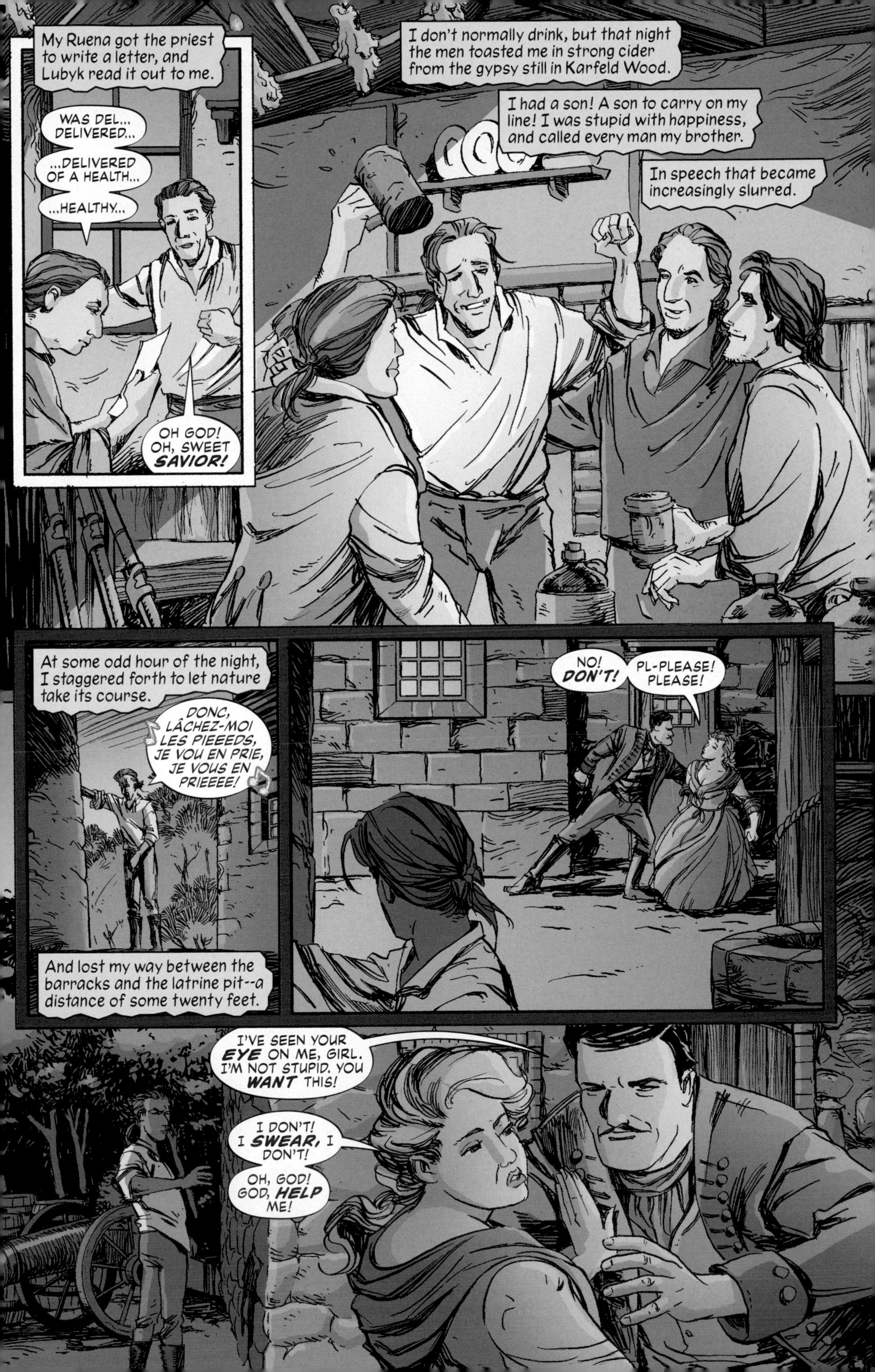
My Ruena got the priest to write a letter, and Lubyk read it out to me.
WAS DEL... DELIVERED...
...DELIVERED OF A HEALTH...
...HEALTHY...
OH GOD! OH, SWEET SAVIOR!
I don't normally drink, but that night the men toasted me in strong cider from the gypsy still in Karfeld Wood.
I had a son! A son to carry on my line! I was stupid with happiness, and called every man my brother.
In speech that became increasingly slurred.
At some odd hour of the night, I staggered forth to let nature take its course.
DONC, LÂCHEZ-MOI LES PIEEEDS, JE VOU EN PRIE, JE VOUS EN PRIEEEE!
And lost my way between the barracks and the latrine pit--a distance of some twenty feet.
NO! DON'T!
PL-PLEASE! PLEASE!
I'VE SEEN YOUR EYE ON ME, GIRL. I'M NOT STUPID. YOU WANT THIS!
I DON'T! I SWEAR, I DON'T!
OH, GOD! GOD, HELP ME!

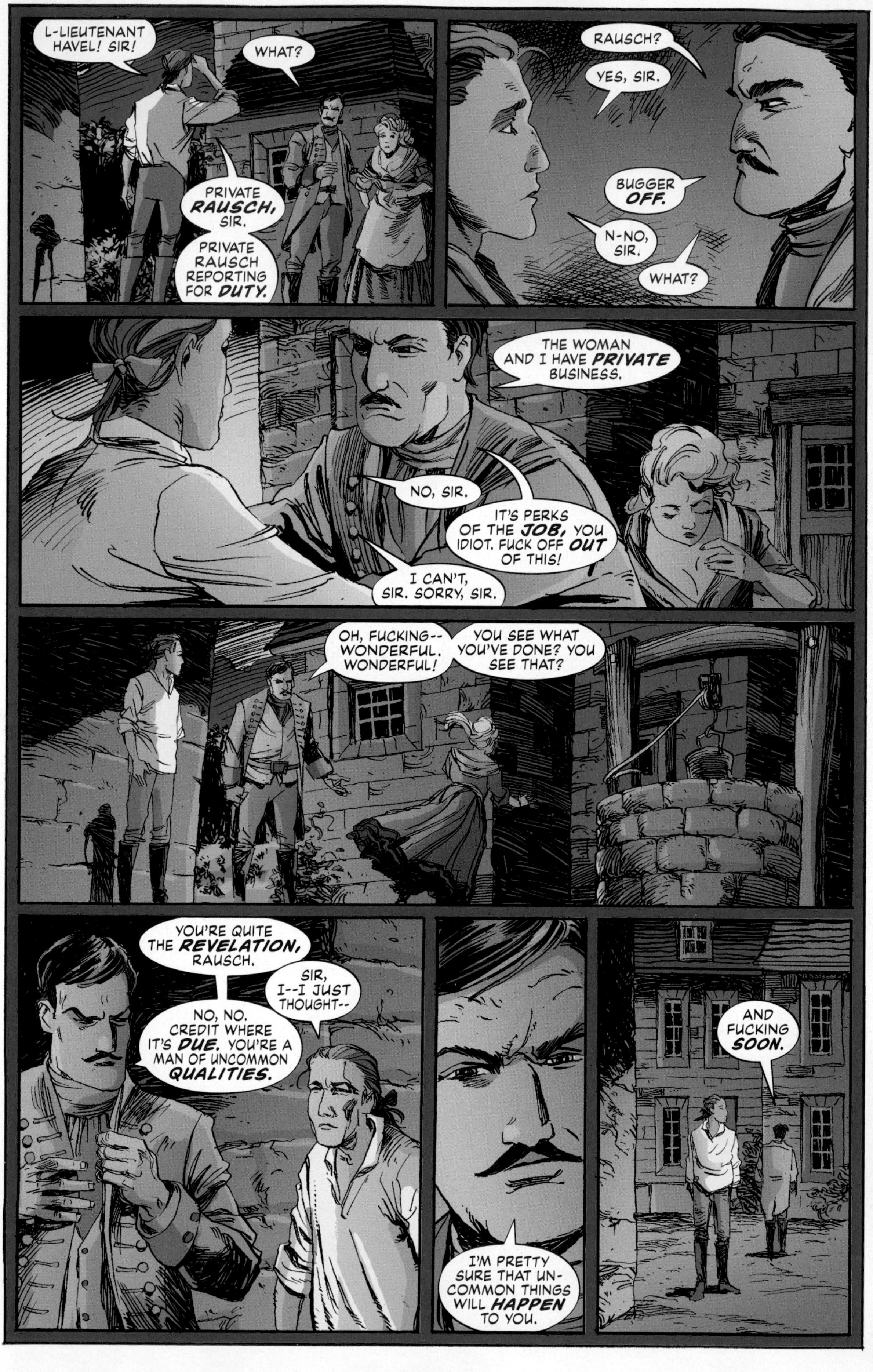
L-LIEUTENANT HAVEL! SIR!
WHAT?
PRIVATE RAUSCH, SIR.
PRIVATE RAUSCH REPORTING FOR DUTY.
RAUSCH?
YES, SIR.
BUGGER OFF.
N-NO, SIR.
WHAT?
THE WOMAN AND I HAVE PRIVATE BUSINESS.
NO, SIR.
IT'S PERKS OF THE JOB, YOU IDIOT. FUCK OFF OUT OF THIS!
I CAN'T, SIR. SORRY, SIR.
OH, FUCKING-- WONDERFUL. WONDERFUL!
YOU SEE WHAT YOU'VE DONE? YOU SEE THAT?
YOU'RE QUITE THE REVELATION, RAUSCH.
SIR, I--I JUST THOUGHT--
NO, NO. CREDIT WHERE IT'S DUE. YOU'RE A MAN OF UNCOMMON QUALITIES.
I'M PRETTY SURE THAT UN-COMMON THINGS WILL HAPPEN TO YOU.
AND FUCKING SOON.

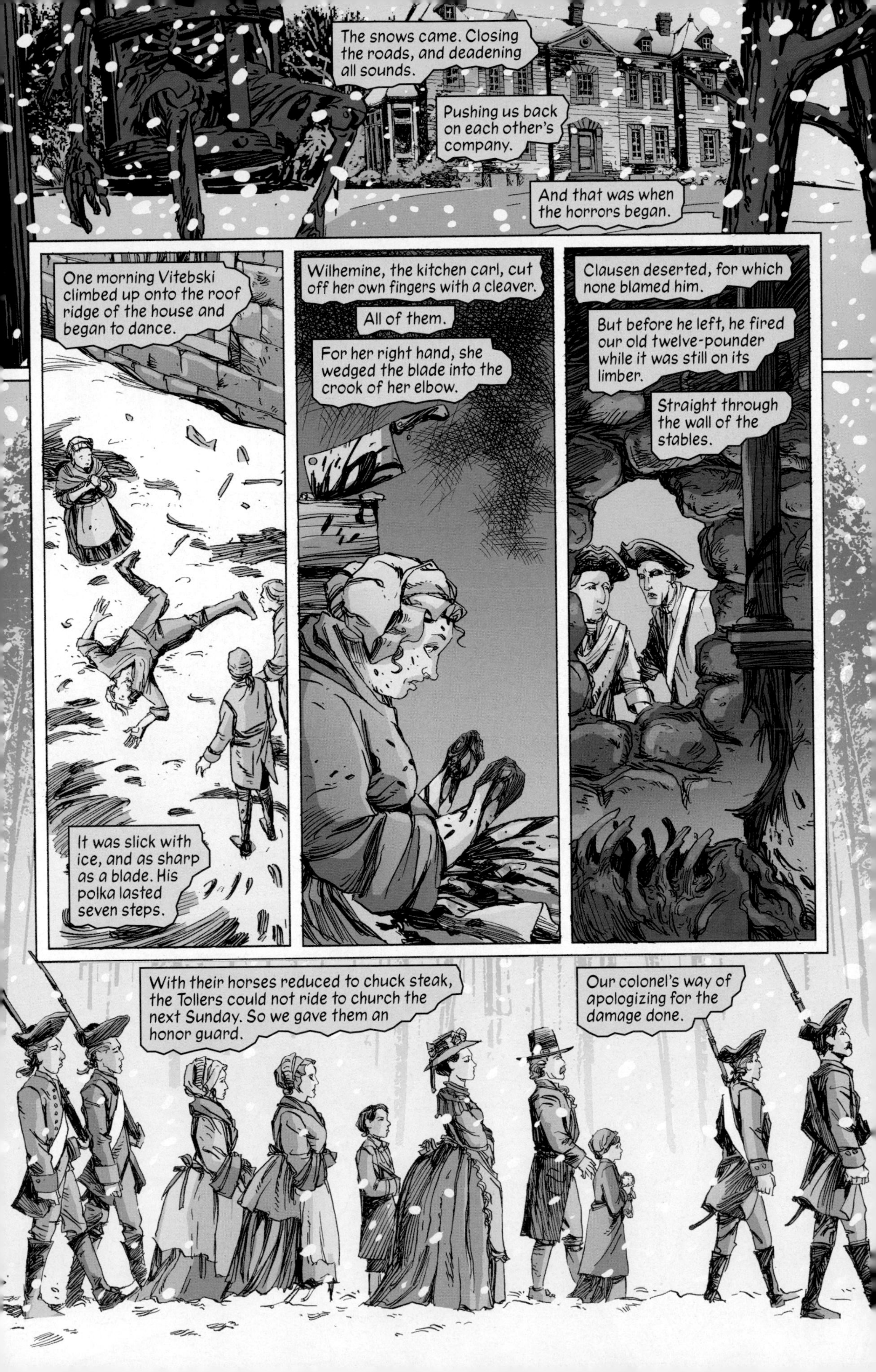
The snows came. Closing the roads, and deadening all sounds.
Pushing us back on each other's company.
And that was when the horrors began.
One morning Vitebski climbed up onto the roof ridge of the house and began to dance.
It was slick with ice, and as sharp as a blade. His polka lasted seven steps.
Wilhemine, the kitchen carl, cut off her own fingers with a cleaver.
All of them.
For her right hand, she wedged the blade into the crook of her elbow.
Clausen deserted, for which none blamed him.
But before he left, he fired our old twelve-pounder while it was still on its limber.
Straight through the wall of the stables.
With their horses reduced to chuck steak, the Tollers could not ride to church the next Sunday. So we gave them an honor guard.
Our colonel's way of apologizing for the damage done.

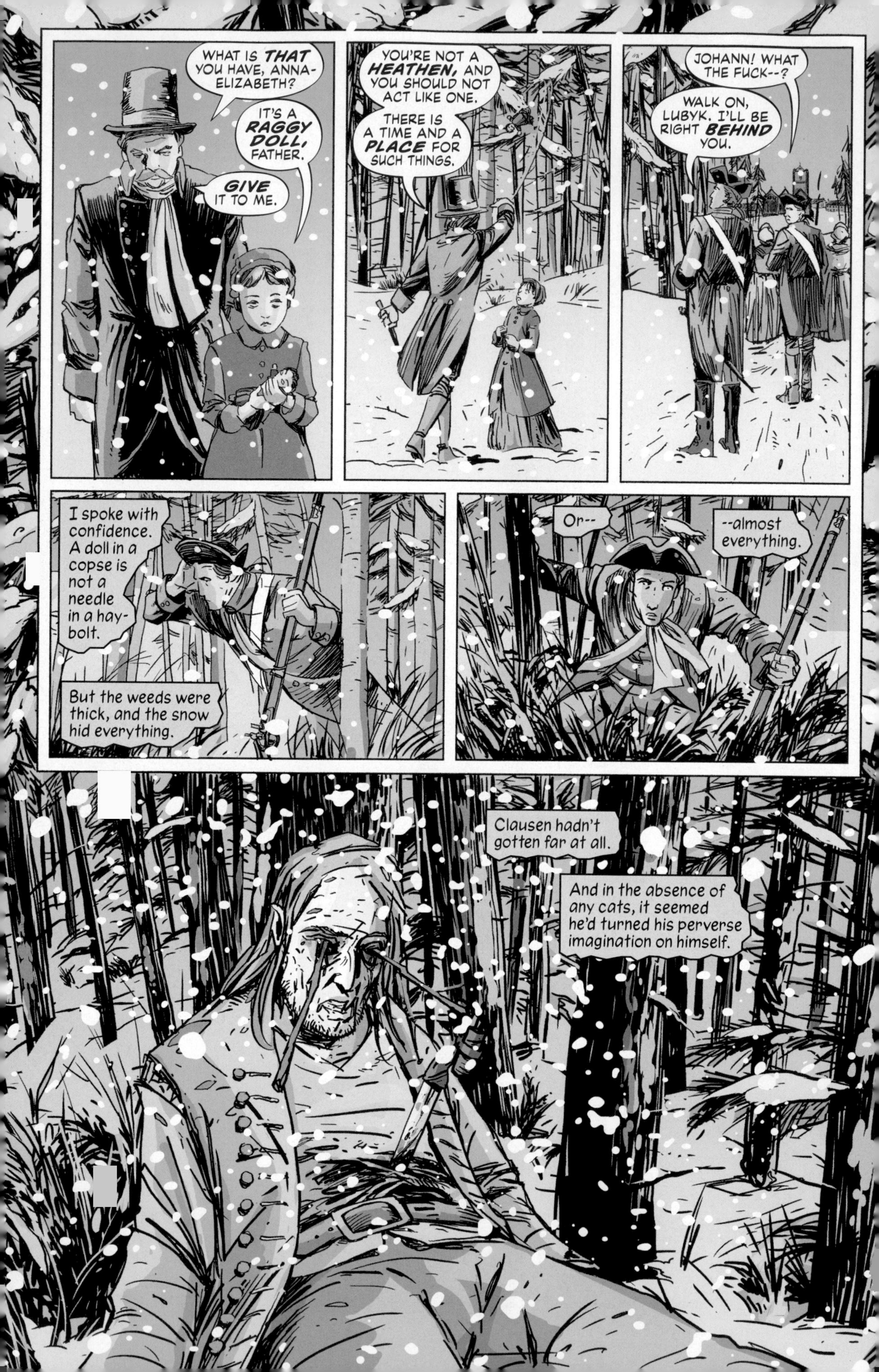

WHAT IS THAT YOU HAVE, ANNA-ELIZABETH?
IT'S A RAGGY DOLL, FATHER.
GIVE IT TO ME.
YOU'RE NOT A HEATHEN, AND YOU SHOULD NOT ACT LIKE ONE.
THERE IS A TIME AND A PLACE FOR SUCH THINGS.
JOHANN! WHAT THE FUCK--?
WALK ON, LUBYK. I'LL BE RIGHT BEHIND YOU.
I spoke with confidence. A doll in a copse is not a needle in a hay-bolt.
But the weeds were thick, and the snow hid everything.
Or--
--almost everything.
Clausen hadn't gotten far at all.
And in the absence of any cats, it seemed he'd turned his perverse imagination on himself.

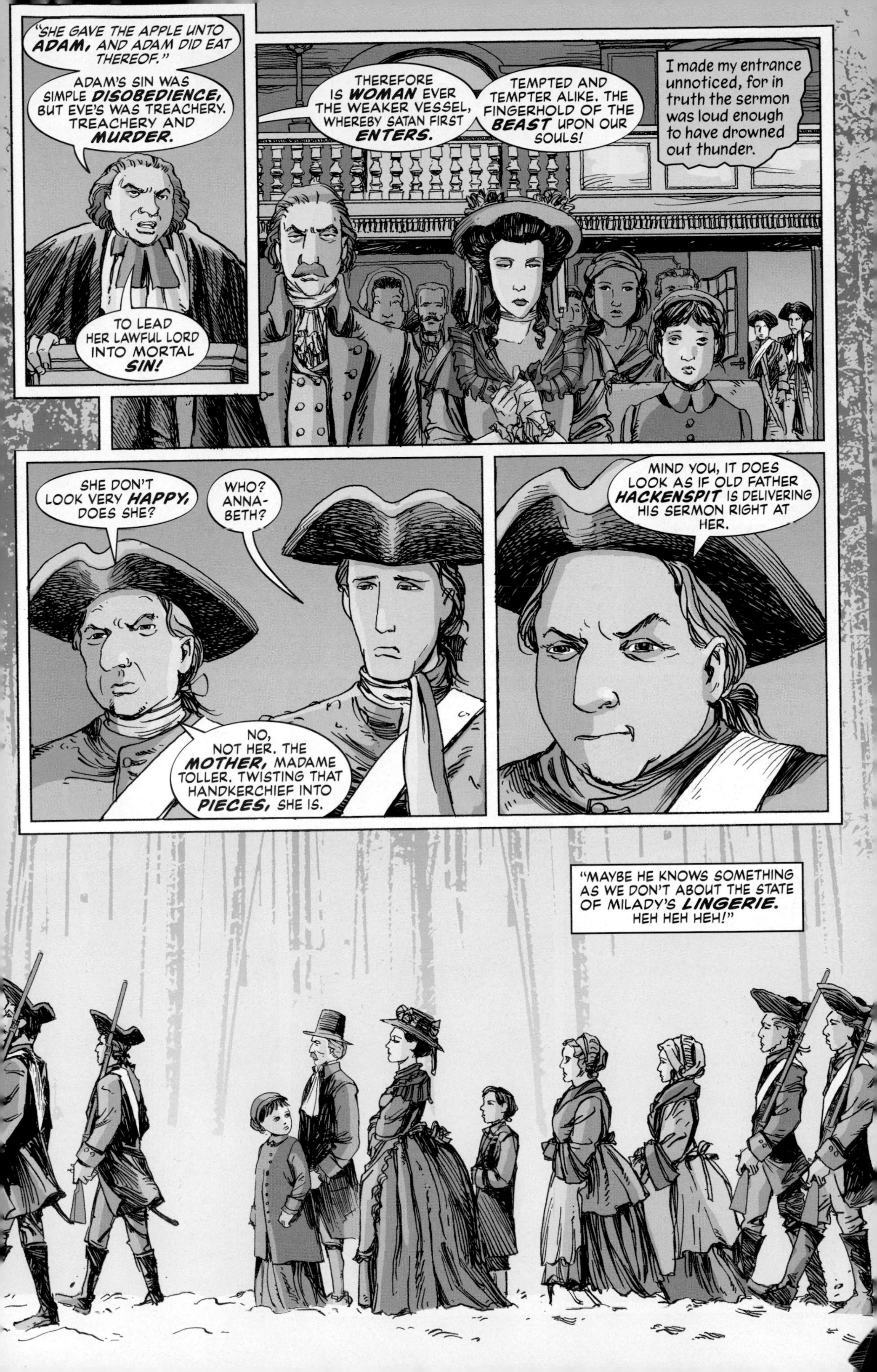
"SHE GAVE THE APPLE UNTO ADAM, AND ADAM DID EAT THEREOF."
ADAM'S SIN WAS SIMPLE DISOBEDIENCE, BUT EVE'S WAS TREACHERY. TREACHERY AND MURDER.
TO LEAD HER LAWFUL LORD INTO MORTAL SIN!
THEREFORE IS WOMAN EVER THE WEAKER VESSEL, WHEREBY SATAN FIRST ENTERS.
TEMPTED AND TEMPTER ALIKE. THE FINGERHOLD OF THE BEAST UPON OUR SOULS!
I made my entrance unnoticed, for in truth the sermon was loud enough to have drowned out thunder.
SHE DON'T LOOK VERY HAPPY, DOES SHE?
WHO? ANNA-BETH?
NO, NOT HER. THE MOTHER, MADAME TOLLER. TWISTING THAT HANDKERCHIEF INTO PIECES, SHE IS.
MIND YOU, IT DOES LOOK AS IF OLD FATHER HACKENSPIT IS DELIVERING HIS SERMON RIGHT AT HER.
"MAYBE HE KNOWS SOMETHING AS WE DON'T ABOUT THE STATE OF MILADY'S LINGERIE. HEH HEH HEH!"

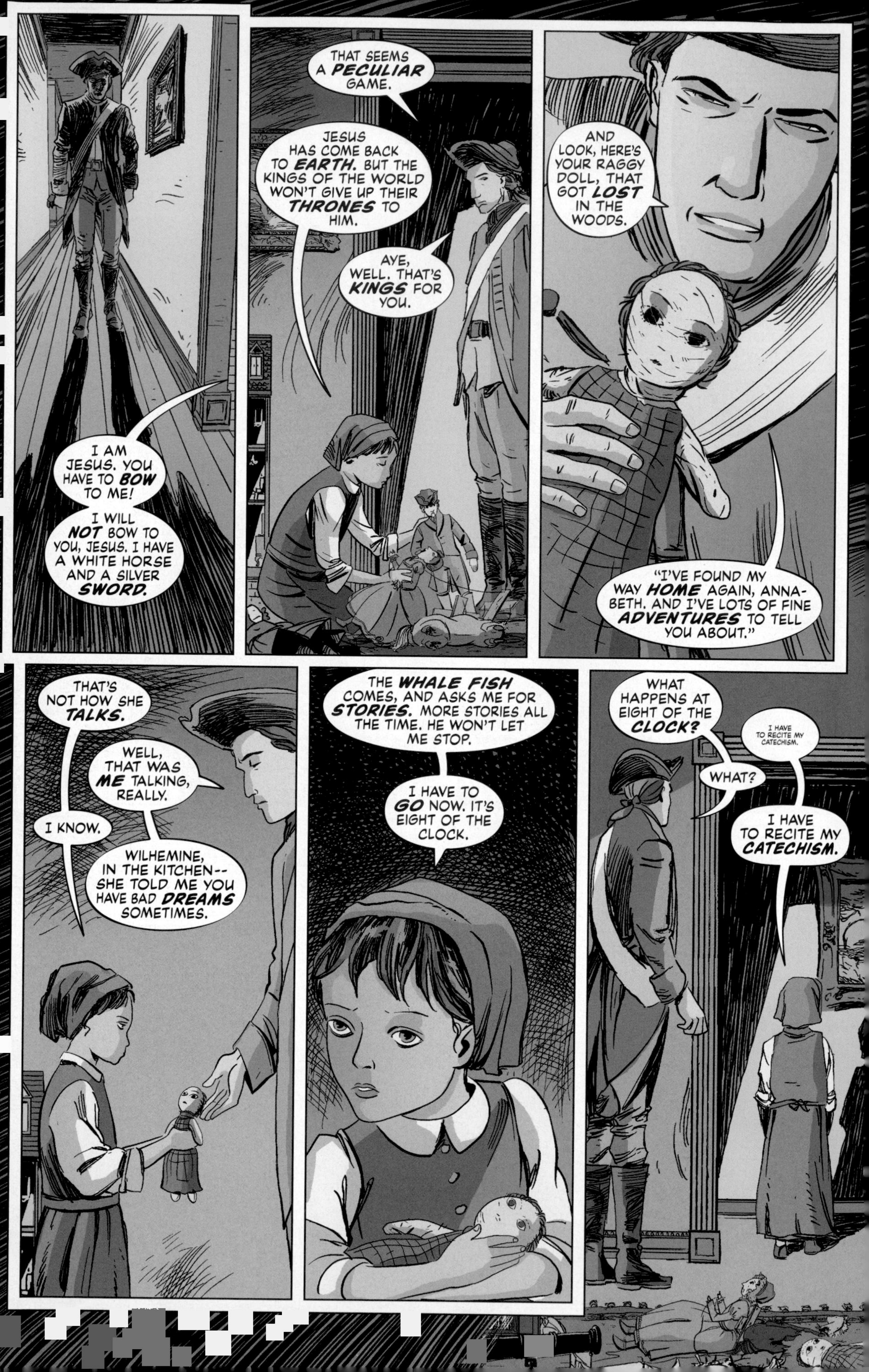
I AM JESUS. YOU HAVE TO BOW TO ME!
I WILL NOT BOW TO YOU, JESUS. I HAVE A WHITE HORSE AND A SILVER SWORD.
THAT SEEMS A PECULIAR GAME.
JESUS HAS COME BACK TO EARTH. BUT THE KINGS OF THE WORLD WON'T GIVE UP THEIR THRONES TO HIM.
AYE, WELL. THAT'S KINGS FOR YOU.
AND LOOK, HERE'S YOUR RAGGY DOLL, THAT GOT LOST IN THE WOODS.
"I'VE FOUND MY WAY HOME AGAIN, ANNA-BETH. AND I'VE LOTS OF FINE ADVENTURES TO TELL YOU ABOUT."
THAT'S NOT HOW SHE TALKS.
WELL, THAT WAS ME TALKING, REALLY.
I KNOW.
WILHEMINE, IN THE KITCHEN-- SHE TOLD ME YOU HAVE BAD DREAMS SOMETIMES.
THE WHALE FISH COMES, AND ASKS ME FOR STORIES. MORE STORIES ALL THE TIME. HE WON'T LET ME STOP.
I HAVE TO GO NOW. IT'S EIGHT OF THE CLOCK.
WHAT HAPPENS AT EIGHT OF THE CLOCK?
I HAVE TO RECITE MY CATECHISM.
WHAT?
I HAVE TO RECITE MY CATECHISM.

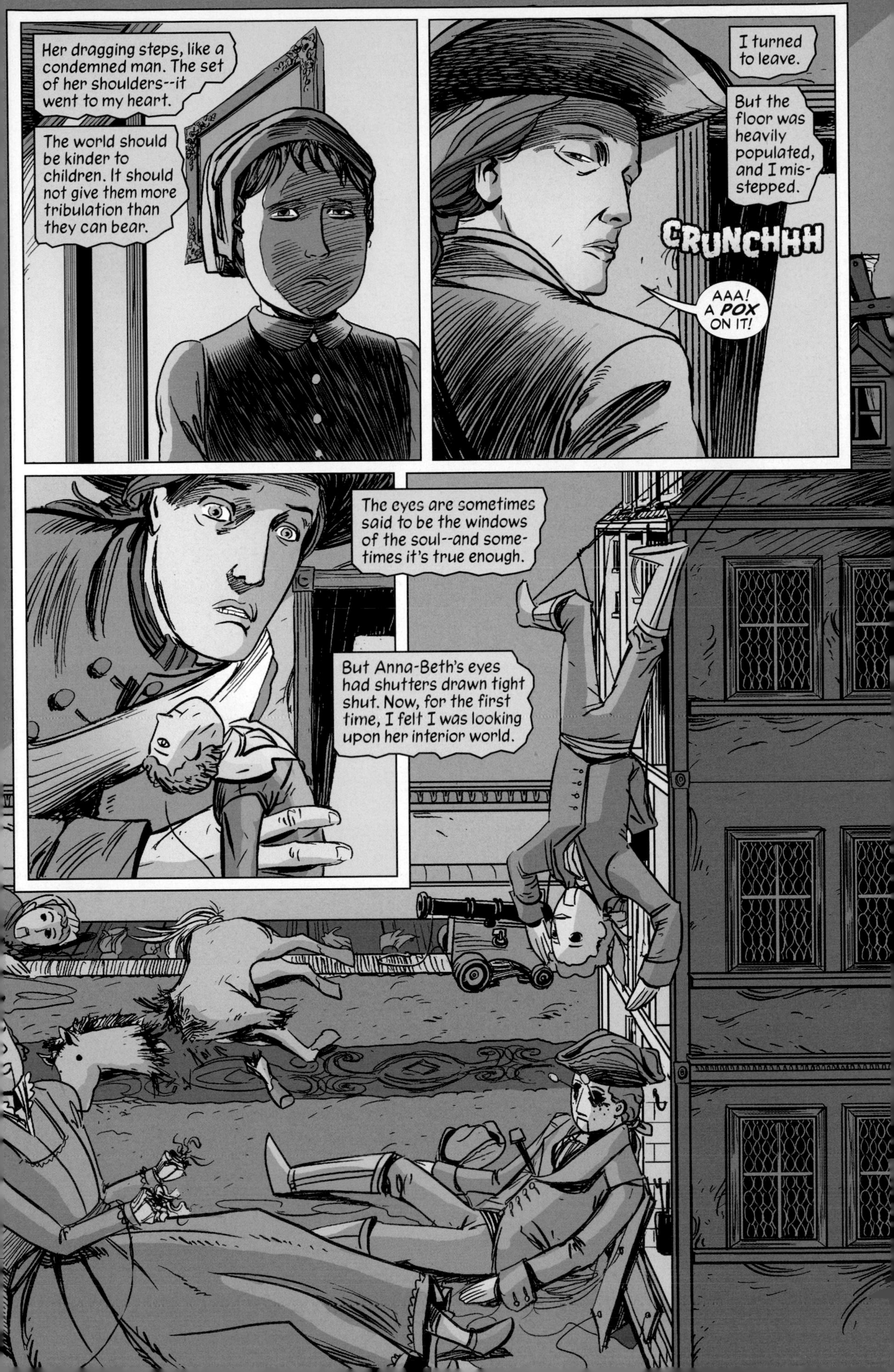
Her dragging steps, like a condemned man. The set of her shoulders--it went to my heart.
The world should be kinder to children. It should not give them more tribulation than they can bear.
I turned to leave.
But the floor was heavily populated, and I mis-stepped.
CRUNCHHH
AAA! A POX ON IT!
The eyes are sometimes said to be the windows of the soul--and some-times it's true enough.
But Anna-Beth's eyes had shutters drawn tight shut. Now, for the first time, I felt I was looking upon her interior world.

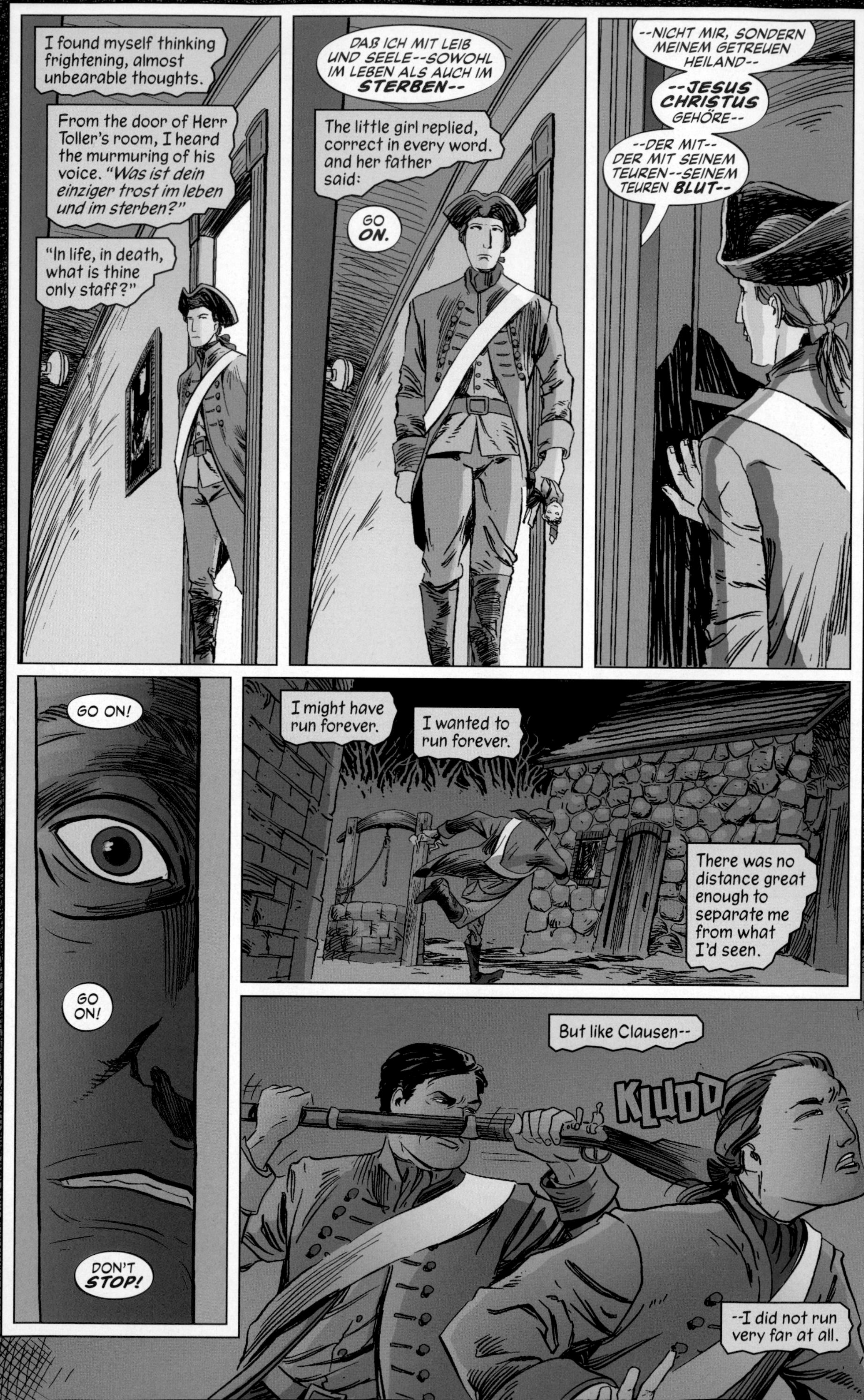

I found myself thinking frightening, almost unbearable thoughts.
From the door of Herr Toller's room, I heard the murmuring of his voice. "Was ist dein einziger trost im leben und im sterben?"
"In life, in death, what is thine only staff?"
DAß ICH MIT LEIB UND SEELE--SOWOHL IM LEBEN ALS AUCH IM STERBEN--
The little girl replied, correct in every word. and her father said:
GO ON.
--NICHT MIR, SONDERN MEINEM GETREUEN HEILAND--
--JESUS CHRISTUS GEHÖRE--
--DER MIT--DER MIT SEINEM TEUREN--SEINEM TEUREN BLUT--
GO ON!
GO ON!
DON'T STOP!
I might have run forever.
I wanted to run forever.
There was no distance great enough to separate me from what I'd seen.
But like Clausen--
KLUDD
--I did not run very far at all.

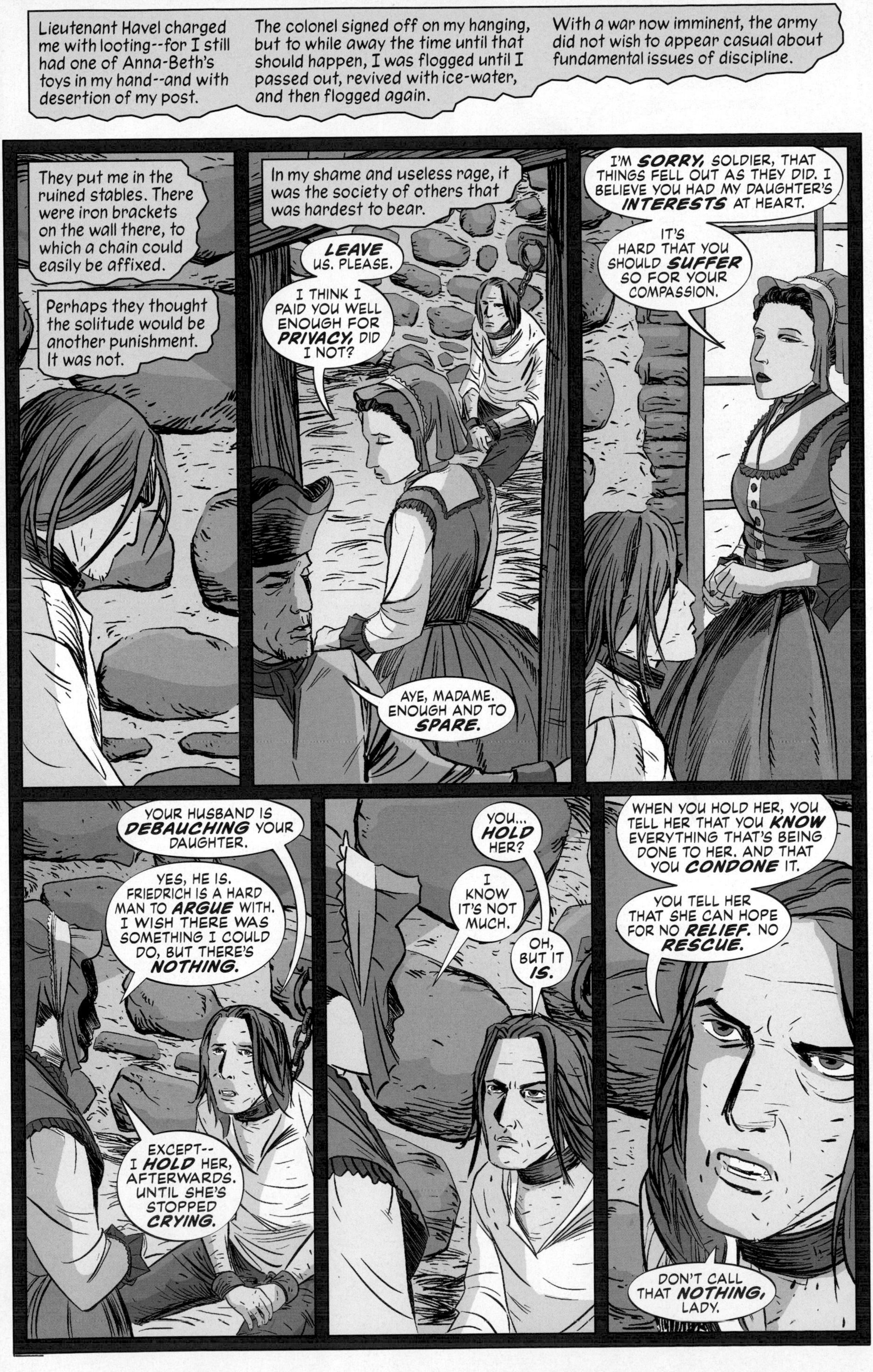
Lieutenant Havel charged me with looting--for I still had one of Anna-Beth's toys in my hand--and with desertion of my post.
The colonel signed off on my hanging, but to while away the time until that should happen, I was flogged until I passed out, revived with ice-water, and then flogged again.
With a war now imminent, the army did not wish to appear casual about fundamental issues of discipline.
They put me in the ruined stables. There were iron brackets on the wall there, to which a chain could easily be affixed.
Perhaps they thought the solitude would be another punishment. It was not.
In my shame and useless rage, it was the society of others that was hardest to bear.
LEAVE US. PLEASE.
I THINK I PAID YOU WELL ENOUGH FOR PRIVACY, DID I NOT?
AYE, MADAME. ENOUGH AND TO SPARE.
I'M SORRY, SOLDIER, THAT THINGS FELL OUT AS THEY DID. I BELIEVE YOU HAD MY DAUGHTER'S INTERESTS AT HEART.
IT'S HARD THAT YOU SHOULD SUFFER SO FOR YOUR COMPASSION.
YOUR HUSBAND IS DEBAUCHING YOUR DAUGHTER.
YES, HE IS. FRIEDRICH IS A HARD MAN TO ARGUE WITH. I WISH THERE WAS SOMETHING I COULD DO, BUT THERE'S NOTHING.
EXCEPT-- I HOLD HER, AFTERWARDS. UNTIL SHE'S STOPPED CRYING.
YOU... HOLD HER?
I KNOW IT'S NOT MUCH.
OH, BUT IT IS.
WHEN YOU HOLD HER, YOU TELL HER THAT YOU KNOW EVERYTHING THAT'S BEING DONE TO HER. AND THAT YOU CONDONE IT.
YOU TELL HER THAT SHE CAN HOPE FOR NO RELIEF. NO RESCUE.
DON'T CALL THAT NOTHING, LADY.

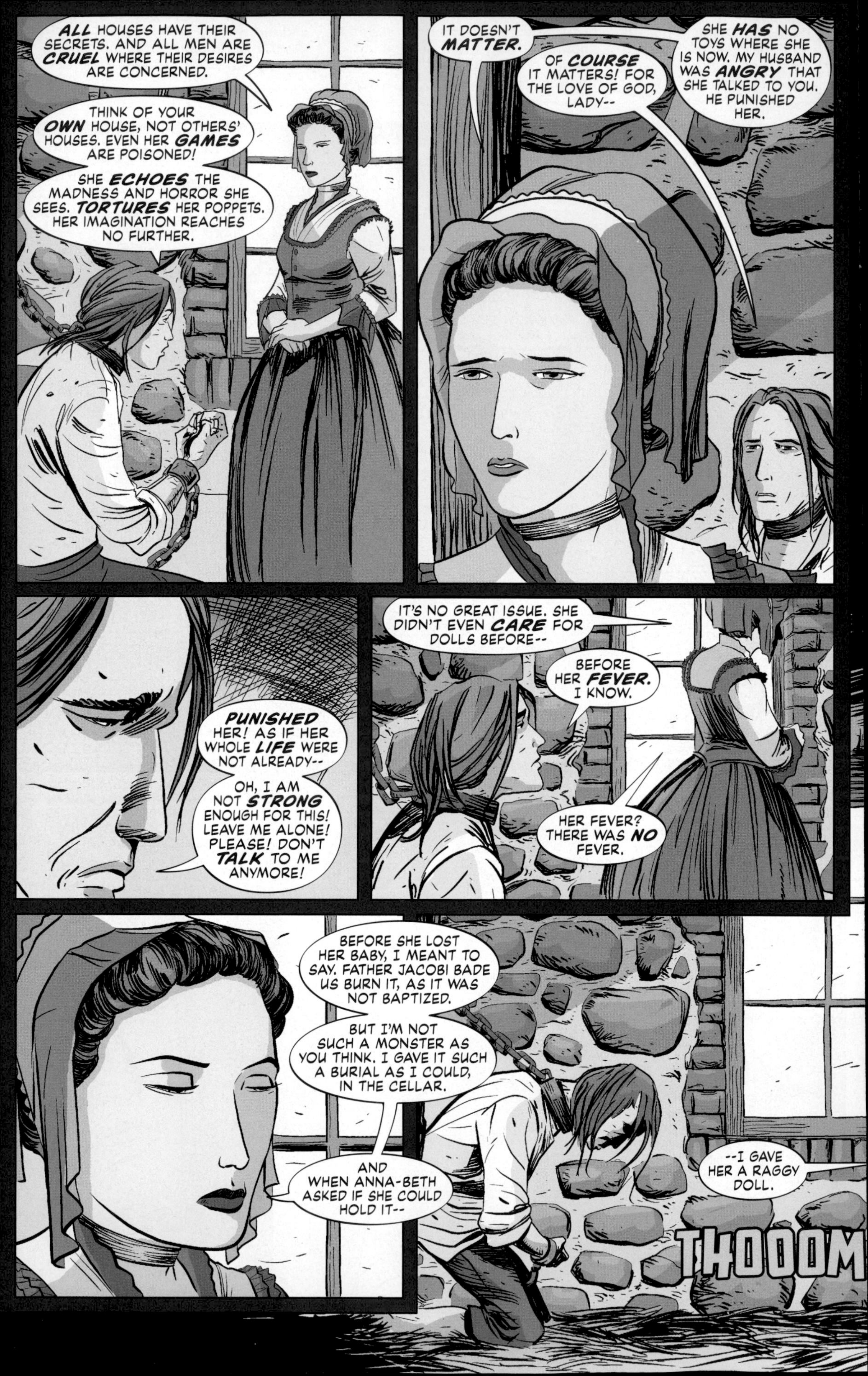
ALL HOUSES HAVE THEIR SECRETS. AND ALL MEN ARE CRUEL WHERE THEIR DESIRES ARE CONCERNED.
THINK OF YOUR OWN HOUSE, NOT OTHERS' HOUSES. EVEN HER GAMES ARE POISONED!
SHE ECHOES THE MADNESS AND HORROR SHE SEES. TORTURES HER POPPETS. HER IMAGINATION REACHES NO FURTHER.
IT DOESN'T MATTER.
OF COURSE IT MATTERS! FOR THE LOVE OF GOD, LADY--
SHE HAS NO TOYS WHERE SHE IS NOW. MY HUSBAND WAS ANGRY THAT SHE TALKED TO YOU. HE PUNISHED HER.
PUNISHED HER! AS IF HER WHOLE LIFE WERE NOT ALREADY--
OH, I AM NOT STRONG ENOUGH FOR THIS! LEAVE ME ALONE! PLEASE! DON'T TALK TO ME ANYMORE!
IT'S NO GREAT ISSUE. SHE DIDN'T EVEN CARE FOR DOLLS BEFORE--
BEFORE HER FEVER. I KNOW.
HER FEVER? THERE WAS NO FEVER.
BEFORE SHE LOST HER BABY, I MEANT TO SAY. FATHER JACOBI BADE US BURN IT, AS IT WAS NOT BAPTIZED.
BUT I'M NOT SUCH A MONSTER AS YOU THINK. I GAVE IT SUCH A BURIAL AS I COULD, IN THE CELLAR.
AND WHEN ANNA-BETH ASKED IF SHE COULD HOLD IT--
--I GAVE HER A RAGGY DOLL.
THOOOM

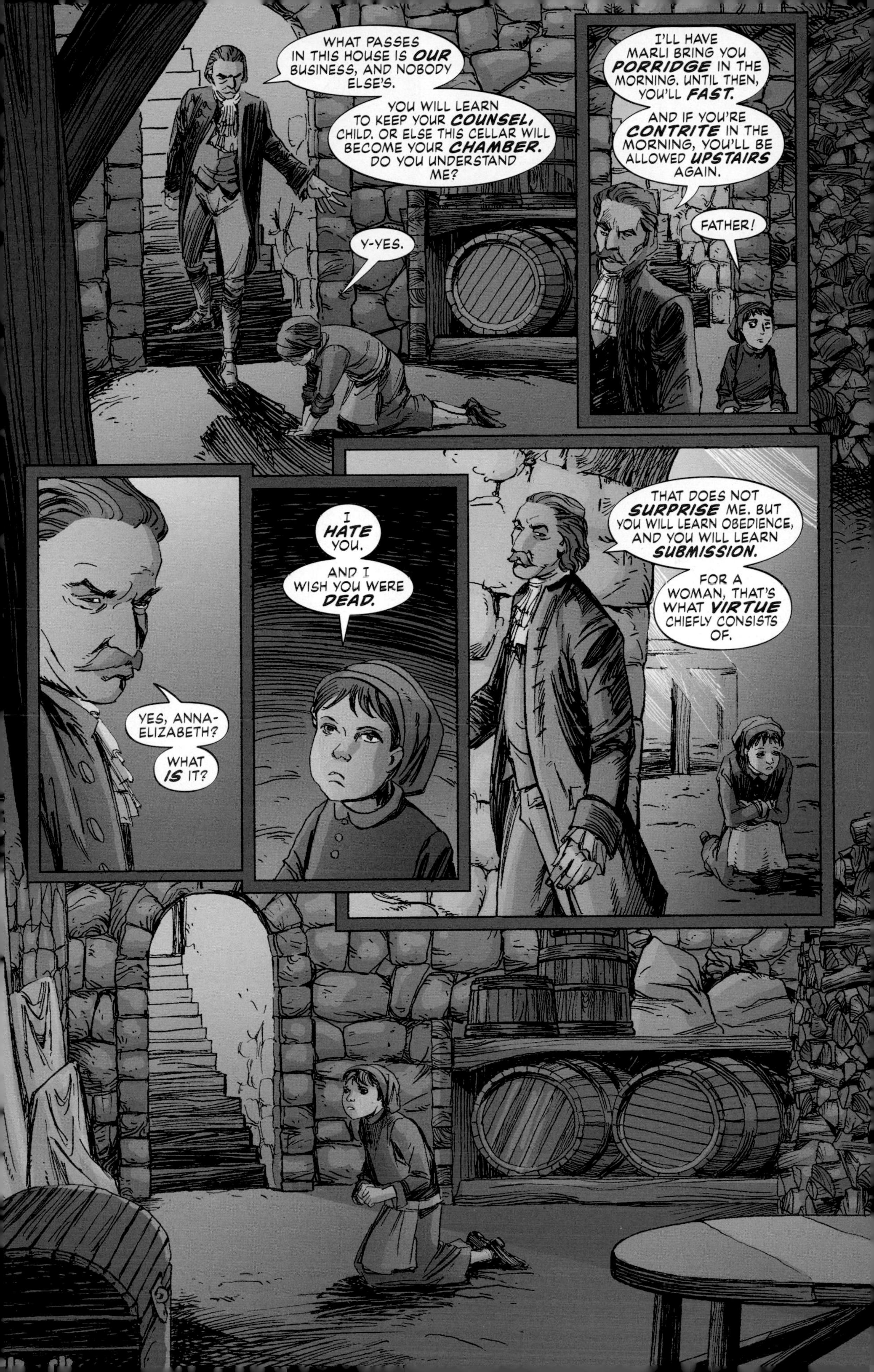

WHAT PASSES IN THIS HOUSE IS ***OUR*** BUSINESS, AND NOBODY ELSE'S.
YOU WILL LEARN TO KEEP YOUR ***COUNSEL,*** CHILD. OR ELSE THIS CELLAR WILL BECOME YOUR ***CHAMBER.*** DO YOU UNDERSTAND ME?
Y-YES.
I'LL HAVE MARLI BRING YOU ***PORRIDGE*** IN THE MORNING. UNTIL THEN, YOU'LL ***FAST.***
AND IF YOU'RE ***CONTRITE*** IN THE MORNING, YOU'LL BE ALLOWED ***UPSTAIRS*** AGAIN.
FATHER!
YES, ANNA-ELIZABETH?
WHAT ***IS*** IT?
I ***HATE*** YOU.
AND I WISH YOU WERE ***DEAD.***
THAT DOES NOT ***SURPRISE*** ME. BUT YOU WILL LEARN OBEDIENCE, AND YOU WILL LEARN ***SUBMISSION.***
FOR A WOMAN, THAT'S WHAT ***VIRTUE*** CHIEFLY CONSISTS OF.

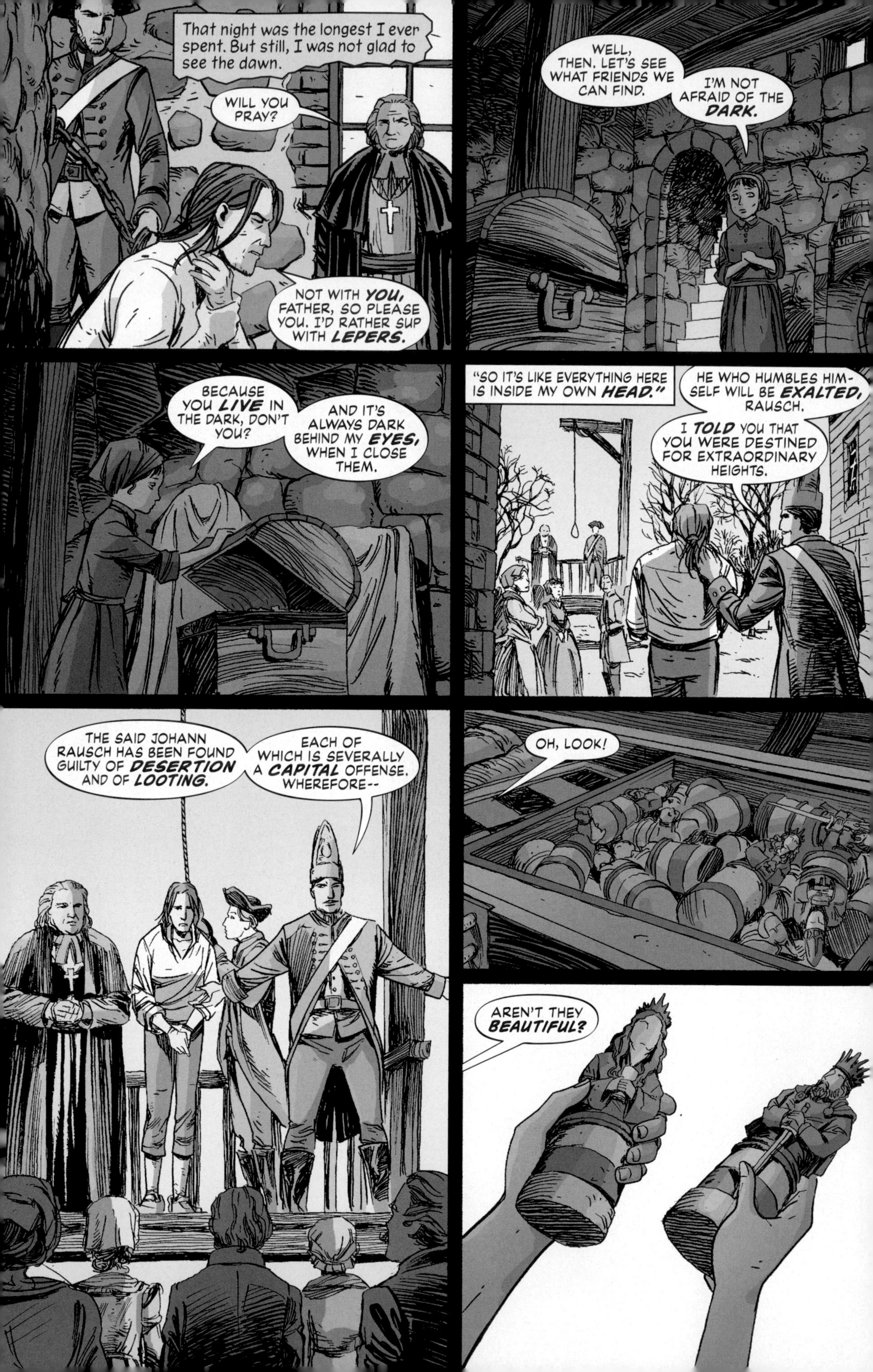
That night was the longest I ever spent. But still, I was not glad to see the dawn.
WILL YOU PRAY?
NOT WITH YOU, FATHER, SO PLEASE YOU. I'D RATHER SUP WITH LEPERS.
WELL, THEN. LET'S SEE WHAT FRIENDS WE CAN FIND.
I'M NOT AFRAID OF THE DARK.
BECAUSE YOU LIVE IN THE DARK, DON'T YOU?
AND IT'S ALWAYS DARK BEHIND MY EYES, WHEN I CLOSE THEM.
"SO IT'S LIKE EVERYTHING HERE IS INSIDE MY OWN HEAD."
HE WHO HUMBLES HIMSELF WILL BE EXALTED, RAUSCH.
I TOLD YOU THAT YOU WERE DESTINED FOR EXTRAORDINARY HEIGHTS.
THE SAID JOHANN RAUSCH HAS BEEN FOUND GUILTY OF DESERTION AND OF LOOTING.
EACH OF WHICH IS SEVERALLY A CAPITAL OFFENSE. WHEREFORE--
OH, LOOK!
AREN'T THEY BEAUTIFUL?

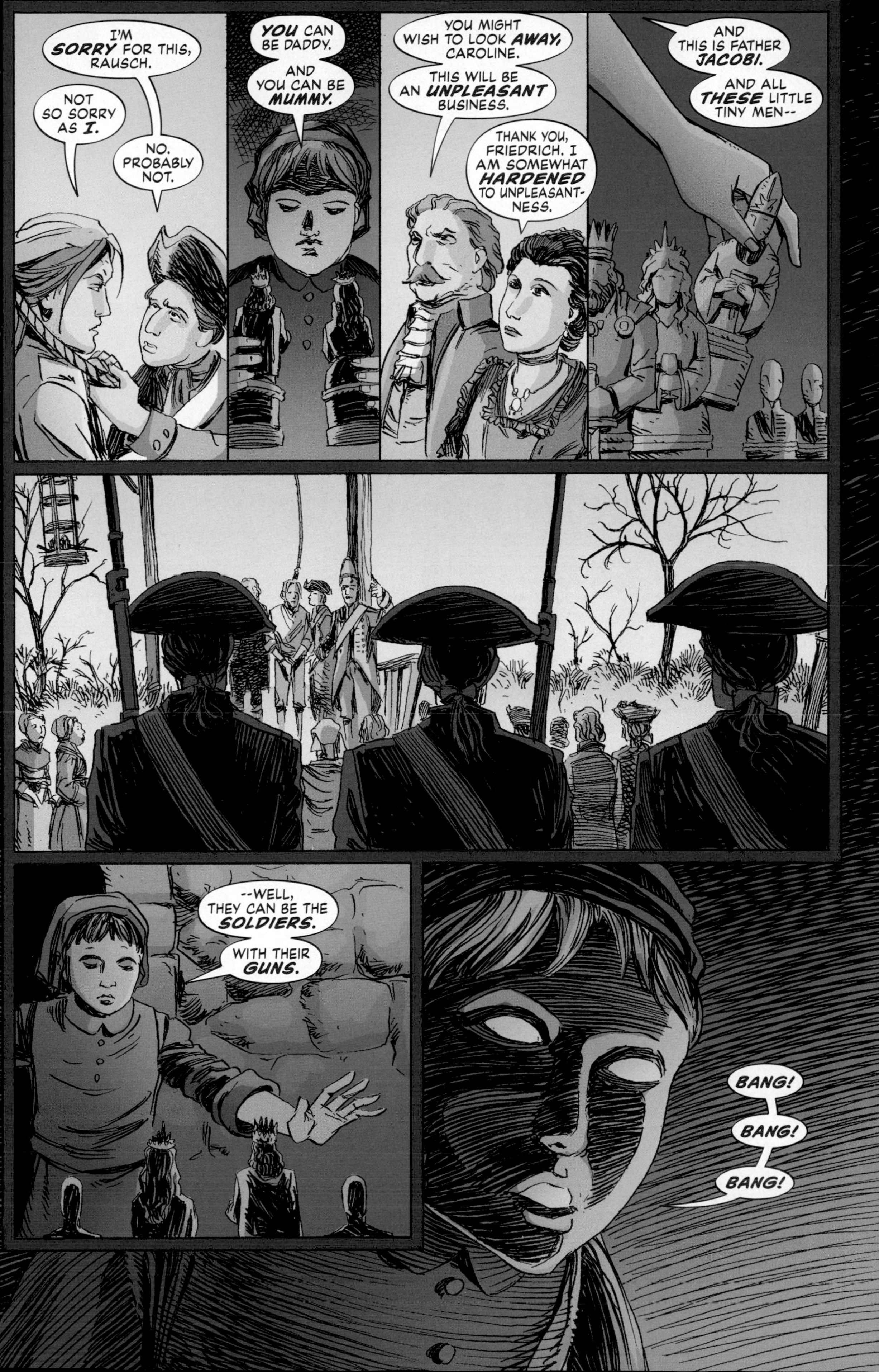
I'M SORRY FOR THIS, RAUSCH.
NOT SO SORRY AS I.
NO. PROBABLY NOT.
YOU CAN BE DADDY.
AND YOU CAN BE MUMMY.
YOU MIGHT WISH TO LOOK AWAY, CAROLINE.
THIS WILL BE AN UNPLEASANT BUSINESS.
THANK YOU, FRIEDRICH. I AM SOMEWHAT HARDENED TO UNPLEASANTNESS.
AND THIS IS FATHER JACOBI.
AND ALL THESE LITTLE TINY MEN--
--WELL, THEY CAN BE THE SOLDIERS.
WITH THEIR GUNS.
BANG!
BANG!
BANG!

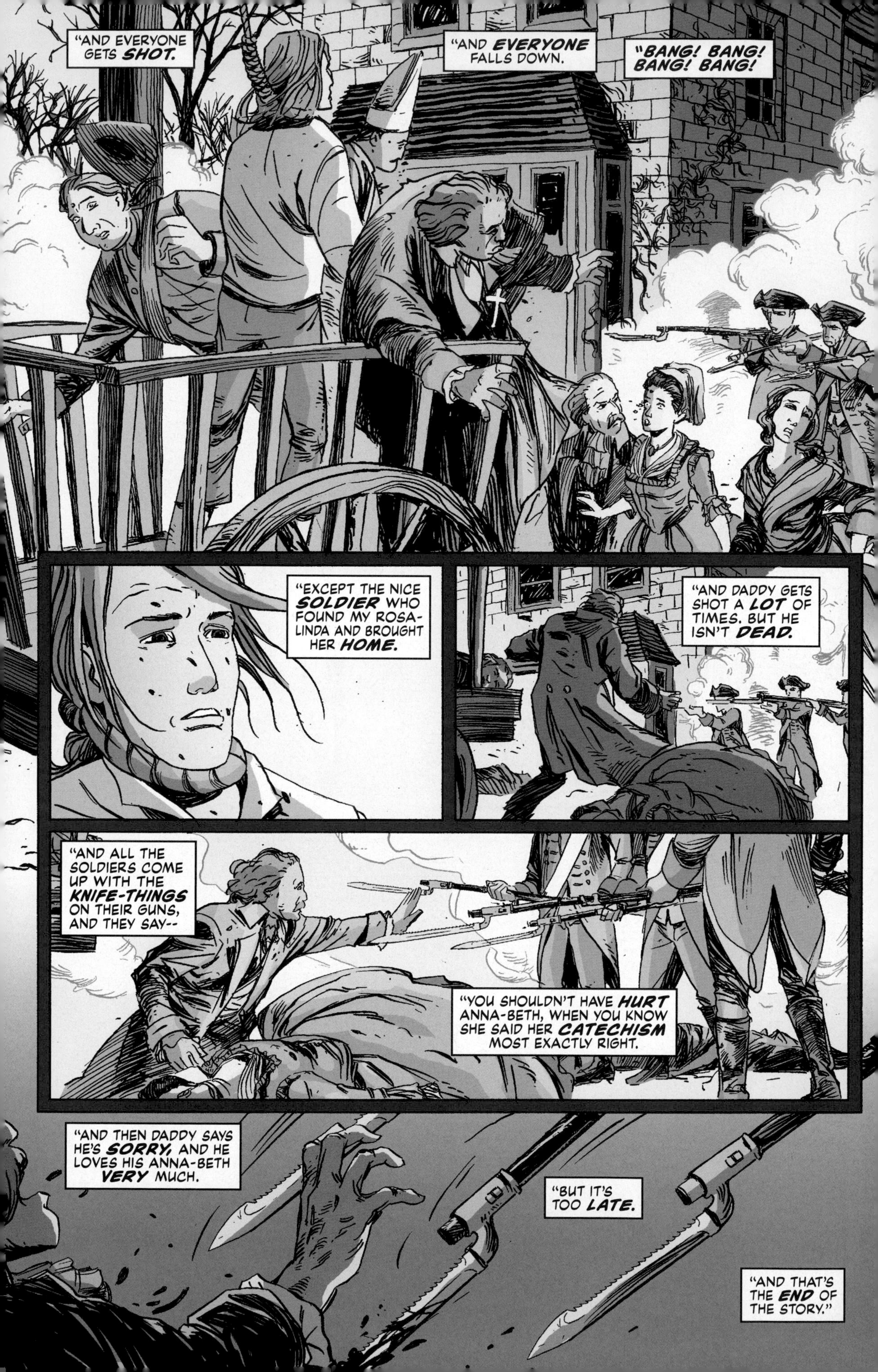
"AND EVERYONE GETS SHOT.
"AND EVERYONE FALLS DOWN.
"BANG! BANG! BANG! BANG!
"EXCEPT THE NICE SOLDIER WHO FOUND MY ROSA-LINDA AND BROUGHT HER HOME.
"AND DADDY GETS SHOT A LOT OF TIMES. BUT HE ISN'T DEAD.
"AND ALL THE SOLDIERS COME UP WITH THE KNIFE-THINGS ON THEIR GUNS, AND THEY SAY--
"YOU SHOULDN'T HAVE HURT ANNA-BETH, WHEN YOU KNOW SHE SAID HER CATECHISM MOST EXACTLY RIGHT.
"AND THEN DADDY SAYS HE'S SORRY, AND HE LOVES HIS ANNA-BETH VERY MUCH.
"BUT IT'S TOO LATE.
"AND THAT'S THE END OF THE STORY."

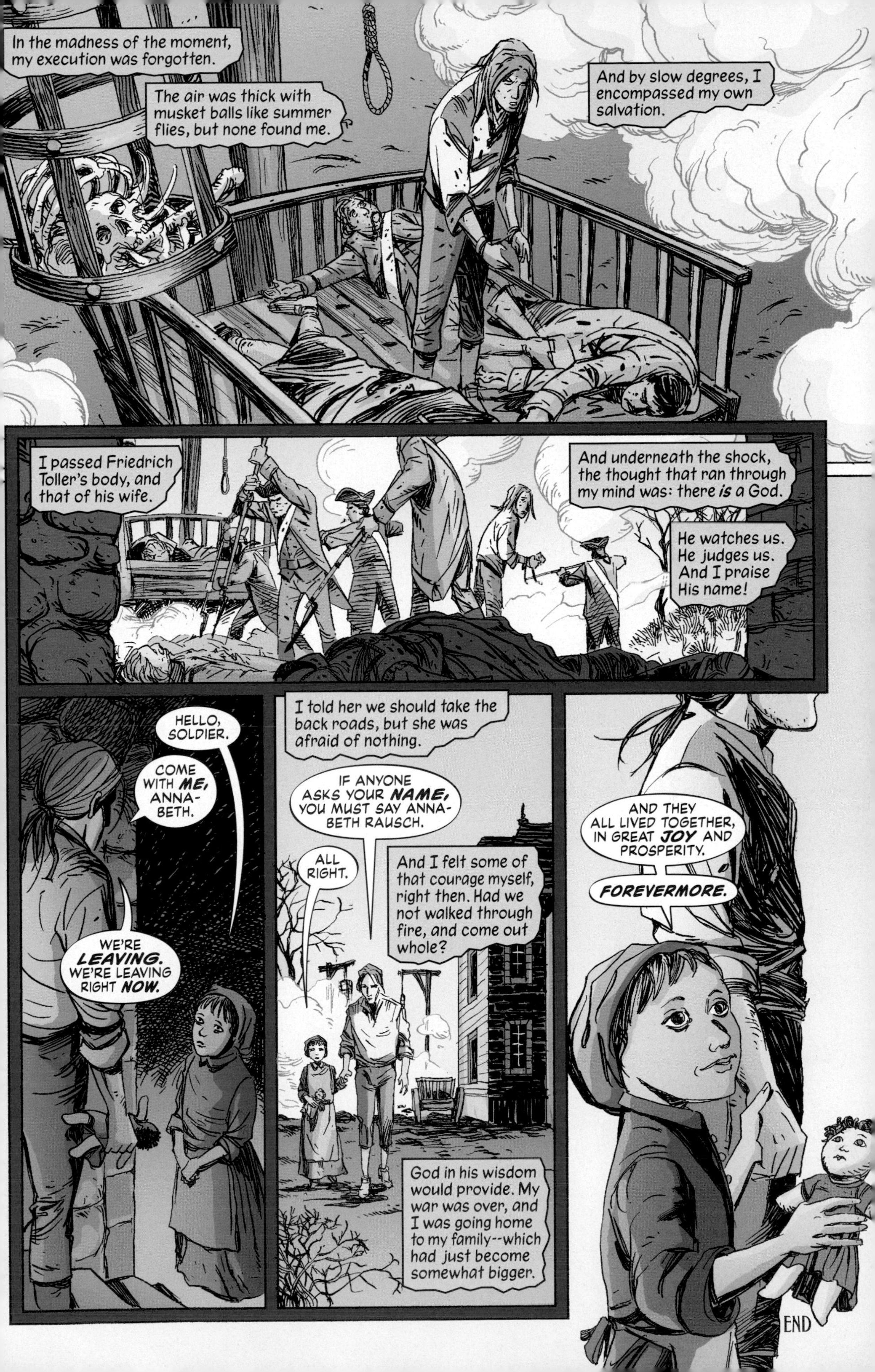
In the madness of the moment, my execution was forgotten.
The air was thick with musket balls like summer flies, but none found me.
And by slow degrees, I encompassed my own salvation.
I passed Friedrich Toller's body, and that of his wife.
And underneath the shock, the thought that ran through my mind was: there *is* a God.
He watches us. He judges us. And I praise His name!
HELLO, SOLDIER.
COME WITH ***ME,*** ANNA-BETH.
WE'RE ***LEAVING.*** WE'RE LEAVING RIGHT ***NOW.***
I told her we should take the back roads, but she was afraid of nothing.
IF ANYONE ASKS YOUR ***NAME,*** YOU MUST SAY ANNA-BETH RAUSCH.
ALL RIGHT.
And I felt some of that courage myself, right then. Had we not walked through fire, and come out whole?
God in his wisdom would provide. My war was over, and I was going home to my family--which had just become somewhat bigger.
AND THEY ALL LIVED TOGETHER, IN GREAT ***JOY*** AND PROSPERITY.
FOREVERMORE.
END

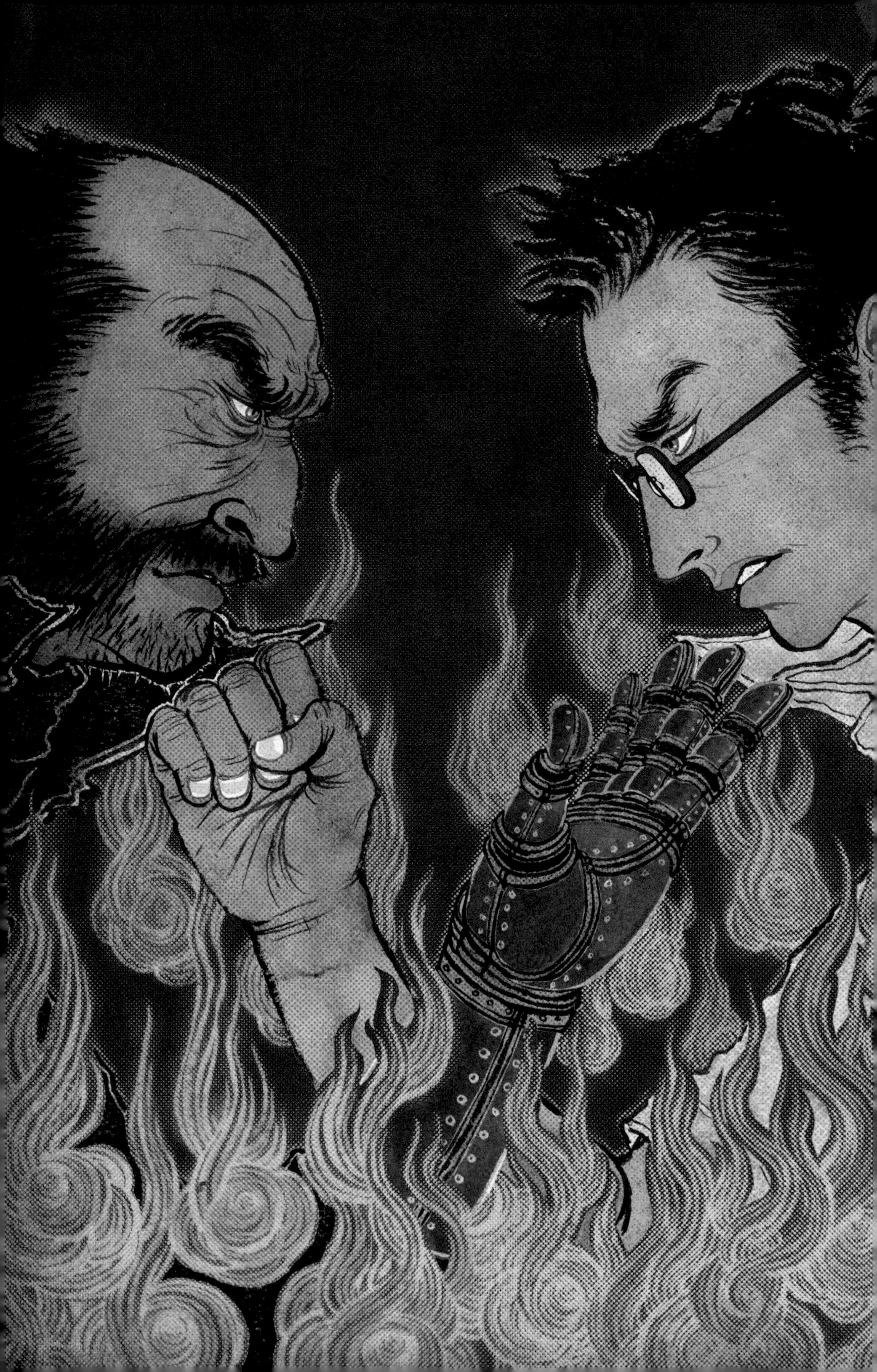

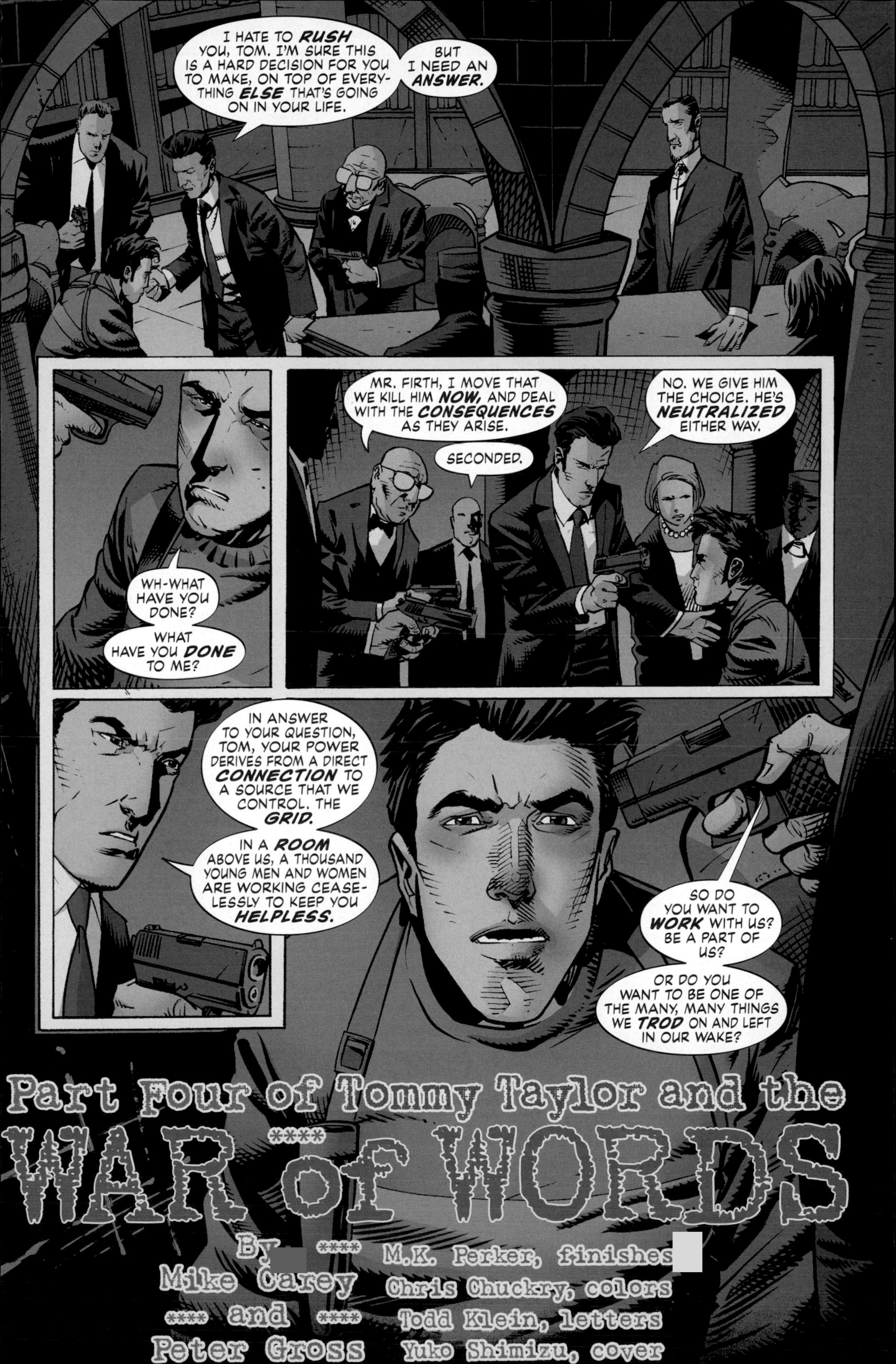

I HATE TO RUSH YOU, TOM. I'M SURE THIS IS A HARD DECISION FOR YOU TO MAKE, ON TOP OF EVERYTHING ELSE THAT'S GOING ON IN YOUR LIFE.
BUT I NEED AN ANSWER.
WH-WHAT HAVE YOU DONE?
WHAT HAVE YOU DONE TO ME?
MR. FIRTH, I MOVE THAT WE KILL HIM NOW, AND DEAL WITH THE CONSEQUENCES AS THEY ARISE.
SECONDED.
NO. WE GIVE HIM THE CHOICE. HE'S NEUTRALIZED EITHER WAY.
IN ANSWER TO YOUR QUESTION, TOM, YOUR POWER DERIVES FROM A DIRECT CONNECTION TO A SOURCE THAT WE CONTROL. THE GRID.
IN A ROOM ABOVE US, A THOUSAND YOUNG MEN AND WOMEN ARE WORKING CEASELESSLY TO KEEP YOU HELPLESS.
SO DO YOU WANT TO WORK WITH US? BE A PART OF US?
OR DO YOU WANT TO BE ONE OF THE MANY, MANY THINGS WE TROD ON AND LEFT IN OUR WAKE?

Part Four of Tommy Taylor and the

WAR of WORDS

By Mike Carey and Peter Gross

M.K. Perker, finishes
Chris Chuckry, colors
Todd Klein, letters
Yuko Shimizu, cover

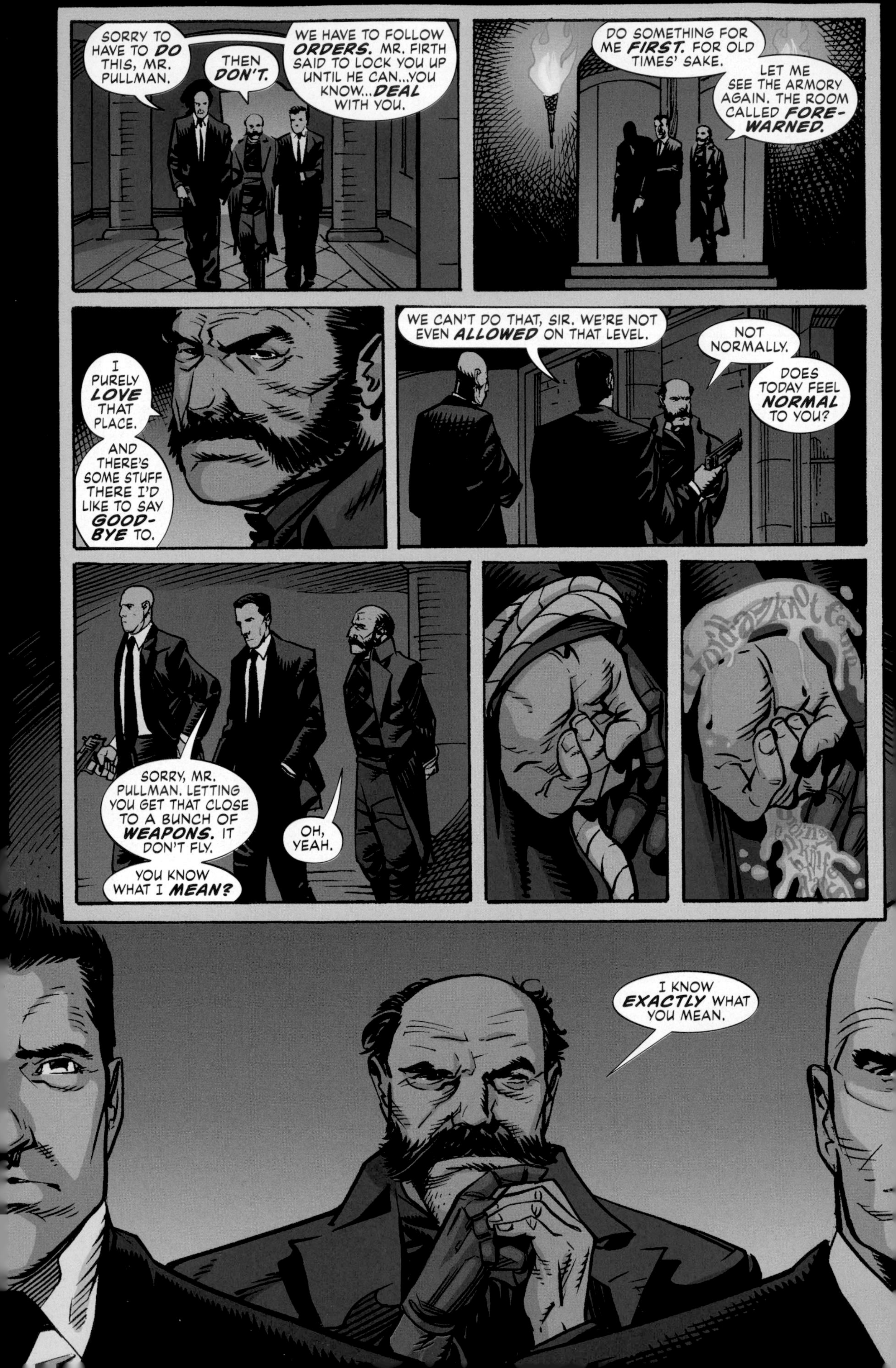

SORRY TO HAVE TO DO THIS, MR. PULLMAN.
THEN DON'T.
WE HAVE TO FOLLOW ORDERS. MR. FIRTH SAID TO LOCK YOU UP UNTIL HE CAN...YOU KNOW...DEAL WITH YOU.
DO SOMETHING FOR ME FIRST. FOR OLD TIMES' SAKE.
LET ME SEE THE ARMORY AGAIN. THE ROOM CALLED FORE-WARNED.
I PURELY LOVE THAT PLACE.
AND THERE'S SOME STUFF THERE I'D LIKE TO SAY GOOD-BYE TO.
WE CAN'T DO THAT, SIR. WE'RE NOT EVEN ALLOWED ON THAT LEVEL.
NOT NORMALLY.
DOES TODAY FEEL NORMAL TO YOU?
SORRY, MR. PULLMAN. LETTING YOU GET THAT CLOSE TO A BUNCH OF WEAPONS. IT DON'T FLY.
YOU KNOW WHAT I MEAN?
OH, YEAH.
I KNOW EXACTLY WHAT YOU MEAN.

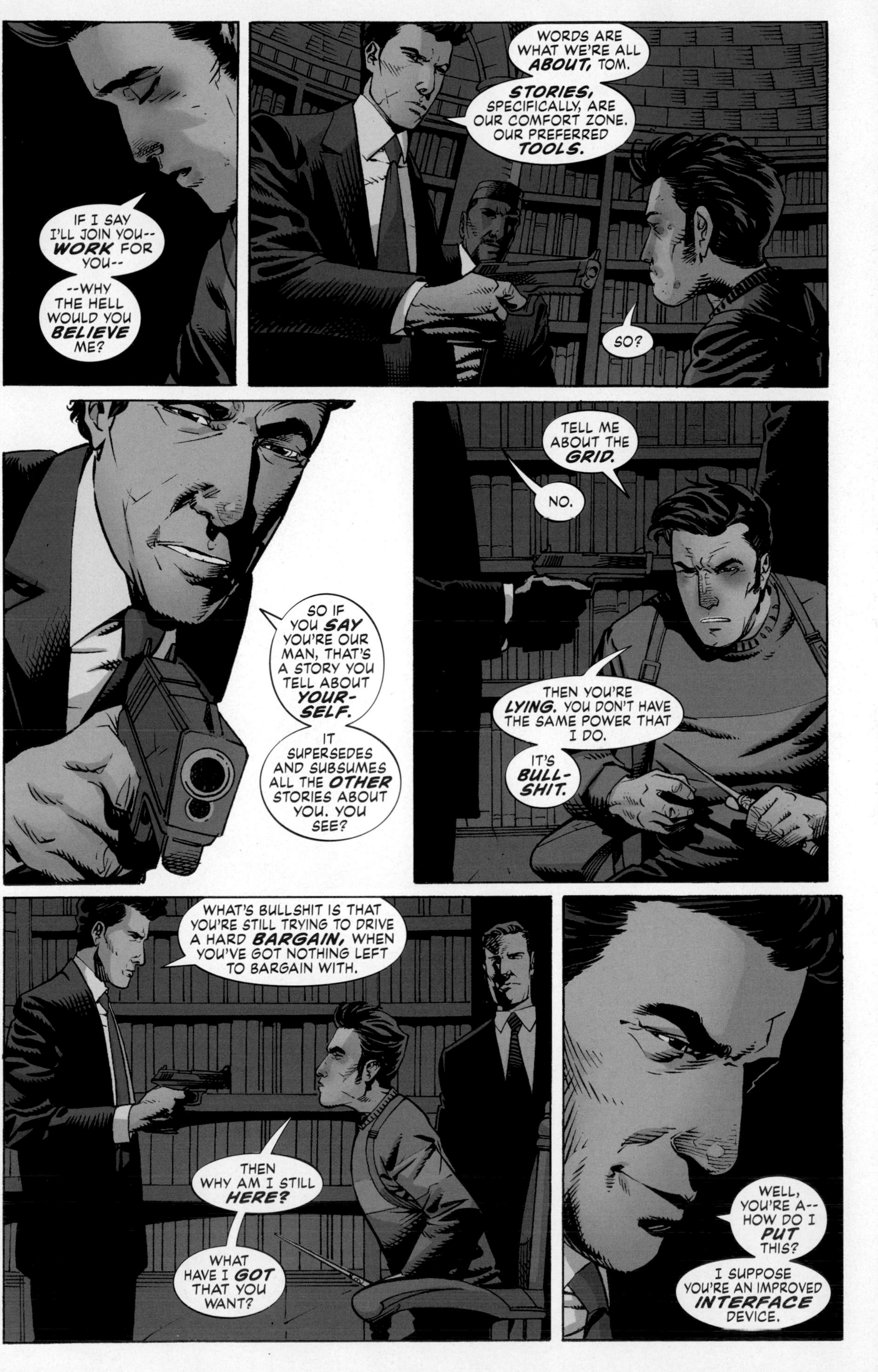
IF I SAY I'LL JOIN YOU-- WORK FOR YOU--
--WHY THE HELL WOULD YOU BELIEVE ME?
WORDS ARE WHAT WE'RE ALL ABOUT, TOM.
STORIES, SPECIFICALLY, ARE OUR COMFORT ZONE. OUR PREFERRED TOOLS.
SO?
SO IF YOU SAY YOU'RE OUR MAN, THAT'S A STORY YOU TELL ABOUT YOURSELF.
IT SUPERSEDES AND SUBSUMES ALL THE OTHER STORIES ABOUT YOU. YOU SEE?
TELL ME ABOUT THE GRID.
NO.
THEN YOU'RE LYING. YOU DON'T HAVE THE SAME POWER THAT I DO.
IT'S BULL-SHIT.
WHAT'S BULLSHIT IS THAT YOU'RE STILL TRYING TO DRIVE A HARD BARGAIN, WHEN YOU'VE GOT NOTHING LEFT TO BARGAIN WITH.
THEN WHY AM I STILL HERE?
WHAT HAVE I GOT THAT YOU WANT?
WELL, YOU'RE A-- HOW DO I PUT THIS?
I SUPPOSE YOU'RE AN IMPROVED INTERFACE DEVICE.

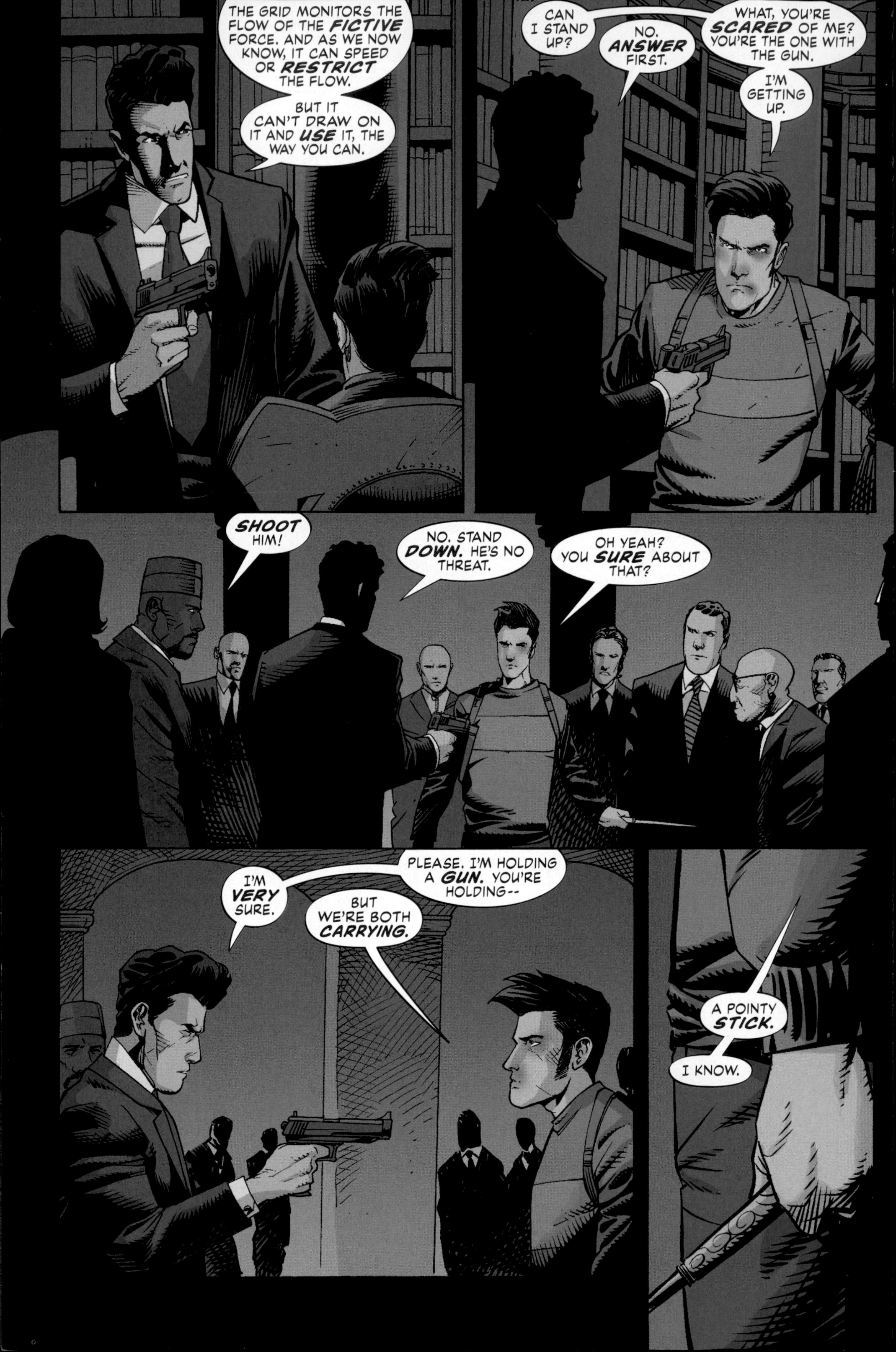
THE GRID MONITORS THE FLOW OF THE FICTIVE FORCE. AND AS WE NOW KNOW, IT CAN SPEED OR RESTRICT THE FLOW.
BUT IT CAN'T DRAW ON IT AND USE IT, THE WAY YOU CAN.
CAN I STAND UP?
NO. ANSWER FIRST.
WHAT, YOU'RE SCARED OF ME? YOU'RE THE ONE WITH THE GUN.
I'M GETTING UP.
SHOOT HIM!
NO. STAND DOWN. HE'S NO THREAT.
OH YEAH? YOU SURE ABOUT THAT?
I'M VERY SURE.
PLEASE. I'M HOLDING A GUN. YOU'RE HOLDING--
BUT WE'RE BOTH CARRYING.
A POINTY STICK.
I KNOW.

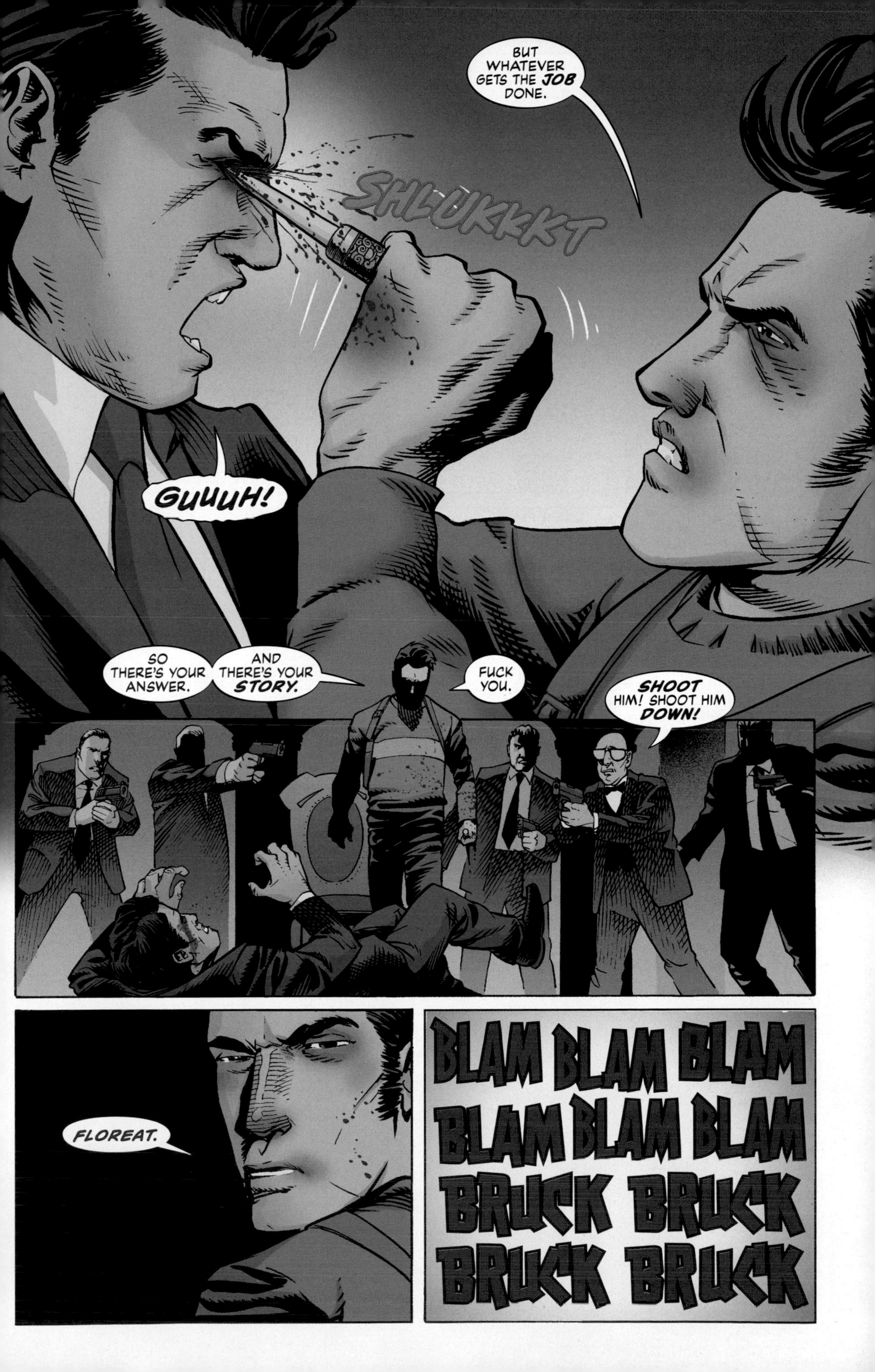
BUT WHATEVER GETS THE JOB DONE.
SHLUKKKT
GUUUH!
SO THERE'S YOUR ANSWER.
AND THERE'S YOUR STORY.
FUCK YOU.
SHOOT HIM! SHOOT HIM DOWN!
FLOREAT.
BLAM BLAM BLAM
BLAM BLAM BLAM
BRUCK BRUCK
BRUCK BRUCK

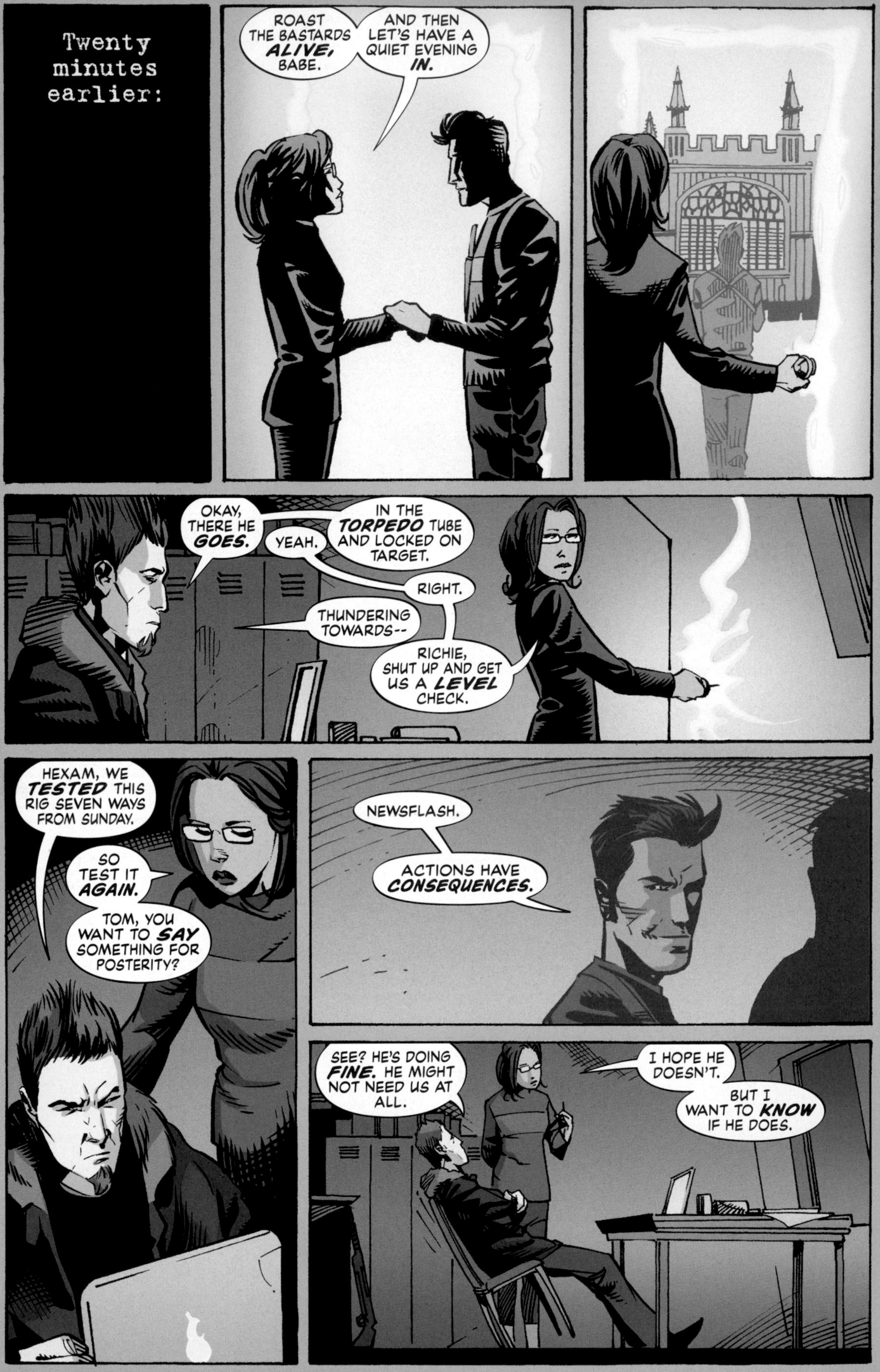

Twenty minutes earlier:
ROAST THE BASTARDS ALIVE, BABE.
AND THEN LET'S HAVE A QUIET EVENING IN.
OKAY, THERE HE GOES.
IN THE TORPEDO TUBE AND LOCKED ON TARGET.
YEAH.
RIGHT.
THUNDERING TOWARDS--
RICHIE, SHUT UP AND GET US A LEVEL CHECK.
HEXAM, WE TESTED THIS RIG SEVEN WAYS FROM SUNDAY.
SO TEST IT AGAIN.
TOM, YOU WANT TO SAY SOMETHING FOR POSTERITY?
NEWSFLASH.
ACTIONS HAVE CONSEQUENCES.
SEE? HE'S DOING FINE. HE MIGHT NOT NEED US AT ALL.
I HOPE HE DOESN'T.
BUT I WANT TO KNOW IF HE DOES.

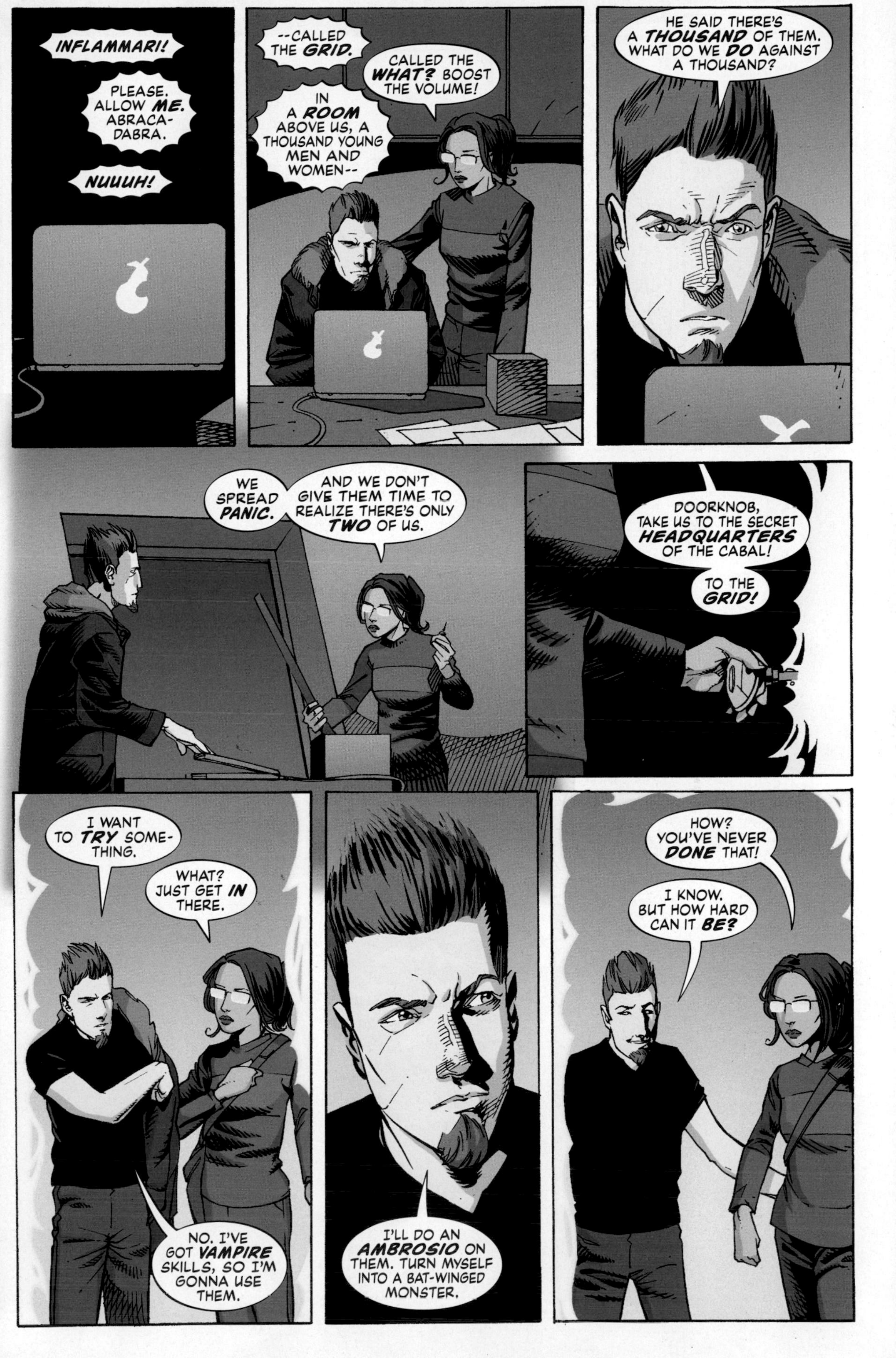
INFLAMMARI!
PLEASE. ALLOW ME. ABRACA-DABRA.
NUUUH!
--CALLED THE GRID.
CALLED THE WHAT? BOOST THE VOLUME!
IN A ROOM ABOVE US, A THOUSAND YOUNG MEN AND WOMEN--
HE SAID THERE'S A THOUSAND OF THEM. WHAT DO WE DO AGAINST A THOUSAND?
WE SPREAD PANIC.
AND WE DON'T GIVE THEM TIME TO REALIZE THERE'S ONLY TWO OF US.
DOORKNOB, TAKE US TO THE SECRET HEADQUARTERS OF THE CABAL!
TO THE GRID!
I WANT TO TRY SOME-THING.
WHAT? JUST GET IN THERE.
NO. I'VE GOT VAMPIRE SKILLS, SO I'M GONNA USE THEM.
I'LL DO AN AMBROSIO ON THEM. TURN MYSELF INTO A BAT-WINGED MONSTER.
HOW? YOU'VE NEVER DONE THAT!
I KNOW. BUT HOW HARD CAN IT BE?

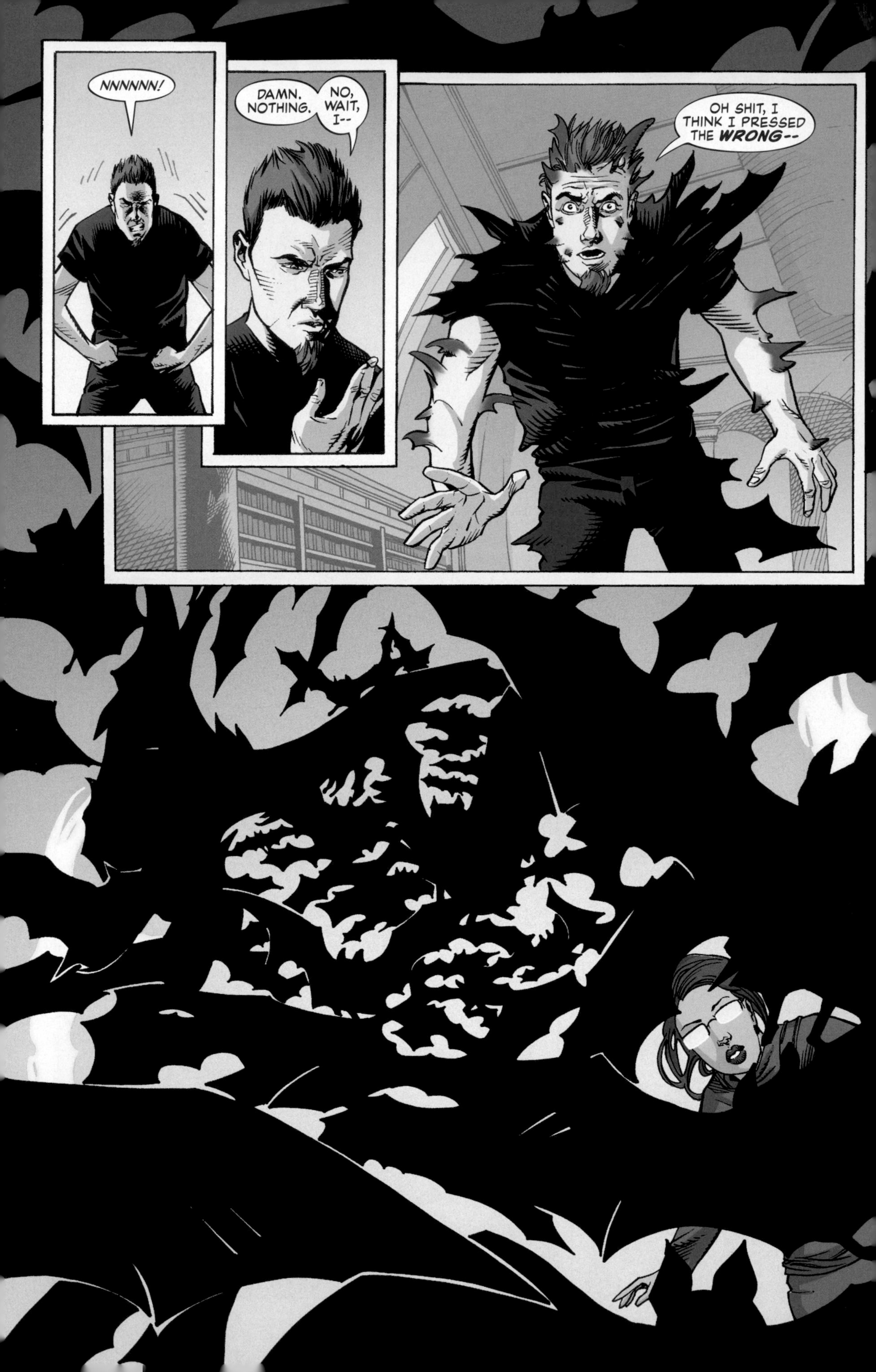
NNNNNN!
DAMN. NOTHING.
NO, WAIT, I--
OH SHIT, I THINK I PRESSED THE **WRONG--**

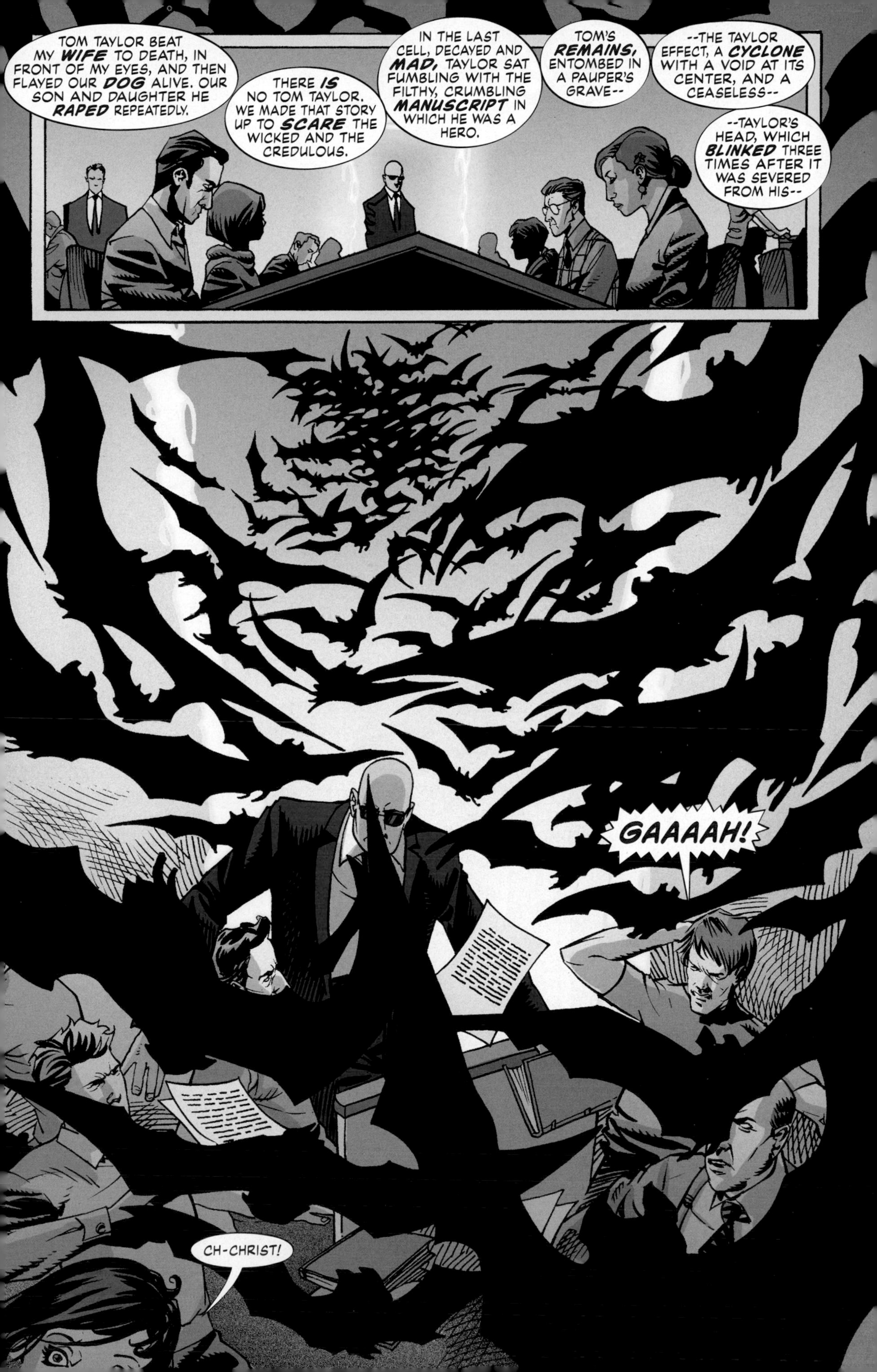
TOM TAYLOR BEAT MY WIFE TO DEATH, IN FRONT OF MY EYES, AND THEN FLAYED OUR DOG ALIVE. OUR SON AND DAUGHTER HE RAPED REPEATEDLY.
THERE IS NO TOM TAYLOR. WE MADE THAT STORY UP TO SCARE THE WICKED AND THE CREDULOUS.
IN THE LAST CELL, DECAYED AND MAD, TAYLOR SAT FUMBLING WITH THE FILTHY, CRUMBLING MANUSCRIPT IN WHICH HE WAS A HERO.
TOM'S REMAINS, ENTOMBED IN A PAUPER'S GRAVE--
--THE TAYLOR EFFECT, A CYCLONE WITH A VOID AT ITS CENTER, AND A CEASELESS--
--TAYLOR'S HEAD, WHICH BLINKED THREE TIMES AFTER IT WAS SEVERED FROM HIS--
GAAAAH!
CH-CHRIST!

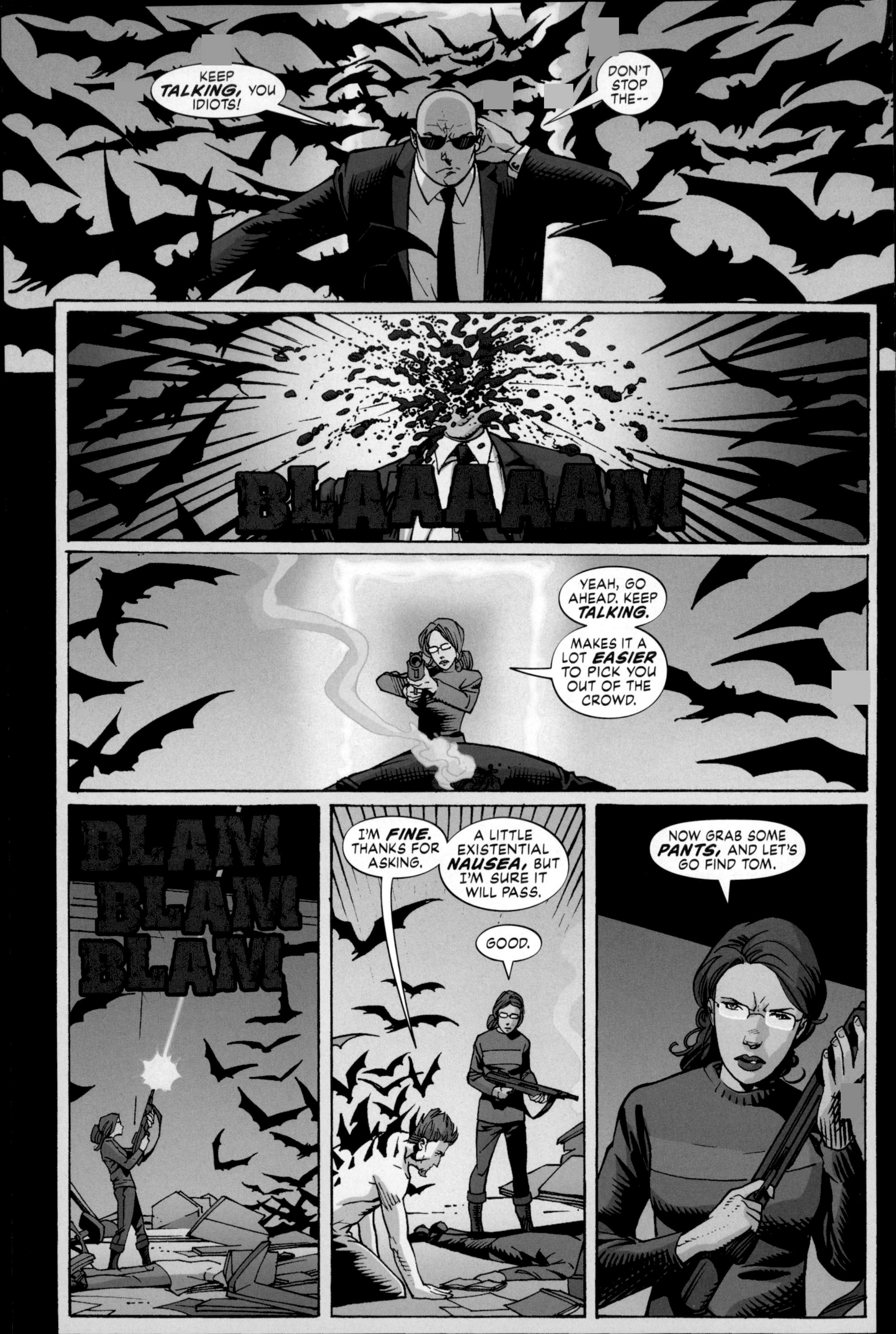
KEEP TALKING, YOU IDIOTS!
DON'T STOP THE--
BLAAAAAM
YEAH, GO AHEAD. KEEP TALKING.
MAKES IT A LOT EASIER TO PICK YOU OUT OF THE CROWD.
BLAM BLAM BLAM
I'M FINE. THANKS FOR ASKING.
A LITTLE EXISTENTIAL NAUSEA, BUT I'M SURE IT WILL PASS.
GOOD.
NOW GRAB SOME PANTS, AND LET'S GO FIND TOM.

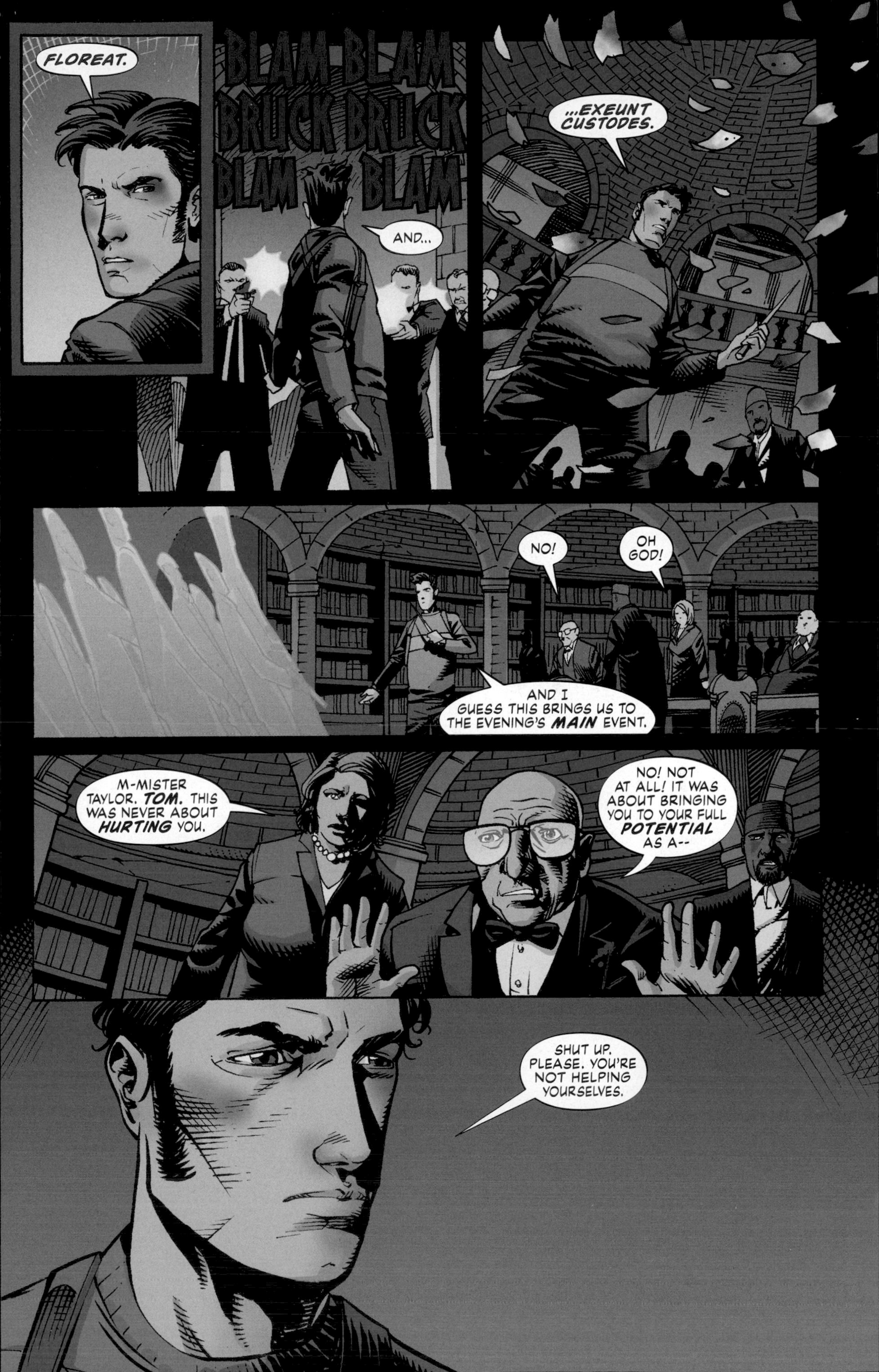
FLOREAT.
BLAM-BLAM
BRUCK BRUCK
BLAM BLAM
AND...
...EXEUNT CUSTODES.
NO!
OH GOD!
AND I GUESS THIS BRINGS US TO THE EVENING'S MAIN EVENT.
M-MISTER TAYLOR. TOM. THIS WAS NEVER ABOUT HURTING YOU.
NO! NOT AT ALL! IT WAS ABOUT BRINGING YOU TO YOUR FULL POTENTIAL AS A--
SHUT UP. PLEASE. YOU'RE NOT HELPING YOURSELVES.

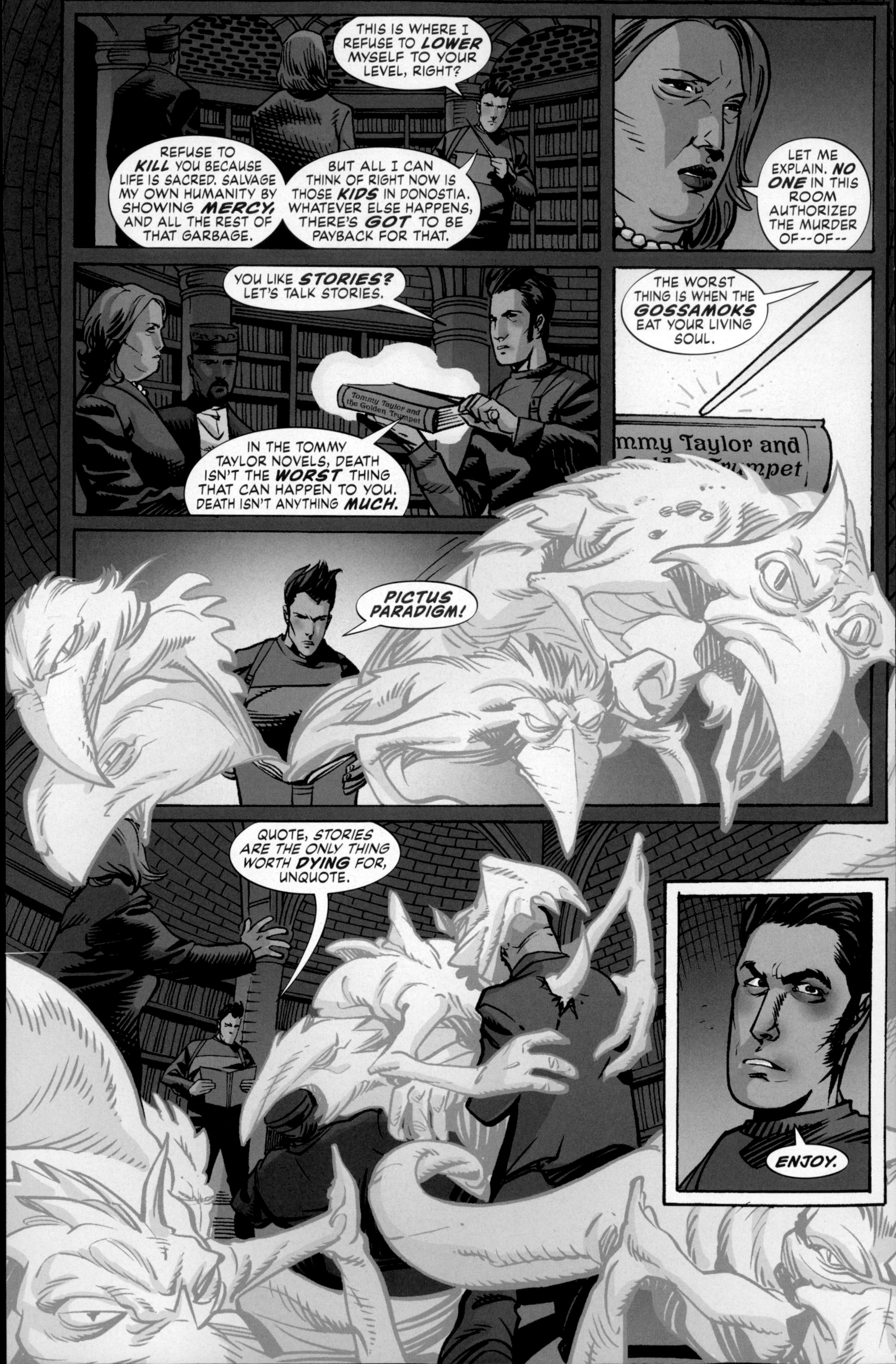
THIS IS WHERE I REFUSE TO LOWER MYSELF TO YOUR LEVEL, RIGHT?
REFUSE TO KILL YOU BECAUSE LIFE IS SACRED. SALVAGE MY OWN HUMANITY BY SHOWING MERCY, AND ALL THE REST OF THAT GARBAGE.
BUT ALL I CAN THINK OF RIGHT NOW IS THOSE KIDS IN DONOSTIA. WHATEVER ELSE HAPPENS, THERE'S GOT TO BE PAYBACK FOR THAT.
LET ME EXPLAIN. NO ONE IN THIS ROOM AUTHORIZED THE MURDER OF--OF--
YOU LIKE STORIES? LET'S TALK STORIES.
Tommy Taylor and the Golden Trumpet
IN THE TOMMY TAYLOR NOVELS, DEATH ISN'T THE WORST THING THAT CAN HAPPEN TO YOU. DEATH ISN'T ANYTHING MUCH.
THE WORST THING IS WHEN THE GOSSAMOKS EAT YOUR LIVING SOUL.
mmy Taylor and
umpet
PICTUS PARADIGM!
QUOTE, STORIES ARE THE ONLY THING WORTH DYING FOR, UNQUOTE.
ENJOY.

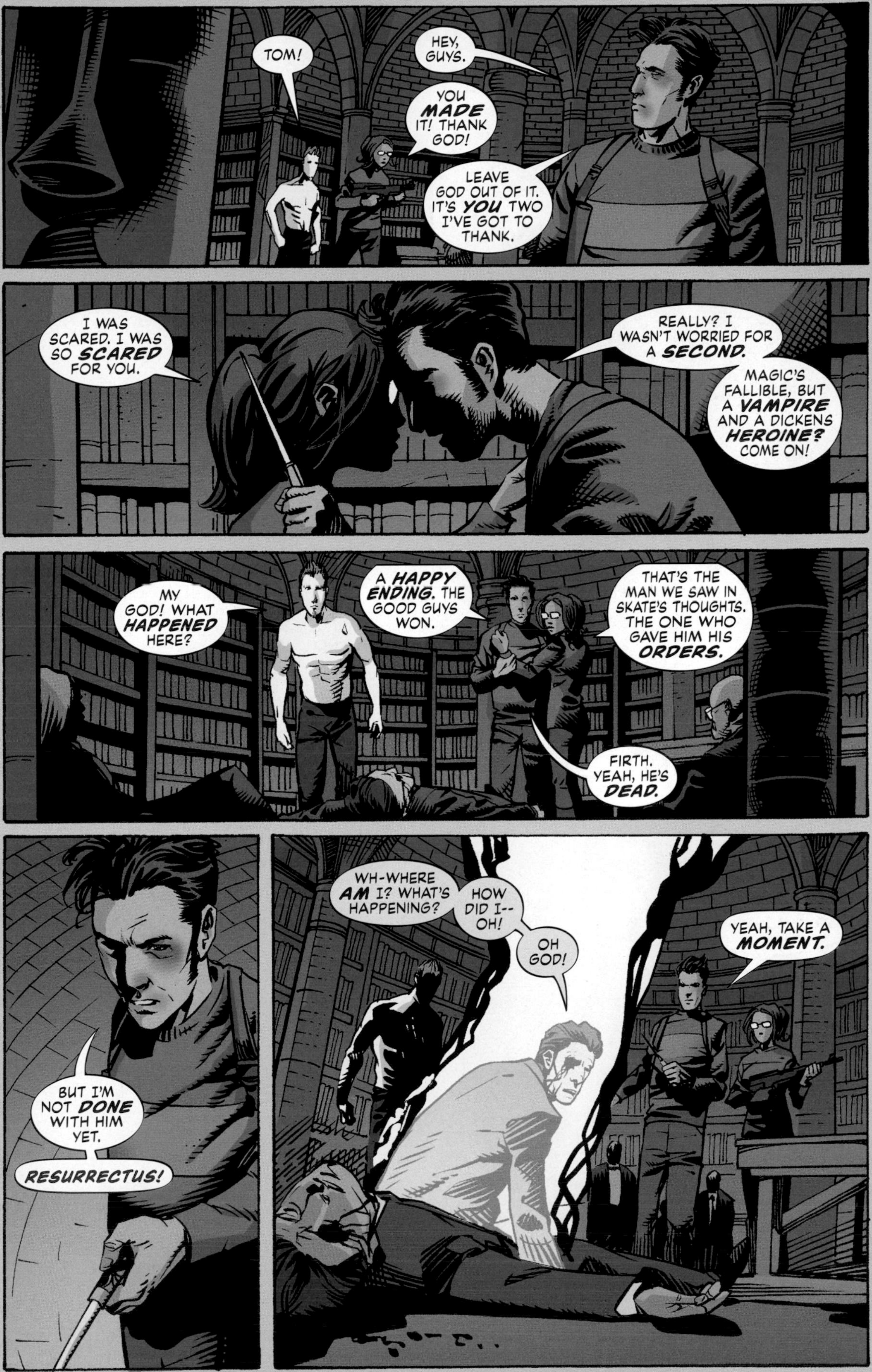
TOM!
HEY, GUYS.
YOU MADE IT! THANK GOD!
LEAVE GOD OUT OF IT. IT'S YOU TWO I'VE GOT TO THANK.
I WAS SCARED. I WAS SO SCARED FOR YOU.
REALLY? I WASN'T WORRIED FOR A SECOND.
MAGIC'S FALLIBLE, BUT A VAMPIRE AND A DICKENS HEROINE? COME ON!
MY GOD! WHAT HAPPENED HERE?
A HAPPY ENDING. THE GOOD GUYS WON.
THAT'S THE MAN WE SAW IN SKATE'S THOUGHTS. THE ONE WHO GAVE HIM HIS ORDERS.
FIRTH. YEAH, HE'S DEAD.
BUT I'M NOT DONE WITH HIM YET.
RESURRECTUS!
WH-WHERE AM I? WHAT'S HAPPENING?
HOW DID I-- OH!
OH GOD!
YEAH, TAKE A MOMENT.

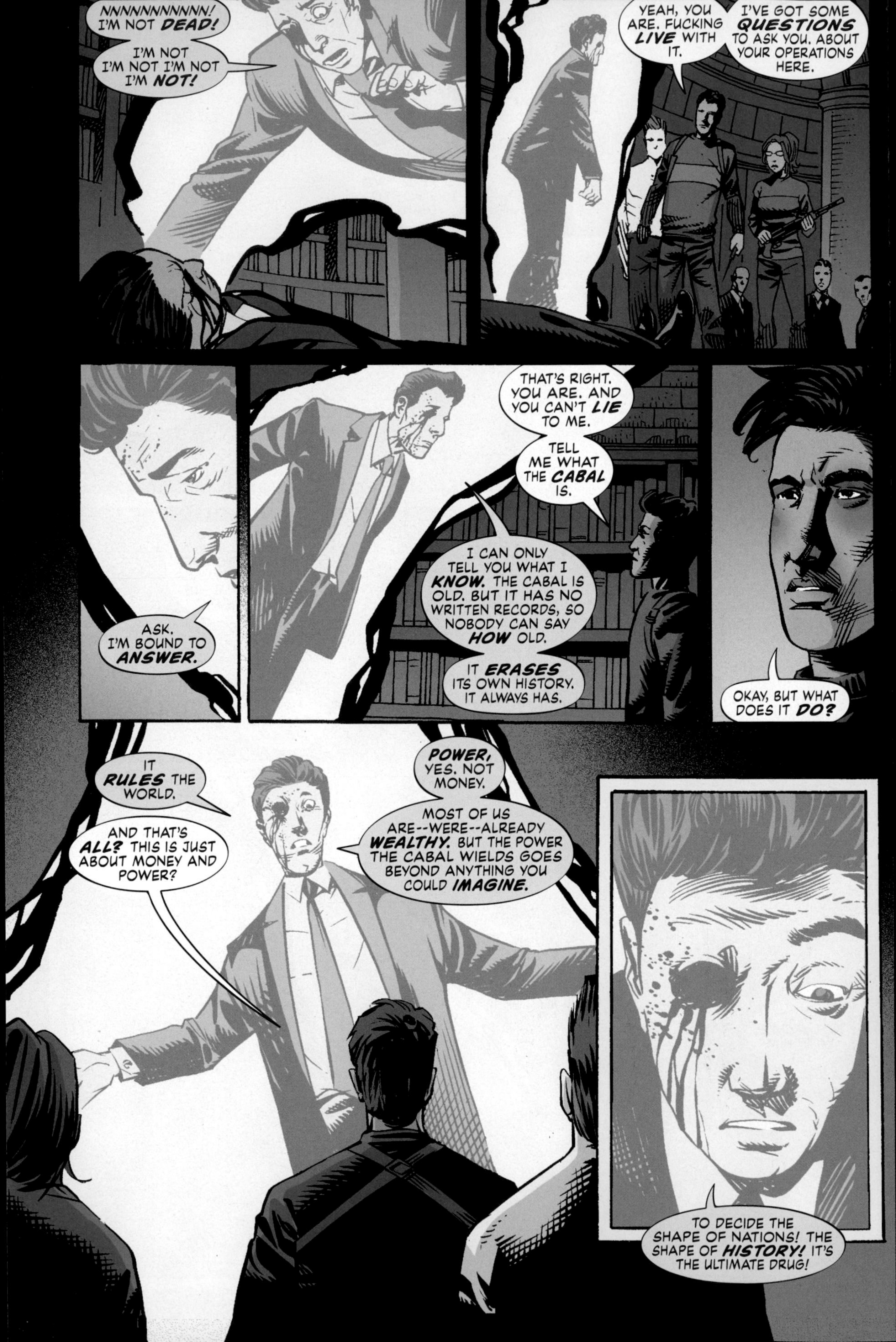
NNNNNNNNNN! I'M NOT DEAD!
I'M NOT I'M NOT I'M NOT I'M NOT!
YEAH, YOU ARE. FUCKING LIVE WITH IT.
I'VE GOT SOME QUESTIONS TO ASK YOU. ABOUT YOUR OPERATIONS HERE.
ASK. I'M BOUND TO ANSWER.
THAT'S RIGHT. YOU ARE. AND YOU CAN'T LIE TO ME.
TELL ME WHAT THE CABAL IS.
I CAN ONLY TELL YOU WHAT I KNOW. THE CABAL IS OLD. BUT IT HAS NO WRITTEN RECORDS, SO NOBODY CAN SAY HOW OLD.
IT ERASES ITS OWN HISTORY. IT ALWAYS HAS.
OKAY, BUT WHAT DOES IT DO?
IT RULES THE WORLD.
AND THAT'S ALL? THIS IS JUST ABOUT MONEY AND POWER?
POWER, YES. NOT MONEY.
MOST OF US ARE--WERE--ALREADY WEALTHY. BUT THE POWER THE CABAL WIELDS GOES BEYOND ANYTHING YOU COULD IMAGINE.
TO DECIDE THE SHAPE OF NATIONS! THE SHAPE OF HISTORY! IT'S THE ULTIMATE DRUG!

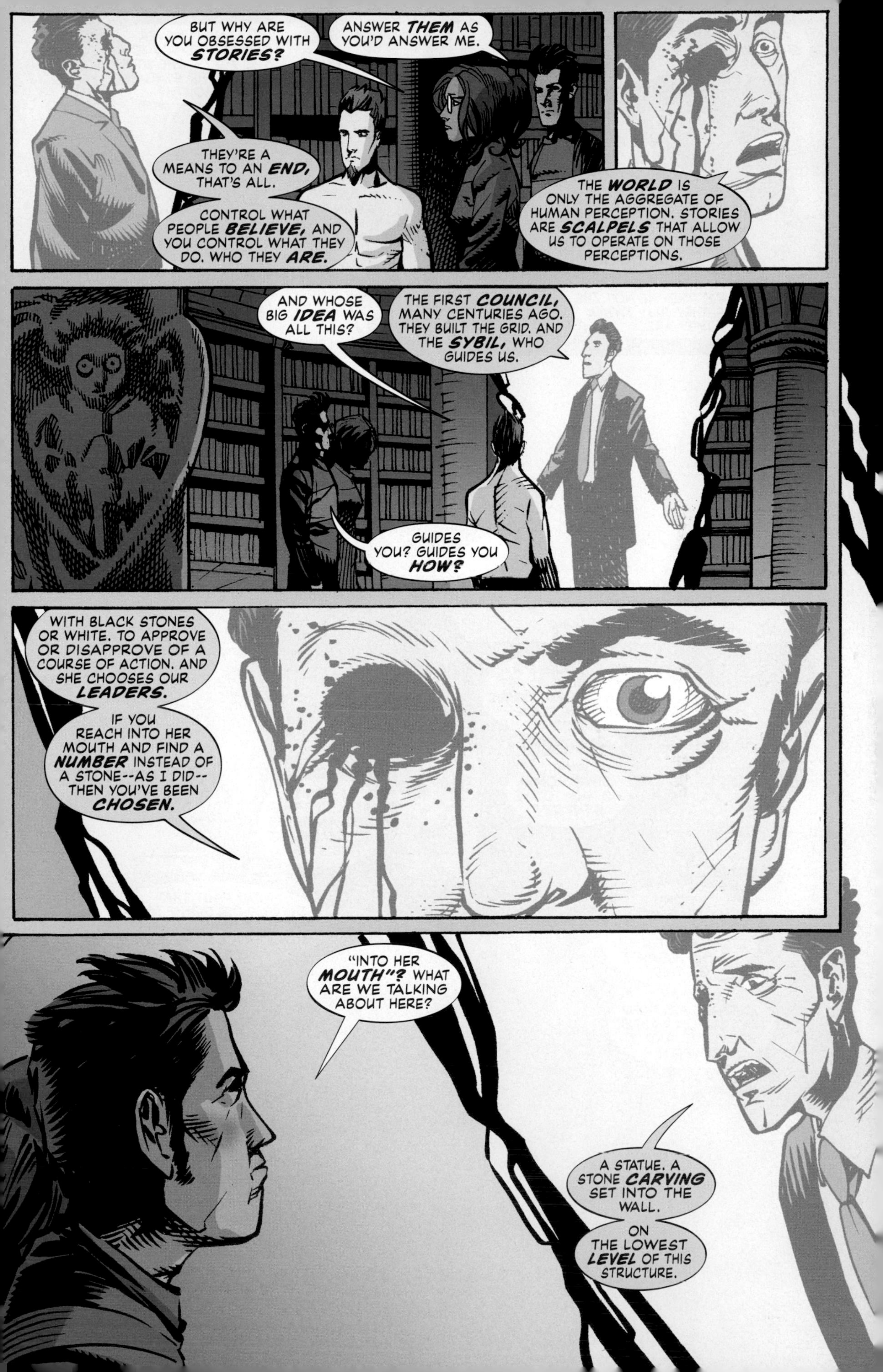
BUT WHY ARE YOU OBSESSED WITH STORIES?
ANSWER THEM AS YOU'D ANSWER ME.
THEY'RE A MEANS TO AN END, THAT'S ALL.
CONTROL WHAT PEOPLE BELIEVE, AND YOU CONTROL WHAT THEY DO. WHO THEY ARE.
THE WORLD IS ONLY THE AGGREGATE OF HUMAN PERCEPTION. STORIES ARE SCALPELS THAT ALLOW US TO OPERATE ON THOSE PERCEPTIONS.
AND WHOSE BIG IDEA WAS ALL THIS?
THE FIRST COUNCIL, MANY CENTURIES AGO. THEY BUILT THE GRID. AND THE SYBIL, WHO GUIDES US.
GUIDES YOU? GUIDES YOU HOW?
WITH BLACK STONES OR WHITE. TO APPROVE OR DISAPPROVE OF A COURSE OF ACTION. AND SHE CHOOSES OUR LEADERS.
IF YOU REACH INTO HER MOUTH AND FIND A NUMBER INSTEAD OF A STONE--AS I DID--THEN YOU'VE BEEN CHOSEN.
"INTO HER MOUTH"? WHAT ARE WE TALKING ABOUT HERE?
A STATUE. A STONE CARVING SET INTO THE WALL.
ON THE LOWEST LEVEL OF THIS STRUCTURE.

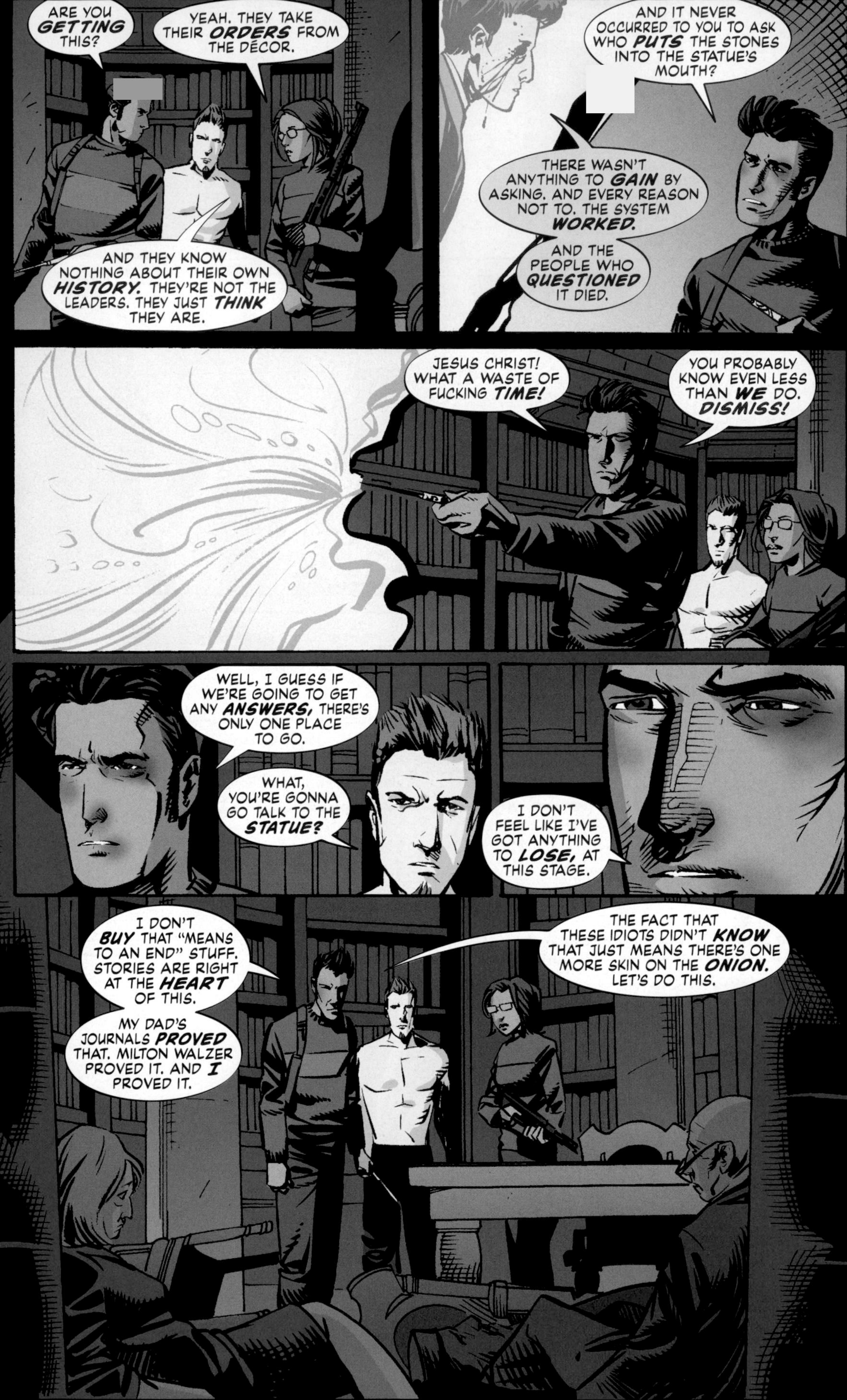
ARE YOU GETTING THIS?
YEAH. THEY TAKE THEIR ORDERS FROM THE DÉCOR.
AND THEY KNOW NOTHING ABOUT THEIR OWN HISTORY. THEY'RE NOT THE LEADERS. THEY JUST THINK THEY ARE.
AND IT NEVER OCCURRED TO YOU TO ASK WHO PUTS THE STONES INTO THE STATUE'S MOUTH?
THERE WASN'T ANYTHING TO GAIN BY ASKING. AND EVERY REASON NOT TO. THE SYSTEM WORKED.
AND THE PEOPLE WHO QUESTIONED IT DIED.
JESUS CHRIST! WHAT A WASTE OF FUCKING TIME!
YOU PROBABLY KNOW EVEN LESS THAN WE DO. DISMISS!
WELL, I GUESS IF WE'RE GOING TO GET ANY ANSWERS, THERE'S ONLY ONE PLACE TO GO.
WHAT, YOU'RE GONNA GO TALK TO THE STATUE?
I DON'T FEEL LIKE I'VE GOT ANYTHING TO LOSE, AT THIS STAGE.
I DON'T BUY THAT "MEANS TO AN END" STUFF. STORIES ARE RIGHT AT THE HEART OF THIS.
MY DAD'S JOURNALS PROVED THAT. MILTON WALZER PROVED IT. AND I PROVED IT.
THE FACT THAT THESE IDIOTS DIDN'T KNOW THAT JUST MEANS THERE'S ONE MORE SKIN ON THE ONION. LET'S DO THIS.

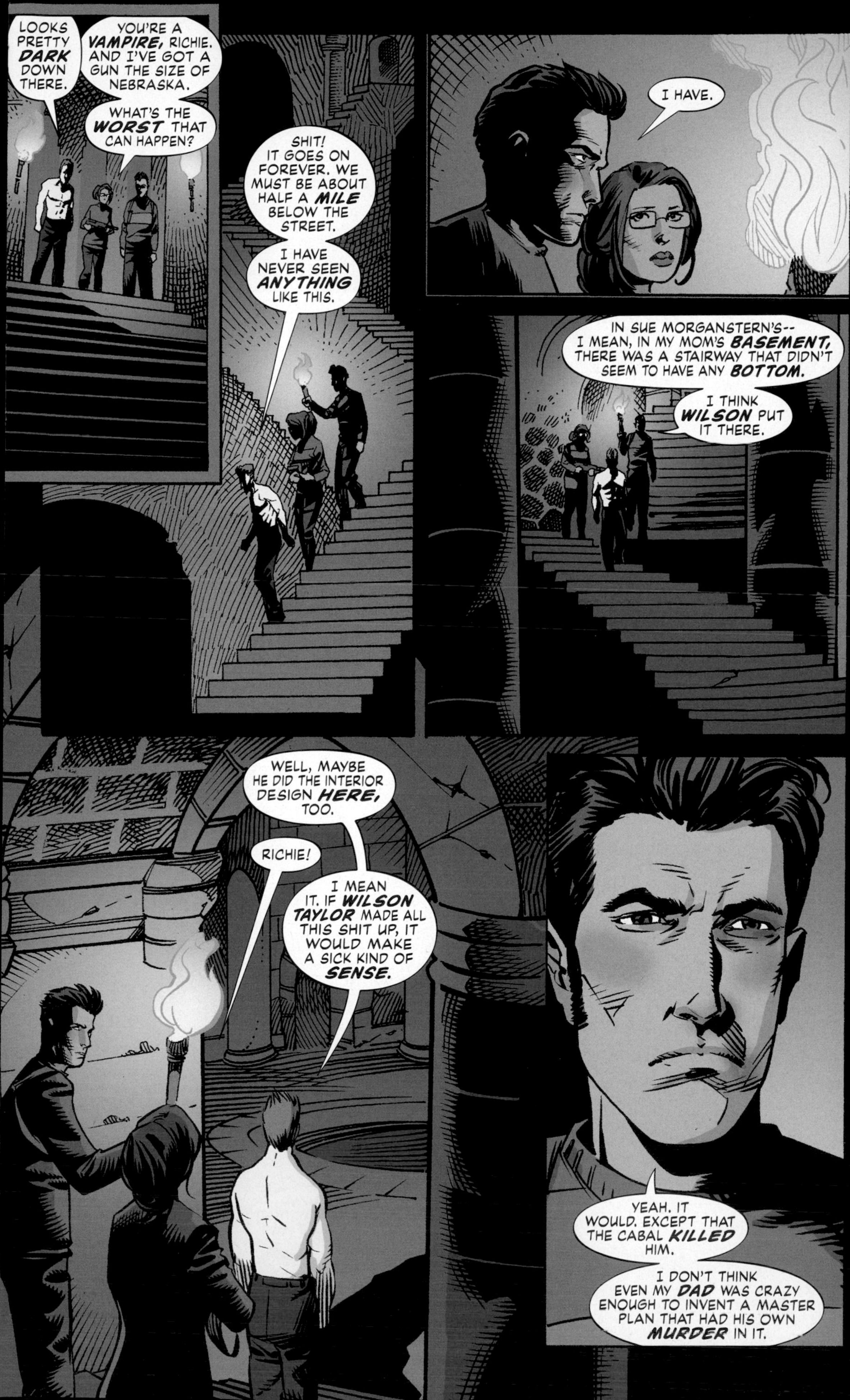
LOOKS PRETTY DARK DOWN THERE.
YOU'RE A VAMPIRE, RICHIE. AND I'VE GOT A GUN THE SIZE OF NEBRASKA.
WHAT'S THE WORST THAT CAN HAPPEN?
SHIT! IT GOES ON FOREVER. WE MUST BE ABOUT HALF A MILE BELOW THE STREET.
I HAVE NEVER SEEN ANYTHING LIKE THIS.
I HAVE.
IN SUE MORGANSTERN'S-- I MEAN, IN MY MOM'S BASEMENT, THERE WAS A STAIRWAY THAT DIDN'T SEEM TO HAVE ANY BOTTOM.
I THINK WILSON PUT IT THERE.
WELL, MAYBE HE DID THE INTERIOR DESIGN HERE, TOO.
RICHIE!
I MEAN IT. IF WILSON TAYLOR MADE ALL THIS SHIT UP, IT WOULD MAKE A SICK KIND OF SENSE.
YEAH. IT WOULD. EXCEPT THAT THE CABAL KILLED HIM.
I DON'T THINK EVEN MY DAD WAS CRAZY ENOUGH TO INVENT A MASTER PLAN THAT HAD HIS OWN MURDER IN IT.

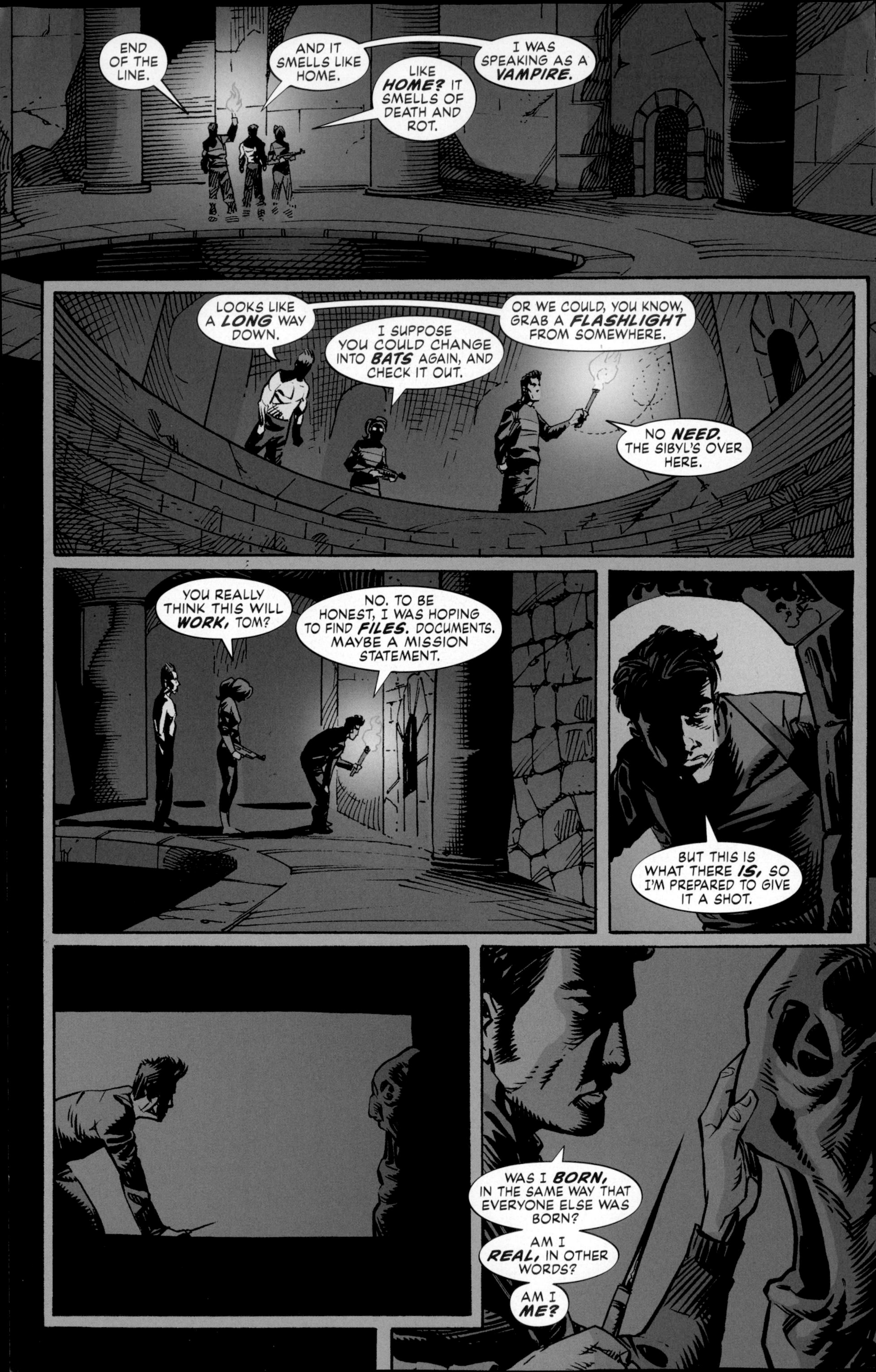
END OF THE LINE.
AND IT SMELLS LIKE HOME.
LIKE HOME? IT SMELLS OF DEATH AND ROT.
I WAS SPEAKING AS A VAMPIRE.
LOOKS LIKE A LONG WAY DOWN.
I SUPPOSE YOU COULD CHANGE INTO BATS AGAIN, AND CHECK IT OUT.
OR WE COULD, YOU KNOW, GRAB A FLASHLIGHT FROM SOMEWHERE.
NO NEED. THE SIBYL'S OVER HERE.
YOU REALLY THINK THIS WILL WORK, TOM?
NO. TO BE HONEST, I WAS HOPING TO FIND FILES. DOCUMENTS. MAYBE A MISSION STATEMENT.
BUT THIS IS WHAT THERE IS, SO I'M PREPARED TO GIVE IT A SHOT.
WAS I BORN, IN THE SAME WAY THAT EVERYONE ELSE WAS BORN?
AM I REAL, IN OTHER WORDS?
AM I ME?

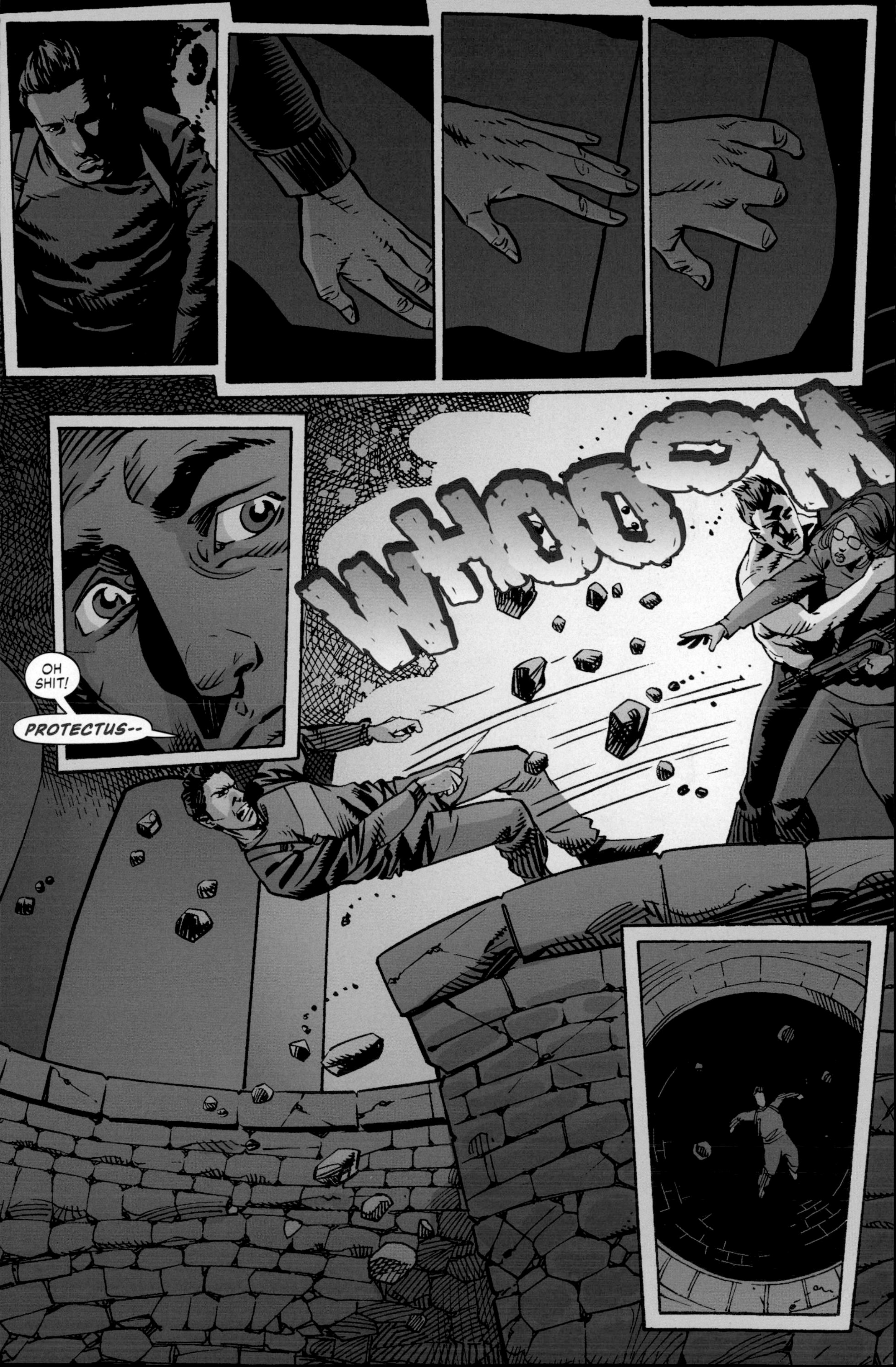
OH SHIT!
PROTECTUS--
WHOOOM

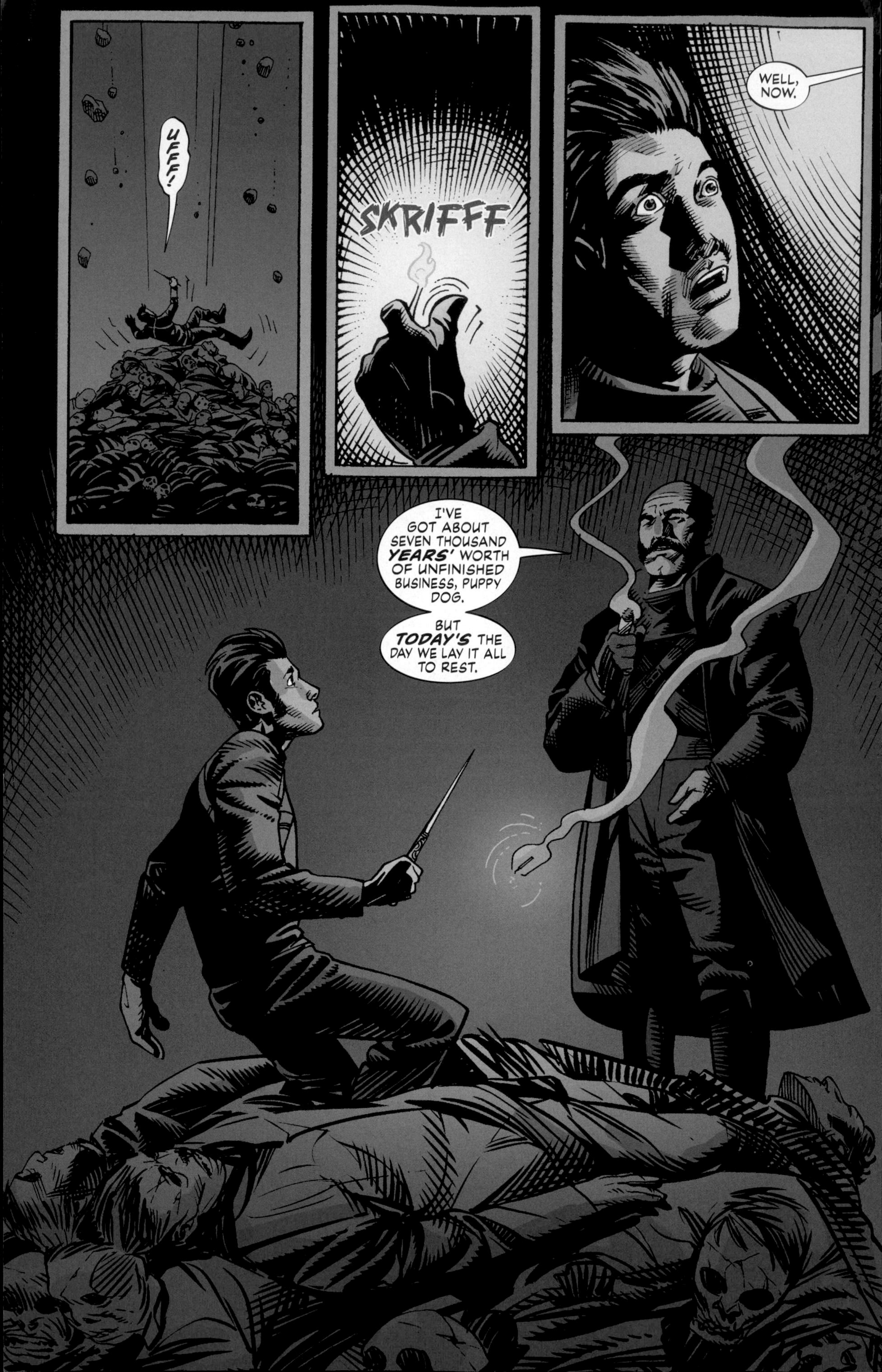
UFFF!
SKRIFFF
WELL, NOW.
I'VE GOT ABOUT SEVEN THOUSAND YEARS' WORTH OF UNFINISHED BUSINESS, PUPPY DOG.
BUT TODAY'S THE DAY WE LAY IT ALL TO REST.

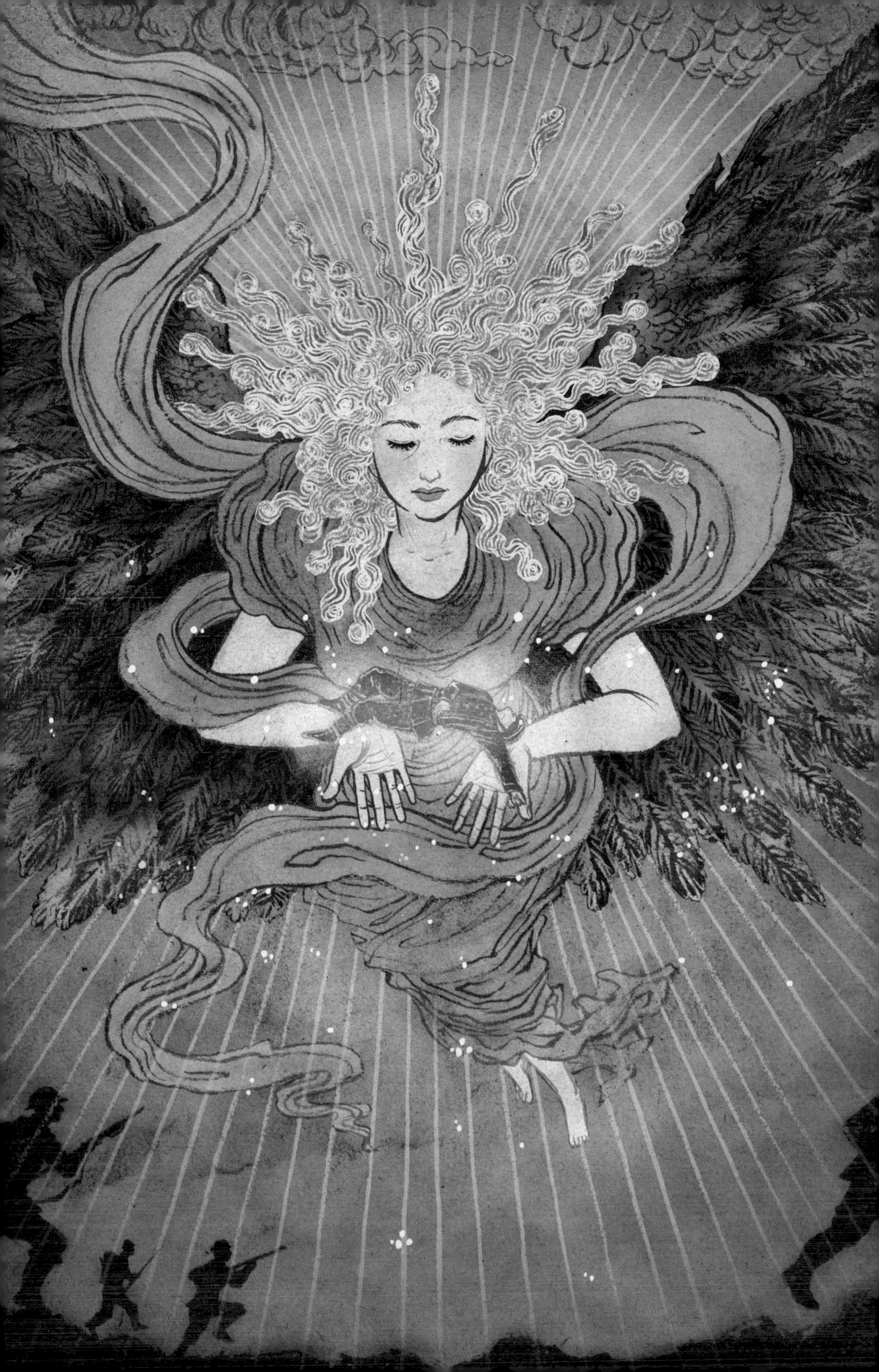

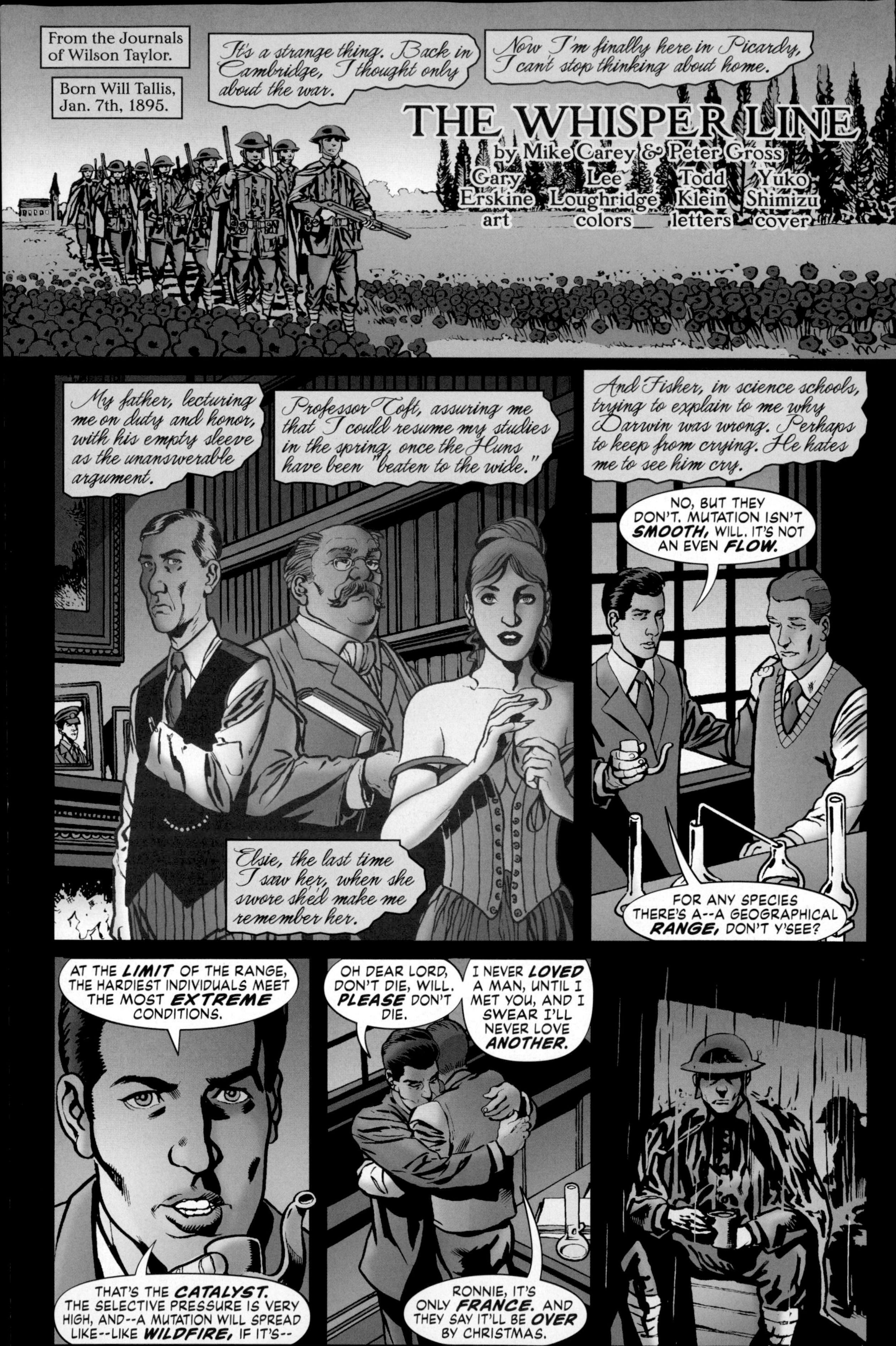
From the Journals of Wilson Taylor.
Born Will Tallis, Jan. 7th, 1895.
It's a strange thing. Back in Cambridge, I thought only about the war.
Now I'm finally here in Picardy, I can't stop thinking about home.
THE WHISPER LINE
by Mike Carey & Peter Gross
Gary Erskine art
Lee Loughridge colors
Todd Klein letters
Yuko Shimizu cover
My father, lecturing me on duty and honor, with his empty sleeve as the unanswerable argument.
Professor Toft, assuring me that I could resume my studies in the spring, once the Huns have been "beaten to the wide."
Elsie, the last time I saw her, when she swore she'd make me remember her.
And Fisher, in science schools, trying to explain to me why Darwin was wrong. Perhaps to keep from crying. He hates me to see him cry.
NO, BUT THEY DON'T. MUTATION ISN'T SMOOTH, WILL. IT'S NOT AN EVEN FLOW.
FOR ANY SPECIES THERE'S A--A GEOGRAPHICAL RANGE, DON'T Y'SEE?
AT THE LIMIT OF THE RANGE, THE HARDIEST INDIVIDUALS MEET THE MOST EXTREME CONDITIONS.
THAT'S THE CATALYST. THE SELECTIVE PRESSURE IS VERY HIGH, AND--A MUTATION WILL SPREAD LIKE--LIKE WILDFIRE, IF IT'S--
OH DEAR LORD, DON'T DIE, WILL. PLEASE DON'T DIE.
I NEVER LOVED A MAN, UNTIL I MET YOU, AND I SWEAR I'LL NEVER LOVE ANOTHER.
RONNIE, IT'S ONLY FRANCE. AND THEY SAY IT'LL BE OVER BY CHRISTMAS.

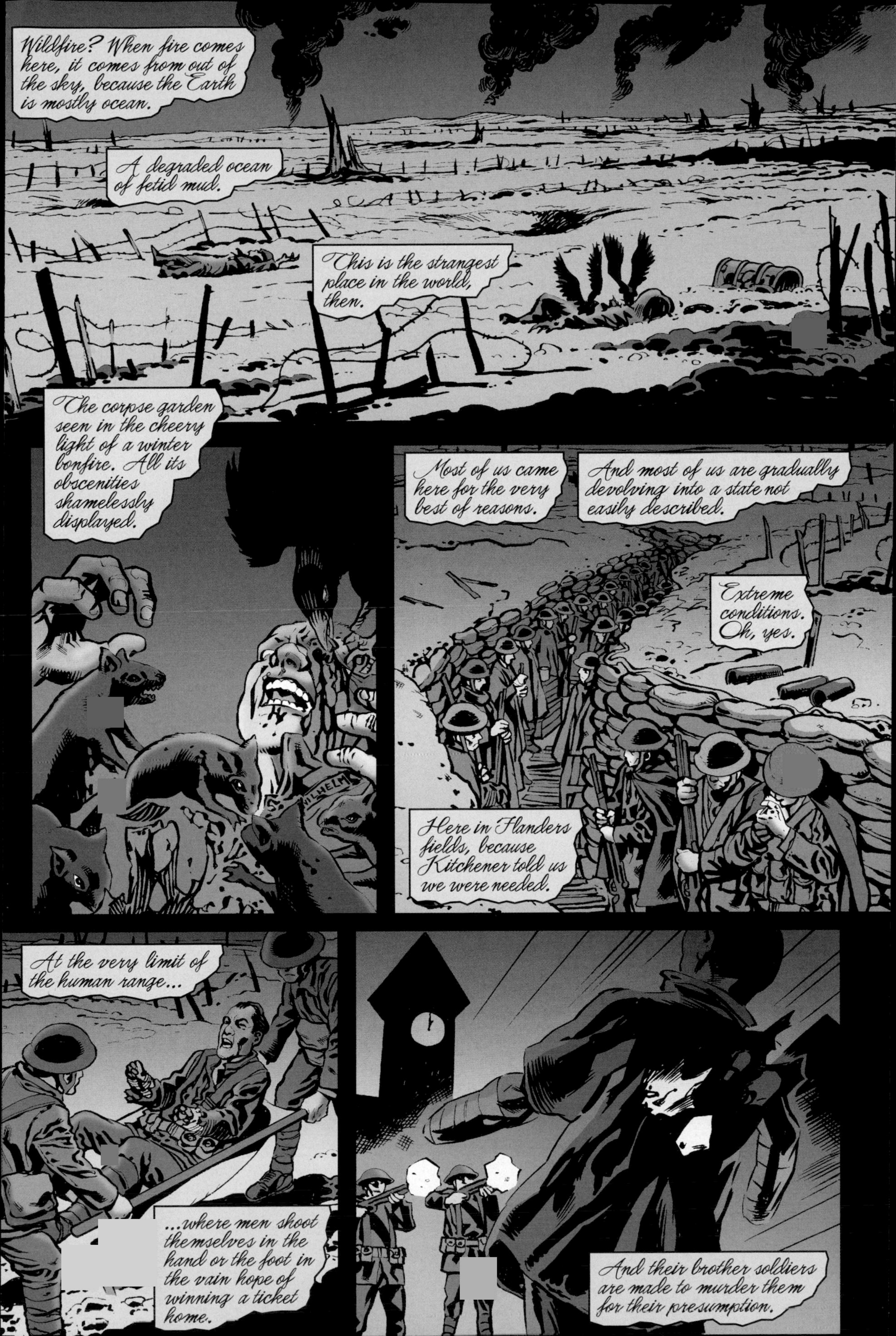
Wildfire? When fire comes here, it comes from out of the sky, because the Earth is mostly ocean.
A degraded ocean of fetid mud.
This is the strangest place in the world, then.
The corpse garden seen in the cheery light of a winter bonfire. All its obscenities shamelessly displayed.
WILHELM
Most of us came here for the very best of reasons.
And most of us are gradually devolving into a state not easily described.
Extreme conditions. Oh, yes.
Here in Flanders fields, because Kitchener told us we were needed.
At the very limit of the human range...
...where men shoot themselves in the hand or the foot in the vain hope of winning a ticket home.
And their brother soldiers are made to murder them for their presumption.

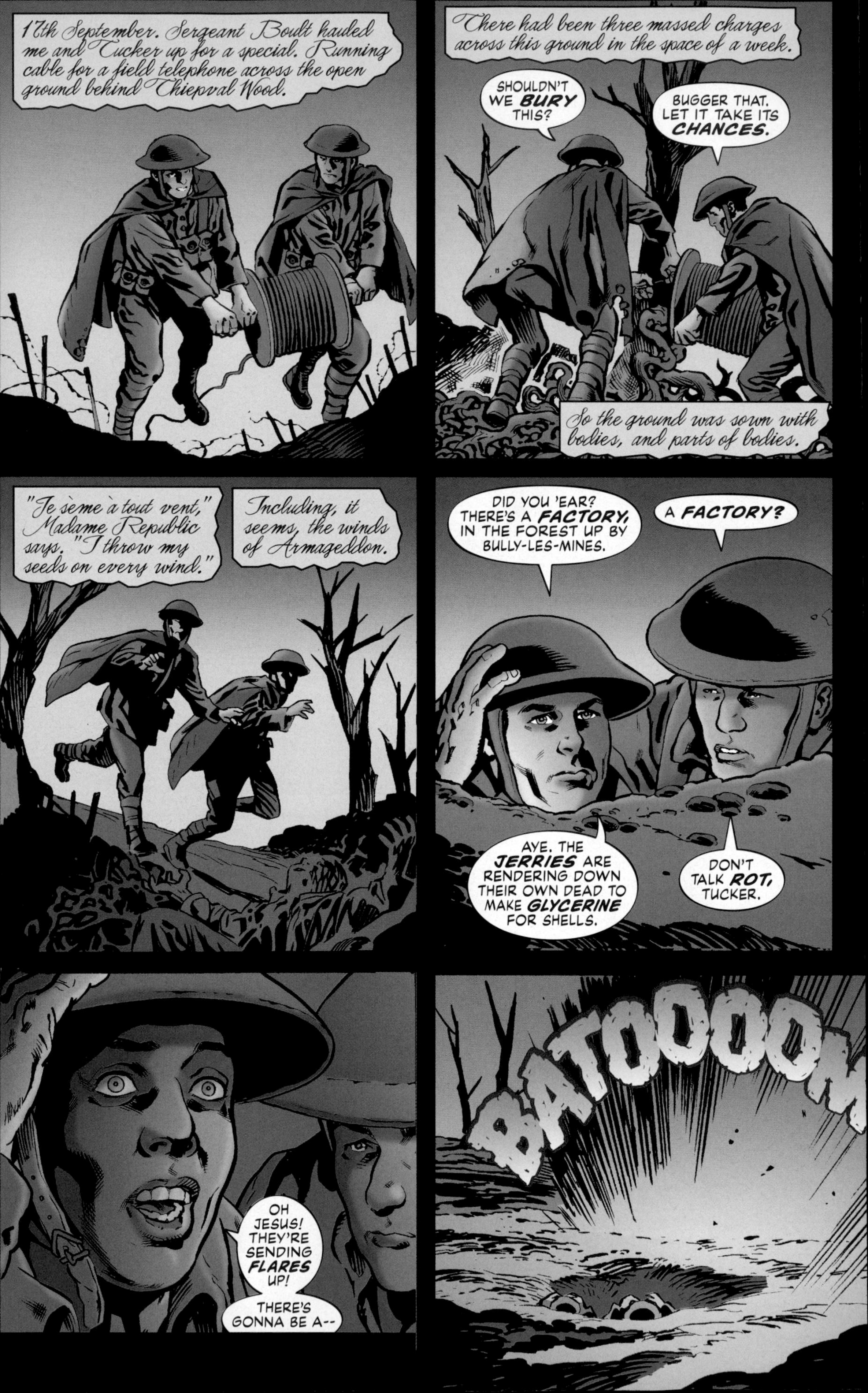
17th September. Sergeant Boult hauled me and Tucker up for a special. Running cable for a field telephone across the open ground behind Thiepval Wood.
There had been three massed charges across this ground in the space of a week.
SHOULDN'T WE BURY THIS?
BUGGER THAT. LET IT TAKE ITS CHANCES.
So the ground was sown with bodies, and parts of bodies.
"Je sème à tout vent," Madame Republic says. "I throw my seeds on every wind."
Including, it seems, the winds of Armageddon.
DID YOU 'EAR? THERE'S A FACTORY, IN THE FOREST UP BY BULLY-LES-MINES.
A FACTORY?
AYE. THE JERRIES ARE RENDERING DOWN THEIR OWN DEAD TO MAKE GLYCERINE FOR SHELLS.
DON'T TALK ROT, TUCKER.
OH JESUS! THEY'RE SENDING FLARES UP!
THERE'S GONNA BE A--
BATOOOOOM

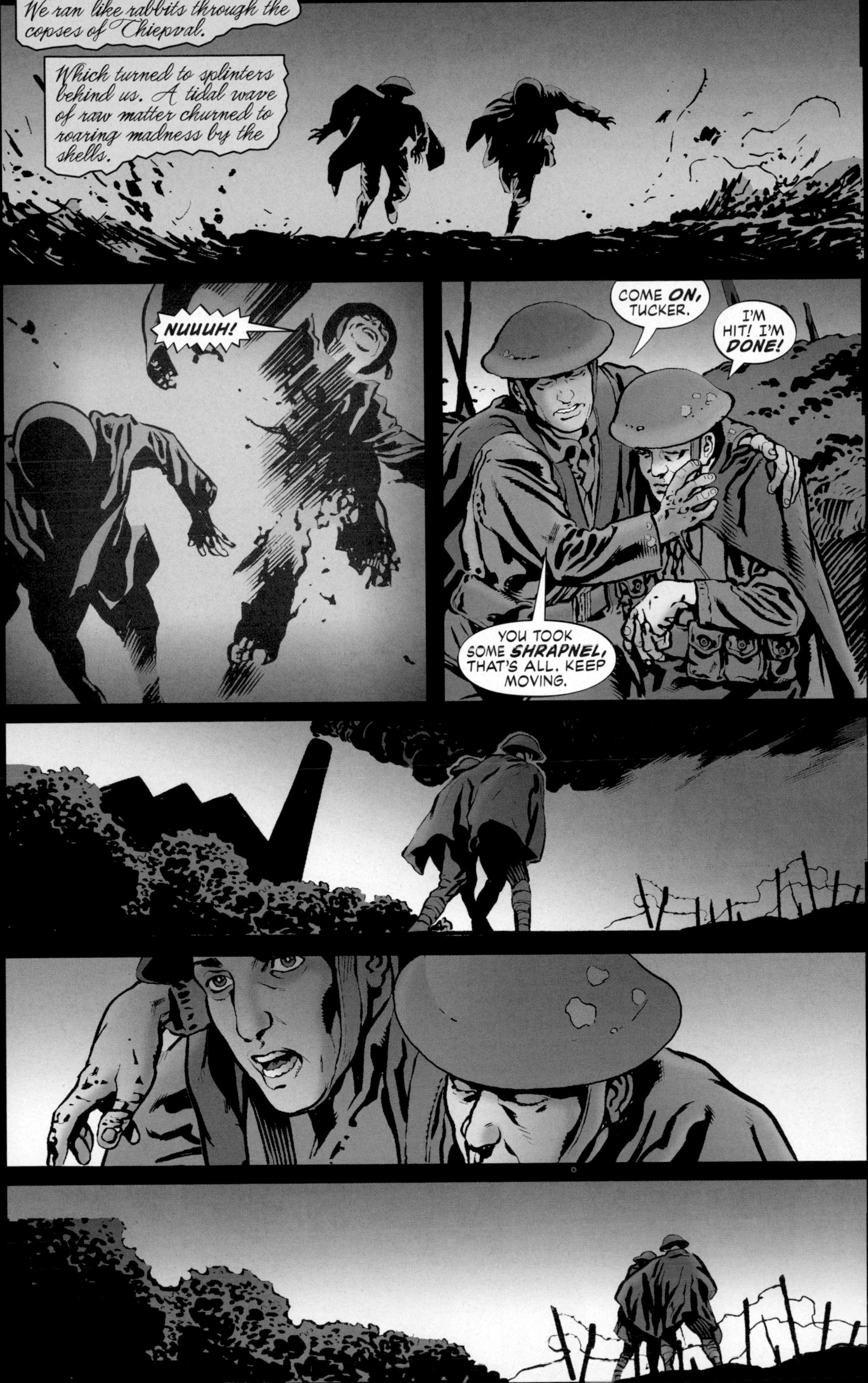

We ran like rabbits through the copses of Thiepval.
Which turned to splinters behind us. A tidal wave of raw matter churned to roaring madness by the shells.
NUUUH!
COME ON, TUCKER.
I'M HIT! I'M DONE!
YOU TOOK SOME SHRAPNEL, THAT'S ALL. KEEP MOVING.

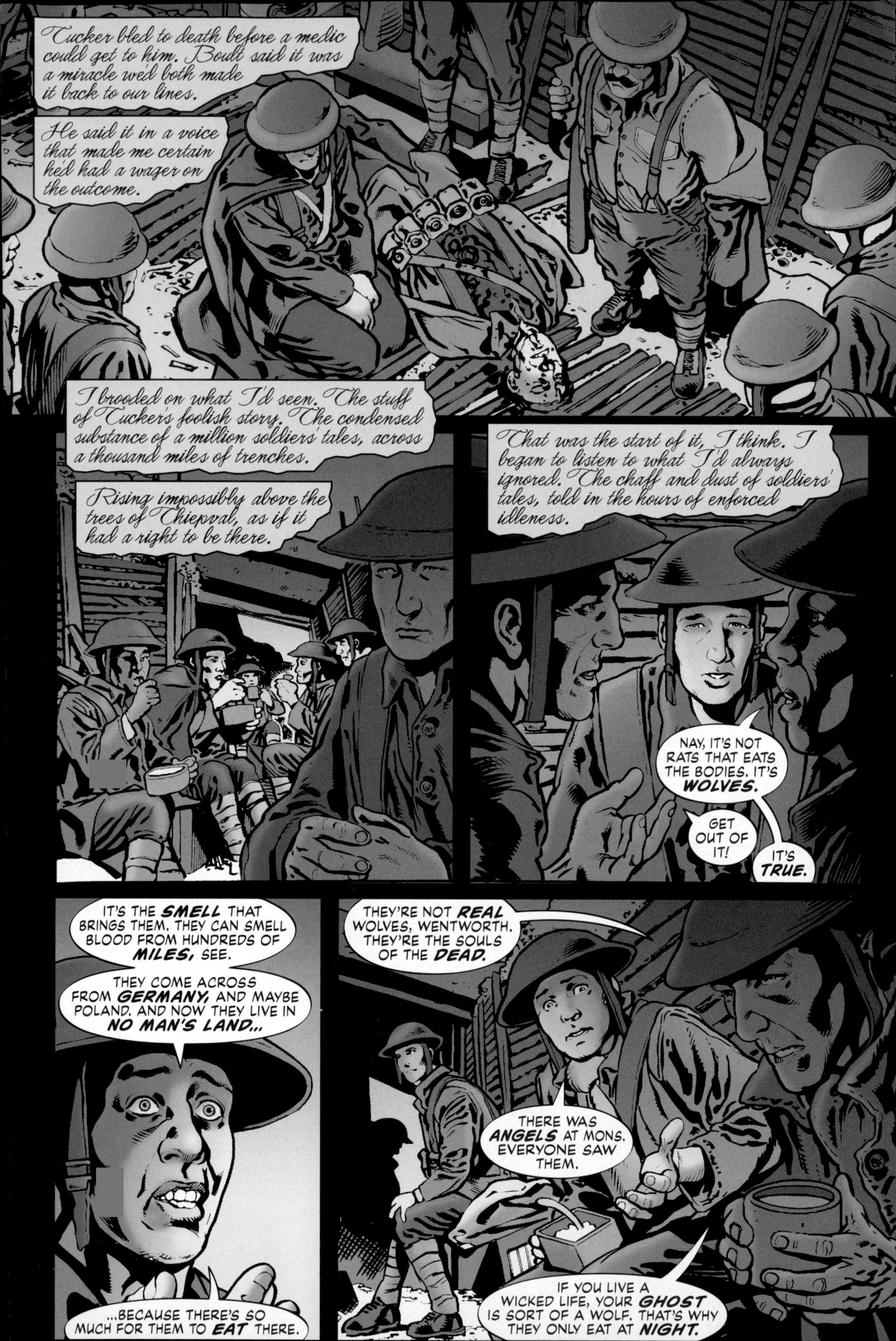
Tucker bled to death before a medic could get to him. Boult said it was a miracle we'd both made it back to our lines.
He said it in a voice that made me certain he'd had a wager on the outcome.
I brooded on what I'd seen. The stuff of Tucker's foolish story. The condensed substance of a million soldiers' tales, across a thousand miles of trenches.
Rising impossibly above the trees of Thiepval, as if it had a right to be there.
That was the start of it, I think. I began to listen to what I'd always ignored. The chaff and dust of soldiers' tales, told in the hours of enforced idleness.
NAY, IT'S NOT RATS THAT EATS THE BODIES. IT'S WOLVES.
GET OUT OF IT!
IT'S TRUE.
IT'S THE SMELL THAT BRINGS THEM. THEY CAN SMELL BLOOD FROM HUNDREDS OF MILES, SEE.
THEY COME ACROSS FROM GERMANY, AND MAYBE POLAND. AND NOW THEY LIVE IN NO MAN'S LAND...
...BECAUSE THERE'S SO MUCH FOR THEM TO EAT THERE.
THEY'RE NOT REAL WOLVES, WENTWORTH. THEY'RE THE SOULS OF THE DEAD.
THERE WAS ANGELS AT MONS. EVERYONE SAW THEM.
IF YOU LIVE A WICKED LIFE, YOUR GHOST IS SORT OF A WOLF. THAT'S WHY THEY ONLY EAT AT NIGHT.

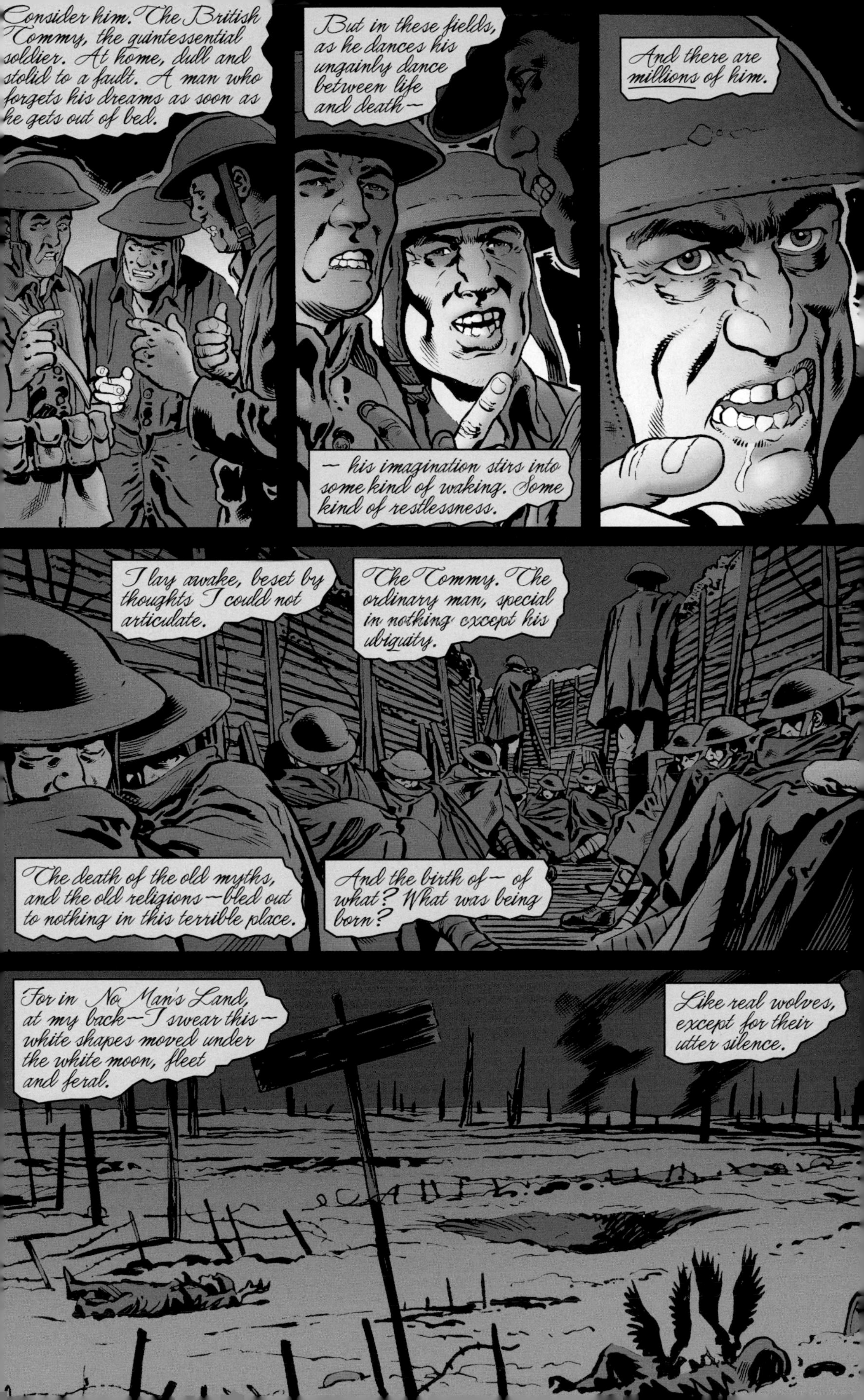
Consider him. The British Tommy, the quintessential soldier. At home, dull and stolid to a fault. A man who forgets his dreams as soon as he gets out of bed.
But in these fields, as he dances his ungainly dance between life and death—
— his imagination stirs into some kind of waking. Some kind of restlessness.
And there are millions of him.
I lay awake, beset by thoughts I could not articulate.
The Tommy. The ordinary man, special in nothing except his ubiquity.
The death of the old myths, and the old religions—bled out to nothing in this terrible place.
And the birth of— of what? What was being born?
For in No Man's Land, at my back—I swear this—white shapes moved under the white moon, fleet and feral.
Like real wolves, except for their utter silence.

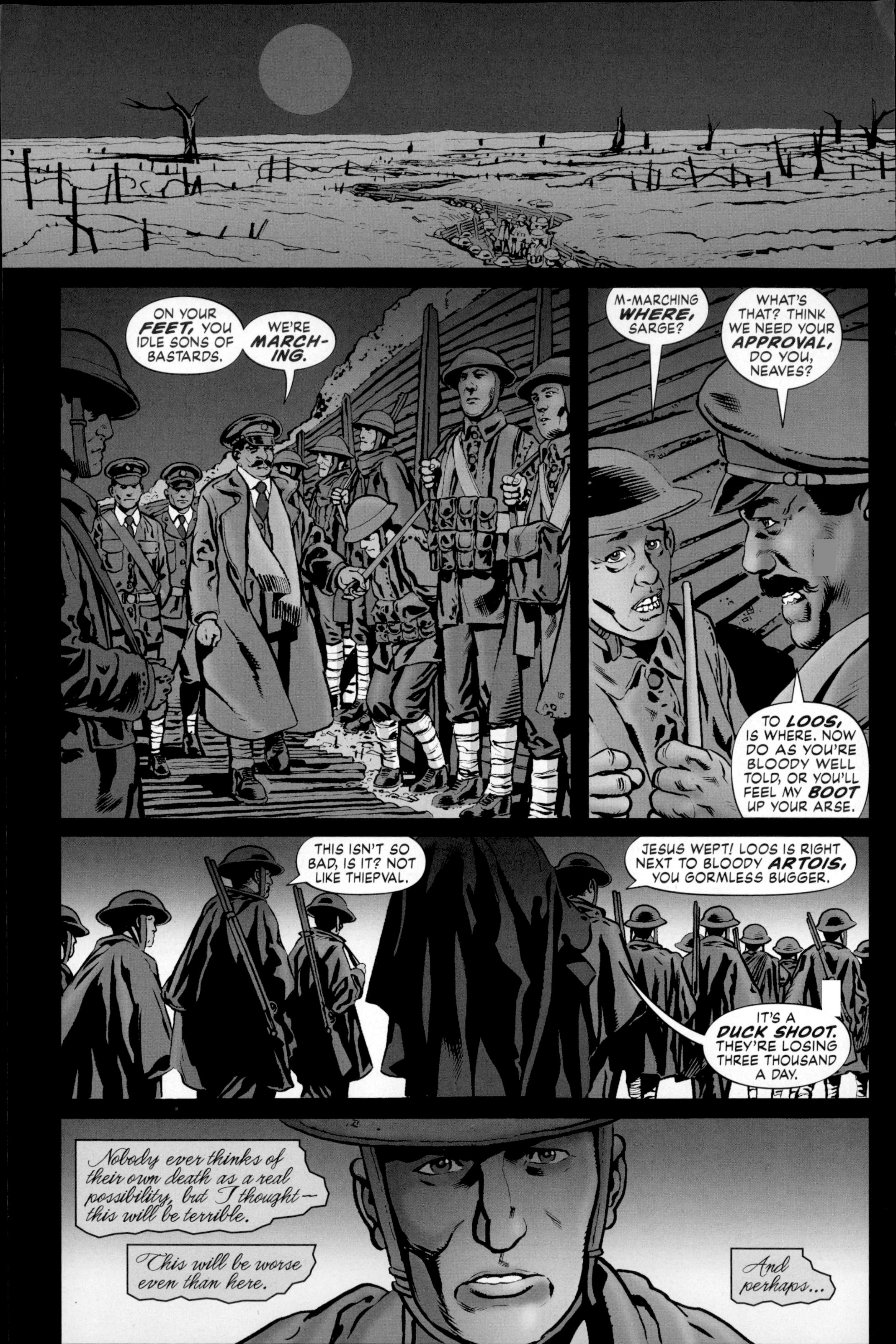
ON YOUR FEET, YOU IDLE SONS OF BASTARDS.
WE'RE MARCHING.
M-MARCHING WHERE, SARGE?
WHAT'S THAT? THINK WE NEED YOUR APPROVAL, DO YOU, NEAVES?
TO LOOS, IS WHERE. NOW DO AS YOU'RE BLOODY WELL TOLD, OR YOU'LL FEEL MY BOOT UP YOUR ARSE.
THIS ISN'T SO BAD, IS IT? NOT LIKE THIEPVAL.
JESUS WEPT! LOOS IS RIGHT NEXT TO BLOODY ARTOIS, YOU GORMLESS BUGGER.
IT'S A DUCK SHOOT. THEY'RE LOSING THREE THOUSAND A DAY.
Nobody ever thinks of their own death as a real possibility, but I thought— this will be terrible.
This will be worse even than here.
And perhaps...

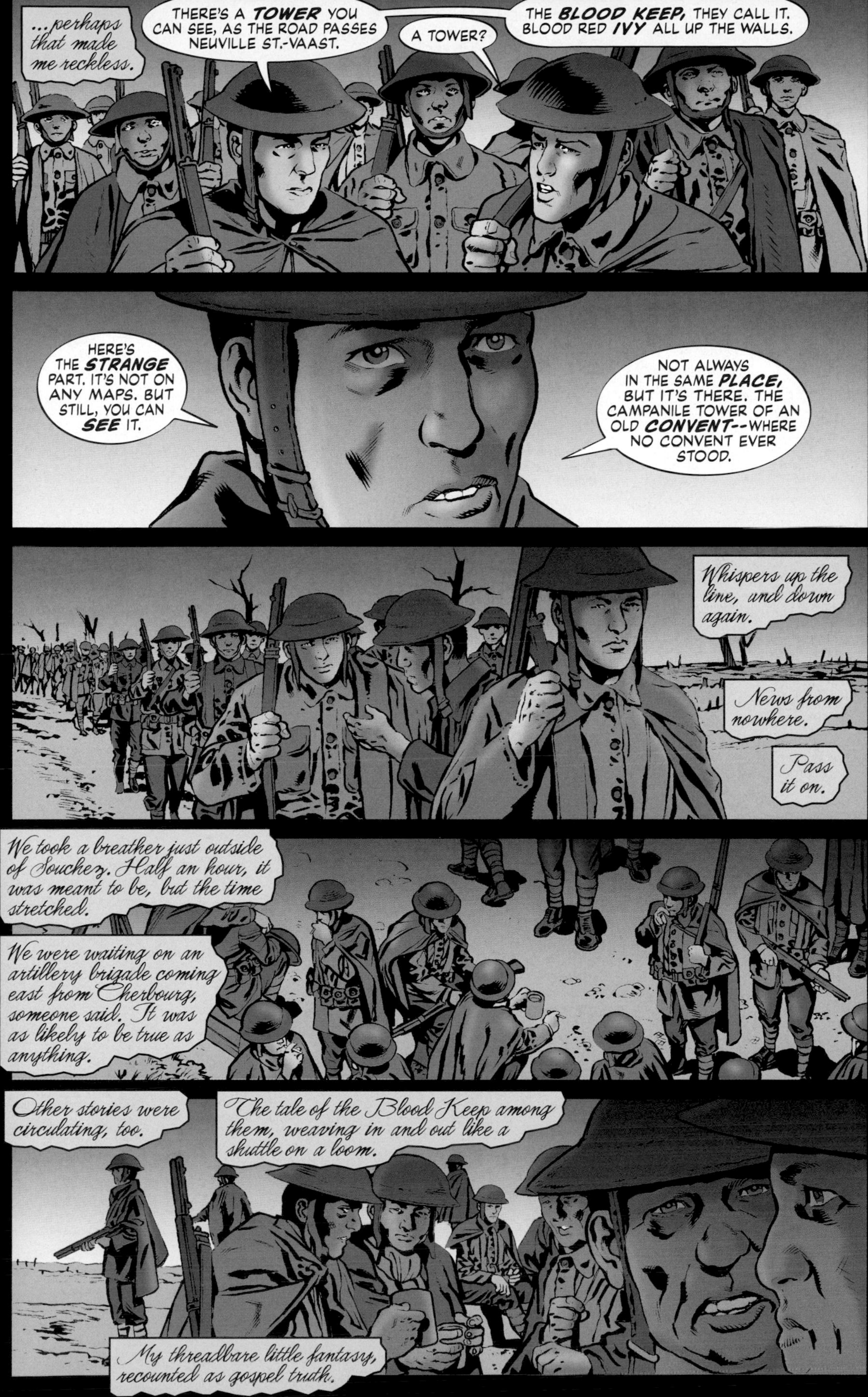
...perhaps that made me reckless.
THERE'S A TOWER YOU CAN SEE, AS THE ROAD PASSES NEUVILLE ST.-VAAST.
A TOWER?
THE BLOOD KEEP, THEY CALL IT. BLOOD RED IVY ALL UP THE WALLS.
HERE'S THE STRANGE PART. IT'S NOT ON ANY MAPS. BUT STILL, YOU CAN SEE IT.
NOT ALWAYS IN THE SAME PLACE, BUT IT'S THERE. THE CAMPANILE TOWER OF AN OLD CONVENT--WHERE NO CONVENT EVER STOOD.
Whispers up the line, and down again.
News from nowhere.
Pass it on.
We took a breather just outside of Souchez. Half an hour, it was meant to be, but the time stretched.
We were waiting on an artillery brigade coming east from Cherbourg, someone said. It was as likely to be true as anything.
Other stories were circulating, too.
The tale of the Blood Keep among them, weaving in and out like a shuttle on a loom.
My threadbare little fantasy, recounted as gospel truth.

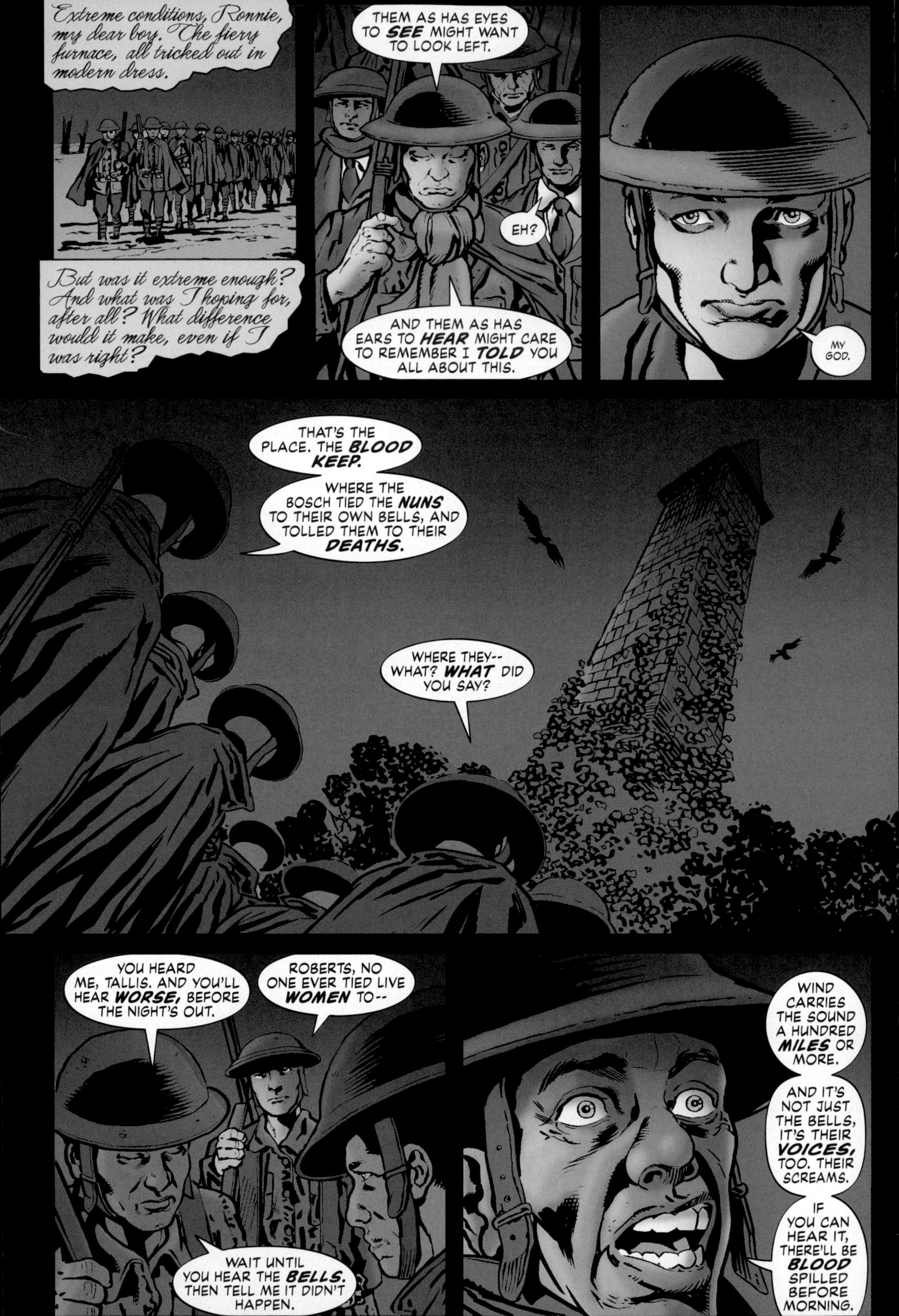

Extreme conditions, Ronnie, my dear boy. The fiery furnace, all tricked out in modern dress.
But was it extreme enough? And what was I hoping for, after all? What difference would it make, even if I was right?
THEM AS HAS EYES TO SEE MIGHT WANT TO LOOK LEFT.
EH?
AND THEM AS HAS EARS TO HEAR MIGHT CARE TO REMEMBER I TOLD YOU ALL ABOUT THIS.
MY GOD.
THAT'S THE PLACE. THE BLOOD KEEP.
WHERE THE BOSCH TIED THE NUNS TO THEIR OWN BELLS, AND TOLLED THEM TO THEIR DEATHS.
WHERE THEY-- WHAT? WHAT DID YOU SAY?
YOU HEARD ME, TALLIS. AND YOU'LL HEAR WORSE, BEFORE THE NIGHT'S OUT.
ROBERTS, NO ONE EVER TIED LIVE WOMEN TO--
WAIT UNTIL YOU HEAR THE BELLS. THEN TELL ME IT DIDN'T HAPPEN.
WIND CARRIES THE SOUND A HUNDRED MILES OR MORE.
AND IT'S NOT JUST THE BELLS, IT'S THEIR VOICES, TOO. THEIR SCREAMS.
IF YOU CAN HEAR IT, THERE'LL BE BLOOD SPILLED BEFORE MORNING.

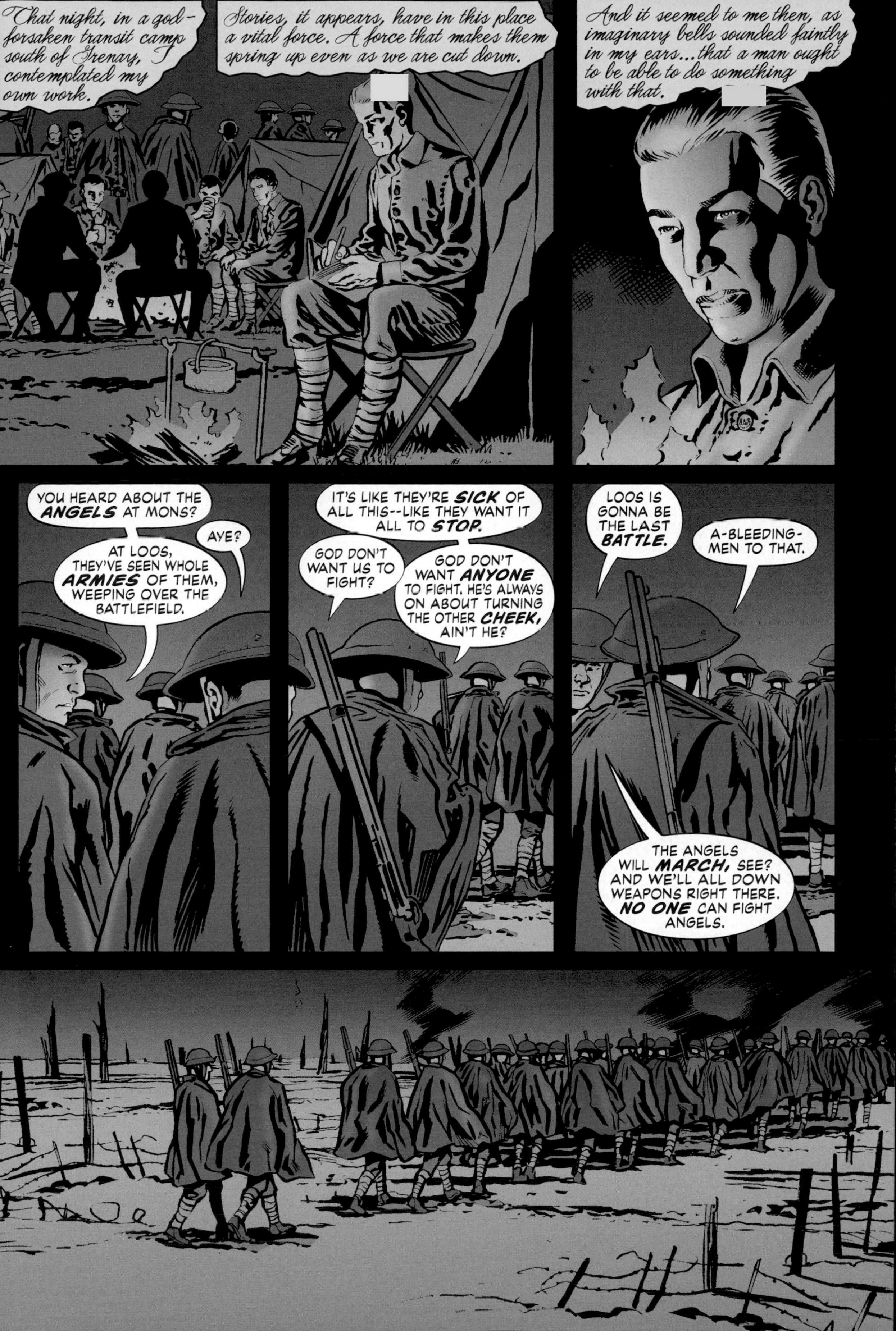
That night, in a god-forsaken transit camp south of Grenay, I contemplated my own work.
Stories, it appears, have in this place a vital force. A force that makes them spring up even as we are cut down.
And it seemed to me then, as imaginary bells sounded faintly in my ears... that a man ought to be able to do something with that.
YOU HEARD ABOUT THE ANGELS AT MONS?
AYE?
AT LOOS, THEY'VE SEEN WHOLE ARMIES OF THEM, WEEPING OVER THE BATTLEFIELD.
IT'S LIKE THEY'RE SICK OF ALL THIS--LIKE THEY WANT IT ALL TO STOP.
GOD DON'T WANT US TO FIGHT?
GOD DON'T WANT ANYONE TO FIGHT. HE'S ALWAYS ON ABOUT TURNING THE OTHER CHEEK, AIN'T HE?
LOOS IS GONNA BE THE LAST BATTLE.
A-BLEEDING-MEN TO THAT.
THE ANGELS WILL MARCH, SEE? AND WE'LL ALL DOWN WEAPONS RIGHT THERE. NO ONE CAN FIGHT ANGELS.

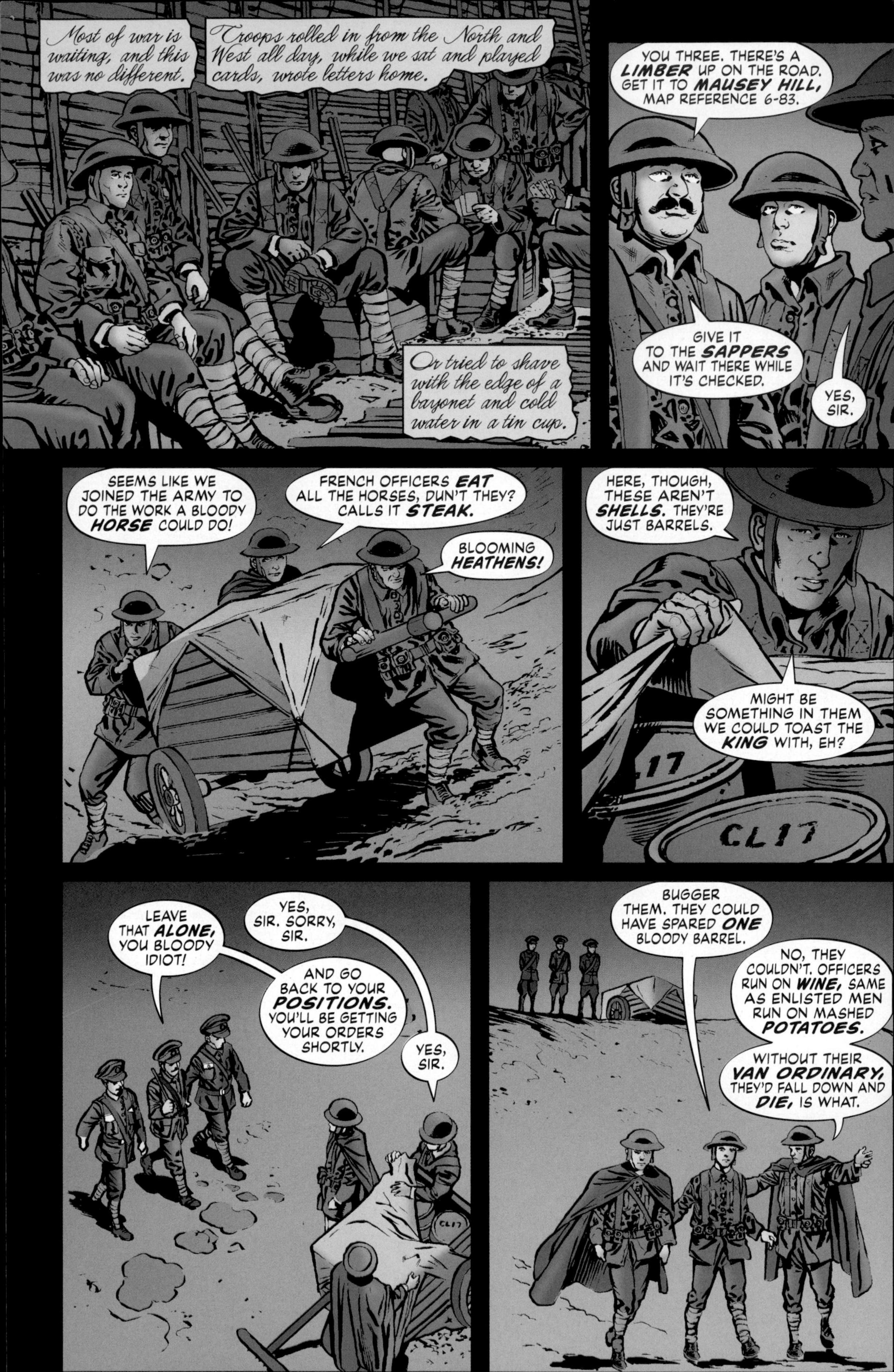
Most of war is waiting, and this was no different.
Troops rolled in from the North and West all day, while we sat and played cards, wrote letters home.
Or tried to shave with the edge of a bayonet and cold water in a tin cup.
YOU THREE. THERE'S A LIMBER UP ON THE ROAD. GET IT TO MAUSEY HILL, MAP REFERENCE 6-83.
GIVE IT TO THE SAPPERS AND WAIT THERE WHILE IT'S CHECKED.
YES, SIR.
SEEMS LIKE WE JOINED THE ARMY TO DO THE WORK A BLOODY HORSE COULD DO!
FRENCH OFFICERS EAT ALL THE HORSES, DUN'T THEY? CALLS IT STEAK.
BLOOMING HEATHENS!
HERE, THOUGH, THESE AREN'T SHELLS. THEY'RE JUST BARRELS.
MIGHT BE SOMETHING IN THEM WE COULD TOAST THE KING WITH, EH?
CL17
CL17
LEAVE THAT ALONE, YOU BLOODY IDIOT!
YES, SIR. SORRY, SIR.
AND GO BACK TO YOUR POSITIONS. YOU'LL BE GETTING YOUR ORDERS SHORTLY.
YES, SIR.
CL17
BUGGER THEM. THEY COULD HAVE SPARED ONE BLOODY BARREL.
NO, THEY COULDN'T. OFFICERS RUN ON WINE, SAME AS ENLISTED MEN RUN ON MASHED POTATOES.
WITHOUT THEIR VAN ORDINARY, THEY'D FALL DOWN AND DIE, IS WHAT.

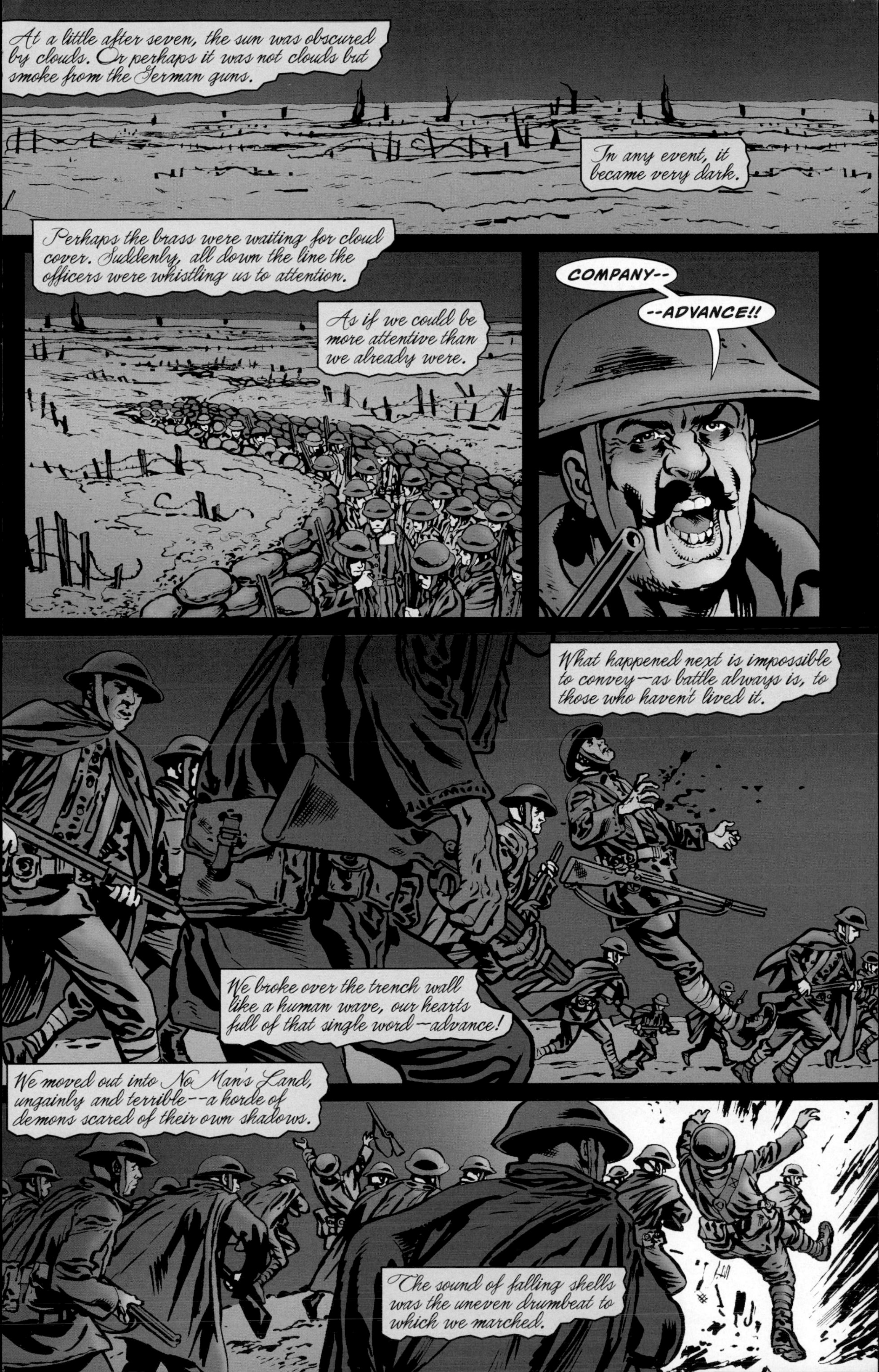
At a little after seven, the sun was obscured by clouds. Or perhaps it was not clouds but smoke from the German guns.
In any event, it became very dark.
Perhaps the brass were waiting for cloud cover. Suddenly, all down the line the officers were whistling us to attention.
As if we could be more attentive than we already were.
COMPANY--
--ADVANCE!!
What happened next is impossible to convey--as battle always is, to those who haven't lived it.
We broke over the trench wall like a human wave, our hearts full of that single word--advance!
We moved out into No Man's Land, ungainly and terrible--a horde of demons scared of their own shadows.
The sound of falling shells was the uneven drumbeat to which we marched.

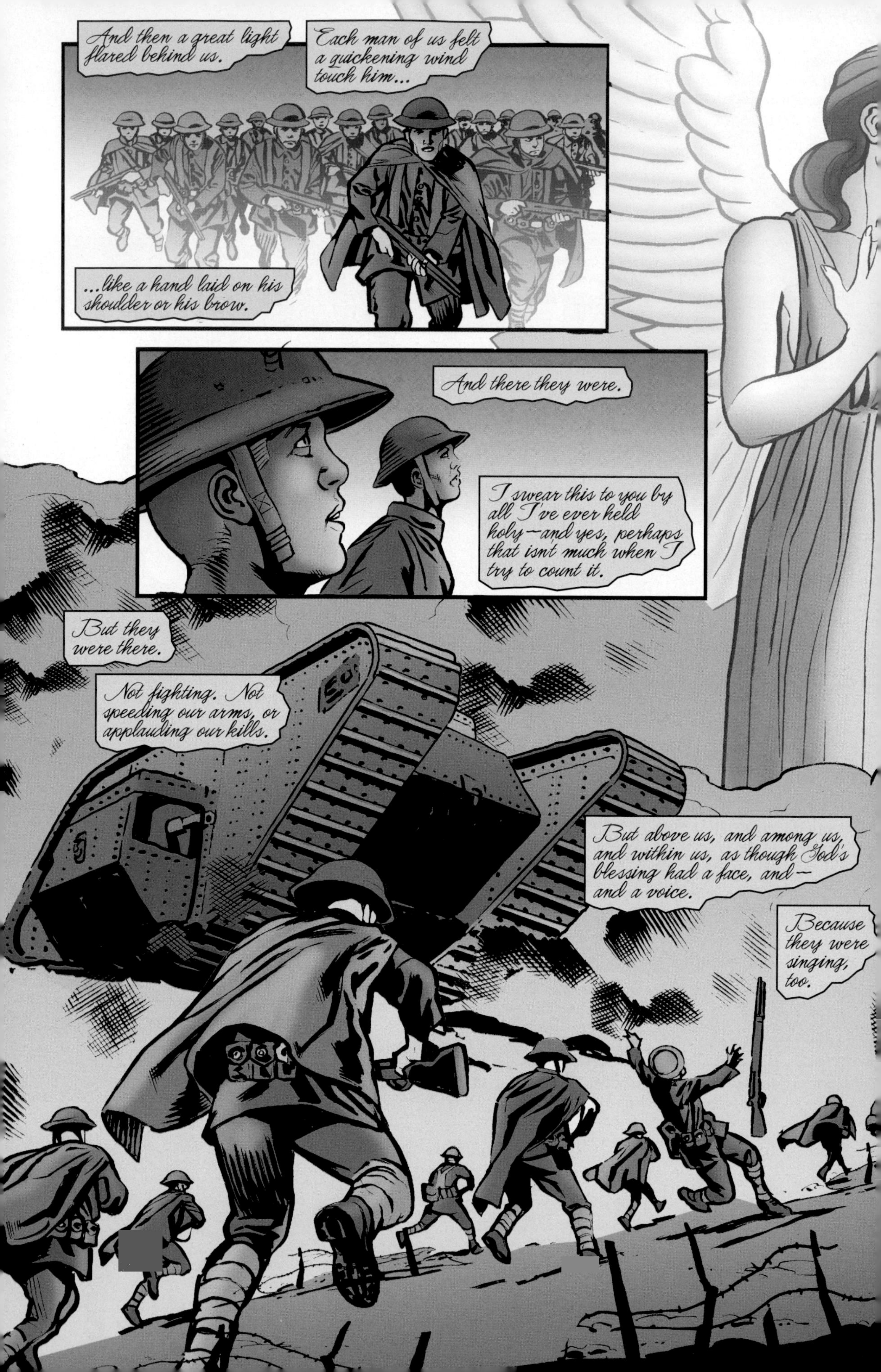
And then a great light flared behind us.
Each man of us felt a quickening wind touch him...
...like a hand laid on his shoulder or his brow.
And there they were.
I swear this to you by all I've ever held holy—and yes, perhaps that isnt much when I try to count it.
But they were there.
Not fighting. Not speeding our arms, or applauding our kills.
But above us, and among us, and within us, as though God's blessing had a face, and—and a voice.
Because they were singing, too.

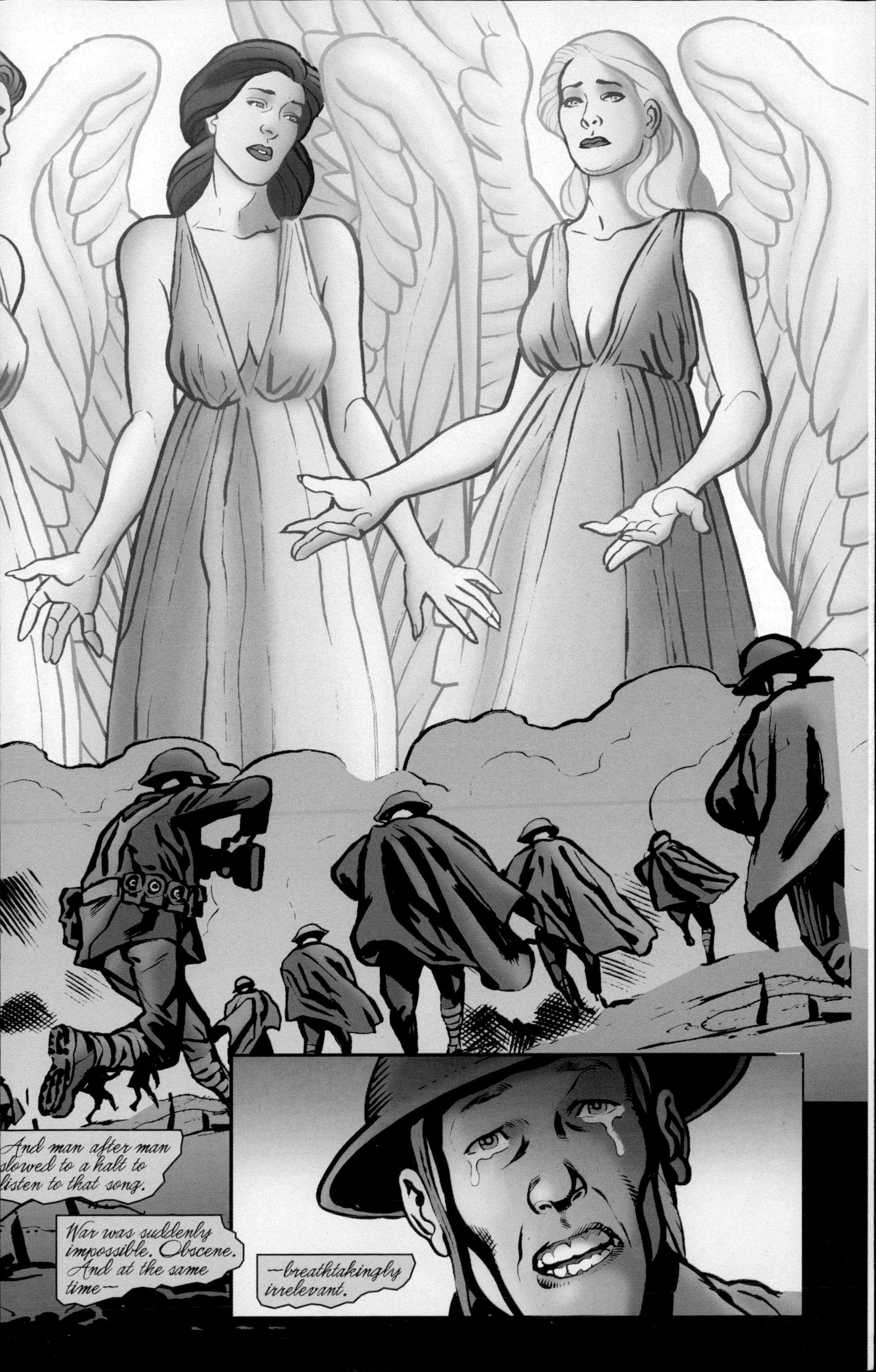
And man after man slowed to a halt to listen to that song.
War was suddenly impossible. Obscene. And at the same time—
—breathtakingly irrelevant.

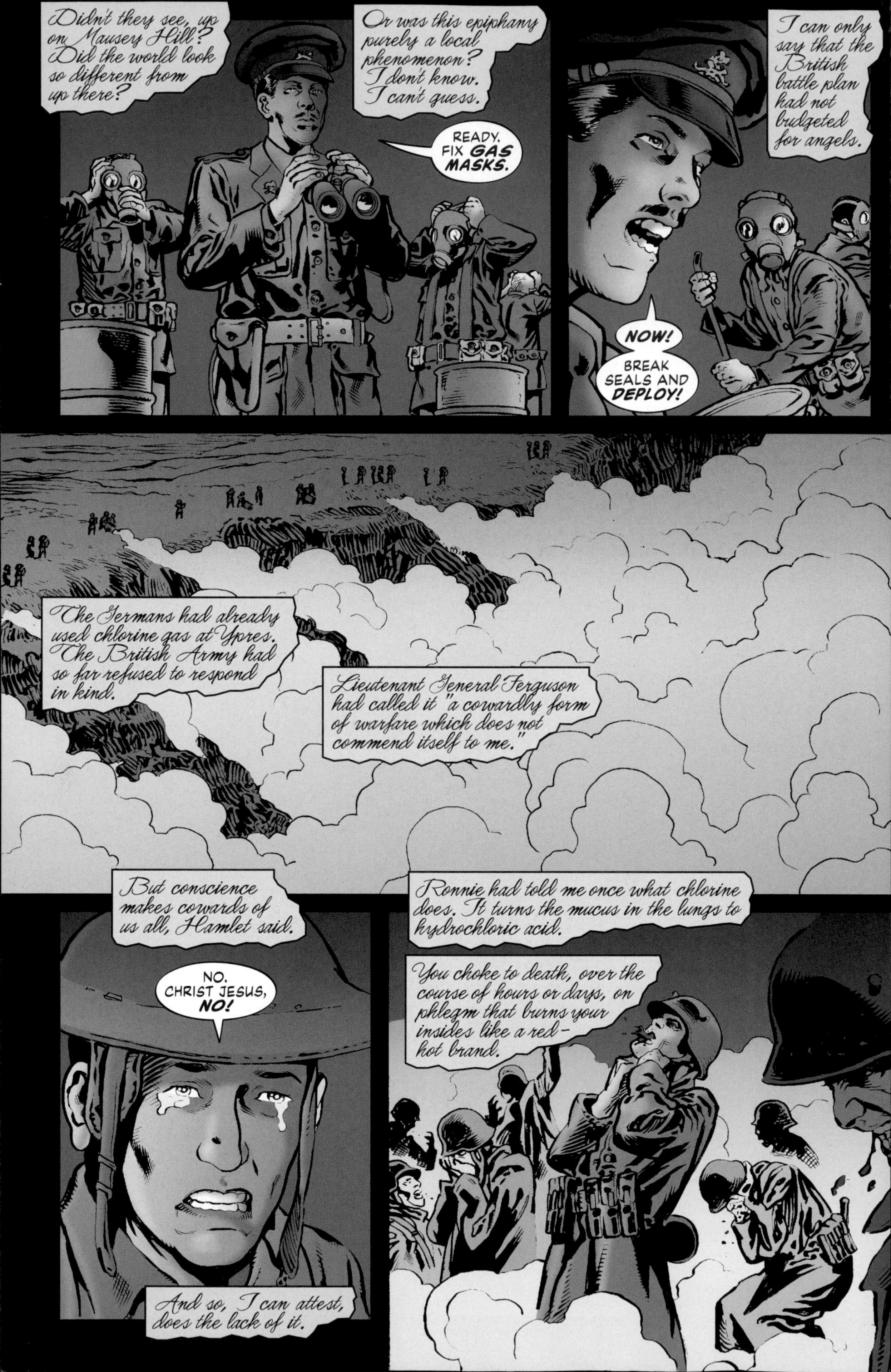

Didn't they see, up on Mausey Hill? Did the world look so different from up there?
Or was this epiphany purely a local phenomenon? I don't know. I can't guess.
READY. FIX GAS MASKS.
I can only say that the British battle plan had not budgeted for angels.
NOW! BREAK SEALS AND DEPLOY!
The Germans had already used chlorine gas at Ypres. The British Army had so far refused to respond in kind.
Lieutenant General Ferguson had called it "a cowardly form of warfare which does not commend itself to me."
But conscience makes cowards of us all, Hamlet said.
NO. CHRIST JESUS, NO!
And so, I can attest, does the lack of it.
Ronnie had told me once what chlorine does. It turns the mucus in the lungs to hydrochloric acid.
You choke to death, over the course of hours or days, on phlegm that burns your insides like a red-hot brand.

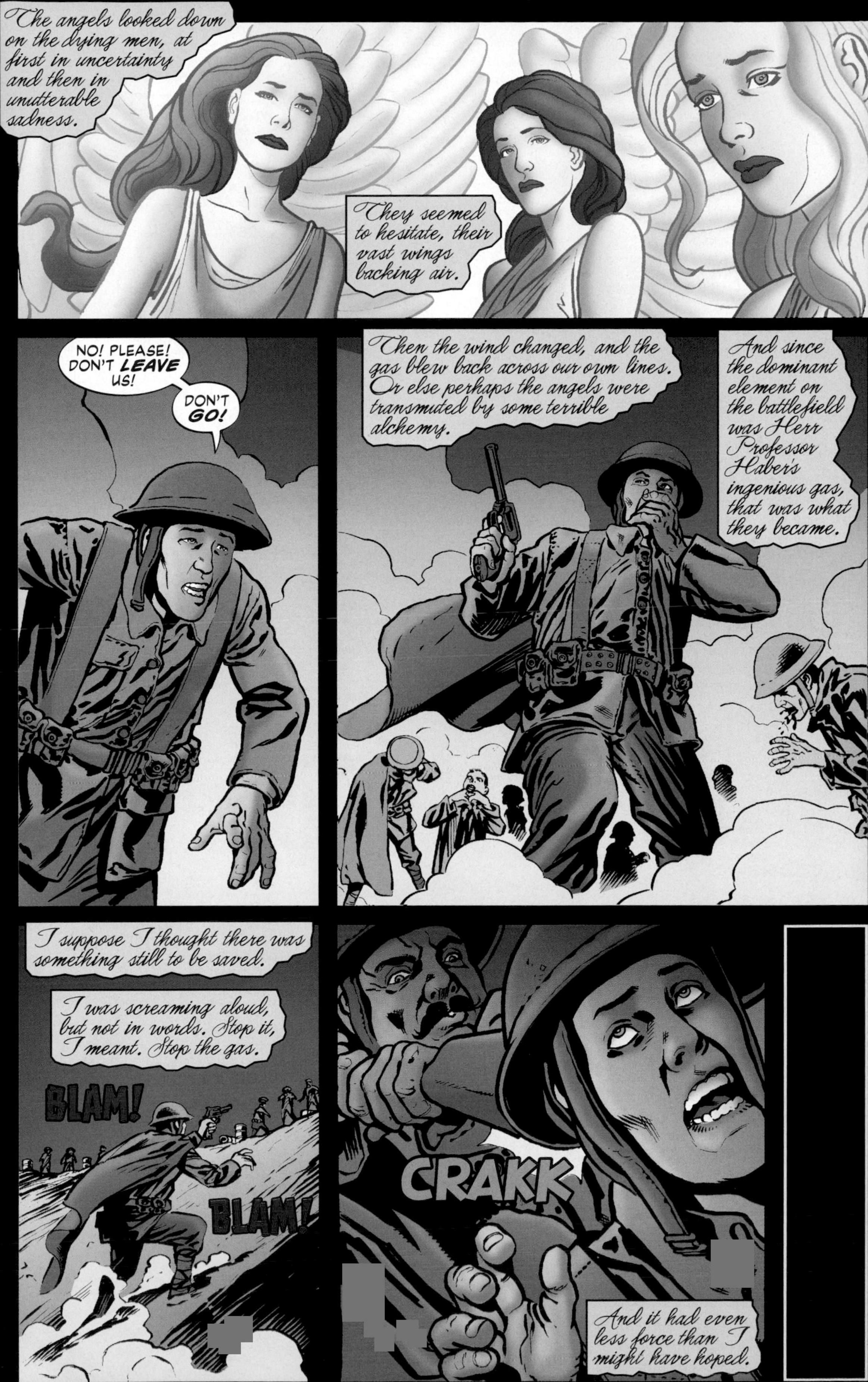

The angels looked down on the dying men, at first in uncertainty and then in unutterable sadness.
They seemed to hesitate, their vast wings backing air.
NO! PLEASE! DON'T LEAVE US!
DON'T GO!
Then the wind changed, and the gas blew back across our own lines. Or else perhaps the angels were transmuted by some terrible alchemy.
And since the dominant element on the battlefield was Herr Professor Haber's ingenious gas, that was what they became.
I suppose I thought there was something still to be saved.
I was screaming aloud, but not in words. Stop it, I meant. Stop the gas.
BLAM!
BLAM!
CRAKK
And it had even less force than I might have hoped.

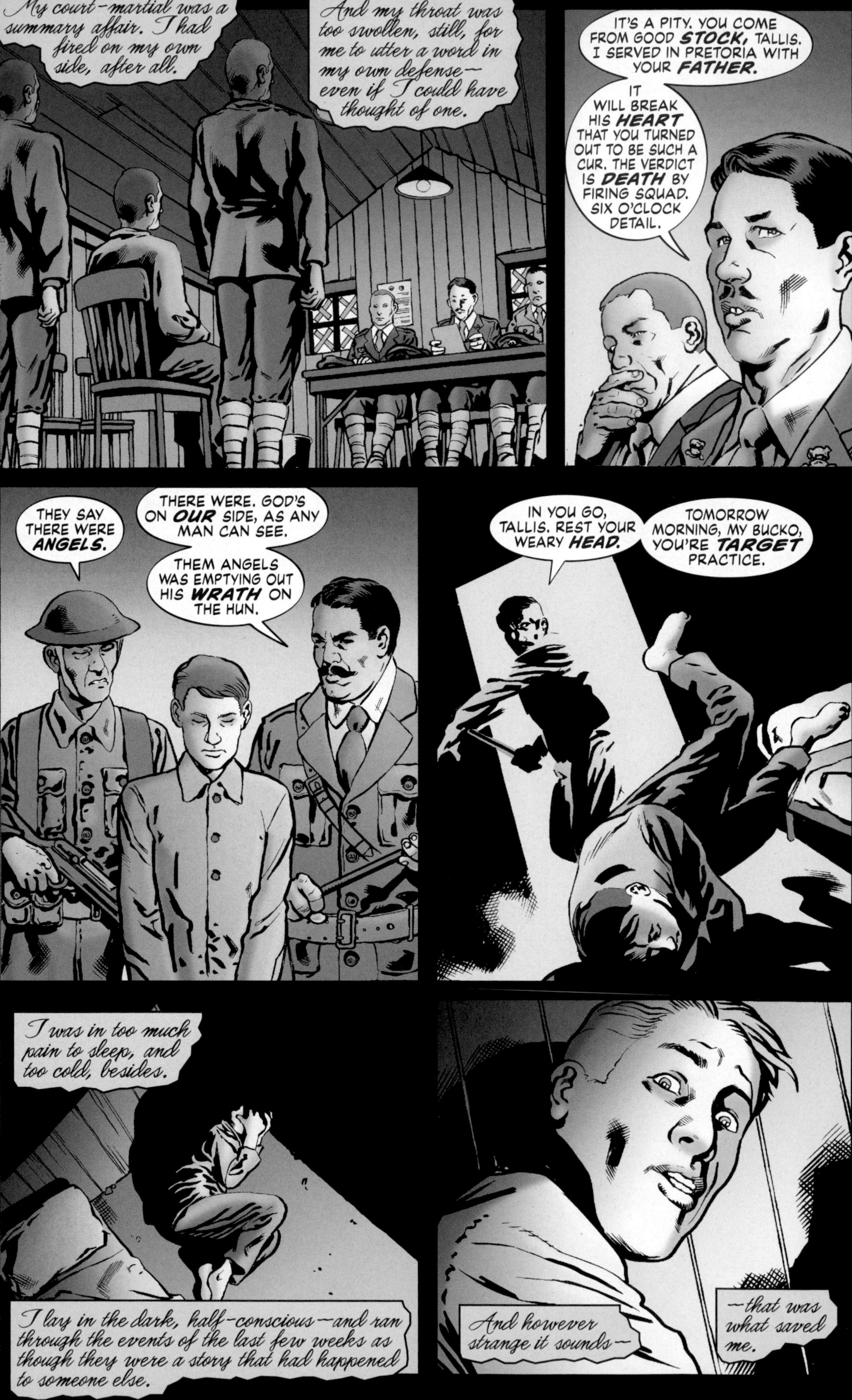
My court-martial was a summary affair. I had fired on my own side, after all.
And my throat was too swollen, still, for me to utter a word in my own defense—even if I could have thought of one.
IT'S A PITY. YOU COME FROM GOOD STOCK, TALLIS. I SERVED IN PRETORIA WITH YOUR FATHER.
IT WILL BREAK HIS HEART THAT YOU TURNED OUT TO BE SUCH A CUR. THE VERDICT IS DEATH BY FIRING SQUAD. SIX O'CLOCK DETAIL.
THEY SAY THERE WERE ANGELS.
THERE WERE. GOD'S ON OUR SIDE, AS ANY MAN CAN SEE.
THEM ANGELS WAS EMPTYING OUT HIS WRATH ON THE HUN.
IN YOU GO, TALLIS. REST YOUR WEARY HEAD.
TOMORROW MORNING, MY BUCKO, YOU'RE TARGET PRACTICE.
I was in too much pain to sleep, and too cold, besides.
I lay in the dark, half-conscious—and ran through the events of the last few weeks as though they were a story that had happened to someone else.
And however strange it sounds—
—that was what saved me.

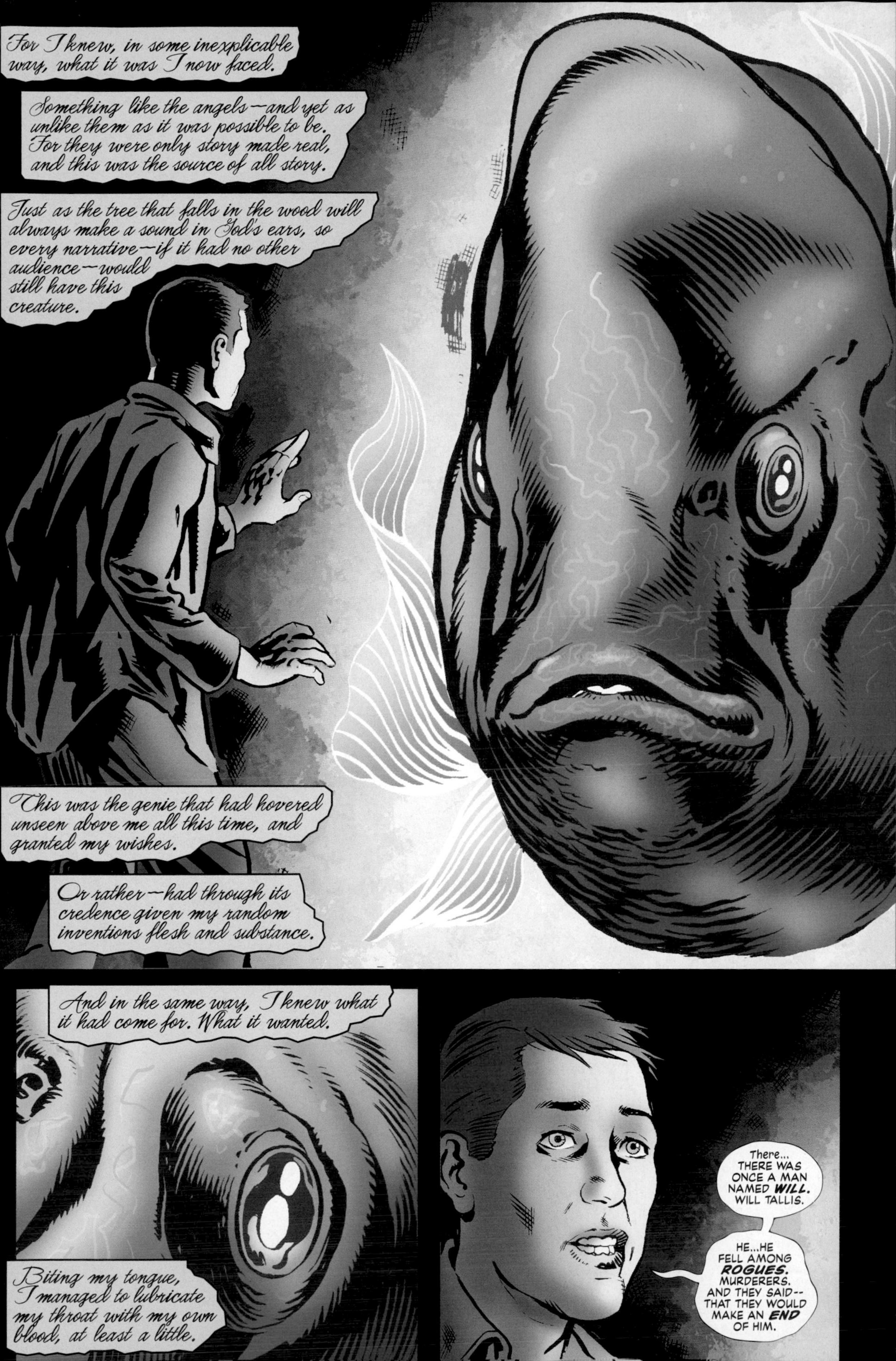
For I knew, in some inexplicable way, what it was I now faced.
Something like the angels—and yet as unlike them as it was possible to be. For they were only story made real, and this was the source of all story.
Just as the tree that falls in the wood will always make a sound in God's ears, so every narrative—if it had no other audience—would still have this creature.
This was the genie that had hovered unseen above me all this time, and granted my wishes.
Or rather—had through its credence given my random inventions flesh and substance.
And in the same way, I knew what it had come for. What it wanted.
Biting my tongue, I managed to lubricate my throat with my own blood, at least a little.
There... THERE WAS ONCE A MAN NAMED WILL. WILL TALLIS.
HE...HE FELL AMONG ROGUES. MURDERERS. AND THEY SAID-- THAT THEY WOULD MAKE AN END OF HIM.

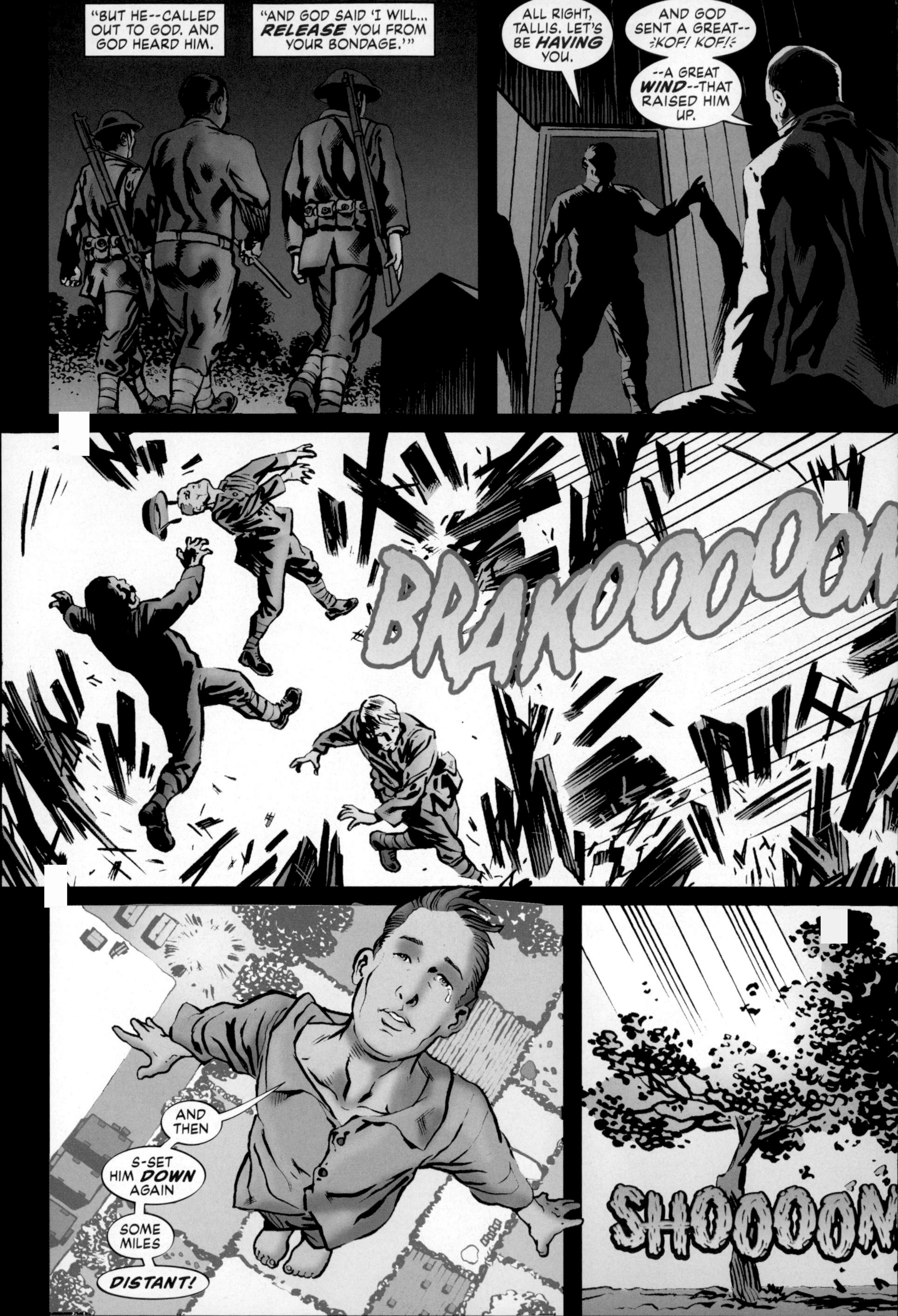
"BUT HE--CALLED OUT TO GOD. AND GOD HEARD HIM.
"AND GOD SAID 'I WILL... RELEASE YOU FROM YOUR BONDAGE.'"
ALL RIGHT, TALLIS. LET'S BE HAVING YOU.
AND GOD SENT A GREAT-- KOF! KOF!
--A GREAT WIND--THAT RAISED HIM UP.
BRAKOOOOOM
AND THEN
S-SET HIM DOWN AGAIN
SOME MILES
DISTANT!
SHOOOOOM

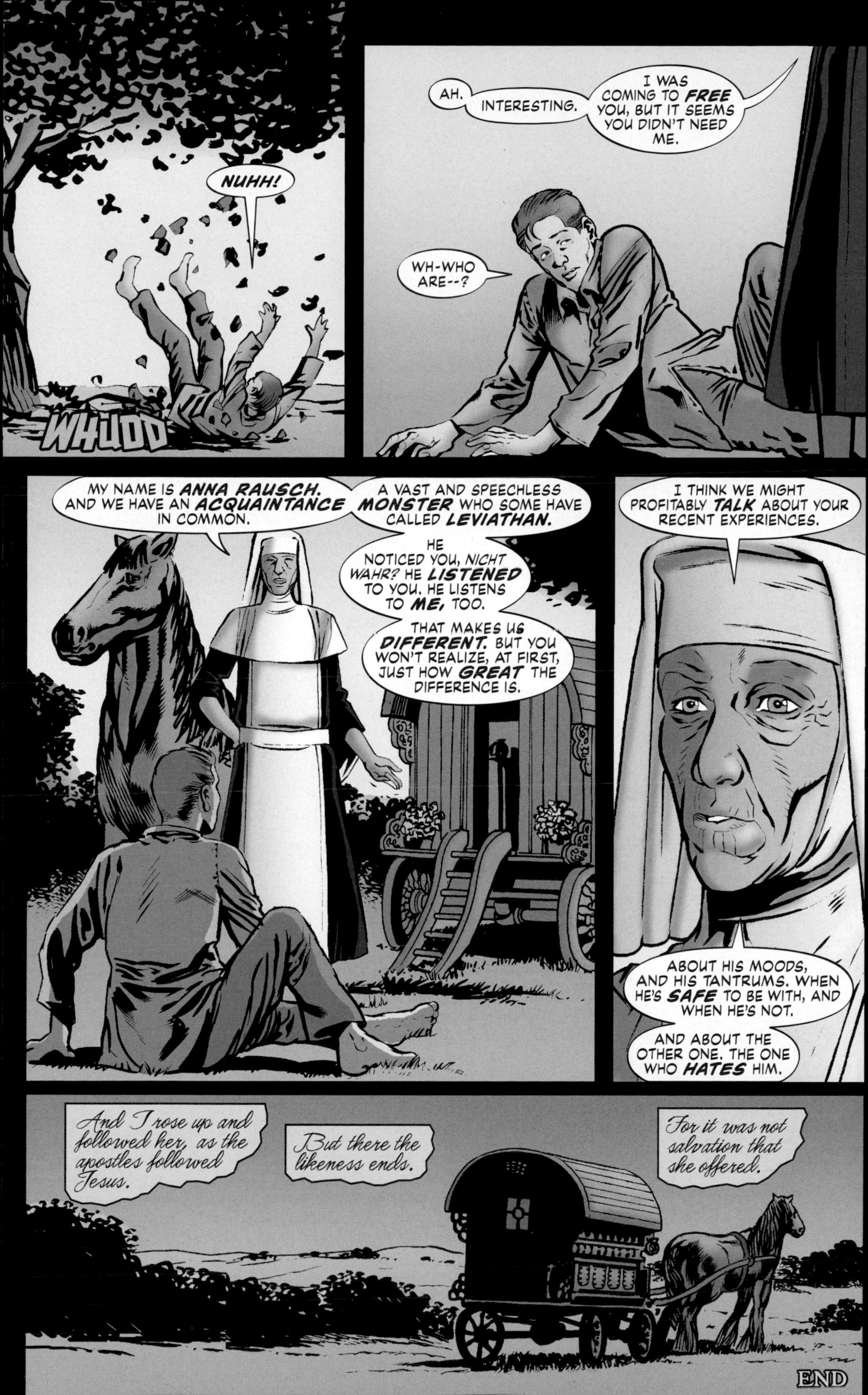
NUHH!
WHUDD
AH.
INTERESTING.
I WAS COMING TO FREE YOU, BUT IT SEEMS YOU DIDN'T NEED ME.
WH-WHO ARE--?
MY NAME IS ANNA RAUSCH. AND WE HAVE AN ACQUAINTANCE IN COMMON.
A VAST AND SPEECHLESS MONSTER WHO SOME HAVE CALLED LEVIATHAN.
HE NOTICED YOU, NICHT WAHR? HE LISTENED TO YOU. HE LISTENS TO ME, TOO.
THAT MAKES US DIFFERENT. BUT YOU WON'T REALIZE, AT FIRST, JUST HOW GREAT THE DIFFERENCE IS.
I THINK WE MIGHT PROFITABLY TALK ABOUT YOUR RECENT EXPERIENCES.
ABOUT HIS MOODS, AND HIS TANTRUMS. WHEN HE'S SAFE TO BE WITH, AND WHEN HE'S NOT.
AND ABOUT THE OTHER ONE. THE ONE WHO HATES HIM.
And I rose up and followed her, as the apostles followed Jesus.
But there the likeness ends.
For it was not salvation that she offered.
END

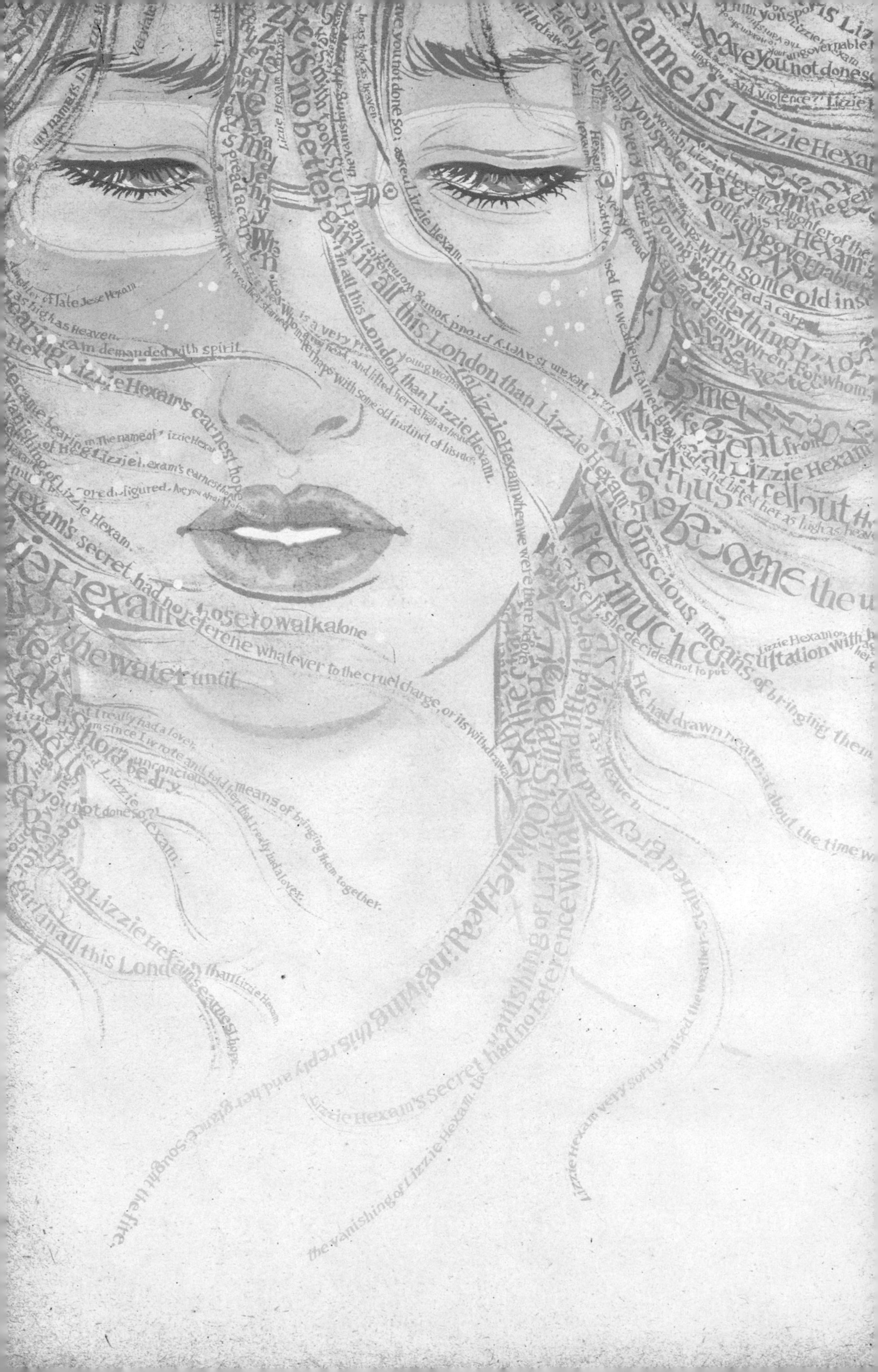

name is Lizzie Hexam
have you not done so
is no better girl in all this London than Lizzie Hexam
the vanishing of Lizzie Hexam
Lizzie Hexam's secret had no reference whatever to the cruel charge, or its withdrawal.
means of bringing them together.
He had drawn nearer at about the time
Lizzie Hexam very softly raised the weather-stained
Lizzie Hexam demanded with spirit
Lizzie Hexam's earnest hope
the vanishing of Lizzie Hexam
this reply and her glance sought the fire
Jenny Wren
whatever to the cruel charge

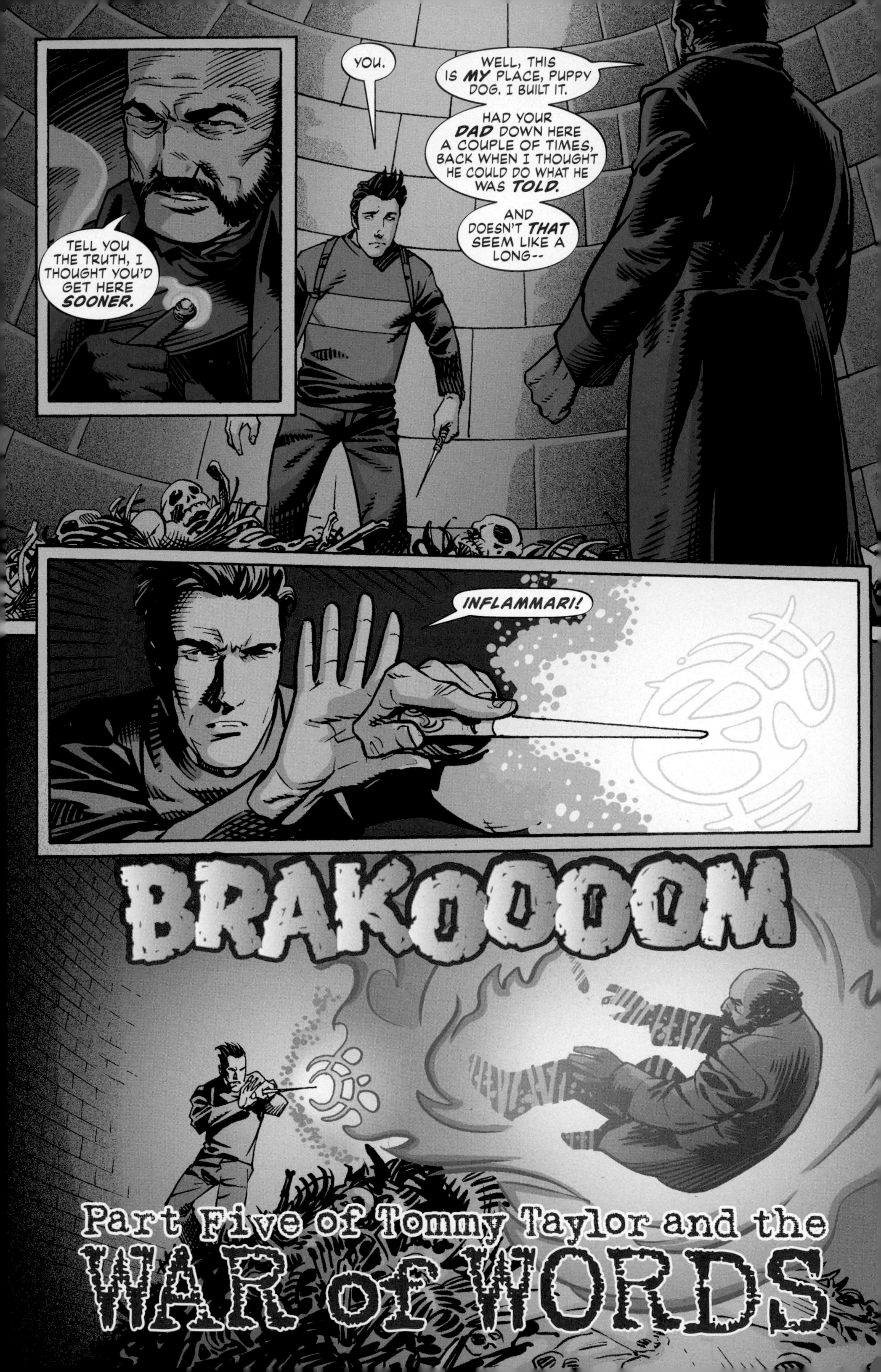
TELL YOU THE TRUTH, I THOUGHT YOU'D GET HERE SOONER.
YOU.
WELL, THIS IS MY PLACE, PUPPY DOG. I BUILT IT.
HAD YOUR DAD DOWN HERE A COUPLE OF TIMES, BACK WHEN I THOUGHT HE COULD DO WHAT HE WAS TOLD.
AND DOESN'T THAT SEEM LIKE A LONG--
INFLAMMARI!
BRAKOOOOM
Part Five of Tommy Taylor and the
WAR of WORDS

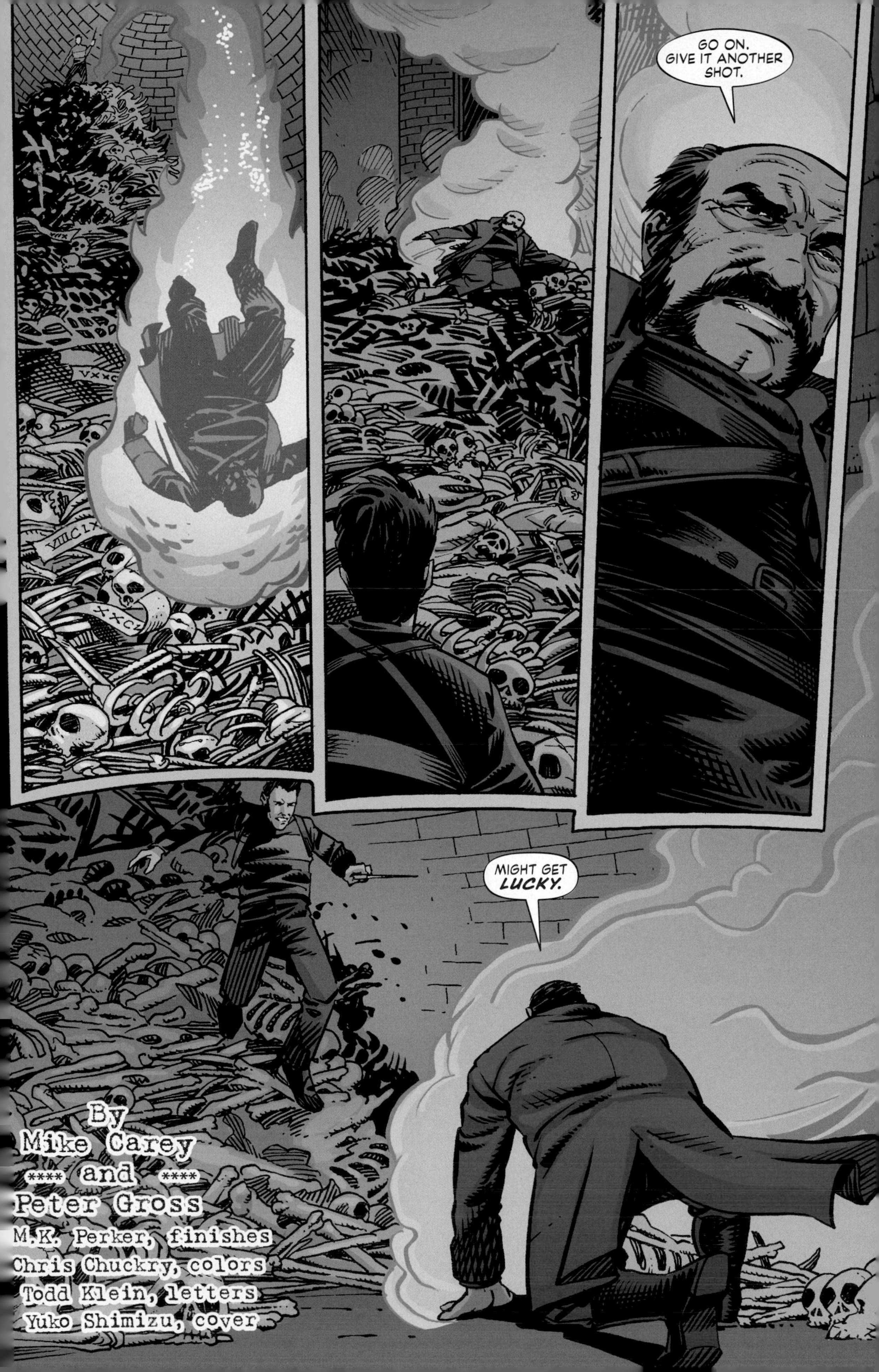

GO ON. GIVE IT ANOTHER SHOT.
MIGHT GET *LUCKY.*
By
Mike Carey
**** and ****
Peter Gross
M.K. Perker, finishes
Chris Chuckry, colors
Todd Klein, letters
Yuko Shimizu, cover

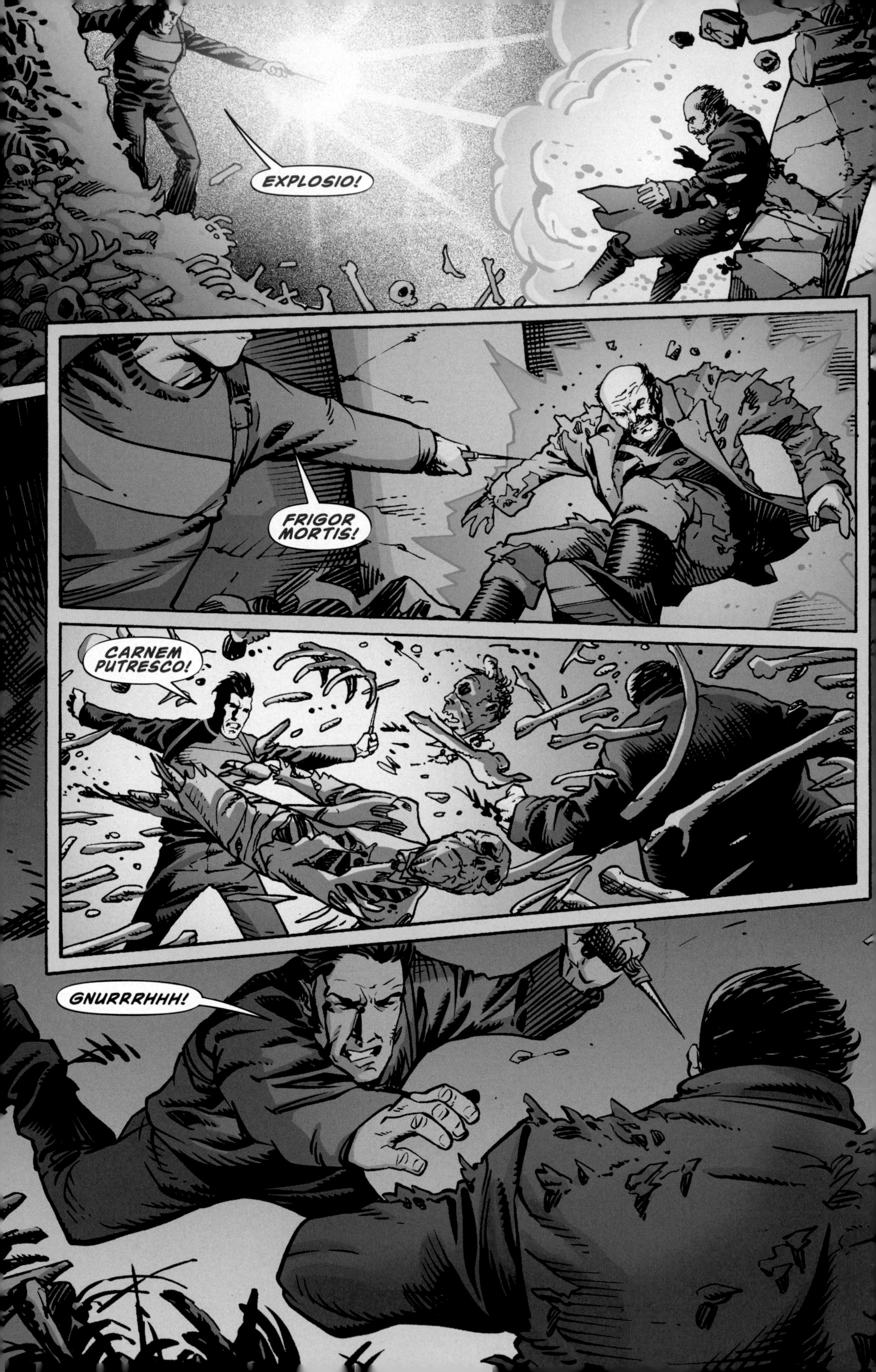
EXPLOSIO!
FRIGOR MORTIS!
CARNEM PUTRESCO!
GNURRRHHH!

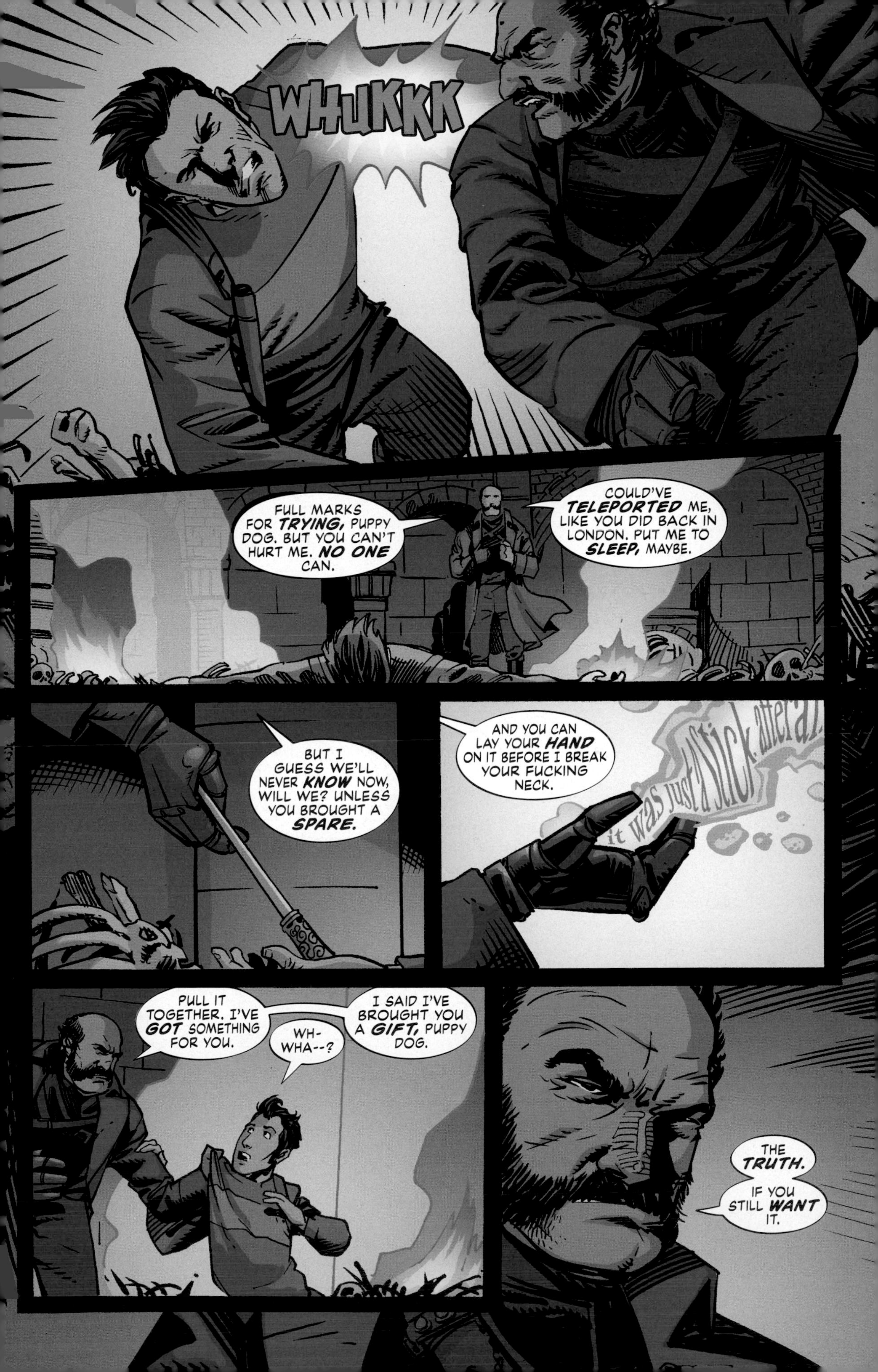

WHUKKK
FULL MARKS FOR TRYING, PUPPY DOG. BUT YOU CAN'T HURT ME. NO ONE CAN.
COULD'VE TELEPORTED ME, LIKE YOU DID BACK IN LONDON. PUT ME TO SLEEP, MAYBE.
BUT I GUESS WE'LL NEVER KNOW NOW, WILL WE? UNLESS YOU BROUGHT A SPARE.
AND YOU CAN LAY YOUR HAND ON IT BEFORE I BREAK YOUR FUCKING NECK.
it was just a stick after all
PULL IT TOGETHER. I'VE GOT SOMETHING FOR YOU.
WH- WHA--?
I SAID I'VE BROUGHT YOU A GIFT, PUPPY DOG.
THE TRUTH.
IF YOU STILL WANT IT.

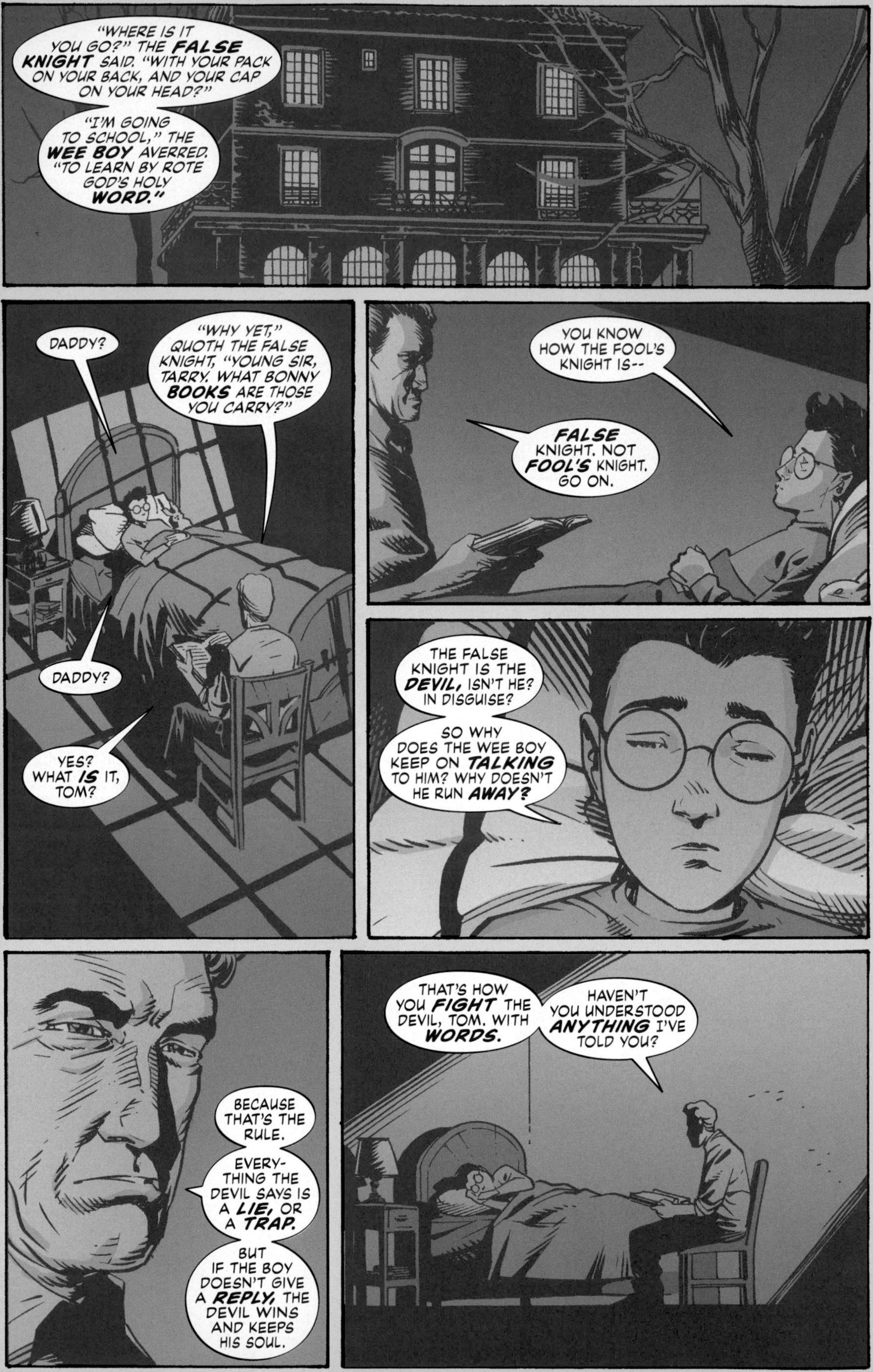
"WHERE IS IT YOU GO?" THE FALSE KNIGHT SAID. "WITH YOUR PACK ON YOUR BACK, AND YOUR CAP ON YOUR HEAD?"
"I'M GOING TO SCHOOL," THE WEE BOY AVERRED. "TO LEARN BY ROTE GOD'S HOLY WORD."
DADDY?
"WHY YET," QUOTH THE FALSE KNIGHT, "YOUNG SIR, TARRY. WHAT BONNY BOOKS ARE THOSE YOU CARRY?"
DADDY?
YES? WHAT IS IT, TOM?
YOU KNOW HOW THE FOOL'S KNIGHT IS--
FALSE KNIGHT. NOT FOOL'S KNIGHT. GO ON.
THE FALSE KNIGHT IS THE DEVIL, ISN'T HE? IN DISGUISE?
SO WHY DOES THE WEE BOY KEEP ON TALKING TO HIM? WHY DOESN'T HE RUN AWAY?
BECAUSE THAT'S THE RULE.
EVERY-THING THE DEVIL SAYS IS A LIE, OR A TRAP.
BUT IF THE BOY DOESN'T GIVE A REPLY, THE DEVIL WINS AND KEEPS HIS SOUL.
THAT'S HOW YOU FIGHT THE DEVIL, TOM. WITH WORDS.
HAVEN'T YOU UNDERSTOOD ANYTHING I'VE TOLD YOU?

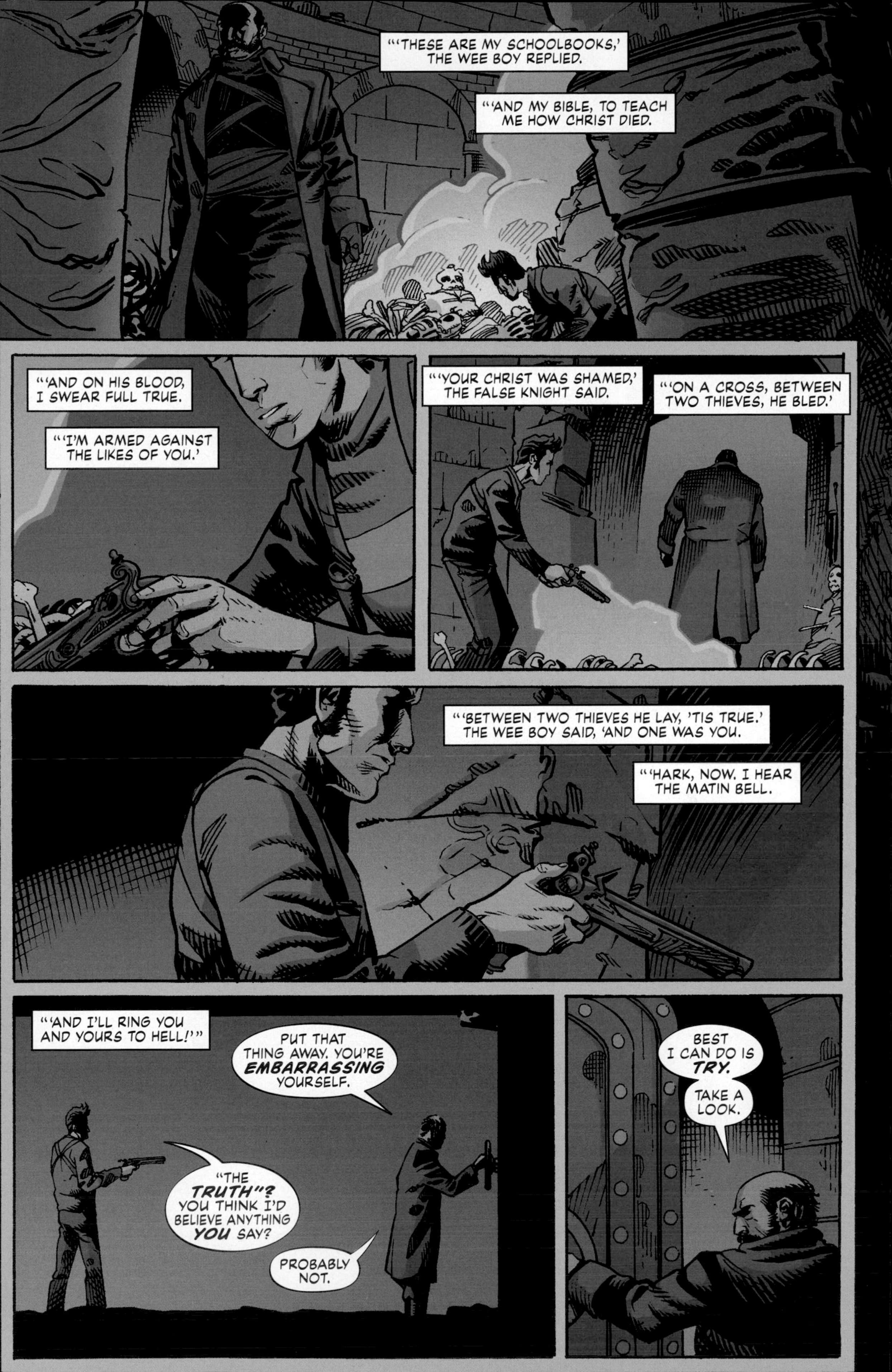
"'THESE ARE MY SCHOOLBOOKS,' THE WEE BOY REPLIED.
"'AND MY BIBLE, TO TEACH ME HOW CHRIST DIED.
"'AND ON HIS BLOOD, I SWEAR FULL TRUE.
"'I'M ARMED AGAINST THE LIKES OF YOU.'
"'YOUR CHRIST WAS SHAMED,' THE FALSE KNIGHT SAID.
"'ON A CROSS, BETWEEN TWO THIEVES, HE BLED.'
"'BETWEEN TWO THIEVES HE LAY, 'TIS TRUE.' THE WEE BOY SAID, 'AND ONE WAS YOU.
"'HARK, NOW. I HEAR THE MATIN BELL.
"'AND I'LL RING YOU AND YOURS TO HELL!'"
PUT THAT THING AWAY. YOU'RE **EMBARRASSING** YOURSELF.
"THE **TRUTH**"? YOU THINK I'D BELIEVE ANYTHING **YOU** SAY?
PROBABLY NOT.
BEST I CAN DO IS **TRY.**
TAKE A LOOK.

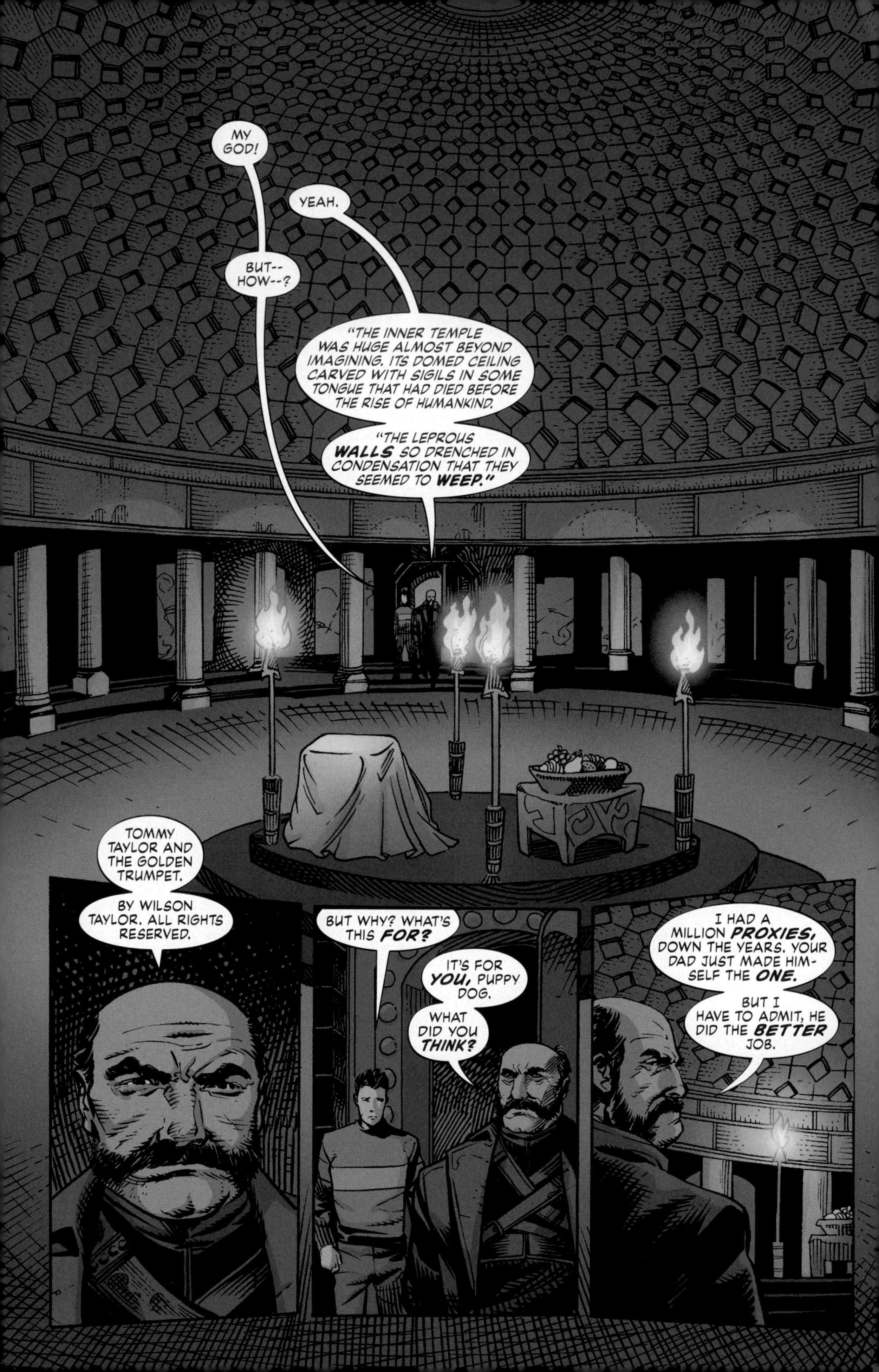
MY GOD!
YEAH.
BUT-- HOW--?
"THE INNER TEMPLE WAS HUGE ALMOST BEYOND IMAGINING. ITS DOMED CEILING CARVED WITH SIGILS IN SOME TONGUE THAT HAD DIED BEFORE THE RISE OF HUMANKIND.
"THE LEPROUS WALLS SO DRENCHED IN CONDENSATION THAT THEY SEEMED TO WEEP."
TOMMY TAYLOR AND THE GOLDEN TRUMPET.
BY WILSON TAYLOR. ALL RIGHTS RESERVED.
BUT WHY? WHAT'S THIS FOR?
IT'S FOR YOU, PUPPY DOG.
WHAT DID YOU THINK?
I HAD A MILLION PROXIES, DOWN THE YEARS. YOUR DAD JUST MADE HIM-SELF THE ONE.
BUT I HAVE TO ADMIT, HE DID THE BETTER JOB.

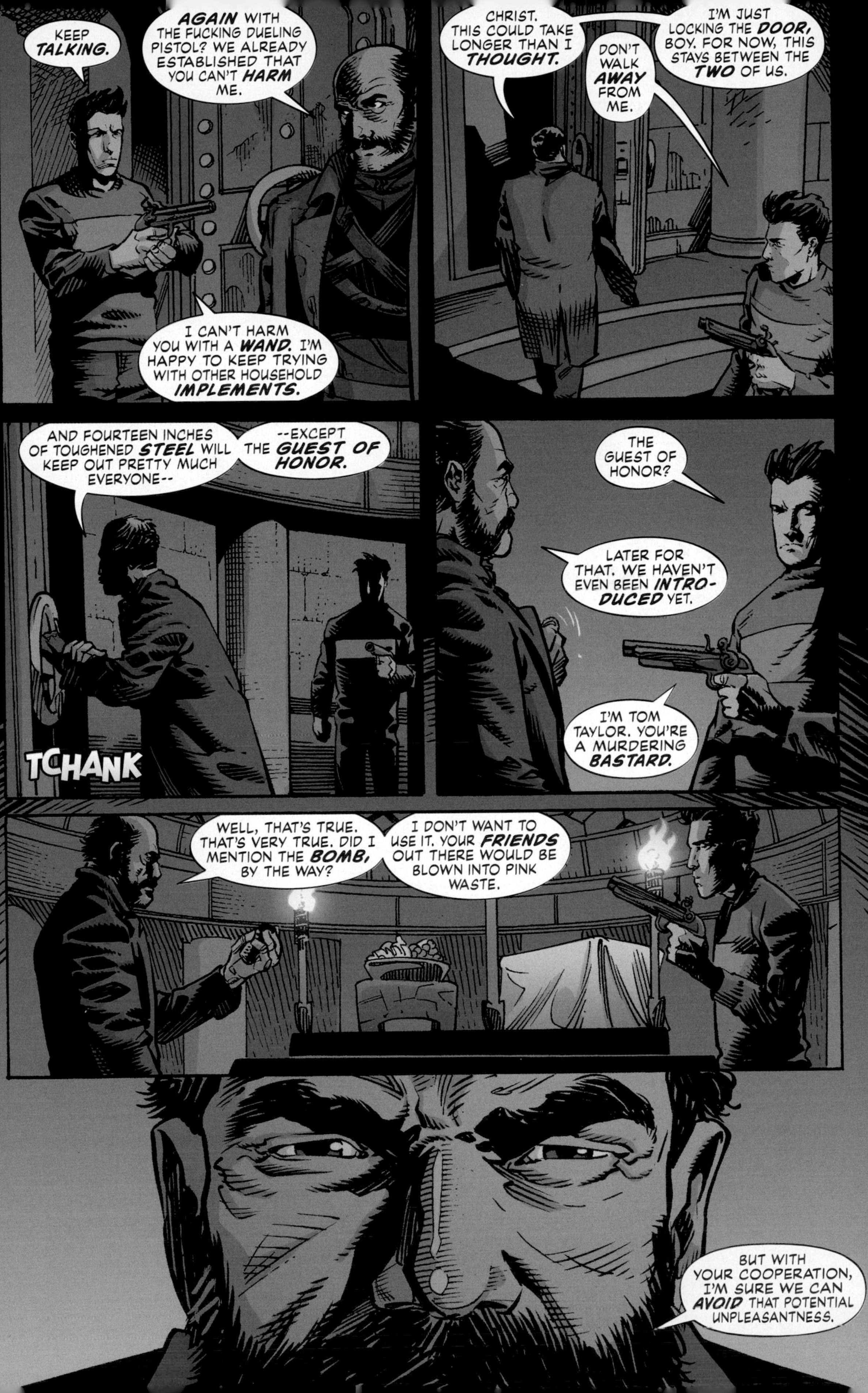
KEEP TALKING.
AGAIN WITH THE FUCKING DUELING PISTOL? WE ALREADY ESTABLISHED THAT YOU CAN'T HARM ME.
I CAN'T HARM YOU WITH A WAND. I'M HAPPY TO KEEP TRYING WITH OTHER HOUSEHOLD IMPLEMENTS.
CHRIST. THIS COULD TAKE LONGER THAN I THOUGHT.
I'M JUST LOCKING THE DOOR, BOY. FOR NOW, THIS STAYS BETWEEN THE TWO OF US.
DON'T WALK AWAY FROM ME.
AND FOURTEEN INCHES OF TOUGHENED STEEL WILL KEEP OUT PRETTY MUCH EVERYONE--
--EXCEPT THE GUEST OF HONOR.
TCHANK
THE GUEST OF HONOR?
LATER FOR THAT. WE HAVEN'T EVEN BEEN INTRO-DUCED YET.
I'M TOM TAYLOR. YOU'RE A MURDERING BASTARD.
WELL, THAT'S TRUE. THAT'S VERY TRUE. DID I MENTION THE BOMB, BY THE WAY?
I DON'T WANT TO USE IT. YOUR FRIENDS OUT THERE WOULD BE BLOWN INTO PINK WASTE.
BUT WITH YOUR COOPERATION, I'M SURE WE CAN AVOID THAT POTENTIAL UNPLEASANTNESS.

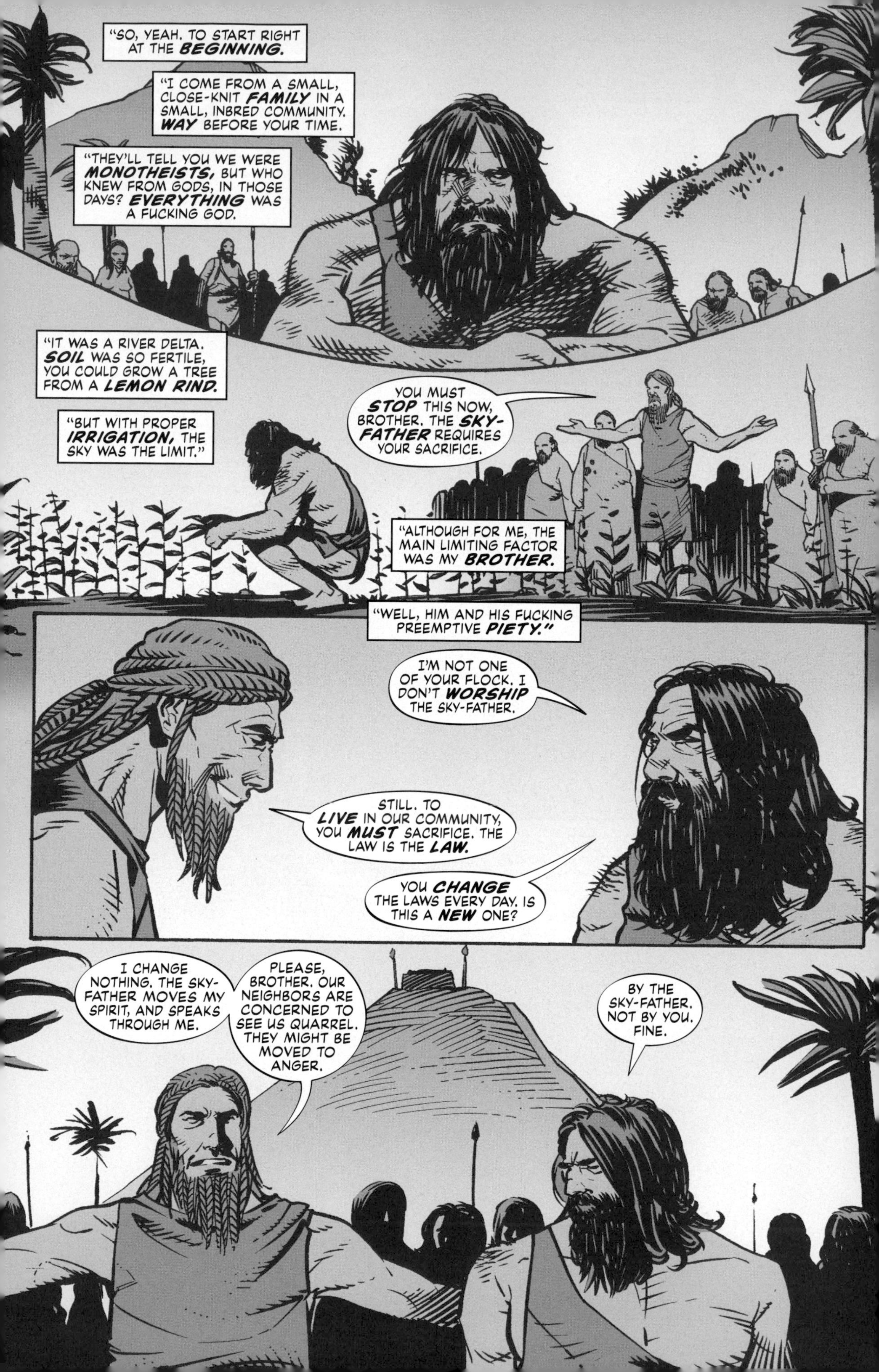
"SO, YEAH. TO START RIGHT AT THE BEGINNING.
"I COME FROM A SMALL, CLOSE-KNIT FAMILY IN A SMALL, INBRED COMMUNITY. WAY BEFORE YOUR TIME.
"THEY'LL TELL YOU WE WERE MONOTHEISTS, BUT WHO KNEW FROM GODS, IN THOSE DAYS? EVERYTHING WAS A FUCKING GOD.
"IT WAS A RIVER DELTA. SOIL WAS SO FERTILE, YOU COULD GROW A TREE FROM A LEMON RIND.
"BUT WITH PROPER IRRIGATION, THE SKY WAS THE LIMIT."
YOU MUST STOP THIS NOW, BROTHER. THE SKY-FATHER REQUIRES YOUR SACRIFICE.
"ALTHOUGH FOR ME, THE MAIN LIMITING FACTOR WAS MY BROTHER.
"WELL, HIM AND HIS FUCKING PREEMPTIVE PIETY."
I'M NOT ONE OF YOUR FLOCK. I DON'T WORSHIP THE SKY-FATHER.
STILL. TO LIVE IN OUR COMMUNITY, YOU MUST SACRIFICE. THE LAW IS THE LAW.
YOU CHANGE THE LAWS EVERY DAY. IS THIS A NEW ONE?
I CHANGE NOTHING. THE SKY-FATHER MOVES MY SPIRIT, AND SPEAKS THROUGH ME.
PLEASE, BROTHER. OUR NEIGHBORS ARE CONCERNED TO SEE US QUARREL. THEY MIGHT BE MOVED TO ANGER.
BY THE SKY-FATHER. NOT BY YOU. FINE.

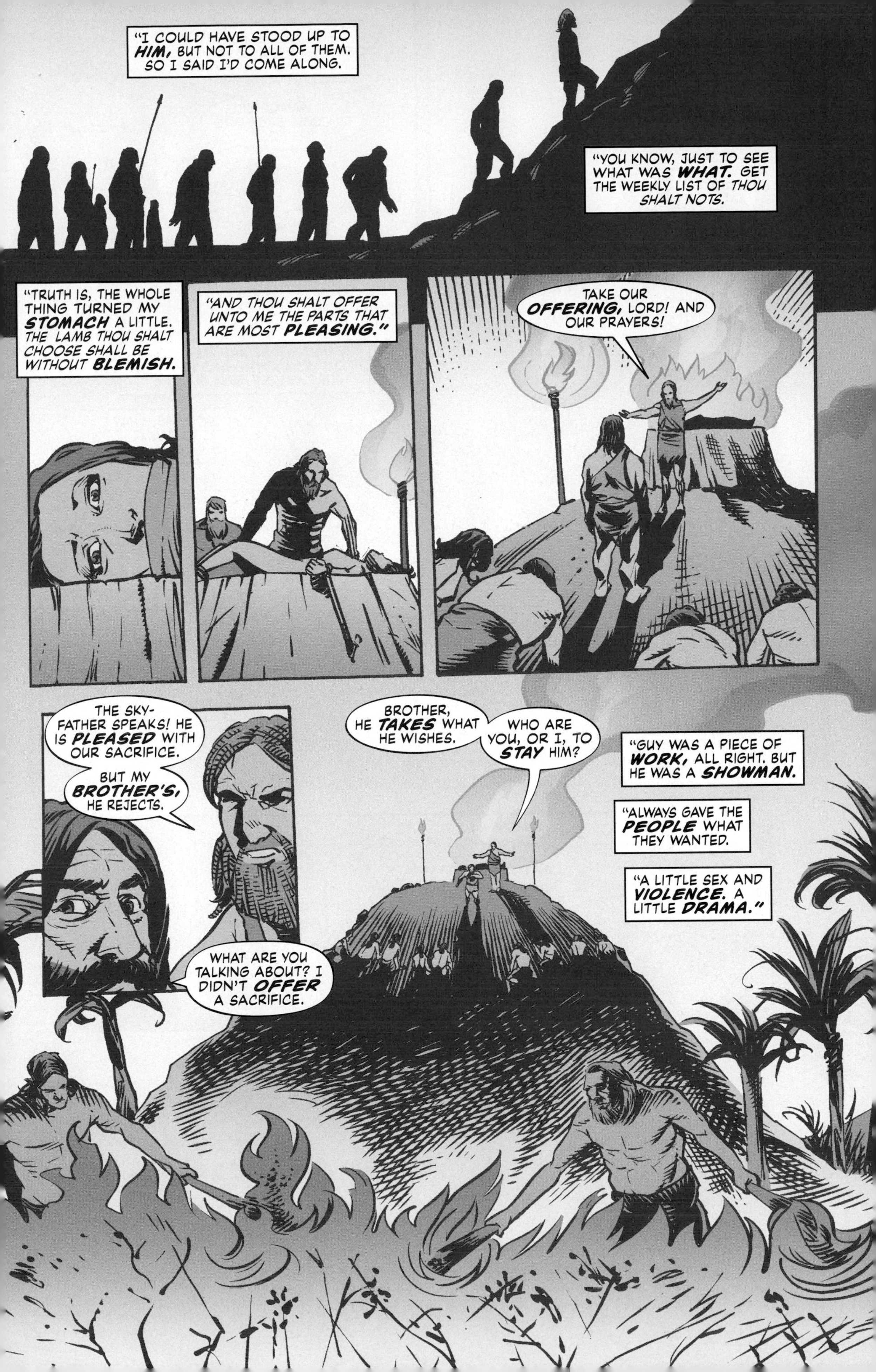
"I COULD HAVE STOOD UP TO HIM, BUT NOT TO ALL OF THEM. SO I SAID I'D COME ALONG.
"YOU KNOW, JUST TO SEE WHAT WAS WHAT. GET THE WEEKLY LIST OF THOU SHALT NOTS.
"TRUTH IS, THE WHOLE THING TURNED MY STOMACH A LITTLE. THE LAMB THOU SHALT CHOOSE SHALL BE WITHOUT BLEMISH.
"AND THOU SHALT OFFER UNTO ME THE PARTS THAT ARE MOST PLEASING."
TAKE OUR OFFERING, LORD! AND OUR PRAYERS!
THE SKY-FATHER SPEAKS! HE IS PLEASED WITH OUR SACRIFICE.
BUT MY BROTHER'S, HE REJECTS.
WHAT ARE YOU TALKING ABOUT? I DIDN'T OFFER A SACRIFICE.
BROTHER, HE TAKES WHAT HE WISHES.
WHO ARE YOU, OR I, TO STAY HIM?
"GUY WAS A PIECE OF WORK, ALL RIGHT. BUT HE WAS A SHOWMAN.
"ALWAYS GAVE THE PEOPLE WHAT THEY WANTED.
"A LITTLE SEX AND VIOLENCE. A LITTLE DRAMA."

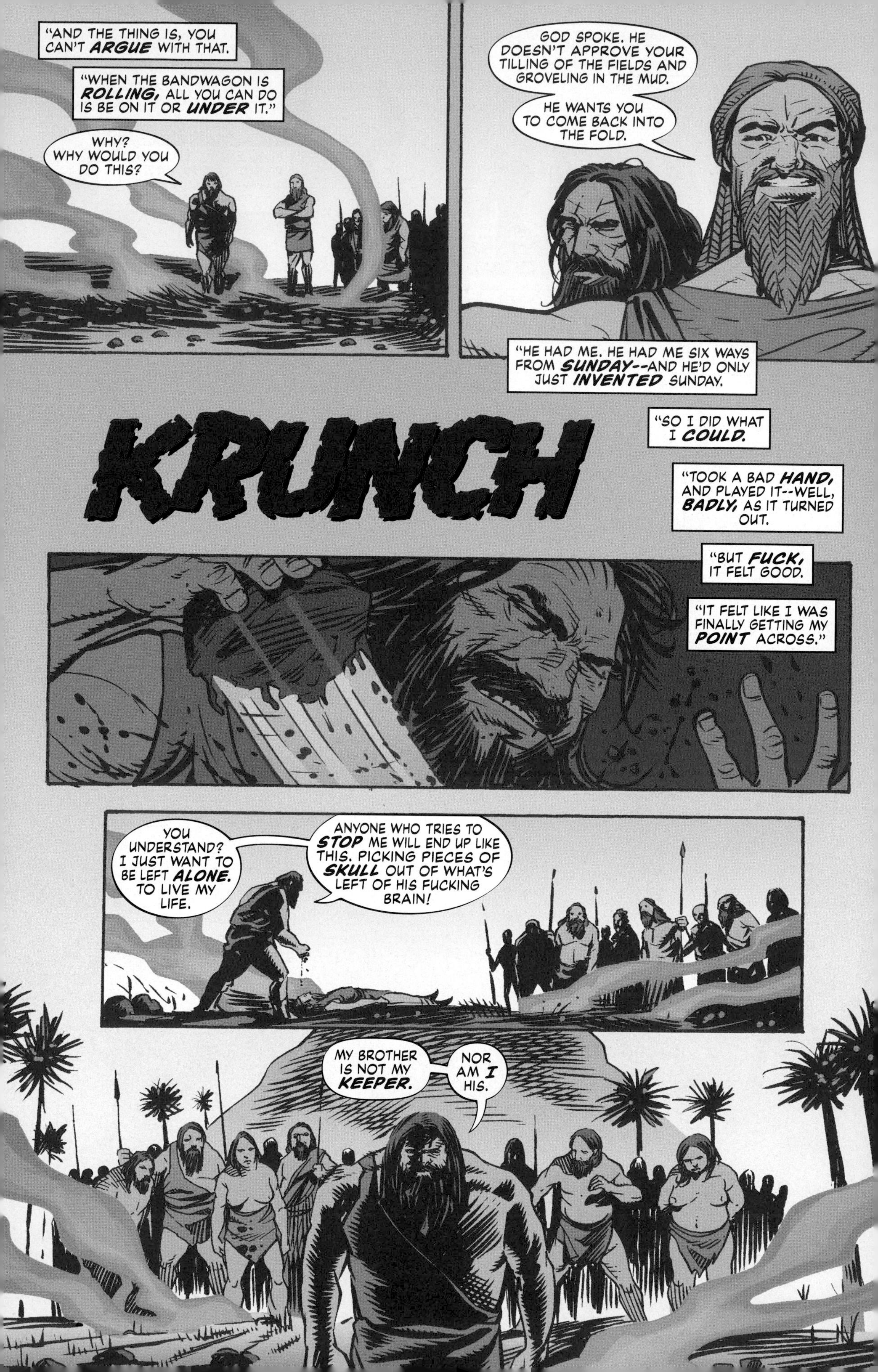
"AND THE THING IS, YOU CAN'T ARGUE WITH THAT.
"WHEN THE BANDWAGON IS ROLLING, ALL YOU CAN DO IS BE ON IT OR UNDER IT."
WHY? WHY WOULD YOU DO THIS?
GOD SPOKE. HE DOESN'T APPROVE YOUR TILLING OF THE FIELDS AND GROVELING IN THE MUD.
HE WANTS YOU TO COME BACK INTO THE FOLD.
"HE HAD ME. HE HAD ME SIX WAYS FROM SUNDAY--AND HE'D ONLY JUST INVENTED SUNDAY.
KRUNCH
"SO I DID WHAT I COULD.
"TOOK A BAD HAND, AND PLAYED IT--WELL, BADLY, AS IT TURNED OUT.
"BUT FUCK, IT FELT GOOD.
"IT FELT LIKE I WAS FINALLY GETTING MY POINT ACROSS."
YOU UNDERSTAND? I JUST WANT TO BE LEFT ALONE. TO LIVE MY LIFE.
ANYONE WHO TRIES TO STOP ME WILL END UP LIKE THIS. PICKING PIECES OF SKULL OUT OF WHAT'S LEFT OF HIS FUCKING BRAIN!
MY BROTHER IS NOT MY KEEPER.
NOR AM I HIS.

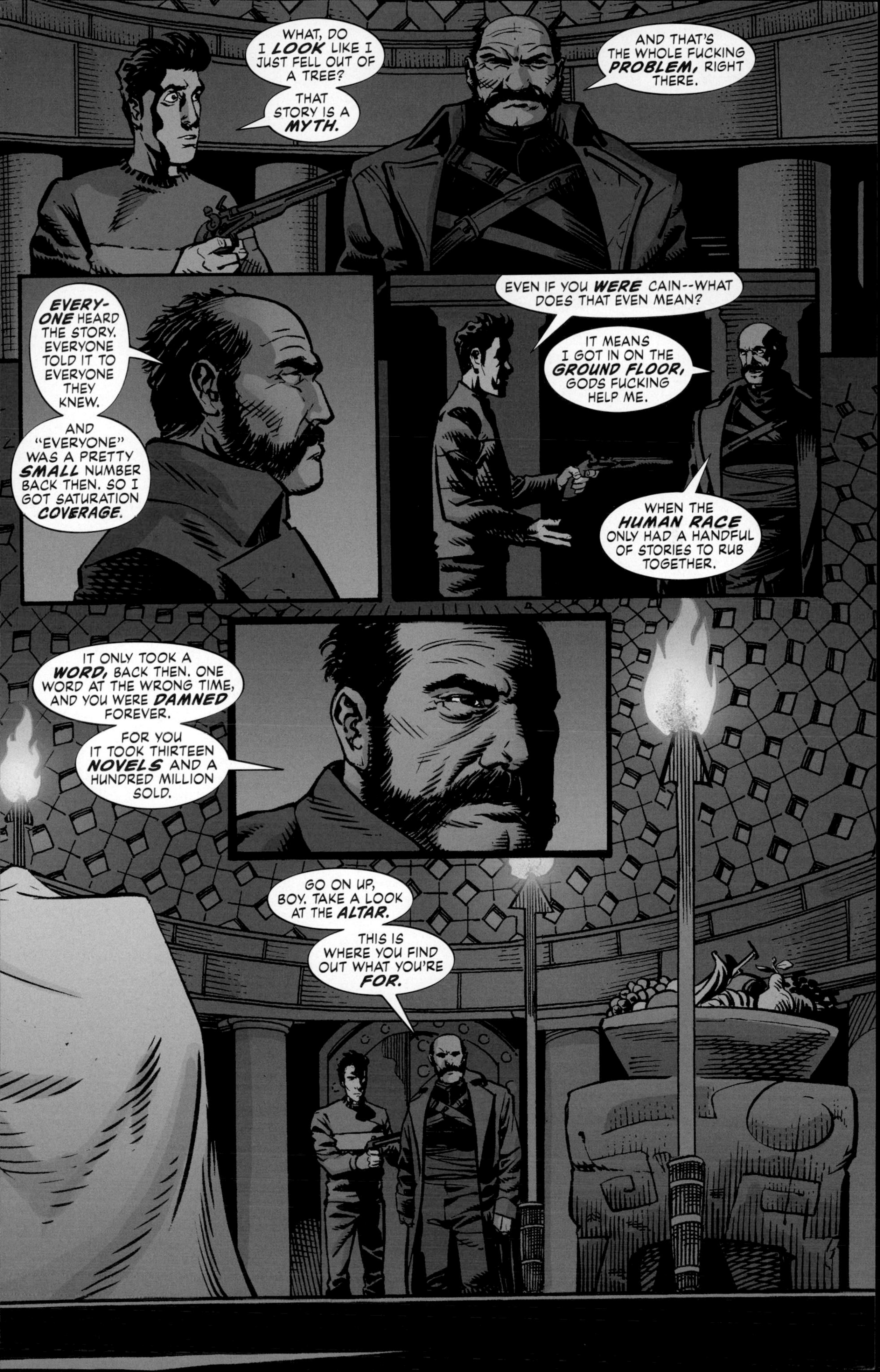
WHAT, DO I LOOK LIKE I JUST FELL OUT OF A TREE?
THAT STORY IS A MYTH.
AND THAT'S THE WHOLE FUCKING PROBLEM, RIGHT THERE.
EVERYONE HEARD THE STORY. EVERYONE TOLD IT TO EVERYONE THEY KNEW.
AND "EVERYONE" WAS A PRETTY SMALL NUMBER BACK THEN. SO I GOT SATURATION COVERAGE.
EVEN IF YOU WERE CAIN--WHAT DOES THAT EVEN MEAN?
IT MEANS I GOT IN ON THE GROUND FLOOR, GODS FUCKING HELP ME.
WHEN THE HUMAN RACE ONLY HAD A HANDFUL OF STORIES TO RUB TOGETHER.
IT ONLY TOOK A WORD, BACK THEN. ONE WORD AT THE WRONG TIME, AND YOU WERE DAMNED FOREVER.
FOR YOU IT TOOK THIRTEEN NOVELS AND A HUNDRED MILLION SOLD.
GO ON UP, BOY. TAKE A LOOK AT THE ALTAR.
THIS IS WHERE YOU FIND OUT WHAT YOU'RE FOR.

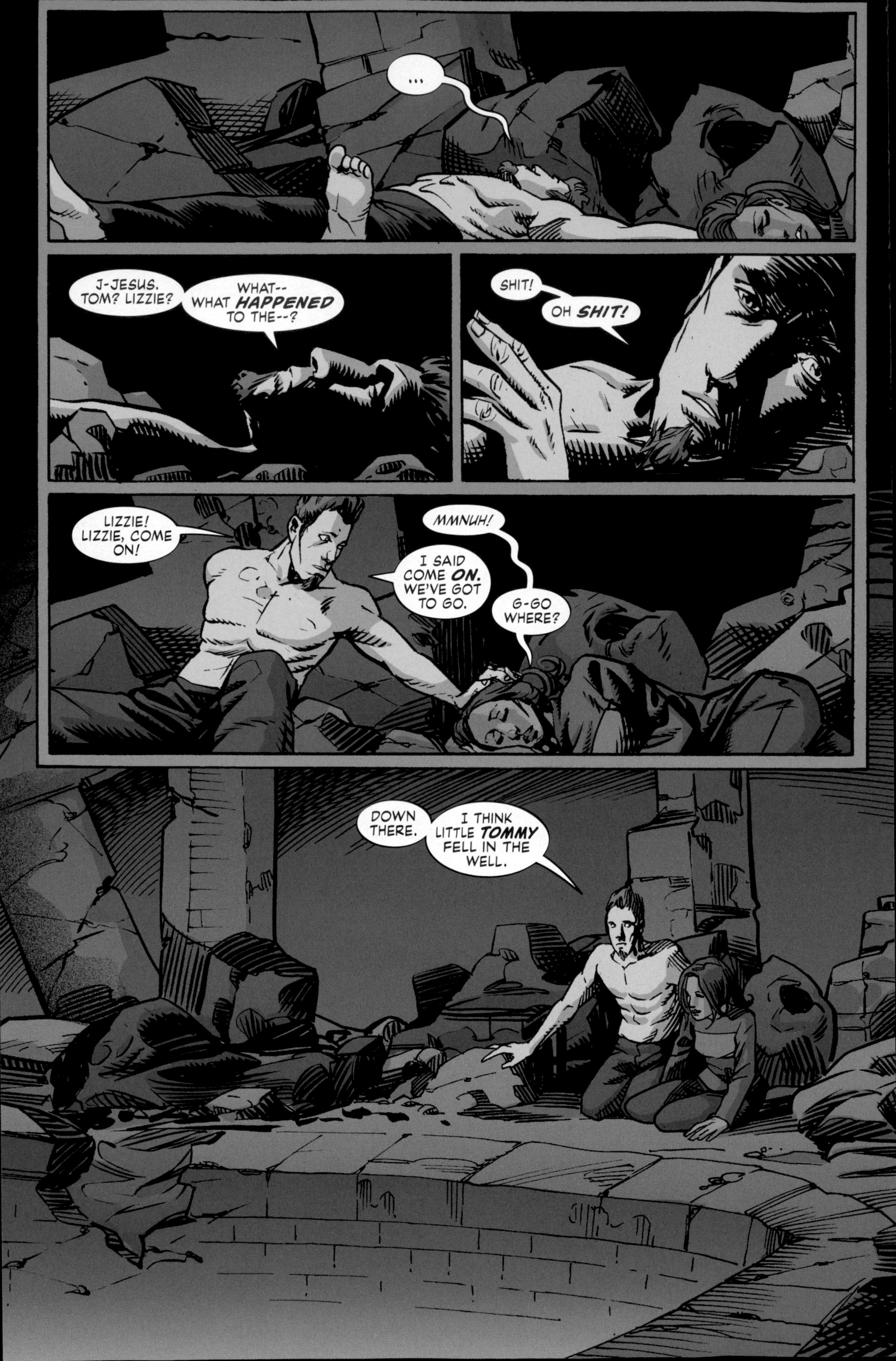
...
J-JESUS. TOM? LIZZIE?
WHAT-- WHAT HAPPENED TO THE--?
SHIT!
OH SHIT!
LIZZIE! LIZZIE, COME ON!
MMNUH!
I SAID COME ON. WE'VE GOT TO GO.
G-GO WHERE?
DOWN THERE.
I THINK LITTLE TOMMY FELL IN THE WELL.

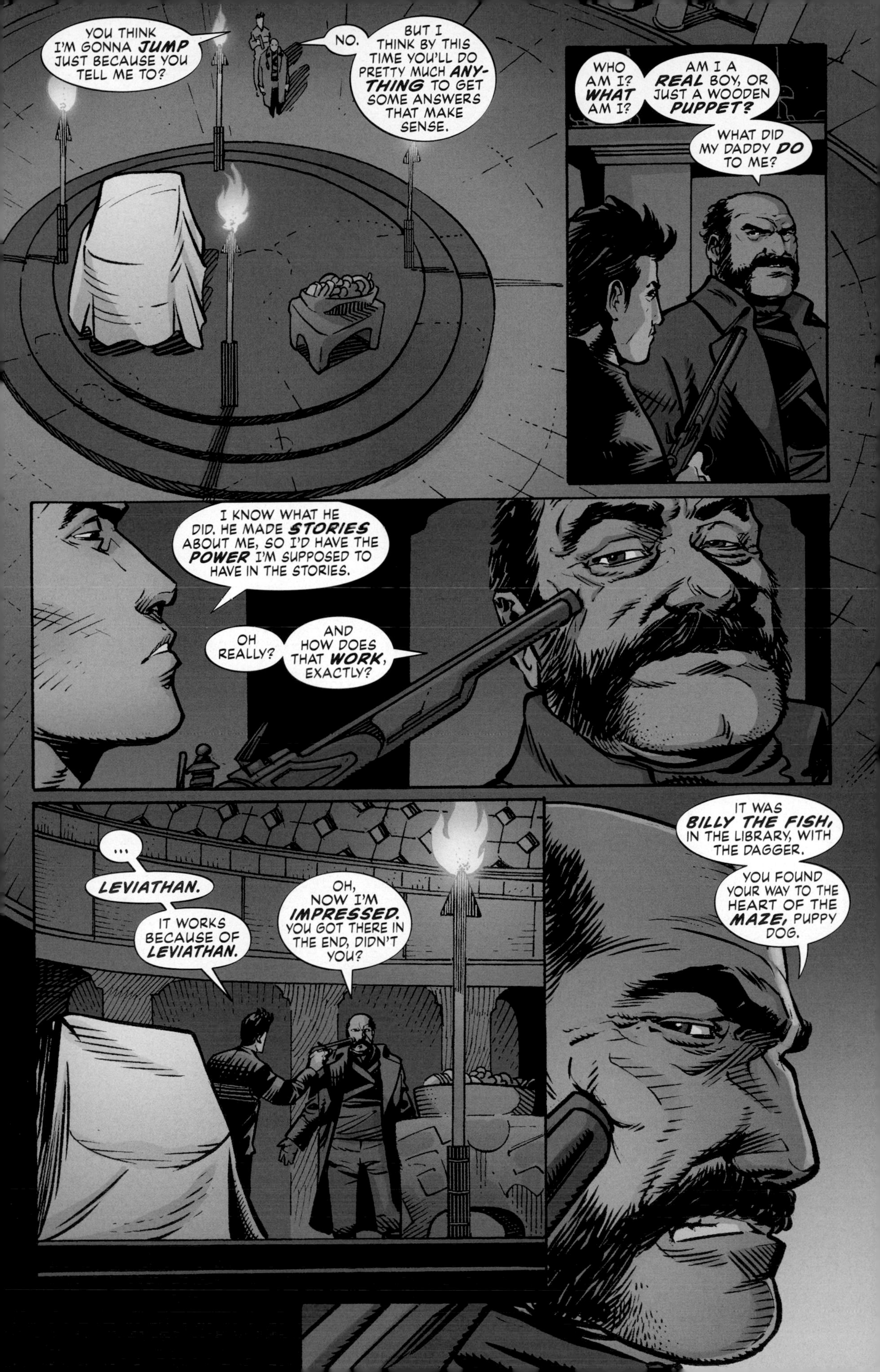
YOU THINK I'M GONNA JUMP JUST BECAUSE YOU TELL ME TO?
NO.
BUT I THINK BY THIS TIME YOU'LL DO PRETTY MUCH ANYTHING TO GET SOME ANSWERS THAT MAKE SENSE.
WHO AM I? WHAT AM I?
AM I A REAL BOY, OR JUST A WOODEN PUPPET?
WHAT DID MY DADDY DO TO ME?
I KNOW WHAT HE DID. HE MADE STORIES ABOUT ME, SO I'D HAVE THE POWER I'M SUPPOSED TO HAVE IN THE STORIES.
OH REALLY?
AND HOW DOES THAT WORK, EXACTLY?
...
LEVIATHAN.
IT WORKS BECAUSE OF LEVIATHAN.
OH, NOW I'M IMPRESSED. YOU GOT THERE IN THE END, DIDN'T YOU?
IT WAS BILLY THE FISH, IN THE LIBRARY, WITH THE DAGGER.
YOU FOUND YOUR WAY TO THE HEART OF THE MAZE, PUPPY DOG.

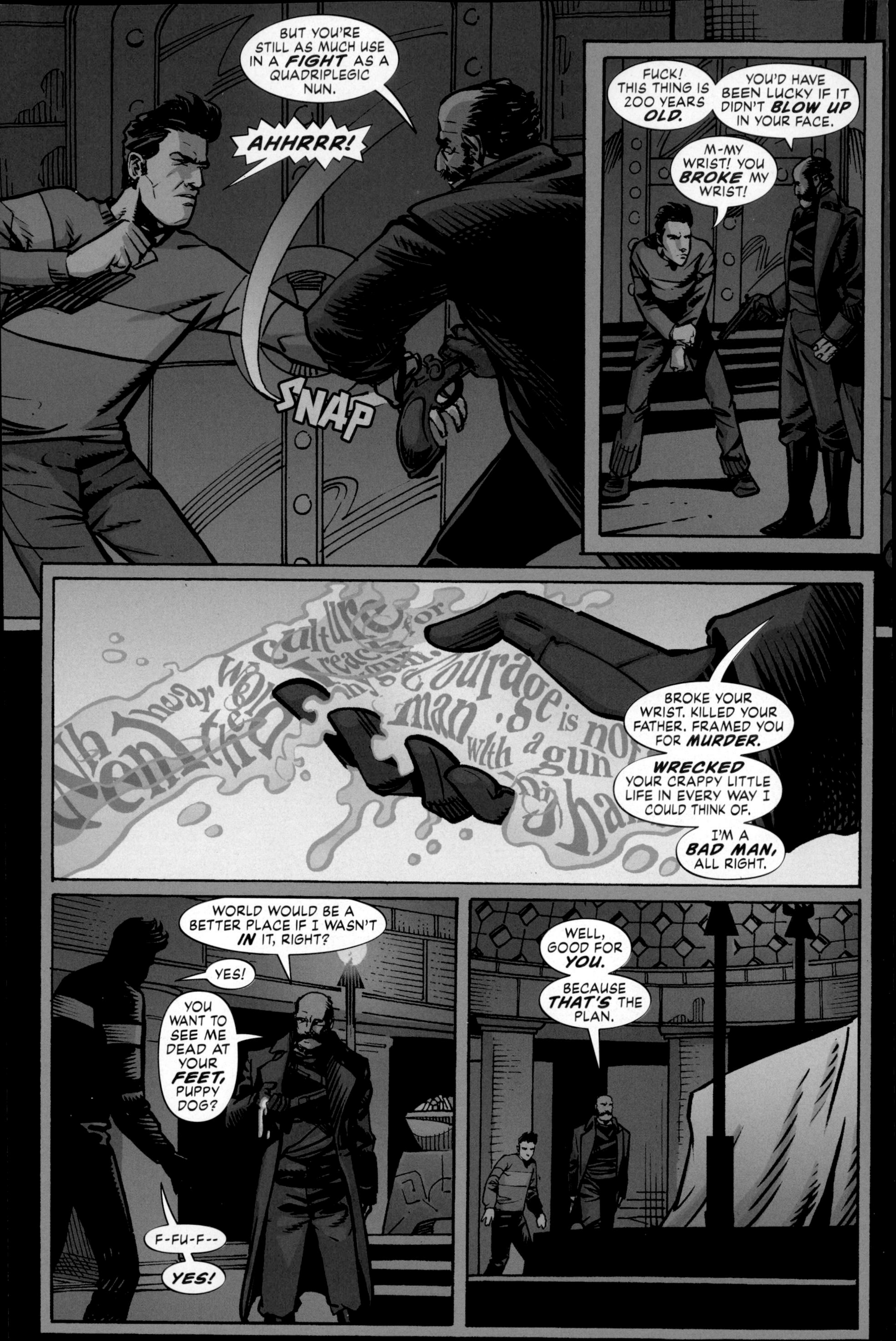
BUT YOU'RE STILL AS MUCH USE IN A FIGHT AS A QUADRIPLEGIC NUN.
SNAP
AHHRRR!
FUCK! THIS THING IS 200 YEARS OLD.
YOU'D HAVE BEEN LUCKY IF IT DIDN'T BLOW UP IN YOUR FACE.
M-MY WRIST! YOU BROKE MY WRIST!
BROKE YOUR WRIST. KILLED YOUR FATHER. FRAMED YOU FOR MURDER.
WRECKED YOUR CRAPPY LITTLE LIFE IN EVERY WAY I COULD THINK OF.
I'M A BAD MAN, ALL RIGHT.
WORLD WOULD BE A BETTER PLACE IF I WASN'T IN IT, RIGHT?
YES!
YOU WANT TO SEE ME DEAD AT YOUR FEET, PUPPY DOG?
F-FU-F--
YES!
WELL, GOOD FOR YOU.
BECAUSE THAT'S THE PLAN.

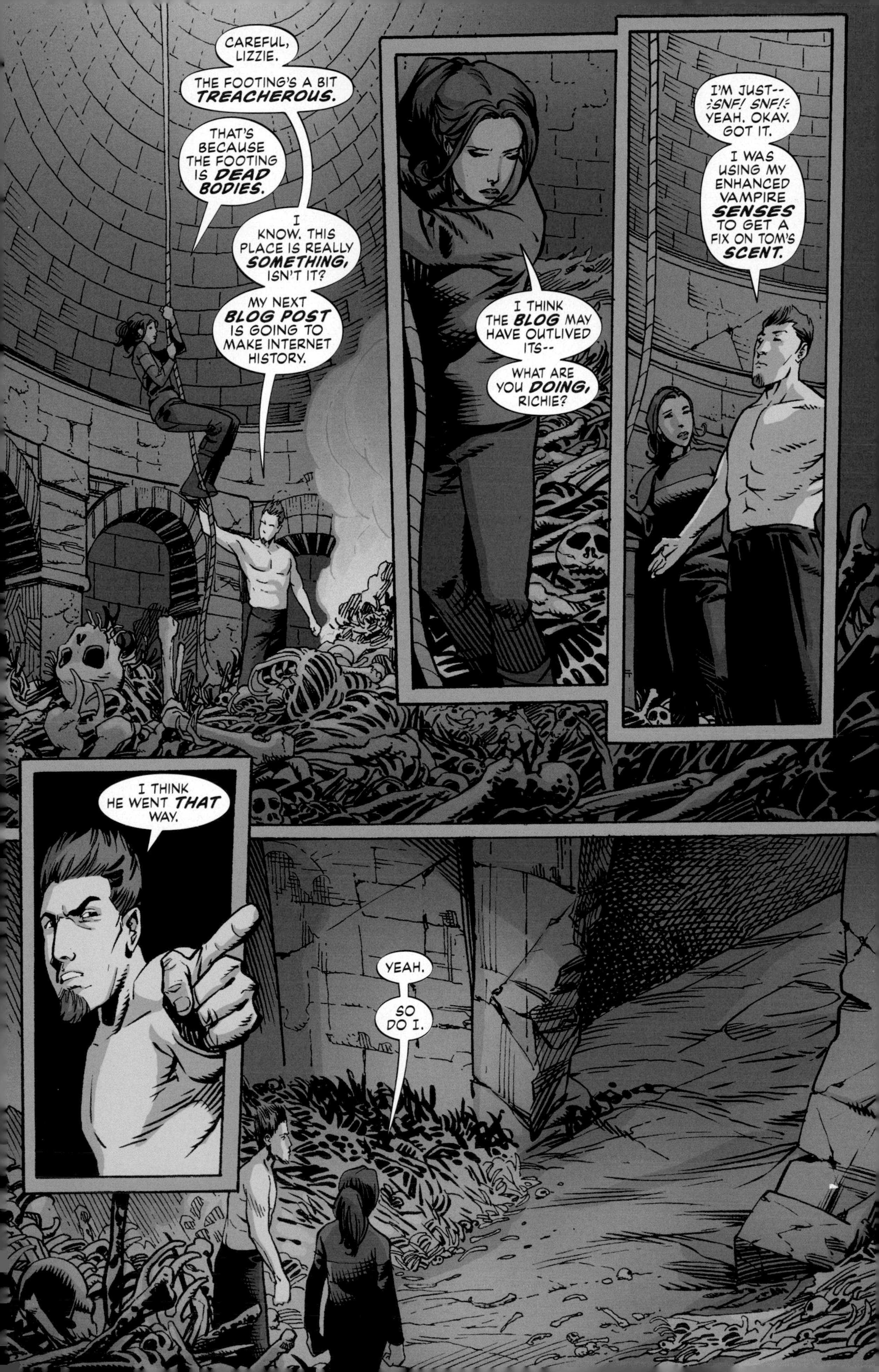
CAREFUL, LIZZIE.
THE FOOTING'S A BIT **TREACHEROUS.**
THAT'S BECAUSE THE FOOTING IS **DEAD BODIES.**
I KNOW. THIS PLACE IS REALLY **SOMETHING,** ISN'T IT?
MY NEXT **BLOG POST** IS GOING TO MAKE INTERNET HISTORY.
I THINK THE **BLOG** MAY HAVE OUTLIVED ITS--
WHAT ARE YOU **DOING,** RICHIE?
I'M JUST-- *SNF! SNF!* YEAH. OKAY. GOT IT.
I WAS USING MY ENHANCED VAMPIRE **SENSES** TO GET A FIX ON TOM'S **SCENT.**
I THINK HE WENT **THAT** WAY.
YEAH.
SO DO I.

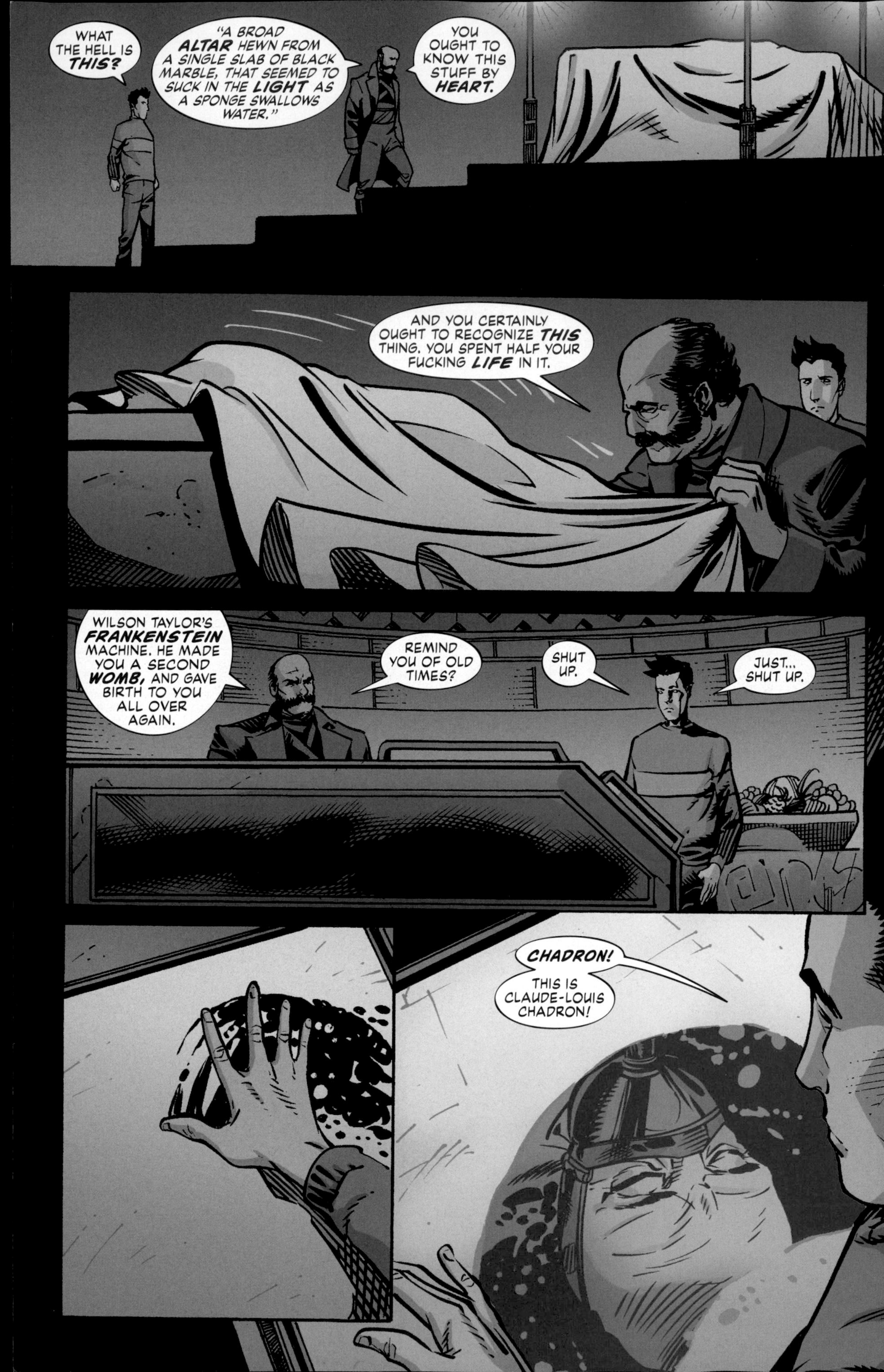
WHAT THE HELL IS THIS?
"A BROAD ALTAR HEWN FROM A SINGLE SLAB OF BLACK MARBLE, THAT SEEMED TO SUCK IN THE LIGHT AS A SPONGE SWALLOWS WATER."
YOU OUGHT TO KNOW THIS STUFF BY HEART.
AND YOU CERTAINLY OUGHT TO RECOGNIZE THIS THING. YOU SPENT HALF YOUR FUCKING LIFE IN IT.
WILSON TAYLOR'S FRANKENSTEIN MACHINE. HE MADE YOU A SECOND WOMB, AND GAVE BIRTH TO YOU ALL OVER AGAIN.
REMIND YOU OF OLD TIMES?
SHUT UP.
JUST... SHUT UP.
CHADRON!
THIS IS CLAUDE-LOUIS CHADRON!

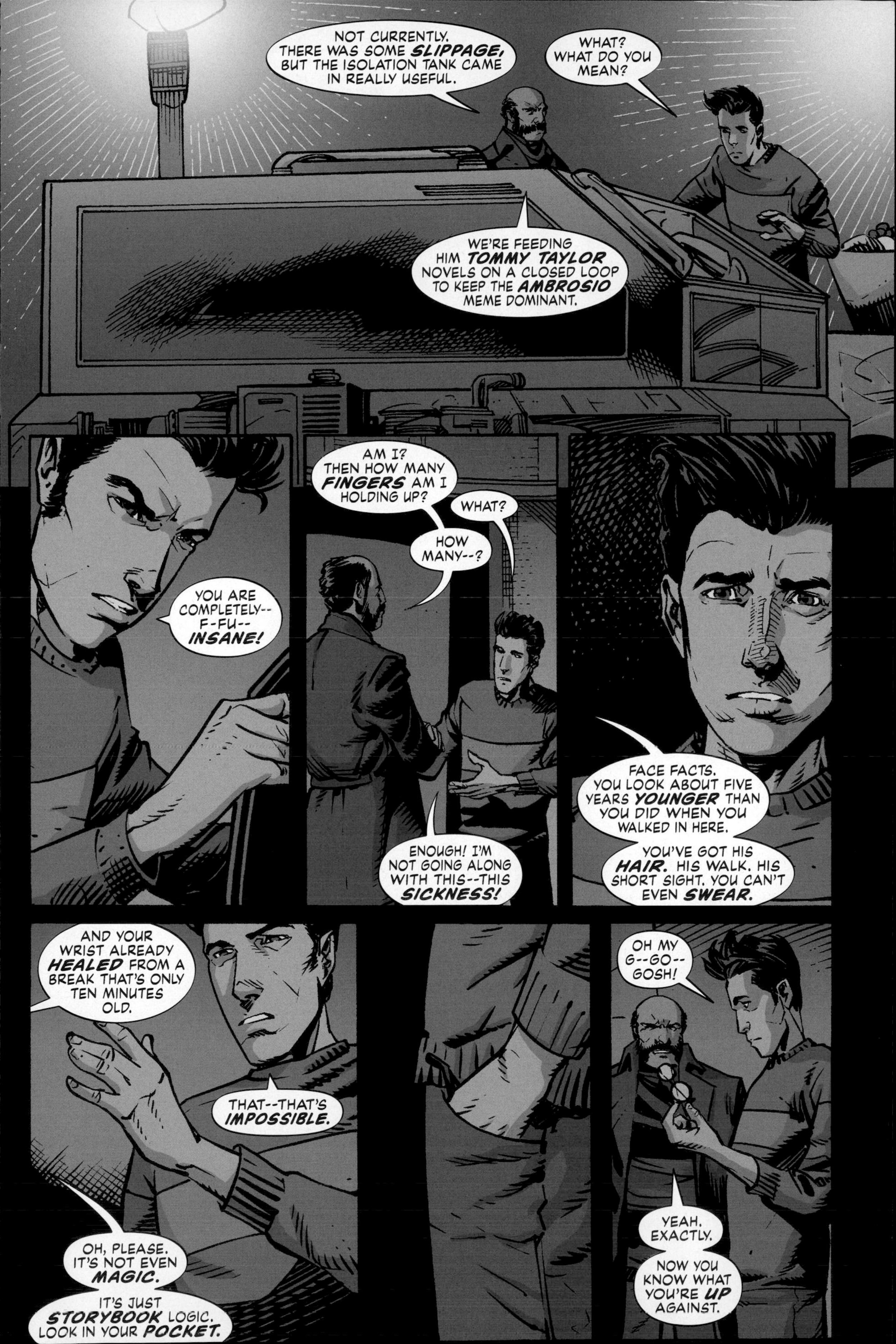
NOT CURRENTLY. THERE WAS SOME SLIPPAGE, BUT THE ISOLATION TANK CAME IN REALLY USEFUL.
WHAT? WHAT DO YOU MEAN?
WE'RE FEEDING HIM TOMMY TAYLOR NOVELS ON A CLOSED LOOP TO KEEP THE AMBROSIO MEME DOMINANT.
YOU ARE COMPLETELY-- F-FU-- INSANE!
AM I? THEN HOW MANY FINGERS AM I HOLDING UP?
WHAT?
HOW MANY--?
ENOUGH! I'M NOT GOING ALONG WITH THIS--THIS SICKNESS!
FACE FACTS. YOU LOOK ABOUT FIVE YEARS YOUNGER THAN YOU DID WHEN YOU WALKED IN HERE.
YOU'VE GOT HIS HAIR. HIS WALK. HIS SHORT SIGHT. YOU CAN'T EVEN SWEAR.
AND YOUR WRIST ALREADY HEALED FROM A BREAK THAT'S ONLY TEN MINUTES OLD.
THAT--THAT'S IMPOSSIBLE.
OH, PLEASE. IT'S NOT EVEN MAGIC.
IT'S JUST STORYBOOK LOGIC. LOOK IN YOUR POCKET.
OH MY G--GO-- GOSH!
YEAH. EXACTLY.
NOW YOU KNOW WHAT YOU'RE UP AGAINST.

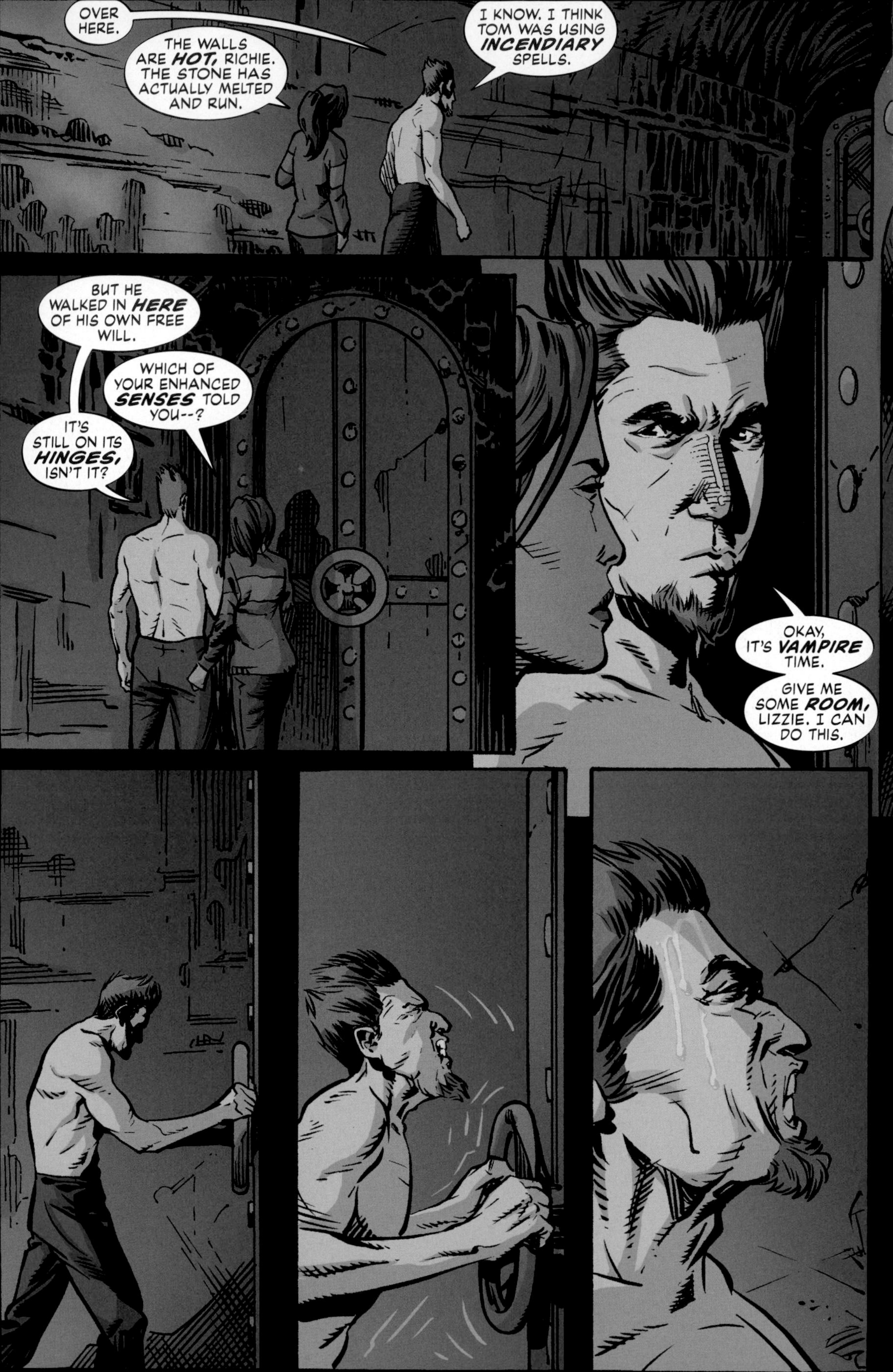

OVER HERE.
THE WALLS ARE HOT, RICHIE. THE STONE HAS ACTUALLY MELTED AND RUN.
I KNOW. I THINK TOM WAS USING INCENDIARY SPELLS.
BUT HE WALKED IN HERE OF HIS OWN FREE WILL.
WHICH OF YOUR ENHANCED SENSES TOLD YOU--?
IT'S STILL ON ITS HINGES, ISN'T IT?
OKAY, IT'S VAMPIRE TIME.
GIVE ME SOME ROOM, LIZZIE. I CAN DO THIS.

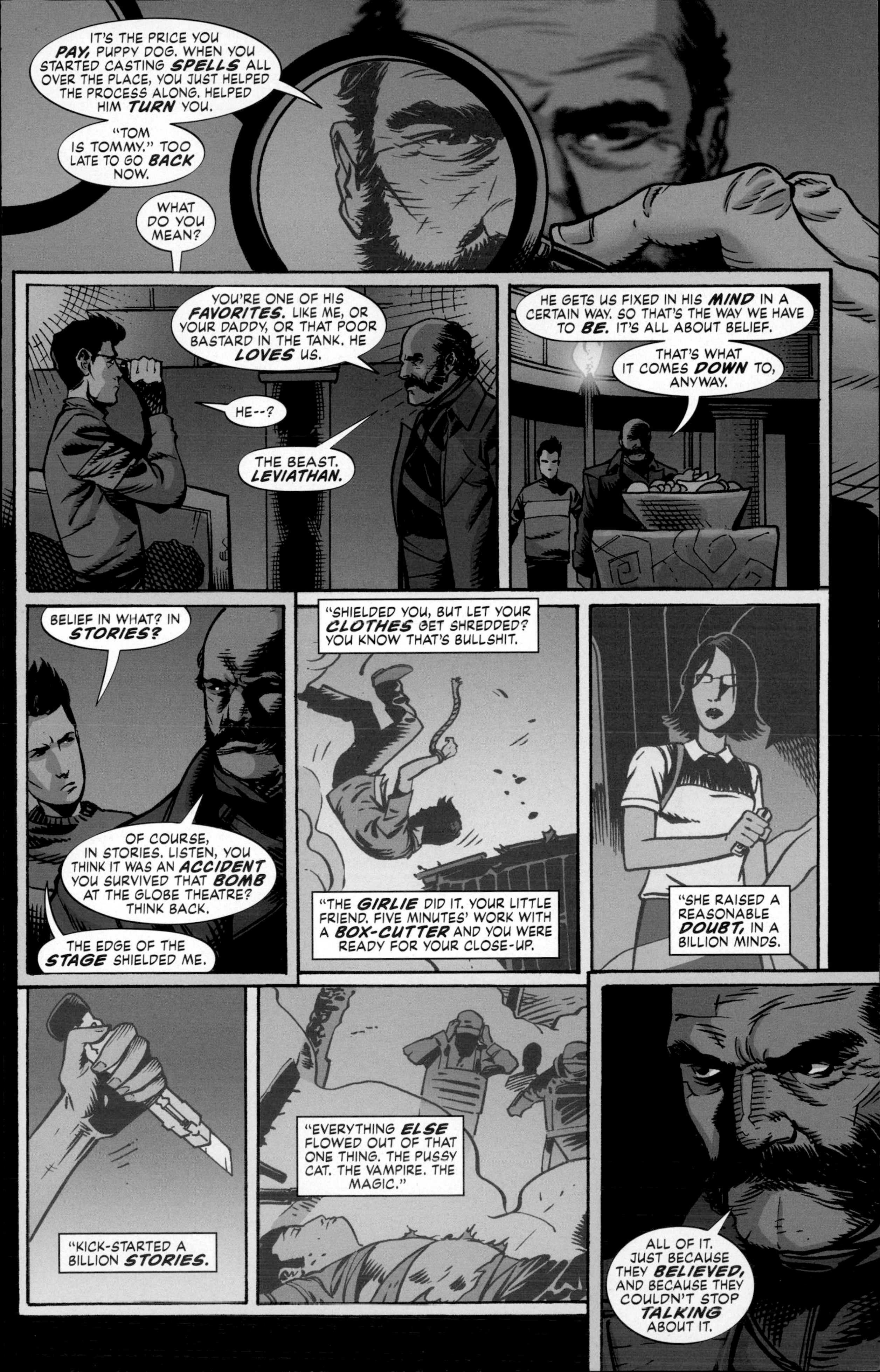
IT'S THE PRICE YOU PAY, PUPPY DOG. WHEN YOU STARTED CASTING SPELLS ALL OVER THE PLACE, YOU JUST HELPED THE PROCESS ALONG. HELPED HIM TURN YOU.
"TOM IS TOMMY." TOO LATE TO GO BACK NOW.
WHAT DO YOU MEAN?
YOU'RE ONE OF HIS FAVORITES. LIKE ME, OR YOUR DADDY, OR THAT POOR BASTARD IN THE TANK. HE LOVES US.
HE--?
THE BEAST. LEVIATHAN.
HE GETS US FIXED IN HIS MIND IN A CERTAIN WAY. SO THAT'S THE WAY WE HAVE TO BE. IT'S ALL ABOUT BELIEF.
THAT'S WHAT IT COMES DOWN TO, ANYWAY.
BELIEF IN WHAT? IN STORIES?
OF COURSE, IN STORIES. LISTEN, YOU THINK IT WAS AN ACCIDENT YOU SURVIVED THAT BOMB AT THE GLOBE THEATRE? THINK BACK.
THE EDGE OF THE STAGE SHIELDED ME.
"SHIELDED YOU, BUT LET YOUR CLOTHES GET SHREDDED? YOU KNOW THAT'S BULLSHIT.
"THE GIRLIE DID IT. YOUR LITTLE FRIEND. FIVE MINUTES' WORK WITH A BOX-CUTTER AND YOU WERE READY FOR YOUR CLOSE-UP.
"SHE RAISED A REASONABLE DOUBT, IN A BILLION MINDS.
"KICK-STARTED A BILLION STORIES.
"EVERYTHING ELSE FLOWED OUT OF THAT ONE THING. THE PUSSY CAT. THE VAMPIRE. THE MAGIC."
ALL OF IT. JUST BECAUSE THEY BELIEVED, AND BECAUSE THEY COULDN'T STOP TALKING ABOUT IT.

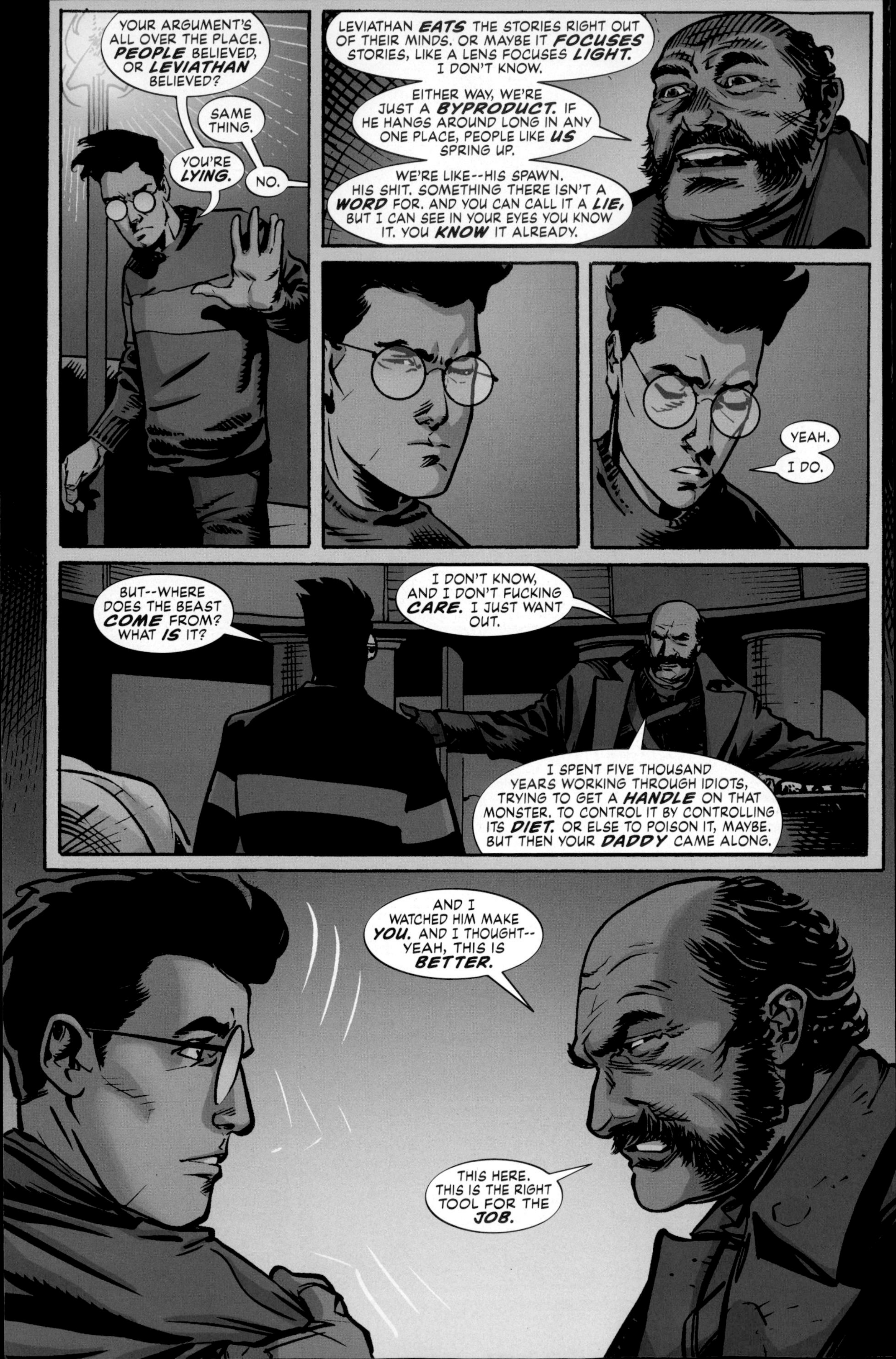
YOUR ARGUMENT'S ALL OVER THE PLACE. PEOPLE BELIEVED, OR LEVIATHAN BELIEVED?
SAME THING.
YOU'RE LYING.
NO.
LEVIATHAN EATS THE STORIES RIGHT OUT OF THEIR MINDS. OR MAYBE IT FOCUSES STORIES, LIKE A LENS FOCUSES LIGHT. I DON'T KNOW.
EITHER WAY, WE'RE JUST A BYPRODUCT. IF HE HANGS AROUND LONG IN ANY ONE PLACE, PEOPLE LIKE US SPRING UP.
WE'RE LIKE--HIS SPAWN. HIS SHIT. SOMETHING THERE ISN'T A WORD FOR. AND YOU CAN CALL IT A LIE, BUT I CAN SEE IN YOUR EYES YOU KNOW IT. YOU KNOW IT ALREADY.
YEAH.
I DO.
BUT--WHERE DOES THE BEAST COME FROM? WHAT IS IT?
I DON'T KNOW, AND I DON'T FUCKING CARE. I JUST WANT OUT.
I SPENT FIVE THOUSAND YEARS WORKING THROUGH IDIOTS, TRYING TO GET A HANDLE ON THAT MONSTER. TO CONTROL IT BY CONTROLLING ITS DIET. OR ELSE TO POISON IT, MAYBE. BUT THEN YOUR DADDY CAME ALONG.
AND I WATCHED HIM MAKE YOU. AND I THOUGHT-- YEAH, THIS IS BETTER.
THIS HERE. THIS IS THE RIGHT TOOL FOR THE JOB.

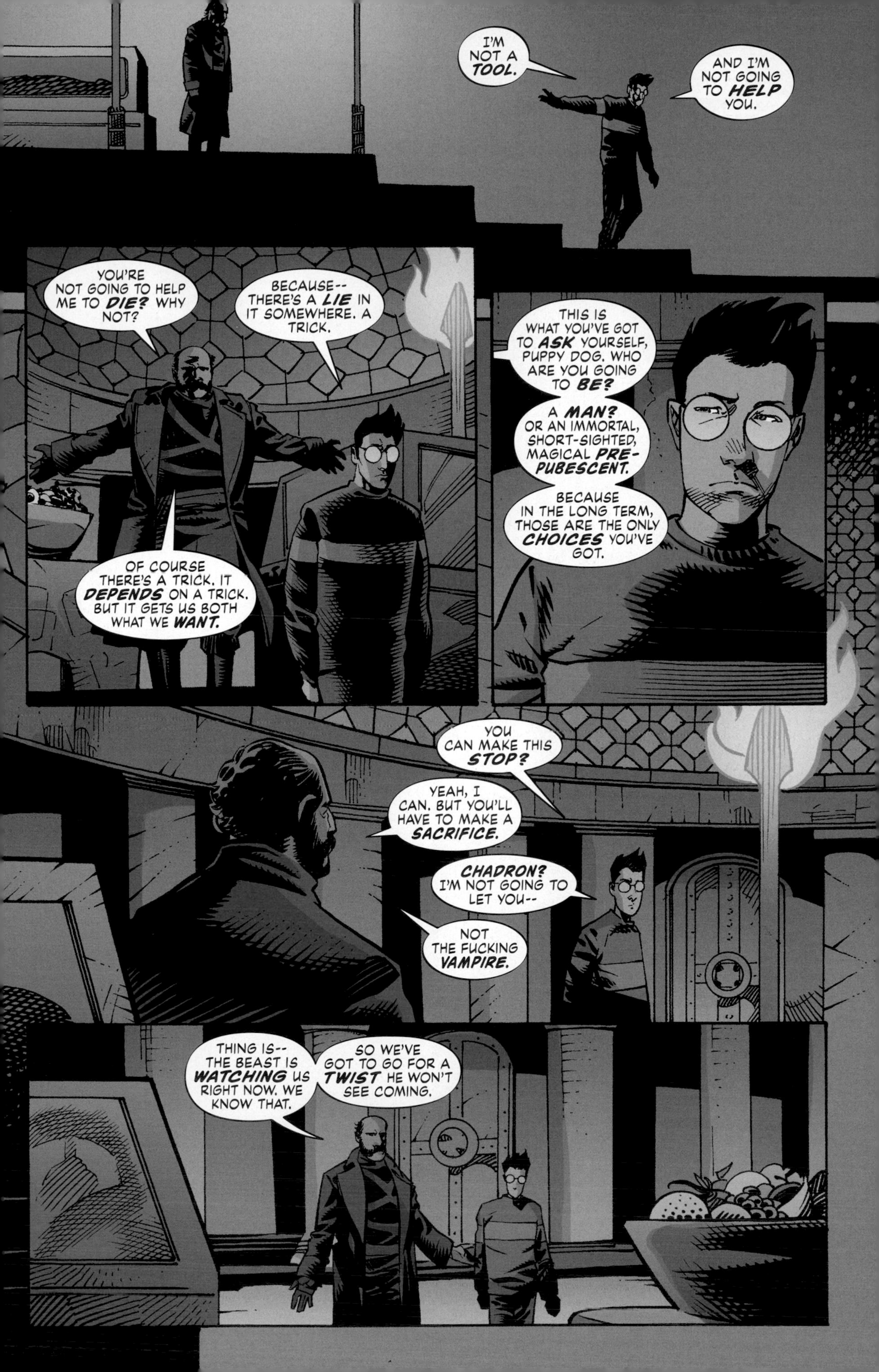
I'M NOT A TOOL.
AND I'M NOT GOING TO HELP YOU.
YOU'RE NOT GOING TO HELP ME TO DIE? WHY NOT?
BECAUSE-- THERE'S A LIE IN IT SOMEWHERE. A TRICK.
OF COURSE THERE'S A TRICK. IT DEPENDS ON A TRICK. BUT IT GETS US BOTH WHAT WE WANT.
THIS IS WHAT YOU'VE GOT TO ASK YOURSELF, PUPPY DOG. WHO ARE YOU GOING TO BE?
A MAN? OR AN IMMORTAL, SHORT-SIGHTED, MAGICAL PRE-PUBESCENT.
BECAUSE IN THE LONG TERM, THOSE ARE THE ONLY CHOICES YOU'VE GOT.
YOU CAN MAKE THIS STOP?
YEAH, I CAN. BUT YOU'LL HAVE TO MAKE A SACRIFICE.
CHADRON? I'M NOT GOING TO LET YOU--
NOT THE FUCKING VAMPIRE.
THING IS-- THE BEAST IS WATCHING US RIGHT NOW. WE KNOW THAT.
SO WE'VE GOT TO GO FOR A TWIST HE WON'T SEE COMING.

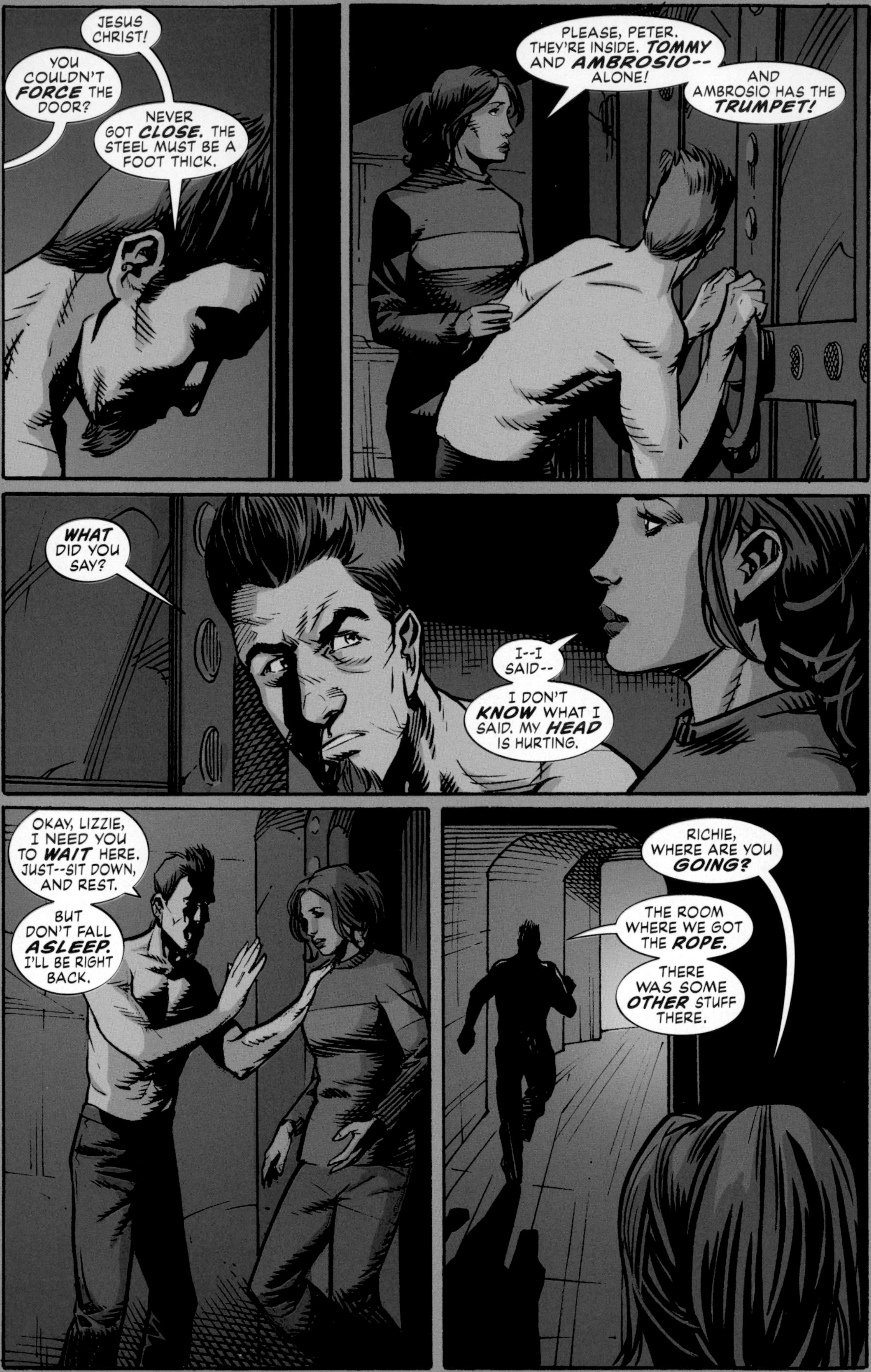
JESUS CHRIST!
YOU COULDN'T FORCE THE DOOR?
NEVER GOT CLOSE. THE STEEL MUST BE A FOOT THICK.
PLEASE, PETER. THEY'RE INSIDE. TOMMY AND AMBROSIO-- ALONE!
AND AMBROSIO HAS THE TRUMPET!
WHAT DID YOU SAY?
I--I SAID--
I DON'T KNOW WHAT I SAID. MY HEAD IS HURTING.
OKAY, LIZZIE, I NEED YOU TO WAIT HERE. JUST--SIT DOWN, AND REST.
BUT DON'T FALL ASLEEP. I'LL BE RIGHT BACK.
RICHIE, WHERE ARE YOU GOING?
THE ROOM WHERE WE GOT THE ROPE.
THERE WAS SOME OTHER STUFF THERE.

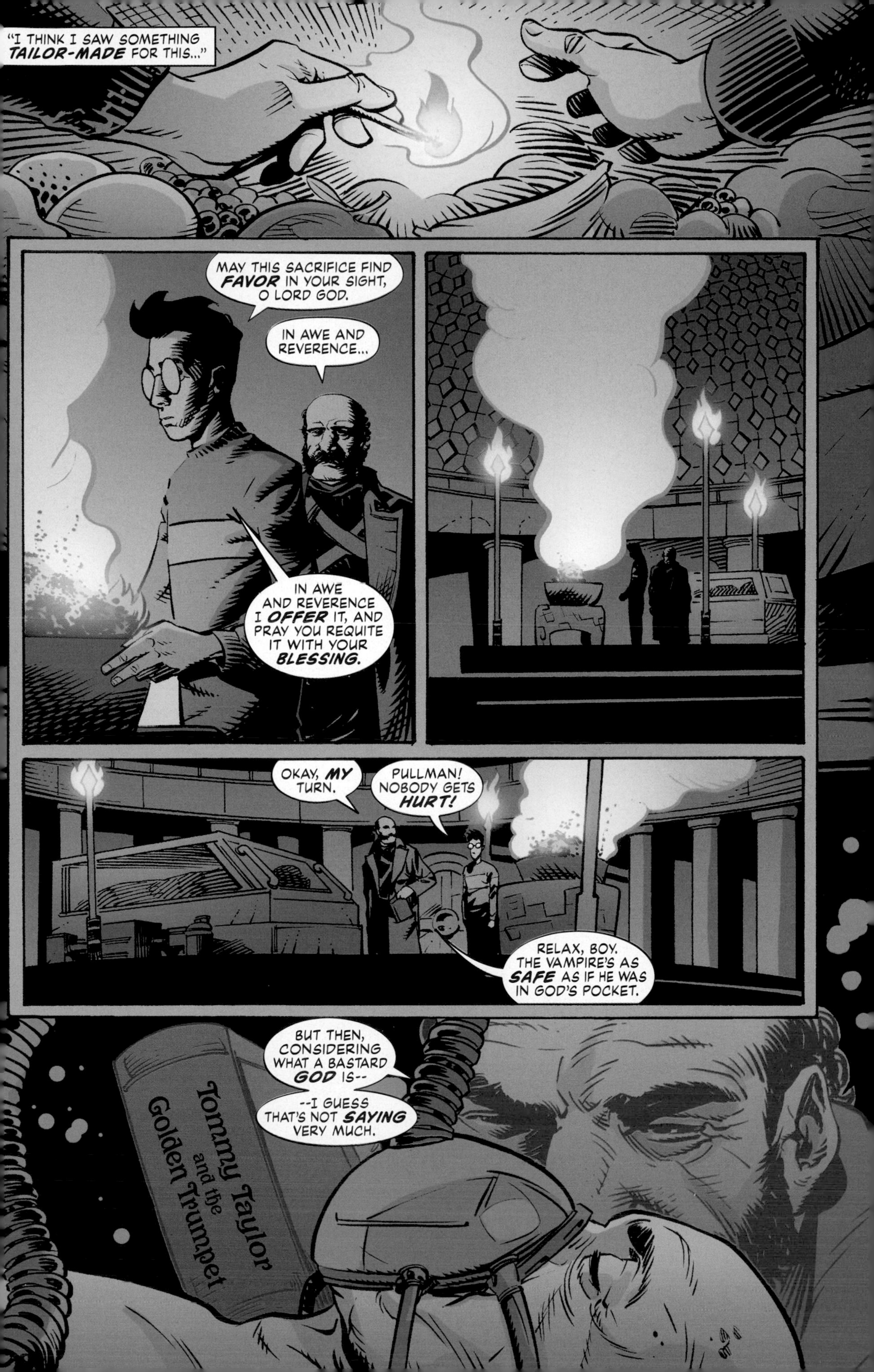

"I THINK I SAW SOMETHING TAILOR-MADE FOR THIS..."
MAY THIS SACRIFICE FIND FAVOR IN YOUR SIGHT, O LORD GOD.
IN AWE AND REVERENCE...
IN AWE AND REVERENCE I OFFER IT, AND PRAY YOU REQUITE IT WITH YOUR BLESSING.
OKAY, MY TURN.
PULLMAN! NOBODY GETS HURT!
RELAX, BOY. THE VAMPIRE'S AS SAFE AS IF HE WAS IN GOD'S POCKET.
BUT THEN, CONSIDERING WHAT A BASTARD GOD IS--
--I GUESS THAT'S NOT SAYING VERY MUCH.
Tommy Taylor and the Golden Trumpet

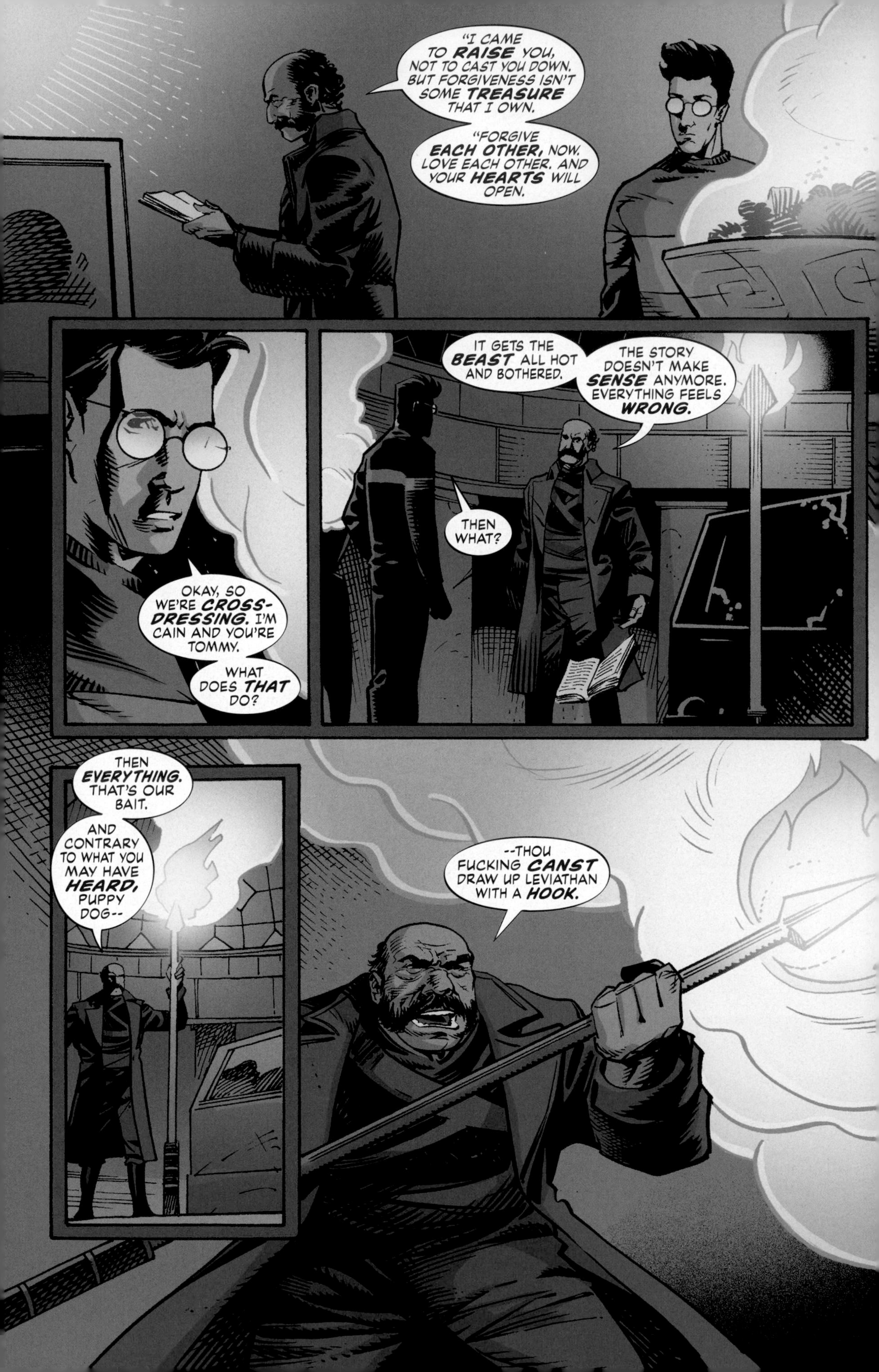
"I CAME TO RAISE YOU, NOT TO CAST YOU DOWN. BUT FORGIVENESS ISN'T SOME TREASURE THAT I OWN.
"FORGIVE EACH OTHER, NOW. LOVE EACH OTHER. AND YOUR HEARTS WILL OPEN.
OKAY, SO WE'RE CROSS-DRESSING. I'M CAIN AND YOU'RE TOMMY.
WHAT DOES THAT DO?
IT GETS THE BEAST ALL HOT AND BOTHERED.
THE STORY DOESN'T MAKE SENSE ANYMORE. EVERYTHING FEELS WRONG.
THEN WHAT?
THEN EVERYTHING. THAT'S OUR BAIT.
AND CONTRARY TO WHAT YOU MAY HAVE HEARD, PUPPY DOG--
--THOU FUCKING CANST DRAW UP LEVIATHAN WITH A HOOK.

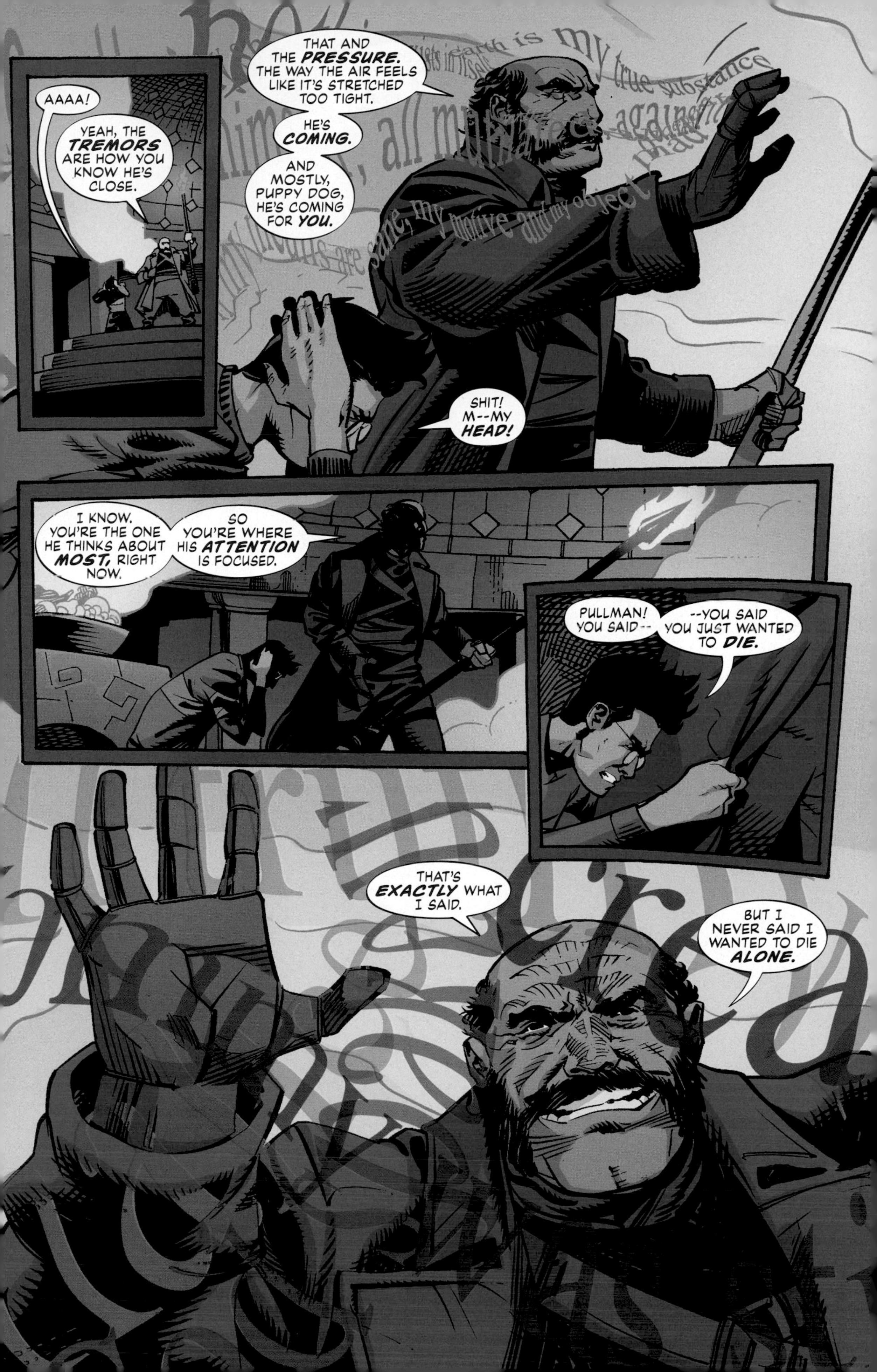
AAAA!
YEAH, THE TREMORS ARE HOW YOU KNOW HE'S CLOSE.
THAT AND THE PRESSURE. THE WAY THE AIR FEELS LIKE IT'S STRETCHED TOO TIGHT.
HE'S COMING.
AND MOSTLY, PUPPY DOG, HE'S COMING FOR YOU.
earth is my true substance
my means are sane, my motive and my object mad
SHIT! M--MY HEAD!
I KNOW. YOU'RE THE ONE HE THINKS ABOUT MOST, RIGHT NOW.
SO YOU'RE WHERE HIS ATTENTION IS FOCUSED.
PULLMAN! YOU SAID--
--YOU SAID YOU JUST WANTED TO DIE.
THAT'S EXACTLY WHAT I SAID.
BUT I NEVER SAID I WANTED TO DIE ALONE.

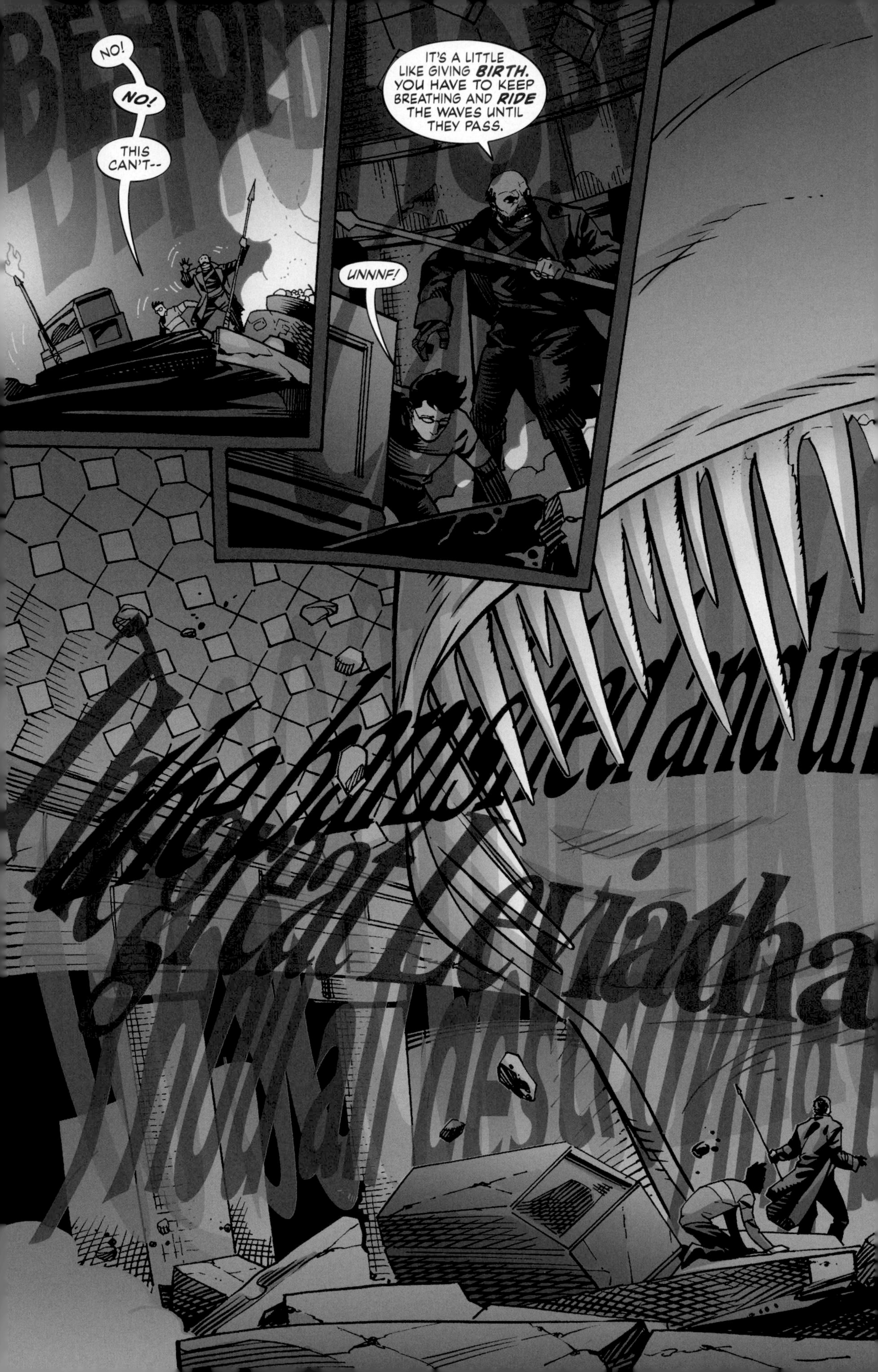
NO!
NO!
THIS CAN'T--
IT'S A LITTLE LIKE GIVING BIRTH. YOU HAVE TO KEEP BREATHING AND RIDE THE WAVES UNTIL THEY PASS.
UNNNF!

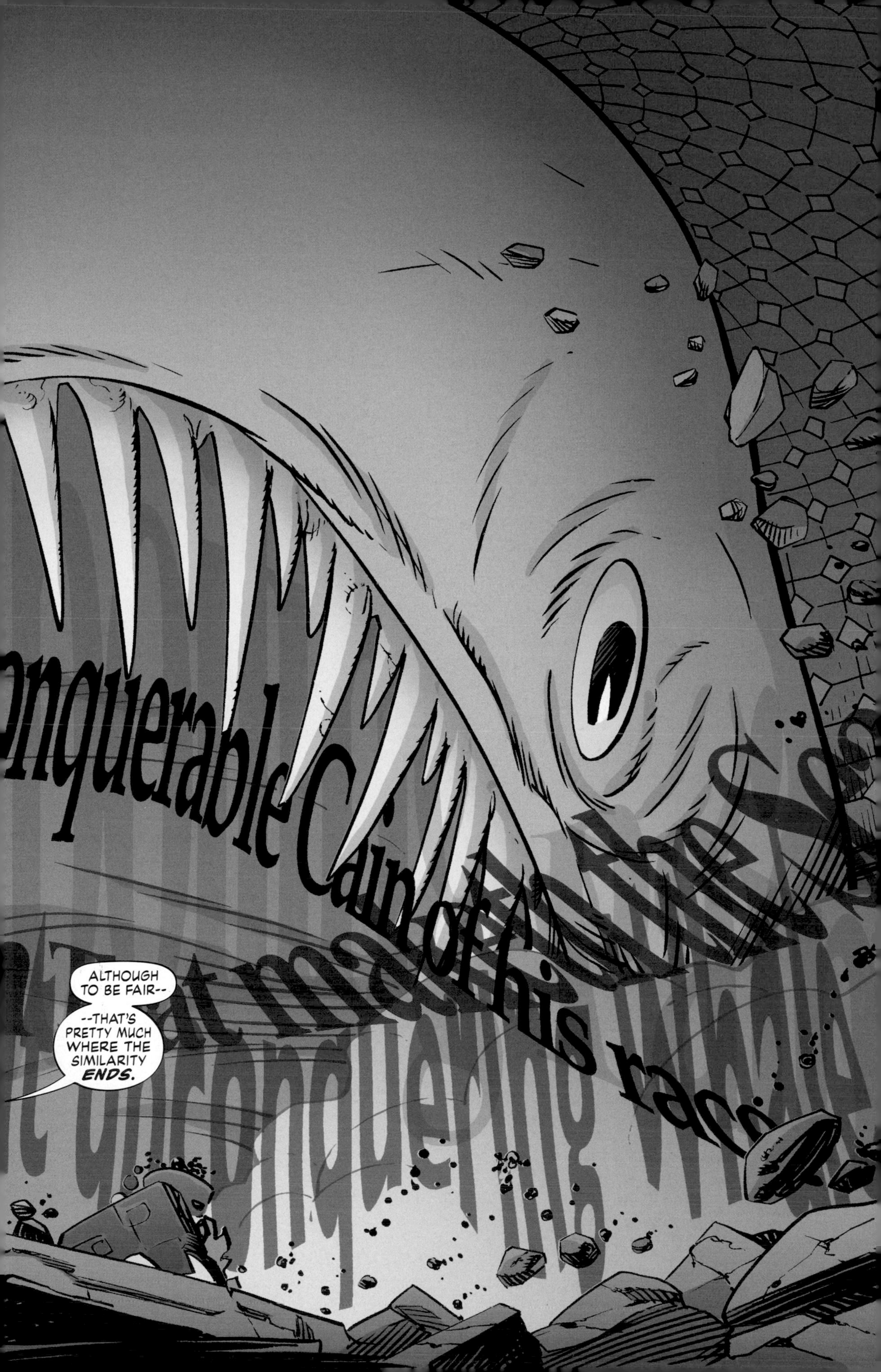
nquerable Cain of his rac
ALTHOUGH TO BE FAIR--
--THAT'S PRETTY MUCH WHERE THE SIMILARITY ENDS.

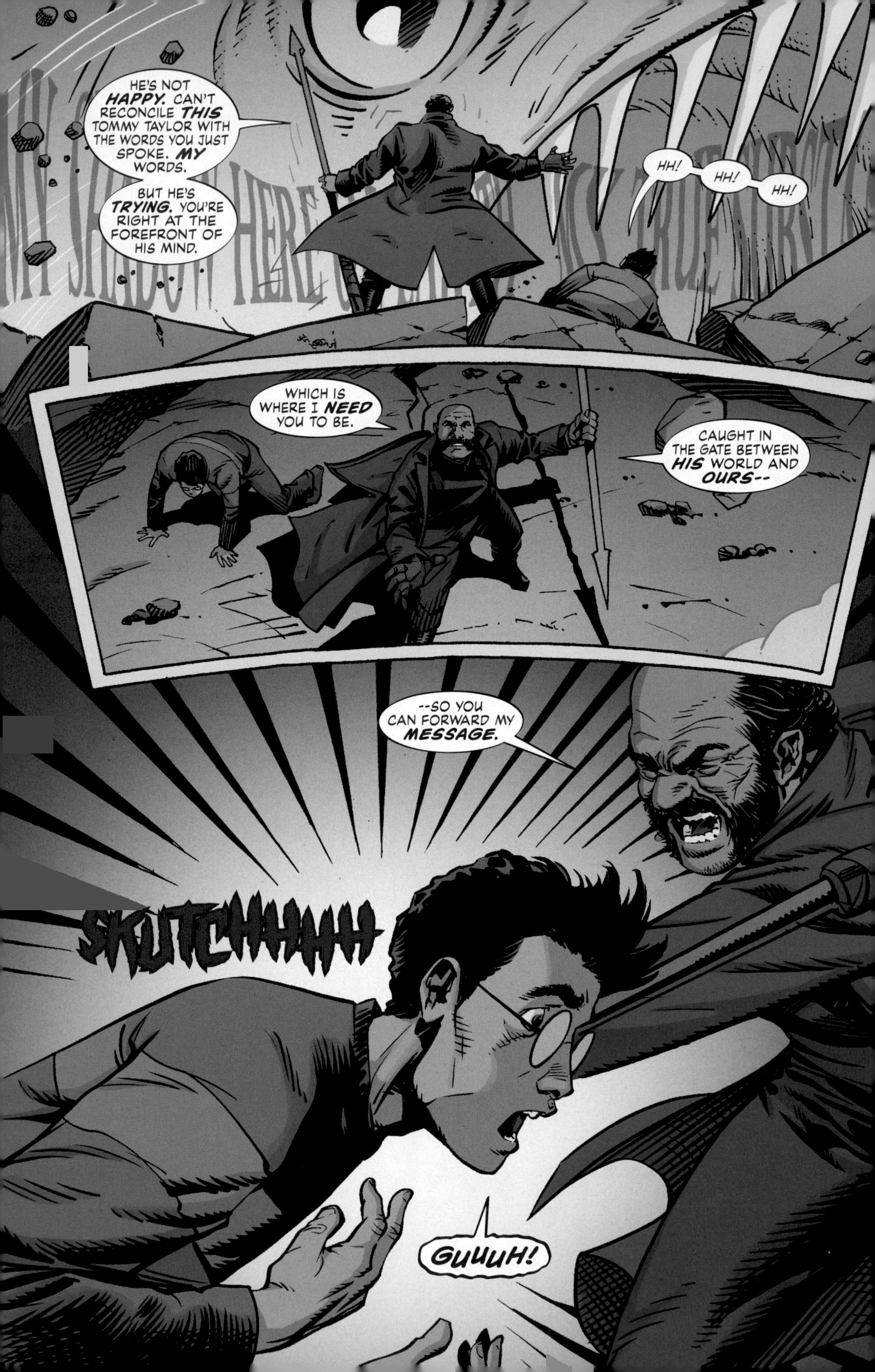
HE'S NOT HAPPY. CAN'T RECONCILE THIS TOMMY TAYLOR WITH THE WORDS YOU JUST SPOKE. MY WORDS.
BUT HE'S TRYING. YOU'RE RIGHT AT THE FOREFRONT OF HIS MIND.
HH!
HH!
HH!
WHICH IS WHERE I NEED YOU TO BE.
CAUGHT IN THE GATE BETWEEN HIS WORLD AND OURS--
--SO YOU CAN FORWARD MY MESSAGE.
SKUTCHHHHH
GUUUH!

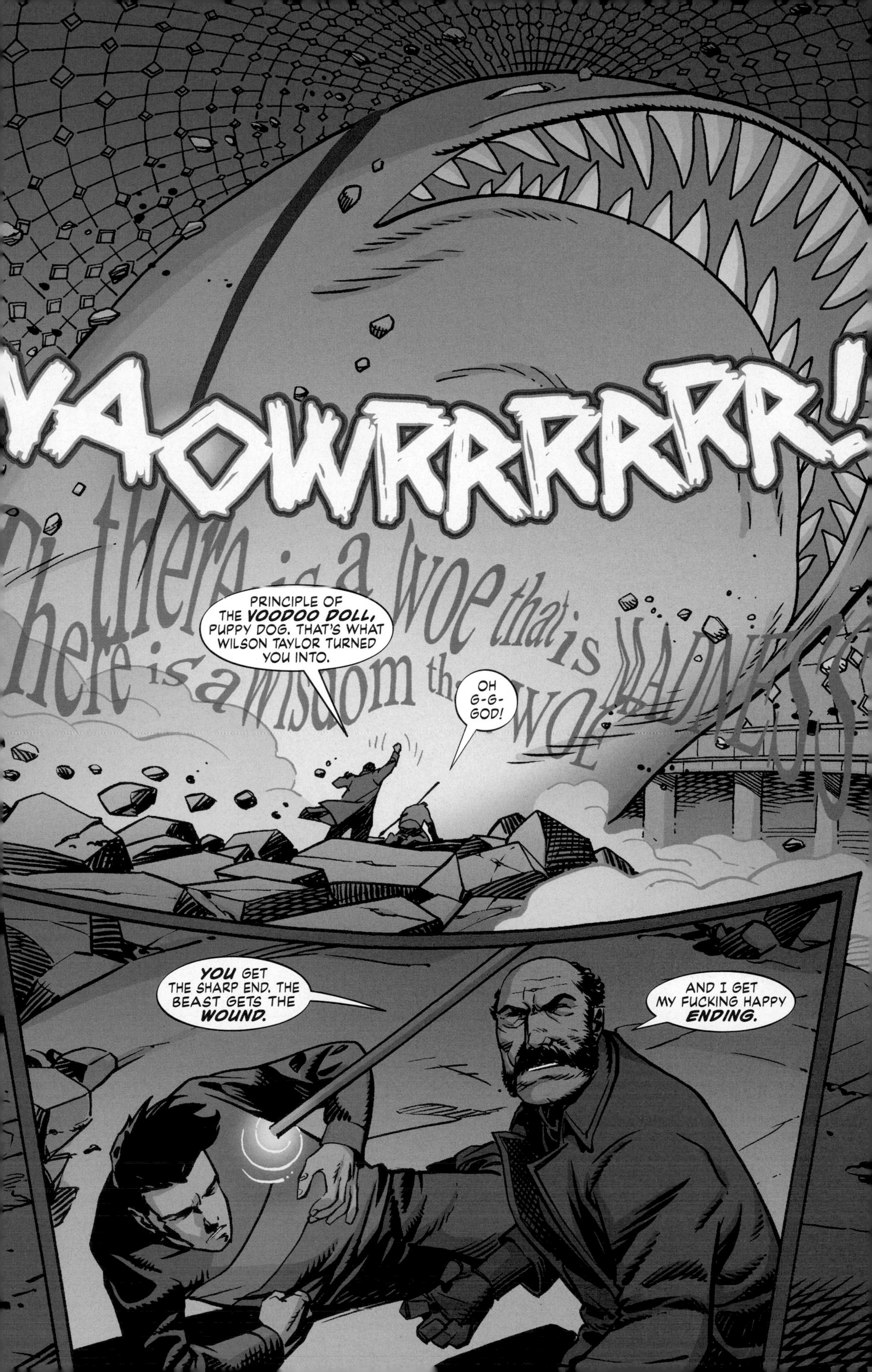

YAOWRRRRR!
there is a woe that is
PRINCIPLE OF THE VOODOO DOLL, PUPPY DOG. THAT'S WHAT WILSON TAYLOR TURNED YOU INTO.
OH G-G-GOD!
YOU GET THE SHARP END. THE BEAST GETS THE WOUND.
AND I GET MY FUCKING HAPPY ENDING.

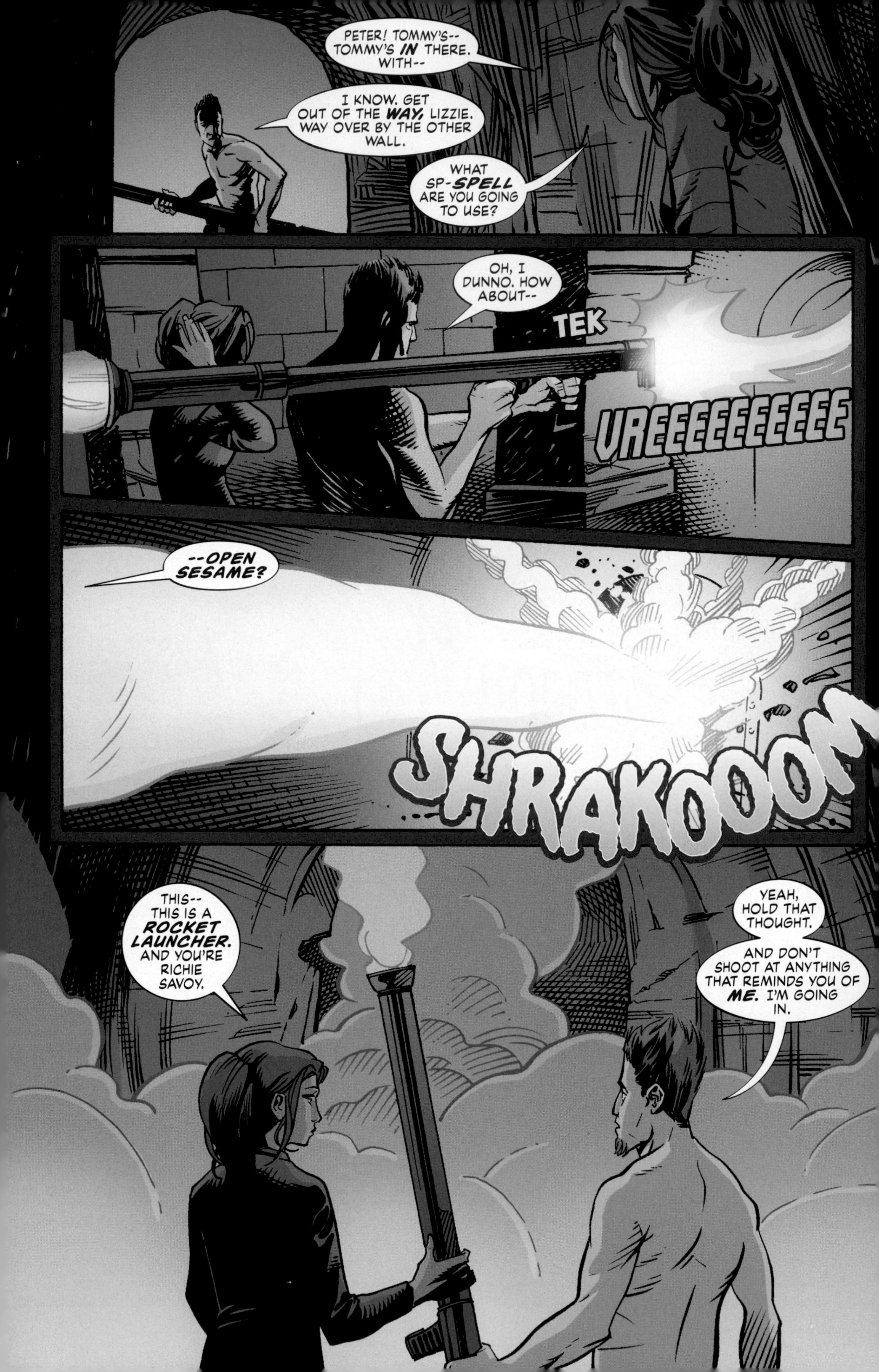
PETER! TOMMY'S-- TOMMY'S *IN* THERE. WITH--
I KNOW. GET OUT OF THE *WAY,* LIZZIE. WAY OVER BY THE OTHER WALL.
WHAT SP-*SPELL* ARE YOU GOING TO USE?
OH, I DUNNO. HOW ABOUT--
TEK
VREEEEEEEEEEE
--OPEN SESAME?
SHRAKOOOM
THIS-- THIS IS A *ROCKET LAUNCHER.* AND YOU'RE RICHIE SAVOY.
YEAH, HOLD THAT THOUGHT.
AND DON'T SHOOT AT ANYTHING THAT REMINDS YOU OF *ME.* I'M GOING IN.

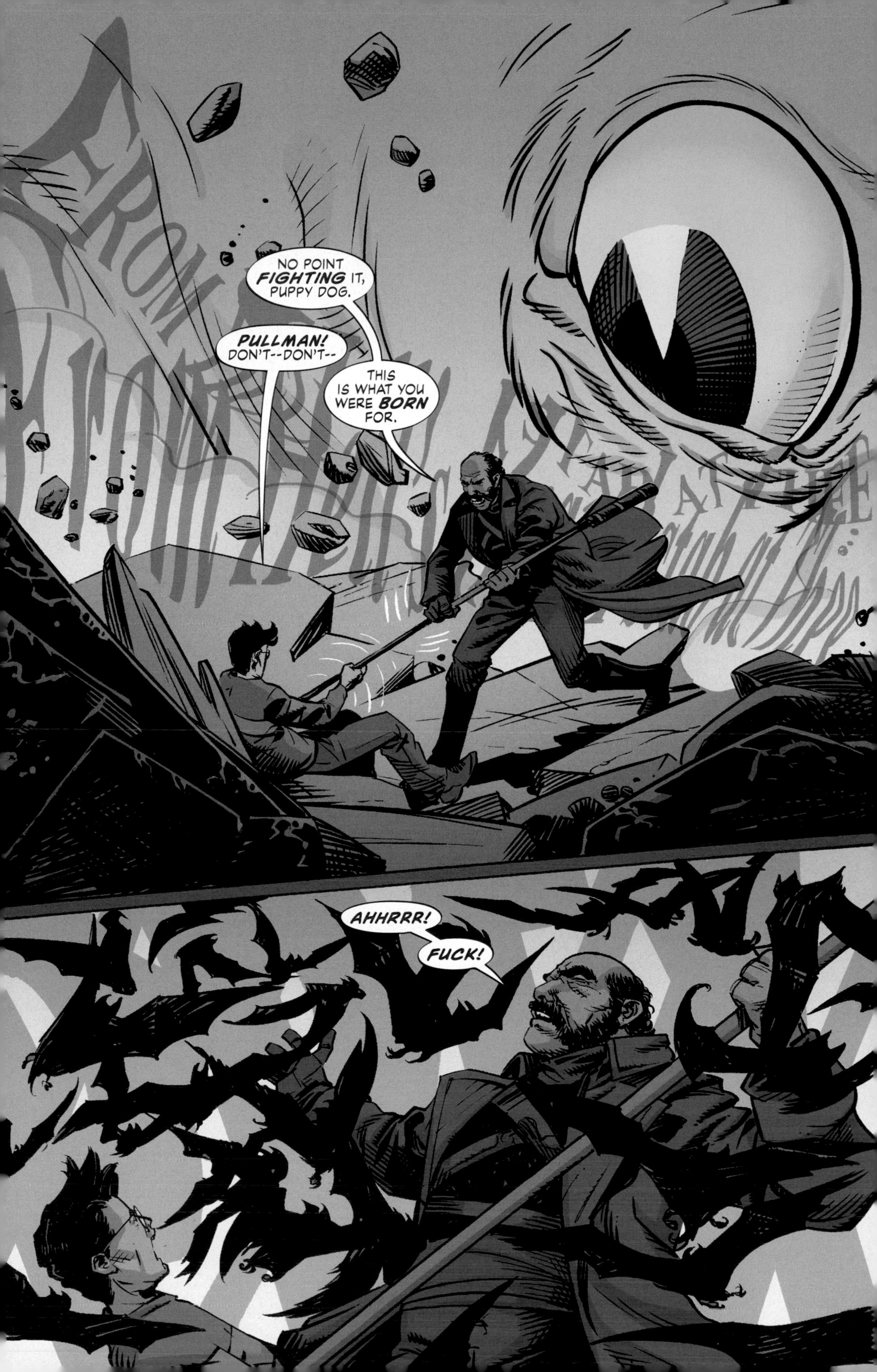

NO POINT **FIGHTING** IT, PUPPY DOG.
PULLMAN! DON'T--DON'T--
THIS IS WHAT YOU WERE **BORN** FOR.
AHHRRR!
FUCK!

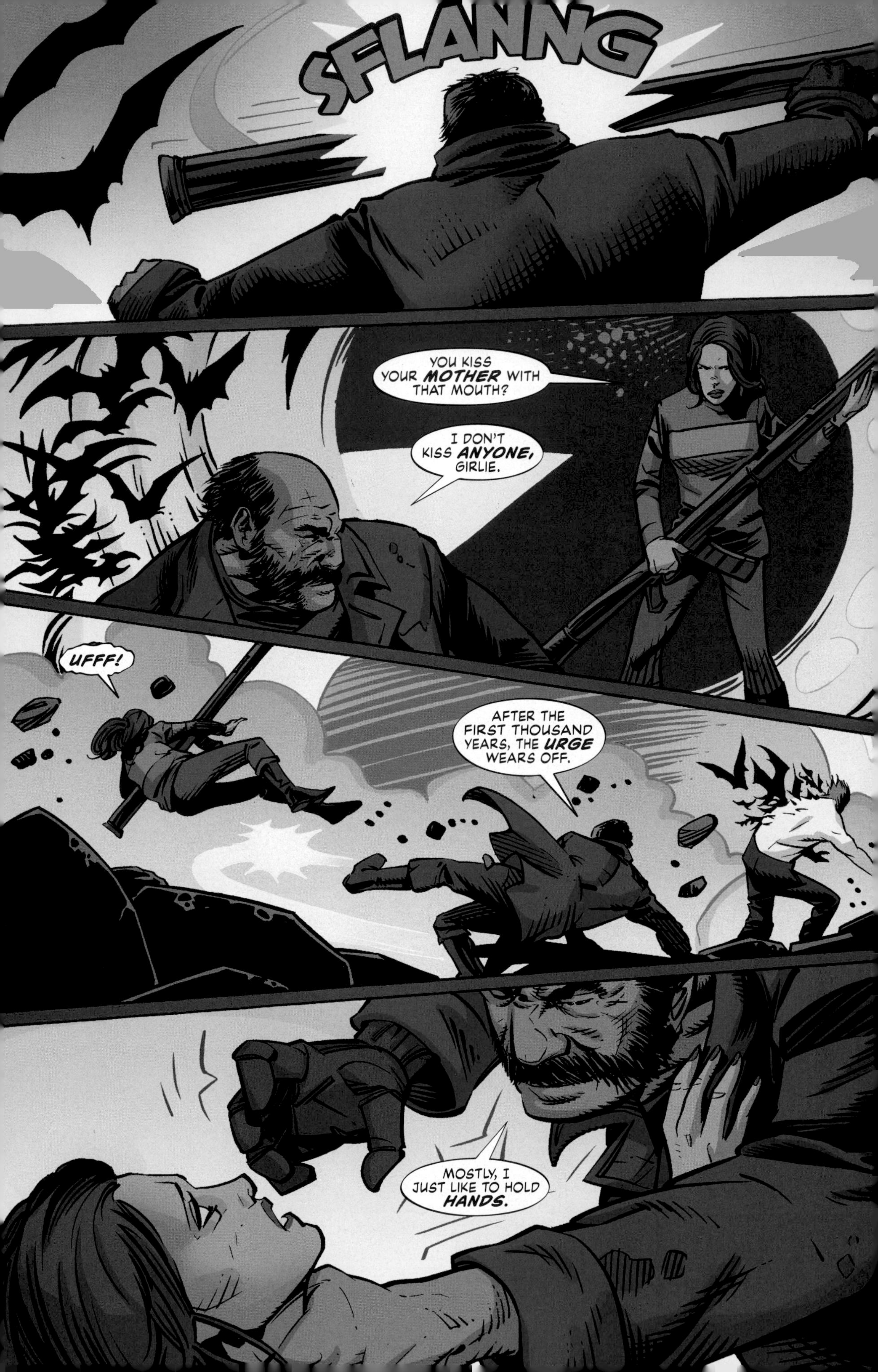
SFLANNG
YOU KISS YOUR MOTHER WITH THAT MOUTH?
I DON'T KISS ANYONE, GIRLIE.
UFFF!
AFTER THE FIRST THOUSAND YEARS, THE URGE WEARS OFF.
MOSTLY, I JUST LIKE TO HOLD HANDS.

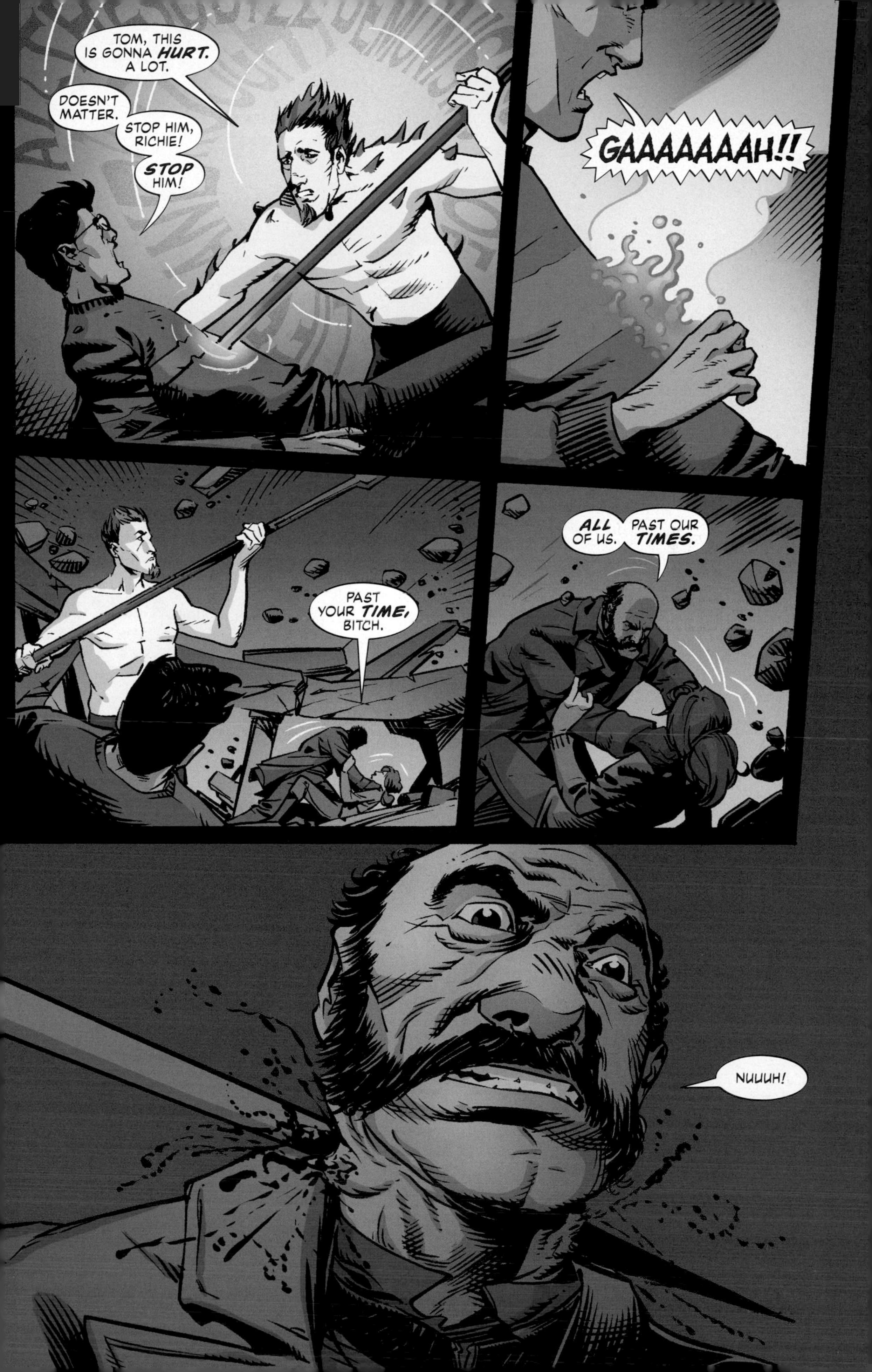
TOM, THIS IS GONNA HURT. A LOT.
DOESN'T MATTER.
STOP HIM, RICHIE!
STOP HIM!
GAAAAAAAH!!
PAST YOUR TIME, BITCH.
ALL OF US.
PAST OUR TIMES.
NUUUH!

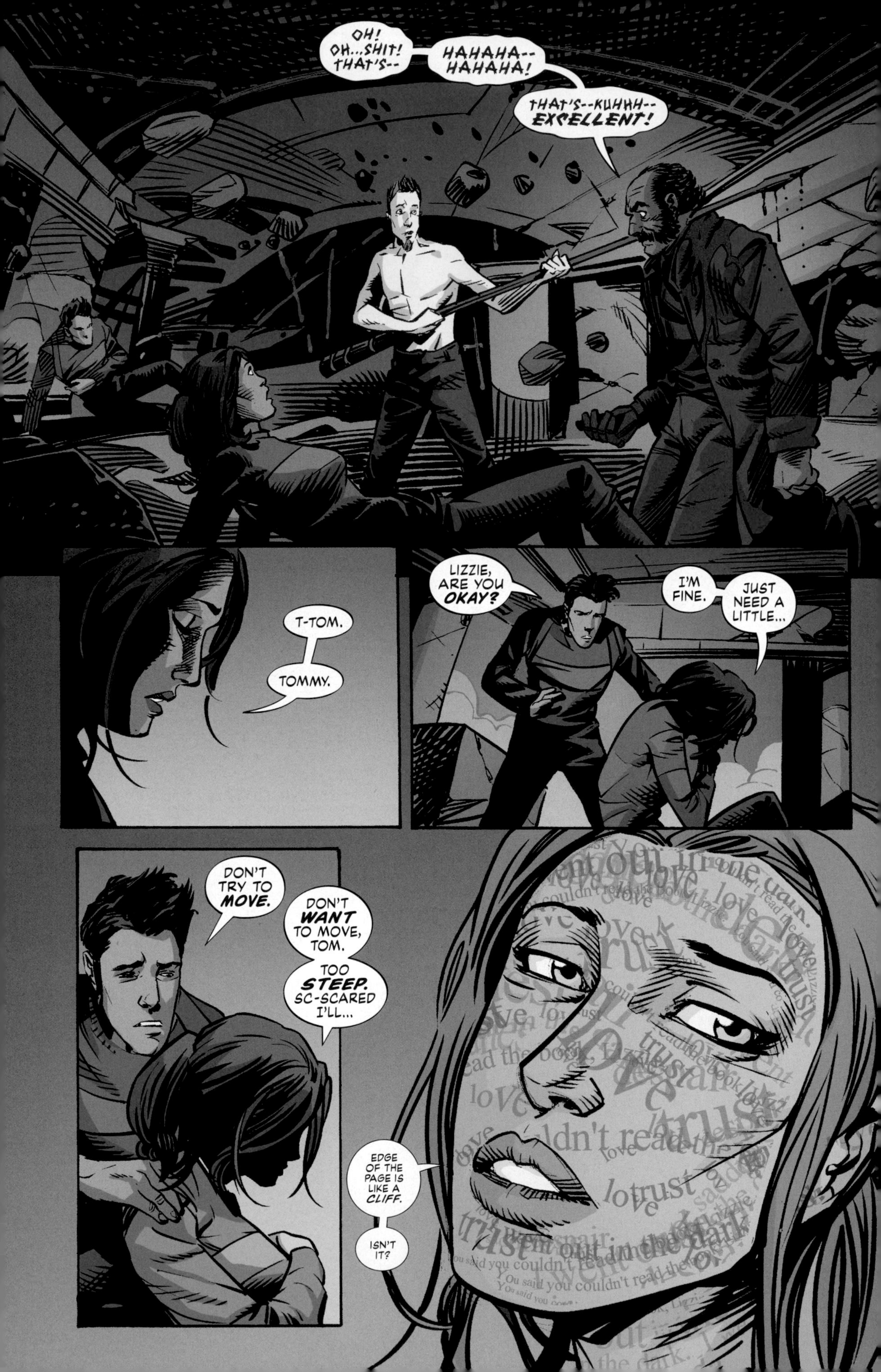
OH! OH...SHIT! THAT'S--
HAHAHA-- HAHAHA!
THAT'S--KUHHH-- EXCELLENT!
T-TOM.
TOMMY.
LIZZIE, ARE YOU OKAY?
I'M FINE.
JUST NEED A LITTLE...
DON'T TRY TO MOVE.
DON'T WANT TO MOVE, TOM.
TOO STEEP. SC-SCARED I'LL...
EDGE OF THE PAGE IS LIKE A CLIFF.
ISN'T IT?

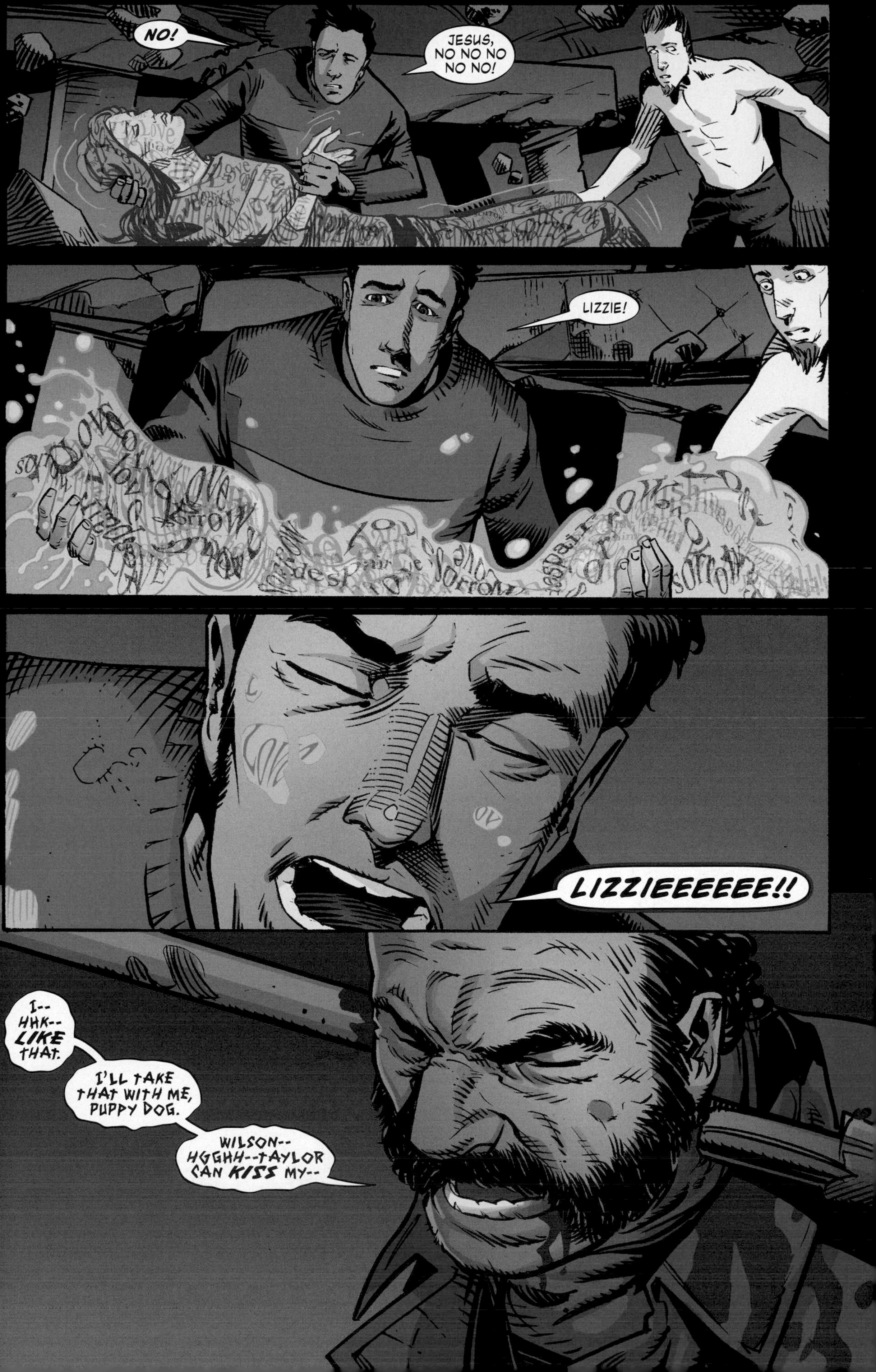
NO!
JESUS, NO NO NO NO NO!
LIZZIE!
LIZZIEEEEEE!!
I-- HHK-- LIKE THAT.
I'LL TAKE THAT WITH ME, PUPPY DOG.
WILSON-- HGGHH--TAYLOR CAN KISS MY--

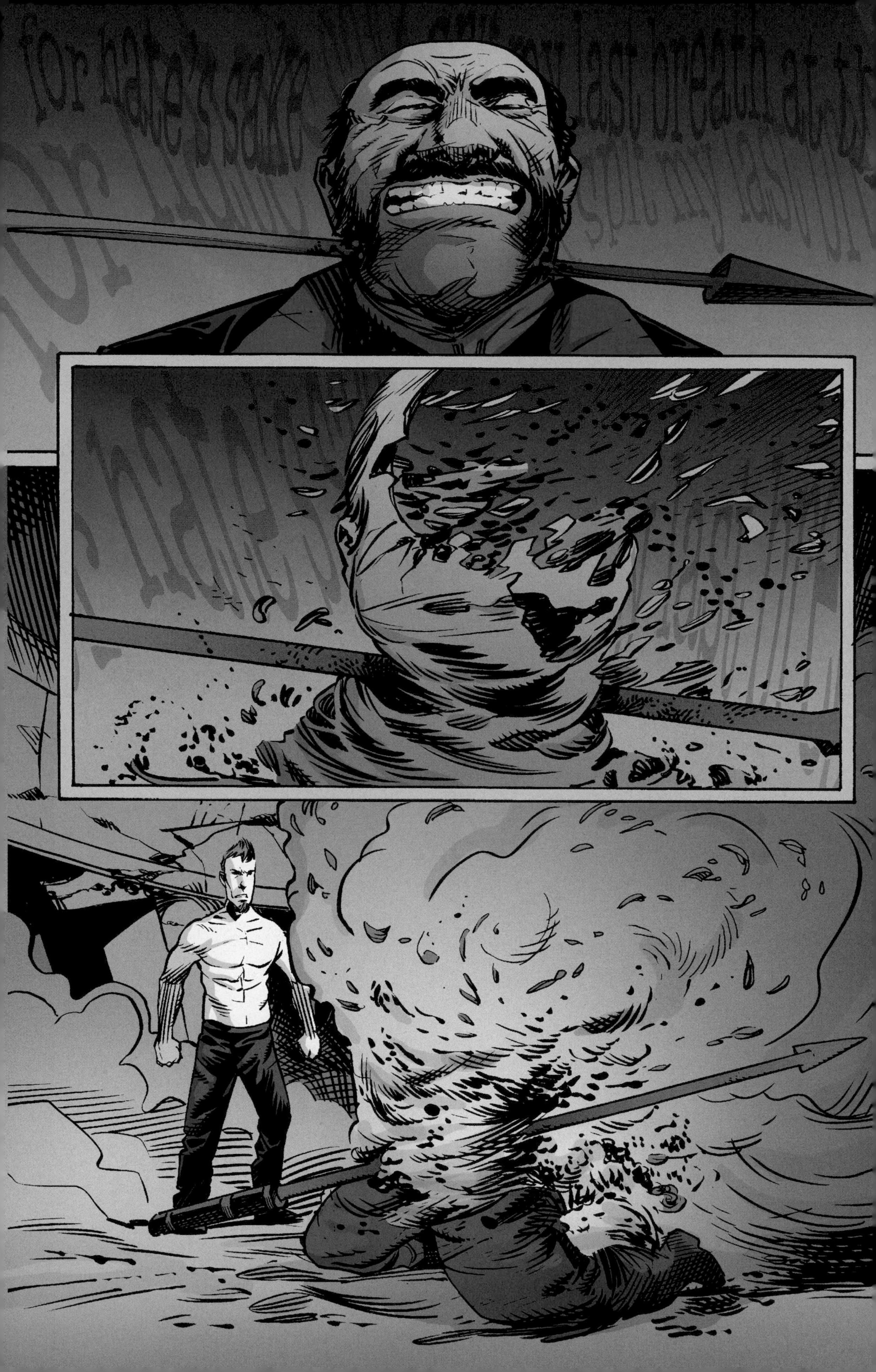
for hate's sake
last breath at

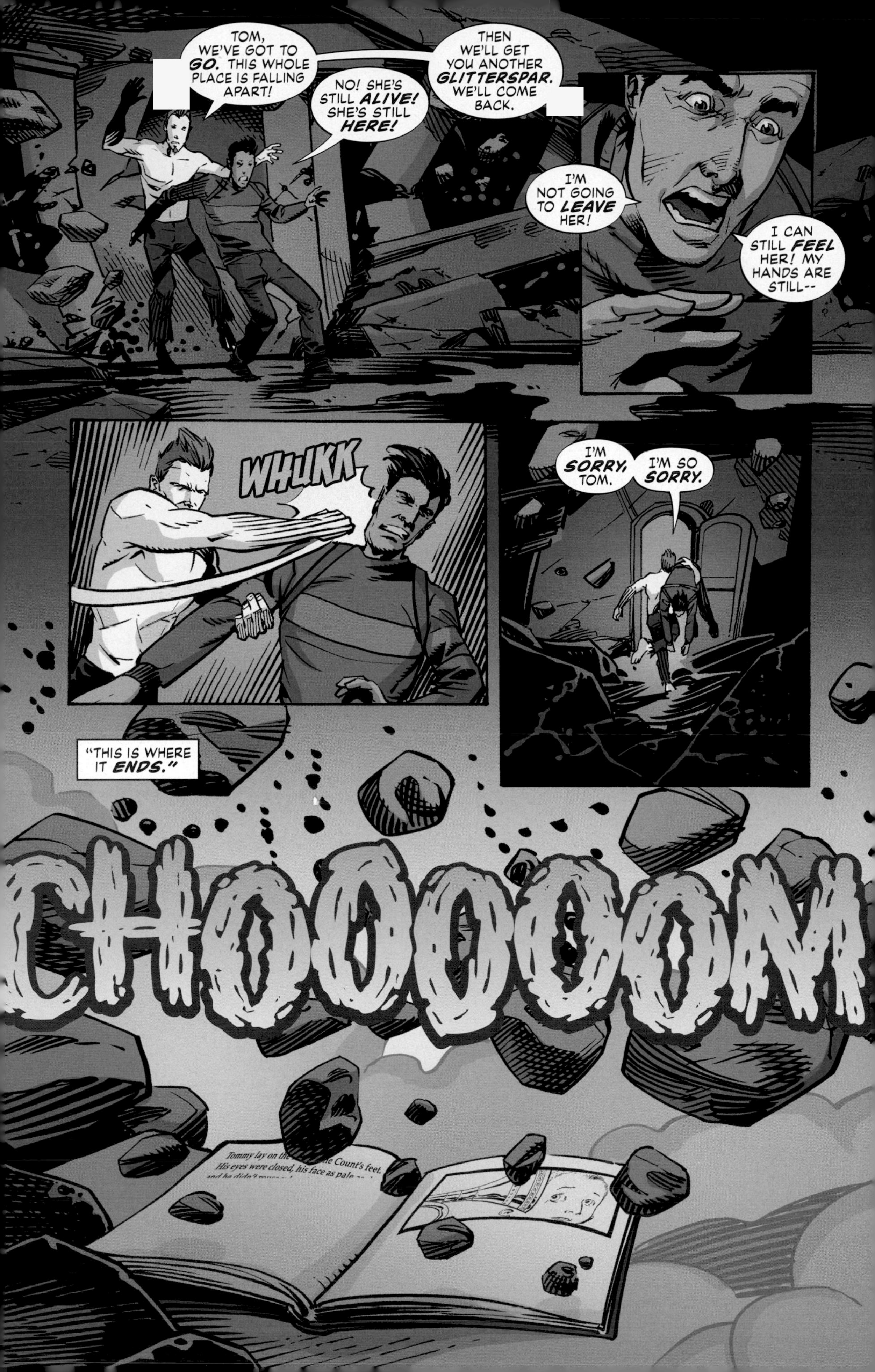
TOM, WE'VE GOT TO *GO.* THIS WHOLE PLACE IS FALLING APART!
NO! SHE'S STILL *ALIVE!* SHE'S STILL *HERE!*
THEN WE'LL GET YOU ANOTHER *GLITTERSPAR.* WE'LL COME BACK.
I'M NOT GOING TO *LEAVE* HER!
I CAN STILL *FEEL* HER! MY HANDS ARE STILL--
WHUKK
I'M *SORRY,* TOM.
I'M SO *SORRY.*
"THIS IS WHERE IT *ENDS.*"
CHOOOOOM
Tommy lay on the
the Count's feet.
His eyes were closed, his face as pale

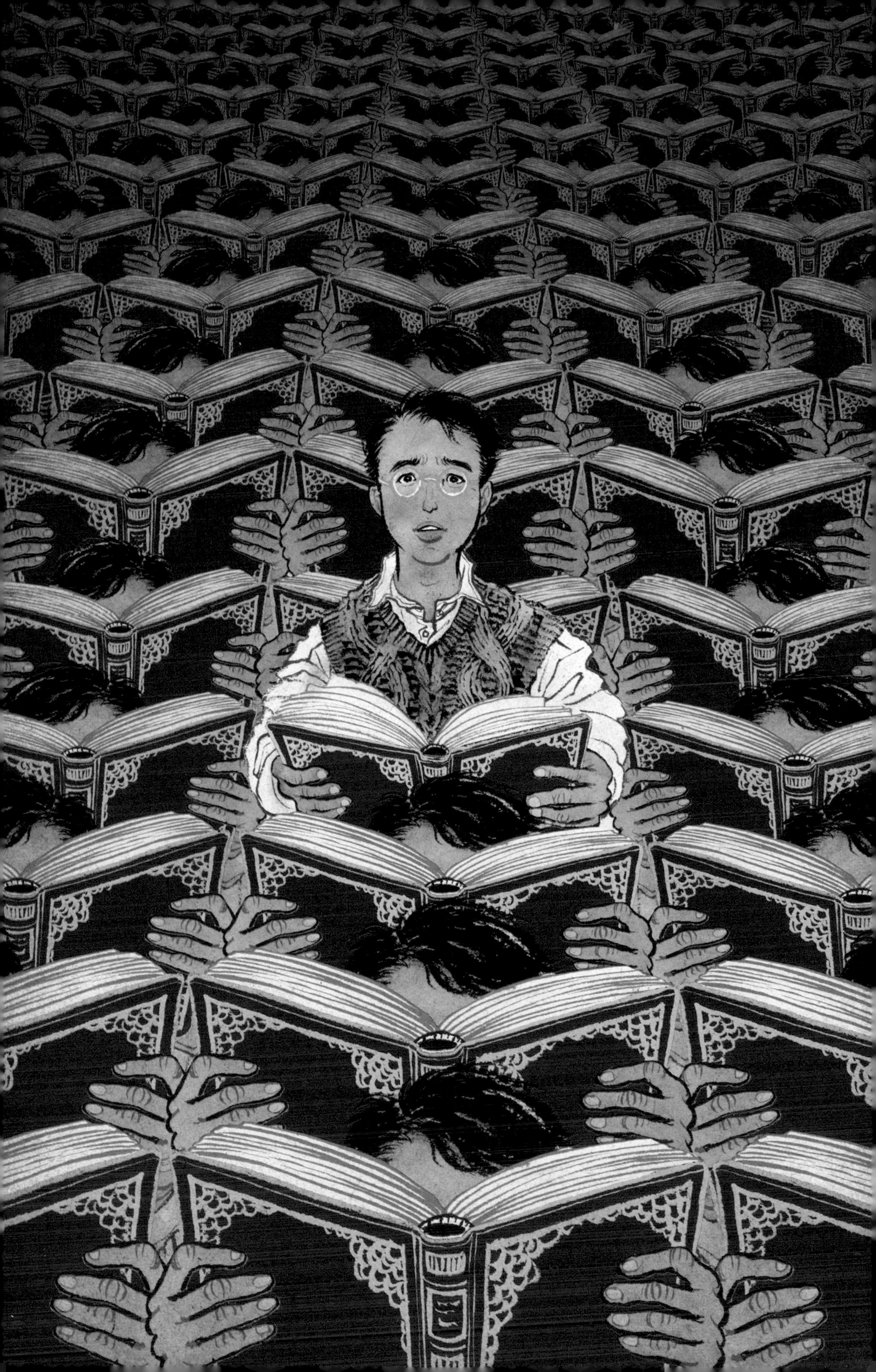

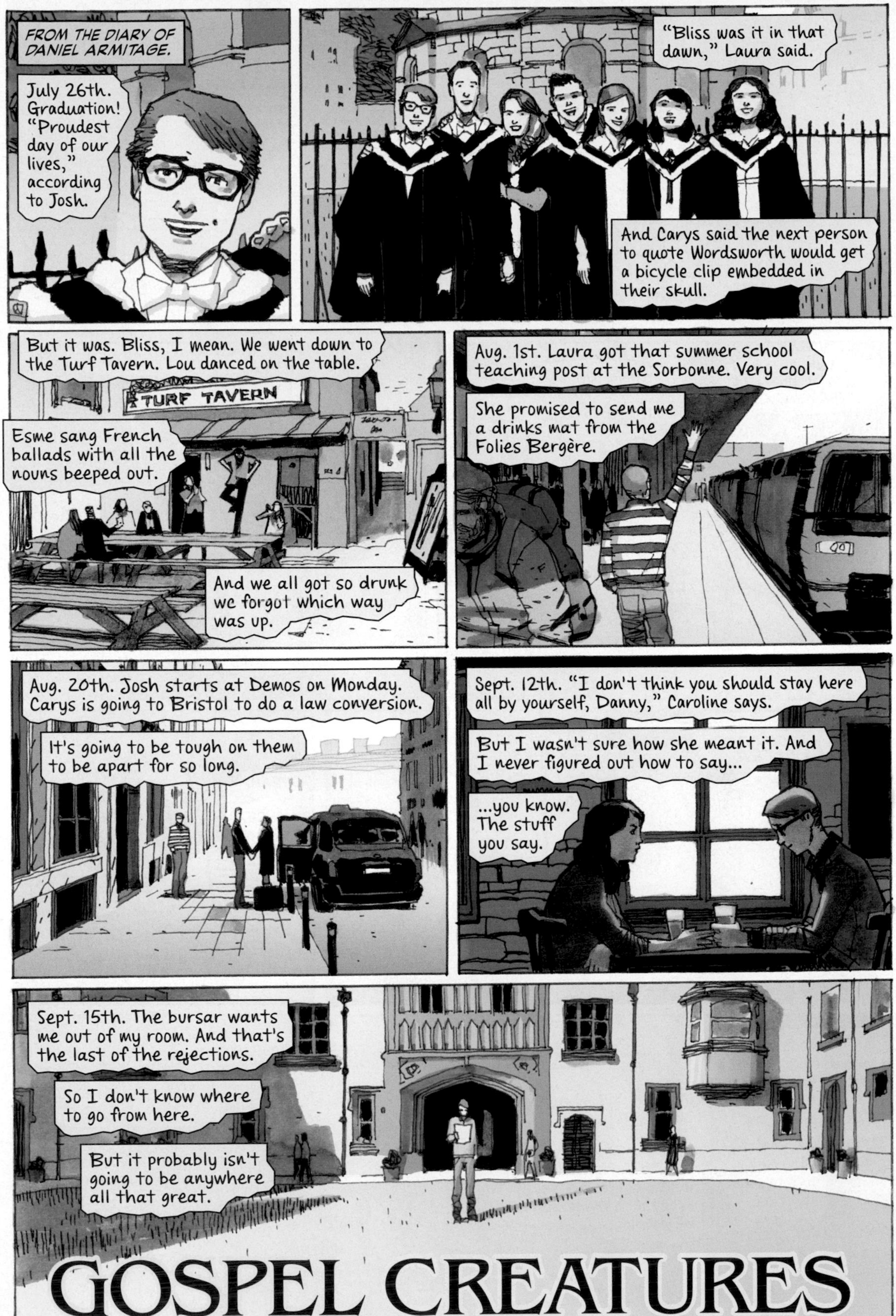
FROM THE DIARY OF DANIEL ARMITAGE.
July 26th. Graduation! "Proudest day of our lives," according to Josh.
"Bliss was it in that dawn," Laura said.
And Carys said the next person to quote Wordsworth would get a bicycle clip embedded in their skull.
But it was. Bliss, I mean. We went down to the Turf Tavern. Lou danced on the table.
TURF TAVERN
Esme sang French ballads with all the nouns beeped out.
And we all got so drunk we forgot which way was up.
Aug. 1st. Laura got that summer school teaching post at the Sorbonne. Very cool.
She promised to send me a drinks mat from the Folies Bergère.
Aug. 20th. Josh starts at Demos on Monday. Carys is going to Bristol to do a law conversion.
It's going to be tough on them to be apart for so long.
Sept. 12th. "I don't think you should stay here all by yourself, Danny," Caroline says.
But I wasn't sure how she meant it. And I never figured out how to say...
...you know. The stuff you say.
Sept. 15th. The bursar wants me out of my room. And that's the last of the rejections.
So I don't know where to go from here.
But it probably isn't going to be anywhere all that great.

GOSPEL CREATURES

by Mike Carey & Peter Gross
Gabriel Hernandez Walta, art

Lee Loughridge colors

Todd Klein letters

Yuko Shimizu cover

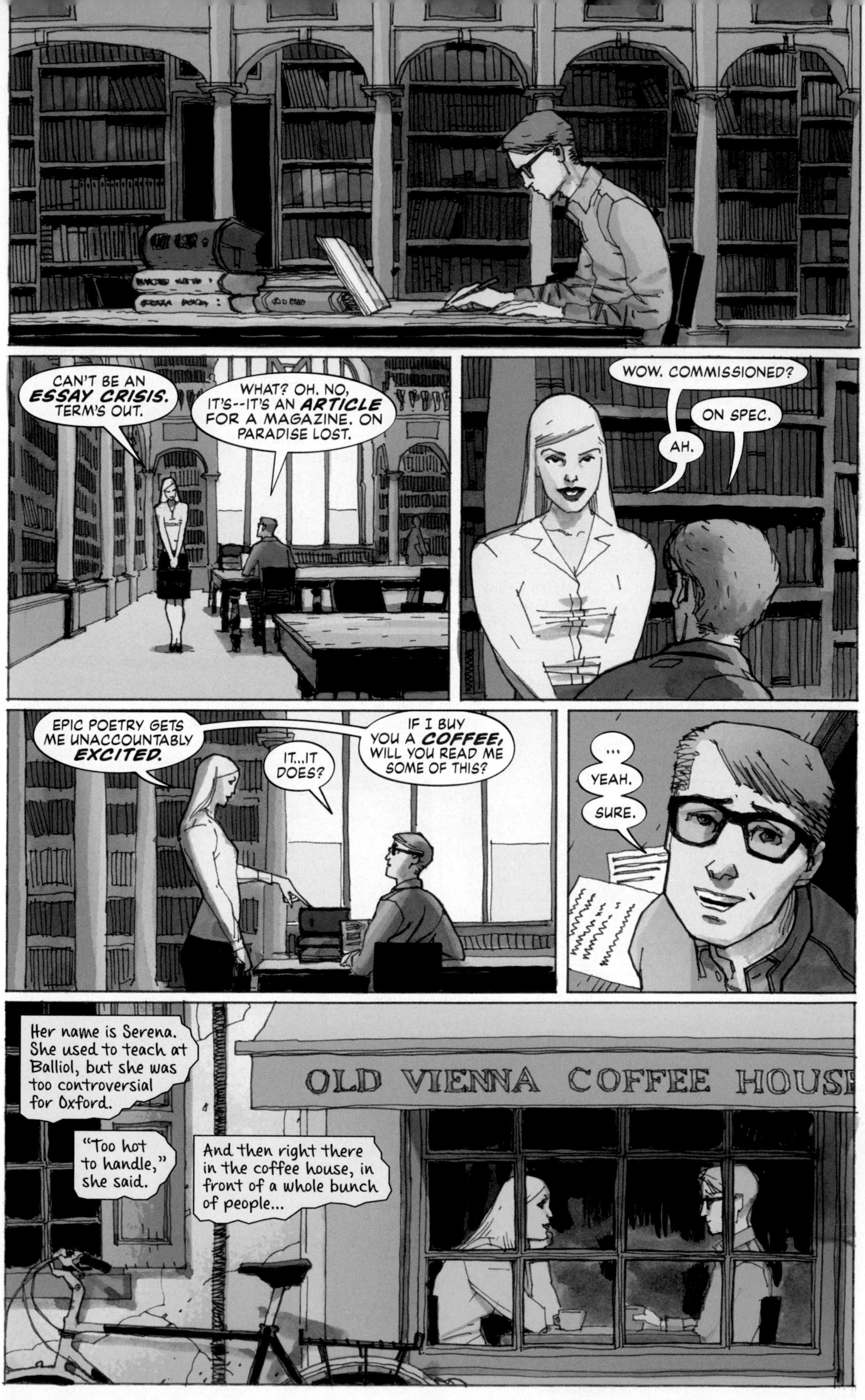

CAN'T BE AN ESSAY CRISIS. TERM'S OUT.
WHAT? OH. NO, IT'S--IT'S AN ARTICLE FOR A MAGAZINE. ON PARADISE LOST.
WOW. COMMISSIONED?
ON SPEC.
AH.
EPIC POETRY GETS ME UNACCOUNTABLY EXCITED.
IT...IT DOES?
IF I BUY YOU A COFFEE, WILL YOU READ ME SOME OF THIS?
...
YEAH.
SURE.
Her name is Serena. She used to teach at Balliol, but she was too controversial for Oxford.
"Too hot to handle," she said.
And then right there in the coffee house, in front of a whole bunch of people...
OLD VIENNA COFFEE HOUSE

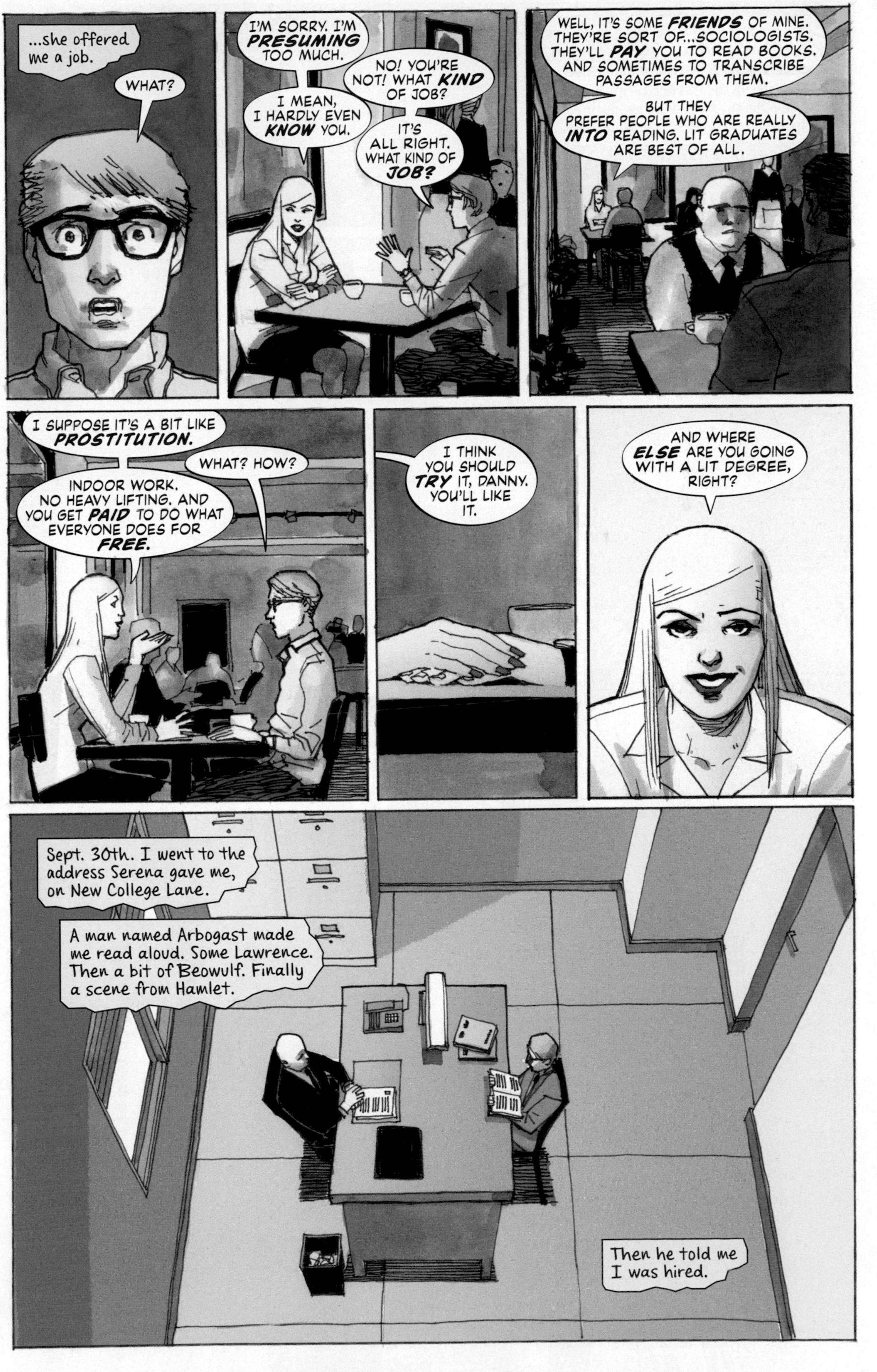
...she offered me a job.
WHAT?
I'M SORRY. I'M PRESUMING TOO MUCH.
I MEAN, I HARDLY EVEN KNOW YOU.
NO! YOU'RE NOT! WHAT KIND OF JOB?
IT'S ALL RIGHT. WHAT KIND OF JOB?
WELL, IT'S SOME FRIENDS OF MINE. THEY'RE SORT OF...SOCIOLOGISTS. THEY'LL PAY YOU TO READ BOOKS. AND SOMETIMES TO TRANSCRIBE PASSAGES FROM THEM.
BUT THEY PREFER PEOPLE WHO ARE REALLY INTO READING. LIT GRADUATES ARE BEST OF ALL.
I SUPPOSE IT'S A BIT LIKE PROSTITUTION.
WHAT? HOW?
INDOOR WORK. NO HEAVY LIFTING. AND YOU GET PAID TO DO WHAT EVERYONE DOES FOR FREE.
I THINK YOU SHOULD TRY IT, DANNY. YOU'LL LIKE IT.
AND WHERE ELSE ARE YOU GOING WITH A LIT DEGREE, RIGHT?
Sept. 30th. I went to the address Serena gave me, on New College Lane.
A man named Arbogast made me read aloud. Some Lawrence. Then a bit of Beowulf. Finally a scene from Hamlet.
Then he told me I was hired.

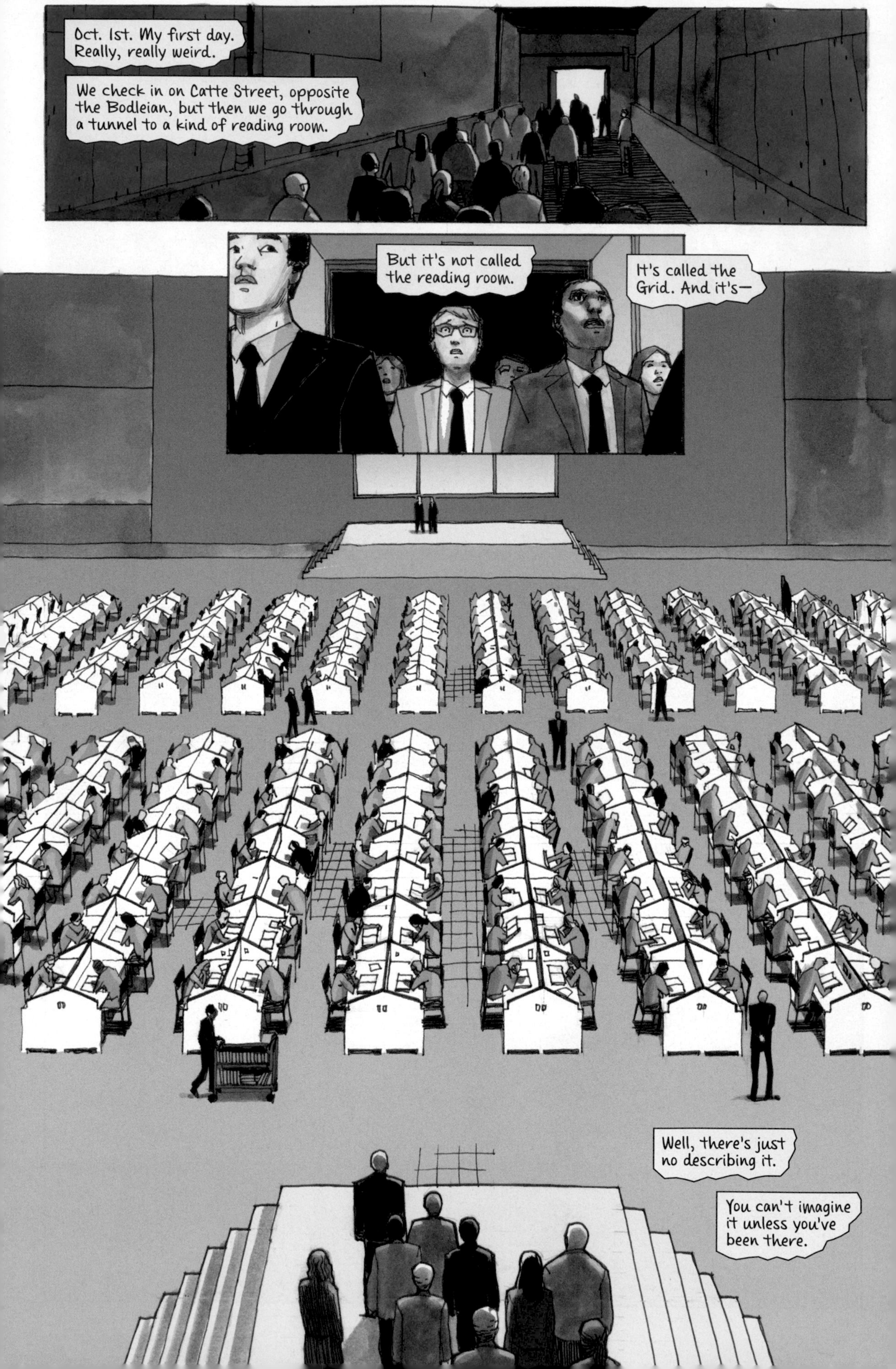
Oct. 1st. My first day. Really, really weird.
We check in on Catte Street, opposite the Bodleian, but then we go through a tunnel to a kind of reading room.
But it's not called the reading room.
It's called the Grid. And it's—
Well, there's just no describing it.
You can't imagine it unless you've been there.

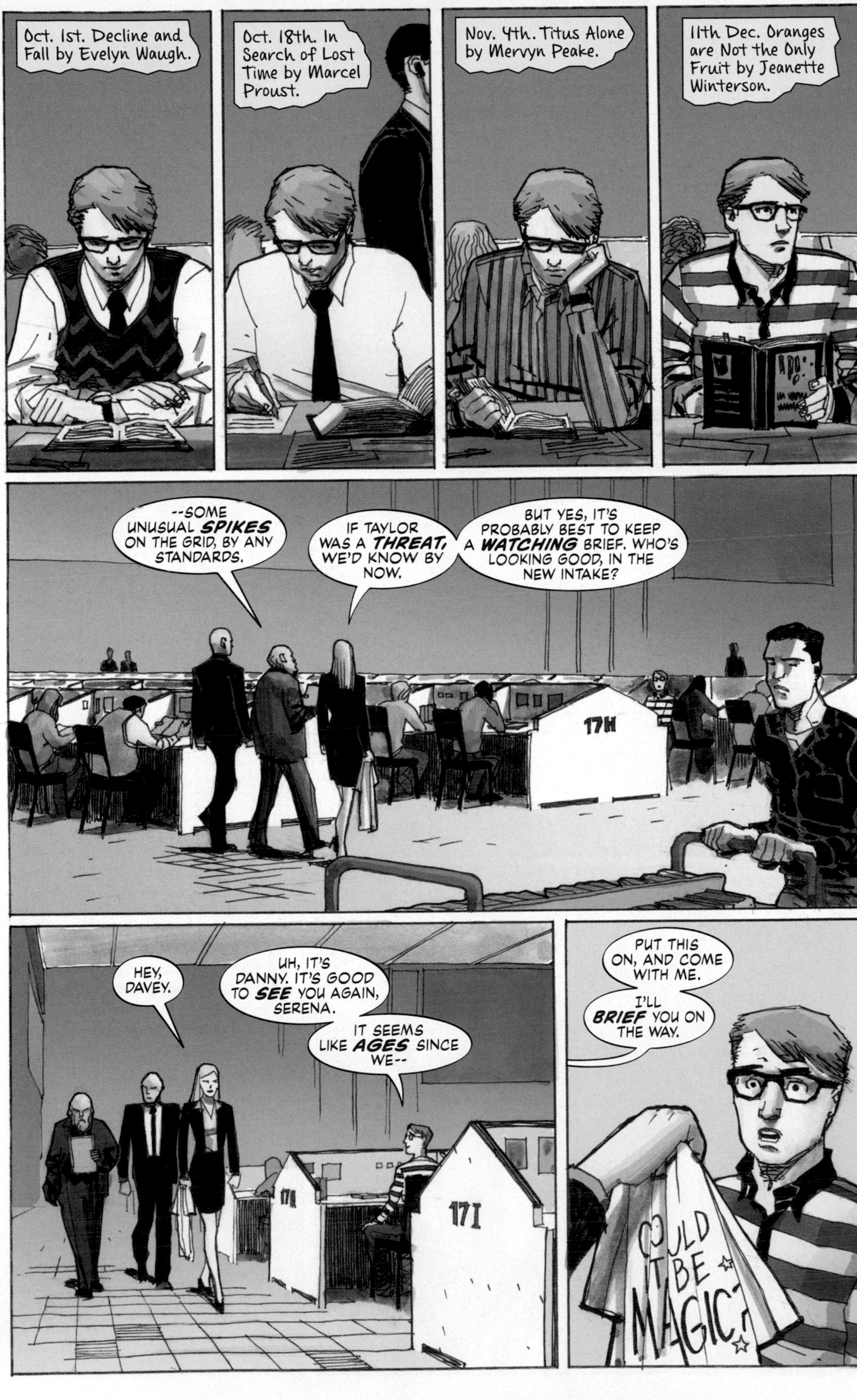
Oct. 1st. Decline and Fall by Evelyn Waugh.
Oct. 18th. In Search of Lost Time by Marcel Proust.
Nov. 4th. Titus Alone by Mervyn Peake.
11th Dec. Oranges are Not the Only Fruit by Jeanette Winterson.
--SOME UNUSUAL SPIKES ON THE GRID, BY ANY STANDARDS.
IF TAYLOR WAS A THREAT, WE'D KNOW BY NOW.
BUT YES, IT'S PROBABLY BEST TO KEEP A WATCHING BRIEF. WHO'S LOOKING GOOD, IN THE NEW INTAKE?
17H
HEY, DAVEY.
UH, IT'S DANNY. IT'S GOOD TO SEE YOU AGAIN, SERENA.
IT SEEMS LIKE AGES SINCE WE--
17H
17I
PUT THIS ON, AND COME WITH ME.
I'LL BRIEF YOU ON THE WAY.
COULD IT BE MAGIC?

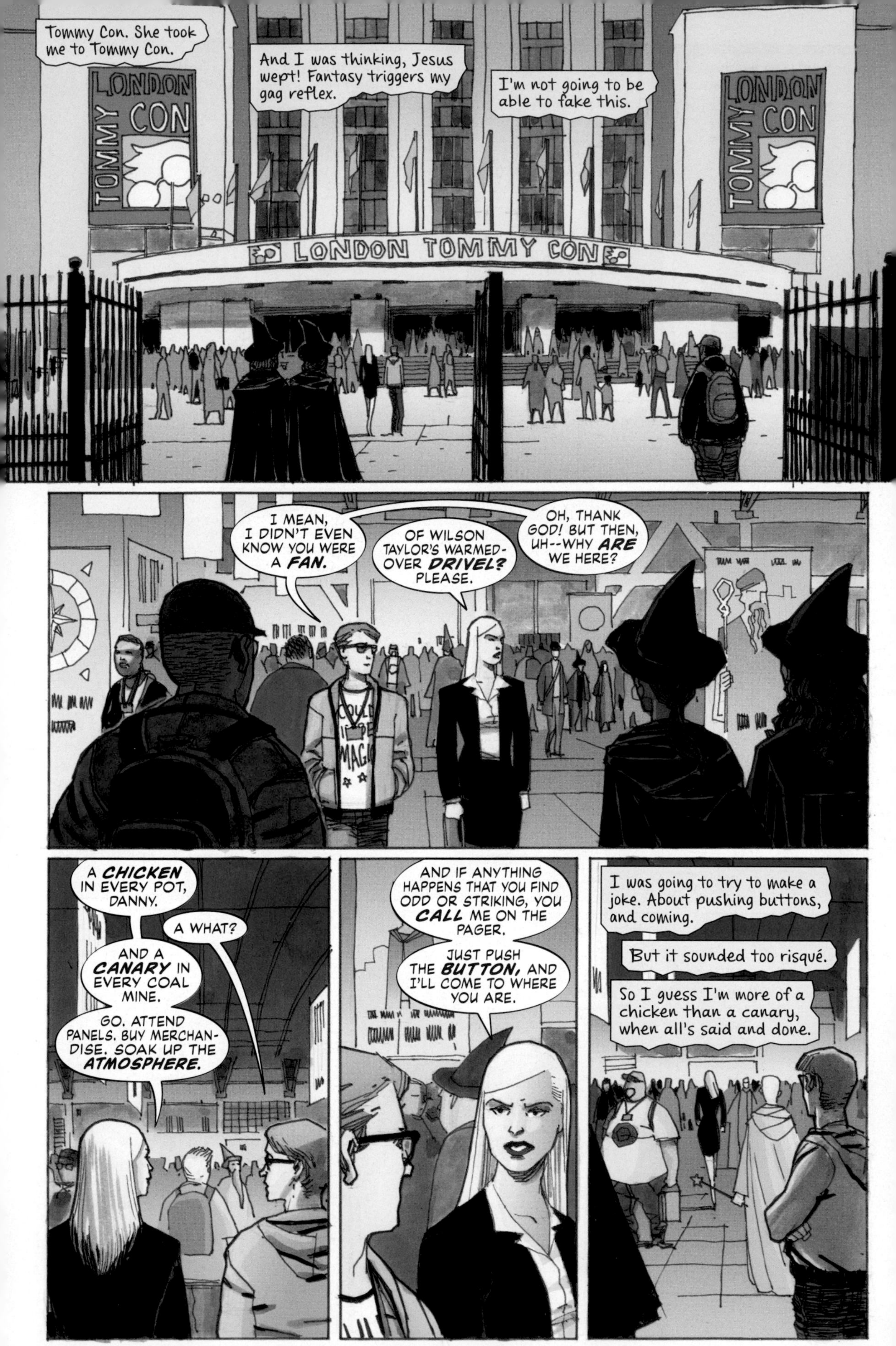

Tommy Con. She took me to Tommy Con.
And I was thinking, Jesus wept! Fantasy triggers my gag reflex.
I'm not going to be able to fake this.
LONDON TOMMY CON
LONDON TOMMY CON
I MEAN, I DIDN'T EVEN KNOW YOU WERE A FAN.
OF WILSON TAYLOR'S WARMED-OVER DRIVEL? PLEASE.
OH, THANK GOD! BUT THEN, UH--WHY ARE WE HERE?
A CHICKEN IN EVERY POT, DANNY.
A WHAT?
AND A CANARY IN EVERY COAL MINE.
GO. ATTEND PANELS. BUY MERCHANDISE. SOAK UP THE ATMOSPHERE.
AND IF ANYTHING HAPPENS THAT YOU FIND ODD OR STRIKING, YOU CALL ME ON THE PAGER.
JUST PUSH THE BUTTON, AND I'LL COME TO WHERE YOU ARE.
I was going to try to make a joke. About pushing buttons, and coming.
But it sounded too risqué.
So I guess I'm more of a chicken than a canary, when all's said and done.

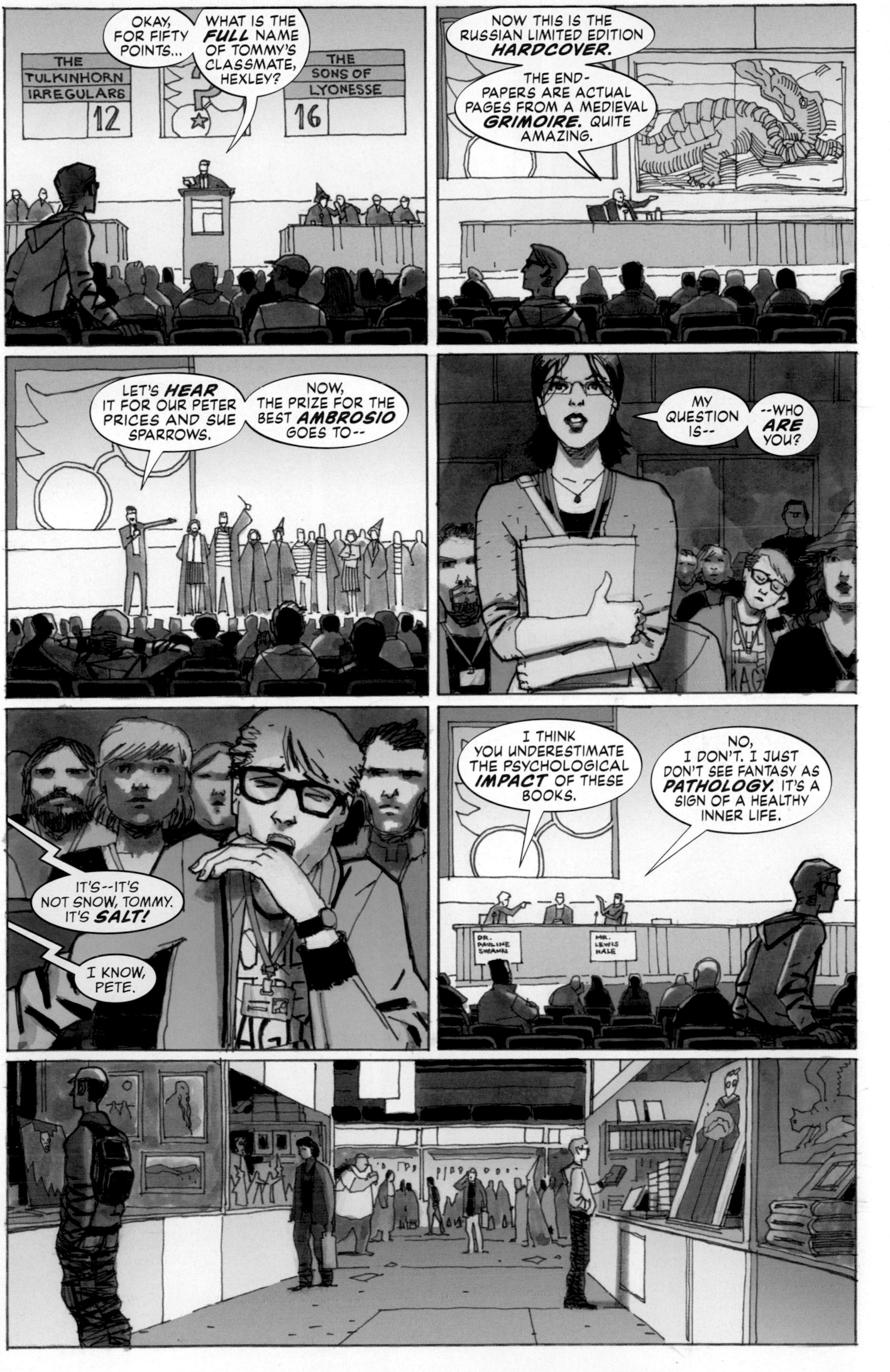
OKAY, FOR FIFTY POINTS...
WHAT IS THE FULL NAME OF TOMMY'S CLASSMATE, HEXLEY?
THE TULKINHORN IRREGULARS
12
THE SONS OF LYONESSE
16
NOW THIS IS THE RUSSIAN LIMITED EDITION HARDCOVER.
THE END-PAPERS ARE ACTUAL PAGES FROM A MEDIEVAL GRIMOIRE. QUITE AMAZING.
LET'S HEAR IT FOR OUR PETER PRICES AND SUE SPARROWS.
NOW, THE PRIZE FOR THE BEST AMBROSIO GOES TO--
MY QUESTION IS--
--WHO ARE YOU?
IT'S--IT'S NOT SNOW, TOMMY. IT'S SALT!
I KNOW, PETE.
I THINK YOU UNDERESTIMATE THE PSYCHOLOGICAL IMPACT OF THESE BOOKS.
NO, I DON'T. I JUST DON'T SEE FANTASY AS PATHOLOGY. IT'S A SIGN OF A HEALTHY INNER LIFE.
DR. PAULINE SWANN
MR. LEWIS HALE

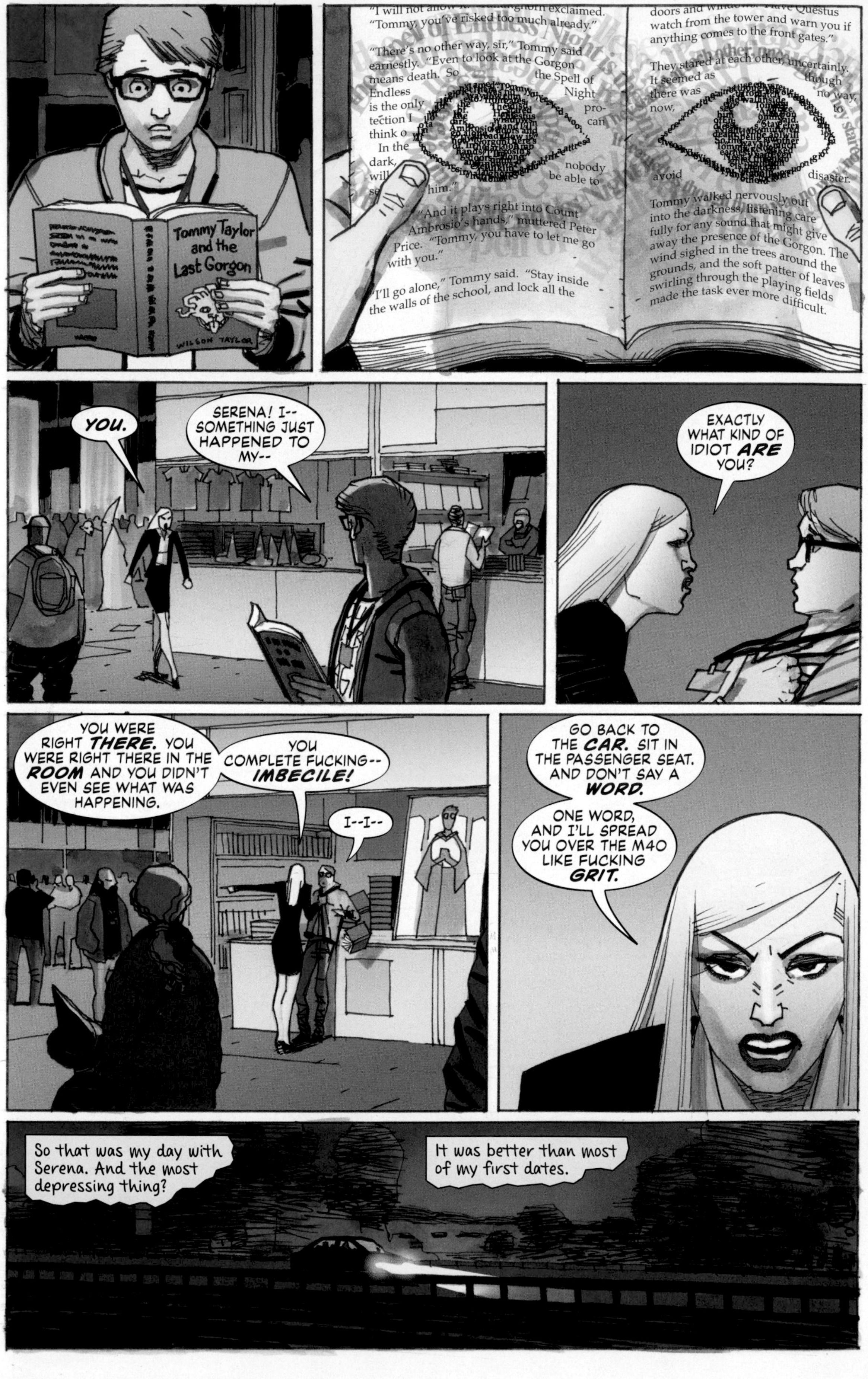

Tommy Taylor and the Last Gorgon
WILSON TAYLOR
“Tommy, you’ve risked too much already.”
“There’s no other way, sir,” Tommy said earnestly. “Even to look at the Gorgon means death. So the Spell of Endless Night is the only protection I can think o
In the dark, nobody will be able to him.”
“And it plays right into Count Ambrosio’s hands,” muttered Peter Price. “Tommy, you have to let me go with you.”
“I’ll go alone,” Tommy said. “Stay inside the walls of the school, and lock all the
doors and windows. Have Questus watch from the tower and warn you if anything comes to the front gates.”
They stared at each other, uncertainly. It seemed as though there was no way, now, to avoid disaster.
Tommy walked nervously out into the darkness, listening carefully for any sound that might give away the presence of the Gorgon. The wind sighed in the trees around the grounds, and the soft patter of leaves swirling through the playing fields made the task ever more difficult.
YOU.
SERENA! I-- SOMETHING JUST HAPPENED TO MY--
EXACTLY WHAT KIND OF IDIOT ARE YOU?
YOU WERE RIGHT THERE. YOU WERE RIGHT THERE IN THE ROOM AND YOU DIDN'T EVEN SEE WHAT WAS HAPPENING.
YOU COMPLETE FUCKING--IMBECILE!
I--I--
GO BACK TO THE CAR. SIT IN THE PASSENGER SEAT. AND DON'T SAY A WORD.
ONE WORD, AND I'LL SPREAD YOU OVER THE M40 LIKE FUCKING GRIT.
So that was my day with Serena. And the most depressing thing?
It was better than most of my first dates.

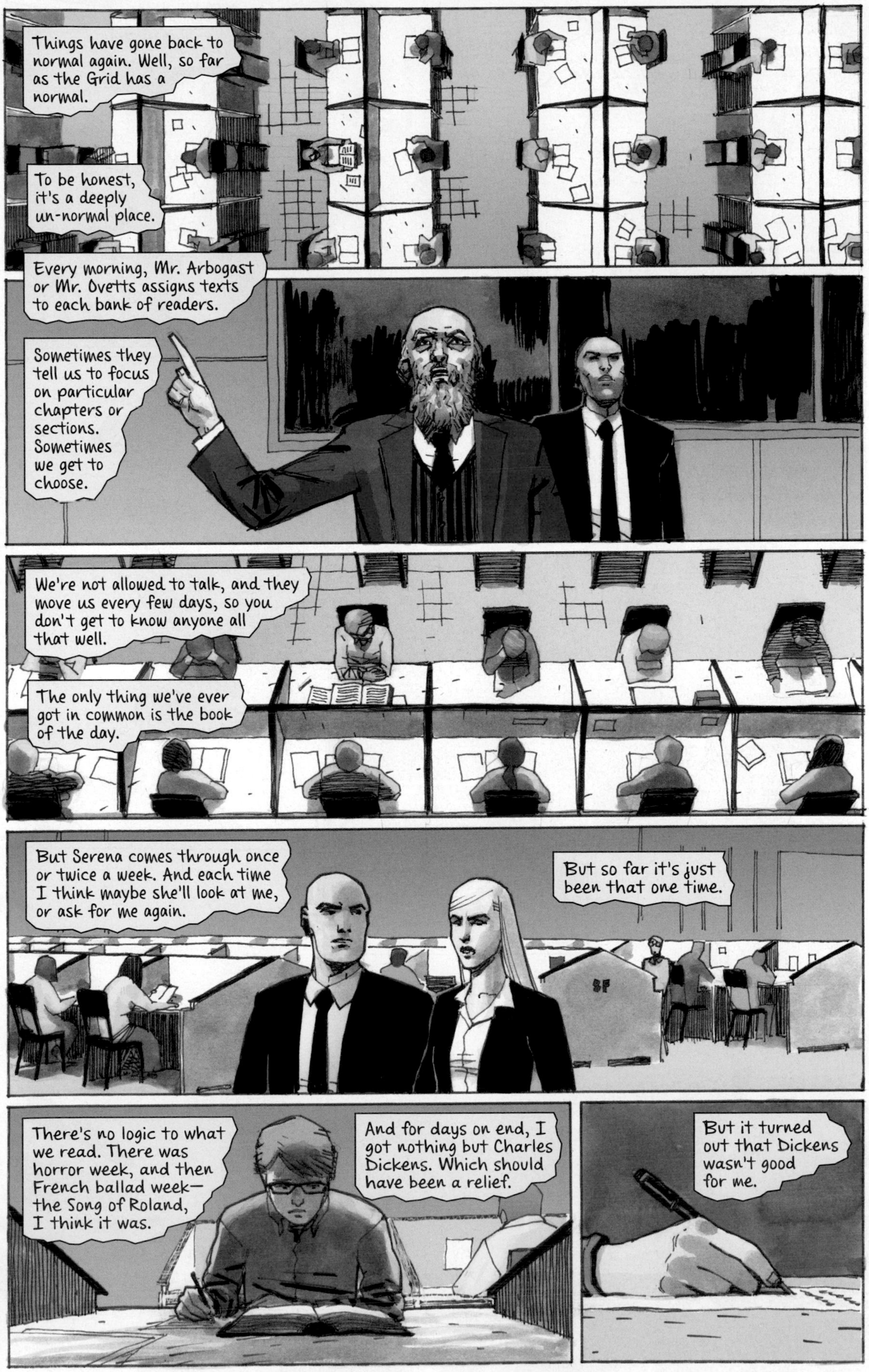
Things have gone back to normal again. Well, so far as the Grid has a normal.
To be honest, it's a deeply un-normal place.
Every morning, Mr. Arbogast or Mr. Ovetts assigns texts to each bank of readers.
Sometimes they tell us to focus on particular chapters or sections. Sometimes we get to choose.
We're not allowed to talk, and they move us every few days, so you don't get to know anyone all that well.
The only thing we've ever got in common is the book of the day.
But Serena comes through once or twice a week. And each time I think maybe she'll look at me, or ask for me again.
But so far it's just been that one time.
There's no logic to what we read. There was horror week, and then French ballad week—the Song of Roland, I think it was.
And for days on end, I got nothing but Charles Dickens. Which should have been a relief.
But it turned out that Dickens wasn't good for me.

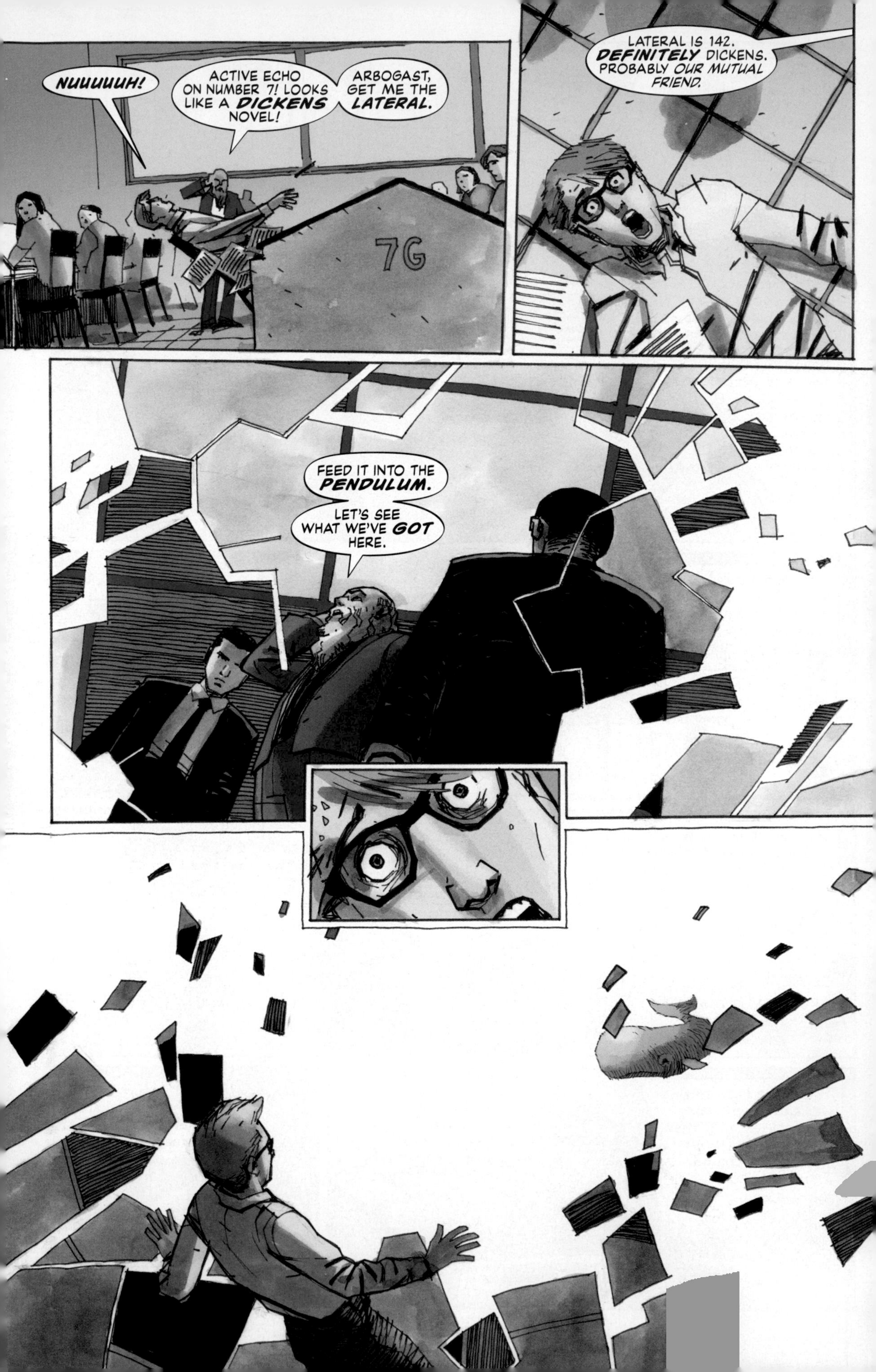
NUUUUUH!
ACTIVE ECHO ON NUMBER 7! LOOKS LIKE A DICKENS NOVEL!
ARBOGAST, GET ME THE LATERAL.
7G
LATERAL IS 142. DEFINITELY DICKENS. PROBABLY OUR MUTUAL FRIEND.
FEED IT INTO THE PENDULUM.
LET'S SEE WHAT WE'VE GOT HERE.

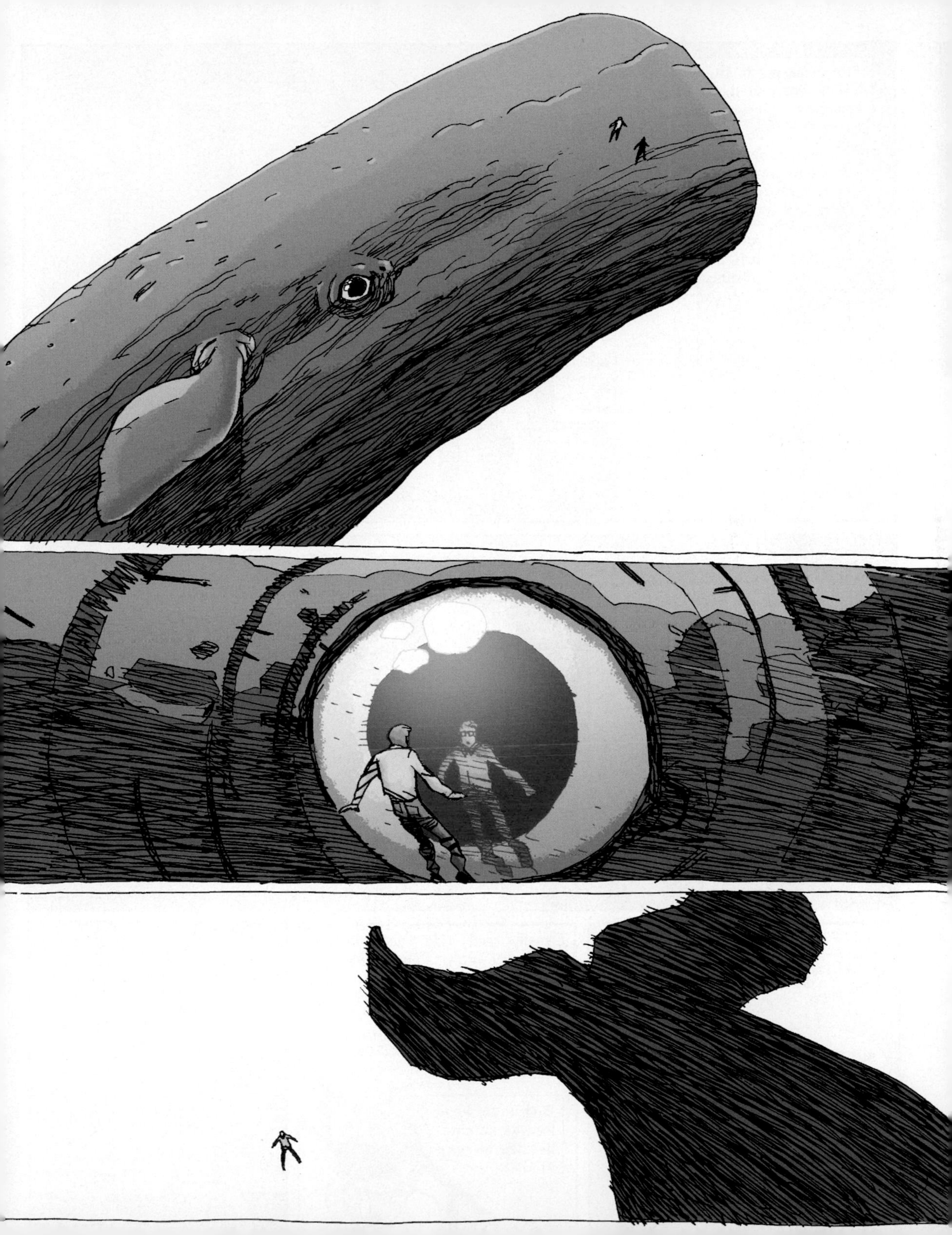

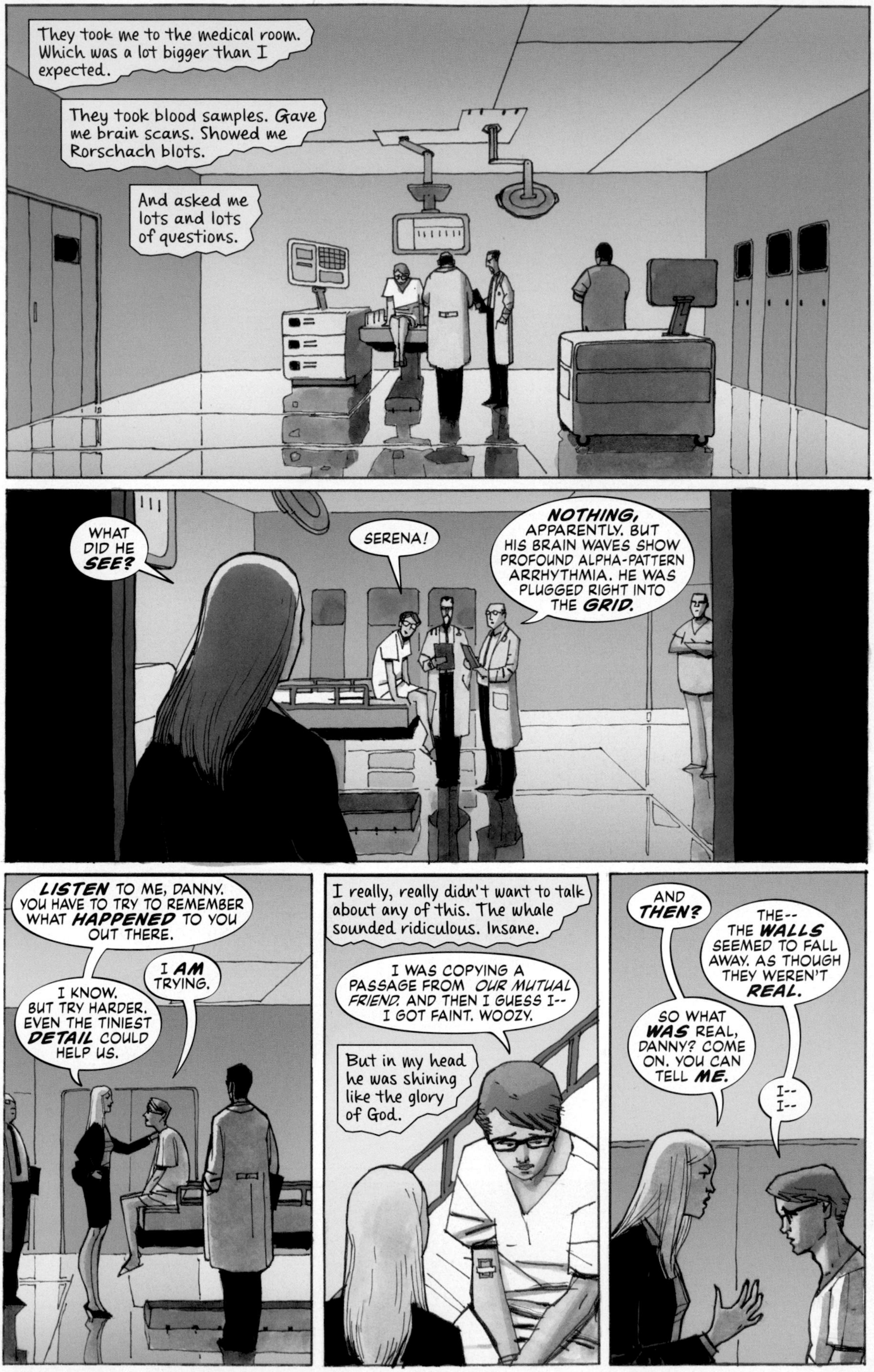
They took me to the medical room. Which was a lot bigger than I expected.
They took blood samples. Gave me brain scans. Showed me Rorschach blots.
And asked me lots and lots of questions.
WHAT DID HE SEE?
SERENA!
NOTHING, APPARENTLY. BUT HIS BRAIN WAVES SHOW PROFOUND ALPHA-PATTERN ARRHYTHMIA. HE WAS PLUGGED RIGHT INTO THE GRID.
LISTEN TO ME, DANNY. YOU HAVE TO TRY TO REMEMBER WHAT HAPPENED TO YOU OUT THERE.
I AM TRYING.
I KNOW. BUT TRY HARDER. EVEN THE TINIEST DETAIL COULD HELP US.
I really, really didn't want to talk about any of this. The whale sounded ridiculous. Insane.
I WAS COPYING A PASSAGE FROM OUR MUTUAL FRIEND, AND THEN I GUESS I-- I GOT FAINT. WOOZY.
But in my head he was shining like the glory of God.
AND THEN?
THE-- THE WALLS SEEMED TO FALL AWAY. AS THOUGH THEY WEREN'T REAL.
SO WHAT WAS REAL, DANNY? COME ON. YOU CAN TELL ME.
I-- I--

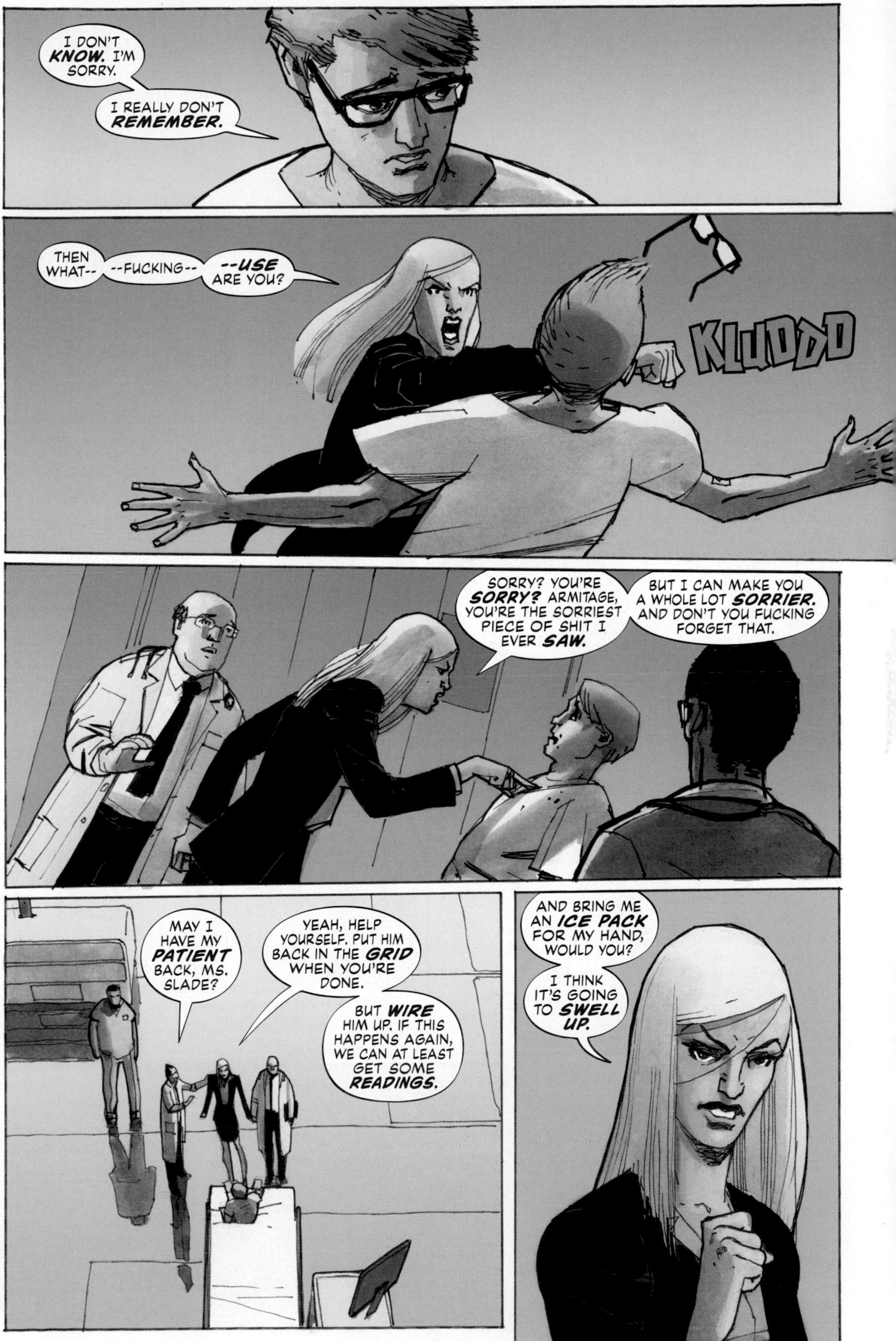
I DON'T KNOW. I'M SORRY.
I REALLY DON'T REMEMBER.
THEN WHAT--
--FUCKING--
--USE ARE YOU?
KLUDDD
SORRY? YOU'RE SORRY? ARMITAGE, YOU'RE THE SORRIEST PIECE OF SHIT I EVER SAW.
BUT I CAN MAKE YOU A WHOLE LOT SORRIER. AND DON'T YOU FUCKING FORGET THAT.
MAY I HAVE MY PATIENT BACK, MS. SLADE?
YEAH, HELP YOURSELF. PUT HIM BACK IN THE GRID WHEN YOU'RE DONE.
BUT WIRE HIM UP. IF THIS HAPPENS AGAIN, WE CAN AT LEAST GET SOME READINGS.
AND BRING ME AN ICE PACK FOR MY HAND, WOULD YOU?
I THINK IT'S GOING TO SWELL UP.

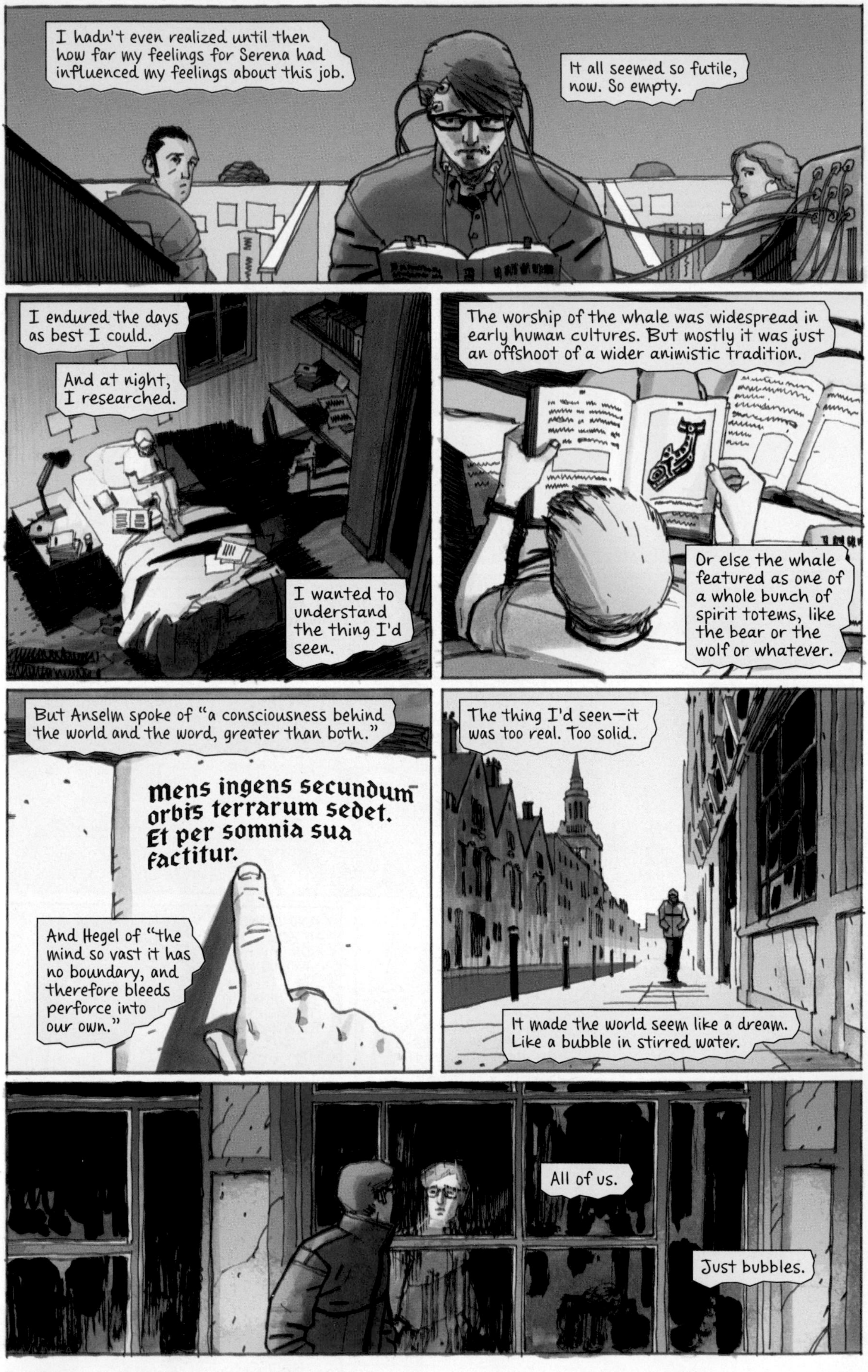
I hadn't even realized until then how far my feelings for Serena had influenced my feelings about this job.
It all seemed so futile, now. So empty.
I endured the days as best I could.
And at night, I researched.
I wanted to understand the thing I'd seen.
The worship of the whale was widespread in early human cultures. But mostly it was just an offshoot of a wider animistic tradition.
Or else the whale featured as one of a whole bunch of spirit totems, like the bear or the wolf or whatever.
But Anselm spoke of "a consciousness behind the world and the word, greater than both."
mens ingens secundum orbis terrarum sedet. Et per somnia sua factitur.
And Hegel of "the mind so vast it has no boundary, and therefore bleeds perforce into our own."
The thing I'd seen—it was too real. Too solid.
It made the world seem like a dream. Like a bubble in stirred water.
All of us.
Just bubbles.

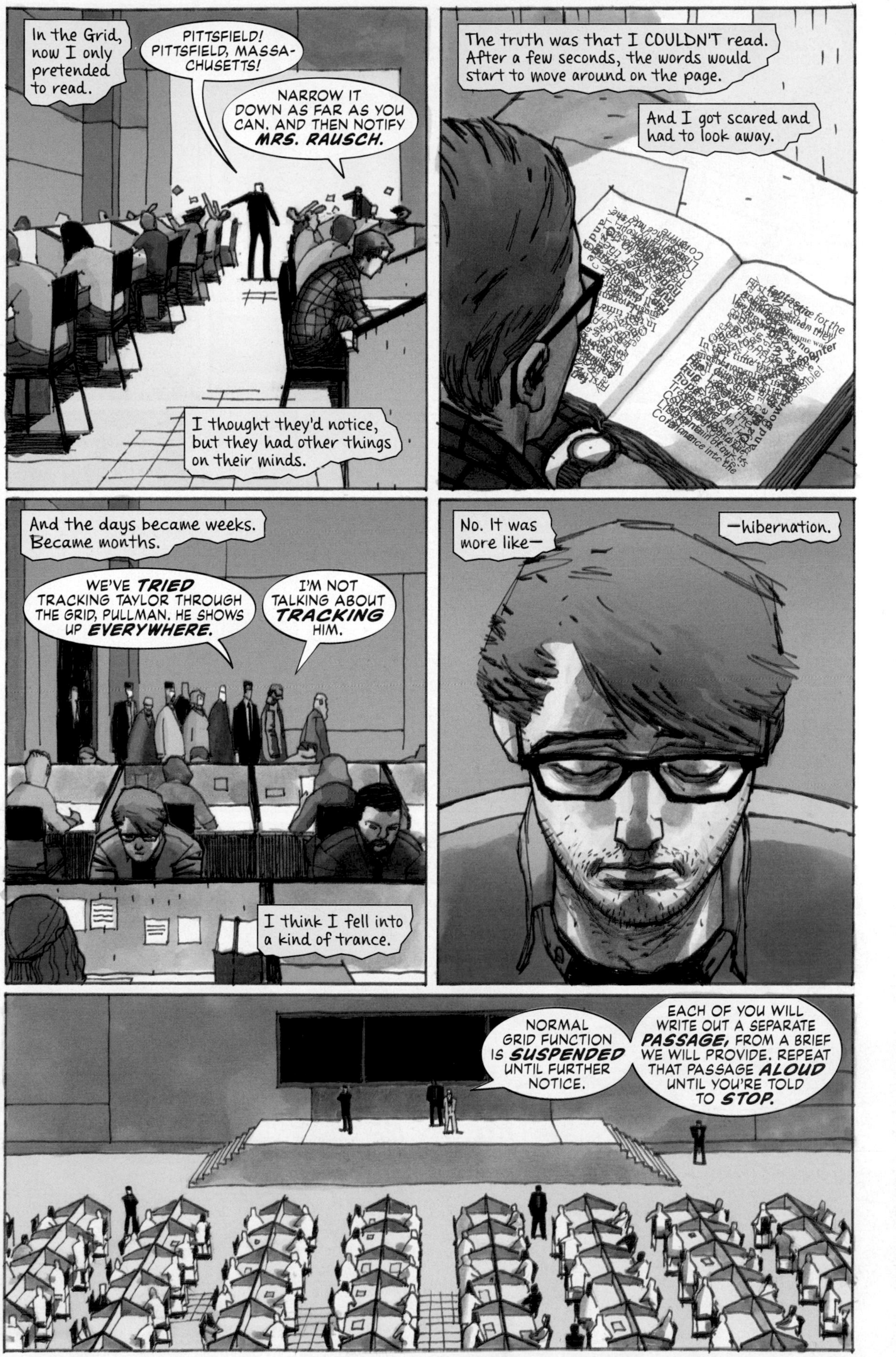
In the Grid, now I only pretended to read.
PITTSFIELD! PITTSFIELD, MASSA-CHUSETTS!
NARROW IT DOWN AS FAR AS YOU CAN. AND THEN NOTIFY MRS. RAUSCH.
I thought they'd notice, but they had other things on their minds.
The truth was that I COULDN'T read. After a few seconds, the words would start to move around on the page.
And I got scared and had to look away.
And the days became weeks. Became months.
WE'VE TRIED TRACKING TAYLOR THROUGH THE GRID, PULLMAN. HE SHOWS UP EVERYWHERE.
I'M NOT TALKING ABOUT TRACKING HIM.
I think I fell into a kind of trance.
No. It was more like—
—hibernation.
NORMAL GRID FUNCTION IS SUSPENDED UNTIL FURTHER NOTICE.
EACH OF YOU WILL WRITE OUT A SEPARATE PASSAGE, FROM A BRIEF WE WILL PROVIDE. REPEAT THAT PASSAGE ALOUD UNTIL YOU'RE TOLD TO STOP.

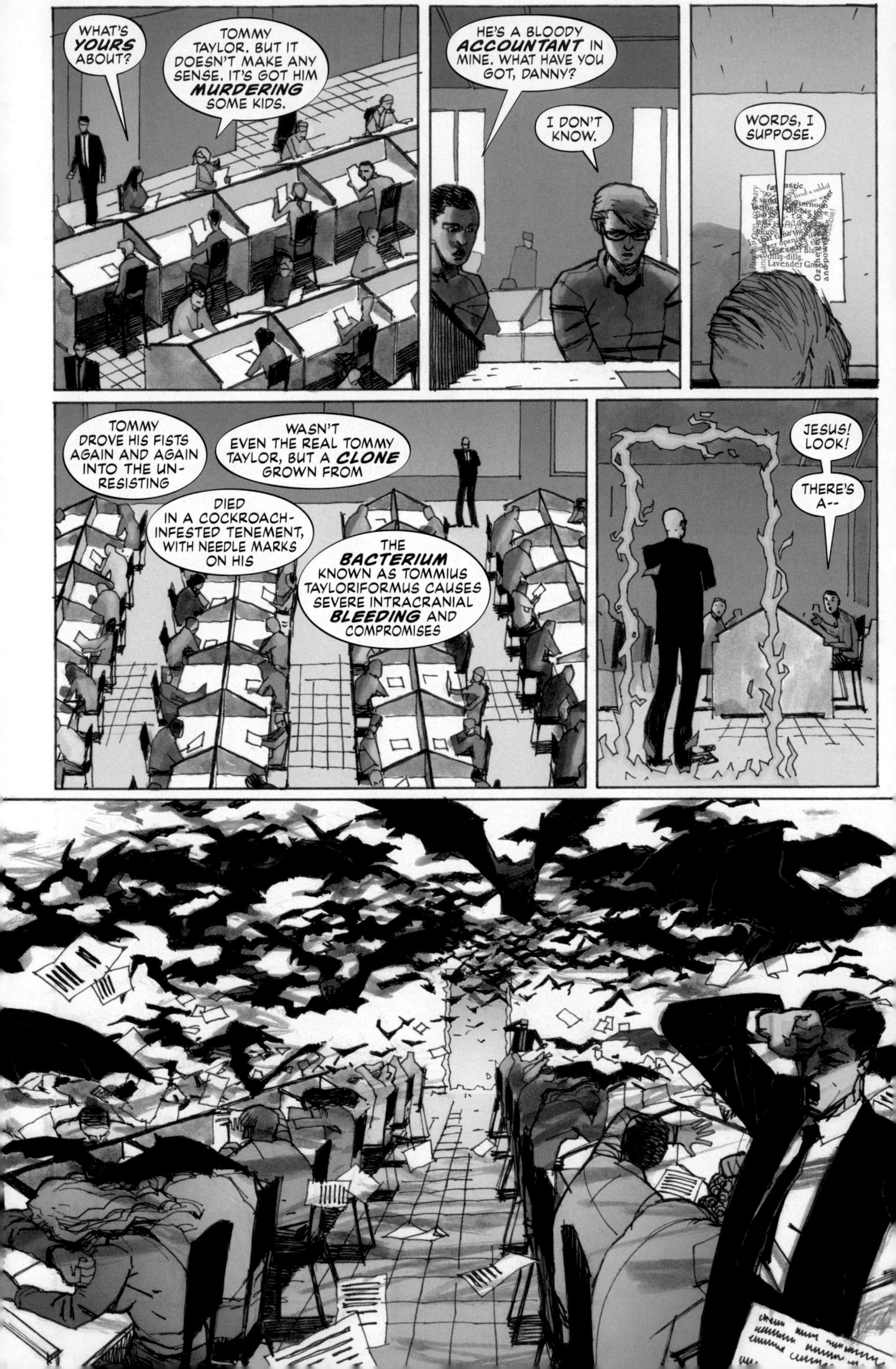

WHAT'S *YOURS* ABOUT?
TOMMY TAYLOR. BUT IT DOESN'T MAKE ANY SENSE. IT'S GOT HIM *MURDERING* SOME KIDS.
HE'S A BLOODY *ACCOUNTANT* IN MINE. WHAT HAVE YOU GOT, DANNY?
I DON'T KNOW.
WORDS, I SUPPOSE.
TOMMY DROVE HIS FISTS AGAIN AND AGAIN INTO THE UN-RESISTING
WASN'T EVEN THE REAL TOMMY TAYLOR, BUT A *CLONE* GROWN FROM
DIED IN A COCKROACH-INFESTED TENEMENT, WITH NEEDLE MARKS ON HIS
THE *BACTERIUM* KNOWN AS TOMMIUS TAYLORIFORMUS CAUSES SEVERE INTRACRANIAL *BLEEDING* AND COMPROMISES
JESUS! LOOK!
THERE'S A--

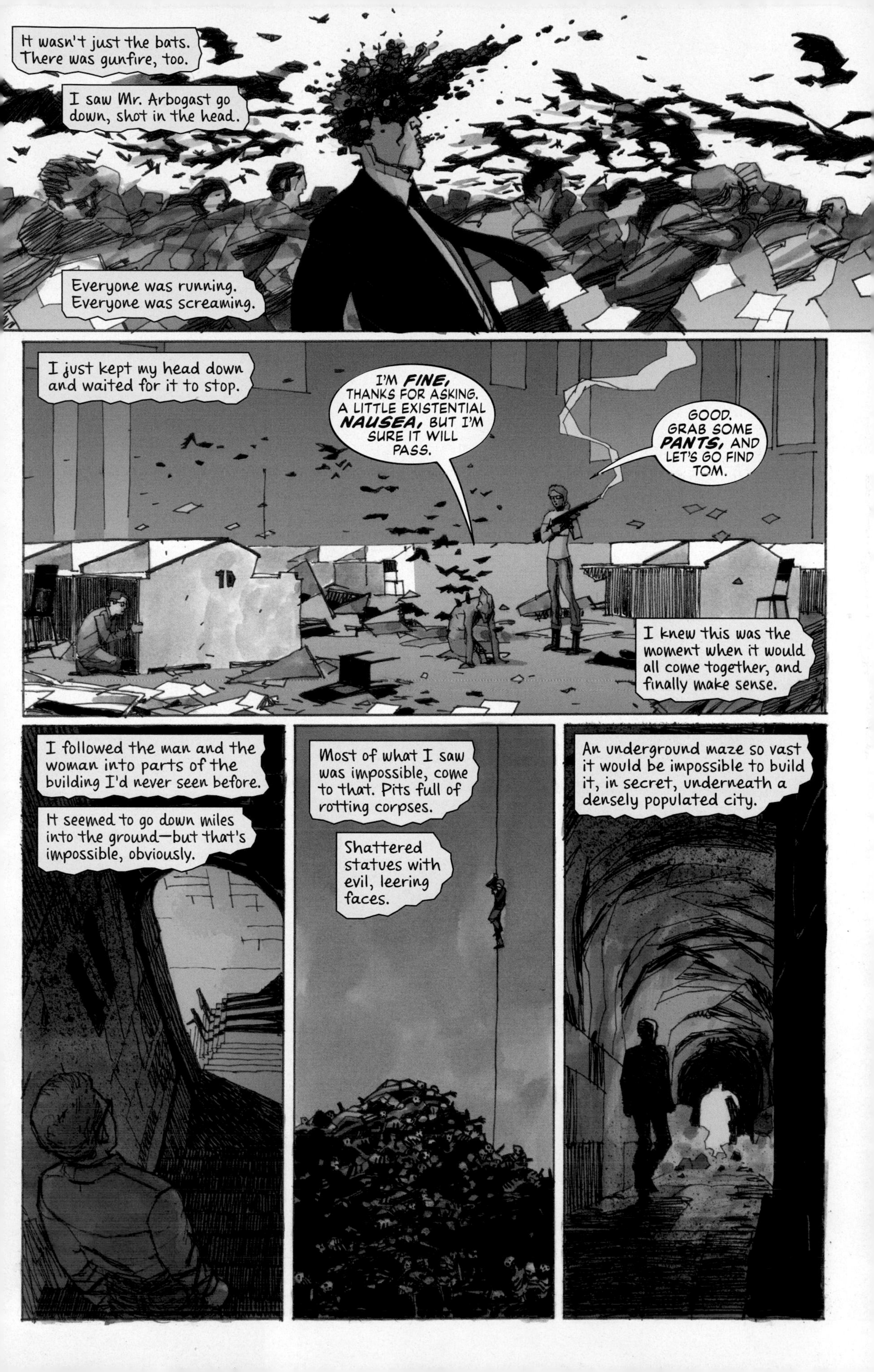
It wasn't just the bats. There was gunfire, too.
I saw Mr. Arbogast go down, shot in the head.
Everyone was running. Everyone was screaming.
I just kept my head down and waited for it to stop.
I'M FINE, THANKS FOR ASKING. A LITTLE EXISTENTIAL NAUSEA, BUT I'M SURE IT WILL PASS.
GOOD. GRAB SOME PANTS, AND LET'S GO FIND TOM.
I knew this was the moment when it would all come together, and finally make sense.
I followed the man and the woman into parts of the building I'd never seen before.
It seemed to go down miles into the ground—but that's impossible, obviously.
Most of what I saw was impossible, come to that. Pits full of rotting corpses.
Shattered statues with evil, leering faces.
An underground maze so vast it would be impossible to build it, in secret, underneath a densely populated city.

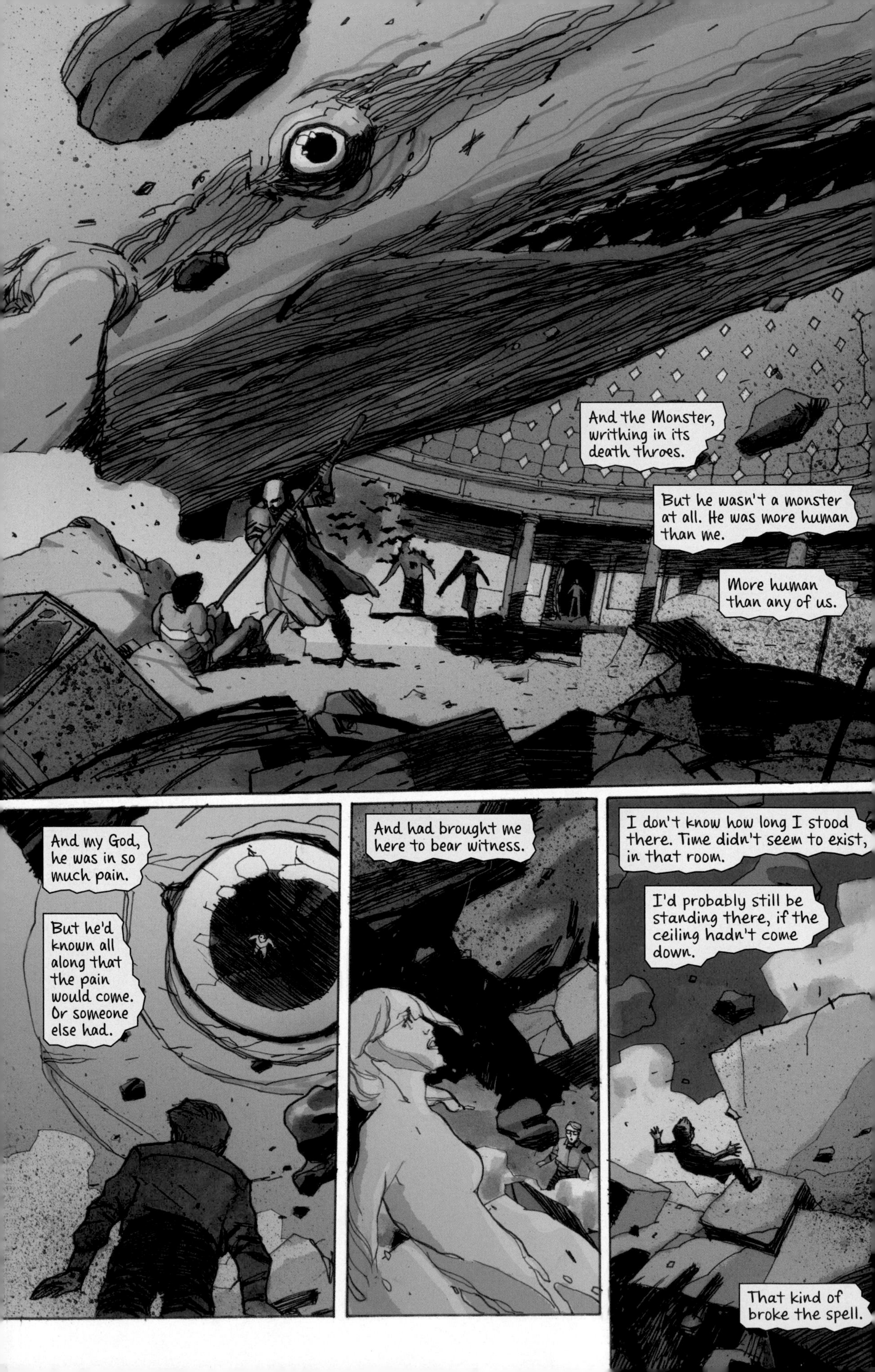

And the Monster, writhing in its death throes.
But he wasn't a monster at all. He was more human than me.
More human than any of us.
And my God, he was in so much pain.
But he'd known all along that the pain would come. Or someone else had.
And had brought me here to bear witness.
I don't know how long I stood there. Time didn't seem to exist, in that room.
I'd probably still be standing there, if the ceiling hadn't come down.
That kind of broke the spell.

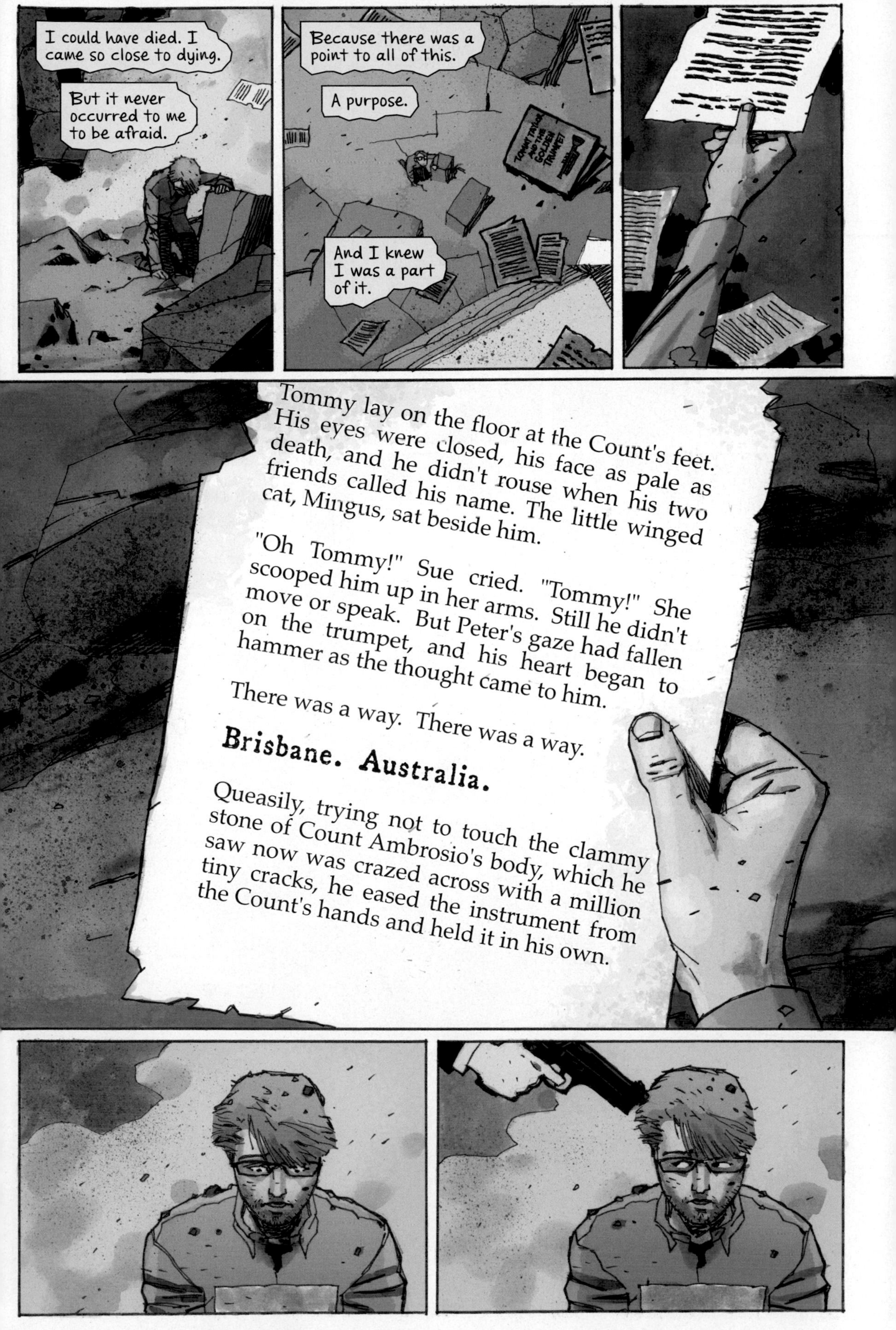
I could have died. I came so close to dying.
But it never occurred to me to be afraid.
Because there was a point to all of this.
A purpose.
And I knew I was a part of it.
Tommy lay on the floor at the Count's feet. His eyes were closed, his face as pale as death, and he didn't rouse when his two friends called his name. The little winged cat, Mingus, sat beside him.
"Oh Tommy!" Sue cried. "Tommy!" She scooped him up in her arms. Still he didn't move or speak. But Peter's gaze had fallen on the trumpet, and his heart began to hammer as the thought came to him.
There was a way. There was a way.
Brisbane. Australia.
Queasily, trying not to touch the clammy stone of Count Ambrosio's body, which he saw now was crazed across with a million tiny cracks, he eased the instrument from the Count's hands and held it in his own.

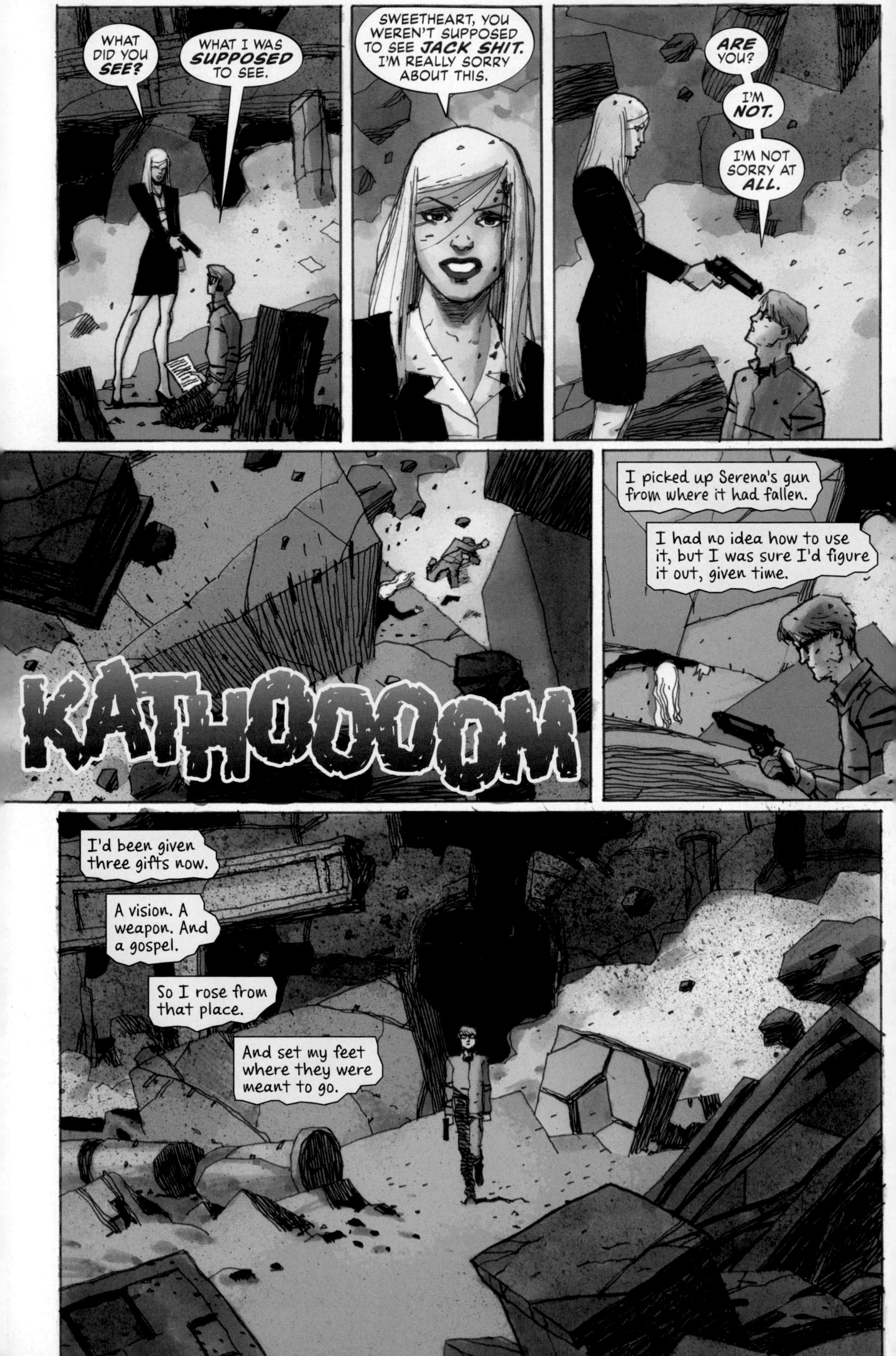
WHAT DID YOU SEE?
WHAT I WAS SUPPOSED TO SEE.
SWEETHEART, YOU WEREN'T SUPPOSED TO SEE JACK SHIT. I'M REALLY SORRY ABOUT THIS.
ARE YOU?
I'M NOT.
I'M NOT SORRY AT ALL.
KATHOOOOM
I picked up Serena's gun from where it had fallen.
I had no idea how to use it, but I was sure I'd figure it out, given time.
I'd been given three gifts now.
A vision. A weapon. And a gospel.
So I rose from that place.
And set my feet where they were meant to go.

VERTIGO

"Incredibly fun and ridiculously addictive."
—USA TODAY.COM

"Ambitious, exciting. Grade A-."
— THE ONION/THE A.V. CLUB

"A wish-I'd-thought-of-it premise, beautifully executed. Highly recommended for anyone who thinks that fantasy can do more than just help you escape the real world."
—BRIAN K. VAUGHAN, Y: THE LAST MAN

FROM THE WRITER OF *LUCIFER* AND *HELLBLAZER*

MIKE CAREY

with PETER GROSS

THE UNWRITTEN VOL. 3: DEAD MAN'S KNOCK

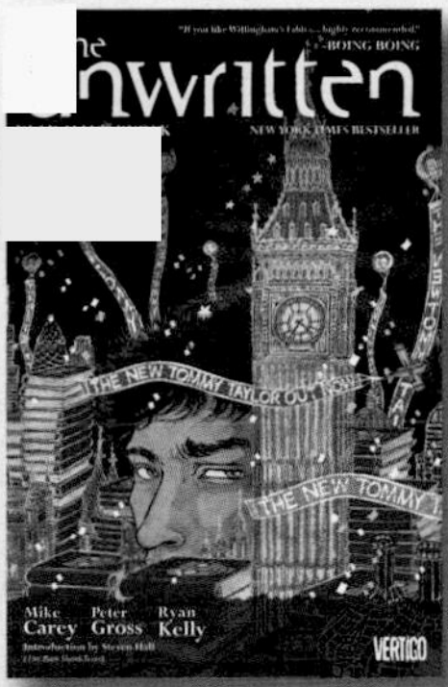

the unwritten
NEW YORK TIMES BESTSELLER
Mike Carey Peter Gross Ryan Kelly
VERTIGO

THE UNWRITTEN VOL. 4: LEVIATHAN

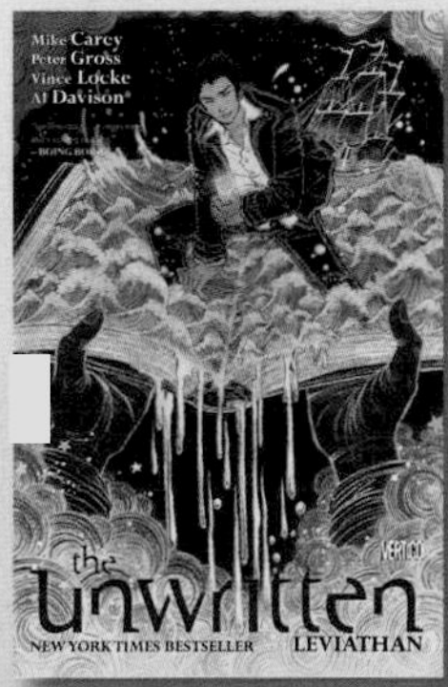

Mike Carey
Peter Gross
Vince Locke
Al Davison
the unwritten
NEW YORK TIMES BESTSELLER
LEVIATHAN
VERTIGO

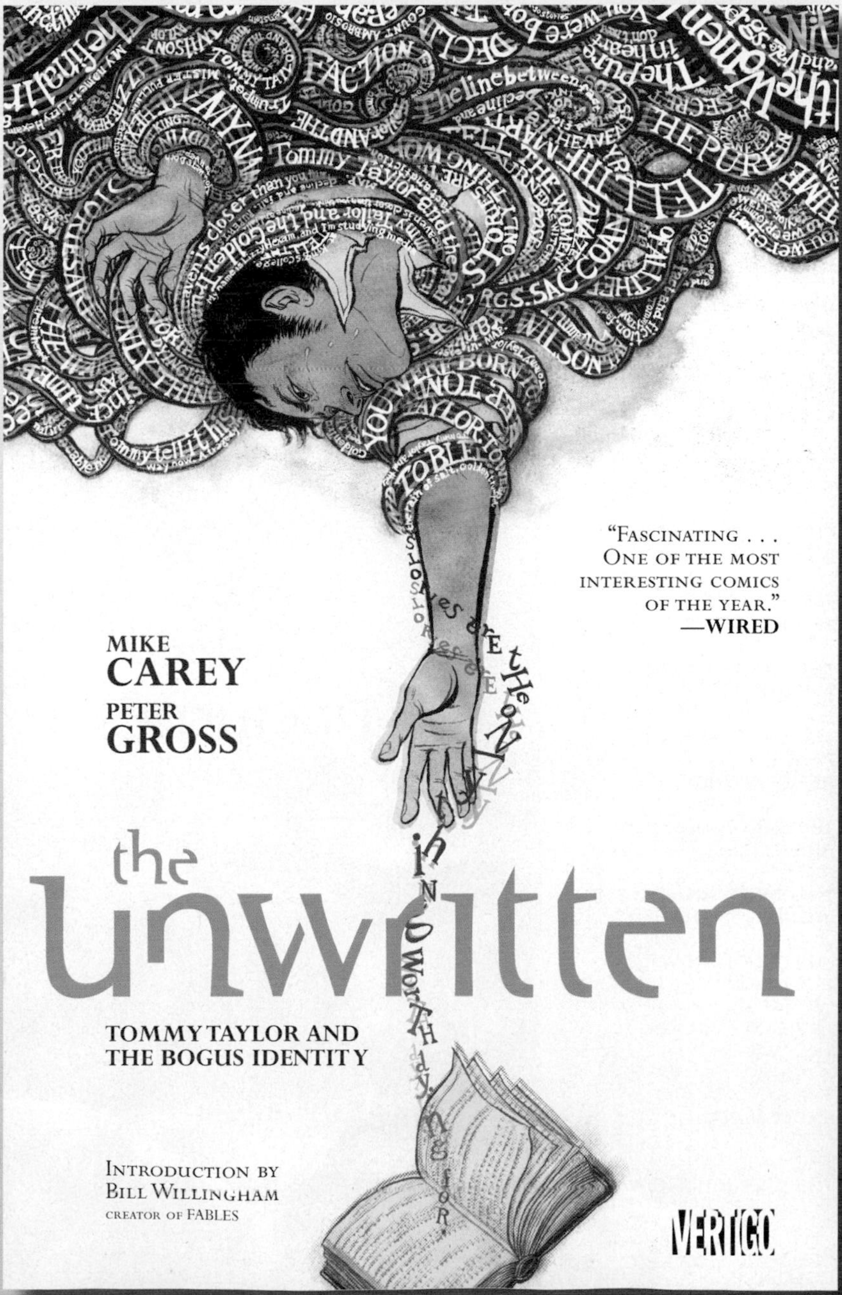

"Fascinating . . . One of the most interesting comics of the year." —WIRED
MIKE CAREY
PETER GROSS
the unwritten
TOMMY TAYLOR AND THE BOGUS IDENTITY
Introduction by Bill Willingham
creator of FABLES
VERTIGO

THE UNWRITTEN VOL. 1: TOMMY TAYLOR AND THE BOGUS IDENTITY

THE UNWRITTEN VOL. 2: INSIDE MAN

THE UNWRITTEN VOL. 3: DEAD MAN'S KNOCK

THE UNWRITTEN VOL. 4: LEVIATHAN

THE UNWRITTEN VOL. 5: ON TO GENESIS

THE UNWRITTEN VOL. 6: TOMMY TAYLOR AND THE WAR OF WORDS

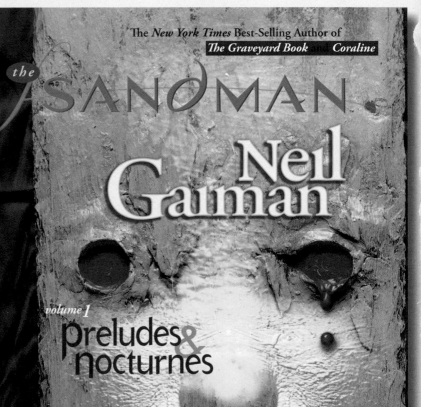